YIRAWALA

To my Mother, woman of the wilderness, who lit a lamp for me to understand the Aborigines of Australia and persevere to right old wrongs. When I was a child, she said, 'In life you may be knocked down many times, but have the courage to get up again and fight back. Nobody is beaten until they admit it.'

And to my dearest friend, Helen Florence Hambley, who gave her life to the Aboriginal cause with passionate endeavour and who encouraged me to write this book.

YIRAWALA

PAINTER OF THE DREAMING

SANDRA LE BRUN HOLMES

Hale & Iremonger

First published by Hodder & Stoughton (Australia), 1992

This edition published in 1994 by
Hale & Iremonger Pty Limited
GPO Box 2552, Sydney, NSW

National Library of Australia Cataloguing-in-publication entry

Holmes, Sandra.
Yirawala, painter of the dreaming.

Bibliography.
ISBN 0 86806 542 0

1. Yirawala, 1894-1976. [2.] Aborigines, Australian — Northern Territory — Arnhem Land — Painting. [3.] Aborigines, Australian — Northern Territory — Arnhem Land — Religion. 4. Painters — Northern Territory — Biography. [5.] Aborigines, Australian — Northern Territory — Arnhem Land — Biography. I. Title.

759.994

Printed by Colorcraft Ltd, Hong Kong

Contents

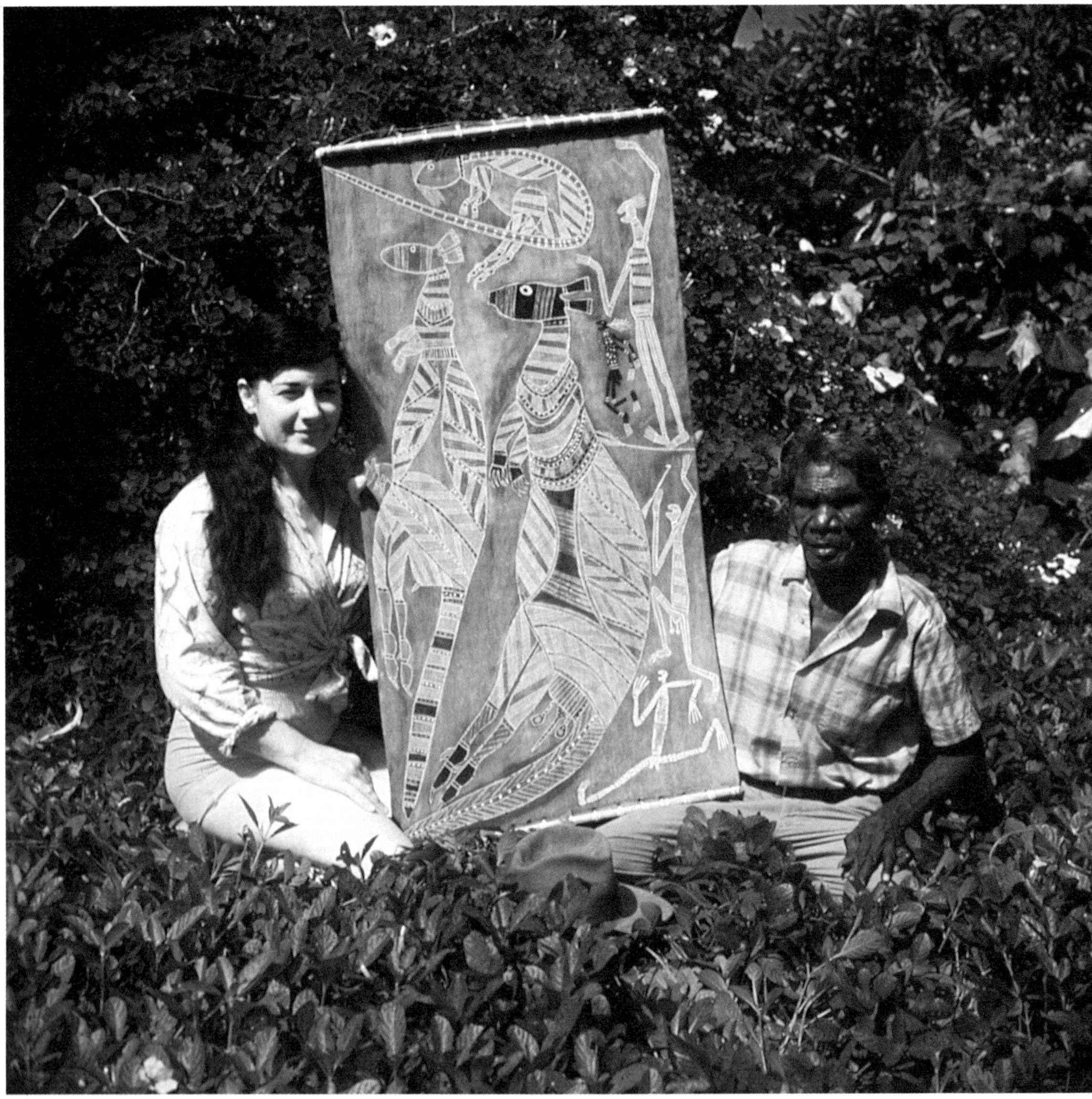

I Yirawala say OK for Sandra to make book of me and all my paintings. I give her the rights to all my drawings and stories painted all my life. When I die she is the owner and the boss always. She will look after them. She is our family. I cut her and lifted her high. I gave her sacred power drawings to say she owns right to copy paintings and nobody else.

YIRAWALA
September 1975

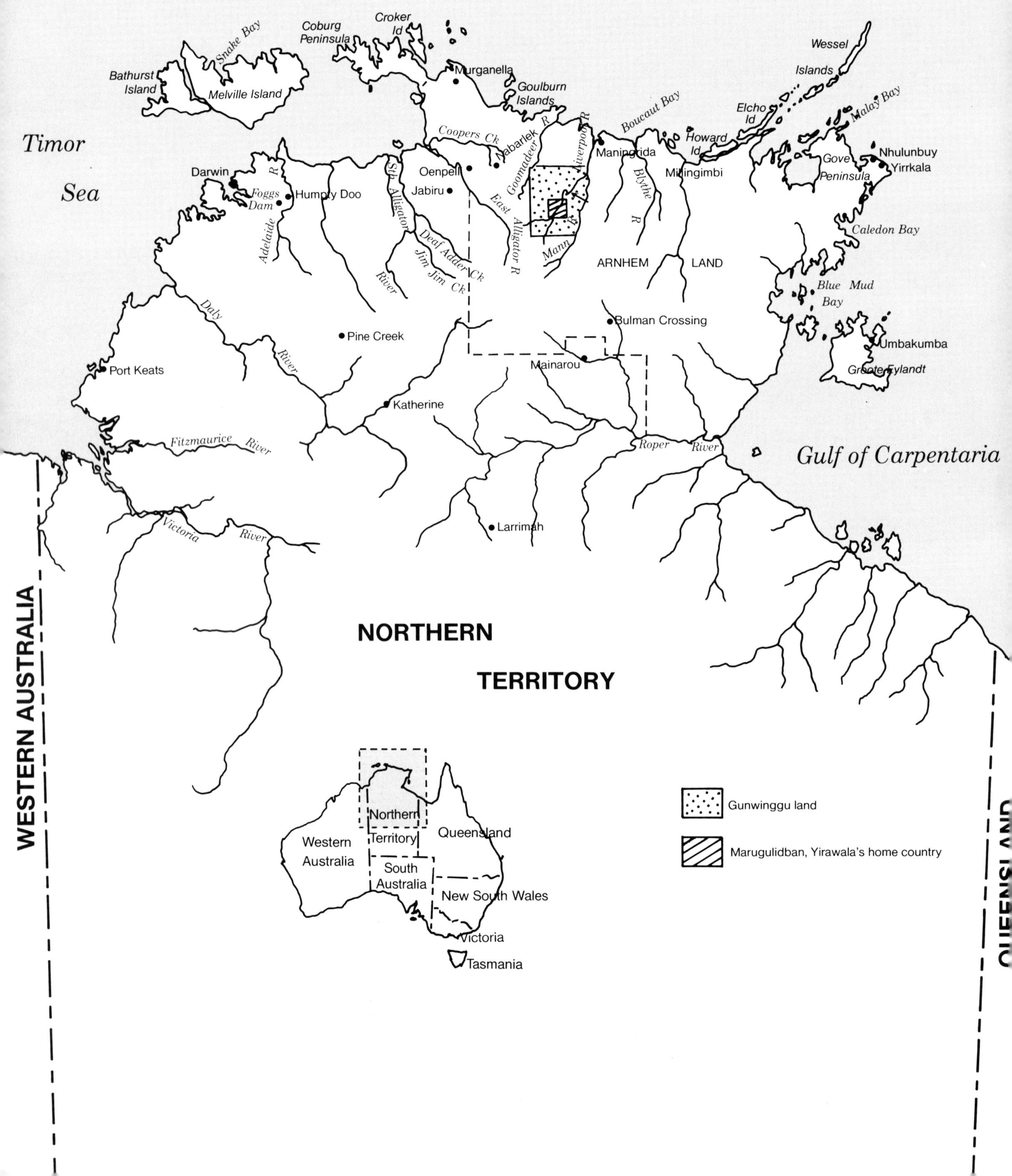

Arafura Sea
Timor Sea
Gulf of Carpentaria
Snake Bay
Coburg Peninsula
Croker Id
Bathurst Island
Melville Island
Murganella
Goulburn Islands
Wessel Islands
Elcho Id
Malay Bay
Boucaut Bay
Howard Id
Coopers Ck
Nabarlek
Goomadeer R
Liverpool R
Maningrida
Milingimbi
Gove Peninsula
Nhulunbuy
Yirrkala
Darwin
Foggs Dam
Humpty Doo
Adelaide R
South Alligator River
Oenpelli
Jabiru
East Alligator R
Deaf Adder Ck
Jim Jim Ck
Mann R
Blythe R
ARNHEM LAND
Caledon Bay
Blue Mud Bay
Daly River
Pine Creek
Bulman Crossing
Mainarou
Umbakumba
Groote Eylandt
Port Keats
Katherine
Fitzmaurice River
Roper River
Larrimah
Victoria River
NORTHERN TERRITORY
WESTERN AUSTRALIA
QUEENSLAND
Northern Territory
Western Australia
Queensland
South Australia
New South Wales
Victoria
Tasmania
Gunwinggu land
Marugulidban, Yirawala's home country

Introduction

Of the work of Australia's greatest traditional painter, Yirawala, Pablo Picasso said, 'That is what I have been trying to achieve all my life.'

In Yirawala's lifetime his ceremonial paintings were eagerly sought by museums and collectors all over the world. He was made a Member of the Order of the British Empire for services to Aboriginal art, and also received the International Art Co-operation Award naming him the best artist in Australia for 1971. Despite all the honours and praise, he was disappointed that his paintings were regarded only as art.

Yirawala was a ceremony leader, law carrier and 'clever man' (medicine man and healer) of the Gunwinggu tribe. Dua moiety, Nubulain skin. He was born around 1894, in Arnhemland, at a place called Marugulidban, where the Liverpool River peters out into a small tributary at the foot of the escarpment country, 65 kilometres from the government settlement at Maningrida. His Dreaming was Dadat, the little red and green lorikeet.

His father, Nowaritj, was a ceremony boss, religious leader, and keeper of sacred symbols and cave galleries of rock paintings — the title deeds of the tribal land.

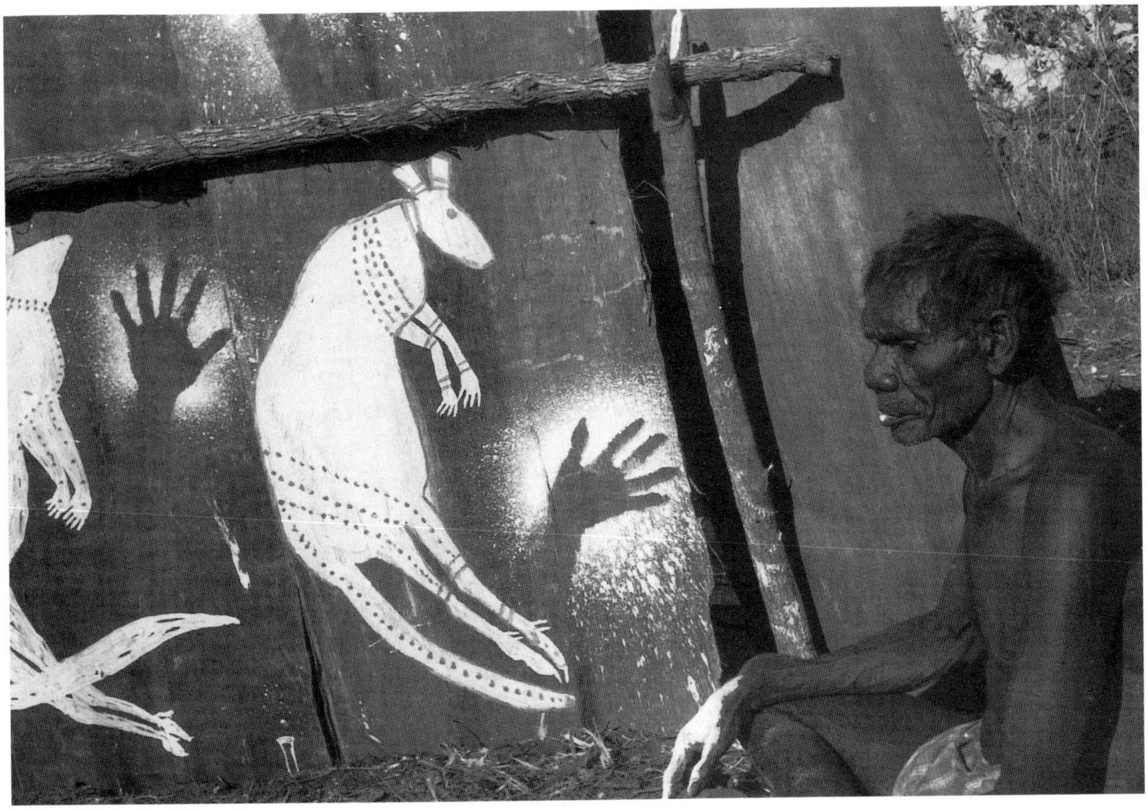

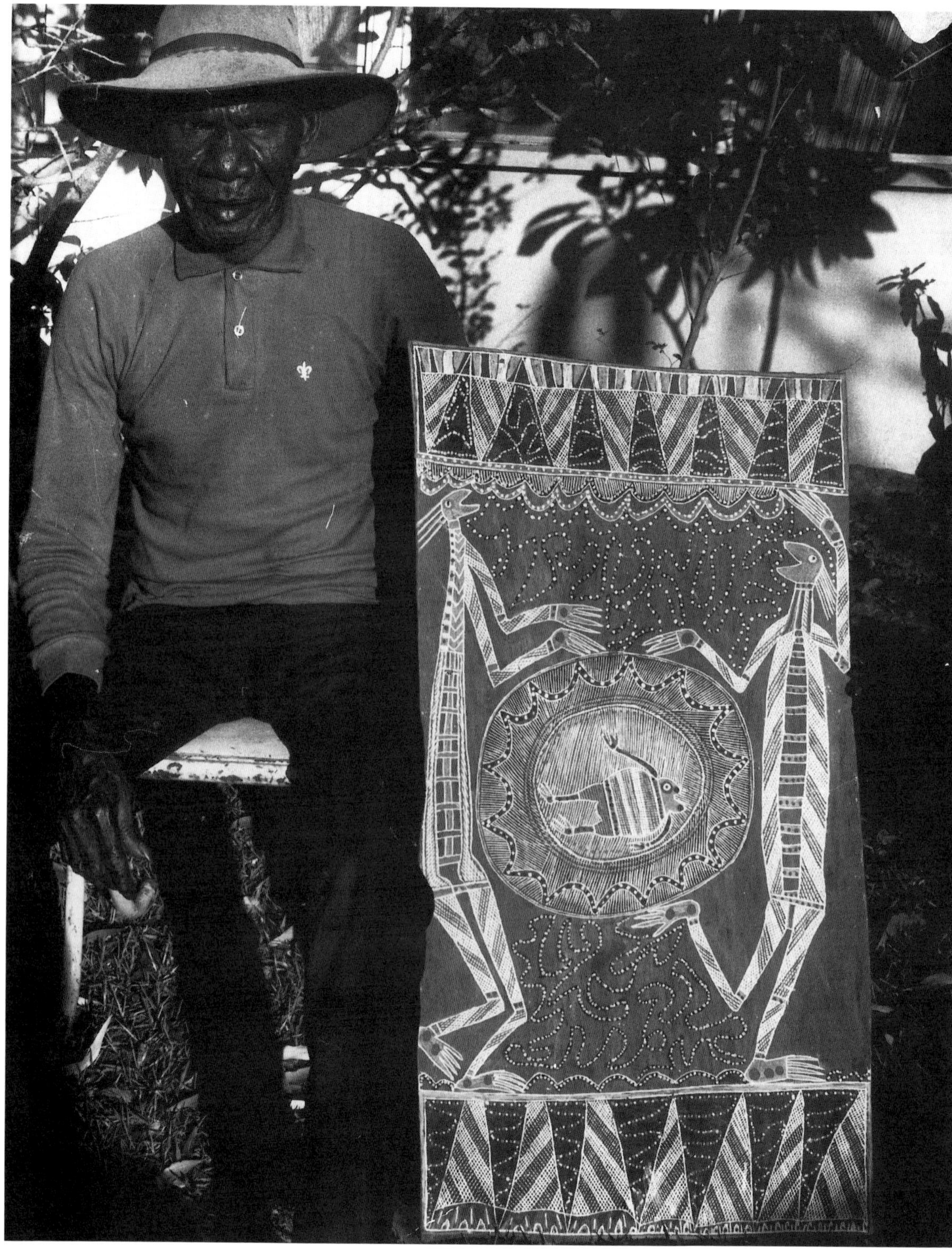

Yirawala with his painting of Barra the wet season man and Jinaroo the dry season man. Barra stamps on the edge of the waterhole and calls the frog king, who will begin the ceremony for the making of rain.

Previous page:
Yirawala — ceremony leader, law carrier and 'clever man' (medicine man and healer) of the Gunwinggu tribe.

As a boy Yirawala travelled over his own country with his family and clan. At that time very few white people ventured into Arnhemland, apart from the odd adventurer, and Paddy Cahill, a buffalo shooter. Paddy Cahill acted as a guide to the famous anthropologists, Spencer and Gillen, who were the first to collect examples of bark paintings from Arnhemland, some of which were donated to the Melbourne Museum.

Yirawala recalled the discovery of the skeletons of two white men and the bones of horses and cattle. Near one of the skeletons Yirawala's father found a rotting saddlebag that contained papers, diaries and faded photographs, wrapped in oilcloth. After burying the skeletons as best he could, Nowaritj decided that the papers and diaries must be very important to the white men, so he set out on a long journey overland to take the saddlebag to a white man at a coastal timber camp opposite Croker Island.

Yirawala inherited his father's sacred designs, songs and stories, all of which he had to be taught as he grew up in the home country.

In this beautiful, bountiful home country of Marugulidban Yirawala made his first kill of a small wallaby. He travelled along the path to manhood by way of the rituals and ceremonies and law, until as a man of forty-five years he was shown the final mysteries.

When Yirawala became a 'proper man' (fully initiated) his first promised wife went to live with him near Oenpelli. Two children were born to this union: Margaret and David Gumaraitj.

When his first wife died, Yirawala went to live elsewhere, working for a time for a Chinese man, cutting timber near Malay Bay.

He had two more promised wives, Mary Malilba and Margaret Monanggu. They went to live with him as his lawful wives. Mary, his number one wife, had three children: Muriel, Bobby Joran (Kadjiba) and Danny Noloman. Margaret had one son: Andrew Millwerriwer.

In the late 1950s Yirawala and his family went to live on Croker Island.

Although the Gunwinggu tribal council was scattered, some living at Maningrida, Oenpelli and Croker Island, Yirawala and his fellow elders came together to discuss important tribal business. They never lost touch with each other or their land and sacred sites.

I met Yirawala while I was engaged in fieldwork for the Australian Institute of Aboriginal Studies. I was to become his friend and biographer, and was taken into his family and clan by special ritual.

Yirawala believed that unless white people understood that Aborigines had their own religion, inseparable from the land, the tribes could be wiped out. He believed that the mindless dealing in Aboriginal art and artifacts degraded Aboriginal religion and law; the old prescribed designs were painted to perpetuate the tribal history and the travels of creator beings — they were not art like the white man's, but were like the pages of a sacred book.

Yirawala asked me to make a collection of his paintings and to write a book illustrating the full collection, explaining their meanings and his struggle to preserve Aboriginal religion, law and land, to make balanda understand.

The text of this book is taken from tape recordings, letters, documents and diaries.

The series of 139 ceremonial paintings is now in the Australian National Gallery, Canberra.

Part I
The painter

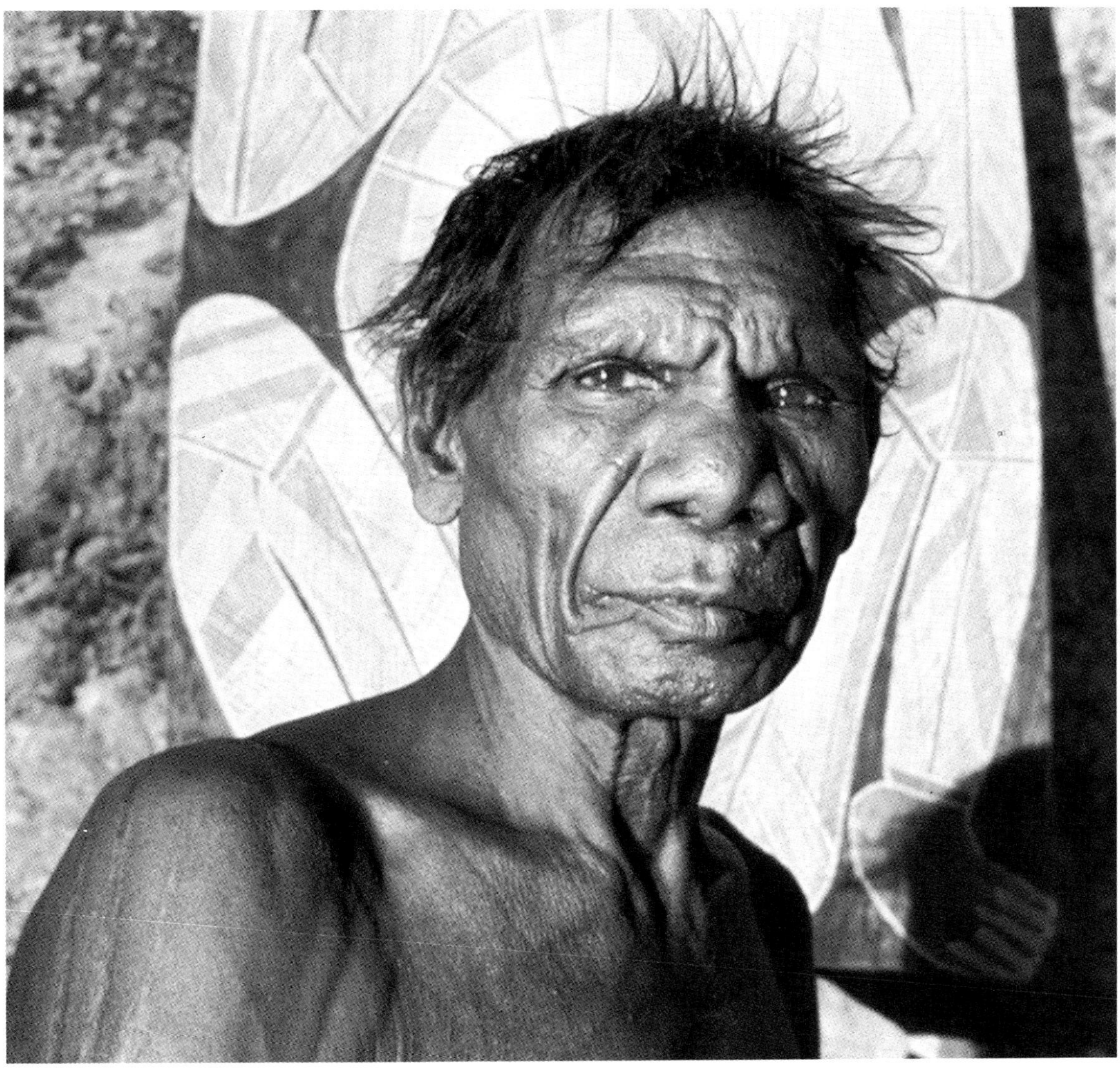

Chapter 1
Like leaves going out on the tide

My first visit to Darwin and Arnhemland was in early 1962. I went there with Cecil Holmes, my husband, to assist with the filming of an Aboriginal mortuary ceremony at Millingimbi Mission. This film, *Djalambu*, was made for the newly established Australian Institute of Aboriginal Studies (AIAS) in Canberra.*

We also made a three-part documentary film called *Faces in the Sun*, researched and written by Cecil Holmes for the Methodist Overseas Missions in Sydney. In the course of making this film I met Mr Lazarus Lami-Lami on Goulburn Island, where we filmed a portion of the Jun-bar-bar giant ceremony. Lazarus was a head man of the Maung tribe and became my friend and informant over a number of years.

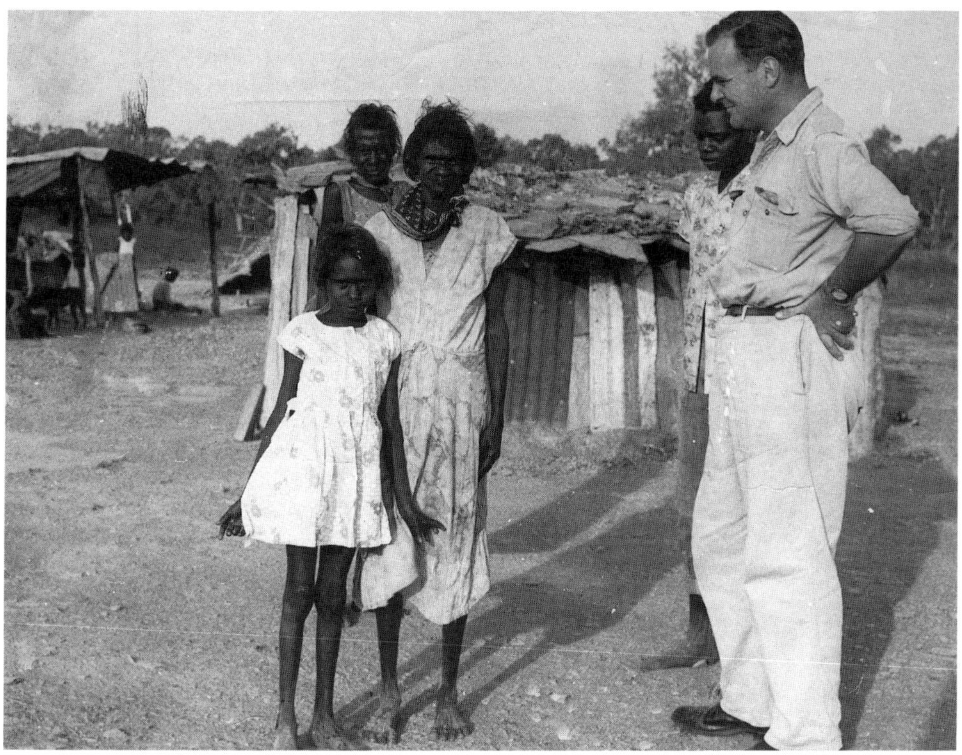

Cecil Holmes, documentary filmmaker and editor of The Territorian *magazine, speaking with Aborigines at Mainarou Station in the Northern Territory.*

* Now called the Australian Institute of Aboriginal and Torres Strait Islanders Studies.

In June 1963 I left Sydney with my husband and two children to live in Darwin, where Cecil would work as editor of *The Territorian*, a magazine owned by News Limited. When time permitted we would film Aboriginal ceremonies for the AIAS archives. I would also work in the field as an anthropological researcher for them.

At that time Aborigines were wards of the State and were not included in official census counts until 1967. In that year they were granted Australian citizenship and became entitled to vote. Federal Government policy was assimilation of Aborigines into white society.

It was apparent that traditional Aboriginal society and culture were disintegrating and would eventually vanish, so the Australian Government through the AIAS wished to save something for posterity, sort of putting a tape recorder under the dying head.

The invasion and occupation of tribal lands by non-Aborigines is a shameful and bloody history, and began with the establishment of a permanent British settlement in 1788. In that century it was roughly estimated that there were 300 000 Aborigines who lived a nomadic existence, sustaining themselves by hunting and collecting over a wide area of land. This land was taken by white settlers who cleared areas of blacks by shooting and poisoning them. Sometimes Aborigines fought back by spearing stock or the odd white man. For even minor retaliation by the Aborigines, punitive forces might wipe out a whole clan — men, women and children.

In the 1830s Christian missions were established to train the remnants of tribes to adopt a settled life according to Christian concepts. The main concentration was training the children, especially in domestic work.

Between 1860 and 1911 Aborigines were placed under local 'protectors', who handled all property and money. Aborigines had no rights at all.

From their pinnacle of ignorance, influential people of the day judged the Aborigines to be brutish and primitive, devoid of moral ethics and spirituality. It was believed that darkness shrouded their savage minds and, because they built no churches, worshipped nothing and had no priests, they had no religion. Certain church men doubted if they had a soul. The white man would bestow a religion on these wretched people and Christianity would save them all.

Such opinions provided excuses down the years for the massacres and on-going barbaric treatment of Aborigines.

From 1911 to 1940 Aborigines were encouraged to stay in designated areas, where they received weekly handouts of food and clothing. If they left the area they received nothing. The ration depots were usually controlled by denominational missions, who had police backup to enforce the institution's rules. Aborigines accepted rations and assistance and gradually became dependent on handouts.

In 1951 the Federal Government established a policy of assimilation and set up an active Aboriginal Welfare Department, with a number of trained district officers. Increased funding was allocated to mission settlements. Education, health and housing were greatly improved.

In all States Aboriginal children were taken from their parents and incarcerated in institutions, such as missions and government settlements, where they were actively discouraged from speaking their own language or trying to contact tribal relatives. The children must be brought up as white. In the Northern Territory only half-caste children were taken from their Aboriginal families.

(In 1954 at Currawang Mission, near Kalgoorlie in Western Australia, I observed some of this assimilation in action. An Aboriginal child was spanked for calling out in language to her parents who were peering through the high wire fence. They and others had walked many miles through burning desert country looking for their children, their little lost ones. In the bush, outside the mission fence, old men were dancing and singing, hoping that some of the children might hear or see them.)

In 1963 Aboriginal old-age pensions were ten pounds ten shillings a week. After the missions and settlements had made deductions for such amenities as accommodation, food

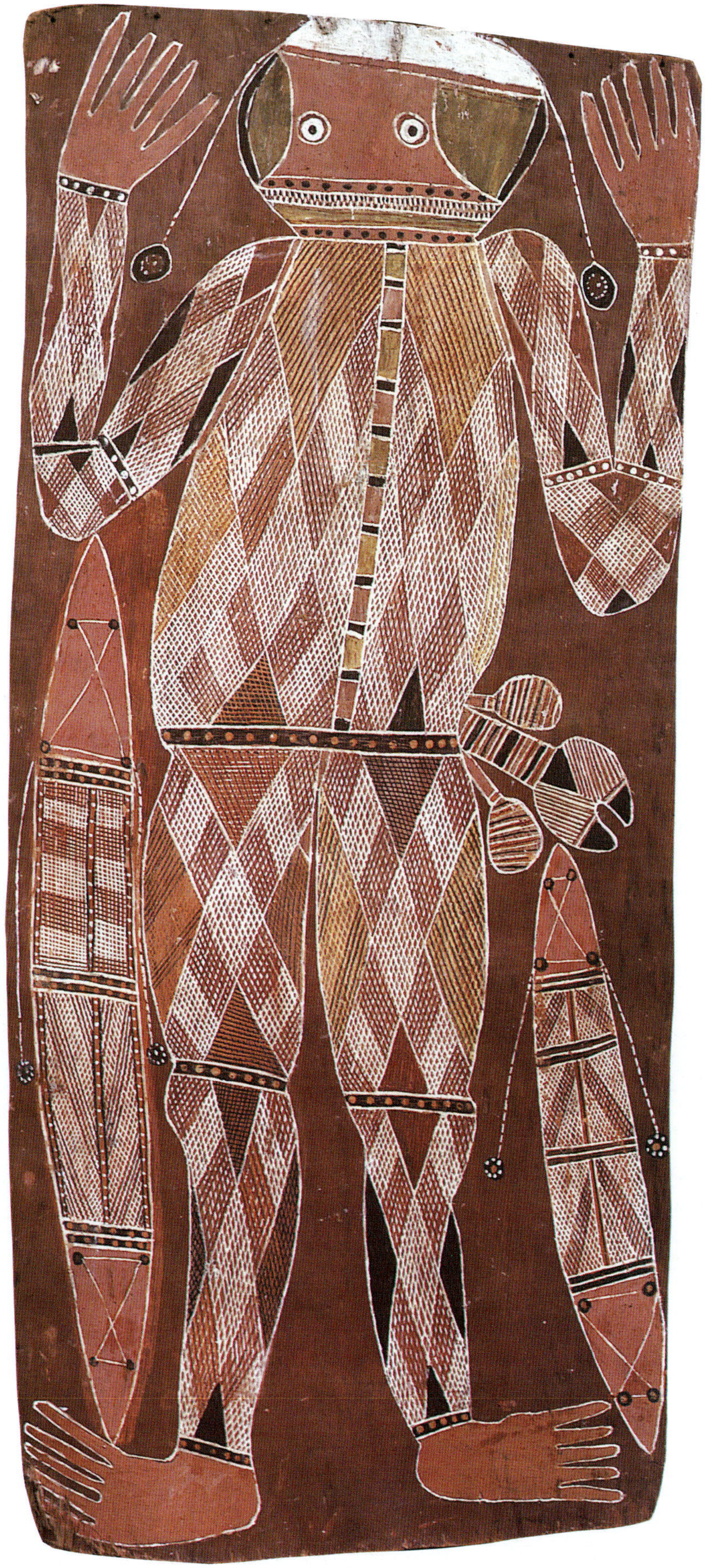

Plate 1 MARAIAN SERIES

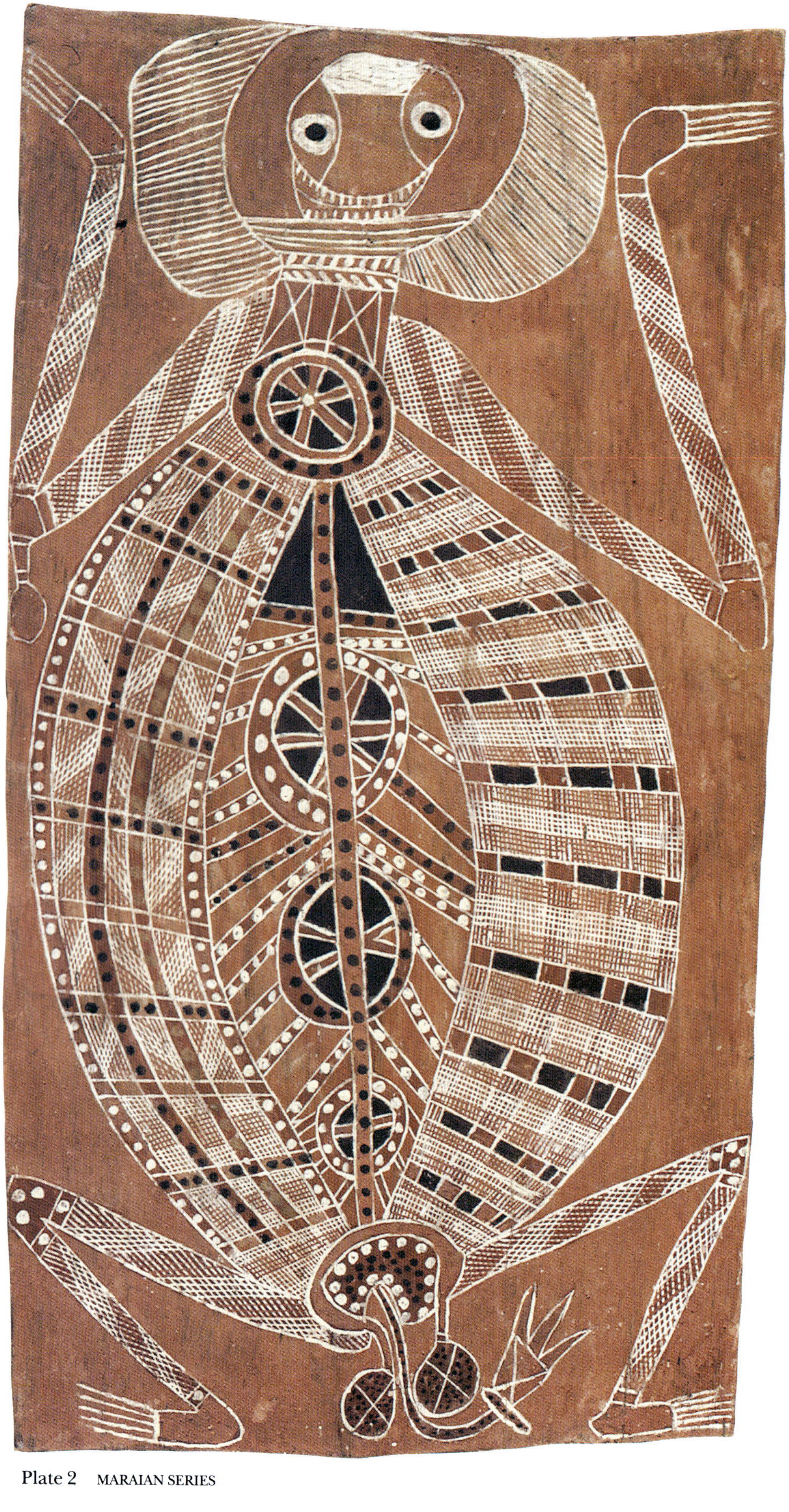

Plate 2 MARAIAN SERIES

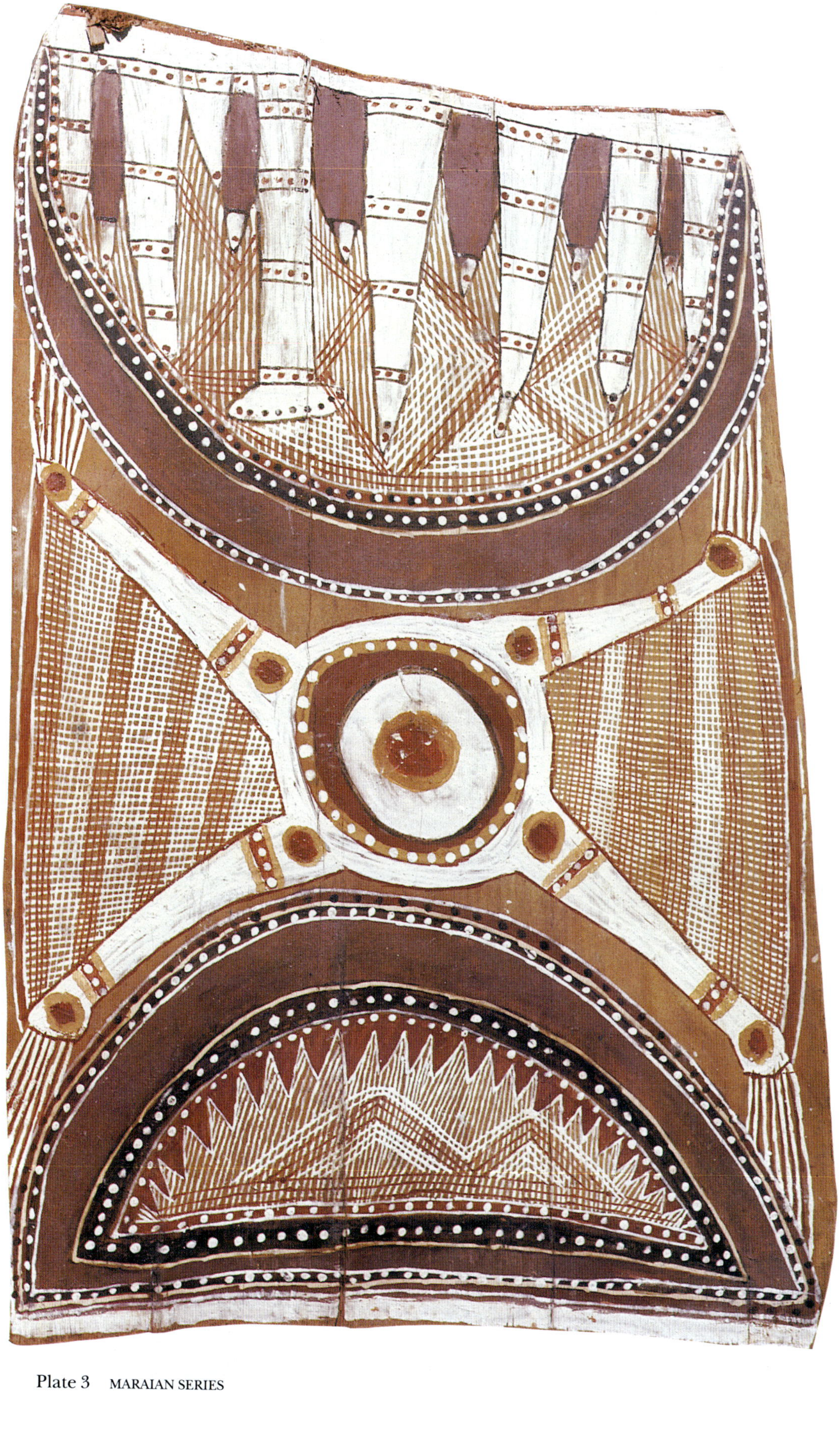

Plate 3 MARAIAN SERIES

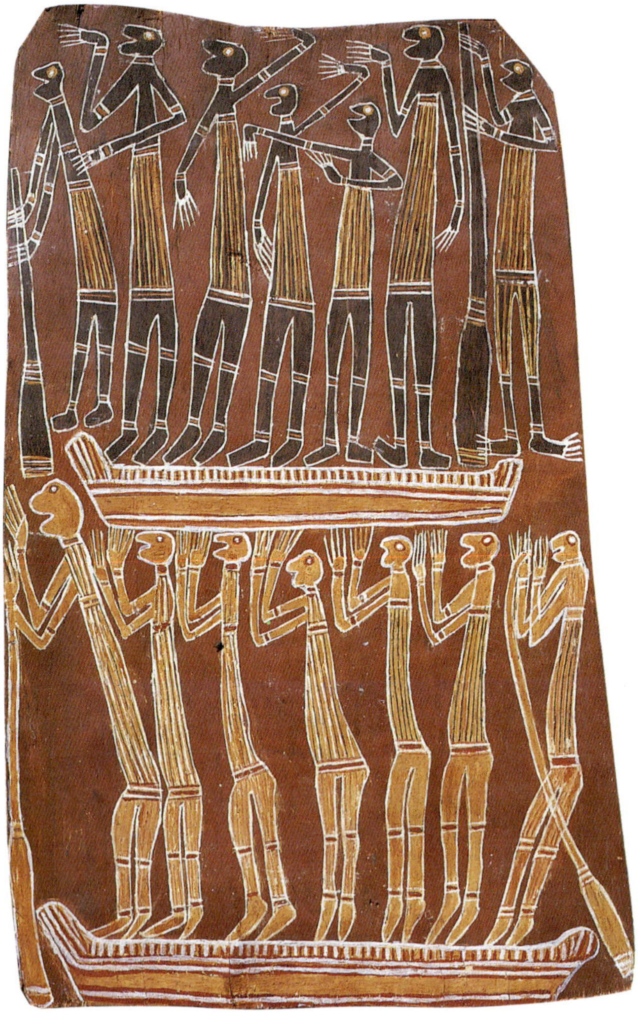

Plate 4 MARAIAN SERIES

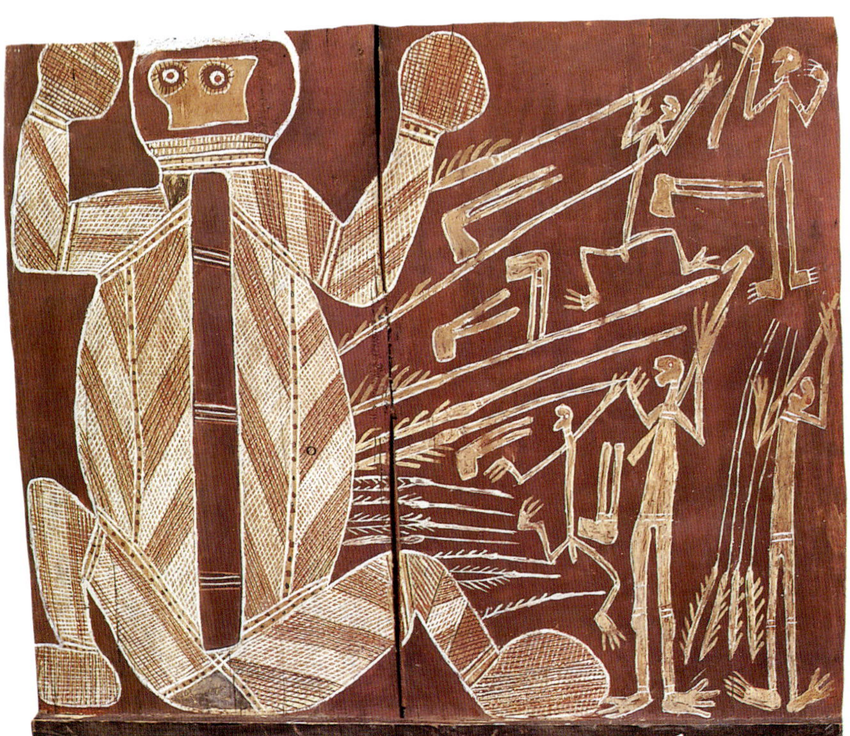

Plate 5 MARAIAN SERIES

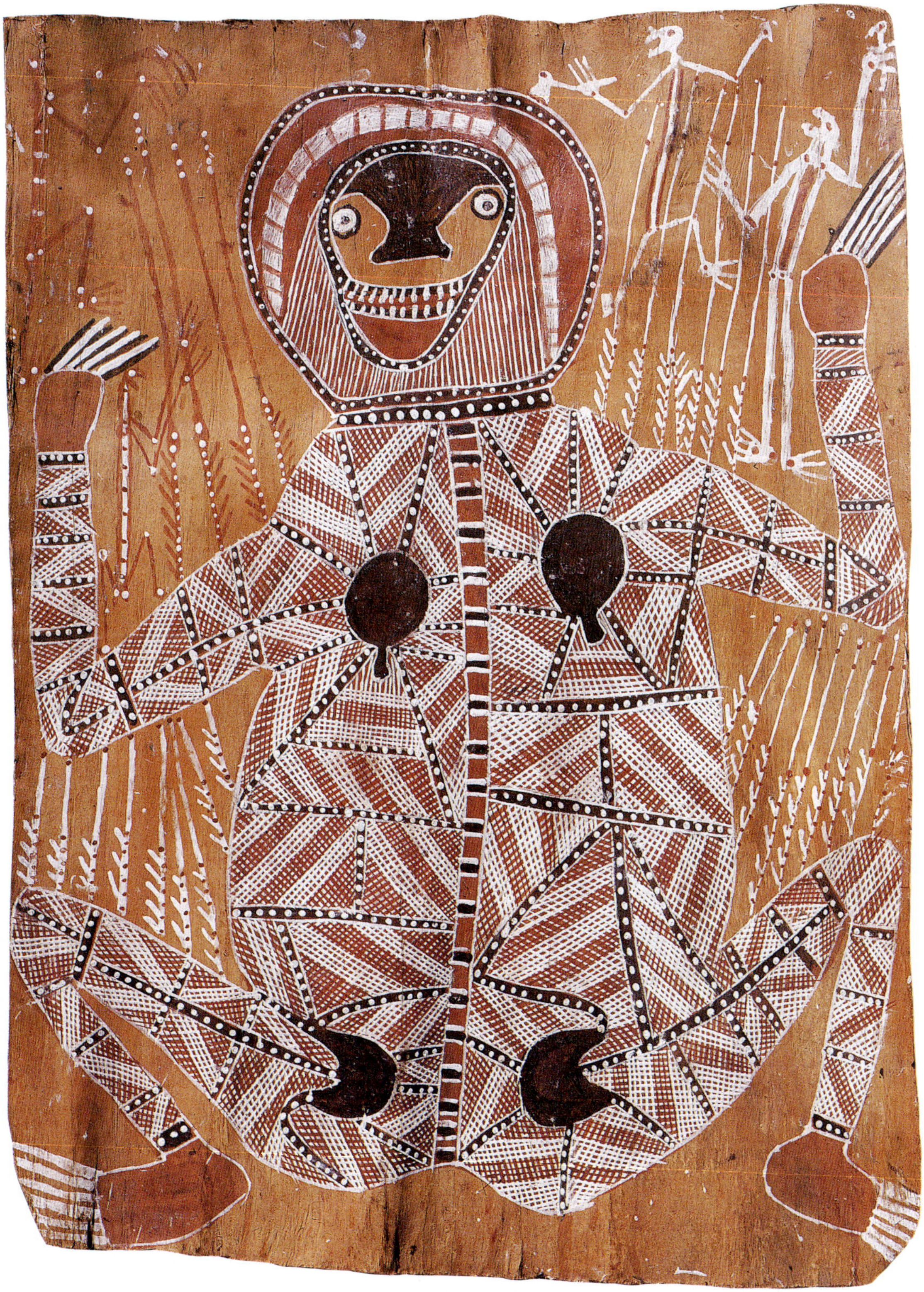

Plate 6 MARAIAN SERIES

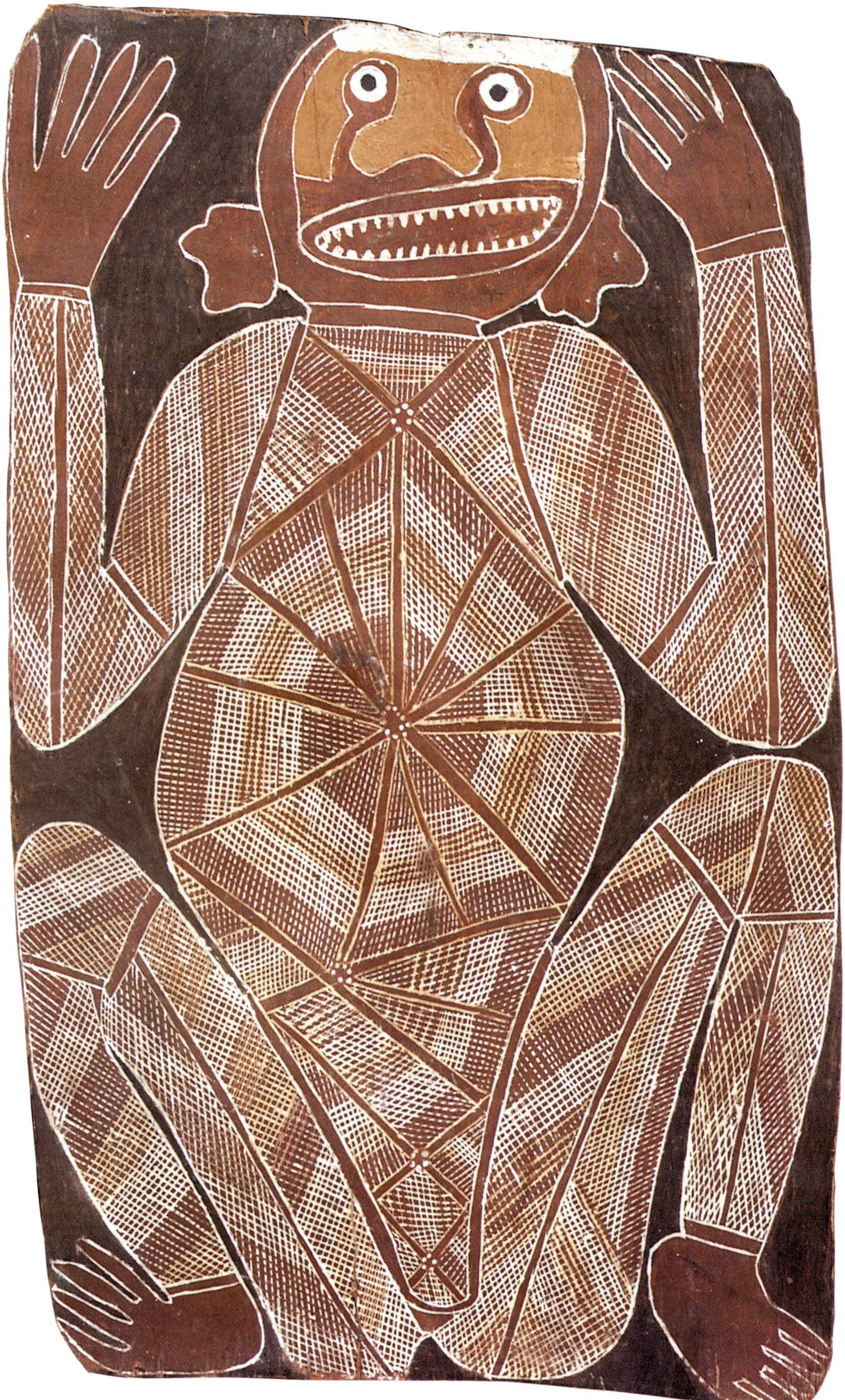

Plate 7 MARAIAN SERIES

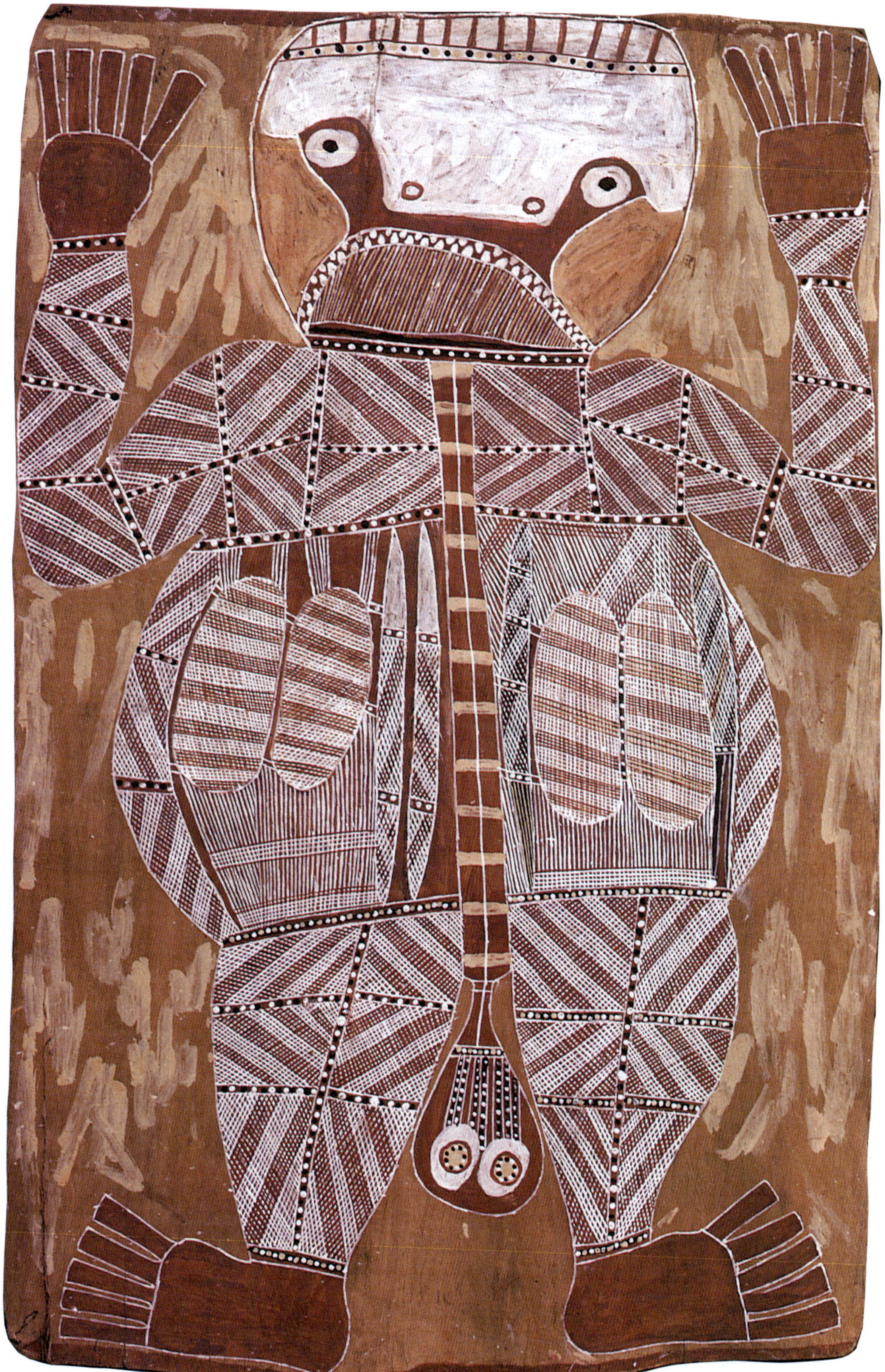

Plate 8 MARAIAN SERIES

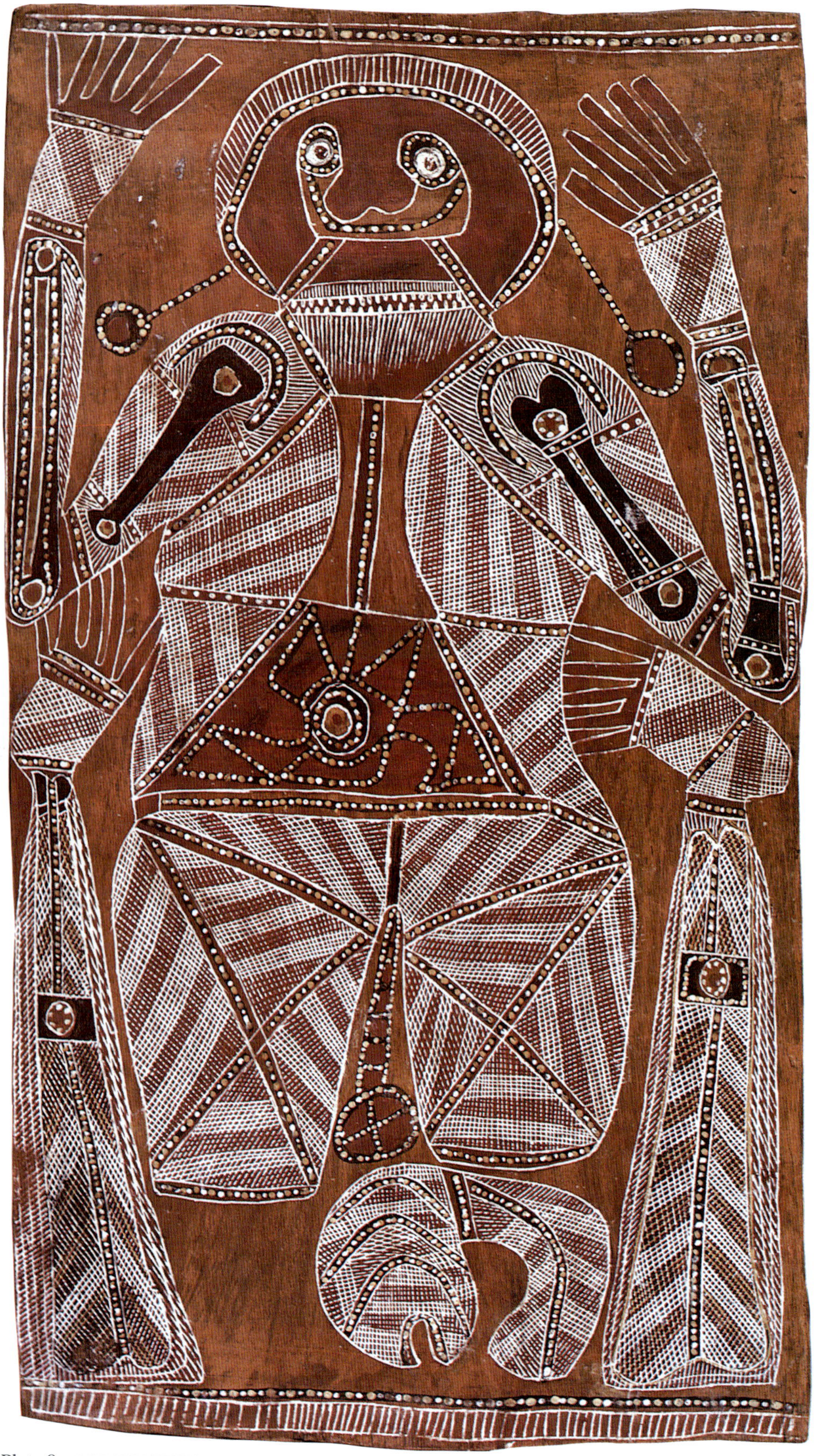

Plate 9 MARAIAN SERIES

and clothing, there was little left for other goods not included in the ration handouts. The local economy on missions and government settlements was boosted by the sale of 'craft'. If there had been better government funding, the eventual mass production and corruption of religious designs and symbols may not have occurred.

My work for the AIAS included collecting rare Aboriginal art and artifacts. I would select suitable items and inform Mr Ted Milliken of Aboriginal Welfare, who would pay the vendors, arrange collection of the pieces, and pack and ship them to Dr Helen Wurm of the AIAS, Canberra.

There was no Federal legislation to encourage the so-called 'craft managers' on the Aboriginal reserves to give priority to the AIAS above the demands of local and overseas dealers. The best was lost forever. Important religious records were sold piecemeal. Falling leaves from a great tree of knowledge. But it was regarded only as art, and Federal policy was assimilation.

In Darwin I visited the Methodist Overseas Mission craft warehouse with its racks of bark paintings, carvings and objects. I noticed a rack of Morning Star (Barnumbirr) ceremonial poles, bedecked with parrot feathers and long strands of feathered string. A mission employee was busily packing a large pile of paintings for an interstate dealer. I asked if I could look at them and was mesmerised by their beauty and power, the delicate web-like designs on human and animal figures, and lines of Mimi spirits that seemed to be prancing right off the bark. This was the work of Yirawala, I was told. Most of these drawings incorporated the sacred Maraian symbols of power and life. I thought it regrettable that such works should be sold like pounds of sugar when they were religious records — ancient prescribed designs preserving and perpetuating the tribal history and stories in the absence of a written language.

Nearby there were other important paintings from Marwulan, Mathaman, Naritjin, Birigitji and others of Yirrkala Mission. The painters of Yirrkala had no idea what became of their paintings and carvings until two or three painters were taken down to a Sydney exhibition as living gimmicks. The men were literate, and when they returned to Yirrkala dissatisfaction spread amongst the 'craft workers', which resulted in a strike for better pay and conditions.

In June 1964, Roy Marika of Yirrkala wrote me a letter asking for some marketing advice and for information on how to obtain fixative to spray their paintings, as they did not want to worry the mission. I replied, saying I would make some inquiries on their behalf and let them know in due course.

Early in August I was summoned to the mission headquarters in Darwin and warned against discussing the marketing of Aboriginal art and artifacts. I must tender a written undertaking in this regard. Also, correspondence about such matters must cease, otherwise I would be banned from visiting Goulburn Island Mission (the inference being that the ban would extend to other Methodist missions).

I gave the written undertaking, as Cecil and I were going to Goulburn Island to film the sacred Uwar (Ubar) ceremony for the AIAS. I received written acknowledgement of my letter.

In late August 1964, I went with my husband and a film crew to film the Uwar ceremony on Goulburn Island. I was pleased to be able to renew my acquaintance with Lazarus Lami-Lami.

Lazarus told me I should visit Croker Island (Minjilang) to meet Yirawala, an important tribal elder and spiritual leader of the Gunwinggu tribe, a man of great knowledge, and keeper of sacred symbols, as expressed in his bark paintings. Yirawala was also a clairvoyant and 'clever man', a medicine man of great power and prestige. 'He is a big boss [ceremony leader] for the Maraian ceremony. He holds the keys that can open doors for you if he wishes.'

Lazarus said that he would soon be going to live on Croker Island where he would work as a carpenter and also study for the Christian ministry. If I came to the island he would introduce me to Yirawala.

I was determined to meet Yirawala and looked forward to documenting his ceremonial designs and accompanying songs, but an opportunity did not present itself until late in 1964. I was kept busy in other areas of the Northern Territory, assisting my husband to film and record other ceremonies for the AIAS. I was pleased to think that in this way I was helping to preserve Aboriginal religion.

In September 1964 the AIAS requested me to go to Croker Island to record and document ceremonial songs and stories from the Gunwinggu and Jiwadja people. At last I would be able to meet Yirawala.

Early one morning I flew out to Croker Island, one and a half hours' flying time from Darwin. The old DC3 droned on along the coast, where green rivers wound snake-like to the Arafura Sea. Over the dull green mangroves white birds drifted like scraps of paper blown by the wind. In the grey-blue distance wisps of smoke floated over the forests, and low-hung clouds cast patches of moving shadow.

Leaving the mainland behind we flew over the blue-green sea until Croker Island came into view. Approaching the red cliffs the plane circled the land then rushed down to the dirt strip with its scatter of trucks and people. We thumped down, engines roaring, turning in a cloud of red dust to halt near a small tin shed.

I clambered down the steps with Aborigines and white people. One young Aboriginal girl carried a new baby and a smiling man ran to meet her. The mission superintendent greeted me and asked for my permit and health clearance from the Aboriginal Welfare Department in Darwin. The permit stated my name, reason for entry to the reserve and the duration of my stay. (This permit could be revoked at any time by the Director of Aboriginal Welfare, with no right of appeal.)

I began collecting my suitcase and recorder as a car pulled up and Lazarus stepped out, hand outstretched and smiling broadly. He was a big, gentle person with a Robeson-like voice. As we waited for the plane to take off he told me that the men were ready for the singing and Yirawala was expecting me.

It was a long drive across Croker Island. The track wound over a wide, green plain dotted with cattle, and in the shimmering distance brolga birds hopped and danced. Leaving the plain we entered a dense forest of ironwood and stringybark trees. Some of the latter had bald patches on their trunks where painters had cut bark.*

Pastor K R Wale of the Methodist Overseas Missions had founded the Croker Island (Minjilang) Mission in 1941. He had chosen a most attractive site on a hillside overlooking the sea. The office and staff houses stood with the hospital, school, church and store; pleasant pathways were shaded by large mango and poinciana trees. Aboriginal huts were dotted on the slope below. Near the little wooden church frangipani flowers fell like a blessing, their sweet perfume blowing on a cool breeze from the sea.

Inside the church hand-made pews stood on a white sand floor. A vase of red flowers had been set on the altar and a pile of worn prayer books lay on a table nearby. The roof beams and uprights were of seasoned bush timber, beautifully decorated with Aboriginal X-ray paintings of fish and lizards, painted by three local artists, Namarardali, Jambalula, and Noganyari. Lazarus was proud of the church and said that one day he would preach here.

After depositing my bags in a cottage called 'Seaview', we made our way down to the beach to meet Yirawala. On the cliff top we passed a large dugout canoe which had once made a long journey around the coast. The dugout had been introduced to coastal tribes by the Macassans, long before the white man came.

A few dinghies and a dugout were drawn up on the white sand. Beyond, the sparkling waves broke and rippled along the shore of the beautiful, tranquil bay. A few tin huts were scattered along the beach and skinny dogs lay in the shade. Some reared up to bark at us and

* At that time only medium pieces of bark were cut; thin surfaces which did not cut into the sapwood. This changed as art dealers demanded large, strong bark paintings. This meant cutting into the sapwood, right around the tree, ringbarking and killing it.

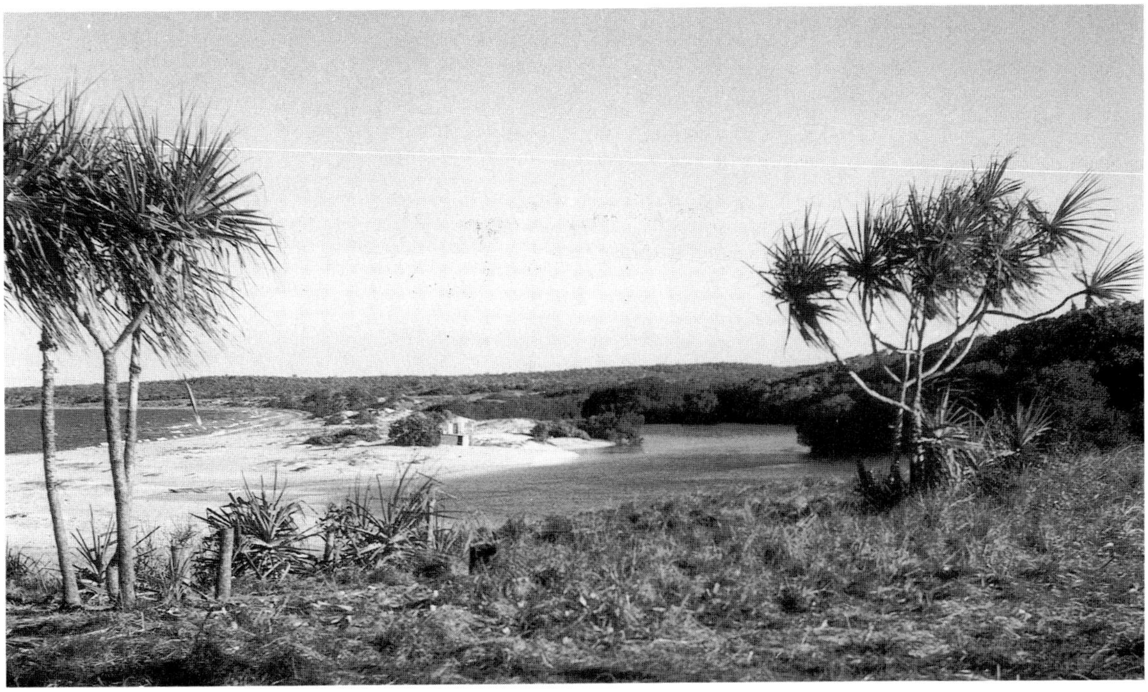

Croker Island beach, 1964. Beyond the pandanus palms and Jap Creek inlet, tin huts were scattered along the beach.

were silenced by shouts and well-aimed sticks.

As we trudged along, Lazarus pointed to a clump of pandanus palms and said that the man sitting in the shade was Yirawala. As we came closer I saw that he was painting on a piece of bark resting across his knees. His head was bowed and he sang softly as he worked. He was painting the figure of a giant with large genitals. From its head hung magic power bags and the Maraian spiderweb design was on the chest and limbs.

Lazarus coughed and Yirawala looked up, putting aside the painting and reaching for an old black pipe, which he relit with a coal from the smouldering fire. Puffing smoke for a few moments, he leaned back and surveyed me quizzically from under his old bush hat. His face was stern and strong.

Lazarus introduced me, speaking gently and respectfully in the Gunwinggu language. Yirawala motioned us to sit down. He said he had heard about my work from old men in other areas. Suddenly he grasped by hand and held it firmly as he looked into my eyes. Though tinged with cataracts his eyes had a burning intensity. The hand that held mine was slender with extremely long fingernails. For some moments his eyes held mine and I could not look away. I felt power flowing from him and I began to tremble. Seeing this he released me and smiled.

I judged Yirawala to be about sixty years of age. His hair was fine, and light brown in colour. His skin was heavily scarred with cicatrices that attest to a man's rank and to his knowledge of tribal law and religious mysteries. As Lazarus had said, Yirawala was a man of high degree and a keeper of sacred symbols.*

Yirawala said he would be happy to record for me later, but for now he must finish his drawing. He tapped the bark with his fingernails. 'This one Lumahlumah, big Maraian man. I make him stand up today.'

We sat watching him at work. He rubbed dark red ochre on a stone palette and splashed water on the little heap of powder, mixing it with a sliver of bark. His brush was a stem of hard

* Aborigines carry their graduation marks on their body; other people preserve theirs on parchment certificates. An Aboriginal man without any marks is ignorant and knows no tribal law or business (ceremonies).

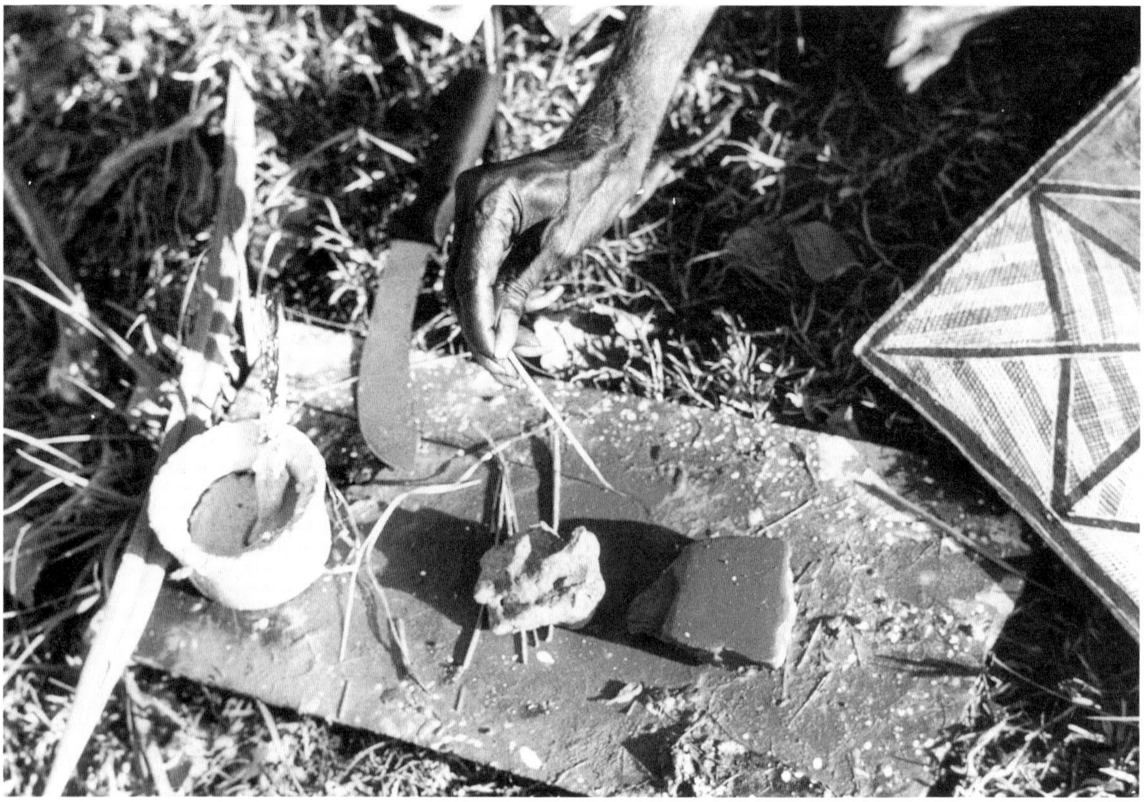

Yirawala's brush was a stem of hard bush grass pared to a long, thin strand at one end. The ochres had to be thin enough to run but not watery, as this would cause blotches. Too little water would result in broken lines. His hand was as steady as a surgeon's.

bush grass pared to a long, thin strand at one end. This was dragged through the paint and carefully applied to the painting. The slender hand of the master delicately pulled the brush to and fro, executing curves and fine sweeping lines, unbroken and without a smudge. Now and then the hand paused, hovering for a few carefully calculated seconds, then swiftly descended with unerring precision, seeming to float over the painting, leaving the fine web of the rarrk design of the sacred Maraian.

As Yirawala painted he sang the story of the giant Lumahlumah, who came from Indonesia way bringing important ceremony and law for the early time people. Lumahlumah walked about all over the country making songs, performing miracles and naming things. When he came to the end of his Dreaming path he began eating people. He had outlived his usefulness so the tribesmen of the East and central Arnhemland coast sent a large number of warriors to kill him.

As he was dying, Lumahlumah sang his last songs to the elders of many tribes, telling them to wait as he had sacred life-giving law and magic to give them. Urgently he shouted at them, 'Don't finish me off yet. Wait'. He snatched up a sharp flint and cut the web-like design on his body, marking out the lines in his own blood, calling the sacred power words.

Finally he told them that the Maraian designs and law that he bequeathed to them was the life force for man and all nature. They must faithfully perpetuate the sacred designs and ritual. If they lost or profaned them, the link to the eternal Dreaming would be broken, the survival of man and the natural species would be jeopardised, and the life after death denied.*

* In this context I use the term 'man' to mean all human beings, male and female.

Finally, as he grew weaker, Lumahlumah instructed the elders of the Dua and Jiritja moieties to take his bones and organs to a certain cave and guard them well. Lifting his arms he sang, 'In dying I give you life, you, the birds, plants and animals. You are all one, dependent on each other. When you paint and call Maraian I will be present, to sustain you with my sacred power and magic. Through this ceremony I will always be with you and you shall have life after death and return to your Dreaming.'

Yirawala sang about the dark red ochre he was applying to the giant's body. This represented the blood Lumahlumah shed when he died, and white clay his bones and flesh. The bones and organs were full of power.

Yirawala gave a sigh and put down his brush. The painting was finished. (Later it would be taken to the mission's craft store from where, unknown to Yirawala, it would be resold to a dealer.)

Yirawala invited us to his house for a lunch of bully beef and bread. The house, which he and his sons had built and which they rented from the mission, was a solid structure of bush timber and sheet iron, divided into two rooms. The furniture consisted of beds and a bench made of bush saplings. The floor was beach sand. Cooking was done outside, behind a tin windbreak. Water was carted from a tap near the base of the cliff. Nearby stood a pan lavatory. Outside the house sheets of bark lay drying in the sun, weighted with stones to stop them twisting and curling.*

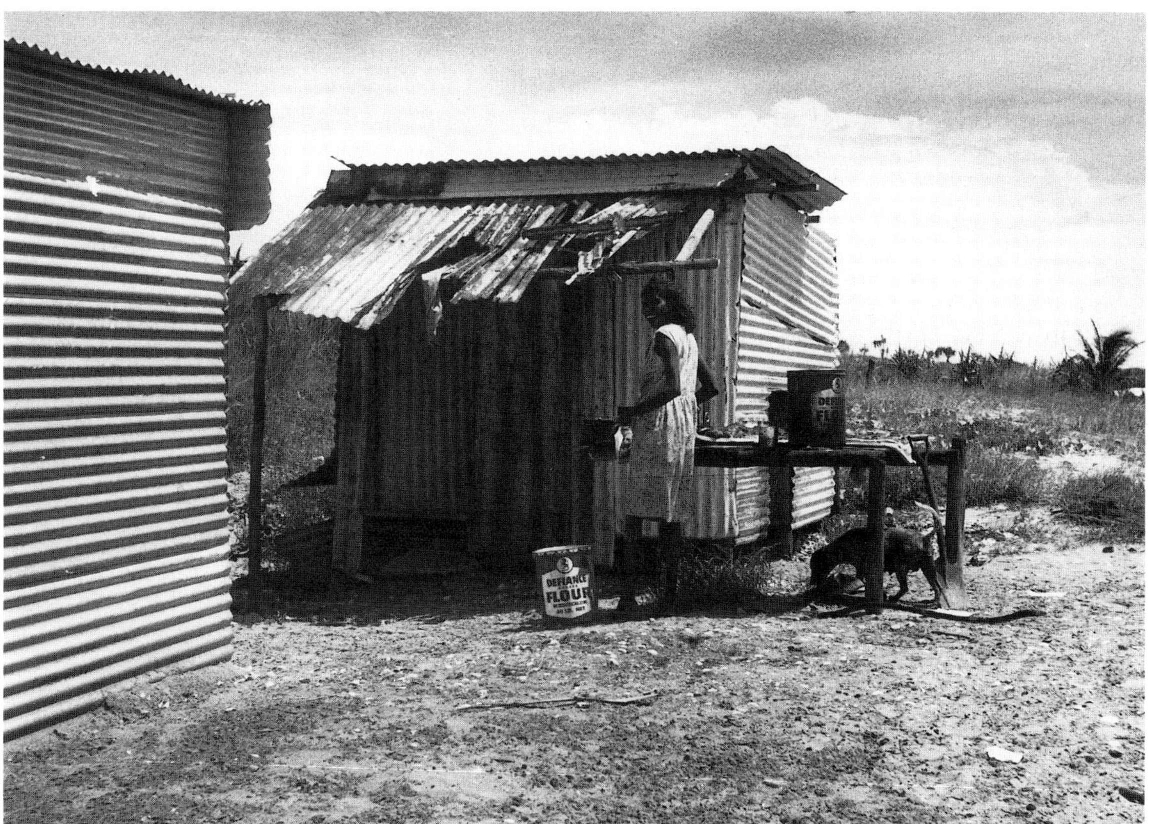

Margaret Monanggu preparing a damper in the 'kitchen' of Yirawala's house, Croker Island, 1964. Yirawala and his sons built the house and rented it from the mission.

* The bark is cured for two or three weeks. Only the smooth inside is painted. If bark is green it will twist later on. Green bark has a tell-tale sap smell. Painters in the Yirrkala (Gove) area flattened the rolled-up bark over a fire, burning off the rough outer bark and partly drying it out.

Lunch was served by Yirawala's wives, Mary Malilba and Margaret Monanggu. As we were drinking black tea, we were joined by two of Yirawala's sons, Bobby Joran (Kadjiba) and David Gumaraitj.

Bobby was a tall, handsome young man, and worked as a carpenter and truck driver. A calm and reliable man, Bobby was devoted to helping his father and would defy any odds. Being literate, he acted as an interpreter for written material and discussions. Later, he would act as a messenger when communications with Yirawala and others broke down.

David was approximately forty years of age, and was Yirawala's eldest son. His mother (Yirawala's first promised wife), had died when he was a boy. He was heir to Yirawala's intellectual property of sacred designs, symbols, songs and stories. He said he still had much to learn from his father, who was the number-one 'boss' of the Gunwinggu tribe. 'Next to him I am like a boy,' he said. David was a stockman for the mission's cattle herd; he also made an occasional painting for the craft store.

Resting after lunch, Yirawala talked about his land. He called the home country Marugulidban. 'That properly my land, mother country — lovely place. Plenty water, cattle, buffalo, fish, geese. Oh, you never know — see my country. One day all family go home, men, women, kid. We make own station, house, school, hospital, fence, radio.' I asked if all the Gunwinggu people wanted to go home to tribal lands. 'Yoh, him all go, whole lot. Not mission, Welfare, him all keep away.' His voice was strong with an undertone of anger.

He was anxious to explain more about his country and called for a pencil and paper. When Bobby gave it to him he began drawing a rough map of his home country. A long fingernail stabbed at the paper. 'There, that my country, my Dreaming place.' He looked up with shining eyes, smiling happily as he gave me the map. 'Might be you help we, all family, go home?' His voice was soft, almost sad. He explained that he had been born and raised in the home country by the Liverpool River, where he had wandered freely with his father and uncles. He had made his first kill of a small wallaby there and began learning about the land, the natural species and becoming a man.

'I stop too long this place. Go home soon, make r'own station, cattle, buffalo, anything. Mining mob might be him come, spoil country, sacred cave.' He puffed his pipe for a while then handed it to David. 'On my land, nobody pay rent, water, nothing. No balanda [white people] pushing us. We keep country, block mining mob.'

Bobby Joran asked me if rumours were true that mining had begun on Gove Peninsula, near Yirrkala Mission. I told him mining would proceed, even though the tribal elders had sent a sacred bark painting petition to Canberra objecting to mining on their lands and pleading for an understanding of their concerns.

Yirawala frowned and sat silent for a while. 'We Gunwinggu mob block mining men. Him keep out. Nobody sell mother country. Money same like water, run away. Our land feed us, look after we all time, like mother. Country there all time.' Mining would ruin the land, profane the sacred waterholes, and endanger sacred sites and caves where sacred life-giving objects were hidden. Yirawala believed that, if this happened, the Aborigines would lose their motivation and become white men in black skins. If the Aborigines lost their land and their Dreaming, they might lose their backbone. He said nobody listened to him on the mission and nobody told him what was really going on elsewhere.

Bobby said there was no future sitting down on the mission. They wanted their own land where they could preserve their own culture and traditions. He did not want his three children to lose it. They needed a government school, but also their own Aboriginal education of language, religion and law. He envisaged a dual education system.

Yirawala agreed. 'Balanda, him never know, never understand my drawing; that my book. All my drawing tell story, long time ago, Dreaming story, that my writing. Mission, him go r'own book, different way.' He smiled with pride. 'Long time, might be eight, nine year, I been make big mob drawing. Him somewhere, might be all locked in big shed.' He waved his arm in the direction of a distant shed.

I looked at Lazarus Lami-Lami and whispered, 'Doesn't he know that his paintings are sold as soon as he makes them?' Lazarus shook his head.

Like most other old painters and sculptors, Yirawala really had no idea where his paintings finished up when they were sold to the mission's craft store. Looking at this impressive, intelligent man I was deeply moved and decided to tell him the truth. Nobody had told him before.

I hesitated, then plunged in explaining the true situation, that all paintings, carvings, objects and artifacts that were sold to craft stores were resold to dealers in Darwin, interstate and overseas. Nothing was saved. His paintings were gone forever.

Yirawala sat quite still, saying nothing for a few moments, then he spoke in language to Lazarus, who confirmed what I had told him. His face was set in grim lines and his eyes burned like coals. Suddenly he stood up and walked out of the house and along the sand. I followed to where he sat on an upturned boat. He dabbed at his eyes with a faded khaki handkerchief, then thrust it into the pocket of his old checked shirt. His voice was almost a whisper. 'All my law, Dreaming story, big mob I make, nine year. I been lose him whole lot, Maraian business, Lorrgon, Ubar, magic, all finish. My eye little bit no good now.'

We were interrupted by the cries of children home from school. Danny and Andrew, Yirawala's youngest sons, ran to their father, who took them by the hand and led them back to the house.

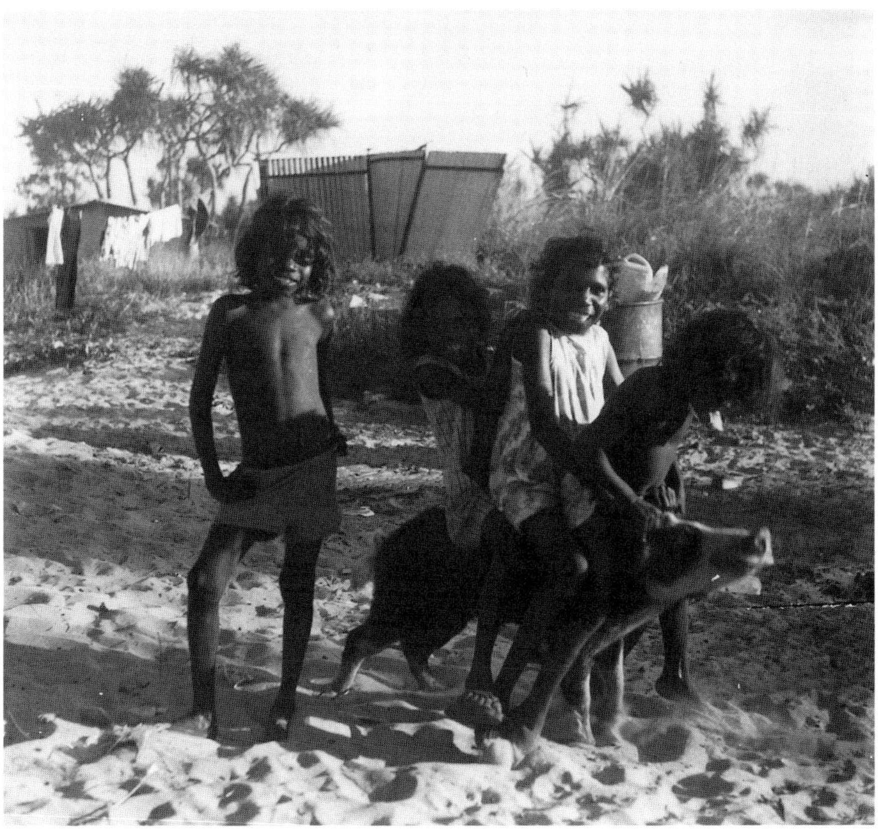

Yirawala's youngest son and grandchildren with Piggy-Piggy. The boar had been captured in the wild and had become a family pet. Left to right: Andrew, Vera, Christine and Shiela.

Bobby introduced me to his wife Aileen, a pretty Tiwi girl, who was an assistant teacher at the local school. She took me to meet their three daughters, Christine, Sheila and Vera, who were playing with a half-grown black boar named Piggy-Piggy. The animal had been captured in the wild and was now a family pet. It followed the children about and allowed them to ride on its back.

Yirawala smiled fondly as he patted the boar's shaggy head, saying that it was a good pig and already a 'nail' (tusk) was growing in its mouth. He said that on the other side of Jap Creek one old man had a female pig, which later on would be wife to Piggy-Piggy, and the litter would be shared.

Early next morning Yirawala and his friend Mijau-Mijau were hard at work, painting on bark. Mijau-Mijau was a fine painter who had inherited different colours and designs.

Yirawala was working on a white barramundi fish design, intricate lines in white, yellow and deep red ochre. He said the fish was Maraian and later he and other Gunwinggu men would perform the rituals associated with it. This drawing was a page from a sacred book. The singers would tell the old story and the dancers would re-enact how the fish was created in the Dreaming time.

He was most anxious to explain the significance of his drawings. 'My drawing like book — we got no writing like balanda. Men sing, dance, tell story for Maraian business. You take my drawing, tape recording, anything, to Canberra gov'ment men, make balanda understand.'

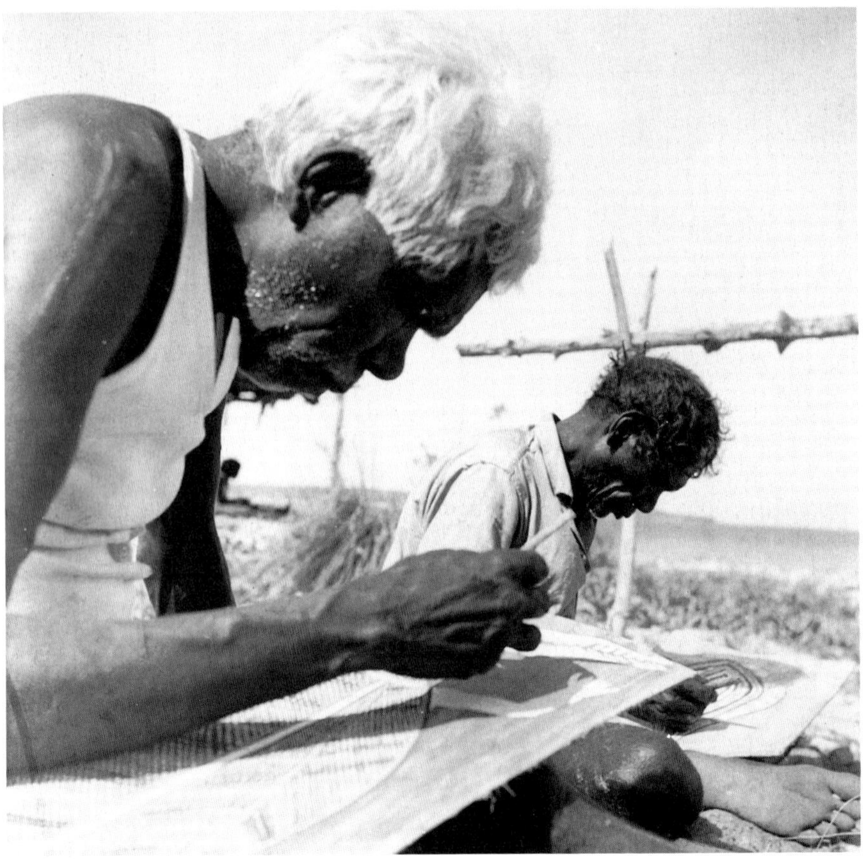

Mijau-Mijau and Yirawala painting for the craft store. Croker Island, 1964. Mijau-Mijau was a fine painter who had inherited different colours and designs. Neither painter would ever have used the colours and designs of another. To do so would have been a serious crime in traditional Aboriginal society.

He felt that white people were very ignorant and arrogant and did not understand that Aborigines had their own religion, inseparable from the land. He was afraid that if the government did not recognise this, then eventually the tribes would lose their land and be scattered. He called it 'leaves falling — going out on the tide'.

That evening I filmed the Maraian barramundi dance and songs. As the story ended Yirawala held the white fish painting, his expression strong and intense as clouds darkened the sky.

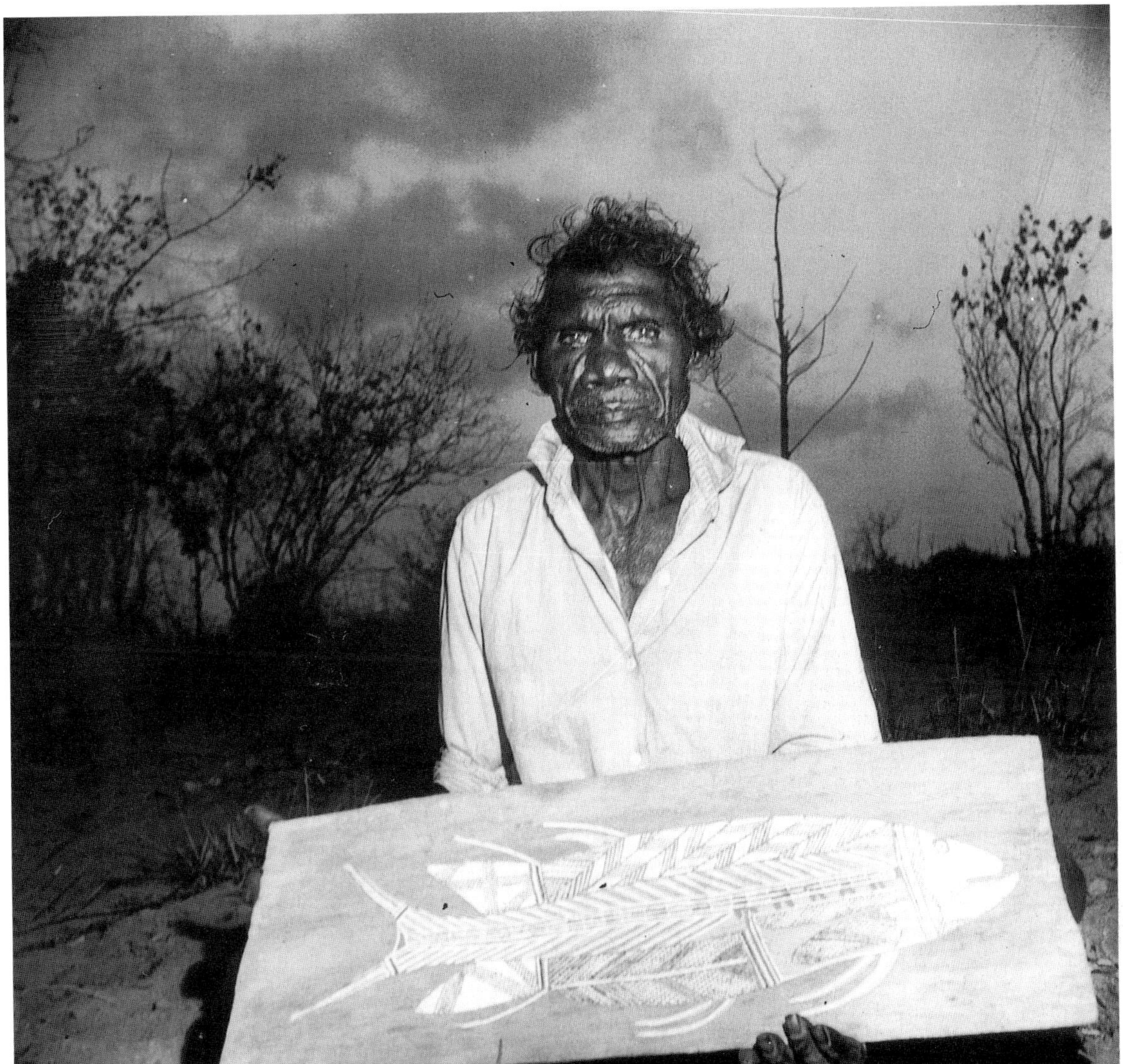

Yirawala with Maraian bonefish painting, Croker Island, 1964. This ceremonial painting was like a page from a sacred book. 'My drawing like book — we got no writing like balanda.'

Old Namarardali sang about the crocodile Dreaming, the barramundi, tortoise and tree sugarbag (wild honey). Mijau-Mijau sang songs from the Ubar ceremony, and Jimmy Jambalula sang seaway song cycles from the Jiwadja and Maung people. Henry Yudbunga of the Jiwadja tribe sang a song from the Ilgarr tribe of Grant Island.

Yirawala and his family invited me to visit him at any time. I laughed and said I would if I could obtain permits from Aboriginal Welfare in Darwin. This was never easy, as my attitudes to the Aborigines were at variance with the established order.

Yirawala said that he would work for me if he could, to make up some of the ceremonial paintings that had been lost. I said I might establish a small museum of his works at my home in Darwin, to teach white people something about Aboriginal religion. This idea pleased

Yirawala. 'Make balanda understand.' He smiled. We shook hands, and I promised to help him to save his land and a record of his religion.

Yirawala saw me as a bringer of information; someone who sat down and listened to him; the first white person who understood and offered to help him. I saw him as a spiritual leader, a man of high degree and defender of the faith, whose drawings were important religious records. I became totally committed to his cause.

Tribal Aborigines recognised Yirawala as a famous painter of ceremonial designs and a religious leader. To the white people on the mission and the world outside, he was just another old blackfellow sitting in the dust producing art and craft — pretty things to hang on the wall.*

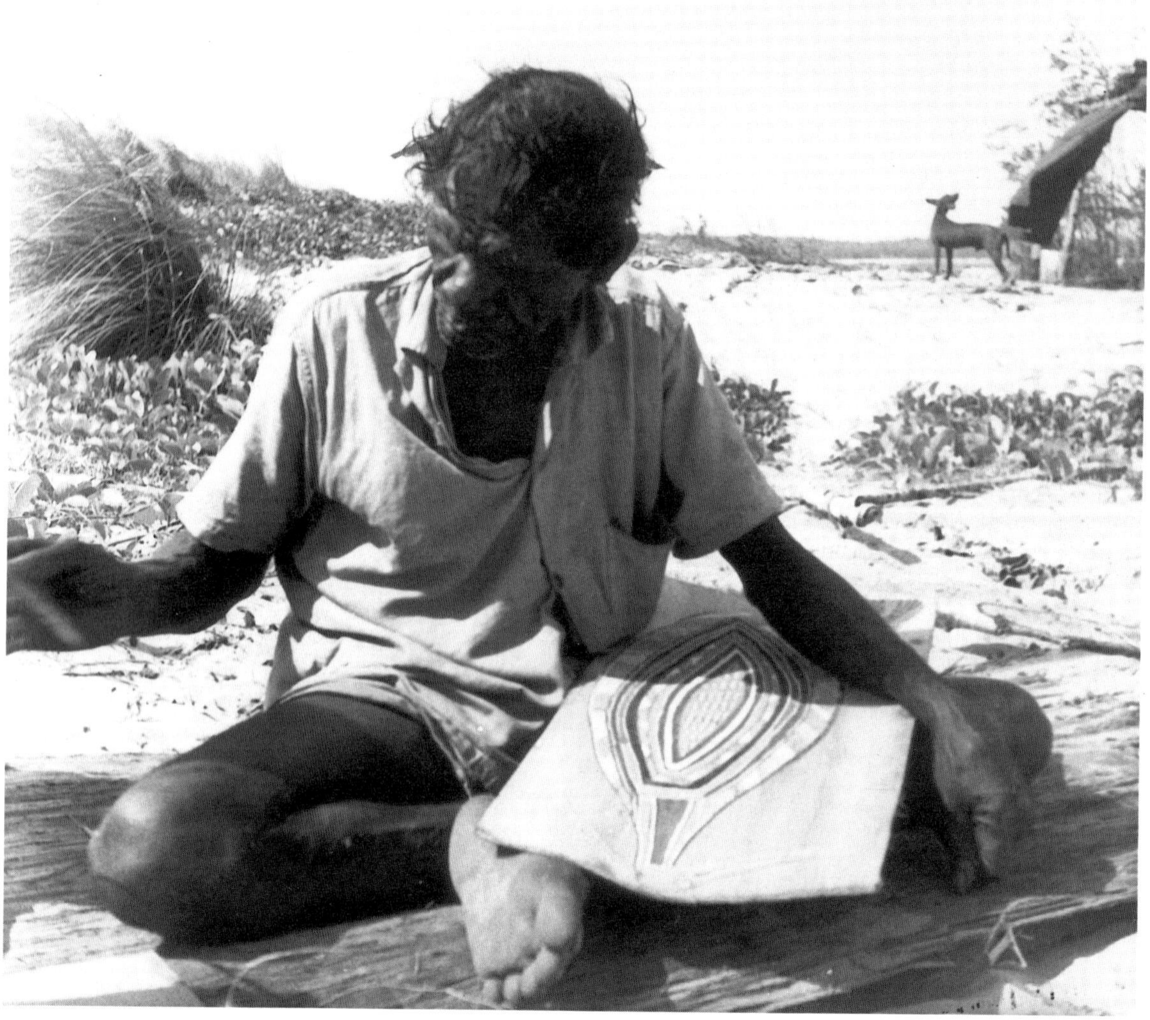

Yirawala painting Oogle the night bird, Croker Island, 1964. Tribal Aborigines recognised Yirawala as a famous painter of ceremonial designs and as a religious leader. To most white people he was just another old blackfellow sitting in the dust producing art and craft.

* This interpretation applied to traditional painters and sculptors elsewhere, and to Noganyari, Mijau-Mijau, Namarardali, and Jambalula who also painted for the Croker Island craft store. There was one missionary on Croker Island who saw some deeper meaning in the local Aboriginal art: the Reverend Jack Goodluck, who with Lazarus Lami-Lami helped me save a few of Yirawala's paintings, which are now in my ceremonial series collection in the Australian National Gallery, Canberra. There are 139 pieces, the only complete collection of Yirawala's works in the world. Goodluck helped me save something for Australia. However, all this changed when he left Croker Island in 1966.

Chapter 2
The Yirawala Museum

As Yirawala could not read or write, we relied on messengers and intermediaries. Early in 1965, Yirawala sent a messenger to see me. I was asked to arrange airfares for him and Mary into Darwin. I gladly complied with his request and picked them up at the airport. On the way home he said he had something for me in his suitcase.*

After lunch he opened the case and took out a stone axe and six exquisite little paintings of giants and Mimi spirits. 'Mission, him never know.' He laughed. Mary giggled and hung onto her husband's arm. They were both happy with their smuggling effort. Aboriginal 'craft workers' were not allowed to market their own work. This was strictly controlled on all missions and government settlements.

These were the first paintings I purchased from Yirawala and formed the foundation of my small house-museum. As time went by more pieces were added from other areas of Arnhemland, much of it purchased from local craft shops and mission warehouses in Darwin. Sometimes Aborigines would bring a painting or carving that they had made at Bagot Settlement, six kilometres from the city.

By June 1965 I established my little museum, which I called the Arnhem Art Gallery. Visitors were asked for a donation, which allowed them to hear a lecture, view traditional Aboriginal paintings and artifacts and listen to non-sacred music and stories. The museum viewing was by appointment only, in between my fieldwork trips.

Yirawala liked meeting visitors to the museum and telling them about his beautiful country and his paintings. American tourists always wanted to photograph him, which he refused, saying he was not a kangaroo in the bush.

Yirawala's visits to Darwin were very infrequent. When he was able to come, he would go and cut a few pieces of bark from a nearby forest and make a few paintings for my museum. He said he would work on a 'book' of three ceremonies, the Ubar, Lorrgon and Maraian. Little by little he would add another bark 'page'.

He would sit in my garden, under the big mango tree near his hut, painting on bark, pausing now and then to drink strong sweet tea prepared by Mary, who always accompanied him to Darwin.

When Yirawala and Mary came to Darwin, a number of relations would come to visit him for a few days. Sometimes there were ten people to be catered for. Occasionally I would object, and Yirawala would say, 'Him all relations, family for you. You look after him properly.'

From time to time corroborees were held in the back yard. If visitors brought alcohol and quarrels broke out (and, once a spear fight) Yirawala relied on me to intervene and take the trouble makers out to Bagot Settlement.

When Yirawala finished work and was paid, he and Mary would go shopping for such things as Erinmore tobacco, axes, blankets, knives, clothing and kitchenware. Mary, a pretty

* During the twelve years in which Yirawala and his family came to visit me in Darwin, I paid for airfares, food and accommodation. Payment to him for his paintings was quite separate.

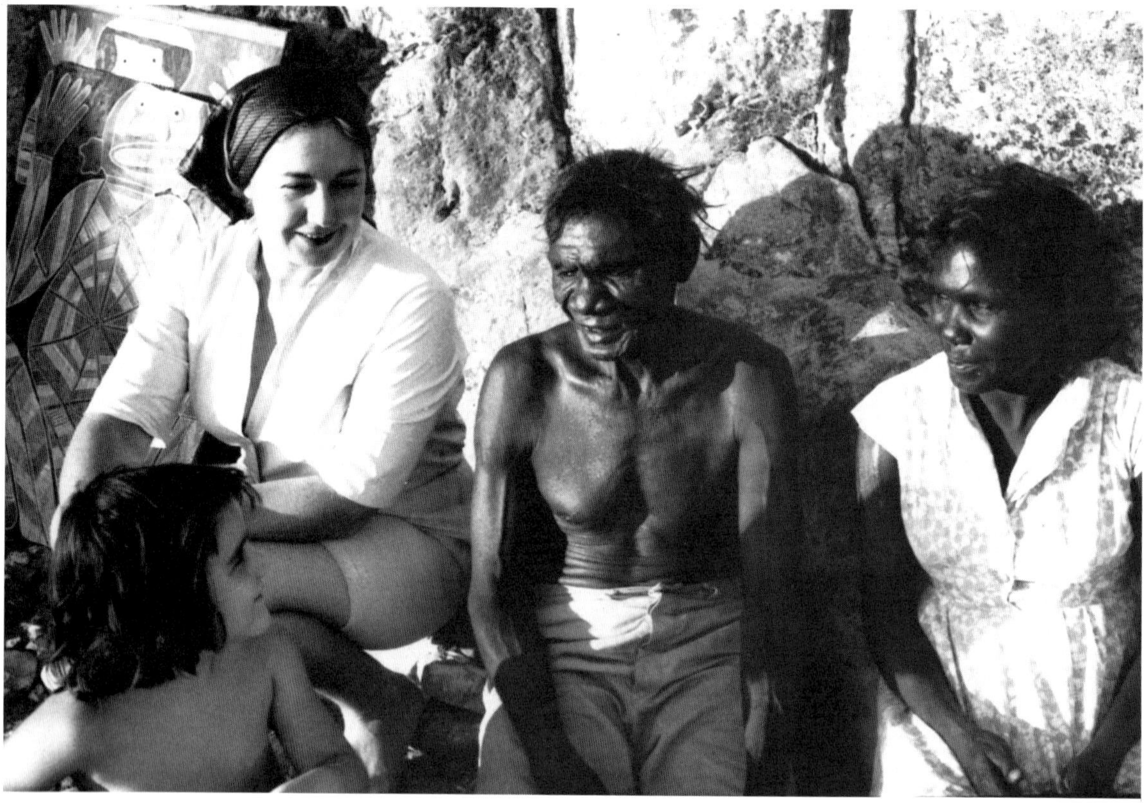

Yirawala and Mary Malilba would come to Darwin and stay at my house. Over the years a strong bond was established between our families. He classed us as relations and gave us our kinship terms. He used a nephew term for me, and called my daughter Amanda his little granny. Left to right: Amanda (aged four), myself, Yirawala and Mary, on Mindil Beach, Darwin.

woman, would buy items of personal adornment such as a red dress, scarves, toiletries and scented Macassar oil. Yirawala grumbled but denied her nothing. They always tried to be one jump ahead of the Aboriginal friends who came for his money.

There were some problems of Yirawala's relatives demanding money from him, which according to kinship rules he could not refuse. When this became excessive he used to leave his wallet with me.

One day I had taken Yirawala and Mary to the plane and came home to find five Aboriginal men running round the back yard looking for Yirawala. They couldn't believe he had gone; they looked behind bushes, under my house and even climbed the mango tree to see if he was hidden there.

Sometimes he brought his son Danny to play with my son Clinton. 'Little boy him play — all same family,' he said.

He was very fond of my daughter, Amanda, and spent a lot of time explaining the names of various birds to her. He would point to an overhead branch and say, 'You see him, black bird, him messenger for thunder man. You listen, when his sing out all time, big storm coming. Him tell you.'

In classificatory kinship terminology he called her his little granny.

At the age of four she was learning ballet and invited Mary and Yirawala to watch her dance. They sat expectantly in the lounge room as she came tripping in, wearing pink ballet shoes and a blue tutu, to the sound of the *Swan Lake* ballet suite. Yirawala was quite overcome and burst into tears.

When Amanda grew older, Mary taught her some Aboriginal dances. Yirawala said they helped to 'grow her up'.

Over the years a strong emotional bond was established between Yirawala's family and

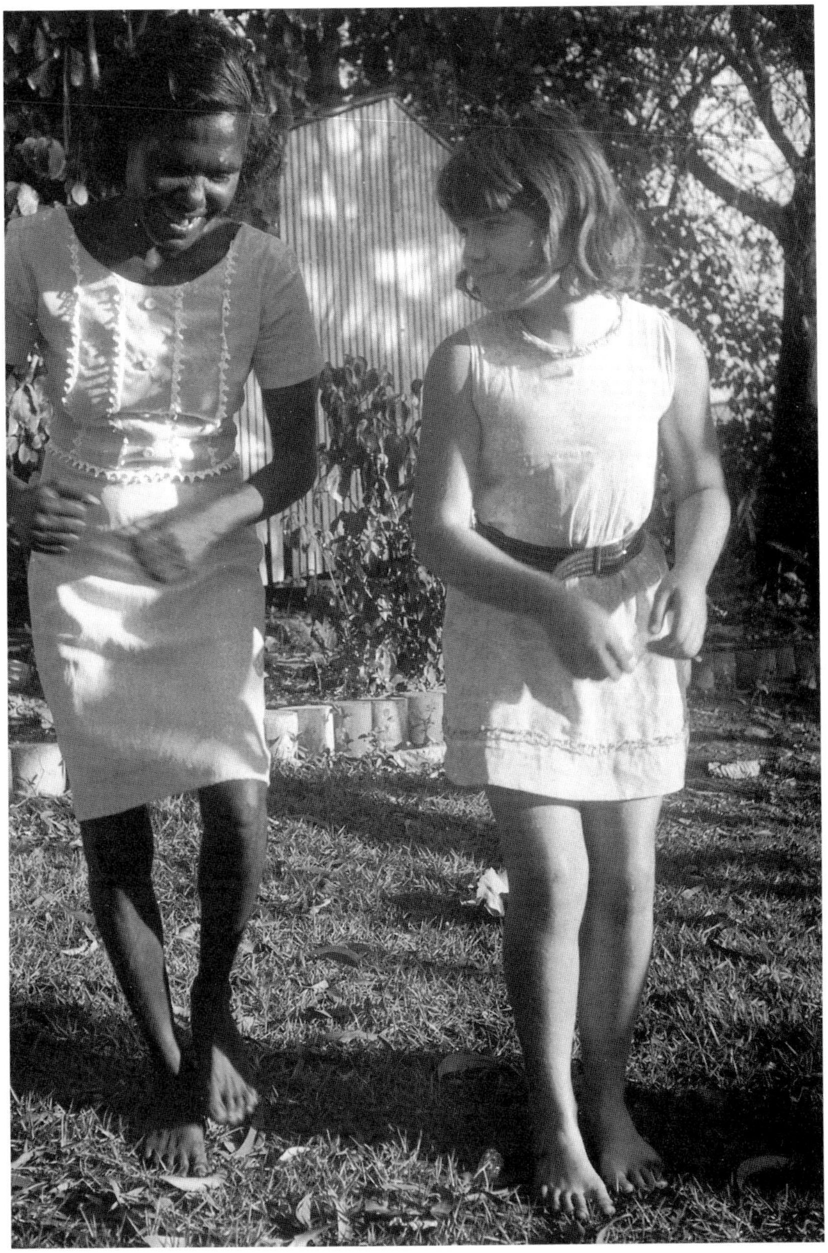

When Amanda grew older, Mary Malilba taught her some Aboriginal dances. Yirawala said they helped to 'grow her up'.

mine. He classed us as relations and gave us our kinship terms. Cecil was Dua moiety and I was Jiritja. He used a nephew term for me and called himself my uncle. We all had responsibilities to each other and I was often called upon to visit family members in hospital, engage legal representatives and pay fines. I would advise and assist them whenever they requested it.

I also assisted Yirawala's friends and relations with legal matters and disputes with local white people. Once an old Tiwi man came up the path dragging a crocodile skin. He said there was another skin with a local skin dealer, for which he had been paid only a small amount. I went with him to argue and obtain a better price. The skin merchant bought the second skin for the going rate, which was small enough. The old Tiwi man grinned and gave me some crocodile teeth.

Through publicity about my museum and articles in the local paper about Yirawala, he was becoming known as an important painter. I also sent reports about him and his work to the AIAS and to various academics. All this caught the attention of the art dealers, who swung in his direction, so that it became increasingly difficult for me to purchase his paintings for my museum. The dealers would approach the Croker Island Mission craft store, and the paintings would be sold. Yirawala had no say in the matter. I wrote to Lazarus, who said there was little he could do to help.

In 1967 Aborigines became legally entitled to be classed as citizens of Australia, the result of a national referendum which voted for changes to the Constitution, giving the Federal Government power to legislate for Aborigines in all States and Territories of Australia and to include Aborigines in official census figures. A Minister for Aboriginal Affairs was appointed, as was an Advisory Council of three to advise the Government on policies for Aborigines.

Aboriginal people were now entitled to vote, but citizenship did not give recognition to tribal marriages and laws of inheritance. Such recognition would have challenged the white status quo. And, as prescribed designs, carvings and sacred objects were the means by which the religion was perpetuated, and were inseparable from clan ownership of the land, it suited the powers that be to class that inheritance as simply craft or art. It suited the Federal Government, who had other plans for the land, the missions, who wanted to make Christians of the Aborigines, and the dealers, who wished to exploit the art and artifacts.

The Reverend Jack Goodluck left Croker Island and it became increasingly difficult to contact Yirawala.

News from Lazarus Lami-Lami was not encouraging. He said that Yirawala's paintings were going to the mission craft store. Lazarus now had no control over the buying and selling. He simply sorted and sprayed the barks.

The demand for Aboriginal art and artifacts increased as the years went by and big exhibitions interstate and overseas were held. Local and overseas exhibitors were applauded for popularising Aboriginal art and craft and assisting them economically.

Significant collections left Australia and were sold overseas. At that time the carvings, objects, paintings and artifacts were of ceremonial significance and were an incalculable loss to Australia.

There existed a Northern Territory Historical Objects Ordinance to protect sacred objects and important paintings, but it seemed to be rarely enforced.

Lazarus wrote in March 1967 to say that with the arrival of the new superintendent he no longer had any authority in the craft store, but he would try to have some barks and spears sent to me. He said that Yirawala was well and was painting for the mission.

In May I received a parcel sent by Lazarus, which contained weapons and three Yirawala paintings.

In June I was able to buy four Yirawala paintings in a local souvenir shop. Two of these were Maraian and were added to my museum display. I was particularly concerned about the Maraian story. I had a few pieces, or 'pages', but there were many gaps. I wanted to make at least one religious record for posterity.

I continued with my research work for the AIAS.

In September Lazarus wrote to say that Yirawala had been to the mainland and had come back in a very bad temper, so was therefore unapproachable for now. Lazarus enclosed a strange little medallion with a sailing ship incised on it, something that had been washed up on a distant beach. He said it was a gift for me.

On 26 December Lazarus wrote again to say that Yirawala wanted to come to Darwin with Mary and work for my museum in January. I would need to send plane tickets. He told me the happy tidings that his wife was expecting another baby, and everyone was well and happy. He expressed his sadness to hear that my husband would soon be leaving Darwin.

Lazarus's next letter informed me that Yirawala would not be coming to Darwin, as he was having family problems. When he sorted them out he would come in with his second wife, Margaret, and their little son, Andrew. Lazarus thanked me for congratulating him on being awarded the MBE.

I wrote to the Superintendent at Croker Island about purchasing some bark paintings from Yirawala. I received a reply to say that nothing was available and they had many outstanding orders to be fulfilled.

In June 1968 I combined with the Darwin Historical Society display and set up my museum in Holtze Cottage, in the Darwin Botanical Gardens. A small admission was charged, which was shared. Holtze Cottage was more secure than my house but had no flywire. All sorts of insects made nests in the exhibits. The wasps preferred the bark paintings, and borers the carvings. A goanna had nested in a hollow log.

I did meet some interesting visitors but finally had to take the collection home and have it fumigated because of insect damage.

I set it up again at home, and changed the name to The Yirawala Museum.

On 14 July Yirawala and Mary came to Darwin, after I had sent plane tickets on request. He apologised for not coming in sooner. I knew he could not help it.

Yirawala had a bad cough and complained of sore eyes and feeling tired, so I took him to see a local GP, who prescribed cough medicine, aspirin and vitamin B tablets. We then visited an eye specialist, who prescribed reading glasses and eye drops and told Yirawala that he had a bad cataract in the right eye which should be operated on as soon as possible. Yirawala sat patiently through the ordeal of drops, bright lights and eye tests. He thanked the doctor, saying 'Nobody cut my eye. Him little bit no good, but can see alright.'

The glasses gave him a headache so he gave them to an old Tiwi man, who lost them in a card game. He liked the vitamin B, however, saying 'Good medicine, alright. Make me walk about.' Mary made sure he took a tablet every day.

In the course of Yirawala's visits to my home he became a close friend of Ali Miller Mungatopi, a painter of religious designs, a great dancer, singer and a leader of the Tiwi people of Melville Island.* Ali had been classed as my father and had named me Tipalamow. Ali was a happy, charismatic man, a famous story teller, with a ready wit and sense of humour, who cheered and delighted Yirawala.

In 1968 Ali's health deteriorated. He told us that he was spitting black blood. I noticed that at meal times he could not eat much. The Darwin hospital began a series of tests and admitted him to a ward. In August Ali's wife Polly came to stay with me, and with Yirawala we visited him every day. Polly said she thought Ali had strained himself when he worked at the Snake Bay timber mill on Melville Island. He and other Aboriginal workers lifted heavy logs without the use of a timber jack.

One afternoon at the hospital Ali managed the ghost of a smile, and whispered that they were sending him home the next day. He would be taken to the medical plane in an ambulance. He had heard the nurse say to the sister, 'What about him in there?' The sister had replied, 'Oh, we might as well send him home to his family.' Yirawala held his hand and tried to comfort him.

Three days after Ali went home to Snake Bay, we received a telegram from Polly to say he had passed away. I went to tell Yirawala the sad news. He put down his brush and went inside his hut to mourn.

That night I was awakened by a thrashing of branches in the tree outside my window. I did not investigate. Half asleep, I imagined that a turkey or goose had escaped from somebody's yard.

* Ali and his wife Polly (Paianamaioo) were my dear friends and informants for some years, interpreting the Tiwi ceremonial life and religion from tapes and film that I recorded for the AIAS. They also greatly assisted me to collect and preserve the Holmes Tiwi collection, now in the Darwin Museum.

In the morning I took Yirawala his breakfast and found him packing his case and rolling his swag. He said, 'You hear him last night, big bird him come? Him sit on my bed, sing out, then fly. Dead man come back, sorry for we. That his spirit. I go home.'

I reminded him that as a medicine man he had the power to send the spirit back to its own country. He agreed to make strong 'business', so we went into the bush to cut bundles of ironwood leaves for the singing.

Yirawala made smoke fires round the house and hut, walking through the heavy acrid smoke, gesturing with burning bunches of leaves to the four corners. The archaic chanting bade the spirit to go home and be at peace, and that it must not worry the living.

After the ritual Yirawala said the spirit had gone home but would only be at peace when the Pukamani mortuary ceremony was performed.

A few days later Polly came to mourn with me and my family. She sang amparoo songs of the Pukamani mortuary ceremony in and around the house for three days, then she returned to Snake Bay.

Over the next few days Tiwi classified relatives called in to mourn with us.

Yirawala and Mary went home soon after. He said he would come back to finish the work at a later date.

The AIAS asked me to film and record Ali Miller Mungatopi's Pukamani ceremony to be held in September.

Many large, beautifully carved and painted Pukamani poles stood in rows near Ali's house. Many painted and plumed male and female mourners sang and danced the beautiful story of Pukamani, the genesis of the Tiwi people. At that time the Tiwi people of Melville Island were strong in their own religion. A death was believed to be like a waning moon, then like a full moon the dead would live again forever in a spirit land. The performance of the Pukamani ceremony guaranteed life after death.

Ali's Pukamani was performed in full, according to ancient tradition, for he was a 'big' man and greatly revered.

In January 1969 word was sent to me that Yirawala wanted to buy a boat. He wanted a few hundred dollars. He would make some paintings for me when he next came to Darwin. I wrote and told him this was acceptable to me.

Four months passed, and I had heard nothing from Yirawala, so I applied for a permit to go out and see him. The permit was issued in June.

He was glad to see me and said that he had just finished painting three ceremonies for my museum: all the remainder of the Maraian series, plus the Lorrgon and Ubar ceremonies. He had told the craft manager to send them to me in Darwin.

The manager had listed the paintings and priced them. I was given the account and Lazarus began packing them up, with my name on the parcels. I explained to the craft manager that I would send a cheque from Darwin as soon as I had obtained another bank overdraft. This would not be a problem. The manager said he would send the barks on the next plane. Yirawala was happy and said I must send extra money for him as well as paying the mission.

On 13 July Lazarus wrote to tell me that when the superintendent returned from holidays Yirawala's paintings were sold to a dealer who came soon after I left. Lazarus said he tried to intervene but had been overruled. He said he was sick for two weeks afterwards. The craft manager also wrote to apologise to me for good faith broken.

Yirawala failed in his efforts to have some say in the fate of his paintings, as no painter was allowed to influence marketing arrangements.

In August 1969 Bobby Joran came to Darwin with his wife and children for a holiday at my house. He said his father was very upset about the loss of the paintings he had made for my museum, and that Yirawala wanted tickets sent out on the plane for himself and Mary.

At Darwin airport we waited for the passengers to file off the plane. I could not see Yirawala and thought he had not come, until Mandy pointed excitedly, 'There he is at the back. I can see his hat.'

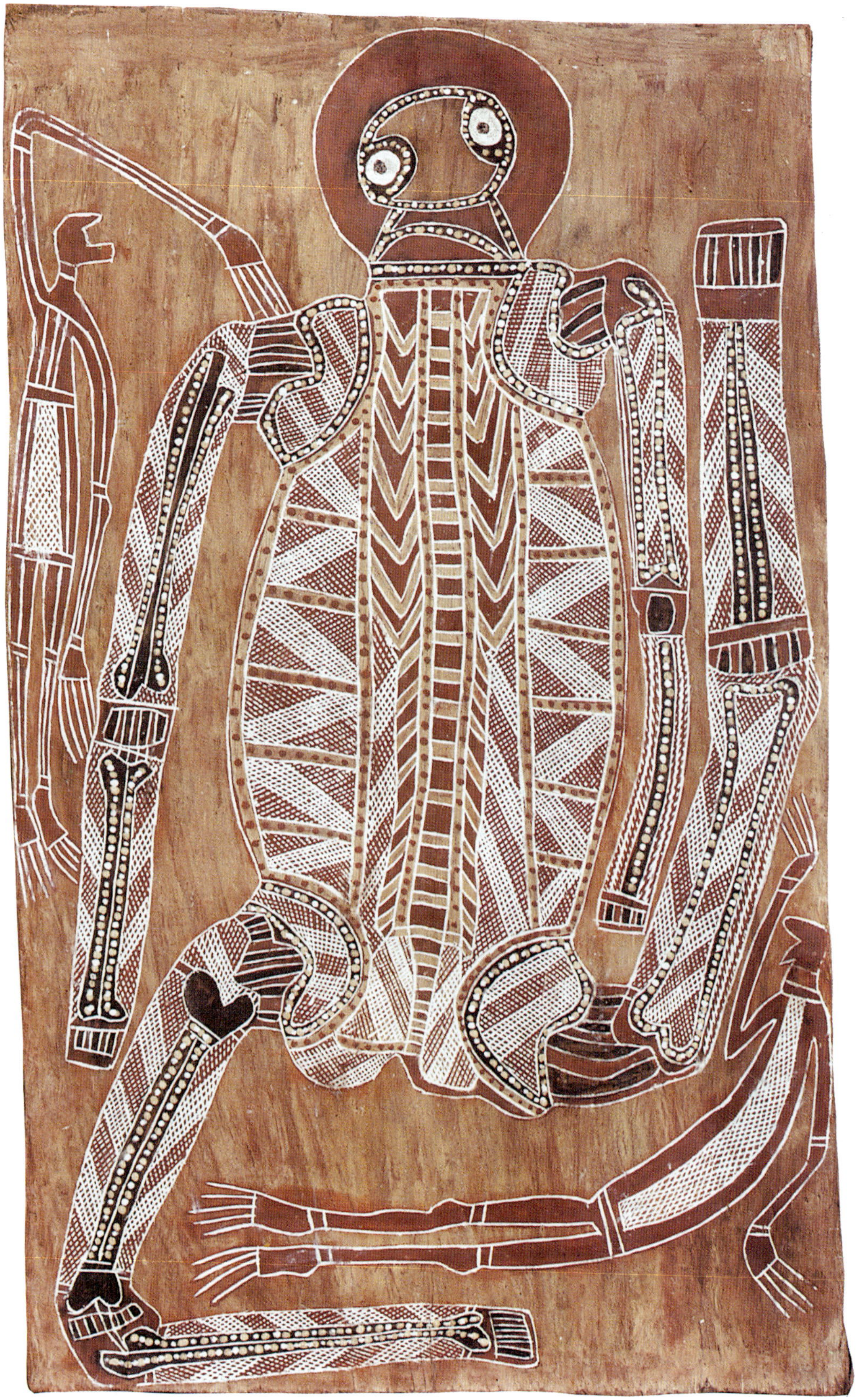

Plate 10 MARAIAN SERIES

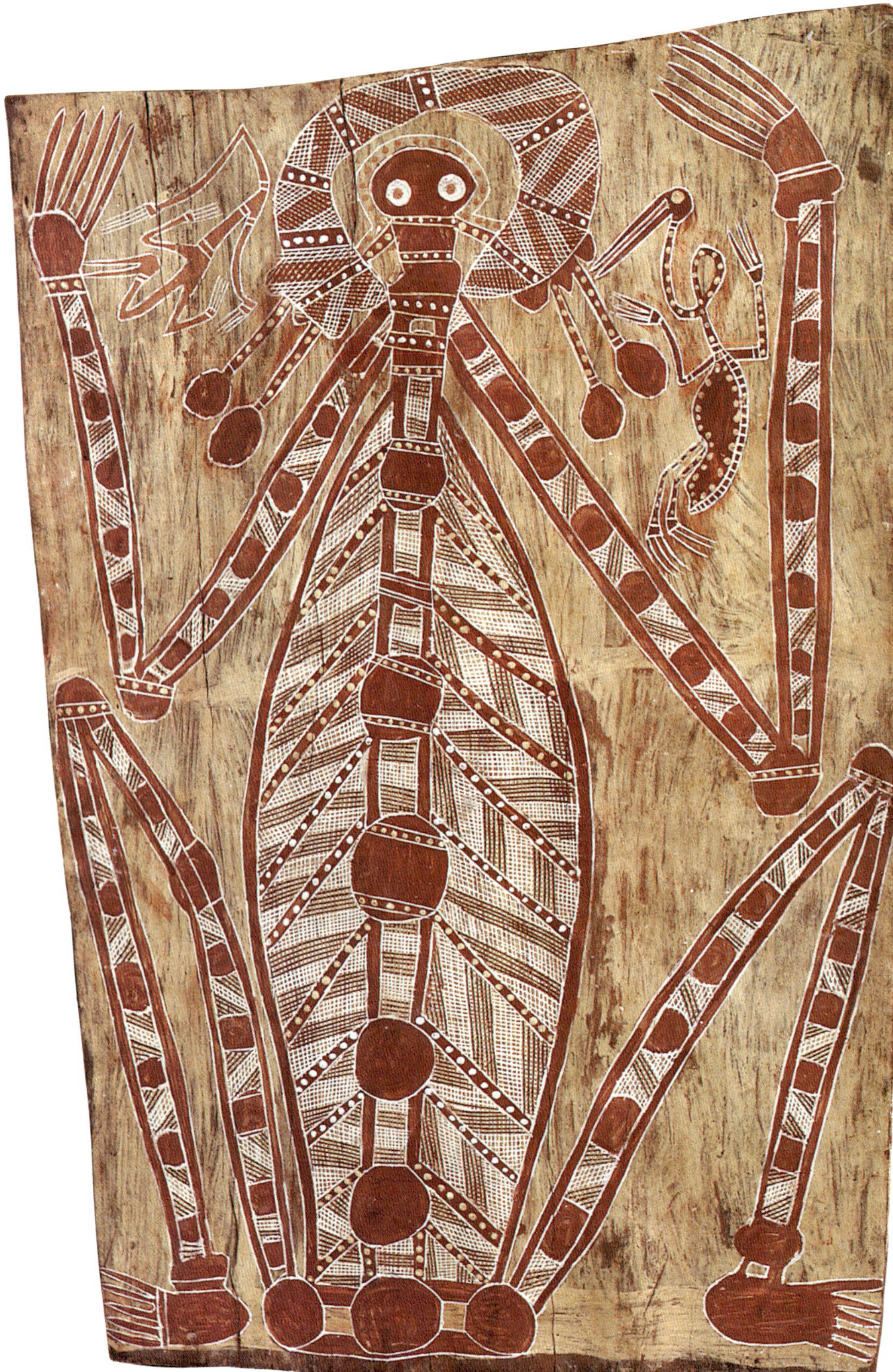

Plate 11 MARAIAN SERIES

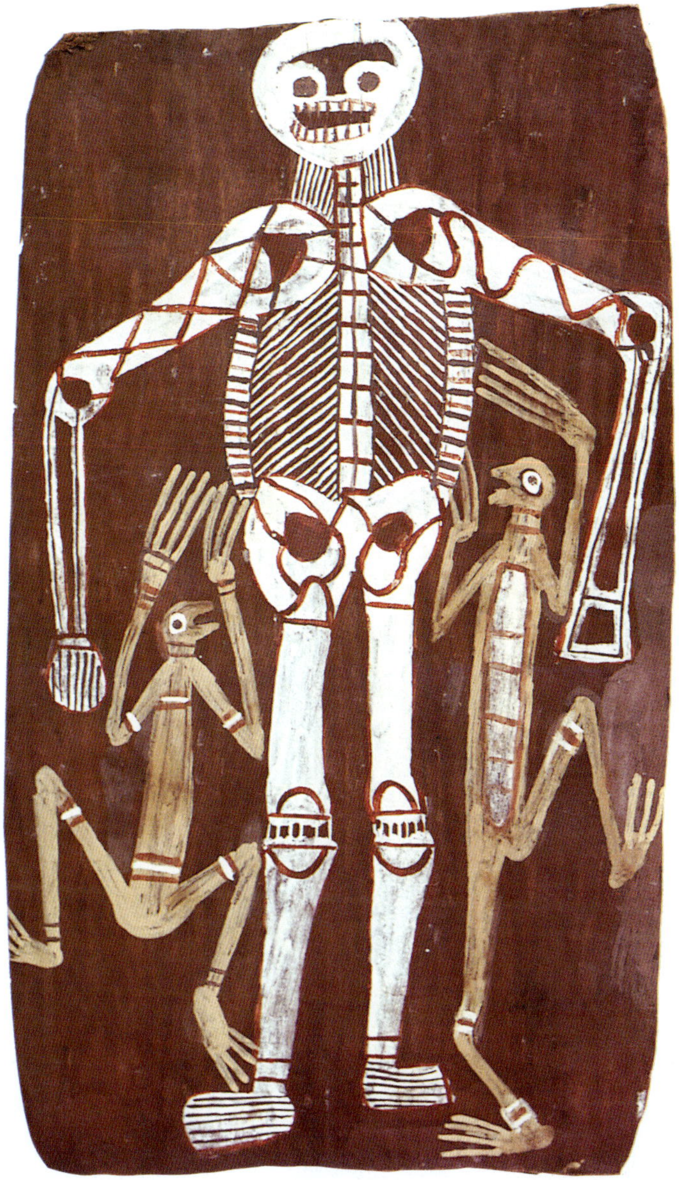

Plate 12 MARAIAN SERIES

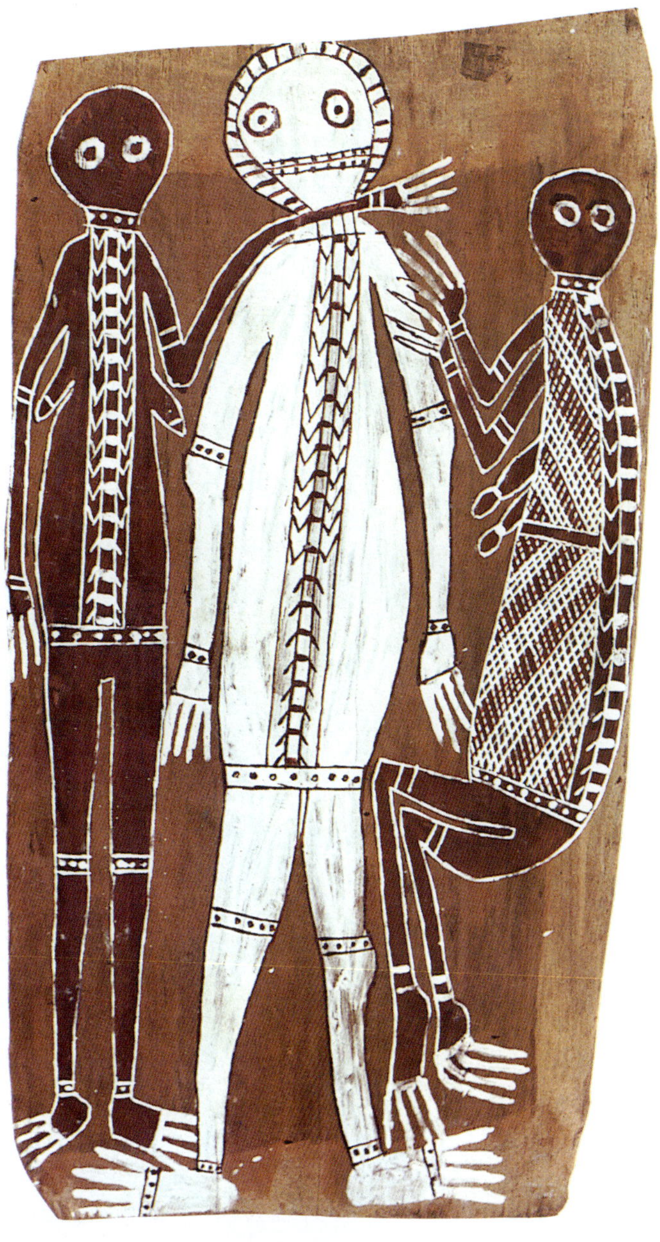

Plate 13 MARAIAN SERIES

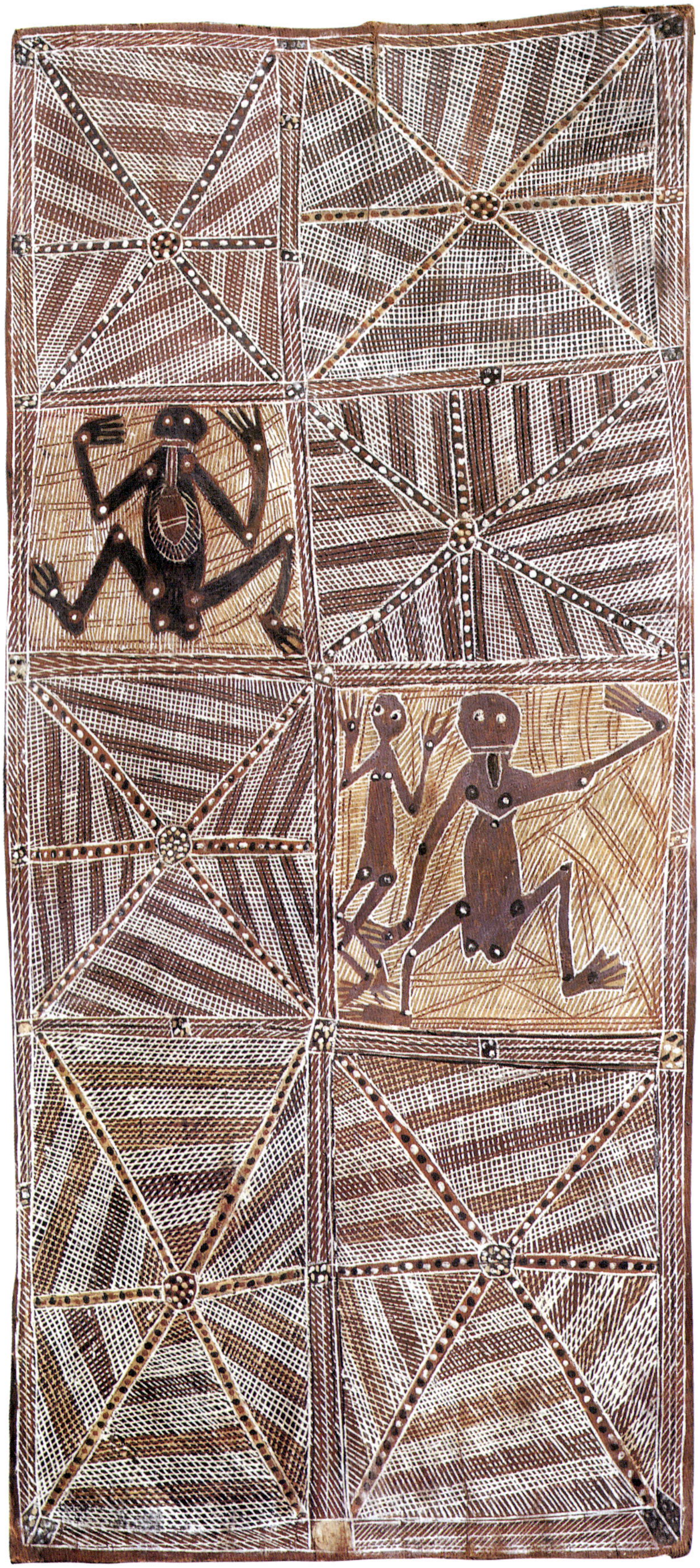

Plate 14 MARAIAN SERIES

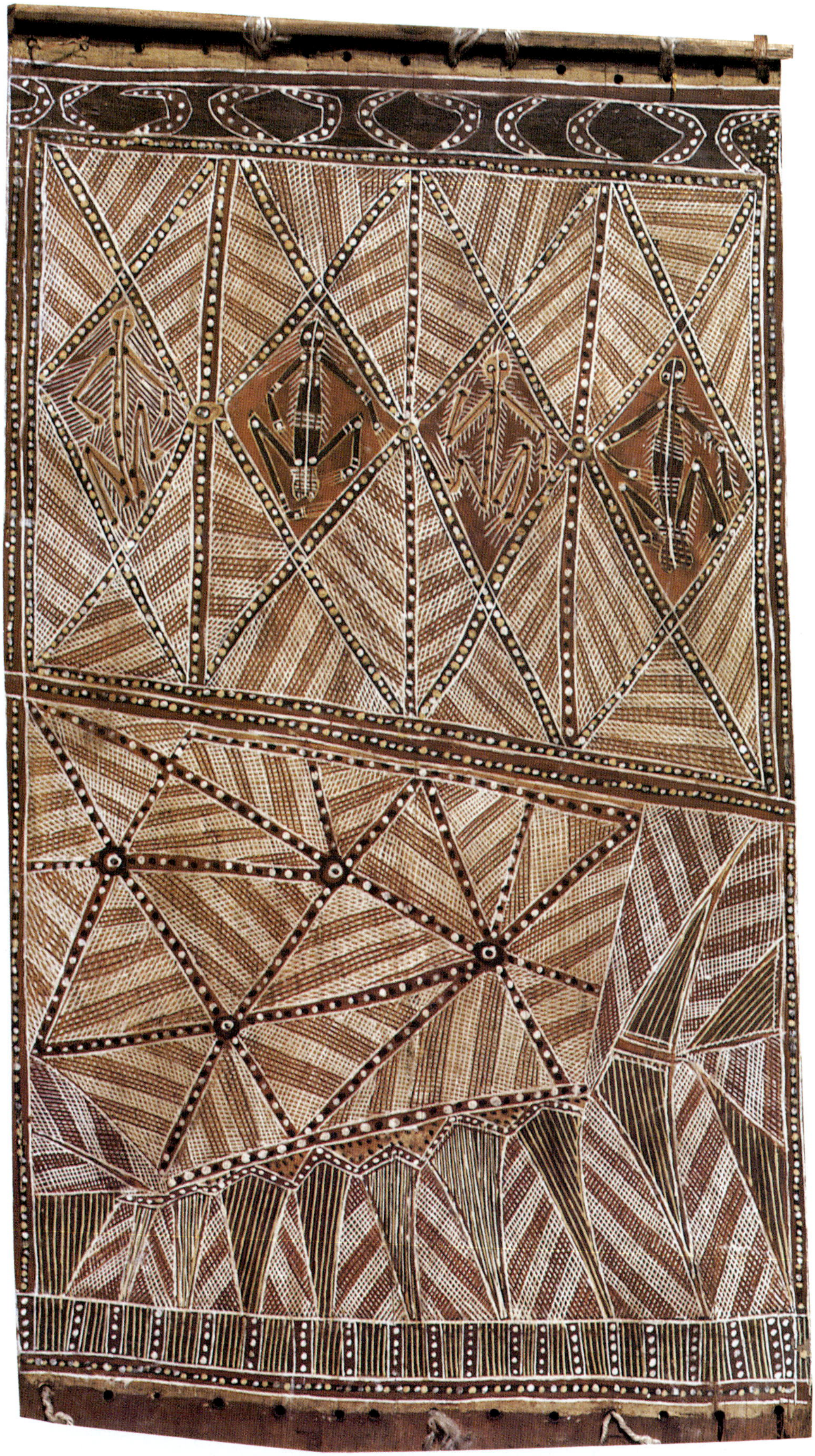

Plate 15 MARAIAN SERIES

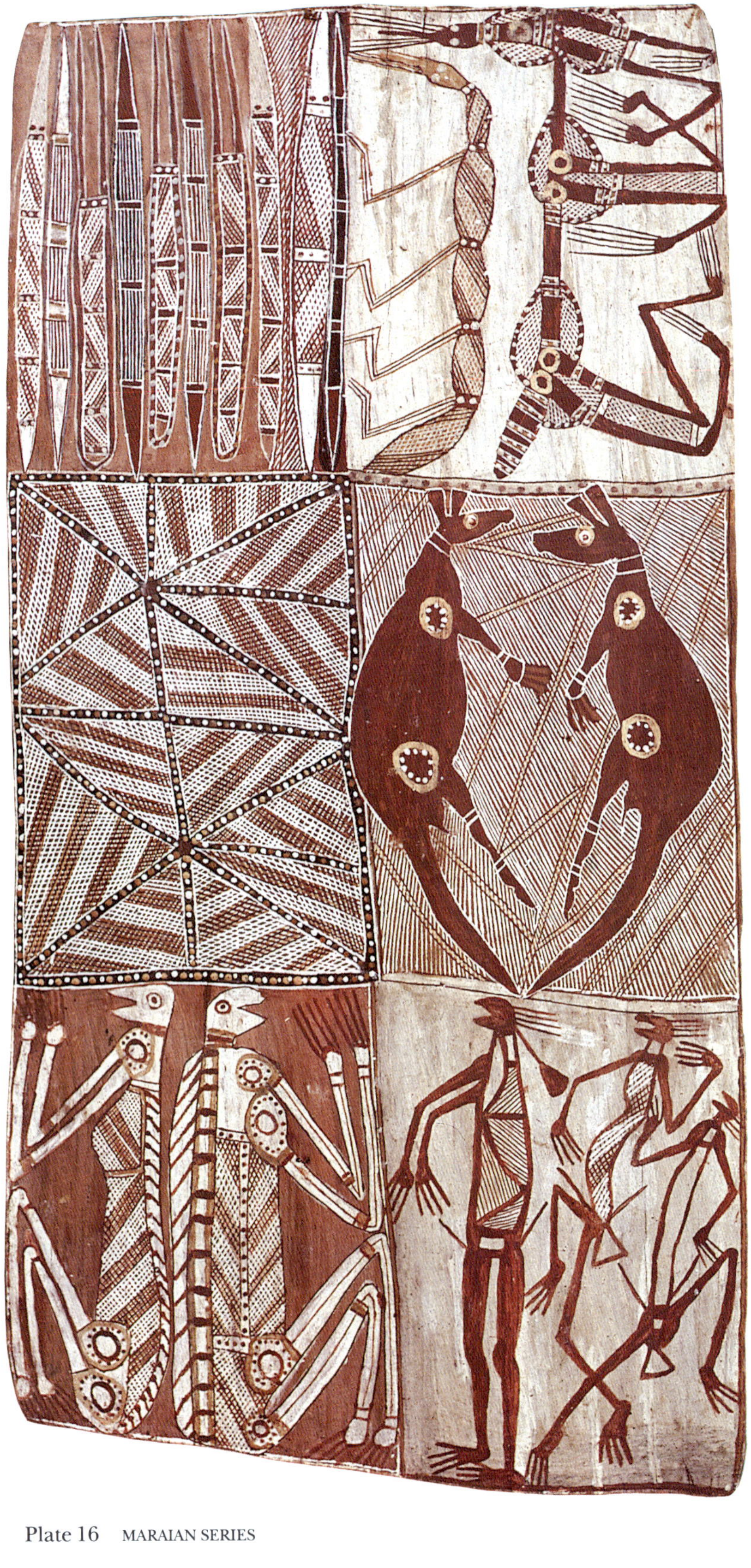

Plate 16 MARAIAN SERIES

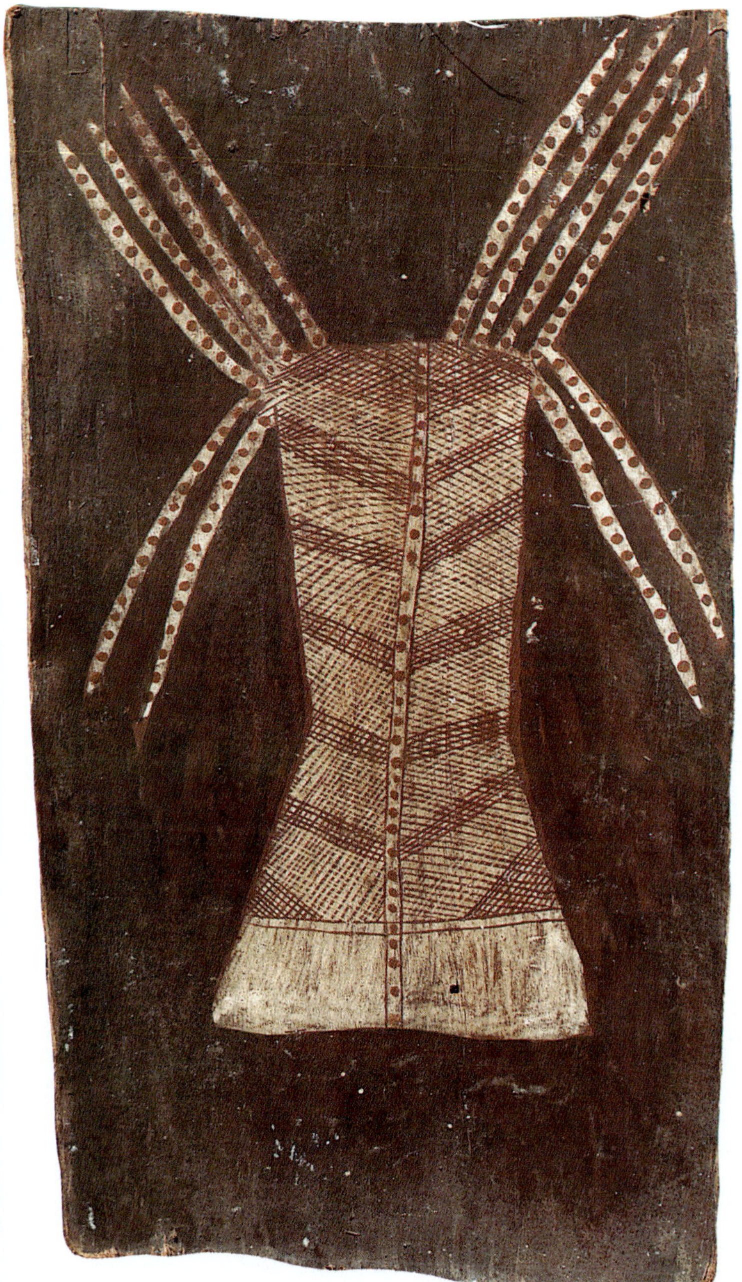

Plate 17 MARAIAN SERIES

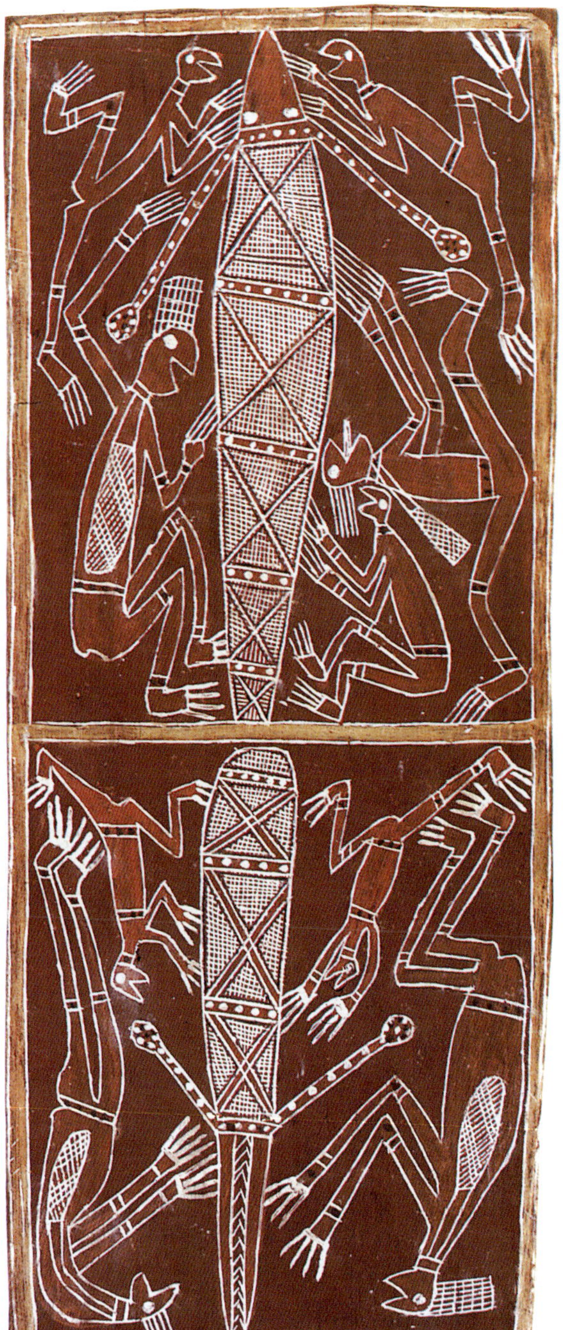

Plate 18 MARAIAN SERIES

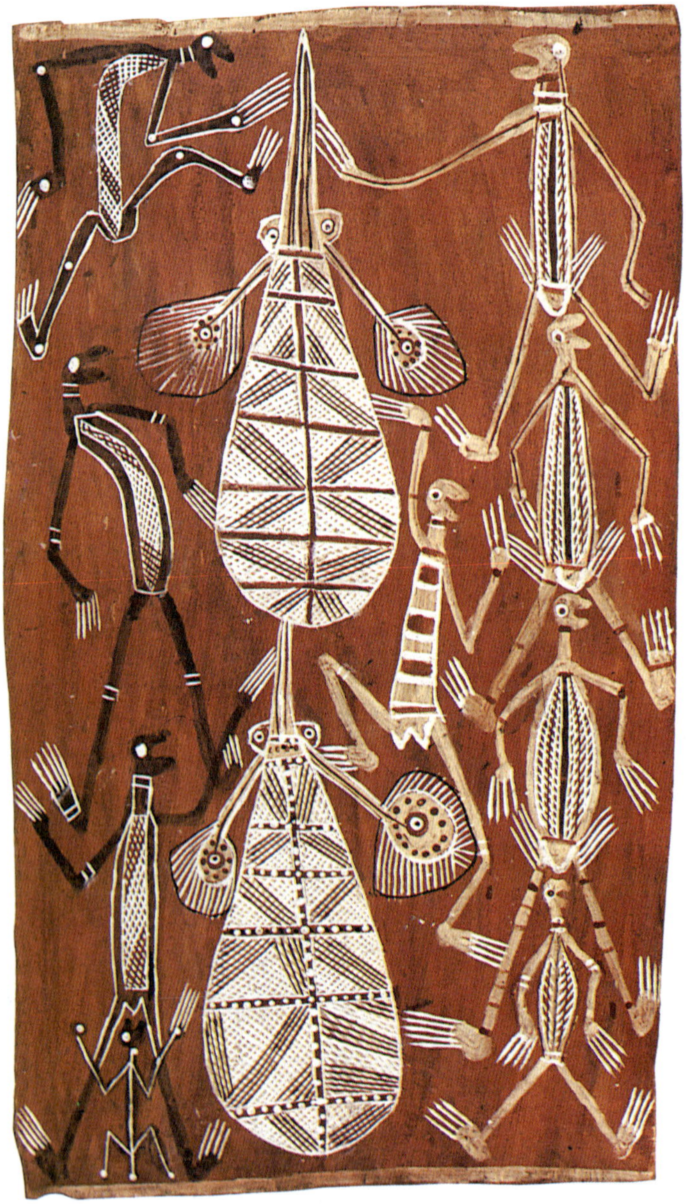

Plate 19 MARAIAN SERIES

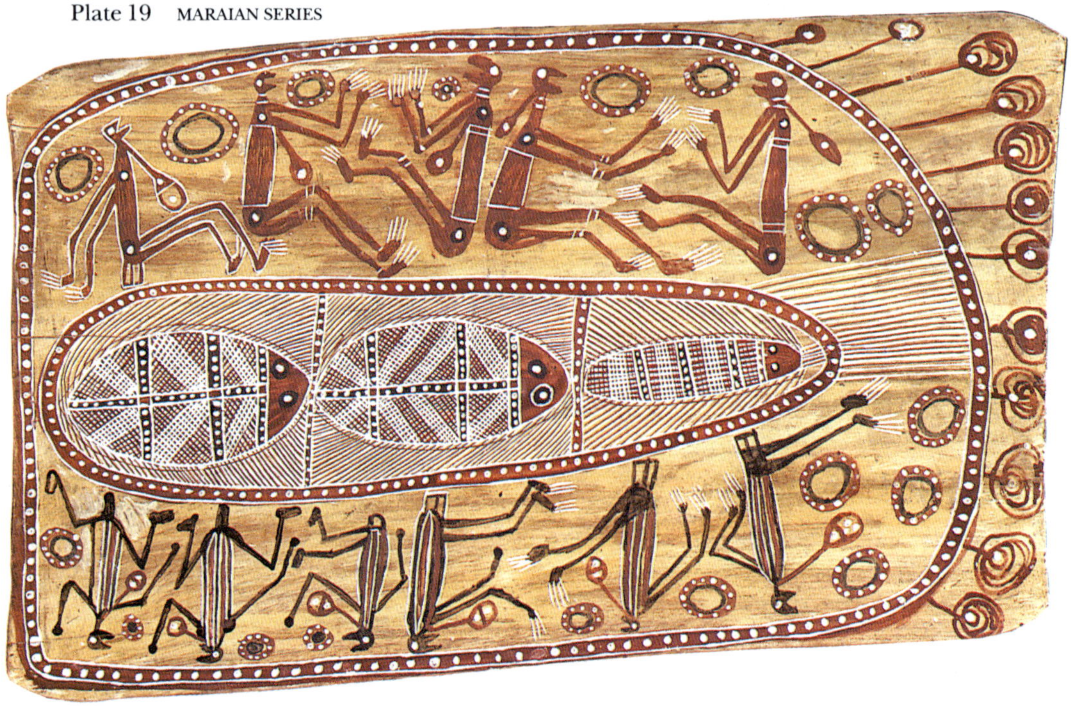

Plate 20 MARAIAN SERIES

Yirawala and Mary kissed Mandy and me, but he was subdued, saying little on the drive home.

Mary had brought my daughter a pretty dilly bag that she had made and a large basket for me, a gift from Margaret.

After lunch, Yirawala jumped to his feet and slapped on his old bush hat, saying, 'Quick, we go mission house. My clean bark, all there. I been sendim on mission barge.'

At the mission headquarters the office girl consulted the bill of lading and said, no, nothing had come in for Yirawala. I asked her to recheck the list. While we were talking, Yirawala ran from the room into the big warehouse. A few minutes later I heard a triumphant cry. 'My bark, him here. I findim parcel.' He was smiling happily as he held the big brown-paper parcel of unpainted sheets of bark.

We were about to leave when we were stopped by an employee, who demanded to look inside the parcel to see if Yirawala had smuggled in any of his own paintings. The blank sheets of bark were strewn on the floor. Seeing no paintings, the white man grunted and walked away. Trembling with outrage, Yirawala picked up the pieces of bark. 'Nobody put me over. I make properly good painting for you.' We carried the bark to my vehicle.

At home we contacted Philip Roberts (Waipuldunja) and Davis Daniels of the Aboriginal Rights Council. They said, Yirawala, like any other citizen, should have a say in his own affairs; such treatment of Aborigines was a denial of human rights. They suggested we contact Dick Ward, a local lawyer and Member of the Legislative Council. He had often taken the MLCs to task concerning the treatment of Aborigines.

After listening to Yirawala's complaints, Mr Ward said that the best approach concerning Yirawala's paintings might be to have a legal contract between him and me, giving me first right of refusal to his works. If I did not want to buy certain paintings of Yirawala's or could not meet his prices, then he would be free to offer them elsewhere.

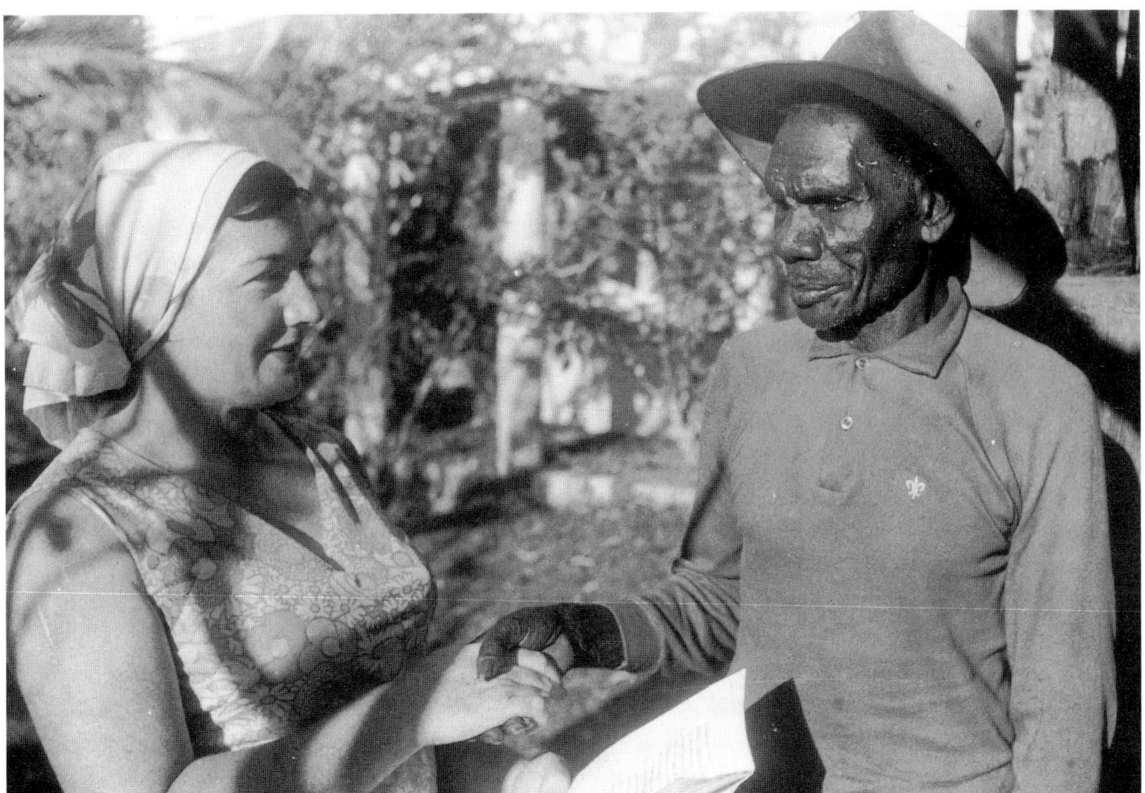

Yirawala and I shake hands after signing the contract that allowed me first option on the purchase of his paintings, Darwin, August 1969.

On 7 August 1969, a Deed was drawn up between Yirawala and me. It required Yirawala to give me first offer of his bark paintings in an attempt to complete a collection of a ceremonial series relating to certain Aboriginal ceremonies. It affirmed that Yirawala was desirous of producing bark paintings and artifacts for such a collection, and that purchase price for each bark painting and artifact was to be agreed upon between Yirawala and me. If within seven days no agreement had been reached between us, then the price would be fixed by the solicitor, upon application by either party. If the prices so fixed were not acceptable to me, then Yirawala would be free to offer his paintings elsewhere.

Another clause in the Deed stated that if at any time Yirawala was prevented from sending his paintings or artifacts to me, or was prevented from leaving Croker Island, or if at any time paintings and artifacts produced by him were seized by any person whatsoever, or taken from his control or custody without his permission or mine, then Yirawala must inform me within twenty-four hours. I would then use my best endeavours to help Yirawala and where possible join with him in taking action against the person or persons or body responsible for the happening of such event or events.

These were the main clauses in the Deed which was registered in the Supreme Court in Darwin.

The interpreters for Yirawala were Philip Roberts and Bobby Joran.

Yirawala was pleased and said nobody could interfere now with his right to market his paintings and artifacts as he chose.

After the Deed had been interpreted, signed and witnessed we went to see Jim Bowditch of the *Northern Territory News.* He shook hands with Yirawala and offered us a beer in his rather ramshackle office. 'Good on you, mate,' he said.

On 16 August an article appeared in the *N T News* under the heading, 'Painter Takes an Independent Course'.

Yirawala was the first Aboriginal painter to take an independent course. A courageous step in those days. He knew it would infuriate other parties but he was unafraid, determined to exercise his rights as a citizen of Australia.

He was satisfied with the Deed, but said he now wanted to talk to the lawyer about his family going back to their home country and making a small settlement there. He desperately wanted a full explanation of citizenship rights and whether it included land rights.

On their own land they would have freedom to determine their own future in their own way, but they would need financial help initially to establish their settlement. Fences would need to be built, huts, a school, a small health centre, a radio room and an airstrip. They would tame scrub cattle and buffalo, make gardens and catch fish.

When Yirawala spoke of these things his face lit up. One day they would all go home to Marugulidban.

In late August Yirawala and I went to see Dick Ward again. We sat near the green glass windows in Mr Ward's old tropical house as he explained citizenship rights to Yirawala, using simple language.

'You have the same rights as I have,' he said. Yirawala sipped tea from a porcelain cup and listened.

When Dick had finished, Yirawala spoke. 'Nobody told me true word 'bout citizen business. If we properly citizen like you, what about permit ask people come see me?' Yirawala was angry now. 'That my r'own house, we build him, me and son. We pay rent. What for?'

Dick explained that Yirawala lived on reserve land owned by the Crown and that the Mission had a long lease. There was also the problem of the permit system.

Yirawala sat in silence for a few minutes then asked if Dick received his letters in his hand. Dick said yes, that was every citizen's right and nobody could interfere with that; all letters were the Queen's mail and if anyone held them back they could go to jail for four years. 'That good law,' said Yirawala. He set down his cup and asked about land rights. Did the Government own Dick's land also? In reply Dick showed him his title deeds. Yirawala held the piece of parchment and tapped the red seal. 'What for this red mark?' There were more explanations. 'Ah, good strong mark alright.' Ever after that, when speaking about his land, Yirawala said he wanted the paper in the hand, with a red mark.

On a Saturday night we took Yirawala and Mary to see the film *2001: A Space Odyssey* at the Parap Theatre. When we sat down, Yirawala refused to remove his hat despite the remarks made by people behind us, who were weaving about like cobras, trying to see the screen.

Yirawala sat enthralled, ignoring offers of refreshments. After the film I asked him what he thought of it. He replied, 'Properly number one film. Man him fly to star, long time him go. Him die, go back to Dreaming.' He understood the deeper meaning of the film.

After ten days of rest, good food and medication, Yirawala wanted to get back to work. He would go next day to cut more bark.

Early Sunday morning he sharpened his axes and knives as Mary sat smoking her old black stub of a pipe which seemed to have sentimental value for her. I recalled the day a fierce skirmish erupted when a woman stole it from her. Mary realised the pipe was missing just as the woman was getting into a taxi. With a loud cry she ran down the path as the taxi began to move. Undeterred she hung onto the back bumper bar, calling out. The driver stopped and got out shouting, 'What's the bloody blue?' Mary wrenched open the back door and grabbed the pipe from the woman's bag. Yirawala had ignored it all.

In the forests 13 kilometres from Darwin city Mary helped Yirawala cut bark, swinging the axe like a man. She followed him as he walked amongst the tall trees, scanning the top branches for fresh looking leaves. If the leaves were dry looking he passed them by, for it meant the trees were not drawing much moisture and the bark would be hard to remove. When he selected a good tree he made a small cut and ripped off a sliver of bark to test its moisture content. When he cut the bark he did not ringbark the tree, but cut only a panel without penetrating the sapwood. His barks were always thin and light.

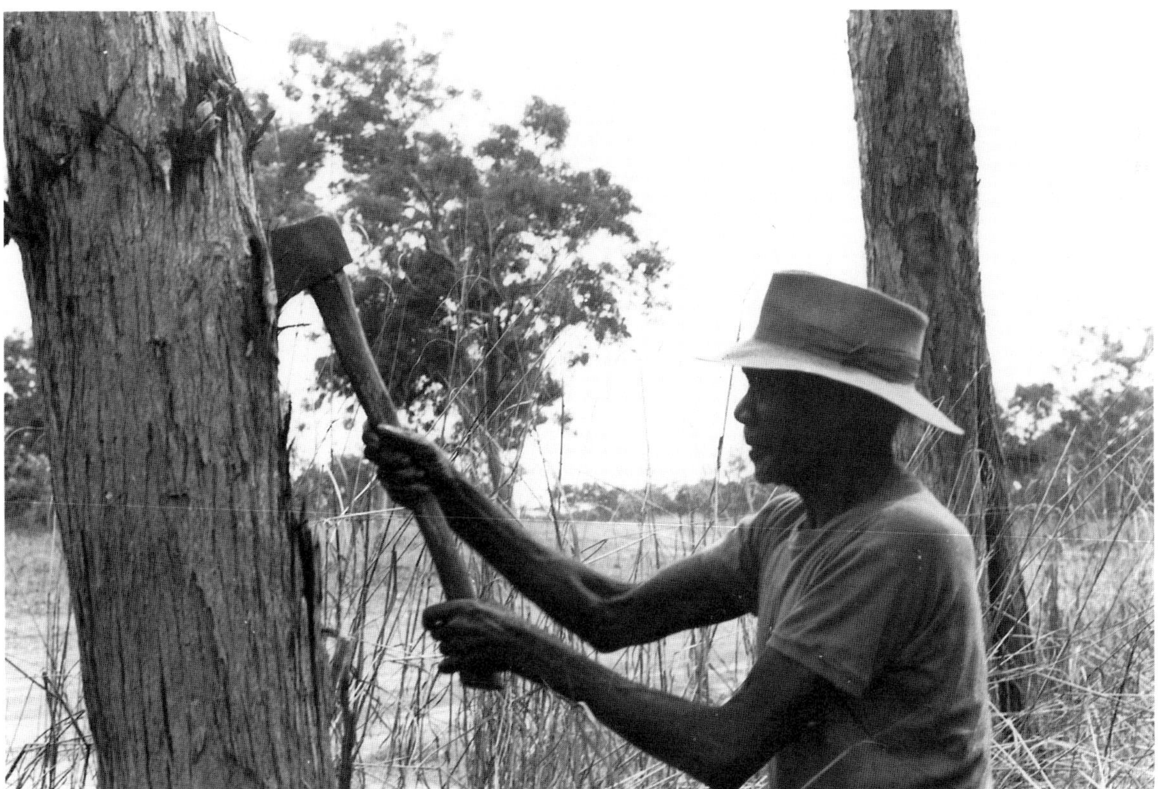

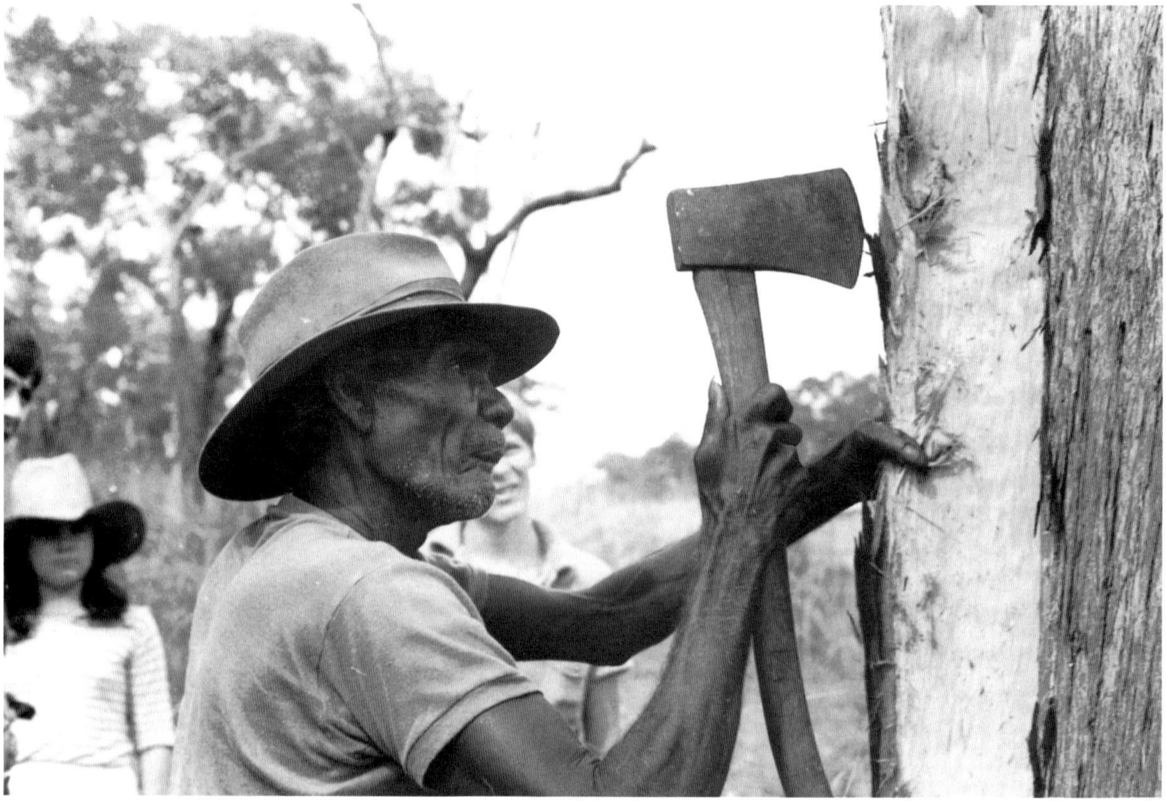

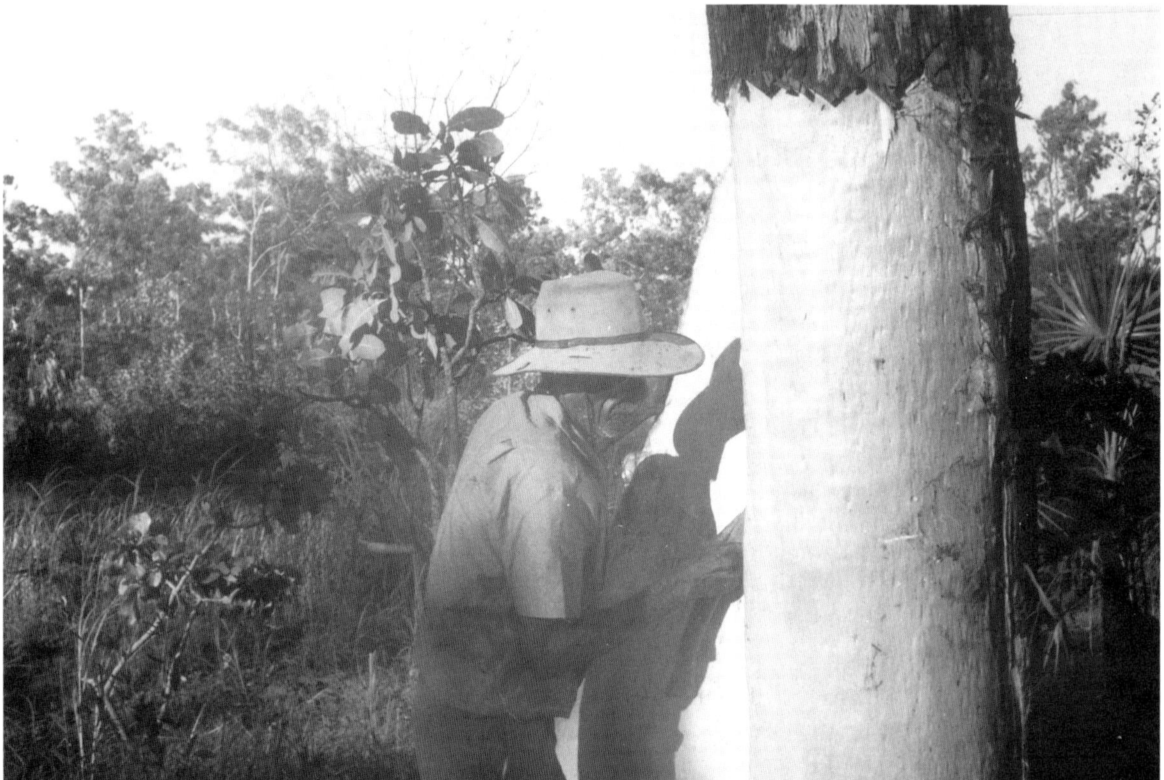

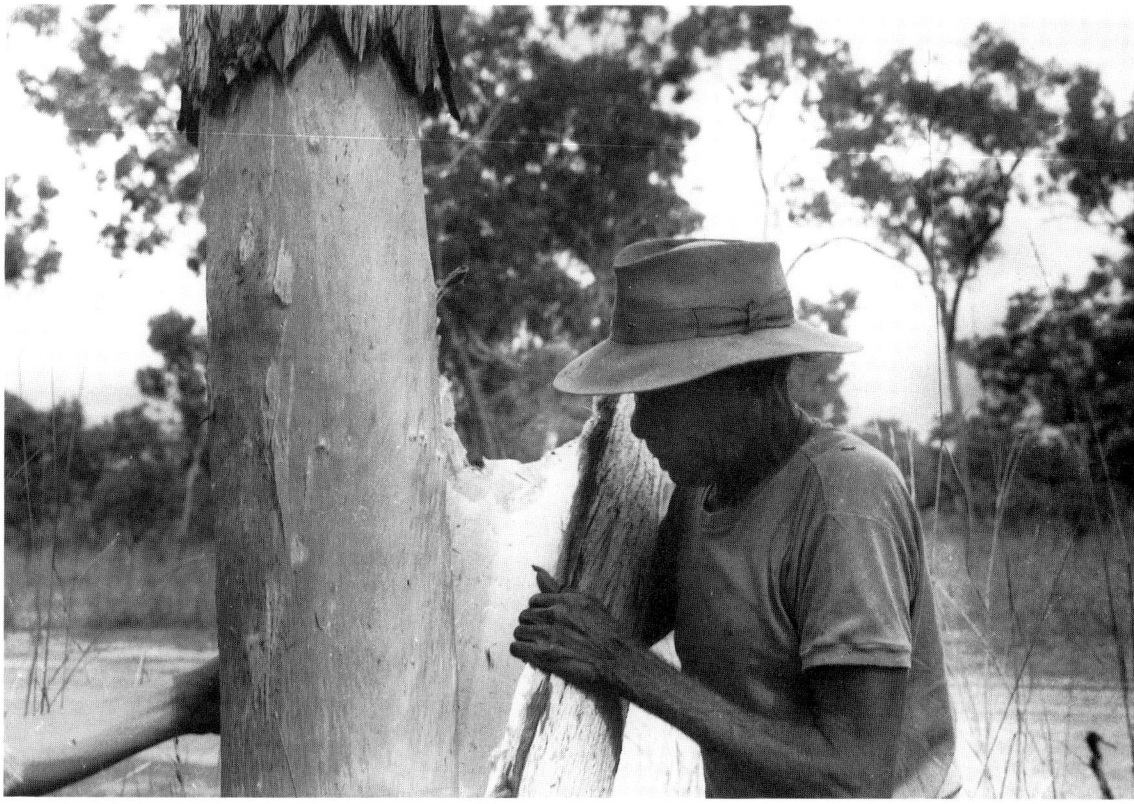

Yirawala would select his bark carefully, cutting only a panel from one side of the tree, without penetrating the sapwood (to do so would have killed the tree). Amanda sometimes helped to strip off the rough outer bark.

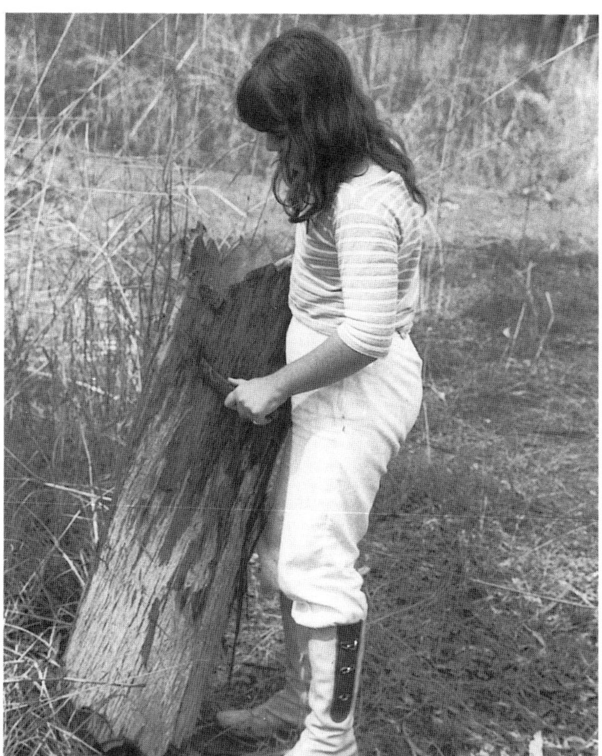

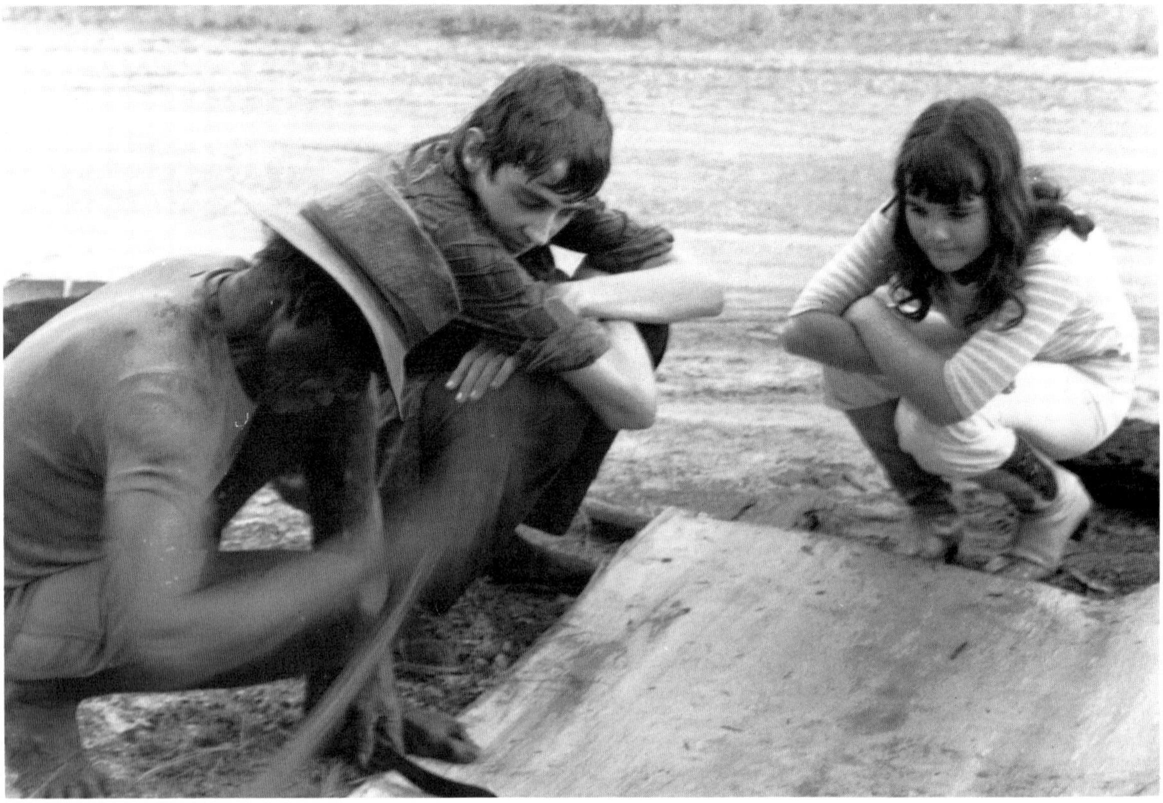

Yirawala cut the bark into sheets with a skinning knife, using an axe-head as a hammer (here he is watched by Clinton and Amanda). Later he would size the bark with bush orchid juice, after chewing the orchid to extract the sticky liquid.

My children and I helped Yirawala and Mary to strip off the rough outer bark, then the damp panels were laid flat on the ground ready for him to cut them into squares with his sharp skinning knife.

At home we spread the pieces of bark in the sun and weighted them with stones. Turning the barks and shifting the stones would cure them in three weeks. Yirawala said only 'rubbish painters' used green bark, which would curl and crack later on. Such painters were only greedy for money, he said.

He was happy with the day's work and would begin painting on the bark sheets he had sent to Darwin on the mission barge. The first painting would be from the start of the Maraian series. He would paint Lumahlumah, the big man who came from Indonesia way, bringing important ceremony and law for the early time people.

This was the beginning of his effort to save the most important Maraian paintings, the core of the religion. Little by little he would add another piece to make the series. He said over the years he had painted many hundreds of paintings for the mission store, but nothing like these. 'Him never got properly sacred drawing. Never get secret or story, no.'

He was very angry about all the paintings that had been sold to the dealers and others that went astray. Trying now to make up for the enormous loss, he would paint only truly sacred works, full of secret power symbols.

As he painted, Yirawala permitted me to record the sacred 'inside' meanings of the painting, which I undertook never to divulge. He said I must keep it all as a record, like a sacred book. I could give the non-sacred 'outside' meanings in any book, but nothing more.

For the big Maraian man, Yirawala selected a large piece of bark, carefully cleaning the back and sanding the surface. After that he raided a clump of bush orchids in my garden and began chewing them to extract the sticky glue which he rubbed all over the bark. When it was dry he began grinding ochres, laboriously rubbing the stones on a large flat rock.

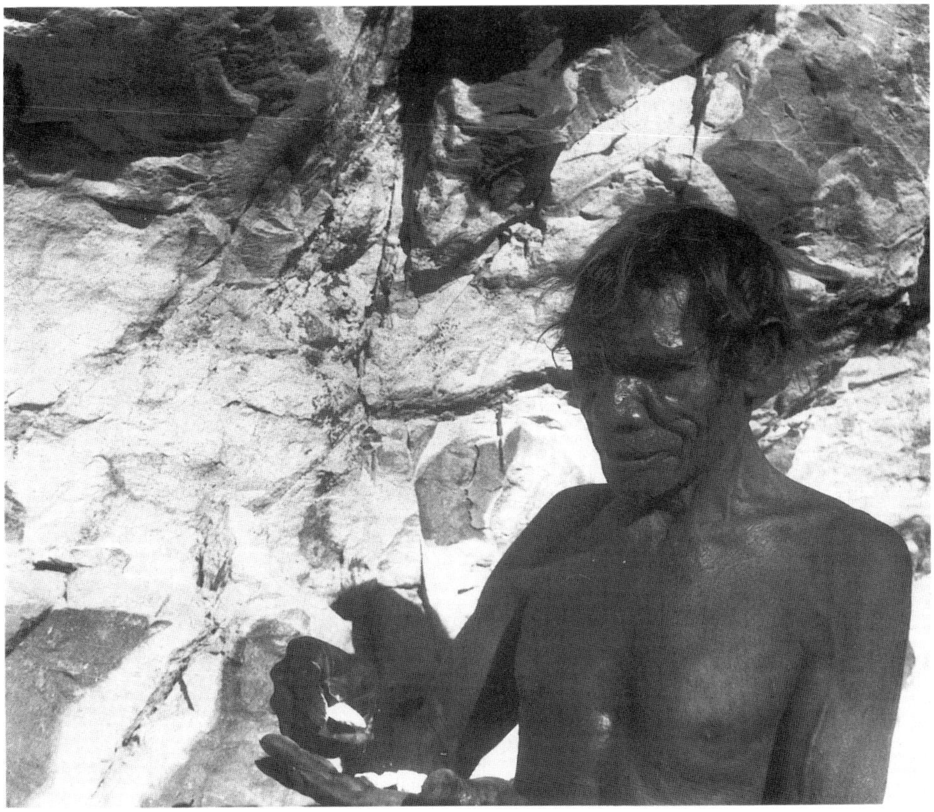

Yirawala collecting white clay from the Dripstone cave area, Casuarina Beach, Darwin.

The background paint was applied with a piece of chewed bark, then the shadowy outline of the figure was made. When this was finished a line was drawn around the figure and the ceremonial sticks.

Patiently he began making the fine white background lines at different angles all over the body and objects. After this came the rows of red, yellow and white lines forming diamond shapes in the form of Maraian crosses. Here and there were touches of dark brown.

The ceremonial sticks showed the power designs of the totemic well and were hung with feathered strings.

From Lumahlumah's head hung power bags filled with magic stones. The mouth was horizontal and filled with teeth. The large phallus was on the left side of the figure.

Yirawala sang as he worked, hardly stopping for food or drink, working day after day until the painting was finished.

After painting the big Maraian man, Yirawala rested for a day. He relaxed by painting little Mimi figures. 'Him all playabout, chasim wallaby.'

The next painting was of Lumahlumah with magic stones in his body. (Some of the Maraian stones were in the keeping of Yirawala, hidden in a sacred site.) Like the first figure, this one had upraised arms, as Lumahlumah sang songs of power and life for all living things. The body design was more powerful, showing the centres of life-giving sacred wells and places. The design has different names which are only called during a big ceremony to summon the life force for the living. Only the old Maraian bosses may use these words on pain of death.

After making this painting Yirawala sat for some time in meditation. He seemed drained but exalted. He would take only a little food that day. Mary slept in the house that night saying, 'Old man stay quiet by self.'

While the sacred work had been in progress, Mary had spent most of her time in the house with me, looking at picture books and smoking her pipe. When the children came home from school she would talk to Amanda or teach her more of the women's dances.

Over the next two weeks Yirawala painted more Mimi and wallaby and a third major work, the death of Lumahlumah. The drawing showed the big Maraian man being speared as he sang songs of life after death. He was filled with male and female fertility from the sacred totemic well. His head was wreathed in rainbows and storms. Inside his head was a skull, a symbol of death and a rising.

On the last two pieces of bark Yirawala painted Maraian male and female crocodiles. The male was covered with intricate power designs and symbols. Some of these were storm centres in the crocodile's head. The painting of the female crocodile was without the lightning and storm centres. She is sacred but has no secret power symbols. She is the mother of all saurians. The paintings are a life force for the increase and survival of the species, inseparable from Lumahlumah and the ceremonial poles.

As Yirawala told the stories I recalled the time we had observed a big crocodile travelling down the East Alligator River in the rain. I had just been for a swim with the children, and was aghast. Yirawala said not to worry as the crocodile had plenty of fish to eat and he was following his own path to find a mate. 'What for him worry for you. Him got big mob fish, too much. Him chasim girlfriend.' He had a relaxed attitude to the natural species, respecting them in the scheme of things, and he had special knowledge of their habits. He went on to say that if the food source was interfered with by too much fishing or power boats, then the crocodiles would attack and eat anything. Like most wild creatures, they preferred to keep away from humans.

When Yirawala had finished painting for my museum collection I paid him his fees as agreed between us. He was very pleased and said he would paint more of Lumahlumah on his next trip to town.

Before going home to Croker Island Mary and Yirawala went shopping. She bought things for the house, such as kitchenware, linen, blankets and furniture. She chose single beds, a table, cupboard and chairs. He selected axes, skinning knives, a pipe and tobacco, plus khaki trousers and checked shirts. Mary also bought personal items, clothing and scented hair oil.

Yirawala insisted on buying a gramophone and records for Danny and Andrew, so we went to Tivoli Music House. The salesman asked them what records they preferred and when they didn't seem to know, he played some rock and roll. Yirawala blocked his ears and cried, 'Stop! That properly rubbish music.' Pop music was also rejected. The salesman waved an LP of the Beatles at Yirawala. 'What that one?' Yirawala asked. The salesman smiled. 'It's the Beatles. You must have heard of them.' Mary giggled and Yirawala frowned. 'What for beetles?' The salesman rolled his eyes. 'You know, it's *the* Beatles — they sing.' Yirawala stared at him. 'I know beetle alright, big mob in my blanket, might be him sing out but we never listen.'

Yirawala finally chose some classical music and an album of Pete Seeger songs. 'Good songman that one,' he said.

Chapter 3
Make balanda understand my drawings

Yirawala liked coming to Darwin where he could communicate with people who gave him information and showed some interest in him and his work. He could satisfy some of the hunger to know what was going on in the large world beyond the reserve. He wanted to know about government legislation that affected him and his people. Cooped up on the missions and settlements, Aborigines were insulated against what was considered to be disturbing influences outside. It was government policy not to over expose them to white contact. A rigid permit system with no right of appeal carefully screened people whose attitudes were at variance with existing government policy. Mining activity and dealer activity was apparently not considered to be disturbing to the Aborigines.

During 1969 Yirawala was anxious to see with his own eyes if rumours were true about there being miners in the Nabarlek area, not far from Gunwinggu land. He said mining helicopters, like blowflies, were sniffing the land. Of the caves and sacred sites and all the wild life, he said, 'Him can't speak — can only die.' Yirawala worried about these things and his own advancing age, also his failing eyesight. He wanted to take Bobby and Danny to the home country to show them the Dreaming places. He would tell his ancestors that he had come home with his sons. He would ask them for power and for help to save the land.

Yirawala was one of the keepers of the Lumahlumah caves and a guardian of sacred symbols, the life force for the clans. That is why he was so afraid of miners roaming over the land. In some areas there were warning signs painted on rocks and understood by Aborigines, who kept away from what they called 'danger places', but the caves were not protected from white people.

Apart from desecrating cave drawings, white people might steal bones and objects as souvenirs or with an eye to selling them. In some areas this had happened.

Yirawala said that if miners blasted and dug the 'yellow mud danger places', everything would blow up. Certainly local clans would be demoralised and break down. He believed that he could prevent this happening.

Yirawala went on to describe the demise of the Crocodile People of Kakadu. An old legend tells of a sacred power cave that was profaned. The link with the Dreaming, the source of life, was then lost forever. Since the blame for this lay with a member of the tribe, the old men decided to punish everyone. Over many days the elders collected yellow and red mud from a danger place and repeatedly put it in the waterhole used by the people. Gradually people sickened, and less children were born, until few people remained.

Today only a few of the original inhabitants remain, but all through the Kakadu area numerous cave drawings of surpassing beauty bear testimony to the large and vigorous tribe which had once inhabited the area.

Yirawala said that in some places yellow mud came up through the ground, and over many years Aborigines had noticed that wildlife was scarce in such areas. 'Might be poison place, kill snake, goanna, whole lot.' Yirawala said that because poison came up through the ground there must be something very dangerous deep down, and if miners dug it up great power and poison would be let out to destroy all living things. 'Everything blow up,' he repeated.

The yellow mud places were at Nabarlek and adjacent to the East Alligator River — areas abundant in uranium.

Sitting beside his hut in my garden, Yirawala and I watched the flying foxes glide across the pink sky, crying as they went. He pointed at them, saying that out on the reserve his voice was like theirs, remote and never understood. He wanted to speak to many people about his fear of mining and the survival of the clans.

I asked if he would like a film record made about taking his sons home. He replied eagerly, 'You and old man make film — tell story.' I agreed to ask my husband, Cecil, and approach the AIAS and others for their support.

Sitting in the twilight, birds twittered in the branches above us and a cool breeze ruffled Yirawala's thin hair. He smiled and held out his hand to me. I vowed that he would take his sons home and we would film it. He was very pleased and said, 'Good, my girl. We make film alright. Later on might be we go all over — show my drawings, make balanda understand.'

He believed that white people needed educating about Aborigines, and that there must be a lot of good white people who would listen and maybe help him to save the land. He was seized with the idea of talking to many white people, getting known to them, then when he 'sang out loud for land', as he put it, they would help him. He was afraid of being wiped out in silent isolation.

In September Yirawala and Mary went back to Croker Island and I wrote to Cecil about the film idea. He had left Darwin by this time to work in Sydney, having resigned his job as editor of *The Territorian* magazine.

I also wrote to Professor A P Elkin, who was delighted with the proposed film. He said the Australian Museum would be interested in photographs and documentation of cave paintings, and that the AIAS would probably participate. He also supported the idea of an interstate tour with Yirawala and a son to lecture and show some of the paintings. He advised me to approach the Australian Council for the Arts. He would also assist us.*

Yirawala had promised to return and finish some of the drawings in a week's time. When nothing was heard from him I decided to write to see if he was all right. I sent the letter on 25 September. There was no reply.

On 12 December I received a letter from the superintendent about a problem with sending a parcel to me from Yirawala. He also said Yirawala was busy building a new house and did not want to come to Darwin. This letter was in reply to one I had written to the superintendent explaining the terms of the legal Deed between Yirawala and me.

On 16 December I wrote to Yirawala and enclosed a plane ticket for 20 December. There was no response.

In January 1970 Danny Noloman, a younger son of Yirawala, wrote to say that his father had sent fifteen bark paintings to me. Danny also mentioned that Yirawala wanted an outboard motor fixed or a new one sent.

I did not receive the paintings.

I wrote again to Yirawala and sent plane tickets for him and Mary to come to Darwin on 3 February. It was a great relief when they came.

Yirawala brought six paintings with him and said he had not broken his contract with me. He had done his best to send parcels to me. If they had gone astray it was not his fault. He said some people wanted him to ignore the contract with me. Individual dealers were also talking to him. He was sick of it.

It seemed our legal contract was really only workable when he came to Darwin and worked at my home.

* A P Elkin, CMG, then Emeritus Professor of the University of Sydney, was a lifelong friend of the Australian Aborigines. He was the first anthropologist to touch the conscience of Australia and win support for Aboriginal rights and dignity. He established deep personal friendships with Aboriginal elders. They honoured him by calling him 'The old man'.

Yirawala said he had a row at the mission office on pension day. He remembered what the lawyer had told him about getting his pension letters in the hand. When it came to his turn to put his mark on the ledger he had refused until he was given his letter. It was a matter of dignity. The man behind the desk told him to put his mark and stop holding up the queue. Yirawala stood fast, then pointing at the white man, said, 'We properly all citizen now. My lawyer told me. That the Queen letter. Nobody can block him. Give me my r'own letter.' When this was refused Yirawala pointed dramatically at the man. 'I put you in jail four year. That new law for we.' The pension letter was given to him. Nobody else was inclined to follow his example.

Yirawala laughed at his own temerity as he recounted this story. This episode and his attempt to market his own paintings did not endear him to those in authority.

Before starting work on the six bark pieces he had brought with him, Yirawala asked to be taken out to East Arm Leprosarium, a few kilometres from Darwin.* He wanted to see Margaret, an older daughter from his first wife who had died. He took with him a little bag. When Margaret opened it, she tipped red earth onto her hand and wept. She held some of it to her lips and whispered, 'My own country. My home.' She kissed her father and Mary, happily telling them that she might be going back soon to Oenpelli.

When we arrived back home, three Aboriginal men were sitting under a tree and cooking something. Yirawala rushed up to them, thinking they were cooking his pet goanna. He called out to Amanda, and they began looking for it. They found the goanna in a rotten, hollow branch of the mulberry tree. The three men stared at the goanna, exchanging meaningful glances. Yirawala ordered them to leave and not return. They were from a different language group in any case.

Yirawala also had three little mice skipping about on a shelf and coming down to eat bread from his hand. He was appalled when I suggested setting traps for them. He told me to leave them alone.

Early next morning he began work on more paintings in the Maraian series. The first showed the sacred totemic wells in Lumahlumah's body and the life force from the Dreaming. Another depicted the clans from all the coastal areas going in canoes to kill the giant. The men were a bit frightened and sang to make themselves brave before attacking and killing Lumahlumah. The painting showing the attack was truly sacred Maraian. Lumahlumah has called upon all his great power to repell his attackers. Lightning flashes around his head and he shows them the face of death. He also shows them that he is man and woman, a giver of all life. (In this painting, Lumahlumah has breasts like a woman.) He sings that fertility and life comes from the totemic wells and that people shall dream about it and multiply.

The next painting depicted Lumahlumah dying. He sings to the elders to wait before they finish him off. In dying he passes on to them his power of life and immortality. As he sings the sacred songs, he cuts the power designs marked out in blood on his own body. Each section relates to totemic beings and the natural species on which man is dependent.

The fourth painting showed Lumahlumah revealing more great mysteries to the elders. His body changed to a towering, shimmering figure revealing all his power and immortality. He sang that his body and organs were sacred; that Dua and Jiritja moieties were each to take parts of his body and place them in certain caves as sacred objects to be venerated ever after in life-giving ritual and ceremonies. They must not profane the sacred songs and designs so bequeathed. If they did the clans would die out and life after death would be denied.

The more Yirawala sang and painted, the greater was his concern for the sacred caves and his desire to go to the home country with his sons, to ask his ancestors for power, and take stock.

After making the power drawings he rested for three days. He asked me about the film and going home to Marugulidban. I was able to report good progress in support. Providing

* Leprosy was introduced to the northern tribes by indentured labourers who came from China to work on the Pine Creek to Larrimah railway line. The disease affected ten per cent of the Aboriginal population of the north.

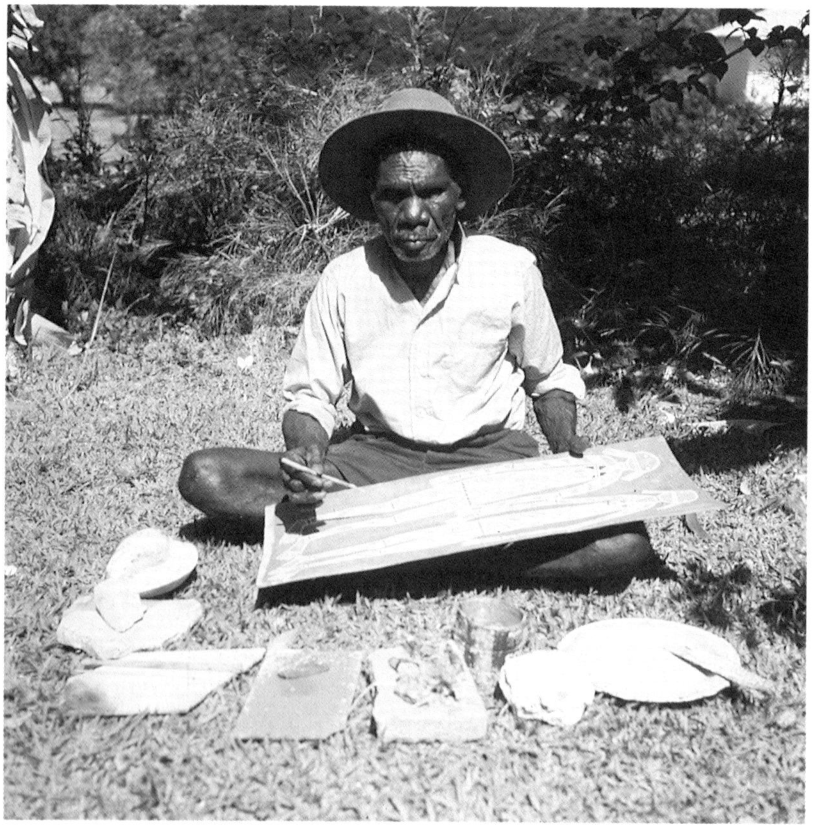

When Yirawala came to Darwin he would sit in the garden, under the big mango tree near his hut, painting on bark, making a few ceremonial paintings for my museum. He wished to save a record of his religion. So many ceremonial paintings had been lost.

permits were available, we would all go in September at the latest. With regard to the interstate tour, an application had been made to the Australian Council for the Arts, who said there could be some funding allocated in 1971. Yirawala was pleased about the prospect of going South to show some of his drawings and lecture with his son, Bobby. They would teach the white people to understand.

Yirawala and Mary went home to Croker Island on 30 May. He said he would come back in a month's time. He would let me know when to send plane tickets.

In April 1970 the Australian Council for the Arts had invited Yirawala to enter a painting in an art competition sponsored by Trans Australian Airlines. He had selected a non-sacred painting, which was duly sent off. The painting won a cash prize, which was forwarded to him on Croker Island. He was pleased about it and received a lot of publicity.

Through the art prize and my Yirawala Museum, his work was becoming widely known and his name increasingly famous. My museum attracted more interstate visitors but also the attention of thieves. I lost about fifteen paintings, including ten by Yirawala. Tropical houses, with their louvred walls, offered little security.

I was offered secure premises in a house next to the notorious Bamboo Lounge in Cavenagh Street. I would make a small charge to cover the rent.

There were not many visitors, who in any case were somewhat put off by raving drunks leering through the bamboo slats of the lounge next door. Sometimes a shouting, screaming tangle of bodies erupted into the street, writhing in a heap until police carted them off. Obscene language and wild juke-box music provided extra sound effects.

One afternoon a drunk reeled into the museum and fell prone. On another occasion a man with the DTs came crawling in on his hands and knees, barking like a dog. All this did not encourage visitors, and finally I was behind with rent payments.

One morning I came to find the land-lady had hurled my art and artifacts out into the street, damaging some of them. She slammed the door as I arrived. A passing Aboriginal man helped me to pick things up and put them in my truck.

I wrote regularly to Yirawala and his family but there was no reply. On 19 June I wrote again to tell him that the beds, mattresses, linen, chest of drawers and mirrors he had asked for would be sent on the barge by the end of the month. These items were always separate from payments I made for paintings. They were gifts from me and my family.

On 22 June an Aboriginal man from Croker Island told me that a dealer from Europe was on the island, buying paintings, and two Australian buyers had been there before him. My heart sank.

On the morning of 10 August I was in the back yard feeding the goanna, when I heard Yirawala calling me. I was surprised, having had no word that he was coming in to Darwin. I looked around but could not see him. Maybe he was playing a trick, hiding from me as he sometimes did. I called out to him but he was nowhere to be found. Something must be wrong. Maybe he was ill?

The next day I sent a telegram to the superintendent at Croker Island: 'If Yirawala ill please hospitalise him. If doctor needed I will send by charter, my expense. Please advise urgently. Phone 3816.'

I received no reply to my telegram, but I knew something was wrong. I would ask for a permit to go and see for myself. The permit was granted only after Mr Ron Withnall, a Darwin solicitor, wrote to the Director of Aboriginal Welfare and I had made a personal appeal to his wife. Whether she spoke for me I do not know.

The permit was issued for 15 August, for half a day. I went by charter to Croker Island.

I found Yirawala sick in bed with some sort of chest infection. He smiled and said, 'Ah, you heard me. Take me Darwin, good doctor.' He went back with me on my charter. Mary accompanied us.

In Darwin the doctor diagnosed a pleurisy infection and prescribed antibiotics. Yirawala was very weak but responded to the treatment.

One afternoon when Mary and I were bathing him, I noticed a large hollow in his head. I asked what had caused it. He laughed and said that when he was a young man they had raided the Malak-Malak people. While he was gazing at a young girl, he was felled by a blow from a stone axe. When he recovered, he sought out the man who had done it and killed him.

On 25 August my husband Cecil wrote to say that the filming of Yirawala taking his sons home would go ahead in September. Channel 7 TV would sponsor it, assisted in a small way by the Australian Museum and the AIAS. I rushed inside the house to tell Yirawala and Mary. He was delighted and Mary smiled happily as she fed him his soup. He told me to contact Bobby and Danny and send plane tickets for them to come in for the film trip.

Cecil would direct the film and I would be sound recordist, field organiser, deal with continuity and liaise with the Aborigines. I would also apply for permits for the film crew.

Professor Elkin wrote to say that the Australian Museum would provide money for photographic stock and tapes. The director of the Museum had written to the Director of Aboriginal Welfare in Darwin asking him to support the film project. The Museum wanted a film record of ancient cave paintings and recorded documentation from Yirawala.

Initially I made a telephone call to the office of the Director of Aboriginal Welfare, outlining the purpose of the film and who would be requiring permits. On 4 September, I followed up with a detailed letter, listing the names of the film crew and four Landrover drivers. I also named the main sponsor, Channel 7 TV of Sydney.

When Bobby came in from Murganella he said that a rumour was already circulating that we were going to the sacred Lumahlumah caves, in Gunwinggu country. Such a rumour could only add to the difficulty of obtaining permits, and made Yirawala very very angry.

Yirawala said he would go and talk to the welfare people himself, but first he would see his lawyer and send a letter to the Director. Here is the text of the letter, dictated by Yirawala on 6 September 1970:

> Dear Mr Giese,
>
> I want to tell you who I am. My name is Yirawala. 73 years old and I belong to the Gunwinggu tribe. Dua moiety. My skin is Nubulain and my Dreaming is the red and green parrot called Dadat.
>
> I want to see you straight away Mr Giese for talk about my country near the bottom of the Liverpool River. My family have three caves there, properly belong to us and nobody else got anything to do with them — only my family. In one cave is my father's bones, and before him for a long time. My father was named Nowaritj and he was a big boss for ceremony business and painting law. My father had job to paint our caves and fix up old ones too, and bones. My job the same too. I am proper law painter and I tell you Mr Giese that these caves are ours and got nothing to do with Mialli, Rambarrnga and other people. Mialli country is long way from my place and Rambarrnga country is near Mainarou, Bulman Crossing.
>
> For long time now I talk to Mrs Holmes to take me back to see caves, my father's bones and drawing. Might be last time for me because I am going blind and getting properly old fella now, and I been very sick and Mrs Holmes save me.
>
> I must go now to my caves and look again at the Dreaming. I want my sons to look and I tell them meaning of old drawings so we don't lose the old law. I asked Mrs Holmes and Mr Holmes to make tape recording of my talk about the cave drawings, and film too. When I die my sons can see these things and nothing lost.
>
> Mrs Holmes and Mr Holmes are my relation, my family now, and their children too. We family trust them all the way and we do not want anybody else making this business for us.
>
> I know TV people helping with the money for Landrovers, the drivers, everything and I know Mr and Mrs Holmes and Professor Elkin look after what I give and nothing inside [sacred] will be seen on TV, that part is for the big museum in Sydney, they keep it, and Mrs Holmes keep copies for my family when I am dead or blind. Mrs Holmes got about two hundred my proper law paintings. I make them get good pay, but still she keep the law paintings for my sons and my daughters, Dreaming drawing. Mrs Holmes has all the law and Maraian business. I give her and her husband same permit from me — and this my business truly. My people can say — nobody else.
>
> All this is Aboriginal business, nothing to do with white man, only for ones we trust. Me, Yirawala and my wife and sons and family ask you not to block us now. We people want Mr and Mrs Holmes to do this film and recording for us quick, and wet season coming soon now.
>
> I know I am going blind and I ask you from me, Yirawala, from my heart. Give these permits for my friends to help us and the other people to work for them driving and making pictures.
>
> Mr Giese, I ask now to come and talk with you straight now — me, my son Bobby if he come in time and Mrs Holmes. I tell you straight where my country is and the caves and I am not crooked man or slack guts. I am big boss for business [ceremonies] and the caves, only my family business.
>
> I want to see you, please.
>
> YIRAWALA

Attached to this letter was a sworn statement of authenticity, signed by Yirawala.

Yirawala sent messages to Gunwinggu elders at Maningrida and Oenpelli, explaining the truth about the film trip. The film unit would not be going near the sacred caves in any part of Arnhemland.

I wrote to the Honourable Mr Fred Chaney, Administrator of the Northern Territory. Mr Bruce Gyngell, the manager of the Channel 7 network, wrote to the Honourable Peter Nixon, Minister for the Interior, to explain the purpose of the film expedition. Mr Jim Bowditch, editor of the *N T News* also weighed in, with an article supporting us.

By 15 September there was still no reply from the office of the Director of Aboriginal Welfare to my letter requesting the issue of permits for myself and the rest of the film crew.

Bobby Joran suggested that we go to Maningrida with his father to discuss the film trip with Gunwinggu elders there. He believed this was vital to clear up any misinformation that might exist about the expedition. So I applied for a permit to go to Maningrida, which was granted for 20 September.

At Maningrida we held talks with Kelly Borgordubhu, Peter Mahlunwunggu and other elders.* After listening to Yirawala and Bobby, the elders said they now understood the true purpose of the film trip, and that they had no objection to us going to Yirawala's family caves,

* Sometimes Kelly's name was spelled Kerly Bagadupu or Curly Borgordupu, and Peter's name as Peter Maralwanga or Peter Malanwanga.

as they knew he would not break the law.

Tommy Yibarra, an Aboriginal liaison officer from the local government office, sat in on the talks and dictated a letter to the Director of Aboriginal Welfare:

> I Tommy Yibarra today talked with Yirawala's relations about his caves, bottom of Liverpool River. Yirawala told me true words and I know now we get mistaken words. Yirawala can go to his family caves they are not sacred. He is boss, and after Yirawala is Peter Mahlunwunggu. He says OK and he will travel back to caves when people go there. All the men say OK and it is all clear. That is true words. Mrs Homes, Mr Holmes and their work man, camera, can go. We trust Mrs Holmes and men say she never break word or trust for us.
>
> Please, it is all clear. They can go. They need not go to Oenpelli. This is enough. Later on we like Mrs Holmes help us again to record and keep for us.
>
> We don't want tourist or other people at the caves.
>
> TOMMY YIBARRA

This letter was witnessed by the tribal elders, who affixed their thumbprints to the letter.

When we returned to Darwin there was a telegram from the Oenpelli superintendent saying that the elders there were against us going to Yirawala's country.

There was also a message that the Director of Aboriginal Welfare would interview us on the following day, 21 September. We would triumphantly present Tommy Yibarra's letter and the signatures, and Yirawala would now be able to meet with the Director face-to-face and 'talk straight', as he put it. I believed we would eventually get the permit but first we would have to go through the wringer.

We sat with our lawyer in the Director's waiting room. The lawyer rustled his papers and made a few notes. Yirawala sat straight-backed on his chair, pulling his hat-brim level. He was trembling but his face was resolute.

We were ushered into the presence of the two senior officers. The Director stood up and ordered Yirawala to sit down. Yirawala looked him in the face and said, 'You sit down, me sit down, level.' We all sat down.

When the documents were read by the Director he said he accepted them, but we must still go to Oenpelli to discuss the trip with Gunwinggu elders there. Yirawala tried to speak but was motioned to be silent. Bobby was given the same treatment.

Wagbara, the interpreter, said that Yirawala's family caves were not secret. The Director still insisted that we must go to Oenpelli.

In the course of the conversation I was asked if we were likely to film a mining venture near Oenpelli, on the reserve. I did not know there was one and replied no, that was not in the script. I pointed out that Yirawala had recently been very ill and was undergoing stress and exhaustion. There was also the matter of increasing expense and the approaching wet season.

Finally we were given permits to go to Oenpelli on 24 September, in a plane provided by Aboriginal Welfare.

At Oenpelli we sat down with Balil-Balil, and other Gunwinggu head men. They wondered what all the fuss was about and thought we had already gone on the trip. They emphatically denied having said we could not go. Bobby recorded interviews from the men and took a signed statement to be forwarded, via our solicitors, to the Welfare Director's office.

Four days later, on 28 September, protracted negotiations began between the Director and our solicitors. The draft permit was lengthy, with pages of conditions laid down, some of them unacceptable. Each clause had to be perused, interpreted and answered. When this was done, a second draft was drawn up and sent. Legal costs were mounting.

Finally, agreement was reached and the permit issued on 6 October. Some of the permit's conditions were:

1 A welfare officer and two Aborigines of the officer's choosing would accompany us.
2 We must pay wages to the Aborigines.
3 The welfare officer would choose our direction and camp sites and could revoke the

permits at any time if he chose to do so.
4 We were not to wander from the chosen route unless in an emergency.
5 The film would have to be shown to the Aborigines concerned before being screened publicly.
6 The Director of Aboriginal Welfare would be given a free copy of the film.

At last. Now we could make real preparations for the trip. Cecil and the camera crew had arrived and the Landrover drivers made ready.

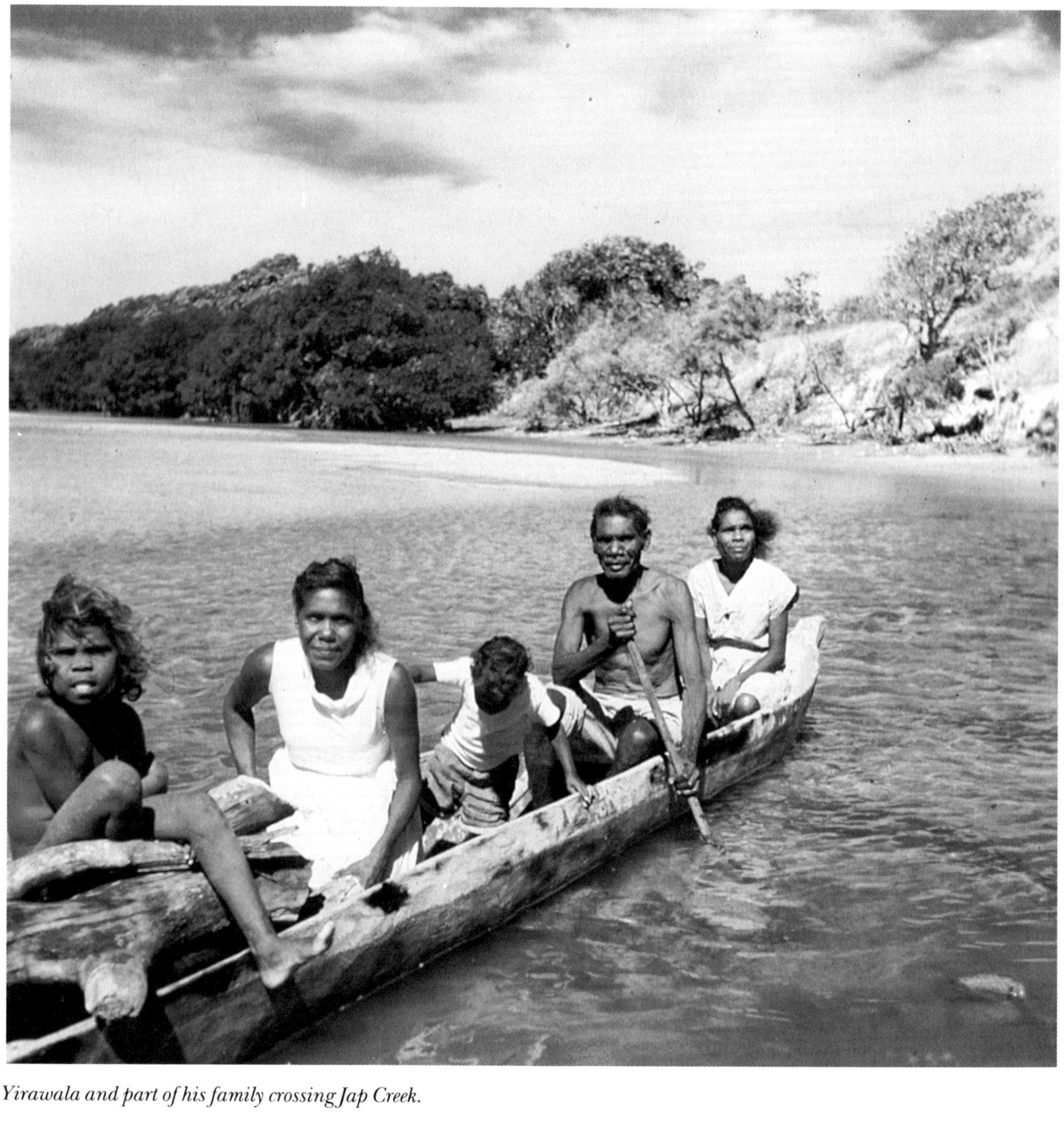

Yirawala and part of his family crossing Jap Creek.

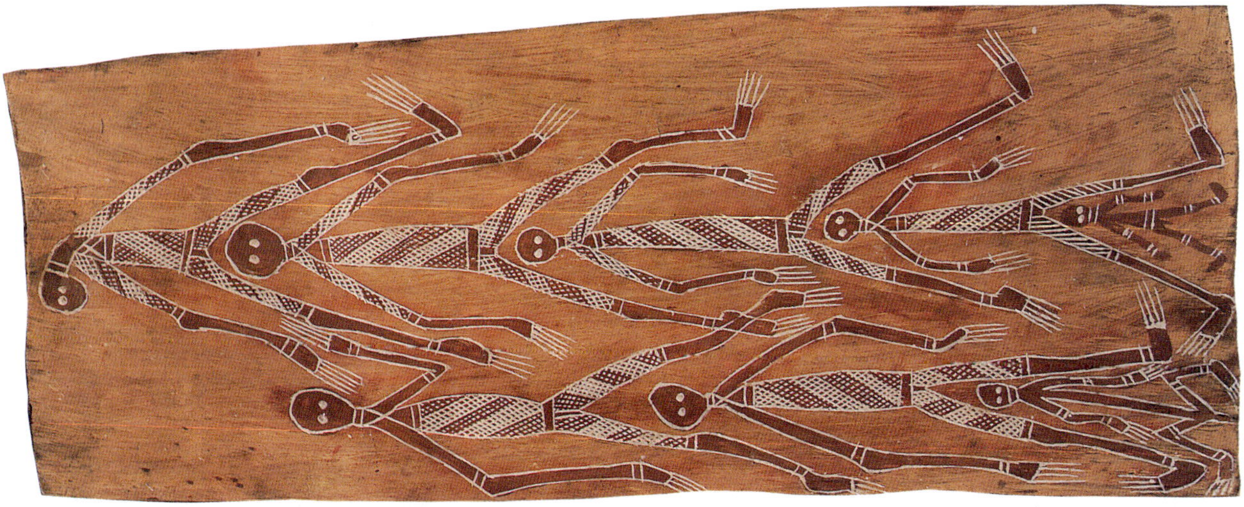

Plate 21 MARAIAN SERIES

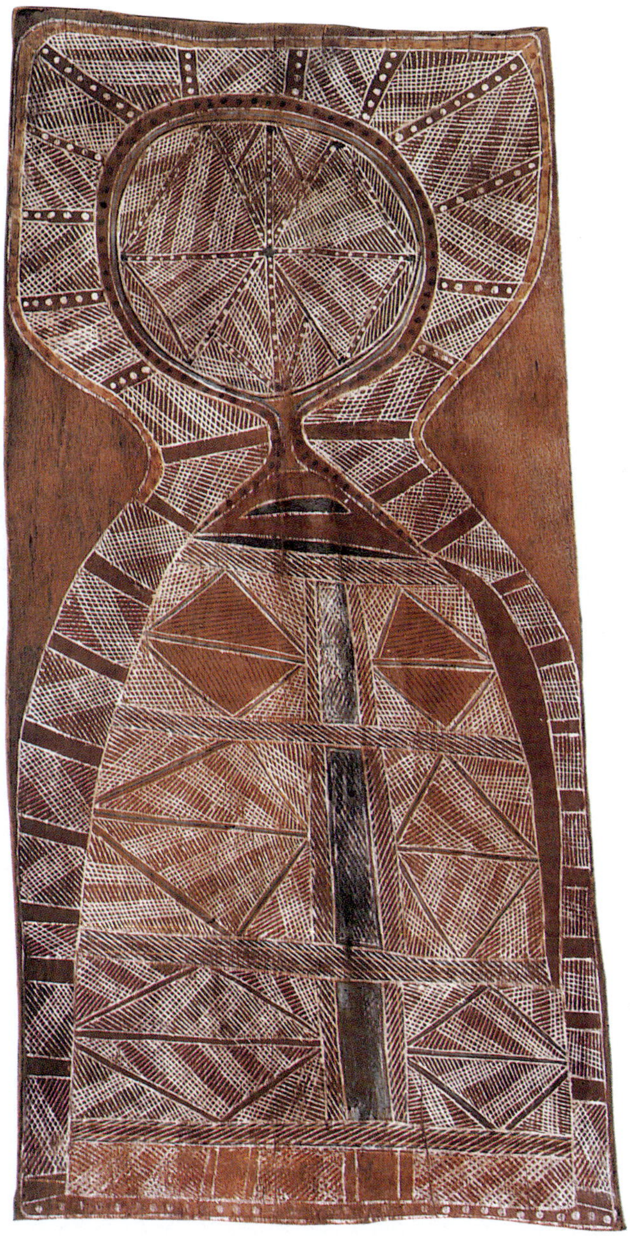

Plate 22 MARAIAN SERIES

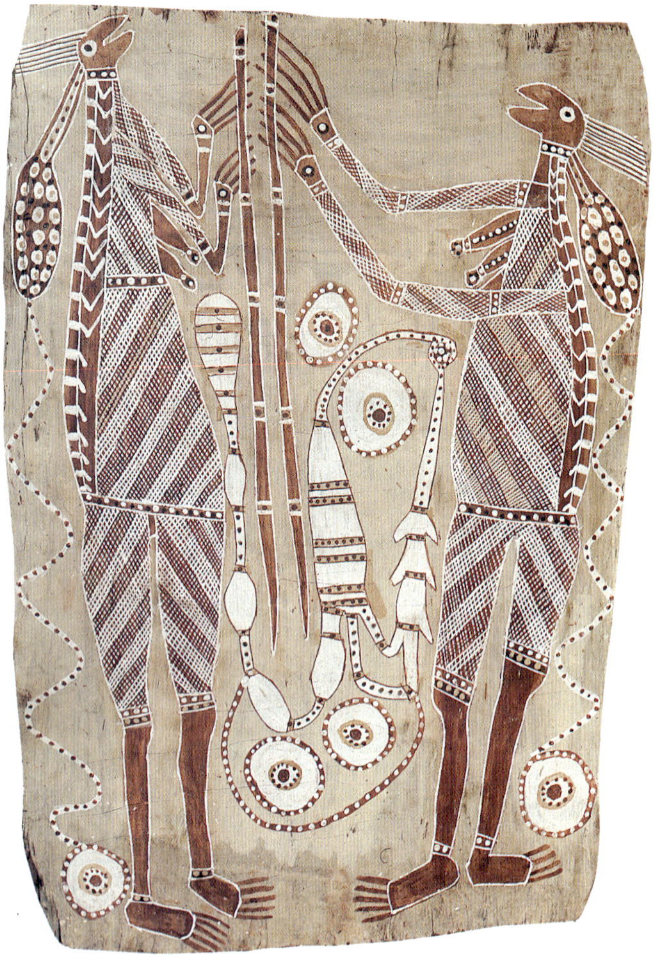

Plate 23 MARAIAN SERIES

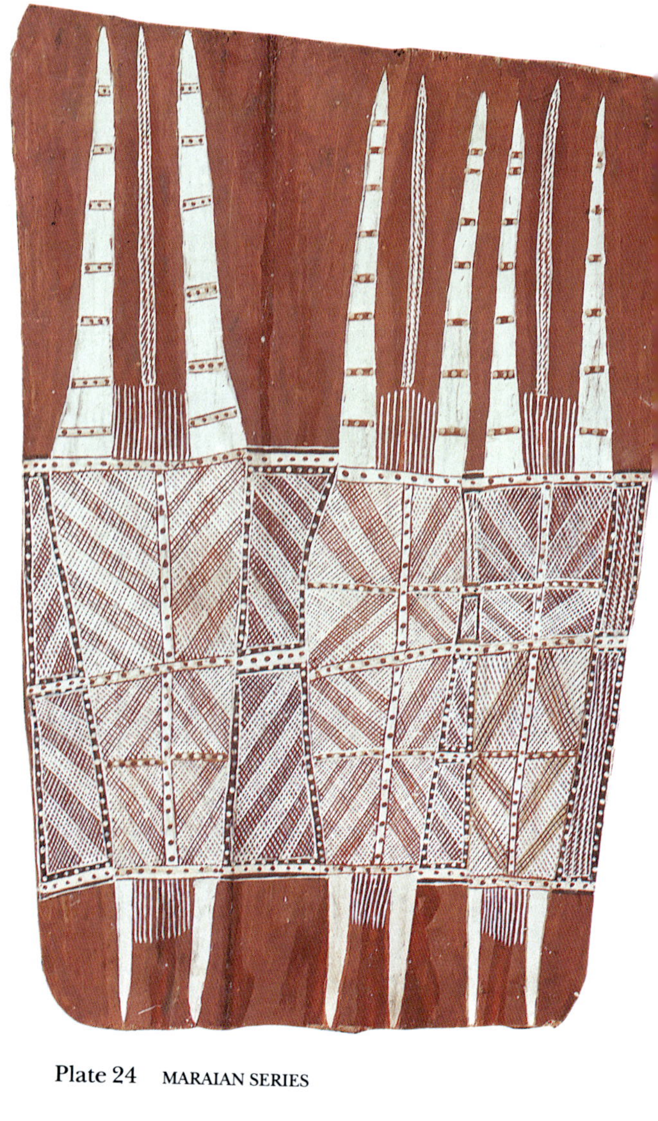

Plate 24 MARAIAN SERIES

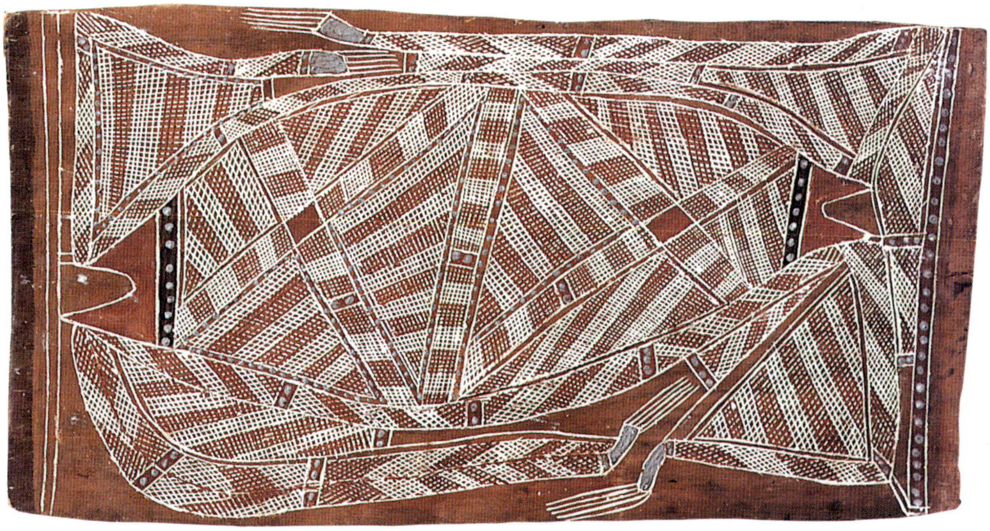

Plate 25 MARAIAN SERIES

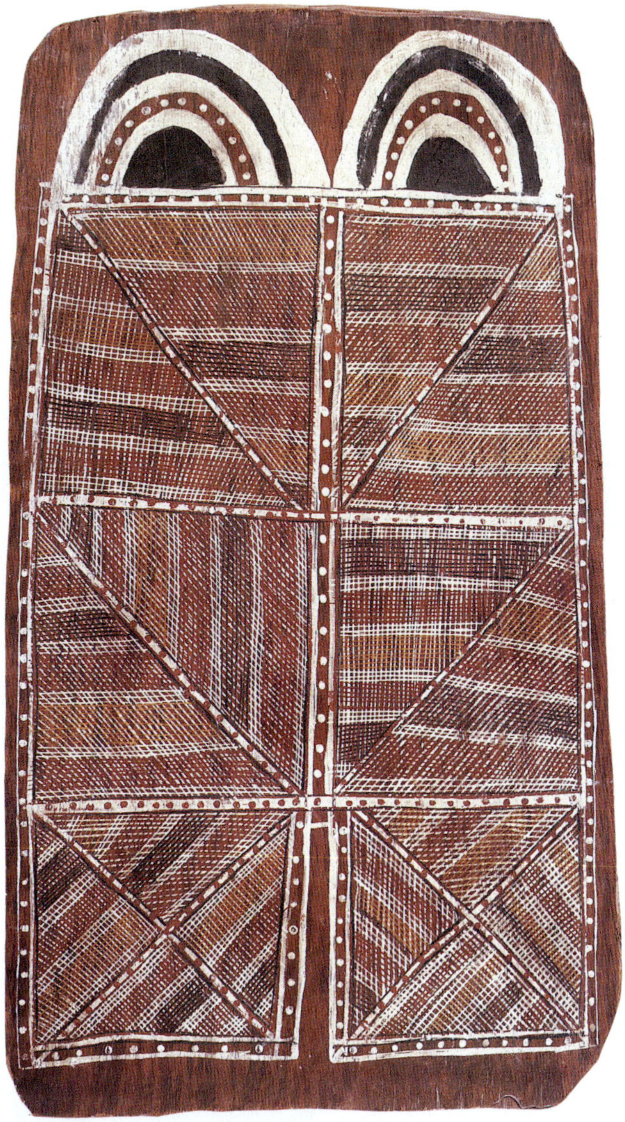

Plate 26 MARAIAN SERIES

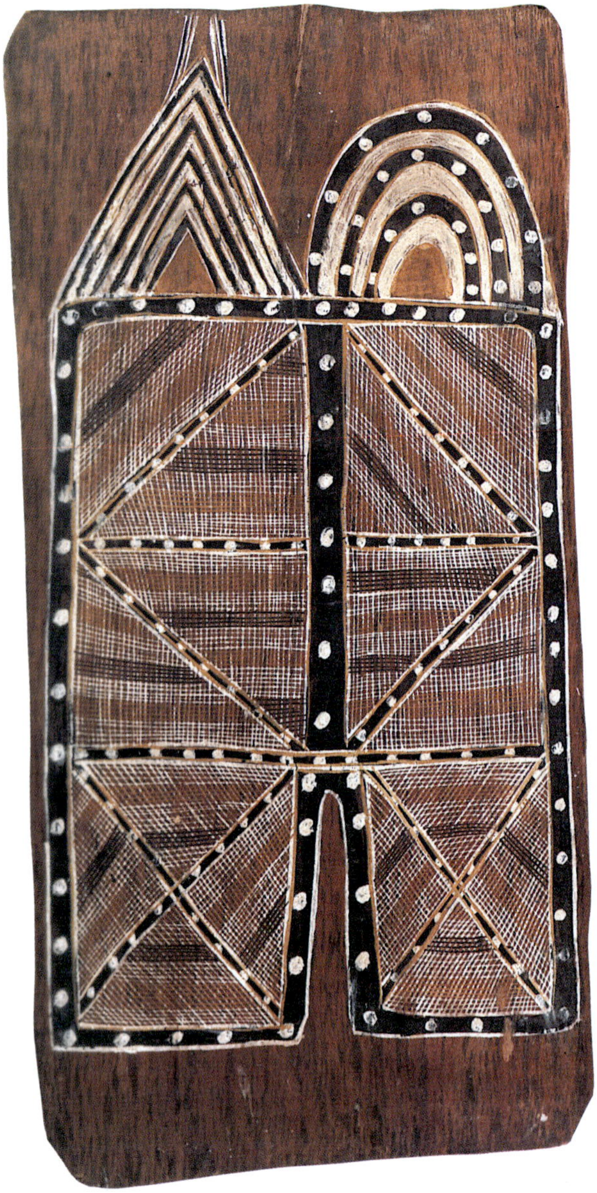

Plate 27 MARAIAN SERIES

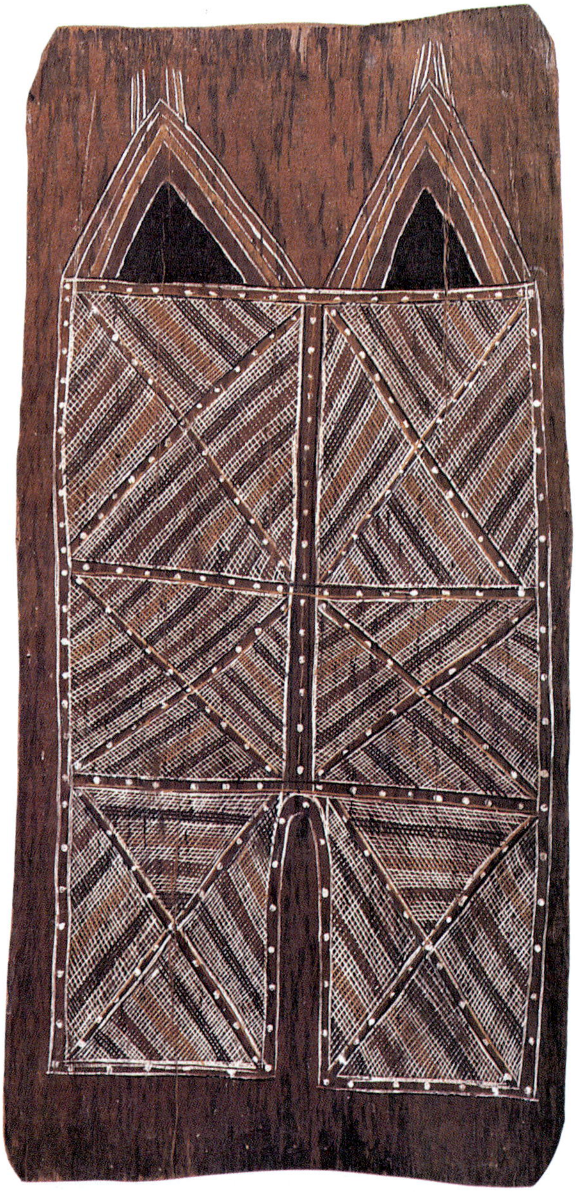

Plate 28 MARAIAN SERIES

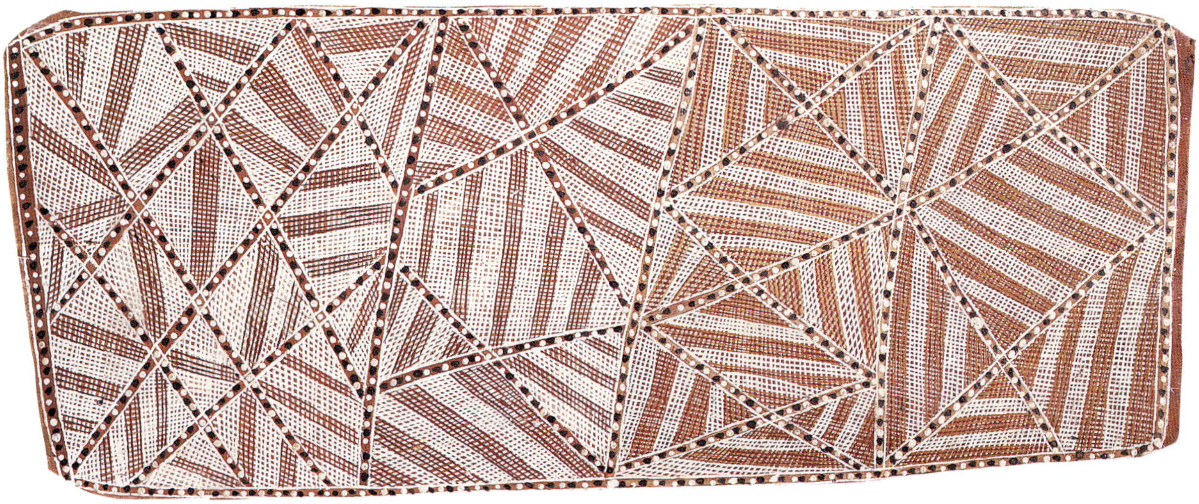

Plate 29 MARAIAN SERIES

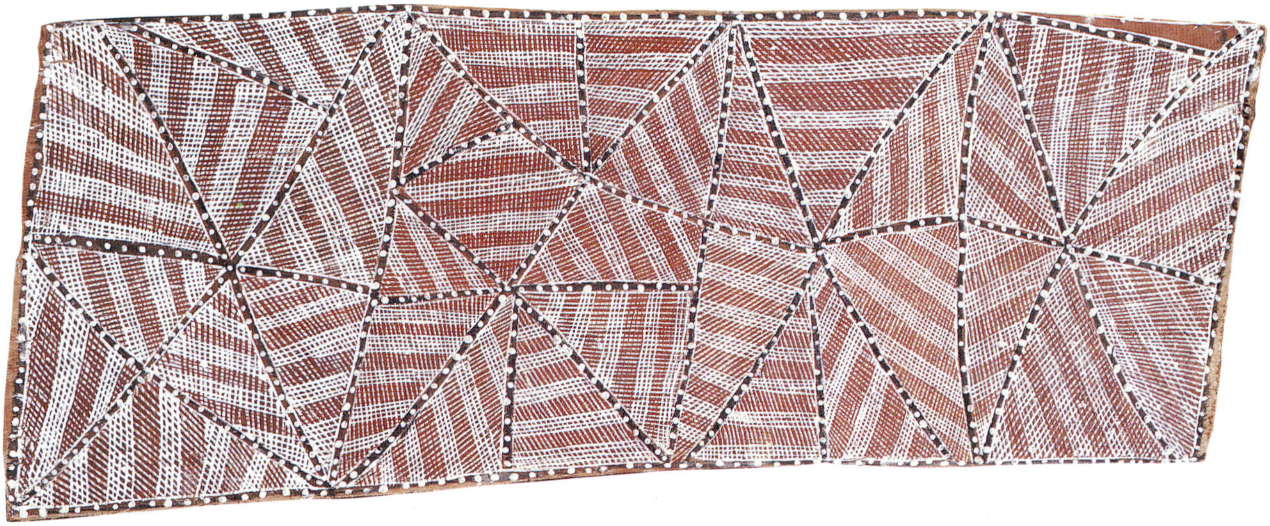

Plate 30 MARAIAN SERIES

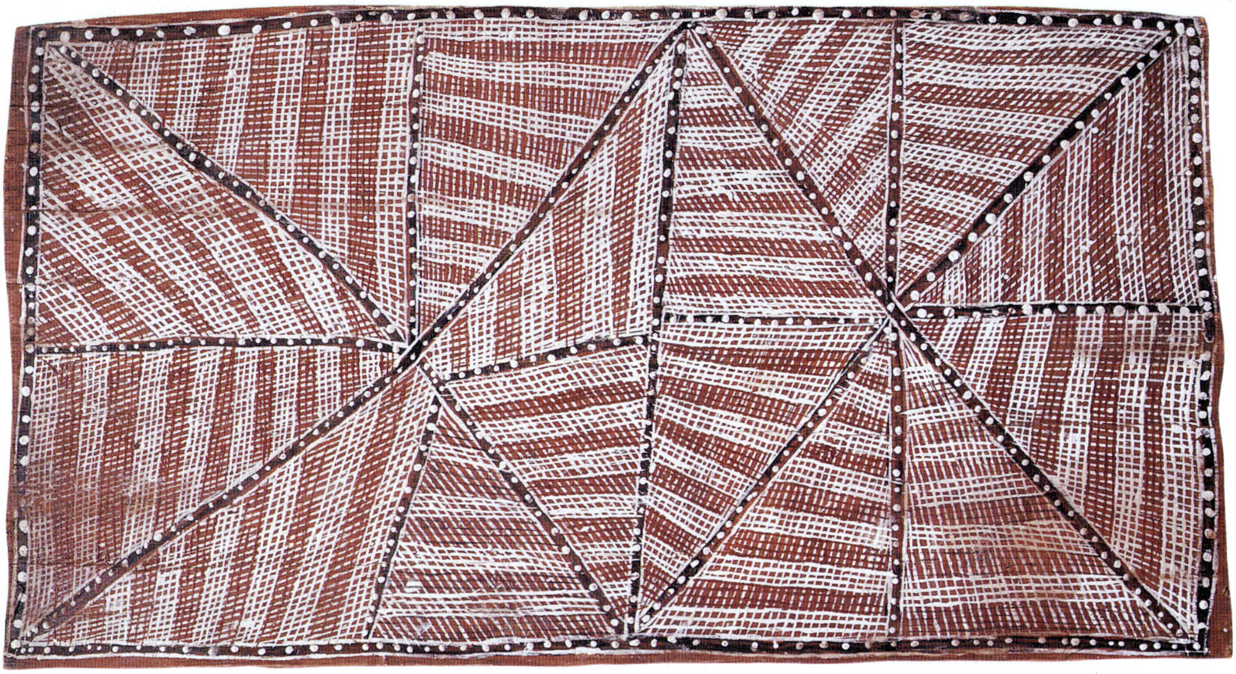

Plate 31 MARAIAN SERIES

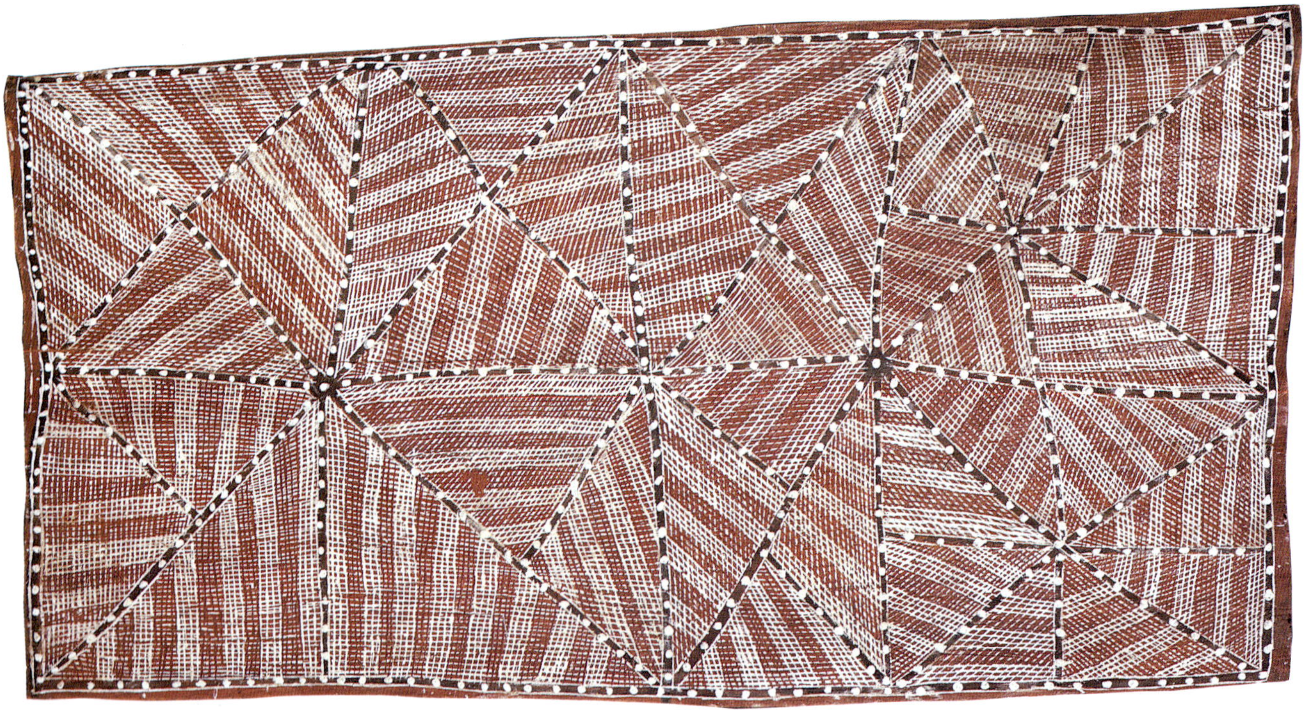

Plate 32 MARAIAN SERIES

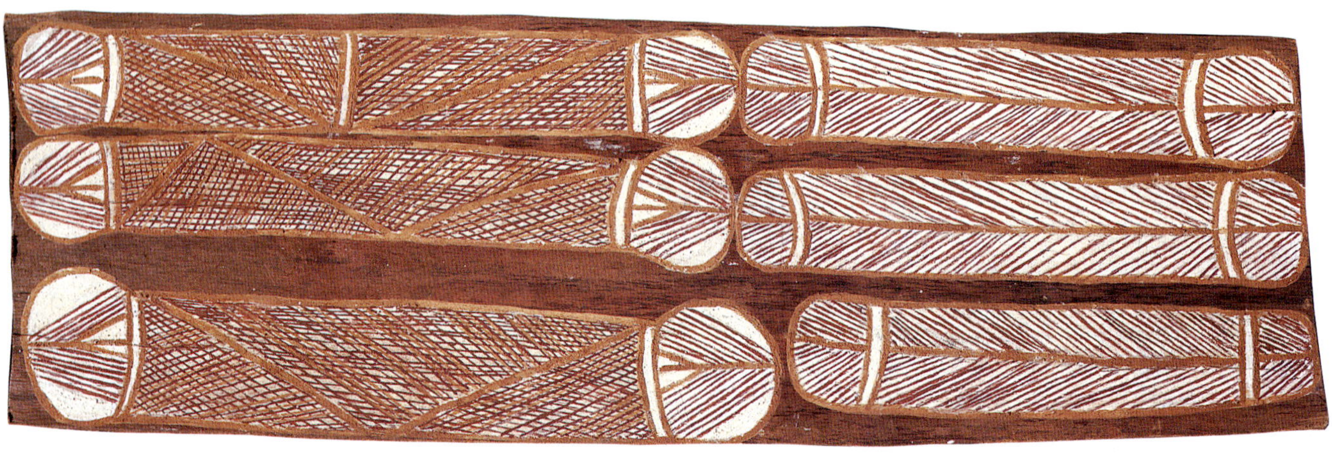

Plate 33 MARAIAN SERIES

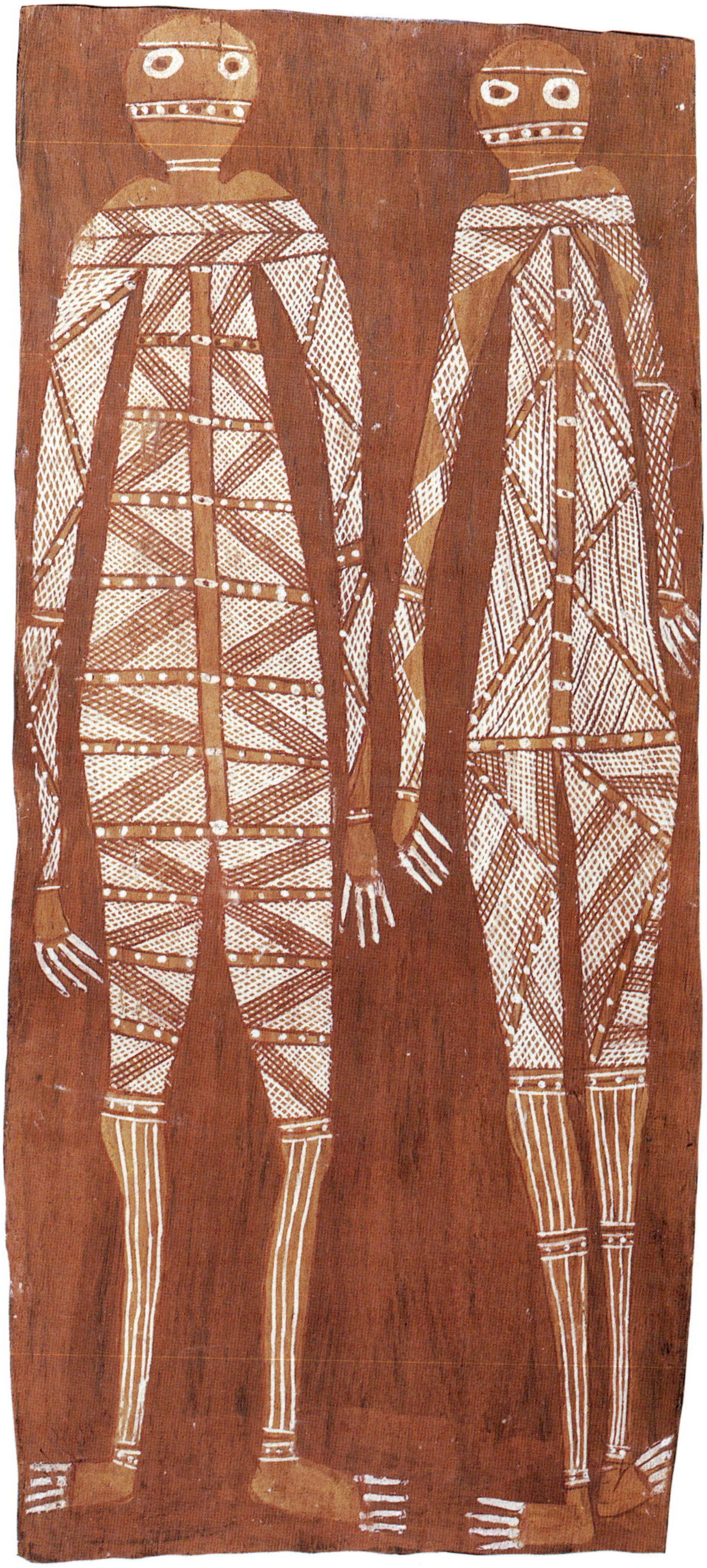

Plate 34 MARAIAN SERIES

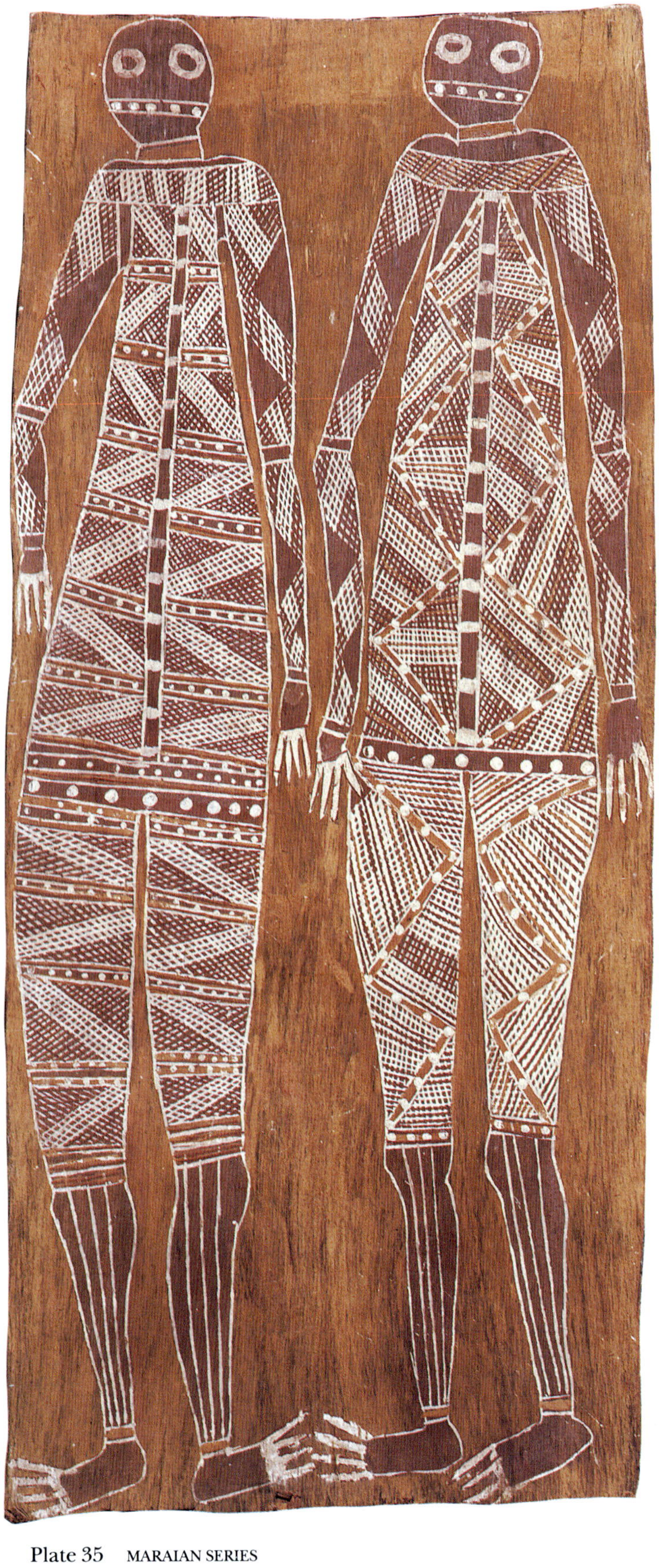

Plate 35 MARAIAN SERIES

Chapter 4
Handprints and signs are our title deeds signed by vanished hands

On 8 October our convoy of four Landrovers set out from Melville Street, Darwin. Yirawala and Mary sat in the first vehicle. They were in high spirits, excited about the trip home and meeting relations on the way. We would meet the welfare officer at Oenpelli Mission.

The heat was suffocating, for the wet season rains were due. Some rain had already fallen near the East Alligator crossing, and we would be extremely lucky to get in and out of Arnhemland. We could become hopelessly bogged if caught in heavy rain.

We proceeded with all speed until the narrow bitumen road gave way to gravel and dirt beyond the Adelaide River. Full-scale mining at Jabiru had not begun and no wide ribbon of bitumen split the forests. The few passing motorists waved as they went by. We carried drums of fuel and supplies in trailers, now dragging and churning through the deep bulldust.

The track wound through paperbark trees on the edge of swampland. This was buffalo country and sometimes we halted to let them pass. A variety of marsupials fled before us, and the bush all around was teeming with bird life.

We stopped to boil the billy near a beautiful billabong surrounded with big trees, where kookaburras gave their harsh, grating calls. They did not laugh like the southern variety. Old timers said this was because there was 'nothing to bloody well laugh about' in the Territory.

Yirawala and Mary sat with their sons on the edge of the water, where little 'Jesus' birds walked on the lily leaves to peer into the water.

The track wound on through sparsely timbered country with a line of blue hills in the distance.

Nearing the South Alligator River, we stopped for refreshment at a small bush pub and store run by Tom Opitz. Yirawala and his family went off to talk with some relations camped near clear, flowing waters. The wind carried smoke from the fire and their happy laughter as they made him welcome.

Crossing the South Alligator River, the sandy soil gave way to stony ground as we neared the hills and drove towards the towering escarpments.

In the late afternoon we reached the East Alligator River store run by Terry Robinson. A few mining company vehicles and utilities were parked under the trees outside. In the bar mining men and buffalo shooters rubbed shoulders with the odd tourist who had managed to get this far. A few Aborigines sat on benches outside, but most of them were encouraged to take their cartons of unchilled beer cans away into the bush. A kilometre or so from the store was a great pile of beer cans. Locals called it 'Terry's tin mountain'. The store also sold some tinned food and Aboriginal bark paintings of good quality.

Yirawala and his sons were mobbed by relatives from Oenpelli. His daughter Margaret who had been in East Arm Leprosarium threw her arms round his neck and wept. Mary and a group of female relatives were also hugging each other and crying. They had been apart for years. The men sat under a tree with Yirawala, talking and passing round the pipe and tobacco pouch. The film crew went into the bar.

We were soon on the road again, as the convoy had to cross the East Alligator causeway before full tide.

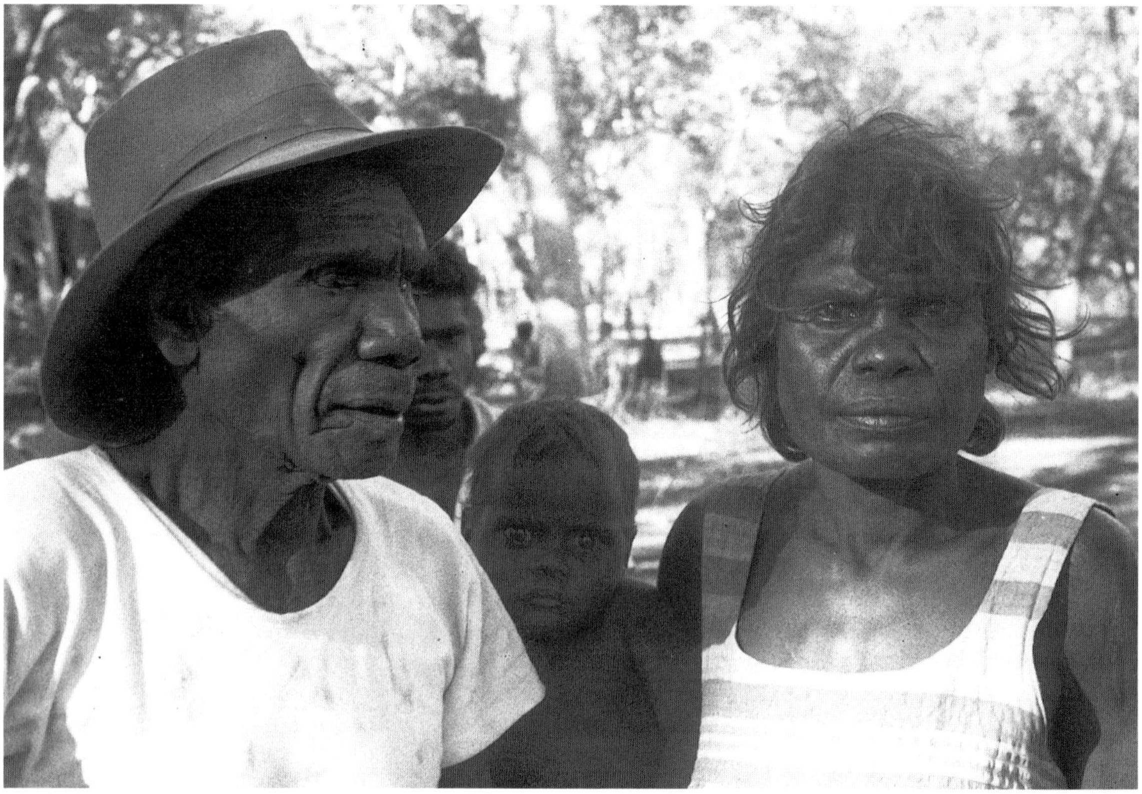

Yirawala and his elder daughter, Margaret, at the Border Store, October 1970. Margaret and David Gumaraitj were the children of Yirawala's first wife, who died before he went to live on Croker Island.

Arriving at Oenpelli Mission we waited for the welfare officer and his Aborigines to join us. Instead of taking two he had selected a group, which greatly angered Yirawala, as some of them had nothing to do with his family cave area. He feared the group might be used to stand over him. I tackled the welfare officer, pointing out the terms of the permit stated that he take only two Aborigines. We had a blazing row, but he had his way.

Finally we were on our way, with the welfare vehicle in front. It wasn't long before arguments developed about which track should be followed. Yirawala became increasingly distressed as his directions were ignored by the welfare party. As friction increased, the welfare man threatened to revoke our permits if we did not obey him. Two of our drivers sided with him and threatened to turn back.

The emotional strain and the fierce inland heat took its toll on Yirawala, who complained of feeling ill. Cecil called a halt and we erected a canopy for Yirawala and Mary.

As Yirawala was resting, an Aboriginal man from the welfare party came to apologise, saying he could not understand what was going on. He knew that Yirawala knew the way home and would not break his own tribal law. He was sorry about the arguments, but he was with the government man's party and must return with him.

Yirawala recovered and steadfastly led our convoy to his family caves.

Gunwinggu country began near Nabarlek and Goomadeer Creek, stretching across to the Liverpool and Mann Rivers, 65 kilometres inland from Maningrida Settlement.

We were now travelling over rocky areas, beneath high escarpments and through heavily timbered valleys. There were no tracks now, but Yirawala knew where he was going.

As the vehicles laboured through lush wet areas, plump brown pigeons walked close by, pecking at spilled grass seeds, oblivious to the crushing wheels. Once we halted to let a huge python pass, its luminous coils flowing through the grass. Yirawala was ecstatic. 'Ah, look, you see him, rainbow snake. Big Dreaming.' He seemed to regard this as a lucky omen.

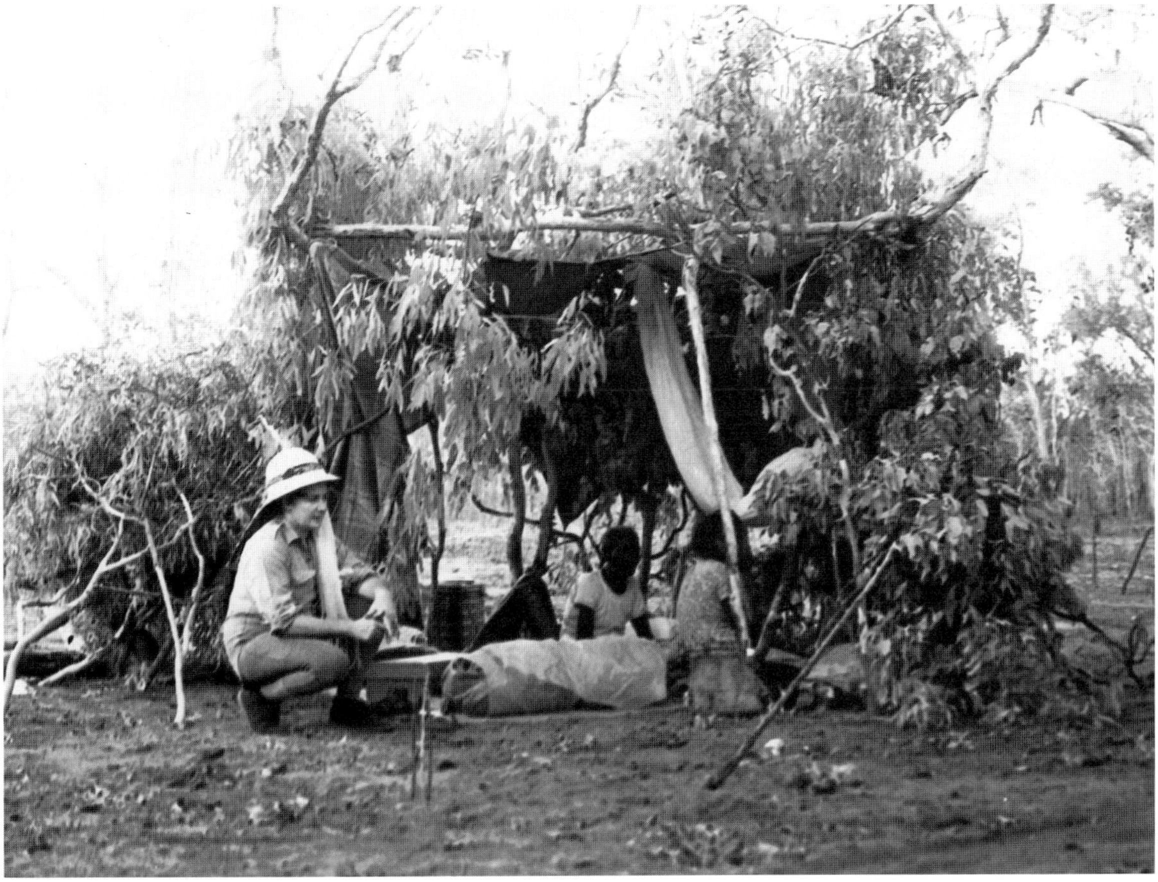

At dusk we made camp.

Perky little wallabies stared through tall grass screens, and flocks of parrots flew swiftly overhead like jewels flung by a giant hand.

At dusk we made camp among the rocky hills. The area was stony, waterless and sparsely timbered. The men pitched the tents while Mary and I prepared food and billies of tea.

We all found it hard to sleep because of the heat.

In the brief coolness of the early morning a variety of bird songs greeted the day. Yirawala was pottering about while billies boiled and fragrant dampers were pulled from the coals. 'Good tucker,' smiled Mary as she handed round large chunks dripping with butter.

As we were eating, Bobby pointed to a distant rocky cleft. Emerging a short distance from it was a big black kangaroo. Yirawala said it was very shy and sacred. 'Belong Maraian business. I paint him later on.' He spoke in language to his sons about the kangaroo.

Some distance away the welfare man was making radio contact with his Darwin base. His group was cooking a kangaroo which later gave some of them indigestion. They were also suffering from infected eyes and were treated from our medical kit.

After breakfast we packed up and moved on, closer to Yirawala's family caves. We travelled through a deep, densely wooded valley where we saw two owls asleep in the heavy foliage. The bird is called Mook-Mook and is a familiar of ghosts, Yirawala said. Emerging from this valley we entered blistering, rocky, scrub country. Here Yirawala called a halt. This was in the heart of his home country, close to his caves.

Early next morning we began filming cave galleries of rock paintings.

Pointing to stencilled hands and symbols, Yirawala told his sons that these were made long ago by tribal elders passing the land to each generation. The drawings, signs and handprints were title deeds signed by vanished hands.

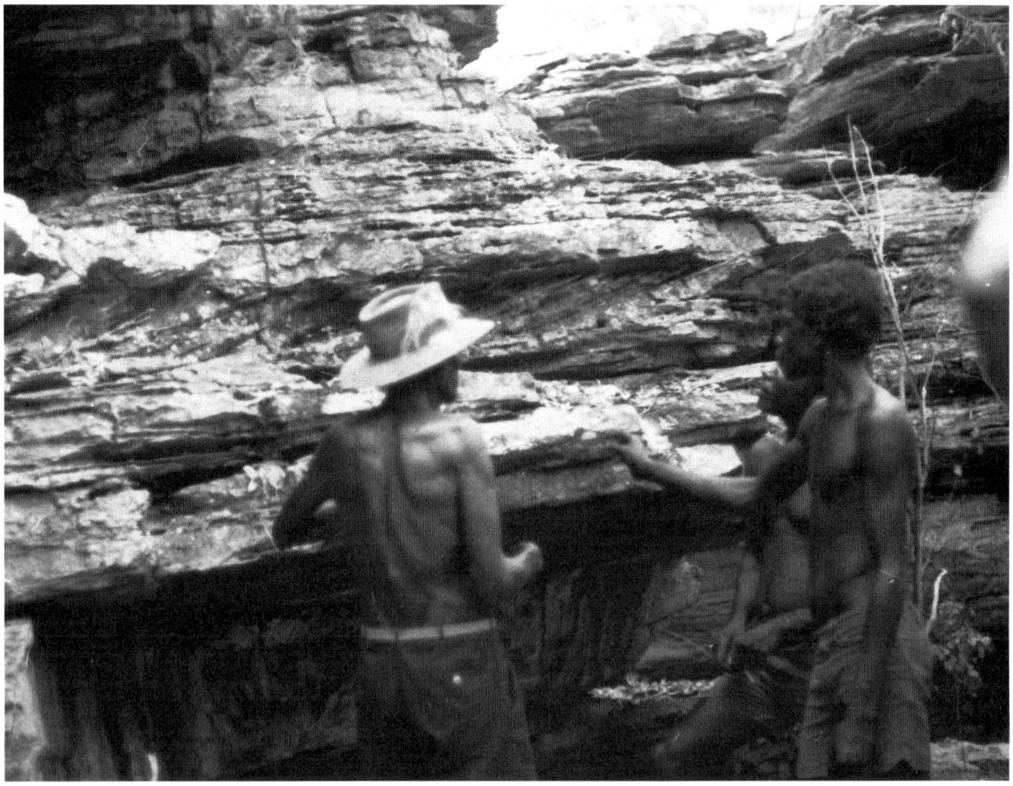

Yirawala in the heart of his home country, showing his family caves to his sons Danny Noloman and Bobby Joran (Kadjiba).

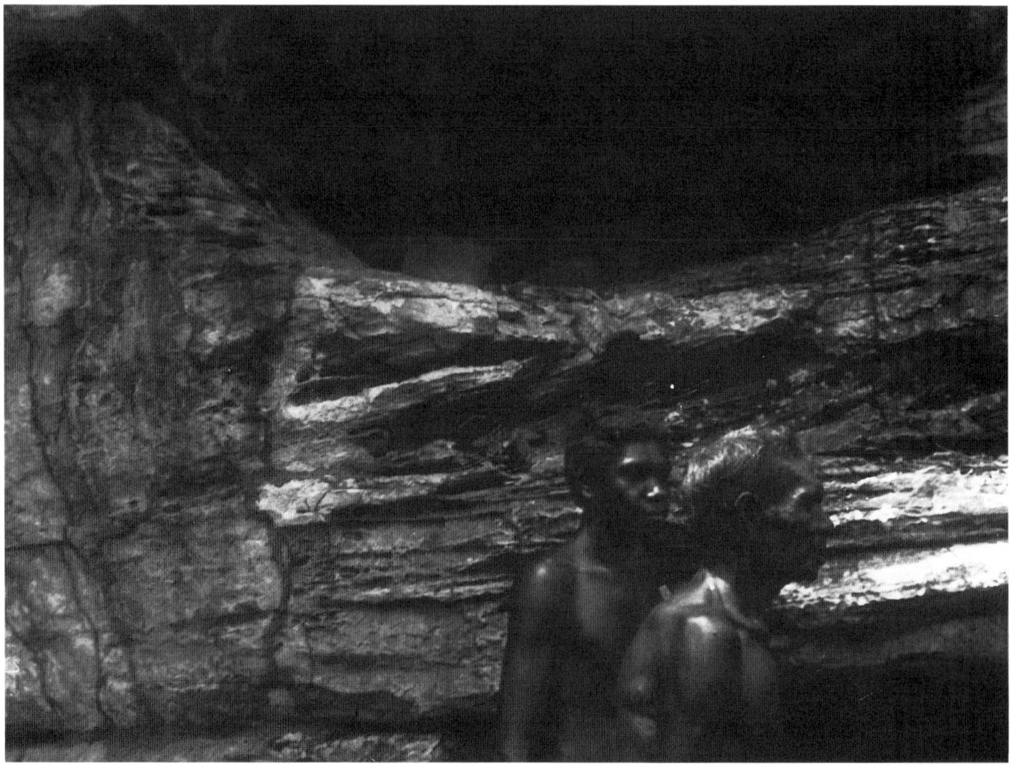

Yirawala and Danny at the family caves. We filmed the cave galleries of rock paintings — title deeds signed by vanished hands.

In one corner of the first cave were painted lines of crouching men with kangaroo heads. This was kangaroo Dreaming and belonged to the Ubar ceremony, he said. Looking upward we filmed the figure of a monster, half human and half crocodile. Yirawala said this was Namarrgine, the evil magician lying in wait for victims. It was also a warning to keep away.

Another painting depicted a woman being attacked by a large fish. This was a cautionary tale of an unfaithful wife who went into the water to gather lily seeds. As she moved into deeper water her husband sang a magic song and turned himself into a large fish which attacked and devoured her.

Yirawala pointed to a large painting of a big man chasing two female figures. He laughed as he recounted the story of Bew-Bew, a lecherous giant who caught two girls and locked them up, forcing them to become his wives. The girls refused him, and Bew-Bew thought it was because he was giving them the wrong food, so he went off to find goose eggs for them. While he was away the girls escaped and ran back to their own people. The giant returned and went in pursuit of his wives. Their clan hastily dug a large pit and Bew-Bew fell into it and was speared to death.

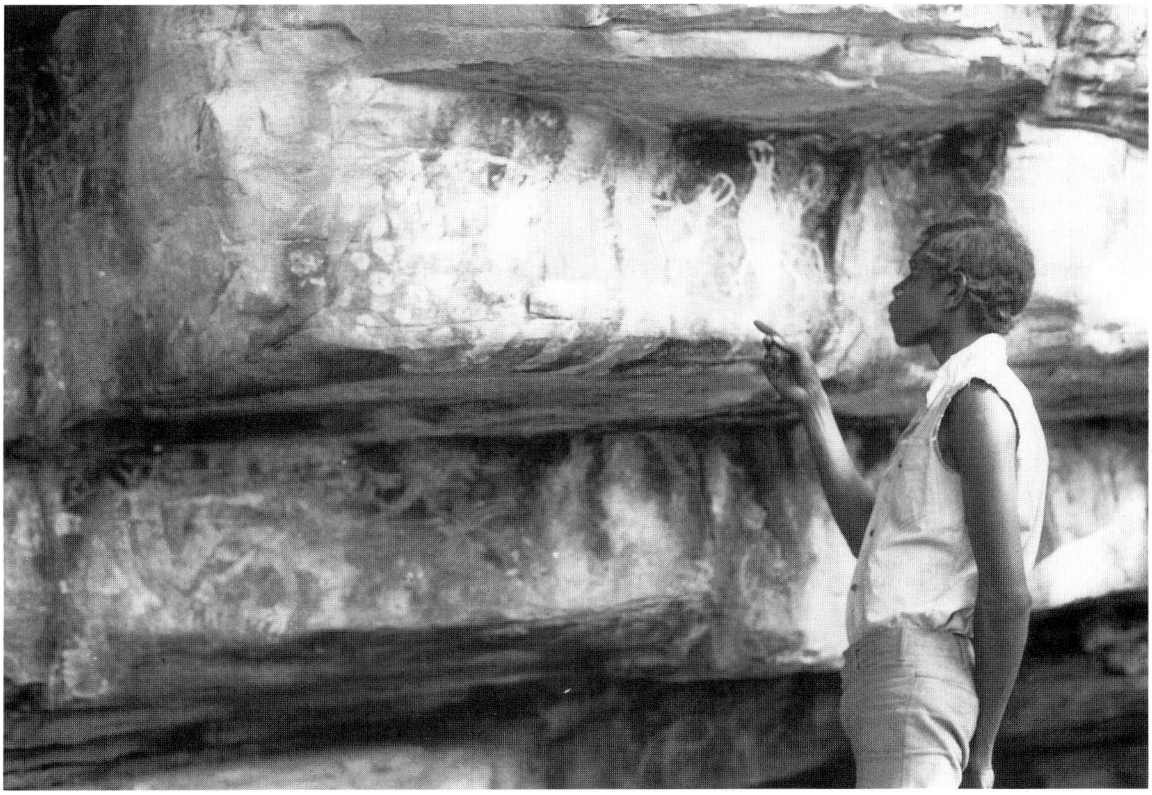

Danny points to the ghost-bird drawings. The owl is called Mook Mook and is a familiar of ghosts.

In the second cave the whole ceiling was covered with a large painting of a woman. This was Maralaitj, the earth mother. While Yirawala was explaining the painting to us, the welfare man was pottering about outside, sometimes picking up stones and putting them in a bag.

The third cave was filled with beautiful drawings and symbols. Near the entrance was a section of flat black rock, pitted with cup-like hollows, worn glass smooth over thousands of years by many hands rubbing the rock in veneration.

We stepped carefully through the cave to avoid treading on stone spear heads scattered about. Yirawala buried some of them in the sandy floor, saying that nobody could take them now.

In a cleft near the floor we noticed the painted bones of what appeared to be the remains of a small marsupial. Yirawala said a ritual had been held there to celebrate a boy's first kill.

Beneath a rocky overhang we filmed drawings of Macassan praus. Yirawala said that long ago Macassans would come down the Liverpool River looking for gold near a place called 'Gold Hill'. Sometimes the boats were wrecked in the river and sometimes the men were speared by Aborigines who resented their intrusion and their taking away bits of the country.

Back at the camp, we found that the small supply of water allotted to us by the Landrover drivers had run out. Also, our box of tinned meat had mysteriously disappeared. The welfare party said they would go to find water. By nightfall they had not returned.

Without water we would not last long in the hot, stony escarpments. Yirawala said there was no waterhole or creek in the area. The following day Bobby took a water bag and said he would go and look for water. He was gone for hours, and towards sunset we began to worry. At dusk he returned with a full water bag and a kangaroo that he had shot. He said he had followed a bird that only ate inland fish, and at sundown it had perched by a small billabong.

Bobby went back with a Landrover and filled two drums with water. Mary and Yirawala prepared and cooked the kangaroo.

Later we returned to the caves. Yirawala took us to a family burial cave. We did not film the bones interred there, only the extended galleries of beautiful paintings: birds, animals and lines of thin running figures called Mimi. Some of these figures were near the cave entrance, with spears upraised as a warning to intruders.

Yirawala said the Mimi were once real people, but always small; they were driven out and killed by new tribes. The Mimi people turned into cave spirits. Some drawings in high places were made by them. The Mimi would stand with upraised arms, sing magic songs to lower the cave ceilings, then they would make their drawings. When they had finished they sang once more then blew on the stone to raise the ceilings up again.

He said the Mimi stay home on a windy day for fear their little heads will snap off like flowers. The Mimi were responsible for yam and wallaby increase. They also hunted Kundaagi the red kangaroo. When they cooked and ate him they never burned his bones but by magic ritual raised him up again, giving him flesh and restoring him to life.

I recalled that the hunting of Kundaagi had been portrayed in the Lorrgon ceremony and asked Yirawala about it. He said that the old Mimi mother in the ceremony had found her son's bones after he had been eaten. She took them away in a dilly bag and made the first Lorrgon ceremony to restore him to life. The same ceremony is made when a human being dies, for they are one with the natural species from the Dreaming time, to ensure life after death.

Early on the day of our departure Yirawala sat some distance away, talking to Bobby and Danny. He told me he was taking them high up to show them to his ancestors. They would see their country and the distant Dreaming sites. Slowly and with bowed head the three men began the ascent.

When they reached the top, Yirawala stood in the centre with raised arms and head thrown back. His mouth was open and at first there was no sound, then his strange chanting cries echoed over the hills and valleys. Birds flew up from below and away towards the darkening sky.

Again and again he raised his arms, calling the Maraian names, calling his ancestors, asking them for power to save the land and sacred places. He had come home to ask for help.

As the last cry faded away it mingled with the sound of distant thunder. On the darkening horizon there was a faint flicker of lightning, like a serpent's tongue. The wet season was about to break over the land.

Yirawala smiled at us. His eyes were shining and his expression radiant. In the shimmering heat he seemed to float down the escarpment.

Bobby carried the heavy Nagra recorder for me as we followed his father. On the way down we paused here and there to peer into smooth, long tunnels. From deep inside we

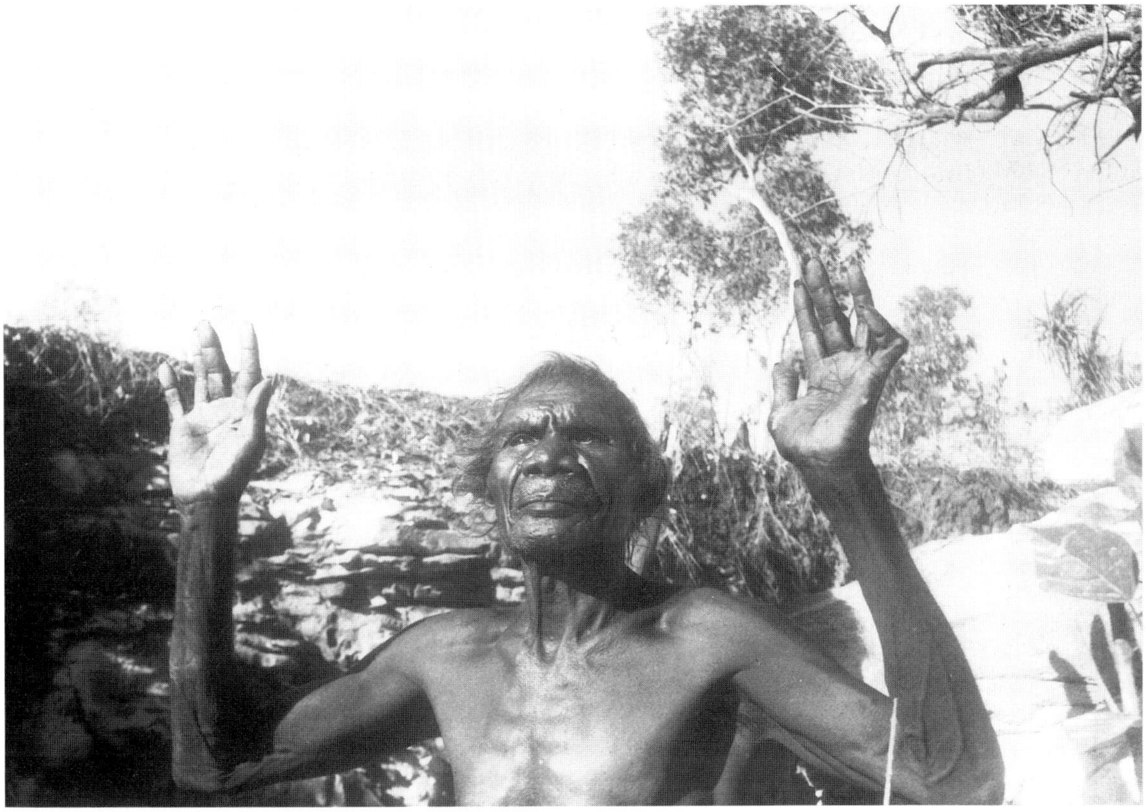

Again and again Yirawala raised his arms, calling the Maraian names, calling his ancestors, asking them for power to save the land and sacred places.

could hear the twittering of bats and saw a few tiny ones clinging to the walls.

One round tunnel was as smooth as glass, with ripples of stone, as if long ago water had been flowing there.

In a rock overhang we inspected fossilised shells embedded in the rock. Some resembled ammonites.

At last we reached the bottom. As our feet crunched in the coarse sand, a rock wallaby darted by and Bobby impulsively picked up a round white pebble and threw it. The stone shattered on the rock face in a rainbow of colour.

We spent the afternoon packing up. Just before sunset the welfare man returned, saying he had been to Oenpelli for water. He brought none for us.

We were all suffering from heat exhaustion and lay down covered with wet towels. Thunder rumbled in the distance and in the breathless heat among the rocks all nature waited for the rain.

That night I dreamed about a big owl sitting next to me. Its eyes were enormous. Looking past it I saw my daughter lying dead. I woke up in fear and told my husband, who said I was under too much strain and not to worry.

Before leaving the area Yirawala wanted to visit a cave which he said was filled with paintings which were important for Mary as well. The welfare man said we must return at once to Oenpelli and Darwin, or he would revoke our permits. The Landrover drivers sided with him. Yirawala pleaded with them, but to no avail.

Late the next afternoon the convoy stopped to rest by a beautiful billabong, surrounded by pandanus palms which cast their reflections in the water, turning it green. Yirawala warned everyone not to break the bushes near the pool, for the area was a sacred home of the Yowk-Yowk, the water women. Anyone who profaned the area would die from storms or drowning.

We boiled the billy and ate the last of the damper. Bobby went off with his rifle and came back with a goose, which he cleaned and roasted in the fire. The best parts were given to his parents.

We were not allowed to burn the bones of the goose for that would destroy its spirit, Yirawala said. He carefully buried the bones away from the pool.

Drinking from his old enamel mug, he told the Yowk-Yowk story.

Deep down in the water live the beautiful, light-skinned water women who rise to the surface on moonlit nights to play and sing, guarded by the old water witch. The water sprites have long black hair and eyes like stars. No man has ever seen them, only heard their wonderful songs. Many wily hunters have sought to capture one of the women for a wife, but at the slightest sound they vanish beneath the water.

There was one famous hunter who longed to capture one. He vowed to other men that one day his dream would be fulfilled, but they only laughed at him.

Twice he tried to get close enough to the water women, and failed, so he consulted his father, who was a 'clever man'. The old man told him that the Yowk-Yowk sprites had acute sense of smell and hearing, so before approaching them he must thoroughly wash all over and then move silently, holding his breath. When close enough, he must move like lightning, grab a girl and place a stone in her mouth to stop her using her shark-like teeth. Next he must bind her hands and feet and carry her home. Once there he must seat her in a smokey fire and place burning bark near her ears to shut out forever the sound of running water. He must also sing a magic song, after which she would forget her origin. Finally the old medicine man warned his son never to let the girl near water, as memory would return and she would dive in and vanish.

The young hunter succeeded in capturing a water sprite and for some months lived

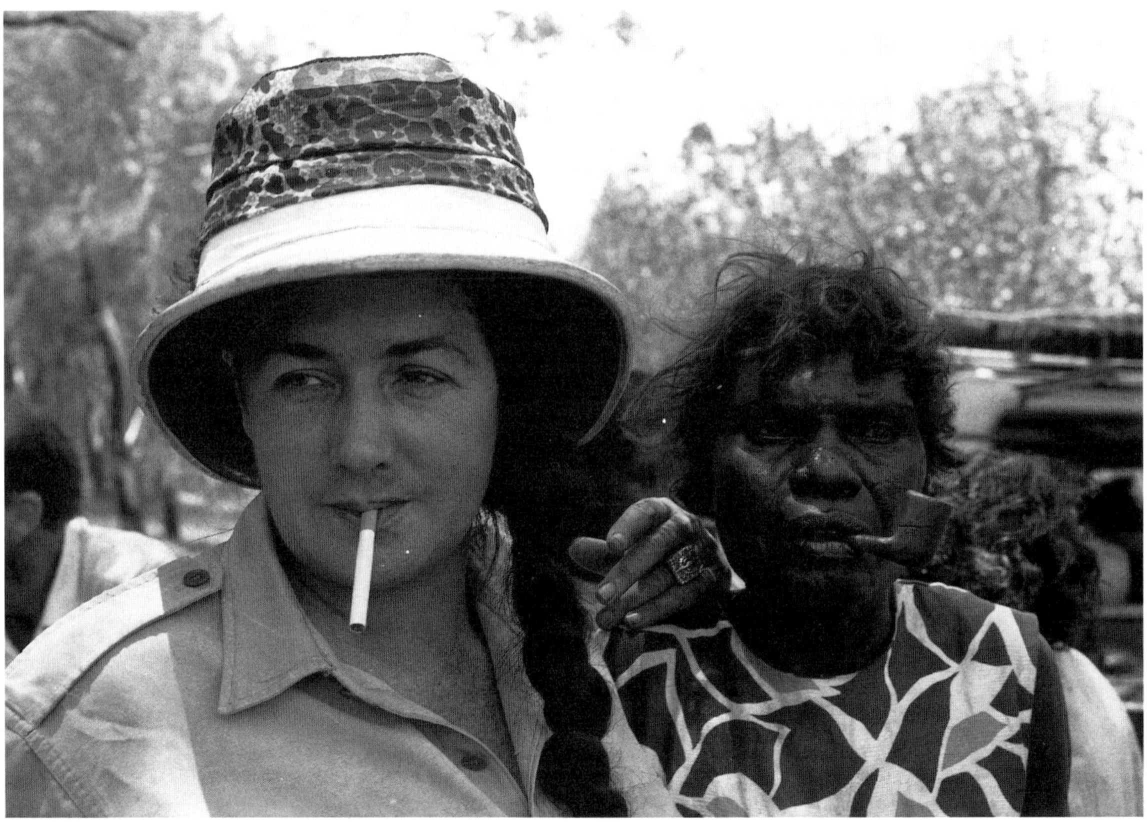

Yirawala's daughter, Margaret, and I at the Border Store after a blazing row with the welfare officer.

happily with her until a jealous wife sent her to fetch water. She dived in and was seen no more.

Late in the evening we reached the East Alligator River and thankfully slaked our thirst at Terry's bar. Ron Withnall, our lawyer, was camped on the river bank and joined us for a drink. He was not surprised to learn of our ordeals and warned there could still be more to come.

We camped by the river and had little sleep due to raving drunks all through the bush. At one stage the assistant cameraman pretended to be a policeman to hunt some of them from our camp.

We moved out early next day and stopped near a large billabong where we all dived in, except Yirawala, who dabbled cannily on the edge, poking at floating leaves with a long stick. He explained, 'Snake, him hot like we. Big King Brown, little snake, death adder, whole lot him swim.' I asked about crocodiles. He shrugged. 'Might be. When big rain come, him walk about.'

Still worried about my dream, I asked the welfare man to call Darwin Hospital. A voice came crackling over the radio. Amanda was in hospital with infectious hepatitus.

We returned to Darwin. After resting for two weeks, Yirawala and his family went back to Croker Island. He was tired but happy that he had shown some of the home country to his sons. Before leaving Darwin the cameraman filmed some of the Yirawala paintings in my museum. I also gave permission for the use of some tracks from my LP *Land of the Morning Star** for the film. The film would be edited in Sydney and a copy sent to us so that we could arrange for certain tribal elders to view it.

In November a letter came from the Australian Council for the Arts to say that our application towards funding a touring art exhibition with Yirawala and Bobby had been

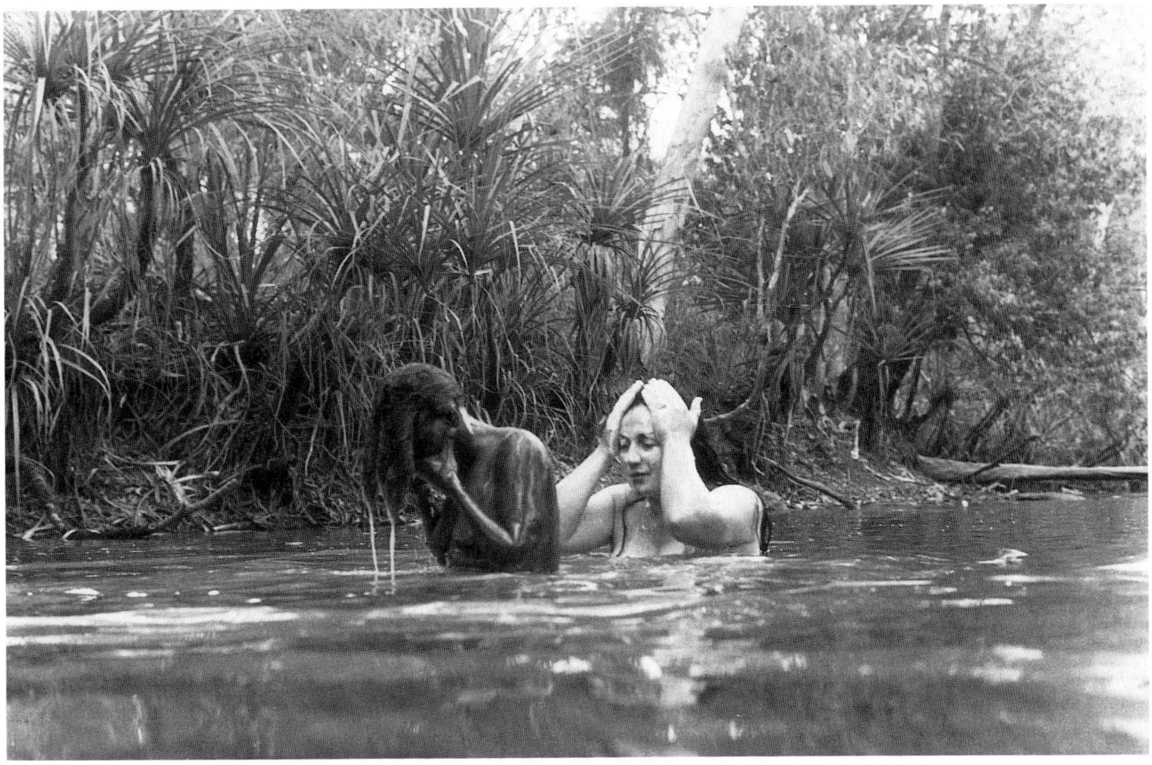

Mary Malilba and I cool off in a billabong.

* Mono. OCLP 7610, EMI 1963 (Aboriginal music).

approved, to enable us to visit Sydney, Melbourne, Adelaide and the Orange Arts Festival, starting in February 1971. I wrote with this good news to Yirawala and his family and to Bobby Joran at a forestry camp where he was employed.

In December problems of communication with Yirawala worsened and there was no reply to telegrams and letters nor acknowledgment of money and goods sent. (Later I learned that a large tent I sent had somehow gone astray.)

Late that month one of Yirawala's relations told me that Yirawala's son David Gumaraitj and a man named Brisbane were cutting and curing bark for Yirawala. He said about sixty paintings were taken to the craft store and sold to a dealer who had approached Yirawala direct. It appeared that our contract was worthless in the eyes of some people.

Chapter 5
Southern art tour, 1971: Paintings and stories inseparable from the land

In January 1971 I began organising the tour south. Trans Australian Airlines generously agreed to be co-sponsors of the tour, providing complimentary seats and carriage of freight.

Our first lecture and exhibition would be held at the Adelaide Museum in mid February. From there we would go to Melbourne for a display at the Ewing Gallery of Melbourne University. The next stop would be Sydney for a display and lecture in the Brennan Room of Sydney University, at which Professor Elkin would give the opening address. The final exhibition would be in Orange.

The month of January was frenetic, arranging venues, accommodation, publicity, interviews, invitations, and my own domestic affairs — and trying to make contact with Yirawala and Bobby. I knew they wanted to go on the tour, but no word came from them. I could only hope that some of my letters or telegrams had reached them.

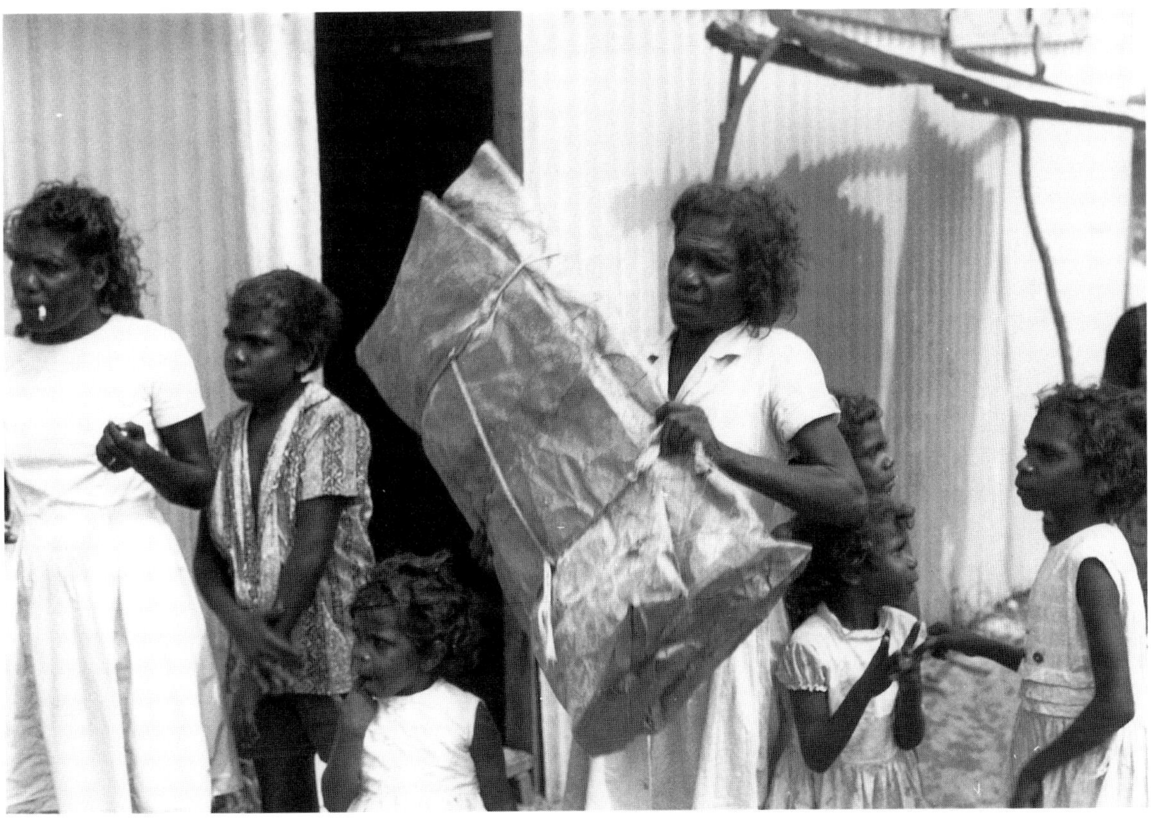

Margaret Monanggu carrying a parcel of paintings for the touring exhibition, February 1971. Mary Malilba is on the left.

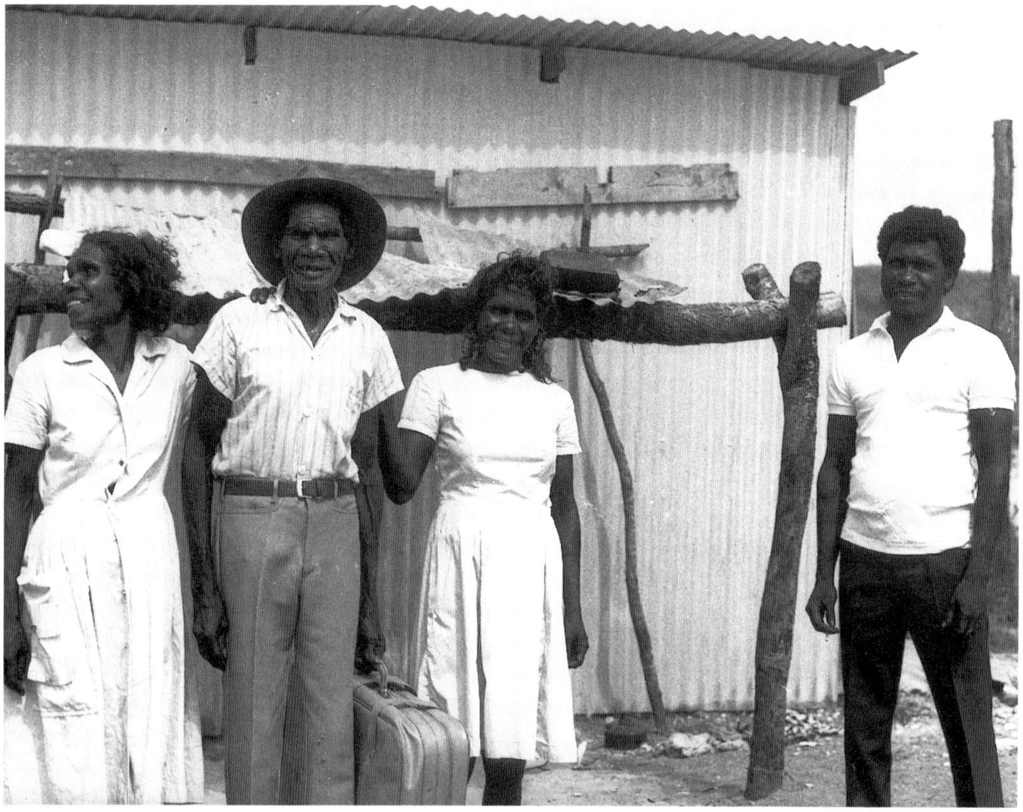

Yirawala and Bobby were anxious to go on tour, and soon made ready. Left to right: Margaret Monanggu, Yirawala, Mary Malilba and Bobby Joran (Kadjiba). Outside their home on Croker Island, February 1971.

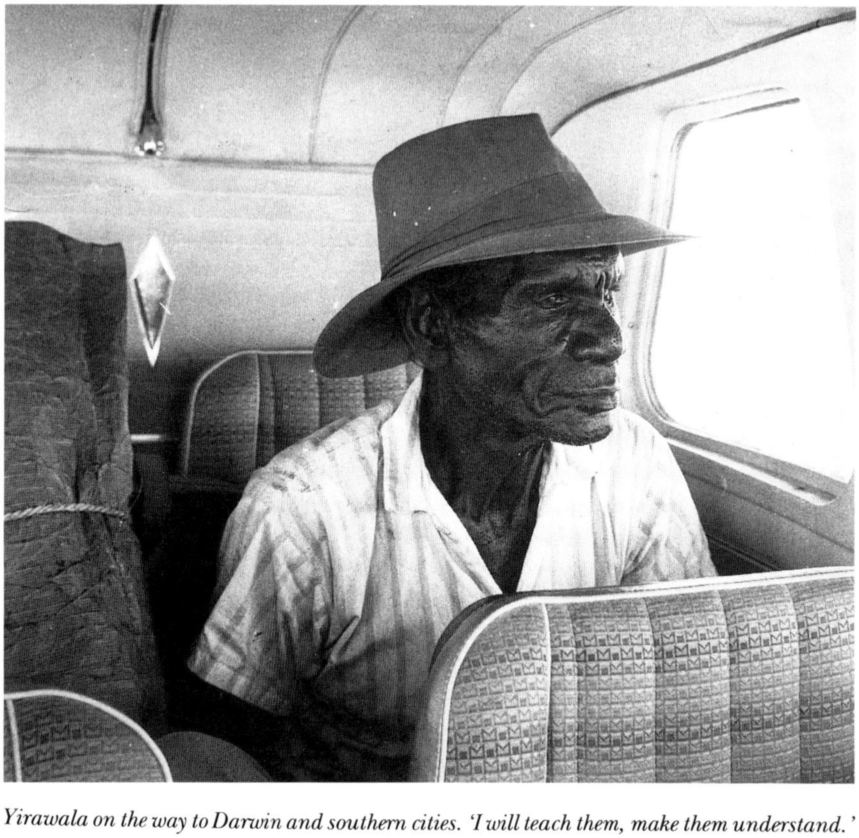

Yirawala on the way to Darwin and southern cities. 'I will teach them, make them understand.'

Early in February I applied for a permit for 9 February to go to Croker Island and pick them up. When I arrived they were anxious to go and soon made ready.

In Darwin, luggage and new sets of clothing had to be bought, including shoes for Yirawala. The new suit and tie did not bother him, but the shoes were a bit of a problem because of his long toenails.

Yirawala and Bobby boarded the jet with complete faith in aeronautical technology. When the plane levelled out Yirawala sat sipping tea, smiling under his old bush hat as the hostess fussed over him. Bobby, tall and handsome in his new suit, sat reading a magazine, relaxed as always. They really had no idea how fast they were travelling or how far.

The Adelaide exhibition caused great interest and attracted a large number of people. Yirawala spoke passionately about his land, desperately grasping at English words, with Bobby acting as his interpreter. He was not at all nervous, and managed to convey that his drawings were religion closely allied to the clan lands, which he was trying to save from mining.

One sour note was the presence of an overseas dealer who had worried us in Darwin. I saw him photographing the paintings with a tiny camera and reading the explanations into a small tape recorder. I reported this to a security guard.

The Lord Mayor of Adelaide, Alderman Porter, invited us for afternoon tea. He was genuinely interested in what the Aborigines had to say. Yirawala and Bobby spoke of their important caves where sacred objects were stored. Alderman Porter then invited them to the small museum of Queen Adelaide's relics in the City Council building. The Aborigines wandered among the glass cases, looking at a tiny pair of slippers, lace and other dainty treasures. When they emerged, the Lord Mayor asked them what they thought of it all. Yirawala said, 'Good. You keep him all in strong room, big lock, guard outside. We got no strong room, lock, guard, in my country.' Bobby explained that before the white people

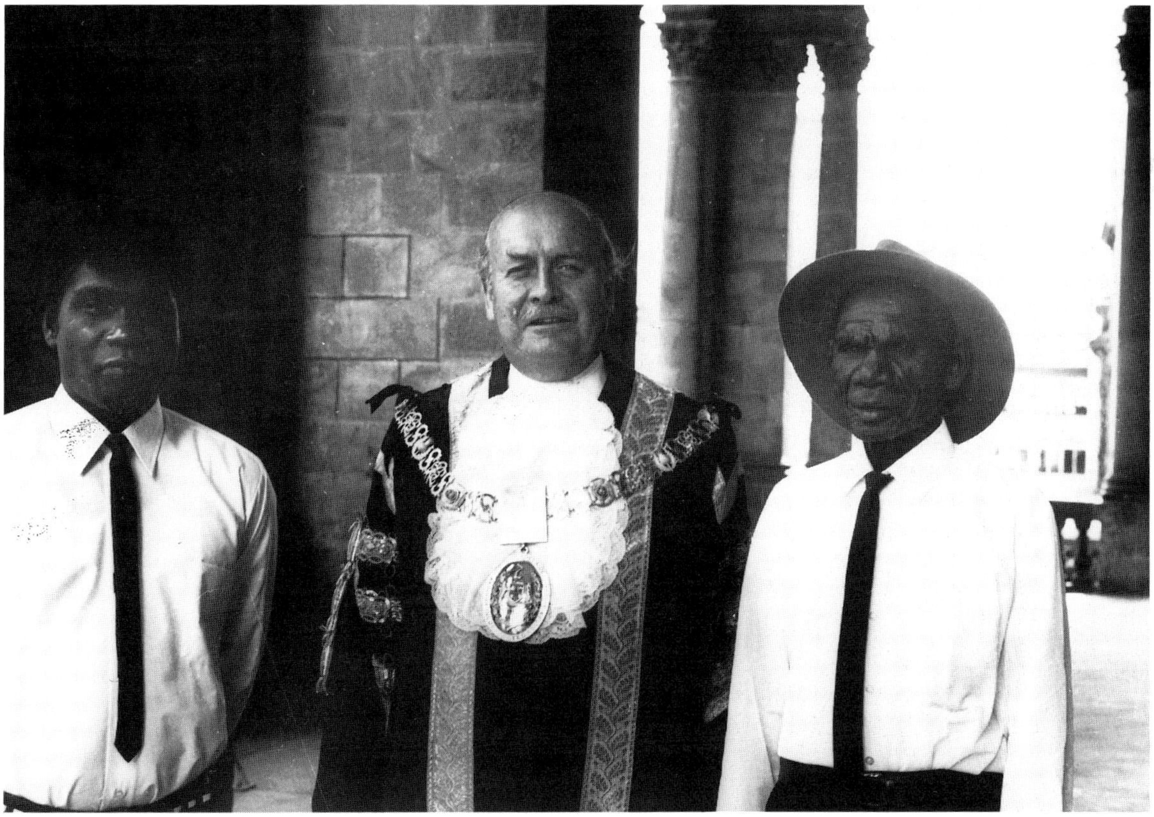

The Lord Mayor, Alderman Porter, welcoming Bobby Joran and Yirawala to Adelaide. He invited them to afternoon tea and was genuinely interested in what they had to say.

came onto their land, Aborigines did not need guards for their caves and objects, but now they needed strong government laws to be made, to protect the sacred sites from vandals and thieves.

Yirawala and Bobby liked the gentle pace of Adelaide and enjoyed going into the hills and picking grapes from the vine. Yirawala said that in some parts of Arnhemland they had wild grapes but very much smaller. They were delighted by their visit to the zoo, and were amazed and amused by the giraffe and monkeys. Yirawala was reluctant to leave the elephants, who stood in the water, squirting each other and washing their own backs to cool off.

Whereas the exhibition in Adelaide had been mounted in a dignified and professional manner, we were to encounter problems in Melbourne.

I booked us into a hotel not far from the university. One hotel had refused accommodation. The manager of the second hotel said that generally there might have been a problem but he had seen the publicity about Yirawala and his art.

The exhibition room at the Ewing Gallery was smaller than we had anticipated and the security could have been better, as two paintings were stolen.

Bobby and I had worked hard putting up posters and giving out leaflets. We had left piles of leaflets here and there where students congregated. Yirawala and Bobby were also interviewed by the media and received a lot of publicity.

The exhibition must have excited the rage of someone, as all our posters were torn down and leaflets ripped up and scattered about.

On the opening night we had a poor attendance, perhaps because of competition from a man who had hired a room on the same floor. We heard the next day that as people approached, he waved a bark painting and called out, 'This way for the Aboriginal art lecture.' Yirawala and Bobby were upset but continued with their lectures to small audiences. We had put up more posters and given out more piles of leaflets, but these were also destroyed.

On the first evening at the hotel we sat in the elegant dining room. Yirawala had ordered a whole grilled fish. For a while he battled with is knife and fork, then picked up a piece of spiny backbone and deftly flicked it across the room. To my horror it landed in the hair of a middle-aged lady, who prattled on oblivious to the decoration in her hair. After that Bobby said his father would order room service.

The Aborigines enjoyed the hotel's room service, its good food and its television. Yirawala liked news programs and the series *Steptoe and Son.* He laughed a great deal at old Steptoe.

A highlight of the visit to Melbourne was a day at the Moscow Circus, organised by Keith Dunstan, then a journalist at the *Sun* newspaper.

Yirawala and Bobby had not seen a big circus before and sat waiting expectantly as the music blared forth and the first act was introduced. It was the Flying Luengos, aerialist acrobats. Swinging high above us were a man and a girl. He was hanging by his ankles and supporting the girl by a bar he held in his teeth. Bobby and Yirawala were thrilled. 'Him got good teeth,' remarked Yirawala.

After that the lions went through their paces, with the whip not far behind them. Yirawala called them 'Clever pussy cats'. He made no comments about the bears, but clucked now and again. Perhaps he felt sorry for them.

Most of all Yirawala loved Popov, the clown with his snake-charming act. Both Aborigines laughed until tears ran down their faces.

After the show Yirawala went to meet Popov. Communication between the two men was instant and they embraced. Popov began clowning for Yirawala and he laughed once more. Through the interpreter Yirawala was introduced as a great artist, which resulted in more embraces and an invitation to drink vodka. This of course was not accepted. The two men embraced once more and parted.

The curator of the State Museum of Victoria invited Yirawala to examine some old bark paintings collected by W B Spencer and F J Gillen in the Oenpelli area. When Yirawala looked at them he became very excited, for he recognised the work as belonging in his

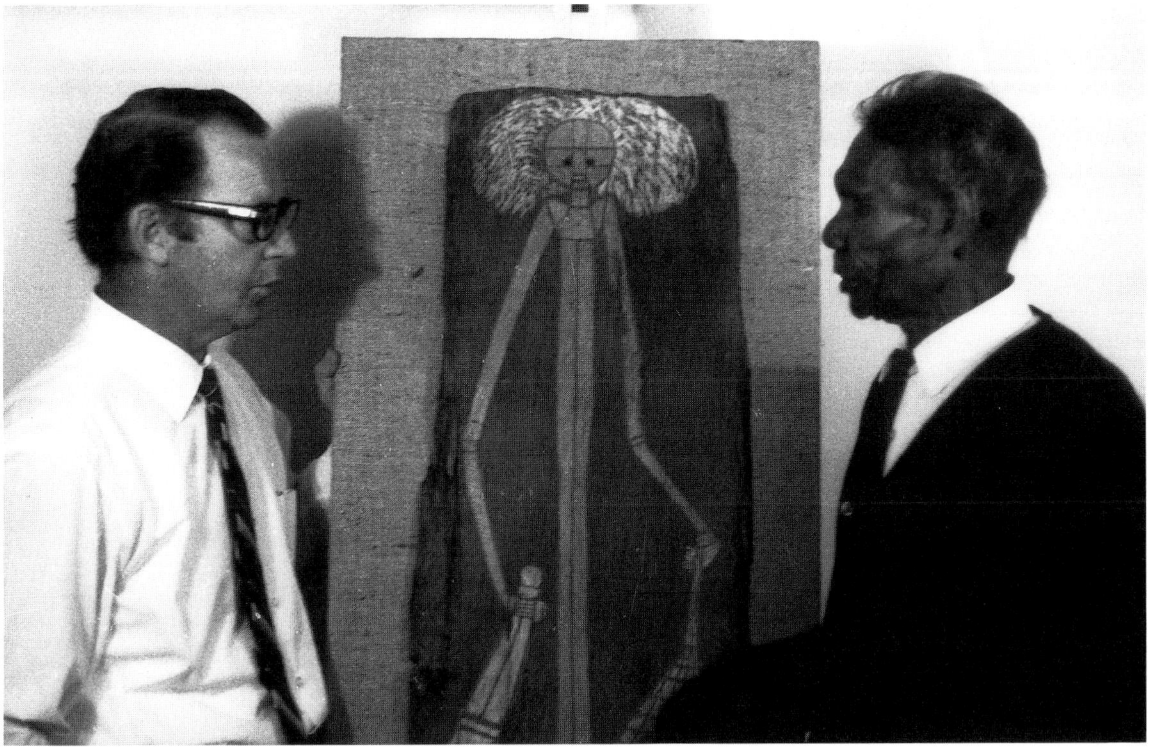

Yirawala at the State Museum of Victoria, talking with the director, Mr White, after identifying the drawings collected by Spencer and Gillen as having been done by his grandfather.

family. They had been painted by his own grandfather. The curator fetched a tape recorder in an effort to have some identification and documentation at last.

Yirawala gave interviews to the media about his caves and how white mining men were moving over the country in trucks and caravans. He said such men stole bones and objects from the caves and had no respect. Some cave paintings had been vandalised as well. He said he wanted to talk to a lot of white people about these things.

Before our leaving Melbourne the National Gallery of Victoria, seeking to honour Yirawala, asked if they could hang five of his paintings for a few days. Yirawala agreed, as long as they were looked after. The paintings were to be sent on in time for the Sydney exhibition. Only three arrived. The curator wrote an apologetic note to say that the paintings had been stolen. That made four paintings stolen in Melbourne.

In Sydney the exhibition opened on 7 March to an audience of distinguished invited guests, including Dr Nugget Coombs and some senior Aborigines from country areas of New South Wales. The opening address was given by Professor Elkin, who praised Yirawala as a man of high degree who had travelled far to present his religious paintings to help us understand their importance and the stories that were inseparable from ownership of the land. Bobby spoke on behalf of his father who, still wearing his bush hat, welcomed people at his exhibition.

In the days that followed, many people came to see the paintings and hear Yirawala and his son. The theme was the same, presenting his paintings like a religious book and needing help to save the land and sacred places from the mining men.

The media treated Yirawala and his son with understanding and respect, and faithfully wrote what they had said about saving their land. When all this was read to Yirawala he was very pleased and said 'Good newspaper men, write true word.'

At night we watched the television news reports. Some featured the exhibition, quoting something of what he had said. He asked me how many people watched television. I told him many people, like ants in a number of nests. He nodded. 'Big mob balanda, him hear 'bout my land. Him all know me, help me when we sing out for land.' He felt that when the battle for his family land began, he could look for support now to the many white people who had heard him speak. He had got his voice out from the confines of the Aboriginal reserve and repressive white authority in the Northern Territory. He was happy.

Some reporters were detailed to show the two visitors around Sydney. Walking along Pitt Street, Yirawala was making swimming motions with his arms. A reporter asked what was wrong, and Yirawala said, 'Too many big houses, can't see. No water, no tree.' Mentally he was trying to pull the buildings down to look at the horizon and the sea. When he came to Australian Square, one reporter pointed with some satisfaction to the tall building and asked Yirawala what he thought of it. He squinted up at it for a while, then said, 'Him alright. Nimbuah Rock in my country him more high.'

The reporters then suggested we have a look at Sydney Harbour Bridge, that would surely impress the old man. It did. Yirawala loved it, admiring the criss-crossed steel of the arch. The journalists smiled and led the way to climb up inside one of the pylons. When we reached the top Yirawala sat on the edge of the stone parapet, his thin hair blowing in the wind. For a while he stared around him then slid down from his perch. He was no longer smiling and whispered to me, 'Too many balanda. Too many house, like ant nest. Big mob balanda. I never know before. Better we go home quick, might be him all come to my country.' He felt overwhelmed and a little threatened by so many buildings and people.

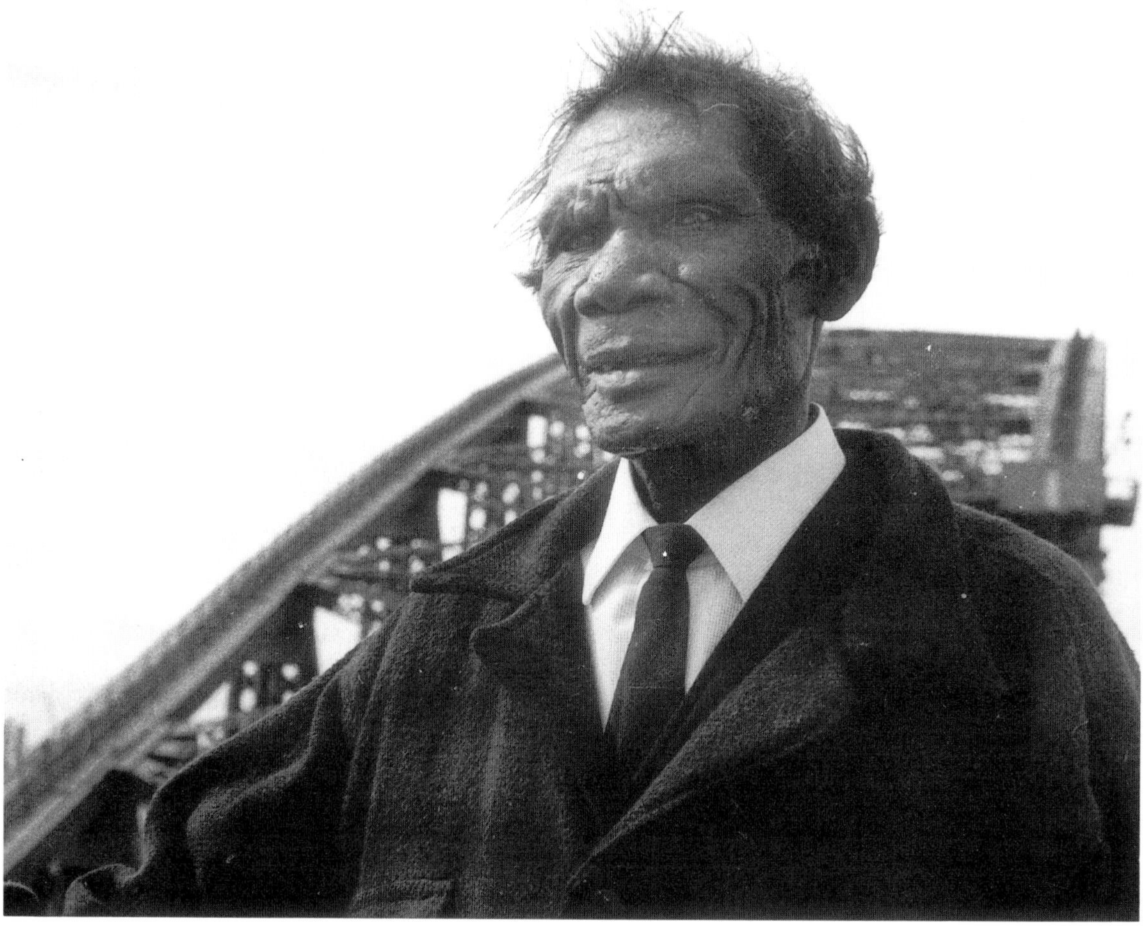

Yirawala looking out at the city and the harbour from the Sydney Harbour Bridge pylon. He was alarmed to see so many buildings. 'Too many balanda. I never know before.'

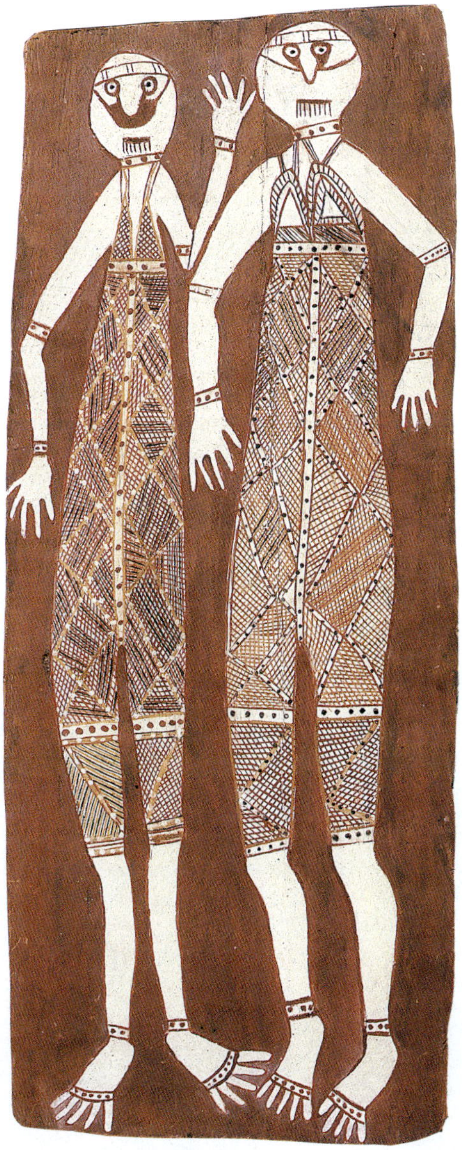

Plate 36 MARAIAN SERIES

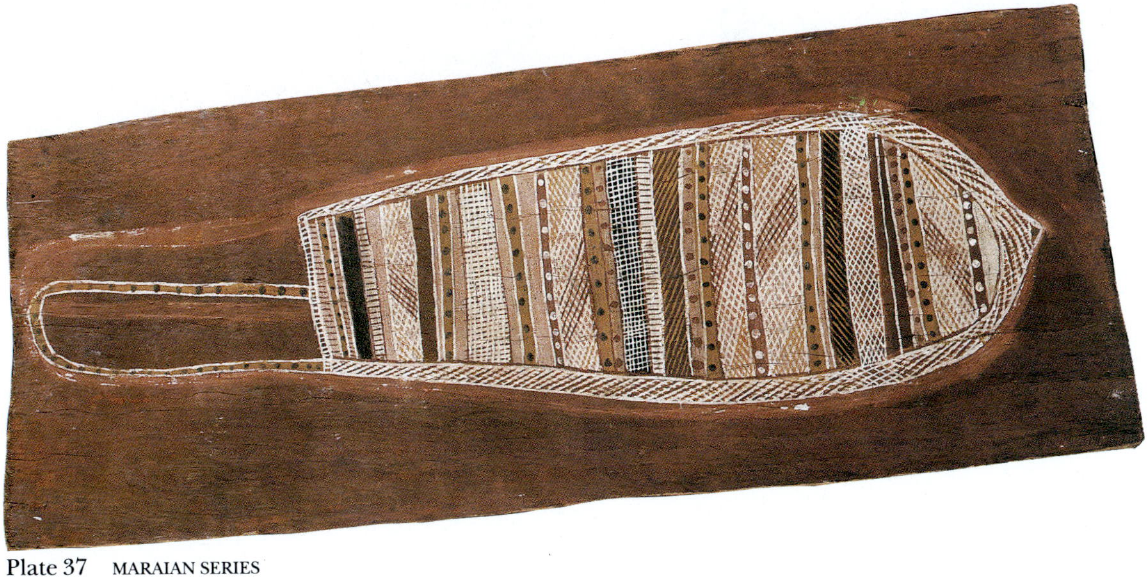

Plate 37 MARAIAN SERIES

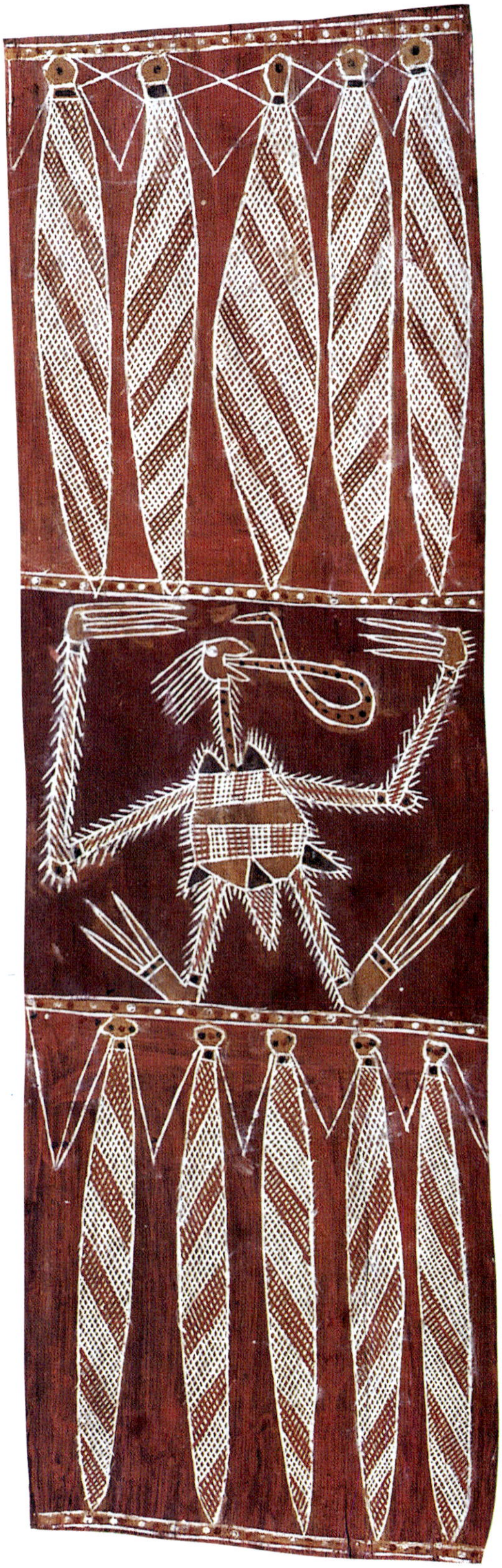

Plate 38 MARAIAN SERIES

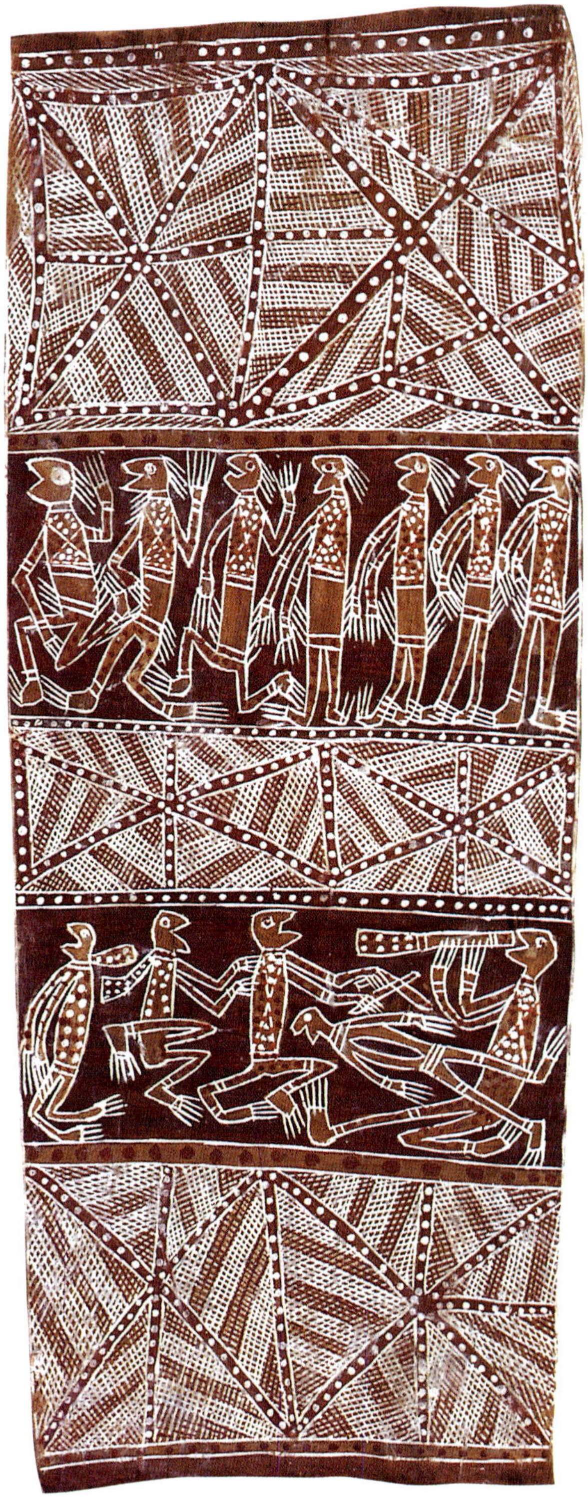

Plate 39 MARAIAN SERIES

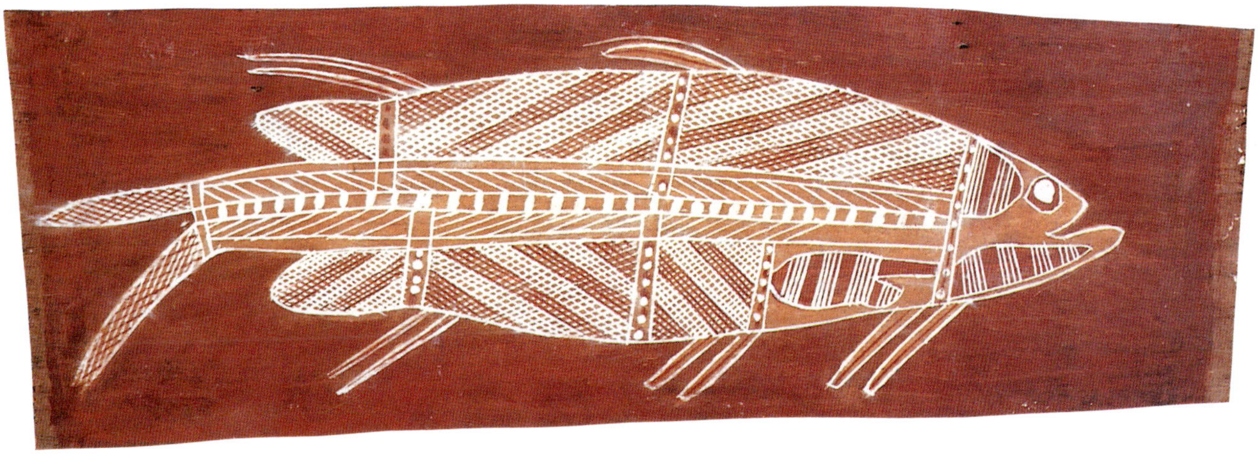

Plate 40 MARAIAN SERIES

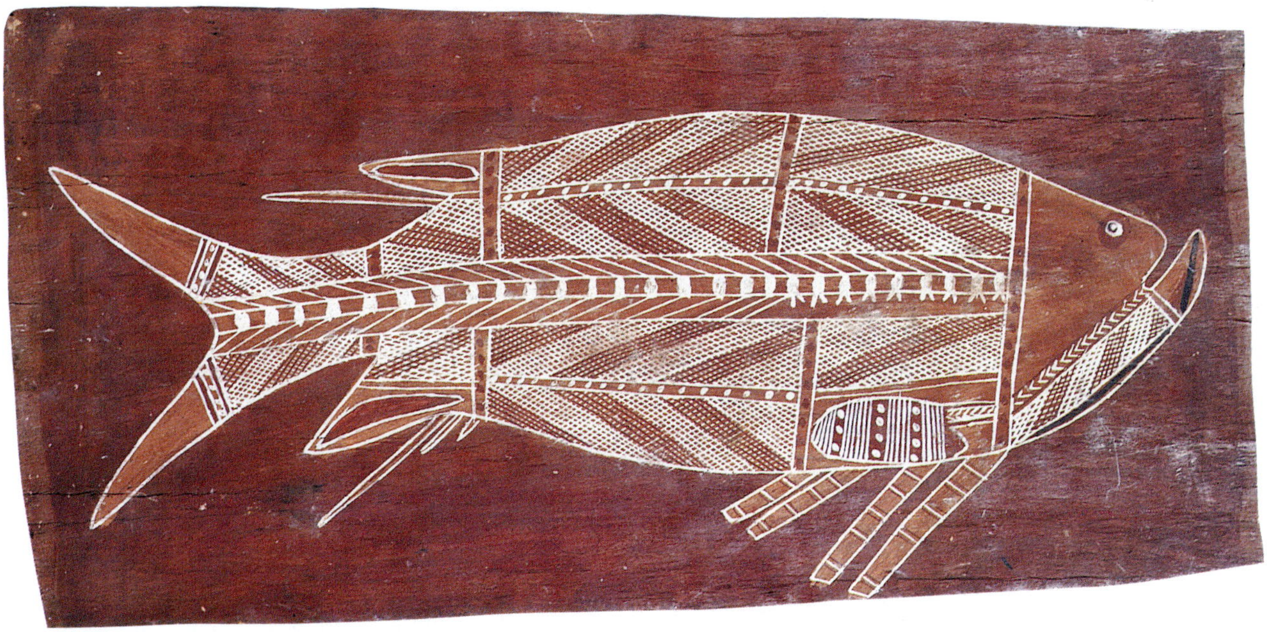

Plate 41 MARAIAN SERIES

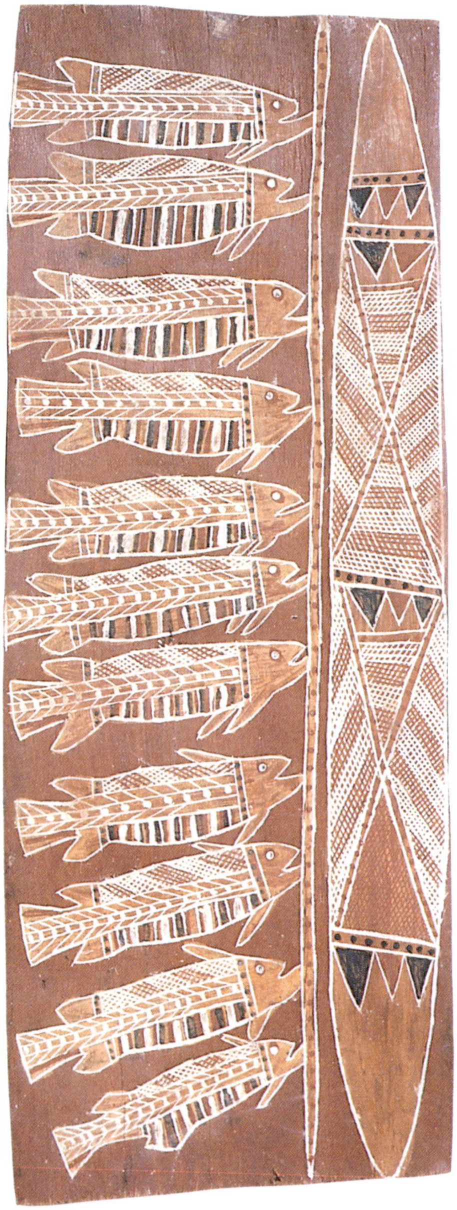

Plate 42 MARAIAN SERIES

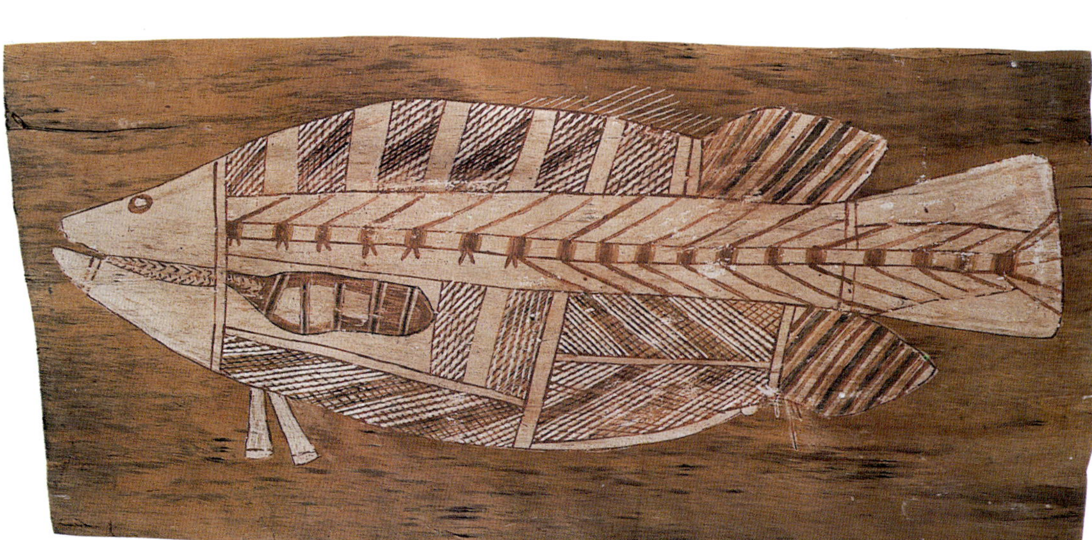

Plate 43 MARAIAN SERIES

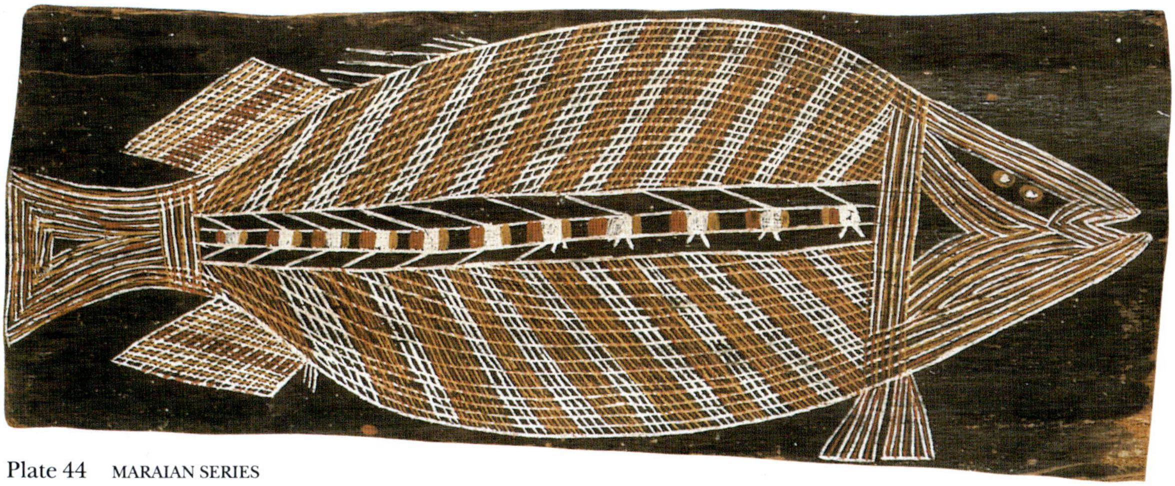
Plate 44 MARAIAN SERIES

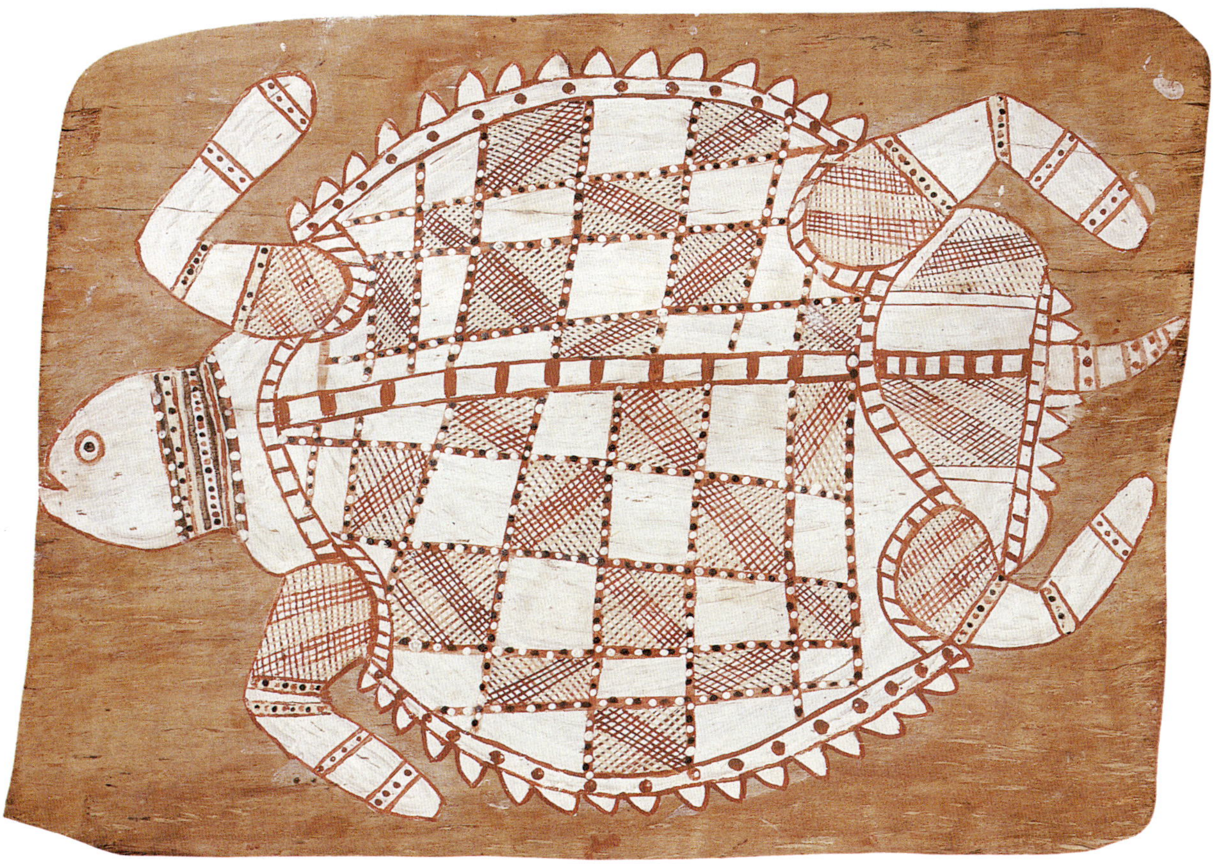
Plate 45 MARAIAN SERIES

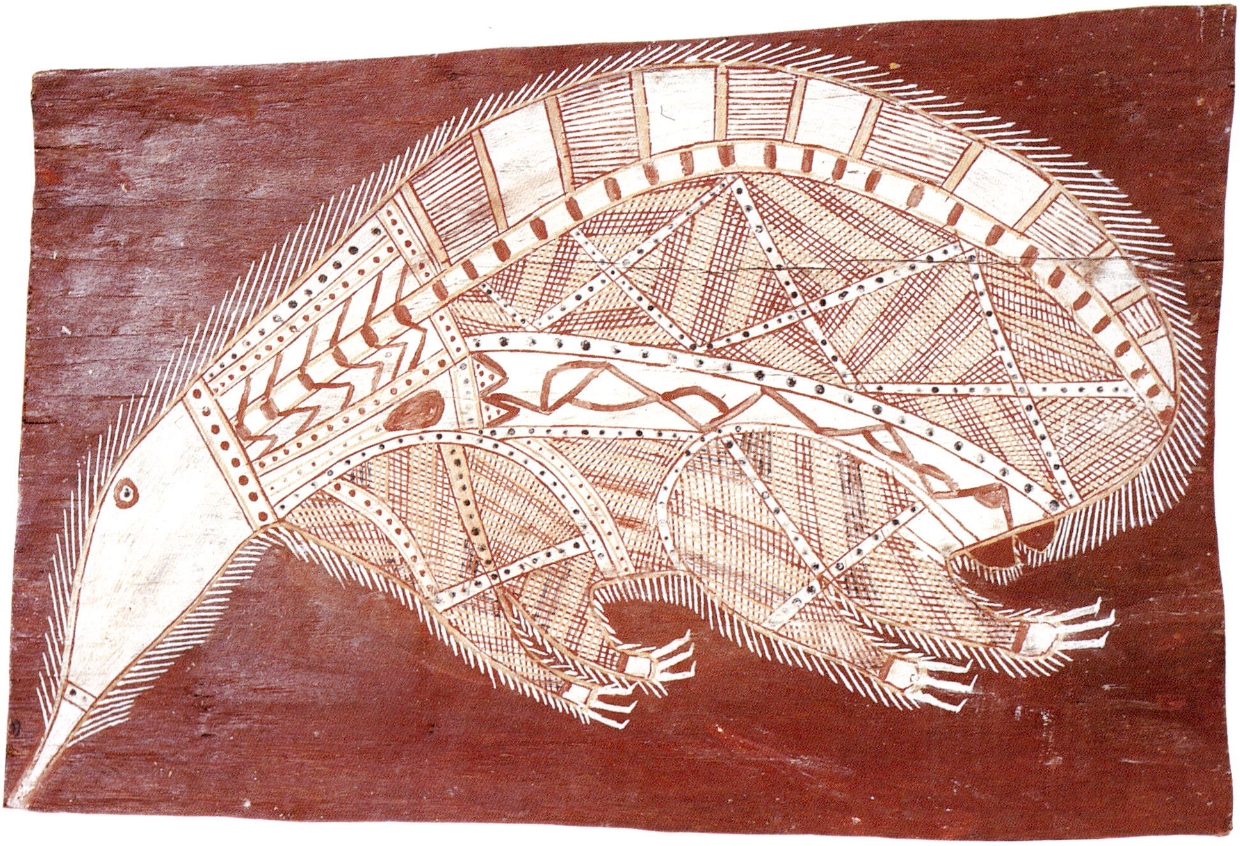

Plate 46 MARAIAN SERIES

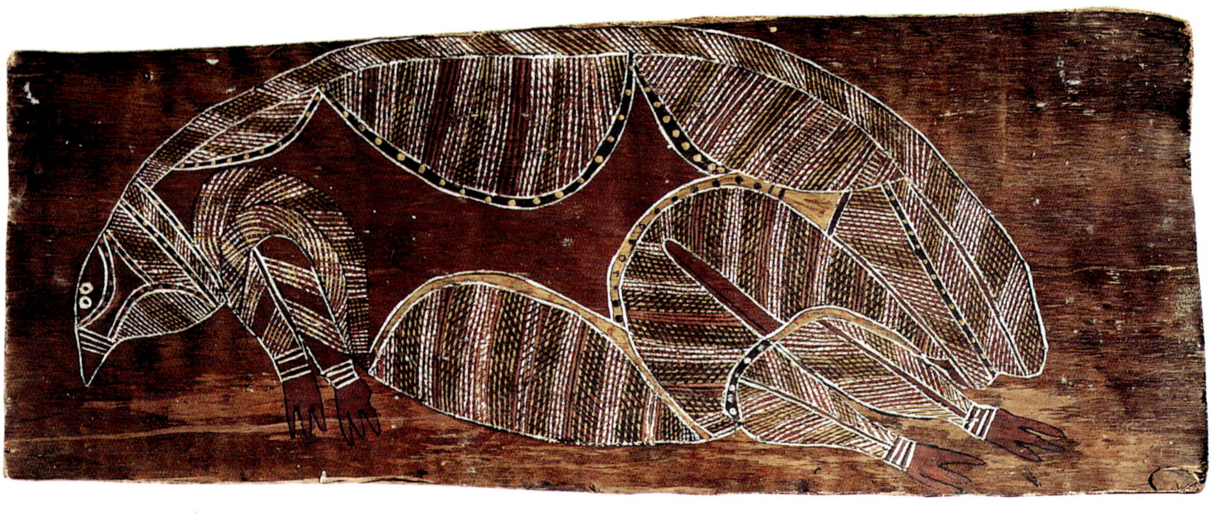

Plate 47 MARAIAN SERIES

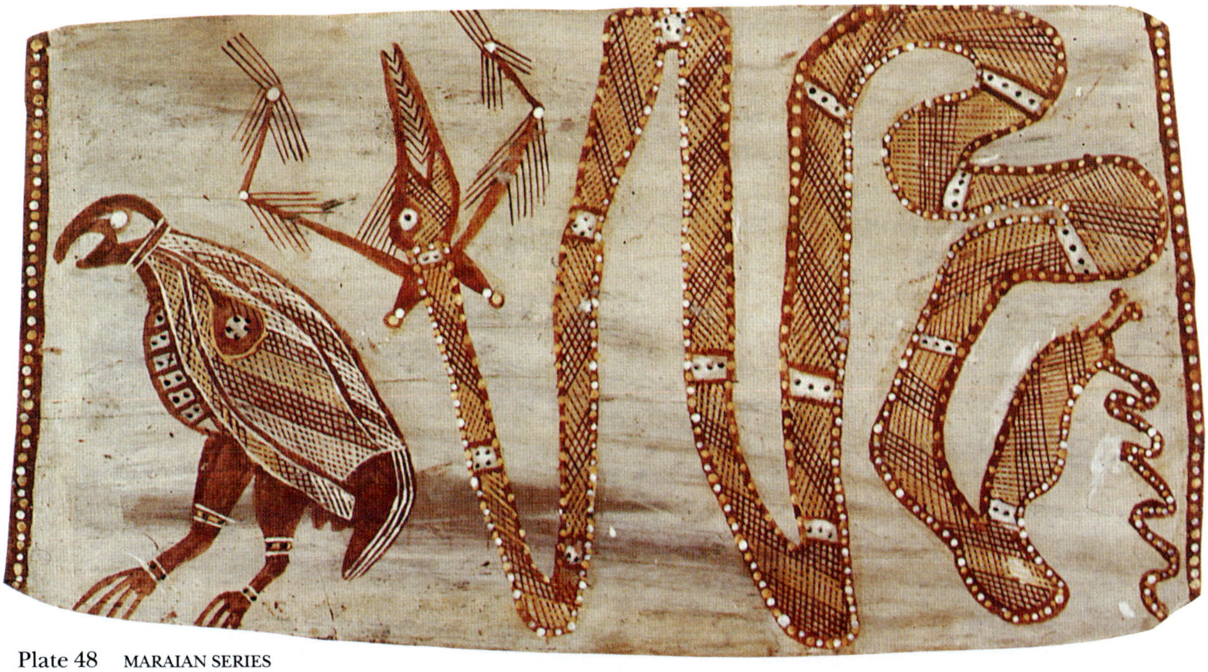

Plate 48 MARAIAN SERIES

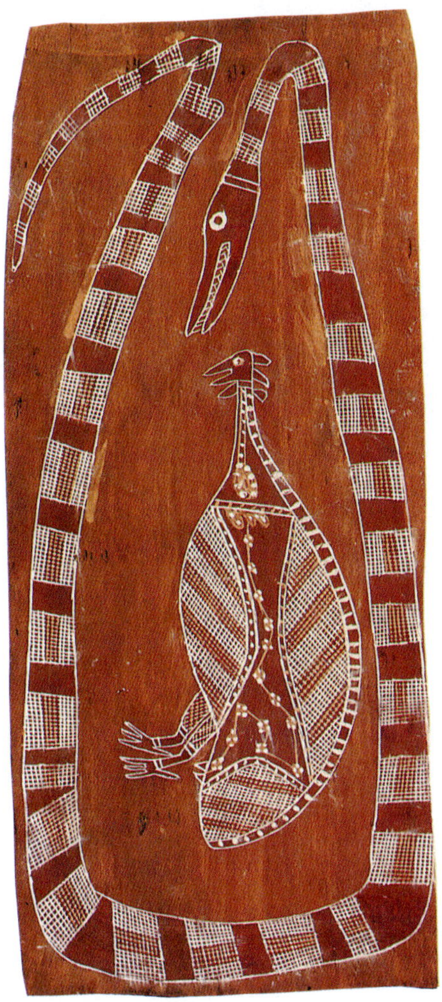

Plate 49 MARAIAN SERIES

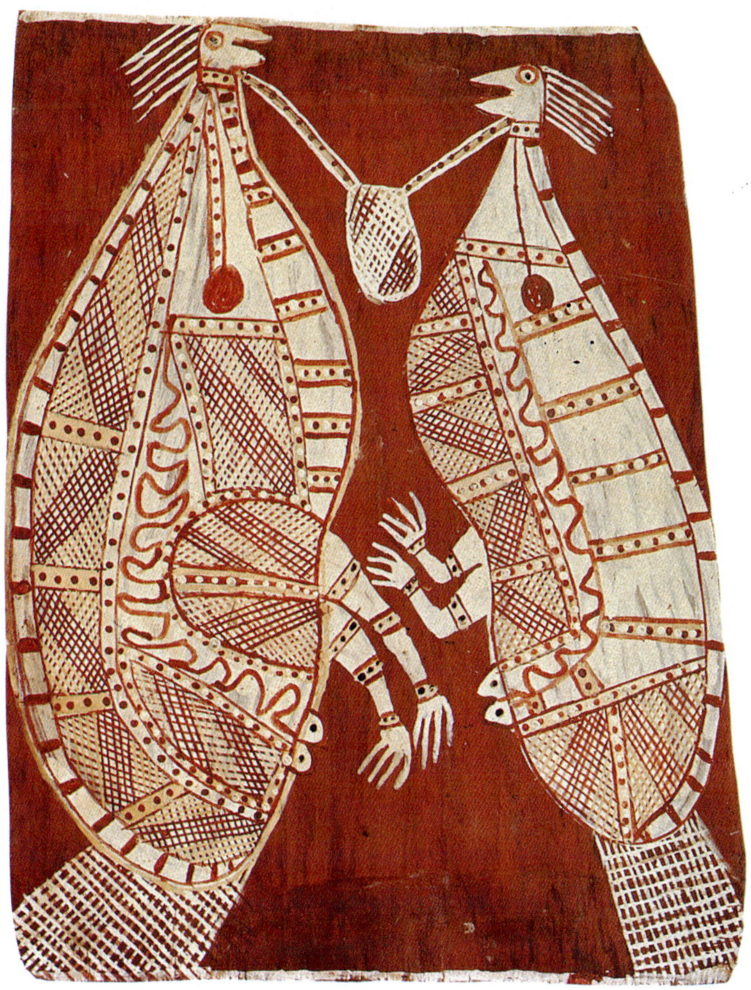

Plate 50 MARAIAN SERIES

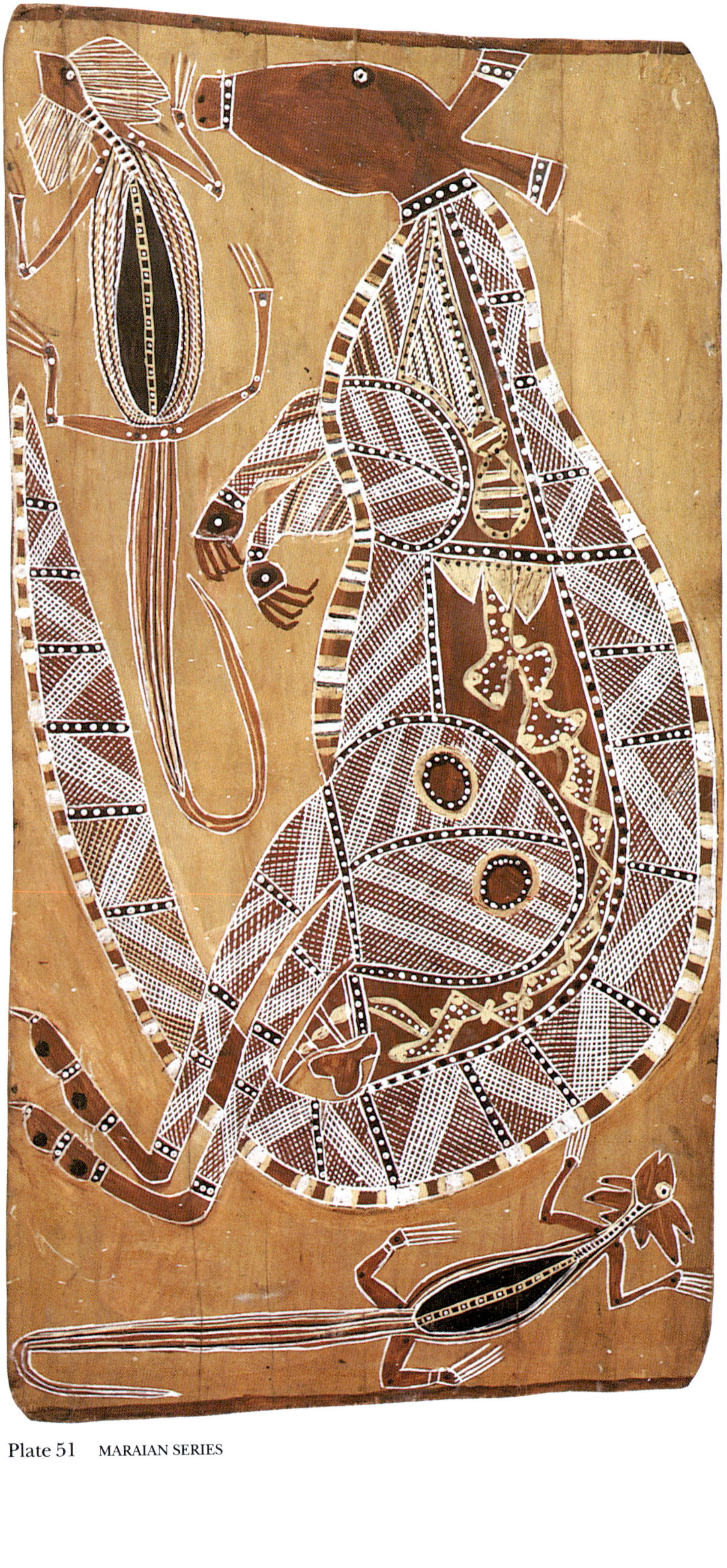

Plate 51 MARAIAN SERIES

After lunch we went to look at the electric trains but Bobby and Yirawala would not travel on them. We went to the zoo by ferry and Yirawala enjoyed seeing the animals, until we came to the caged dingo dogs. He was upset and said, 'Poor bugger in jail. What for?' He did not like to see native animals in cages. He was also sorry for the black cockatoos, saying we should take them back to their home country in the Territory.

Before leaving Sydney Yirawala was contacted by Dr Henry Rathgeber, a physicist from Sydney University, who invited him to inspect some Aboriginal rock carvings at Kuringai Chase, north of Sydney.

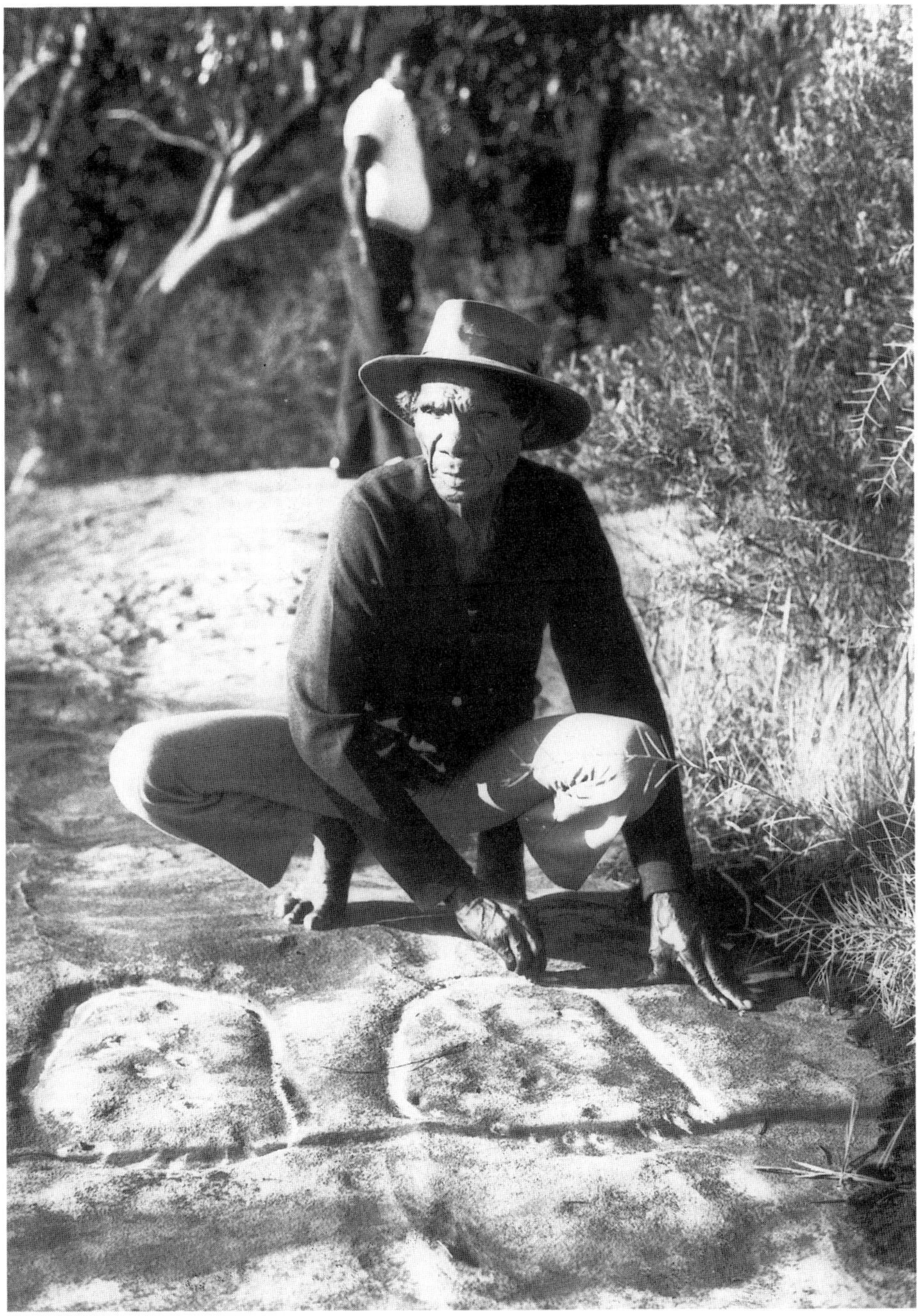

Yirawala at Kuringai Chase, Sydney. He is examining the carved footprints from Lumahlumah and his daughters' travels. 'Long time ago they come, sit down this place, full moon time.'

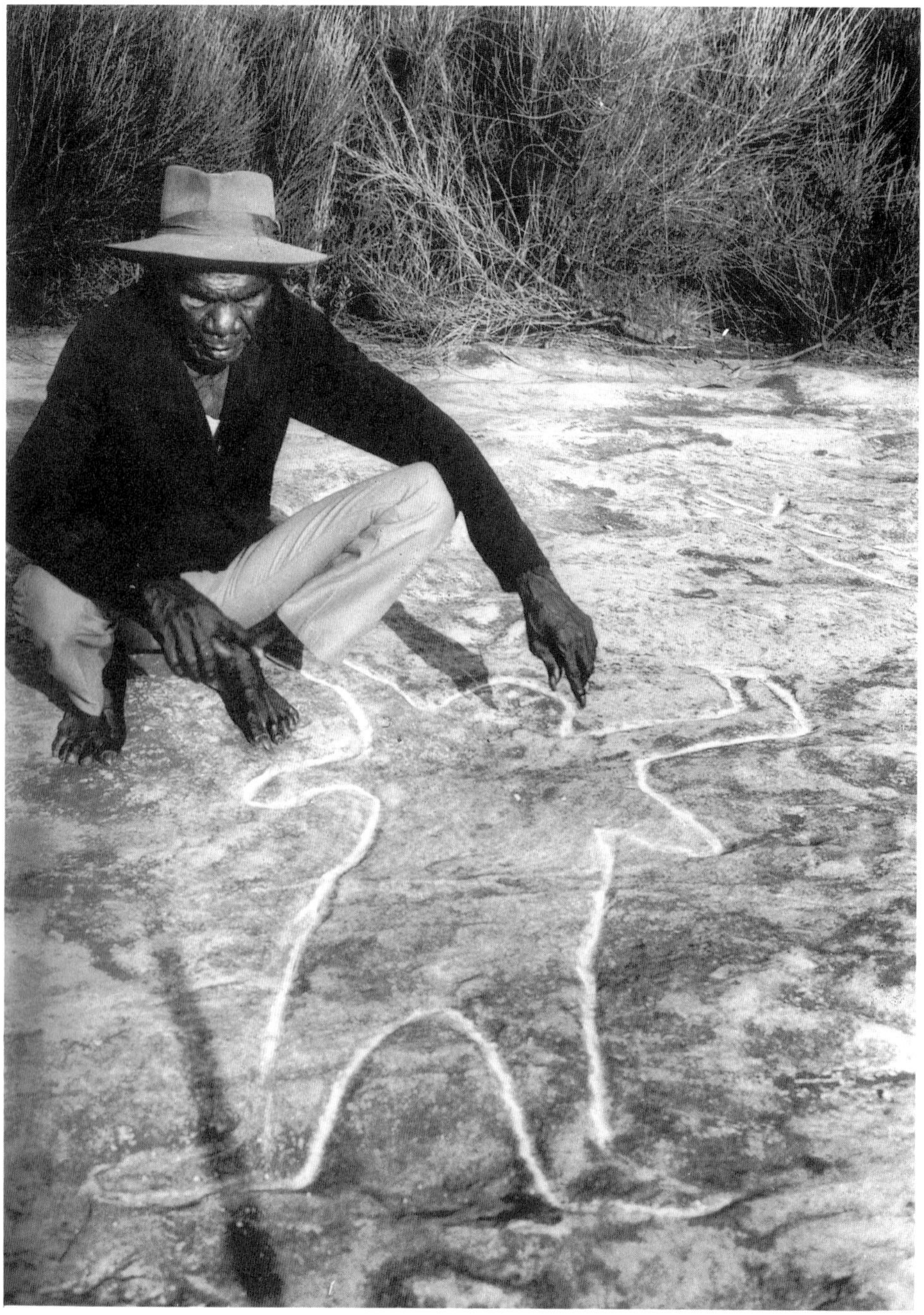

Yirawala blew white sand onto the female figure then carefully blew some of it away. She was a creator ancestress and daughter of Lumahlumah.

As we climbed the stony ridge at Kuringai Chase, a train roared past a short distance away. When we reached the top Yirawala pointed to the large human figures cut into the rock face. There were two females and one male, with numerous carved footprints around them. Yirawala examined the figures eagerly, talking in language to himself. He followed the footprints into the bushes and returned to the figures, running his hands over them, then sat down in silent contemplation. After a while he spoke, 'This man, Lumahlumah, got two daughter. Long time ago they come, sit down this place, full moon time. Sit down little bit wait for new moon.' Yirawala pointed to the crescent moon shape above the male figure's head, then he crawled over the rocks, scraping away sand and leaves among some bushes.

'Must be full moon some place.' Then a triumphant cry. 'Here, findim moon alright, him here.' Where he had cleared sand and leaves, we saw a circle etched in the rock. The circle had two bars across it. Yirawala continued searching among the bushes, saying there must be a canoe somewhere. He had progressed to the edge where the rock had been cut and blasted away to make way for a road. He looked across the road, where the rocky ridge rose again near some houses. He pointed and said that the road had taken the canoe, but Lumahlumah and his daughters had travelled that way and their footprints would be on the rocks near the houses.

Returning to the figures, he sprinkled white sand on their torsos, then carefully blew some of it away. Some of the sand remained in fine lines cut on the man's body. Yirawala gently ran his fingers over them and said they were Maraian cicatrices on the big man's chest.

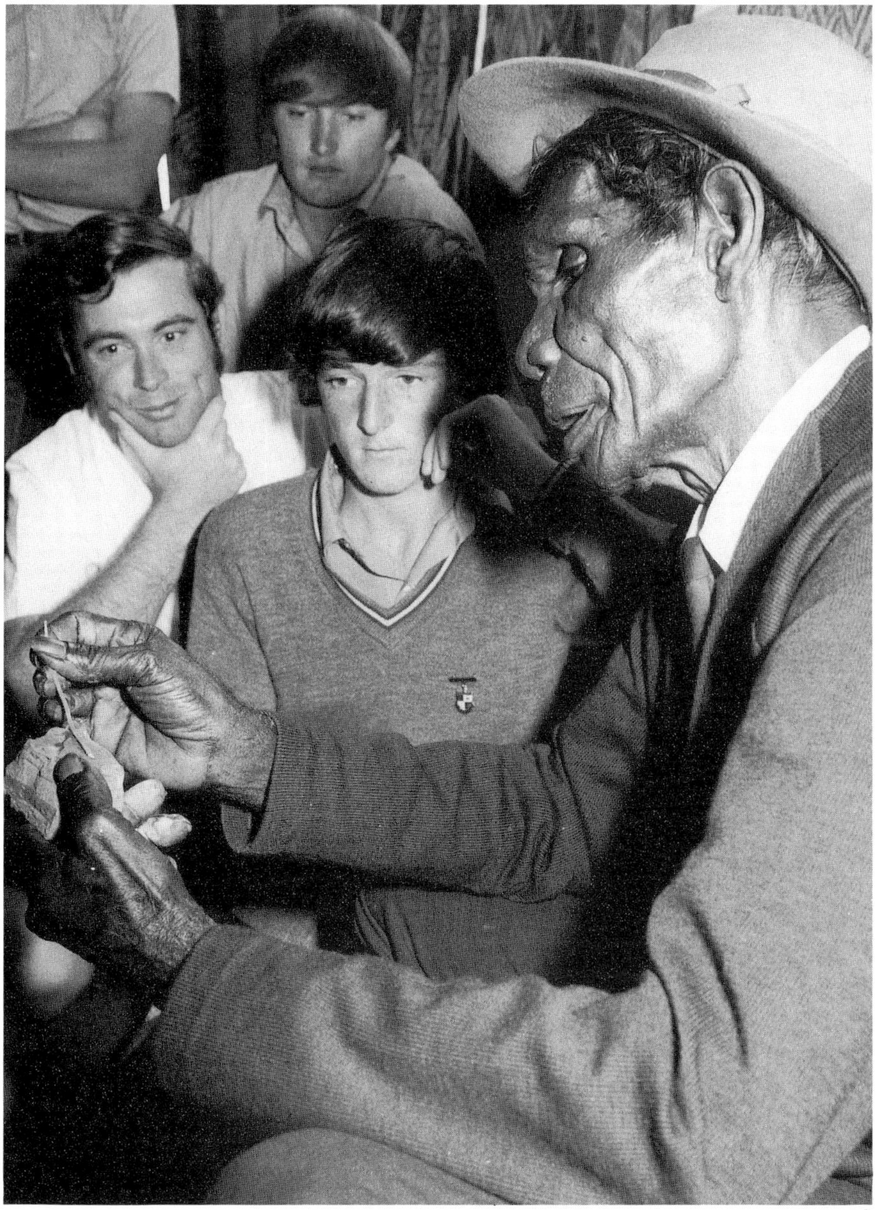

Yirawala showing a brush and ochre to students at Orange, NSW. He demonstrated painting techniques to the many school children who came to meet him. Some school classes came two or three times. (Photo: Central Western Daily)

Using the same procedure on a female figure Yirawala marked out the womb and the chest cuts from 'women's business'.

Weeks later, Dr Rathgeber wrote to say that the carved footprints did continue near the houses across the road, just as Yirawala had said.

The final exhibition on the tour was in the town of Orange in New South Wales, where Yirawala's lectures and display were included in the annual arts festival.

Yirawala demonstrated painting techniques for the many school children who came to meet him. He was very patient with them and let them handle ochres and bark. A few received small samples of yellow ochre and were delighted.

Some school classes came two or three times, and their teachers said they had learned more from these visits than any textbooks could teach them.

Bobby made string figures for the children and played the didjeridu. One morning when he had finished playing, a little girl of five looked up at him and said, 'Mister, what makes you so black?' Bobby laughed and said it was because he was an Aborigine.

Yirawala sat on the floor, surrounded by a number of children. He spoke gently to them, telling stories about his beautiful country and all the wild life, rivers and forests. He said it was in danger and he was trying to save it all. The two Aborigines were relaxed and happy among the children, all the sweet innocent faces, so attentive, listening and asking simple questions about birds and animals.

On our final day at Orange a group of little children made a special visit to talk to Yirawala. A teacher said the children had been thinking about what Yirawala had said about his land. A little girl and boy stepped forward with a bunch of bush flowers which they held out to Yirawala. The little girl shuffled her feet then asked Yirawala how they could help him save his land. The old painter's eyes filled with tears as he stretched his hands out over their heads and whispered his thanks.

Both Aborigines were deeply moved and never forgot the little children of Orange. Years later, when his strength was failing, Yirawala remembered them and said, 'Only little children try help me save my land.'

Chapter 6
Honoured for the art he considered a sacred book

When we arrived back in Darwin at the end of March, there was an invitation from the University of Papua New Guinea inviting Yirawala and me to participate in the first Nuigini Festival of Arts with lectures and a display of his paintings. The festival would be held at the University in Port Moresby in May. Yirawala was keen to go for a week, so we accepted the invitation.

Bobby went back to his wife and family and his job in the forestry camp, and Yirawala went back to Croker Island. The two men had enjoyed their tour, and the shopping expedition in Sydney, and took home a number of gifts from well wishers.

Yirawala returned to Darwin in April to inspect a long wheel base Landrover that I had promised to buy him. This would enable him to be driven about to talk to tribal elders about their land and how to keep the miners out. He also wanted to discuss an application to the Federal Government for land rights. He wanted to own his family land, with the paper in the hand and a red mark (seal).

First we would go to New Guinea for the lectures and art display. TAA would kindly assist us once again. Yirawala was curious about the 'New Guinea men', what sort of country they lived in and also about their ceremonies.

When we arrived at the University, we were told that a headman from the Highlands had journeyed down from the mountains to meet the 'Australian man' whom he assumed to be the same status as himself.

In a grassy clearing we waited for him. Yirawala gasped as he appeared. A splendid sight in full regalia. The two men approached each other, both a little wary. Standing face-to-face, the headman held out gifts for Yirawala. A wide, carved armlet and a knife made of cassowary bone. Yirawala accepted them and gave him two large, gold lipped pearl shells. The ice was broken. The two men smiled at each other and began talking in pidgin, which Yirawala understood.

Yirawala gave the gifts to me, saying they might contain harmful magic.

Each night we watched the colourful spectacle of dancers from different villages. Yirawala was thrilled by them and asked many questions. He was particularly interested in dances from the Gulf of Papua. One of these mimed the hunting and spearing of a kangaroo, while a performer blew a long pipe which resembled a didjeridu.

The New Guinean people treated Yirawala with great respect, almost reverence. Many came to see the exhibition and talk to him. He talked about his land and asked them about theirs. He would have liked to learn more from the people, and was sorry to leave.

On our return to Darwin Yirawala said he would stay in town for a while as he wanted to visit clan members at Oenpelli for information about prospecting. He told me to write to his family at Croker Island to ask them to send word to Paddy Compass, an old Gunwinggu medicine man, for information about some mining agreement that the Maung people of Goulburn Island had agreed to with some Aborigines at Maningrida. Yirawala knew that some discussions had taken place before he went away and he was worried about the outcome.

No word came back from Paddy or the other people involved with discussions on mining exploration on four areas of Aboriginal land, including Yirawala's.

Yirawala then sent word for Bobby to come to Darwin and drive him to Oenpelli. Bobby came in with two other relations and drove off with his father.

Soon afterwards a full-page article appeared in the *NT News* (3 June 1971), under the heading: 'A Deal is Done and the Dancing Begins', in which it was reported that the general-manager of Ocean Resources NL, Mr George Alcorn, announced that exploration would begin that month on the prospecting authorities in Arnhemland held by the ORMAC (Ocean Resources MacIntyre Mines) Aboriginal joint venture. The article continued:

> The highlight of the celebration was the exchange of tangible symbols, representing the agreement. Mr Alcorn and Mr George Dowling, representing MacIntyre Mines, presented the Aboriginals with a miner's dish and pick. One of the Goulburn Island elders, Nungoloman, presented them with a piece of rock, symbolising the handing over of the land to the mining companies.

Visitors came from interstate to attend the celebration and barbecue. The article went on to report that Mr Alcorn said that vehicles and caravans were in Darwin waiting to be barged to Maningrida, and that a program of geological mapping and stream sampling would be initiated plus an airborne spectrometer survey as well as aeromagnetic and very low frequency electromagnetic surveys; plans for the East Alligator region would be made after the airborne radioactive data became available.

On 4 June 1971, Yirawala had just returned from Oenpelli with Bobby when a letter was sent to my address for Yirawala, from Mr M L Tyrrell, Official Secretary to the Governor-General, informing him that Her Majesty the Queen would be graciously pleased to appoint him a Member of the Civil Division of the Most Excellent Order of the British Empire for his services to Aboriginal art. The letter went on to ask him to inform the Governor-General's office if the honour was acceptable to him.

Yirawala said yes, he would be pleased to be honoured by the big white queen, and asked me if it would help him to get his land.

He was very unhappy about the mining agreement that had been signed on Goulburn Island, especially after Bobby read him the newspaper article of 3 June. His face registered grief and fury. He remarked that nobody had asked him, and that some Aborigines had signed away other people's land to the miners.

Bobby said there could be trouble and divisions created between those Aborigines who seemed greedy for money and those like his father who sought to protect the land and sacred sites. Yirawala said, 'What for we travel all over, talk about my land, ask balanda help?'

In August Channel 7 TV sent a copy of the film we had made,* and requested clearance from the Gunwinggu elders concerned with it.

I needed to apply for another permit, and I knew this would mean more expense and trips away from home. The latter was of great concern because we had been receiving abusive phone calls and threats to burn the house down. As it was, there had been another break-in and more paintings stolen.

Yirawala agreed that it would be better to put the paintings somewhere safe for the time being. At the suggestion of the Australian Council for the Arts, I approached the Australian Museum in Sydney, who agreed to store the collection for a limited time.

Having attended to this I contacted Oenpelli Mission requesting a permit to screen the Yirawala film there for clearance from the Aborigines who belonged to Yirawala's clan. Permission was refused.

I wrote to the Director of Aboriginal Welfare advising him of the refusal and that I would therefore have to make other arrangements.

This resulted in a flurry of hand-delivered letters and telegrams. We would screen the film at Terry Robinson's Border Store on the East Alligator River and invite only those men

* *Return to the Dreaming* (director Cecil Holmes, sound recordist and advisor Sandra Holmes, camera Oscar Scherl).

concerned with the content of the film, the Gunwinggu elders.

The Director advised me that I would be breaking the original permit agreement if I screened the film at Terry Robinson's store, and that the film must be shown to Aboriginal communities at Oenpelli Mission and Maningrida Settlement.

This letter overlooked the fact that Oenpelli had refused permission for us to go there, and the screening at the East Alligator would be private and only for the Gunwinggu elders.

More letters were written to Aboriginal Welfare to say the screening at the Border Store would go ahead. Yirawala and Bobby advised Maningrida relatives of the true situation and invited them to the screening.

The Director of Welfare replied, warning of the consequences if we went ahead with our screening. He suggested that a copy of the film should be given to them and they would show it to the people at Maningrida and Oenpelli, after which we would be advised whether the film had been cleared for general public screening.

Then the superintendent at Maningrida informed us that the three Gunwinggu elders would not be able to get to our screening.

Bobby and Yirawala said we must go ahead with our screening or the film might never be cleared even though it contained nothing sacred or offensive to Aborigines. Yirawala was angry and disgusted. 'Too much humbug. Might be Welfare mob block film.'

We hired a film projector in Darwin and set out in Yirawala's vehicle, my son Clinton doing most of the driving.

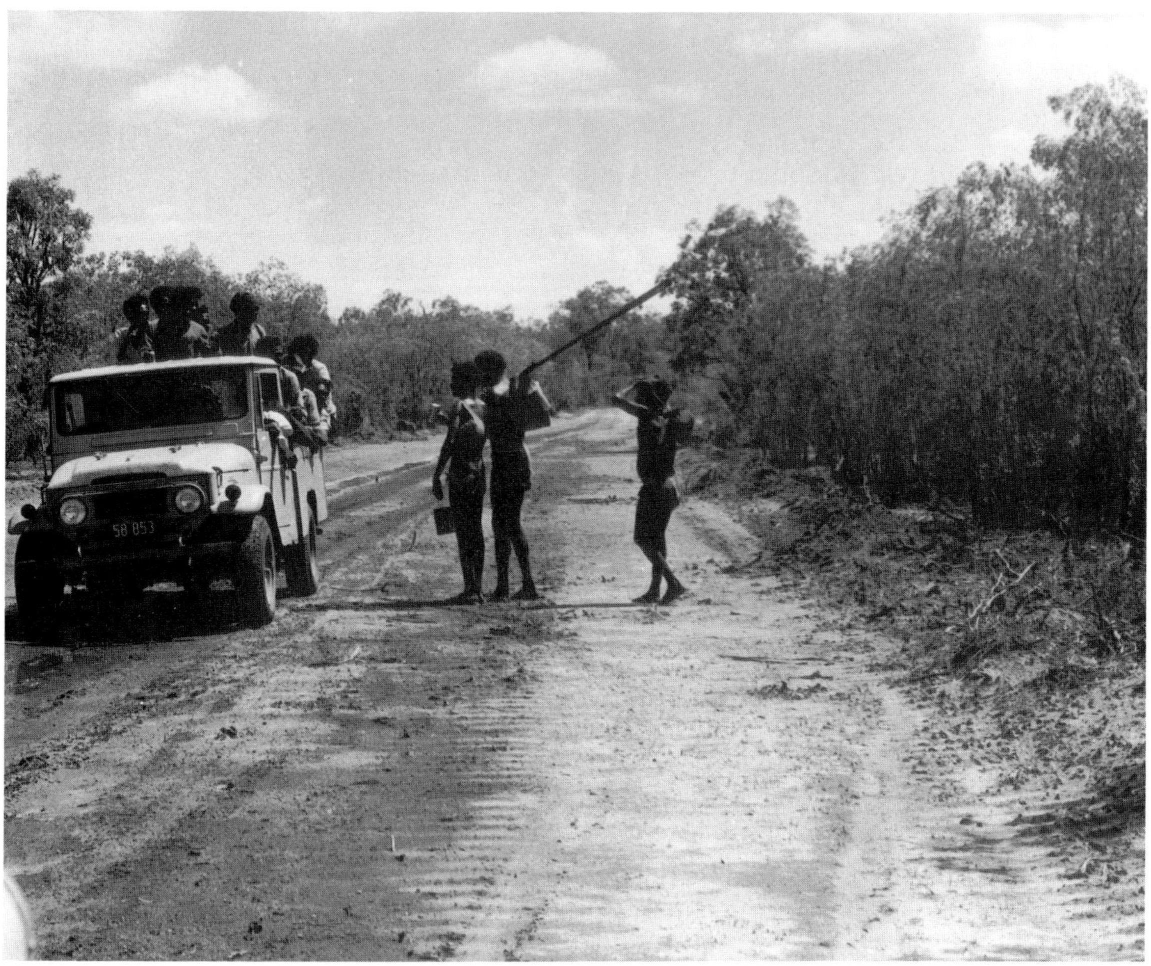

Yirawala's old Landrover on the way to the East Alligator River for the screening of the documentary on Yirawala and his sons returning to their home country. This photograph, taken in 1971, shows Arnhemland prior to the Jabiru town and mine.

The truck played up all the way as it lurched over rocky ground, roared through deep bulldust and squelched through boggy plains. The engine was making a strange noise and smoke was coming from under the bonnet. Clint pulled up and groaned. 'Looks like we've had it.' He lifted the bonnet and was enveloped in smoke and steam. Yirawala yelled to him, 'Look out, little boy. Might be engine blow up.' Just then two jeeps roared alongside and stopped in a swirl of dust. Four men got out. One of them, a lanky Texan, said he was a mechanic, and crawled underneath the truck. After a few minutes he wriggled out again, shaking his head. Then with a laconic grin said, 'Well, ma'am, looks like that little old engine 'bout to fall on the ground. Reckon the engine mounting is broken clear away.'

We limped on to the Border Store, where Bobby said the truck would never make it across the causeway to Oenpelli to pick up other Gunwinggu elders. Fortunately a battered old sedan pulled up full of Aborigines. He persuaded the driver to take him to Oenpelli.

We sat down to wait in the so-called beer garden near the bar. Black and white drunks reeled around, shouting and laughing, with tinnies clutched in their hands. Leaning on the bar and staring at us was a welfare officer. Well, we were not on the reserve.

By 9.30 p.m. Bobby had not returned and his father was worried. Maybe there had been an accident, or some trouble at the mission?

About 10 p.m. a mission vehicle pulled up and a white man leaned out to talk to some Aborigines. One of the group came over to our table to tell us that the missionary wanted to talk to us about the screening. We could all go back with him to Oenpelli Mission to show the film. We declined the offer, fearing more obstruction. In any case Clinton and I had no permits from the Director of Welfare.

At 10.30 p.m. Bobby returned with the Gunwinggu elders and we set up the projector at the back of the store, only to find that the power supply was inadequate.

The only alternative was Geopeko mining camp about thirty kilometres away.

The Aborigines climbed on the back of the truck and we were off on a very rough track. Half way we broke down again, with a broken accelerator. I got out to try and walk to the mining camp for help. Half an hour later the truck came chugging behind me. Bobby had wired the broken accelerator together.

We reached the camp at 12.30 a.m. and were met by a crowd of drunken miners wanting to know what a mob of 'bloody boongs' was doing at their camp. 'This is our club,' one shouted, 'and until now it was a bloody clean club.' More swearing and racist remarks followed. I went over and sat down with them, accepting a drink, trying to calm them down, explaining the reason for our visit. A man began pawing me, so in desperation I said the manager in Darwin had given permission for the screening and if anything went wrong he would not be happy. I went on to say that Yirawala was a famous artist and an MBE. This impressed a Dutch foreman and a German rouseabout. They gave permission for the screening and helped us put up blankets for privacy away from the drunken miners.

The film was shown to and approved by all the elders present. They signed a document to say that there was nothing sacred in the film and it was all right for general release.

Yirawala was very tired, so the German invited him to sleep in an airconditioned demountable. I was allotted a hut nearby and warned to lock the door. My son camped in the bush with the Aborigines.

In the morning I scrounged food and tea for us all, then went to see the site manager, who had been asleep the night before. He agreed that many miners were hostile to the Aborigines and needed educating. He was helpful to us and arranged to transport the Aborigines back to the Border Store. A mining truck would take us and our broken-down truck back to Darwin.

Drinking tea on my verandah, Yirawala suddenly burst out laughing, as he relived some aspects of our ghastly trip. He said. 'Nobody put me over. We win all the way, my girl. Might be welfare man and mission him cry now.' He was very tired but exultant that we had beaten the bureaucracy again.

A copy of the approval document that the elders had signed was sent to the Director of Aboriginal Welfare, and we heard no more about it.

The painting collection remained in storage, safe from thieves. We needed a sound, brick building to house the collection or some financial assistance to upgrade my house in Darwin to make it burglar proof, and we continued to explore avenues of possible support from government departments.

Although no financial help was forthcoming, I retrieved the collection from storage in Sydney, as having it locked away was not fulfilling the purpose for which the paintings were made, to inform and educate.

Before Yirawala went back to Croker Island we received a letter from Aileen Joran, Bobby's wife, saying that arguments had increased about the prospecting agreement that had been signed between Goulburn Islanders and Ocean Resources MacIntyre Mines. She said some people were very angry about it and divisions between some Aboriginal groups had increased.

Yirawala puffed his cigarette and said, 'All the silly people, greedy for money, that's all.' His face was grim. He said that under tribal law any unauthorised person near a sacred cave would be speared by the guardians. No Aborigine would go near 'danger places', but this did not apply to the white people now roaming all over the country. If Aborigines took them to sacred sites and caves they would be punished later. He also said that no one man or two could sign away the land, as all the people were traditional owners and must be consulted.

As a guardian of sacred caves and sites, Yirawala must consult with other tribal councillors who held the land in trust for all the Gunwinggu.

Yirawala believed that somehow the Gunwinggu must go home to their home country and make a settlement where they would control the permit and their own lives. They must have the power to keep the miners out. If this was not accomplished the social cohesion of the clans would be destroyed along with their land, culture and identity.

He knew that divisions among the tribal groups were fostered by white people. Yirawala said some Aborigines wanted the money promised by the mining men and thought only about trucks and motor cars.

I received word that the presentation of Yirawala's MBE would take place on 22 September at Government House, Darwin. He flew in from Croker Island on the 21st and we went shopping, as he needed new clothes. He favoured black, formal trousers and a white shirt. The tie he selected was very conservative.

That evening he wanted to know why the big white queen wanted to give him a medal and would she help him to get his land. I explained that the award was for his services to Aboriginal art and the Queen could not help him about his land. It was simply an honour that lifted him high. It indicated respect and recognition of his work.

The following day Yirawala was up early, anxious to make ready for the ceremony. He sat down to breakfast and I helped him with his tie. He seemed a bit nervous and kept fiddling with his collar, saying he might choke.

I asked him if he wanted to go in a taxi but he declined, saying he preferred the Landrover.

At Government House an usher guided us to the large room where a number of Service personnel and members of the public were assembled. We sat at the back and watched Mr Fred Chaney, the Administrator of the Northern Territory, take his place at the rostrum, flanked by officers of the Army, Navy and Airforce, all in dress uniform, standing stiffly to attention with swords upraised.

One by one the recipients of awards in the Queen's Birthday Honours list were called to the rostrum and presented with their medals by the Administrator, with due pomp and ceremony.

When Yirawala's name was called he trembled all over, then slowly walked down to the front. Mr Chaney welcomed him, then picked up the medal from a red velvet cushion. Smiling he leaned over and pinned it on Yirawala's shirt and shook his hand. The officers of the three Services marched up and saluted him, presenting their swords, which flashed in a ray of sunlight coming through a window. Yirawala stood proud and straight as the servicemen marched back to their places, then he walked back to his seat with head held high.

He had not sought fame for its own sake, but he liked being treated with respect. Maybe now his voice would be heard.

His was the only MBE awarded that day. The other recipients received the British Empire Medal. After the ceremony everyone relaxed with champagne and a chat with Mr and Mrs Chaney.

Yirawala knew that he had been honoured for the art that he considered a sacred book. He thought that now, with such recognition, land rights would follow. Everyone would know him now and he would have more influence when he asked for the rights to clan land.

After Yirawala went back to Croker Island an invitation came from Mr Martin Finger, President of the Royal Commonwealth Society of the Northern Territory, inviting him to a reception on 19 October for recipients of the Queen's Birthday Honours for 1971.

Yirawala attended the function and wondered why all the government men treated him so nicely at medal ceremonies, but otherwise seemed to ignore him.

When he went home, Bobby and Danny came in to pick up his Landrover, which had been thoroughly repaired. They planned to drive it to Murganella forestry camp then ferry it across to Croker Island.

After loading drums of petrol, cans of oil and other supplies they set off on the long journey. Two weeks later a telegram came from the Border Store asking me to send a new clutch plate for the Landrover. Bobby and Danny were still in the East Alligator area with relatives who wanted to use the truck. Some men had been driving the truck and had not attended to putting in oil.

When Yirawala heard about it he sent a messenger in to contact his sons and tell them to fix the truck then bring it back to Darwin, where I would consign it to Croker Island on Perkins' Barge. He said not to attempt a crossing from Murganella as the seas were too rough.

Terry Robinson came to Darwin and told me that drunken people were driving the truck all over the place. I had no vehicle, as mine had been repossessed, and could not go and investigate. I could only send a strong message.

During this same month I received a letter from Mrs Edna Edgar, Secretary of the International Art Co-operation Award, offering Yirawala their award. A panel of distinguished fellow artists, including Dr Lloyd Rees, had voted him the best Australian artist for 1971. They wanted to arrange a date to present the medallion to him and wished to be advised whether a display of Yirawala's paintings could be arranged.

Yirawala sent word that he would be pleased to accept the award, and asked for a plane ticket to come in to Darwin.

Terry Robinson sent word that the Landrover was at the Border Store in a useless condition. The engine had seized up.

On hearing this, Yirawala was enraged, and when drunken relations came he said they could stay.

When neighbours complained about the nightly noise I tried to evict the drunks without success. Finally a neighbour called the police and they took them away. When they had gone, Yirawala said he was sorry he had invited them to stay. He'd been upset about losing his truck. He said he would make a painting then go home to Croker Island.

Yirawala had not left when, on 20 November, I noticed two strange Aboriginal men in the yard. When I asked Yirawala what the strangers wanted, he said they had come to tell him that a close relation was sick somewhere in town. The men were not drunk, so I left them talking with Yirawala.

Next morning when I took a breakfast tray to Yirawala's hut he was not there. Perhaps he had walked to the shop for more tobacco? When he had not returned by 11 a.m., Clinton and I went to look for him. We called at Bagot Settlement and local fringe camps, but nobody had seen him. After that we rang the police station. They knew nothing of him.

When Darwin Hospital said nobody named Yirawala had been admitted, I decided to make a ward-by-ward search. When I came to Intensive Care, the sisters said that nobody named Yirawala was in the ward. At that point I broke down and asked a nurse to go in and check to see if there was an old Aboriginal man in there. I said he always wore a bush hat.

The nurse came back and said, yes, there was an old Aboriginal in there, who had been admitted under the name George Edwards. He had been picked up in a back lane opposite the Don Hotel in Cavenagh Street. He had a broken arm and head injuries. I was permitted to look at him. It was Yirawala.

I immediately sent telegrams to Croker Island and Oenpelli to advise his close relations, then I went to the police station to discover the full circumstances concerning Yirawala's injuries. They said a police van was cruising down the lane when they saw a body lying near a half-demolished building. An Aboriginal man was standing nearby. They asked him what was going on and he said that the man on the ground was named George Edwards and he had fallen from the second floor of the building. The police called an ambulance. They assumed he had sustained the injuries when he fell.

Each day I sat by Yirawala's bed praying for his recovery. I also took in some power paintings and symbols to place near his bed.

One morning he opened his eyes and lifted a trembling hand. He recognised me. The doctor said he was out of danger and would be going into a ward to recover fully.

Yirawala's wives came to stay at my house until he was well enough to be sent home. Each day we all went in to see him. His sons also came in to Darwin.

After some days in hospital he was very much better but still weak. The doctor said his right arm would need continued physiotherapy and he might not regain full use of it.

When he recovered he told me that he had been tricked into climbing to the top of the building. He was told that a sick relation was up there. When he reached the top somebody pushed him off, onto the concrete below. It had been an attempt on his life, made to look like an accident.

Yirawala went back to Croker Island in January 1972; he was still rather weak.

I wrote to him frequently, sending his pension cheques. He had requested the Department of Social Security send them to him at my address. I also sent parcels of clothing, food, tobacco and other goods. When pension cheques were sent to him I sent covering letters and telegrams to advise him.

Lazarus wrote to say that Yirawala was well and painting again.

In early March we were advised the presentation of the International Art Co-operation Award would be made on 24 March 1972 at Trans Australian Airlines headquarters in Sydney. Yirawala was not well enough to undertake such a long journey and requested that I act for him. Professor Elkin agreed to accept the medallion on his behalf.

I took the medallion back to Darwin, and applied for a permit to take it out to Yirawala. The permit application was made to the Deputy Administrator, a fair and reasonable man, who now had some say in issuing permits. (I was told that a senior public servant had warned him that I was 'the most dangerous woman in the Northern Territory'!)

The other reason for going to Croker Island was to try and persuade Yirawala to come back to Darwin to receive treatment for an ulcerated cornea of the left eye. So far he had refused to board two Air Medical planes.

When I arrived he was sitting on his bed with half his face bandaged. He said he felt weak and was glad I had come. 'Nobody cut my eye. You take me good doctor.' He had been afraid that people he did not know might order some sort of eye operation. I explained that no operation was contemplated and I would see that nothing was done without consulting him. He was relieved and told Mary to pack his case. He agreed to go on my charter plane. Bobby came with us.

I told Yirawala about the ceremony in Sydney and that his old friend Elkin had received the medal for him. He smiled. 'Ah, good old man.' He said I could give him the medal later, when he felt better.

In hospital his eye was treated with antibiotics and after eight days the bandages were removed. He said he felt good and wanted to see his medal. Bobby presented it to him in the hospital. He was very happy to receive it and, even though his drawings were not art like the white man's, he was proud of the medal.

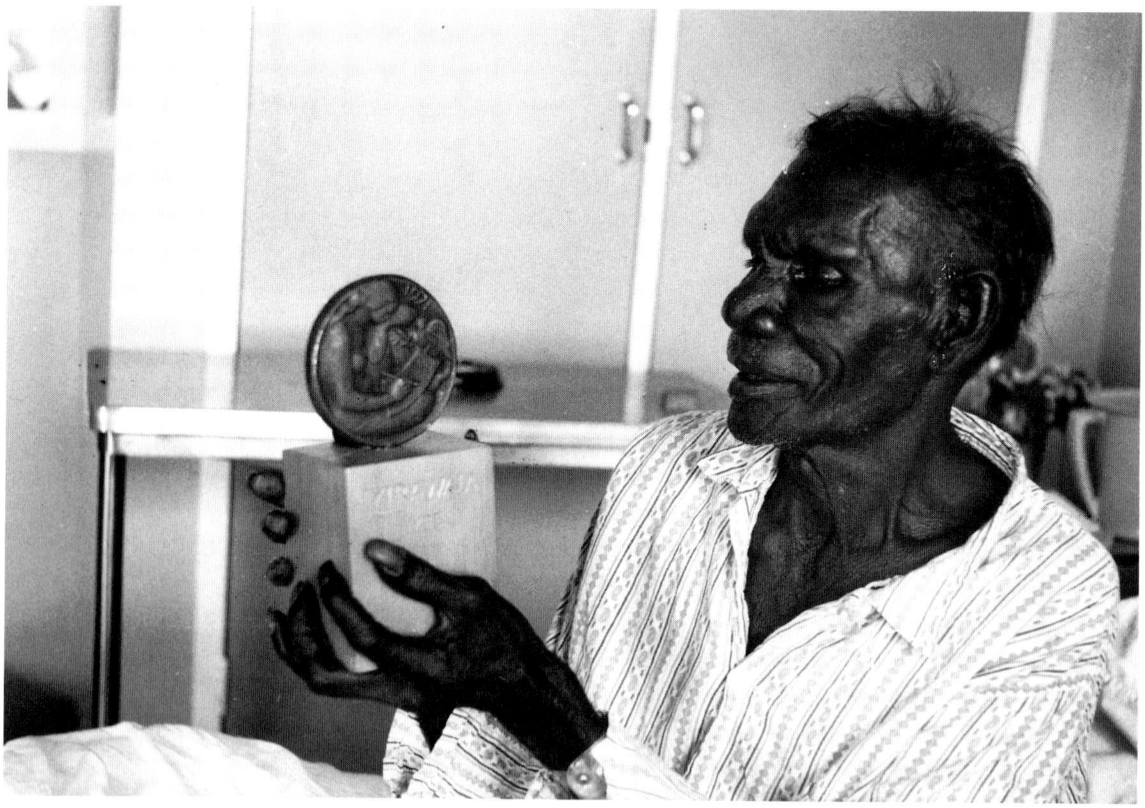

Yirawala on receiving the International Art Co-operation Award for 1971, naming him the best Australian artist for that year. Bobby presented it to him in hospital. He was happy to receive it and, even though his drawings were not art like the white man's, he was proud of the award.

Chapter 7
Battle for the land

While Yirawala was in hospital, his lawyer came to see him on request. Yirawala wanted to apply properly for his land. The lawyer provided a document which Bobby and his father signed. This was only a preliminary application. The whole Gunwinggu council of elders would have to discuss everything, mark their land area on maps, and provide details of what their special-purpose lease would be used for. Finally all the elders would have to sign proper documents applying for leasehold of their land.

One morning Bobby went to the hospital to see his father and found he had suddenly been sent back to Croker Island. He was upset that nobody had told him.

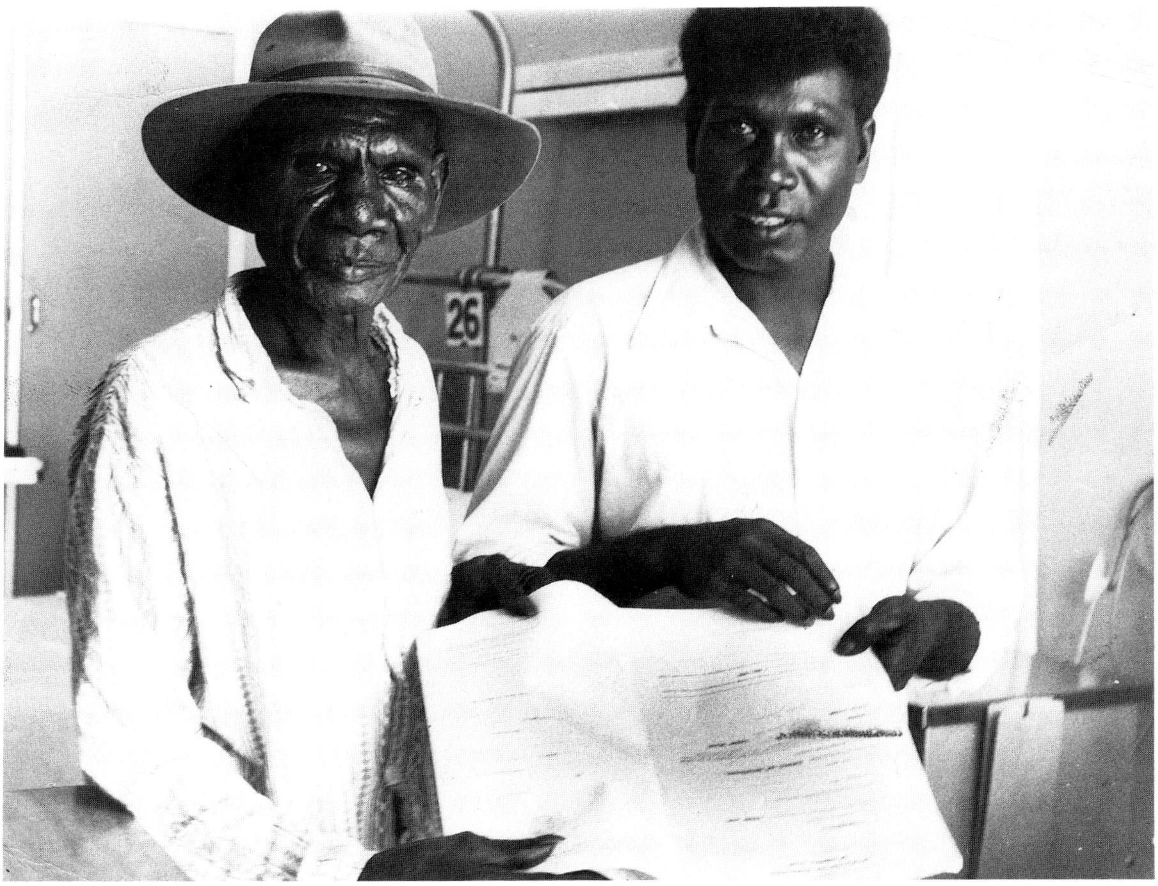

Yirawala and Bobby Joran with a preliminary land application, Darwin Hospital, 1972.

Communication problems began again, and a messenger was sent to Croker Island. The messenger reported that Yirawala was well and working on some bark paintings for an overseas dealer out there.

On 29 May a mechanic from Jabiru wrote to say that Yirawala's Landrover would cost a fortune to fix and was only suitable for parts. I advised David and Bobby and they came in to discuss things. They sold the truck for $250.00

Yirawala came in to Darwin a month later for a medical check up and for discussions about the land application. I did not take him to task about anything that happened on the Mission, because it was beyond his control.

The lawyer reminded Yirawala that Aborigines could only apply for special-purpose leases on the Reserve, not ownership. He also said they would have to provide full details of the enterprise they envisaged and some evidence that it would be viable. They would have to form a proper Association and have it registered. In this case, the Marugulidban Pastoral and Agricultural Association. A board would have to be elected and hold regular meetings. At the time it was the only way the tribal people could apply to live on their own land, be self-supporting and steer an independent course.

Yirawala had always wanted to break free from the yoke of white authority and with his tribe claim their land, and until now he had not known how to do it.

On 11 July 1972 the lawyer submitted the Gunwinggu land application to the Chairman of the Northern Territory Land Board in Darwin.

The application gave detailed information on the land area, a full description of the country, the purpose for which the land was to be used, the number of people who would be living and working on the land, and the names of all the Gunwinggu tribal elders in order of status and authority.

The application pointed out that if the land was granted it would certainly be made the land of the people already bound by ethnic ties, and that the present disintegration of tribal groups and the drift of young people from them could be stemmed by giving to the people a lease which they could work and land which they would know to be their own. To comply with covenants incorporated in the lease, the applicants could apply for funds to the Aboriginal Trust Fund or to grants in aid. Finally, the application stated that if the NT Land Board required the individual people listed in the application to sign the application, arrangements would be made. A map was enclosed with the Gunwinggu land area marked out in red ink.

Signatures of the tribal elders listed on the application were required, so a few days later Bobby, Amanda and I went to the Border Store and obtained the signatures of the Gunwinggu elders who came to meet us there. The men signed even though an Aboriginal working for the Mission tried to prevent them, saying everyone must stay on the Mission and let the mining go through.

Danny asked for a lift back to Darwin and a plane ticket back to Croker Island.

We still had to obtain signatures of other tribal elders at Maningrida, so I applied for a permit to go there with Bobby. The permit was issued for 25 July.

When we arrived at Maningrida the superintendent said unfortunately the elders had suddenly left the Settlement. The visit was a waste of time and money, and I returned to Darwin. Bobby stayed behind with the documents in the hope of finding the men.

The men had still not returned when Bobby went back to Croker Island more than two weeks later. He sent word that the elders were in the Marugulidban area and we would have to go there for the signatures. He still had the documents intact and he would come to Darwin in two weeks' time.

In the meantime, Professor Elkin sent me more cuttings from *Alchuringa* magazine, which were the cause for some unease. The first, from March-May 1972:

> Yet a continuing disregard for Aboriginal art is shown by the fact that the works of a major traditional artist such as Yirawala are allowed to remain under the control of a private individual. Couldn't an Aboriginal Art Trust or some similar body be set up to hold such treasures until such time as the Aboriginal people apply to use them in their own museums and galleries?

Another little piece appeared in the June-July issue:

> Senator Jim Keefe rang the Rocks Gallery in June with a message for *Alchuringa*. It seems that he is instigating a move for all Yirawala's paintings to become the property of the Nation. Excellent. It is wrong that such great Aboriginal art should remain in the hands of an individual and be subject to her whims.

Elkin warned me that there were rumours of seizure of my collection and said it would be tragic if it fell into the wrong hands. He strongly advised me to seek a safe national institution in which to place the Yirawala collection. The alarm bells were certainly ringing, but I did not want to lose my collection. I wanted support for a Yirawala museum in the Northern Territory so that Yirawala and his family and other Gunwinggu people would be involved in it.

On 20 August 1972, I received a letter from Yirawala and his family, written by Aileen Joran. She said that Peter Mahlunwunggu, the tribal elder second to Yirawala, was at Oenpelli and wanted to talk to Yirawala about a missionary from Oenpelli visiting Marugulidban. Bobby would not let Yirawala go to Oenpelli alone. Peter would have to come and see him at Croker Island. When Yirawala was stronger he would go with his sons to show the men where to make the airstrip.

A few days later the lawyer sent a letter asking that the land application forms be signed by the Gunwinggu elders so the full lease application could be submitted to the Land Board in Darwin.

Bobby came to Darwin on 4 September to assist with collecting the rest of the signatures from the Gunwinggu elders. We would have to journey to Oenpelli and Marugulidban as soon as possible.

Four days later Yirawala and Mary sent a telegram to Bobby, asking him to send the pension cheques. He had already sent them by registered letter, but they had not received them. Bobby was at a loss to understand the on-going communication problems.

In September 1972 campaigning had begun for the Federal elections in December. Labor, Liberal and Country Party members scurried around the Territory, promising much to voters, particularly the Aborigines. We were excited about the prospect of a Labor victory, as the ALP had adopted at its 29th Federal Conference the previous year a most enlightened platform in relation to Aborigines. In part, Aborigines would receive: equal pay for equal work; the right to receive Social Service benefits; better educational opportunities including pre-school for Aboriginal children and adult education where possible; a health offensive to be launched against leprosy, hook worm, tuberculosis, eye disease and the high infant mortality rate. All discrimination was to end. Regarding land rights and ownership, all Aboriginal lands were to be vested in a public trust, and no Aboriginal lands were to be alienated except with the approval of both the trust and of Parliament.

All this was encouraging and long overdue, and could be a basis for more democracy on missions and settlements and perhaps lead to Aboriginal ownership of land. If a Labor government came to power at the next elections, perhaps Yirawala's dream of the Gunwinggu establishing a settlement on their own land might become a reality.

To assist with our campaign to obtain signatures for the land application, Bobby had brought with him a document, signed by Yirawala, David, Brisbane and other Gunwinggu people, stating that I was their official secretary and represented them in all their affairs, so they therefore requested the Northern Territory Government to issue me with a permit to enter the Arnhemland Reserve on their behalf whenever they had need of my services.

I applied for a permit to visit Oenpelli and beyond to obtain signatures for the Gunwinggu land application.

When there was no response from Aboriginal Welfare, Yirawala's lawyer wrote to the Deputy Administrator to request a permit for me, explaining the reasons for my application and enclosing evidence from the Gunwinggu elders who had requested my visit.

The reply raised a number of hurdles. The village council at Oenpelli would need to be consulted, as would the Gunwinggu people at Goulburn Island, Croker and Maningrida. A meeting would have to be held for all concerned at Oenpelli to discuss my visit and whether or not I could proceed to Marugulidban. If the decision was favourable from all these groups, I would have to obtain authority from Darwin Administration to travel beyond Oenpelli. Dates and places to be visited were to be indicated on my application. I would have to wait at Oenpelli for the permit authority.

Bobby said things seemed to be getting more complicated all the time. The Gunwinggu elders had the say, not a lot of people down the line. We were doing things according to tribal rules. The Administration seemed to be making a big fuss which could result in people getting stirred up or being put under pressure by others with vested interests in the land. People we needed to talk to might be whisked off somewhere.

It seemed to us that the application by Gunwinggu people for control of their own land would be strongly resisted by miners, missions, and cattle graziers, all of whom had greater power than the Gunwinggu elders. Yirawala knew the odds were overwhelming, and told his sons that this was the last big fight.

With his fellow elders he wanted to draw the tribe together, men, women and children, young and old and with them all establish a viable settlement where they could become self sufficient in time. They would hold their own religion and culture, teaching the young, passing it on from hand to hand, like rare and precious gems. There would be a dual education system for children and young adults. Learning and preserving tribal law and language, as well as education in government schools and hopefully universities.

Yirawala said they did not want to be segregated but did not want to be crushed and swallowed by the white man, who so far had almost destroyed the tribes. He resented being treated like a child or an old fool and forced to watch the destruction of tribal culture and social cohesion.

He said if they did not make a stand now the clans could only be broken down. They would lose their anchor, as he put it, and drift into a twilight world of alcoholism and morbidity. A slow painful death would follow loss of their Dreaming.

When we had last spoken to Yirawala he had placed his hands on Bobby's head and mine, saying, 'You two men go — travel all over, get good word, mark on paper from Gunwinggu big men. You take my law, my word on tape recorder all over — we sing out loud now for land. We win.'

On 9 November 1972 Bobby and I made a preliminary trip to the Border Store. As yet I had not been issued with a permit to visit Oenpelli and Marugulidban, so Bobby drove my old Landrover across the East Alligator River causeway to bring the Gunwinggu elders out for talks. We had a number of signatures from the tribal elders but had to obtain Peter Mahlunwunggu's and Kelly Borgordubhu's. When the men came across the river we told them the purpose of the trip we proposed to make regarding the application for a Gunwinggu lease of land. The Gunwinggu men were annoyed by all the bureaucratic fuss being created. One man said some people were running about like ants after sugar. A lawyer had been to Oenpelli talking to Aborigines about their land. The men thought the lawyer must be working for the Mission.

Ten Gunwinggu elders said they had no objection to my going into their country in the course of helping them apply for land. They all signed a document to this effect, which was witnessed by Bobby Joran.

Back in Darwin this document was sent to our lawyer to assist with my application for a permit. A letter signed by David Gumaraitj and Bobby Joran was also sent to the Deputy Administrator of the Northern Territory, and to Aboriginal Welfare, about the Gunwinggu plans to establish their own little settlement on their own land. They requested that I be recognised as a friend and secretary, and given permits to continue my work of assisting them.

Bobby and I received telegrams from Oenpelli Mission councillors saying they did not want me to visit Oenpelli. One telegram bore Bluey's name. He had already signed our document requesting that I be given a permit.

Eventually I was issued with a permit to visit Oenpelli on 18 November for talks with

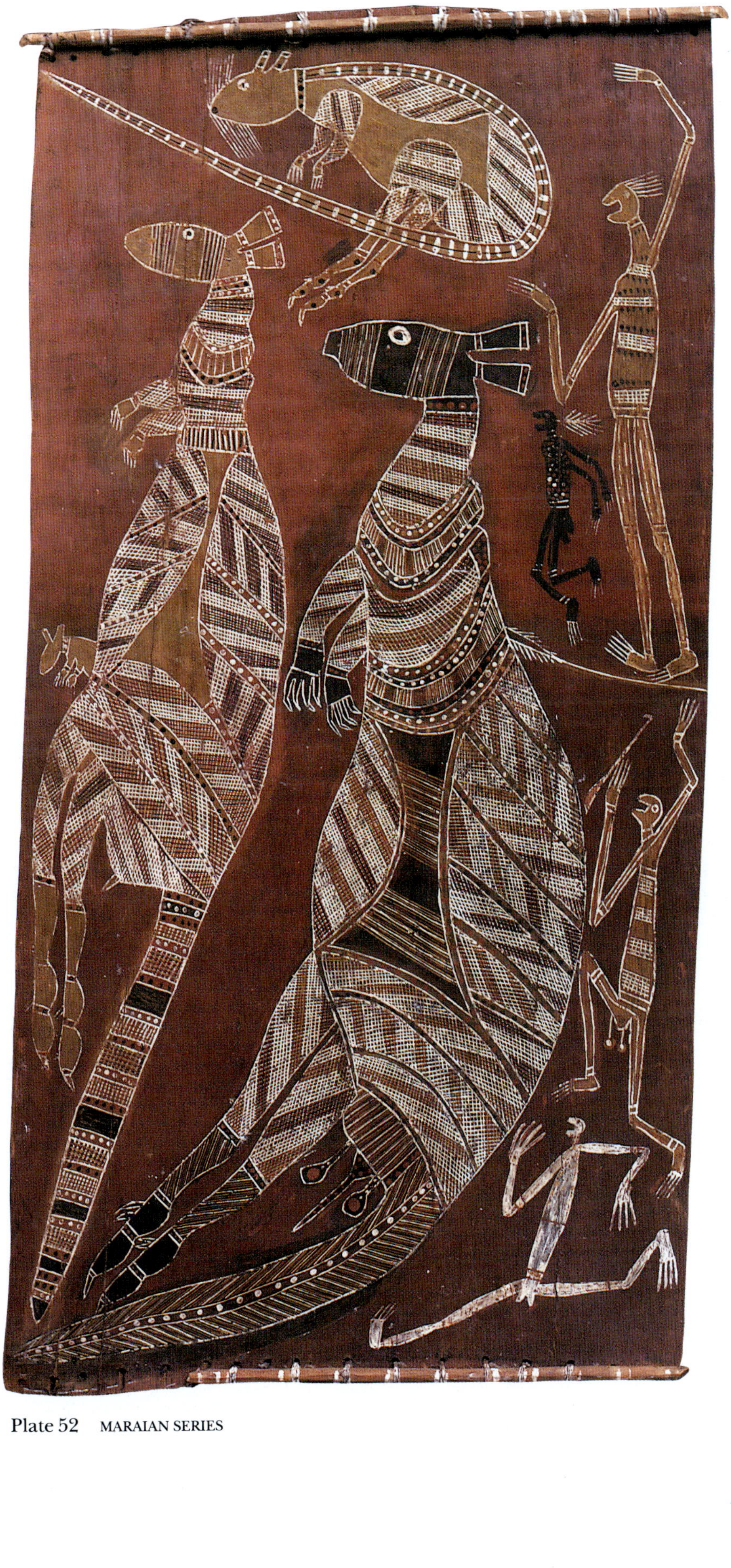

Plate 52 MARAIAN SERIES

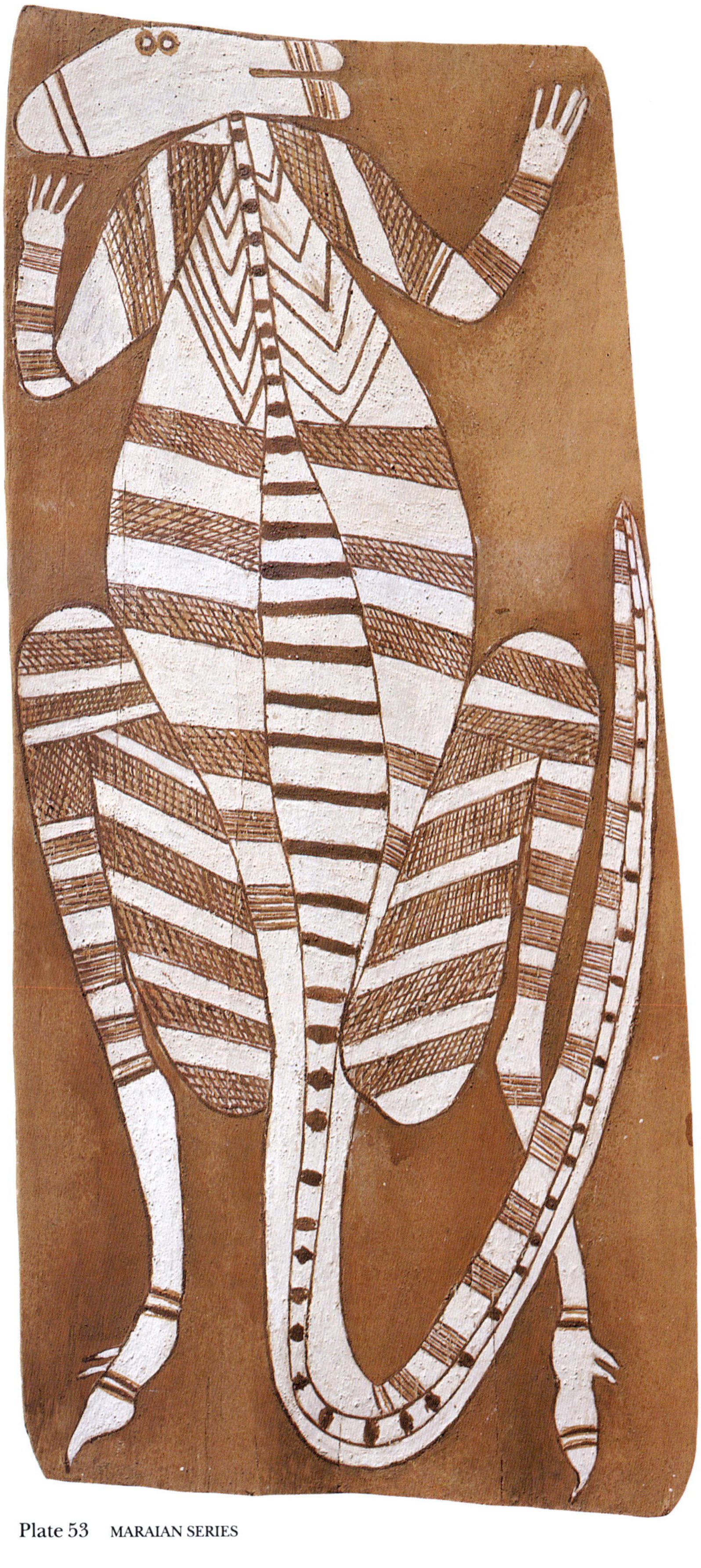

Plate 53 MARAIAN SERIES

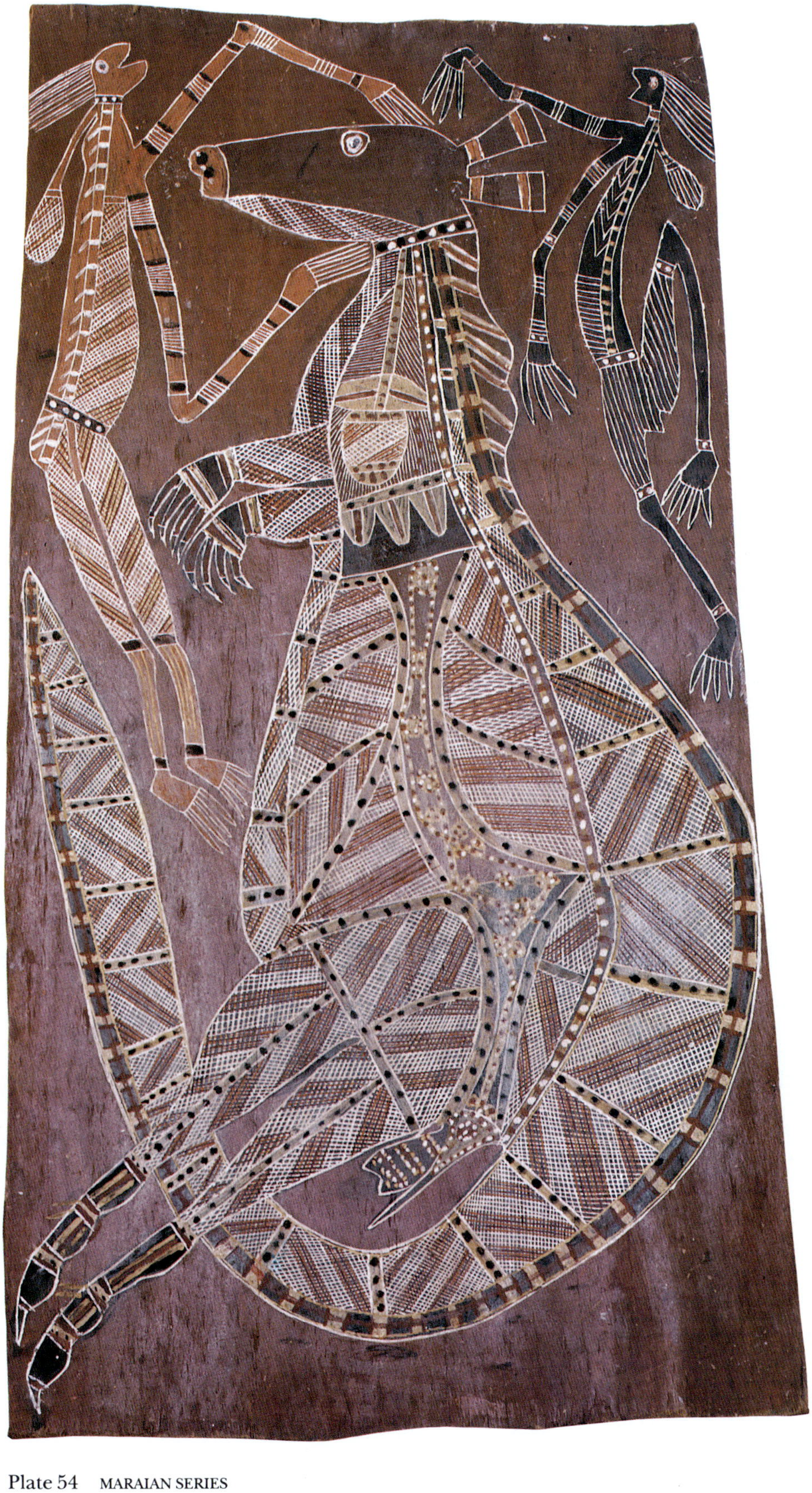

Plate 54 MARAIAN SERIES

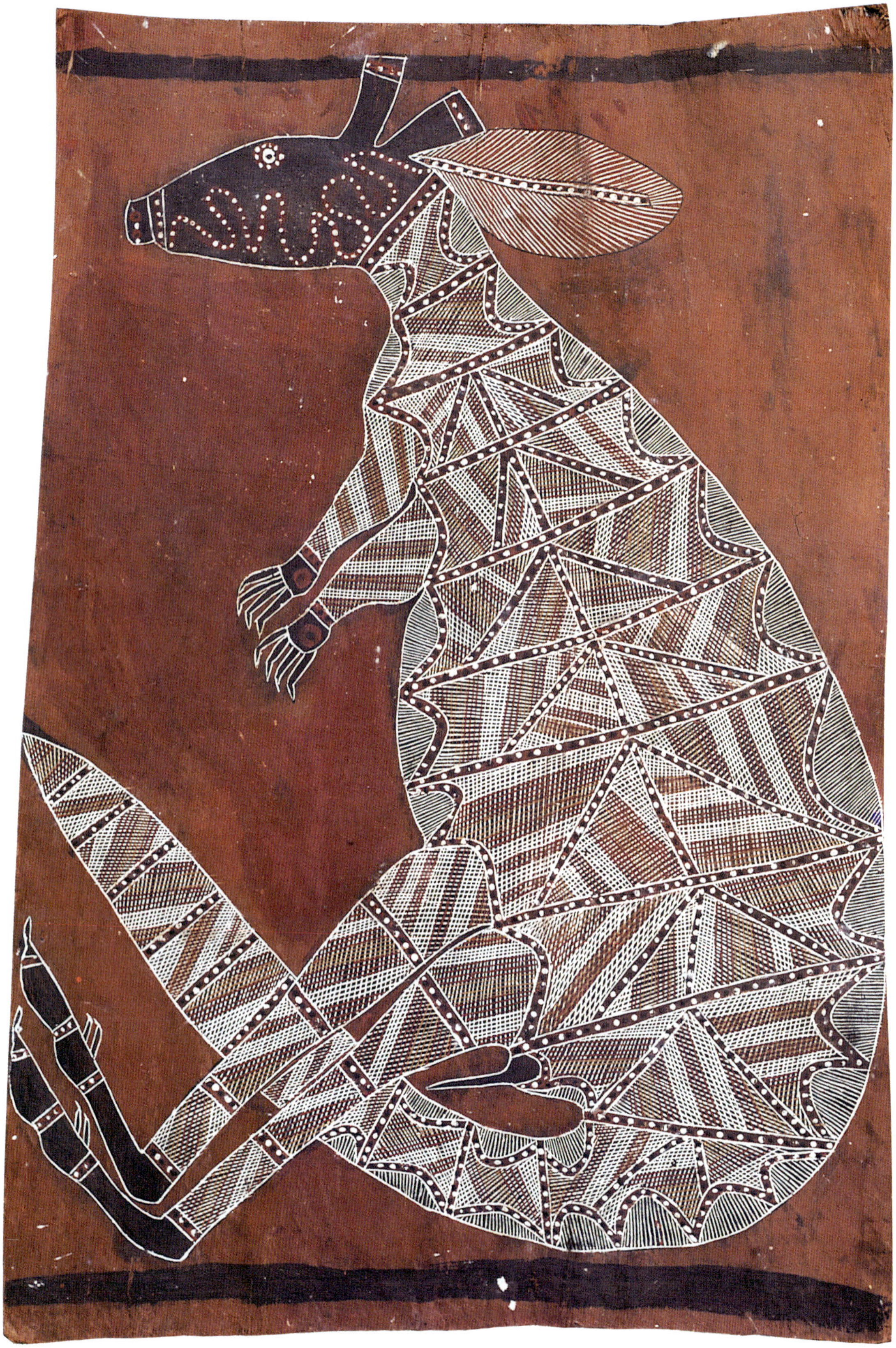

Plate 55 MARAIAN SERIES

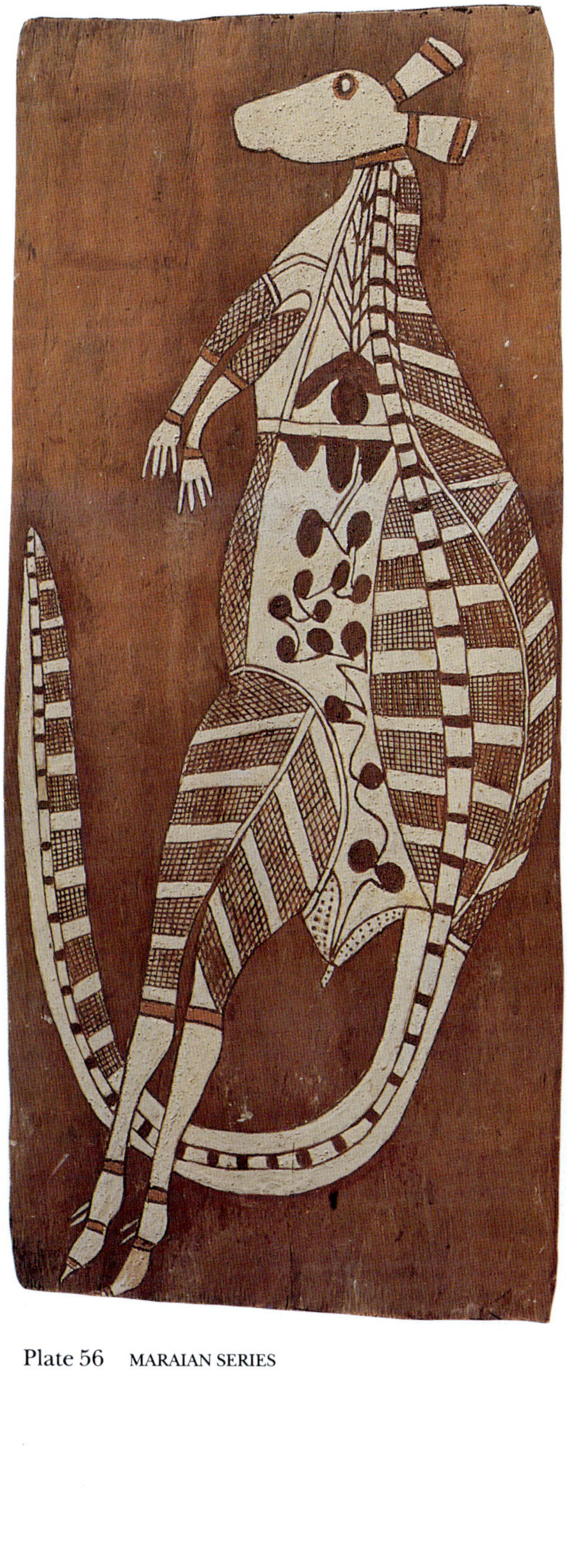

Plate 56 MARAIAN SERIES

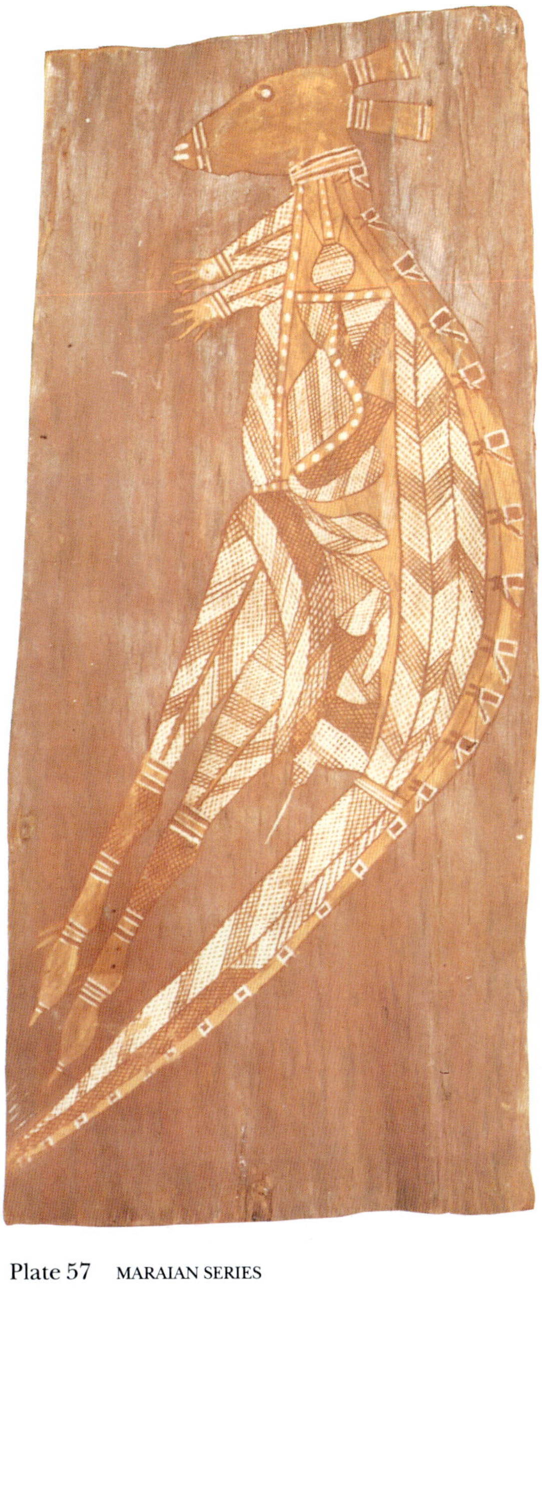

Plate 57 MARAIAN SERIES

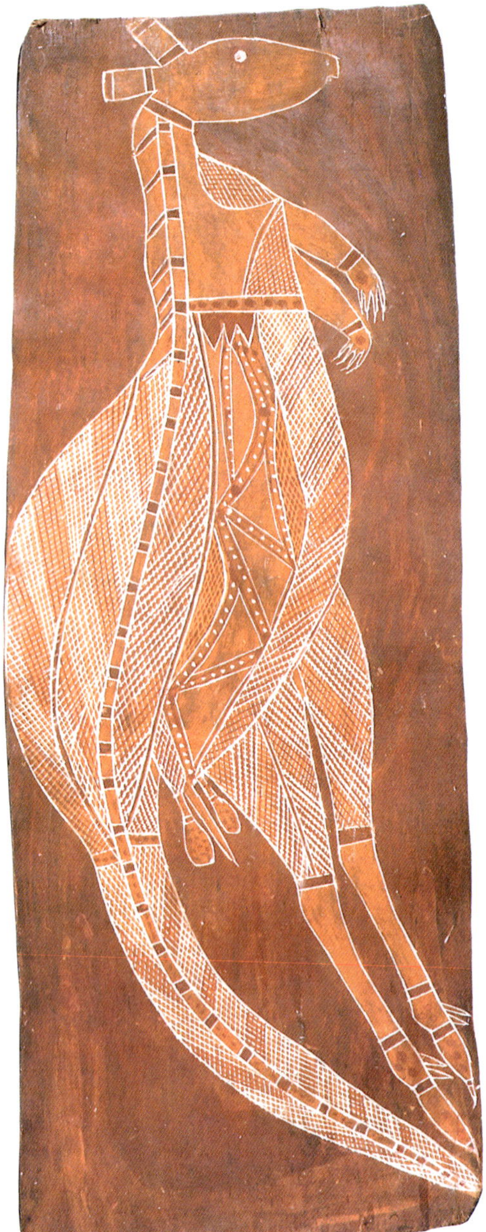

Plate 58 MARAIAN SERIES

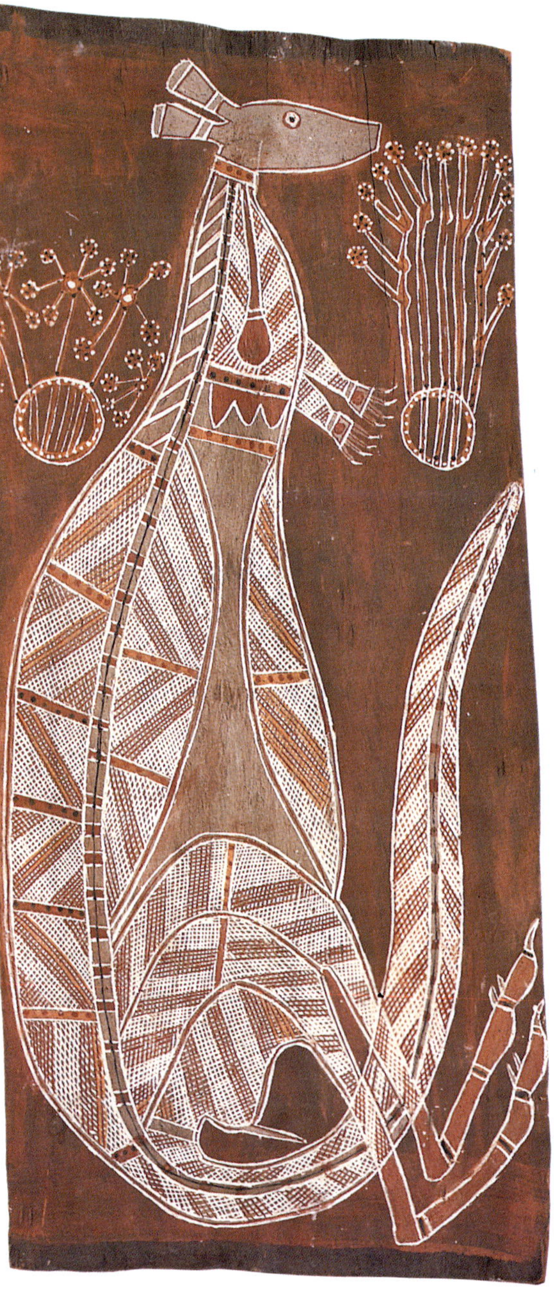

Plate 59 MARAIAN SERIES

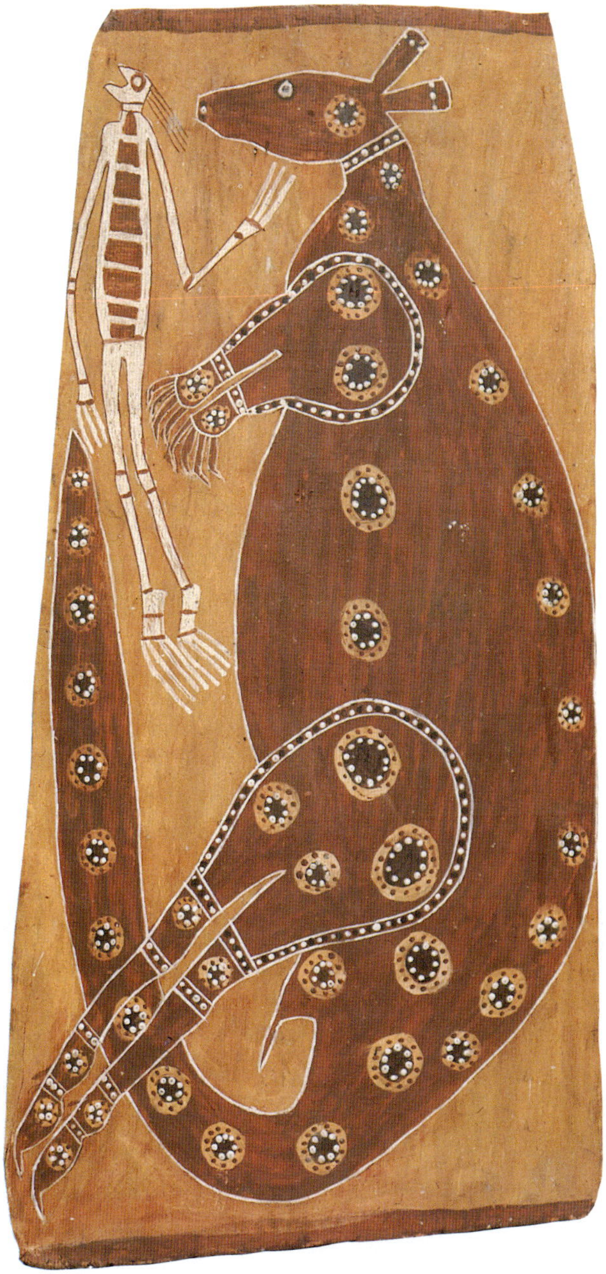

Plate 60 MARAIAN SERIES

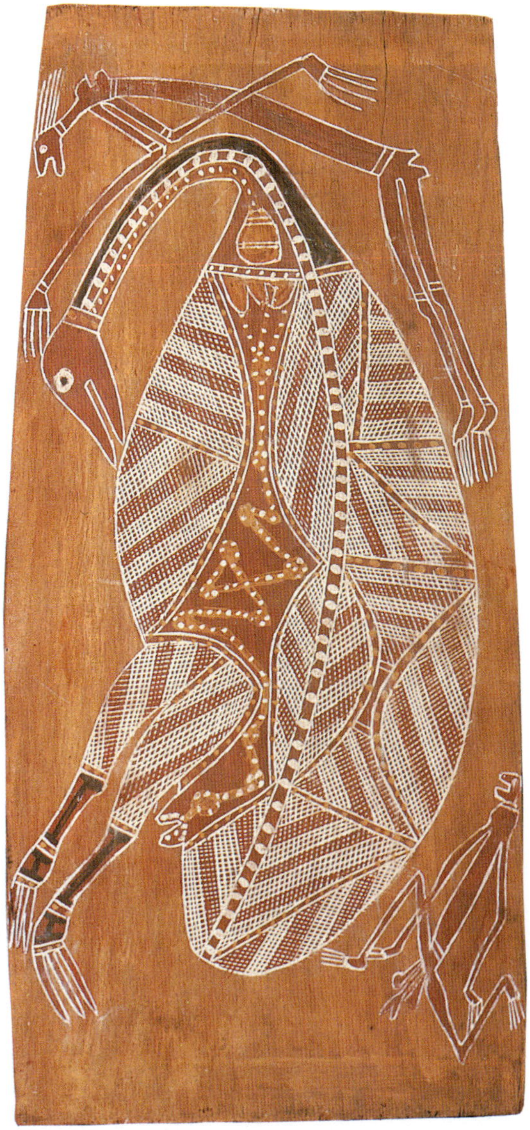

Plate 61 MARAIAN SERIES

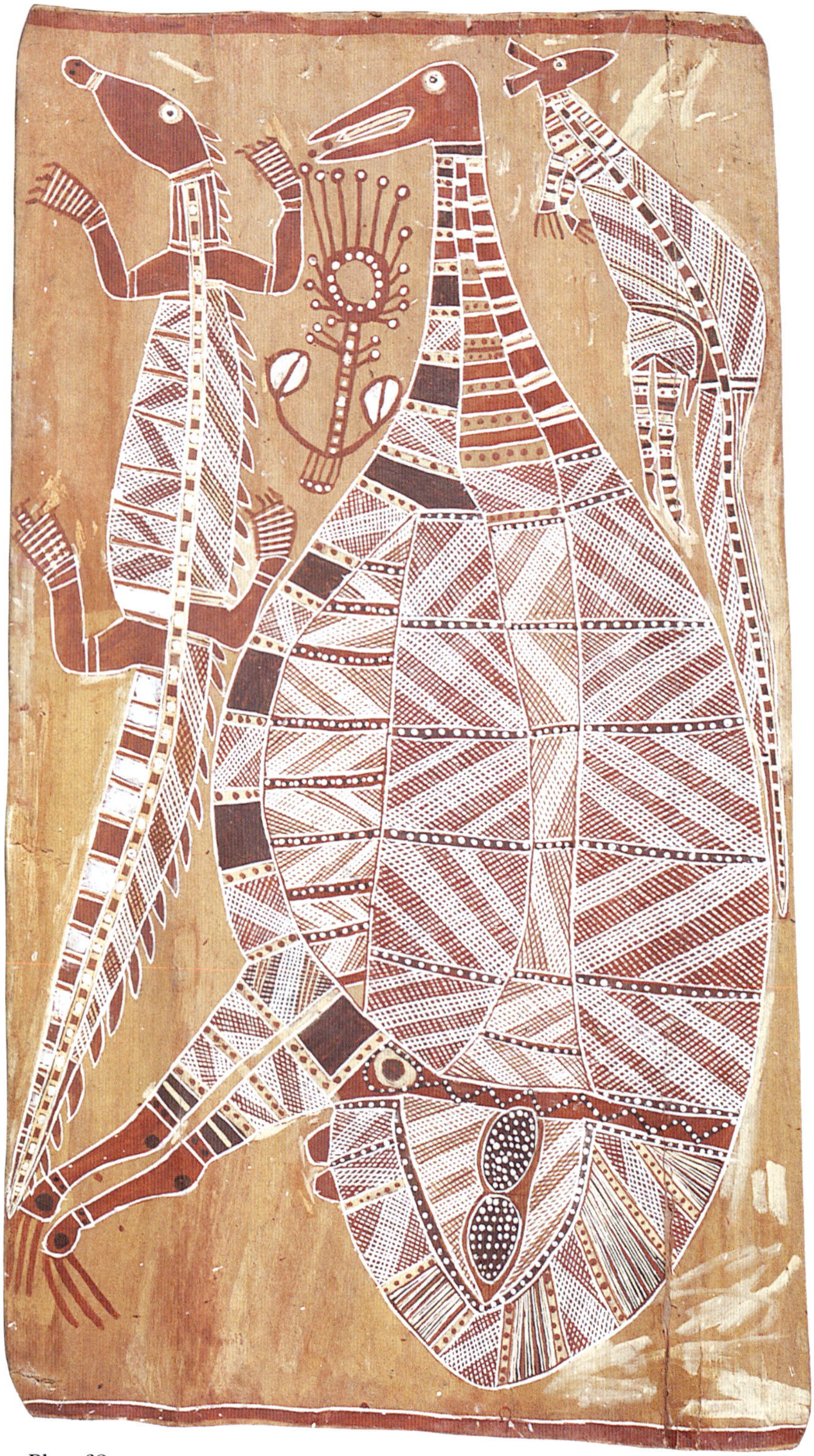

Plate 62 MARAIAN SERIES

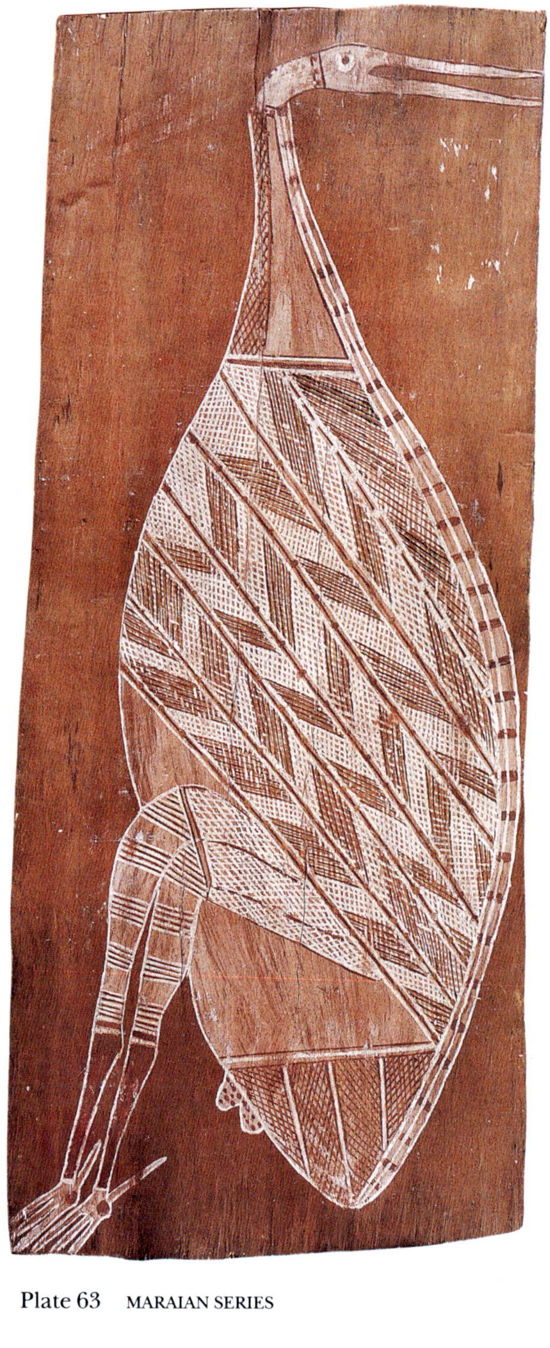

Plate 63 MARAIAN SERIES

Aborigines. I was not to proceed past Oenpelli until full discussions had been held with Oenpelli councillors and Aborigines elsewhere. If they all agreed that I should proceed to Marugulidban, this would be relayed to the Administrator's Department in Darwin, who would then issue me with authority to proceed further.

The lawyer advised me to carefully document everything and make sure people thoroughly understood what they signed. Also, we would have to hurry as the deadline for applications expired in four days' time.

We set off at first light. Bobby did all the driving as I was sick with pleurisy.

We arrived at Oenpelli in the late afternoon and pulled up in the sparse shade of some spindly trees. Bobby spread a blanket on the ground and I filled my felt bush hat with water and put a wet towel around my neck to counter the fierce heat.

A straggle of Aborigines came over to talk to Bobby as we waited for the main group of Gunwinggu elders.

The missionary and some of his Aboriginal councillors drove past us, ignoring our presence. They had been advised of our coming and the reason for the visit. Bobby said that like most Aborigines, the councillors were frightened of white authority, often with good reason, and so they found it easier to go along with the decisions made by white authority.

With what seemed like hostility from the mission, I wondered how there could be proper discussion and decisions as to whether or not I could proceed to Marugulidban.

We waited in vain for some contact from white staff or Aboriginal mission councillors. I felt ill and made a futile attempt to drive away dogs who were wetting on our gear.

As the sun was going down, a group of Gunwinggu elders approached us, led by old Balil-Balil. He spoke to Bobby in language, which was recorded, then translated.

Balil-Balil said, 'I am a big boss of Gunwinggu people here. I am the boss for everyone present. The mission council is made up of different tribal people, they cannot interfere or speak for us about our land. We say who can visit us and our land. We did not say no, you could not come.'

Balil-Balil said he would like to go with us to Marugulidban, but he was too old for such a long, rough journey. Bluey and Dudley Jollom could go instead and look after us.

Bluey said a lawyer from Darwin had been to Oenpelli the day before we arrived, asking the elders about their application for land and showing them a map. The lawyer had also questioned them about me. Was I going to take pictures and what was I going to do?

Balil-Balil began talking again, mostly in language. Finally he said that I was welcome to go on beyond Oenpelli. He and the other elders gave me their permission. Dudley and Bluey would guide us. He told us to get going as it would soon be dark.

Bobby agreed we should get moving. He said nothing would be gained by waiting for the mission people to organise a meeting to discuss whether I could proceed beyond Oenpelli or not. In any case, they appeared to have snubbed us. We should therefore take the advice of Balil-Balil. I could explain to the Deputy Administrator and Aboriginal Welfare when we returned to Darwin.

I hesitated, saying that I had no permit to go past Oenpelli and could be arrested, jailed or fined. The law allowed for both.

Bobby grew angry. 'Whose law do you listen to? You were taken into our family, you and yours. My father is your uncle. You made a promise to that old man. You going to back out now?'

I said I was not backing out, just thinking of what might happen to me, that was all. Dudley and Bluey said not to worry. I had their permission to go.

It was a terrible track to Nabarlek mining camp, and we decided to call in and ask for hospitality. I could not go any further without a rest. I was afraid of becoming too ill to go on. The mining site manager kindly allocated some tents for us and allowed me to take a shower. It was midnight when I lay down on the camp stretcher.

I awoke at 5 a.m. to the early morning chorus of birds. From my tent I could see a pink sky and the large trees surrounding the camp. There was dew on the ground and a cool breeze that would vanish all too soon. The country looked fresh with its heavy foliage — so different from the starkness of Oenpelli. The country all round that area had been dry; by empty waterholes lay dead buffalo and cattle, kites and crows astride them.

After all the men had showered I went with Bobby to fill the water drums and ask about buying petrol. We had barely a jerry can left, as the Border Store had only been able to sell us four gallons. The site manager was generous. He gave us petrol and sat down with the Aborigines to work out the best track to follow. Then we boiled the billy and ate bread and cheese for breakfast.

Something had been nagging at Bobby and he asked Bluey to tell him straight. Did he sign a telegram at Oenpelli telling us Sandra Holmes could not go to Gunwinggu country? Bluey hotly denied it.

It was very rough country, deep ruts with sharp tree roots protruding that could slice tyres right round. We only had one spare.

In the distance we could see a mighty rock. The men said it was old man Nimbuah, in Mialli country. Bluey explained, 'This Nimbuah. He old man. He was Yirdu tribe. His wife same. These two old people sit down and old man say to his wife, "I'll sit down here. You too old. I stay here turn myself into big rock. You go over there make yourself into little stone." They too old so they both turned into stone.'

The old man was a cult hero of the Yirdu people. Both he and his wife had come to the end of their Dreaming path, so he sang magic songs to turn himself and his wife into stones.

As we drove on Bluey pointed to a camp site we had made on the film trip. I recalled that Mary had dived for cockles in the lovely waterhole. Now there was a fence. Bobby asked who had put it there. Dudley replied it was made for the mission.

As we travelled on, the track got worse. We lurched up a rocky incline and there below was an expanse of deep white sand, rocks and debris. Bluey said this was the Nimbuah River, when it was running.

We churned and bumped through the riverbed, following a track that ran close to Nimbuah Rock, which rose to a dizzy height like a mighty column. The top was rounded, as if a huge boulder had been set down there. On top of this some trees were growing. Bluey said the round part was the old man's head and the trees were his hair. Dudley said that sometimes mining company helicopters landed like blowflies in Nimbuah's hair.

I took note of the country as we progressed. Some of it looked like good grazing or gardening country. There were fat cattle and buffalo wandering about. Dudley got quite excited, pointing to some white bullocks that he had not seen before. There were also sightings of fine-looking wild horses. Bobby said they planned to catch some of them for stock work when they got their own station.

At 2 p.m. we arrived at Goomadeer River, where the mission had established a settlement. There was a gravel airstrip, some huts and gardens.

Dudley said this was the start of true Gunwinggu country. We stopped to have a meeting and boil the billy.

When we were all seated under a tree with the men of the settlement, Bobby spoke to a man named Peter Nungiliwah. Peter informed us that this place was leased to the mission at Oenpelli. I asked him if he had signed papers to okay the lease and he said yes, it had been done through a senior man in Aboriginal Welfare. He did not know the size of the lease and had no copy of the papers. As far as he knew, the Gunwinggu council of elders had not been consulted. Dudley confirmed this. We told the men that we would see them on the way back.

We had to get to Marugulidban before dark.

From this point we started to keep a count of the kilometres on the odometer to give some idea of the size of the Gunwinggu country.

A few kilometres from the settlement we were confronted with a wide expanse of mud, deep river-sand and rocks. Bobby reminded me this was where some of the vehicles got bogged on the film trip. I was worried it would happen again, and we had no winch or any other help. Bobby smiled and patted my hand. 'We'll get through. I'm driving.' Bluey laughed. 'We can't get bogged.' The Landrover roared through the mud and into the sand. 'Don't say "hooray" yet,' said Bobby. The men repeated, 'Don't say "hooray" yet.'

We roared up the other side, to see a deep riverbed with some water lying in it and steep, slippery sides. We roared into it and almost got bogged in the middle, slowly pulling out, wheels churning, then slowly up the river bank.

Some areas were worse, so we skirted around them until we came to the lovely pool of the Yowk-Yowk, the water sprites, now surrounded by chopped trees, cans and bottles. We stopped to pick up all the rubbish. The men filled plastic bags which would be taken back to Darwin. They were upset. 'Too many balanda ruining our country, all the way.' They said they wanted the government to put up a notice declaring it a sacred place to Aborigines.

Rocks near the waterhole had been moved to widen the track, possibly for bigger vehicles. The men thought mining people must have done it.

Bobby reflected, 'Why do they make it so hard for you to come through, when many white men are going all over the country and spoiling it?'

The track wound through a dark, swampy area with a rocky hill on one side. Bobby said this was the home of the giant Numoroto. I asked him if this giant was the same as Jun-Bar-Barr. Bluey said yes, but Numoroto is the Gunwinggu name for him. The jungle country was his home. This area was called Numullgarong. Aborigines did not go in there for fear of getting lost and eaten by Numoroto. Nobody was allowed to hunt there or set fire to the scrub, as this would anger the giant.

At 4.15 p.m. we came to a few leaf shelters near the track. Some Gunwinggu were camped there. One old man was painting on bark. Dudley called out to them in language and we stopped to rest for a short time and eat something. Bluey introduced me to a man named Jacki Numarraraba, who said he wanted to talk to me about his land. He was trying to establish something for his wife and children. Bobby explained the purpose of our visit and Jacki said he was glad. The people had been waiting for a long time.

Just over an hour later we arrived at Marugulidban, a scatter of leafy shelters by a clear river, with big trees all round. The trees were filled with cackling geese that suddenly took off in a great cloud as hunters disturbed them. I had never seen so many. The men said they would catch one later for supper. We had run out of food and were all hungry.

The people made us welcome and said we would have a meeting later, when Kelly Borgordubhu and others arrived on the evening tide from Maningrida. They would come down the Liverpool River at high tide and beach the canoe on a sandbar where a branch of the river petered out, about 6.5 kilometres away. They would walk from there.

I was invited to lie down in a leaf shelter while the men went hunting. They came back with a goose which we roasted on the fire. A little girl bought me a barramundi which she had caught.

As the sun went down the mosquitoes arrived, droning like a distant plane. We were also attacked by march flies.

As the light began to fade distant shouts heralded the arrival of Borgordubhu and his party.

He was glad to see us, and asked if Yirawala had received his letter saying they had started to clear an area for an airstrip. He had also written me a letter asking us to come and have a look. Both letters had been received. Bobby said his father was pleased and had sent a taped message.

I went to lie down and Bobby played tapes from Balil-Balil and Yirawala. He also recorded the discussions about land and the application. The meeting went on till 3 a.m.

I went to sleep to the sounds of a camp corroboree performed to welcome Kelly Borgordubhu.

The elders present also dictated a letter to the Darwin Administration asking for their land and stating that they wanted me to be their go-between for their land application. Bobby made sure the men understood fully what was set down before they signed it. The statement from the elders was also recorded on tape. Finally they marked out their land area on a Land Board map.

They said they had never said they did not want me, and were sick of being kept in the dark and being given wrong information. They wanted to make their own settlement and would all come in to Darwin to talk to their lawyer and the Land Board.

Early next morning after breakfast we had final talks and the statements were gone over once more. The only thing added was that they requested Administration to acknowledge that I was their official helper and should be given a permit at all times.

Each man who signed the statement also recorded their expertise in different fields. One man was experienced in professional fishing, others were stockmen, saddle makers and generally trained in the cattle industry. Some were buffalo shooters, some gardeners.

Before we left, Borgordubhu showed us the airstrip clearing, grassy plains for cattle, and sites where they planned to build houses and erect a water tank. He was full of hope and proudly spoke of their plans to have a place of their own. Near a creek he planted the mango trees we had bought.

On the return journey Bobby travelled as fast as the rough terrain allowed. This was our third day on the track. It was Sunday and the application had to be submitted on Monday.

Travelling on a long stretch of deep, white sand Bluey said there was a light aircraft flying above us. He smiled. 'Might be that Welfare boss, looking for you?' They all laughed. I knew I could be arrested, and I couldn't appreciate the joke. There was only one chance of reprieve: if a Labor Government came to power in the forthcoming Federal elections, all existing Administration machinery would be on hold and the present policies and practices of Aboriginal Welfare could be frozen.

At 2 p.m. we reached the Goomadeer settlement and stopped for meeting. We obtained more signatures from a man called Captain and old Roorgoorla, who was married to Muriel, Mary and Yirawala's daughter.

Roorgoorla was sick and asked us to take a message on to Darwin to have him flown out. He was too ill to go with us in the truck. The people seemed to be in poor condition and were doing it hard. Bobby said he would pass all this on.

We gave them our remaining sugar, tea, bread and tinned milk.

We were making good time and arrived at Oenpelli at 5.30 p.m. We said goodbye to Dudley and Bluey, who said they would tell Balil-Balil and the others about the trip. Bobby told them not to sign any papers because they could not understand them. They said they would wait for news from him.

We raced on for the East Alligator River crossing only to find the stone causeway blocked by a huge mining company truck carrying a demountable house. The driver had stopped in the middle, very close to the edge of the causeway. Bobby said the tide would be coming in soon.

Frantic at this unforeseen obstacle I got out and went down to talk to the driver, who was swearing horribly. An American foreman was waving his arms about and shouting at him to 'get the goddamn thing moving', and yelled at me to 'get the hell out of the way' as they were coming through. The driver thought otherwise, saying to the foreman, 'Listen mate. If you want the whole bloody lot in the drink, I'll take her forward.' The foreman bent down to look at the wheels. By now the water was over his shoes, making the rocks more slippery. He looked up and shouted at the driver, 'I reckon you can make it.' The driver just sat there.

I spoke to the American foreman, pleading with him to tell the driver to back up onto solid ground, then have another go at the crossing. I told him of our desperate journey on behalf of Yirawala. We just had to get through tonight, and it was a long drive back to Darwin. 'Hey!' he cried. 'I read about that old man. An MBE and a famous painter. Well, hell, sure we can let you by.' He shouted at the driver to back off the causeway. Then turning to me, 'That's a terrible trip you've been on. Reckon you got a lot of guts.'

Slowly, the big truck backed off, with men all round shouting instructions to the driver. It took over half an hour to clear the causeway.

As we drove across the American gave us a big grin and the thumbs-up sign.

It was getting dark and we were exhausted. We did not stop at the Border Store but hurried on. Bobby patted the dashboard of the Landrover and praised it for getting us through without a breakdown. The problem now was buffalo on the track, and our weariness. Bobby was almost asleep at the wheel and ran off the track. I took over for a while and also nodded off. He grabbed the wheel just in time to avoid our hitting a big paperbark tree. A number of times we almost hit buffalo and the truck was lurching to right and left. Tired as I was, I worried that the police might be waiting for me when I got home.

We drove all night and by daylight were on the bitumen beyond the experimental farm near Foggs Dam. By 7 a.m. we had reached Humpty Doo and I phoned Ron Withnall to tell him we had gone on past Oenpelli and we had all the signatures. 'I know,' he said in a flat voice. 'You've done it now. I can't help you if they pick you up.' I said all the documents and tapes would be delivered to him by my son, before 9 a.m.

I went to have a sleep, after instructing my children not to open the door to anyone.

Although an order for my arrest had been signed it was decided to wait for the outcome of the Federal elections.

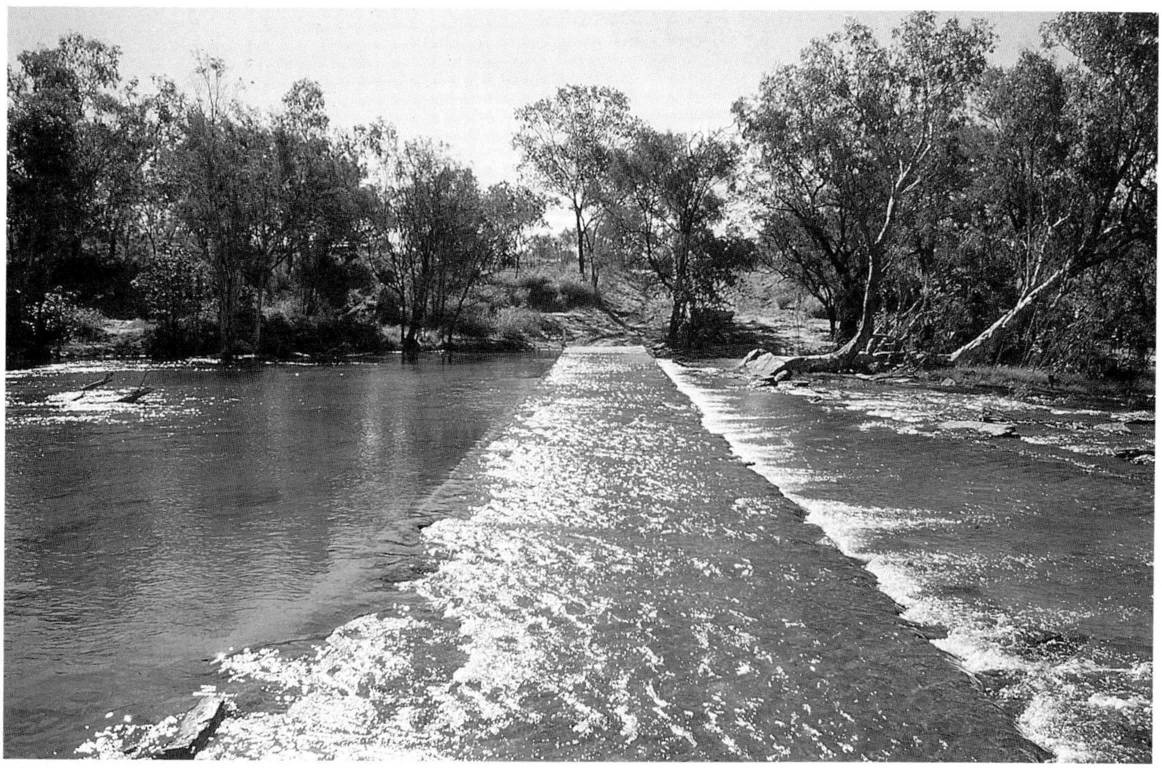

The East Alligator River crossing.

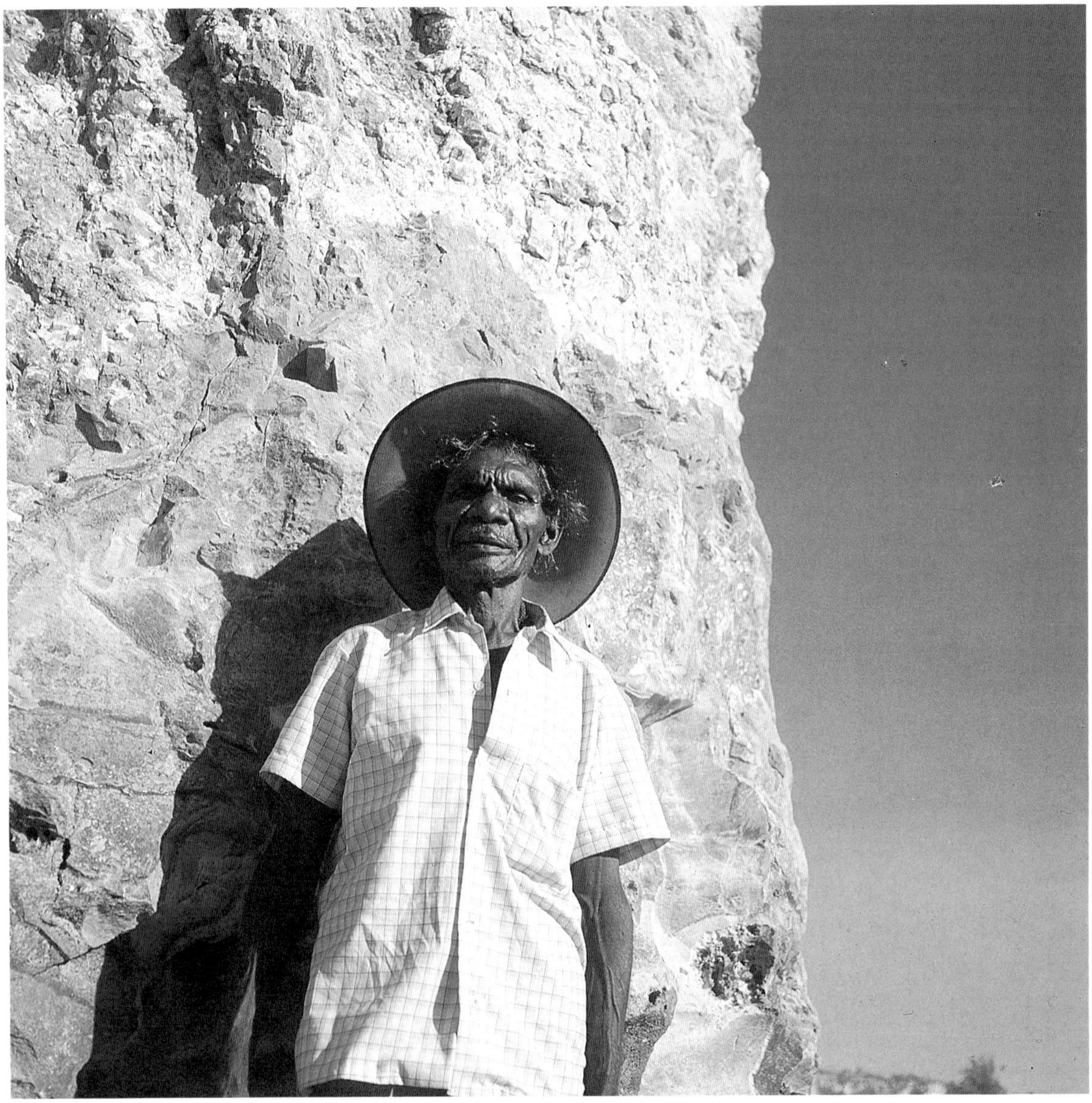

Chapter 8
We all stand up straight today

The Whitlam Labor Government came to power in December. Their election slogan had been 'It's time'. Well, it was time for a lot of changes.

Under the new Labor Government, the name Aboriginal Welfare was changed to the Department of Aboriginal Affairs, and the first Labor Minister for Aboriginal Affairs was appointed, The Honourable Gordon M Bryant.

All existing land leases and mineral exploration licences in the Northern Territory were frozen, pending a land rights enquiry by Mr Justice A E Woodward, the first Commissioner for Aboriginal land claims hearings.

Funds for Aboriginal programs were greatly increased.

The official Federal policy for Aborigines would be Self Determination, instead of Assimilation. This was a step in the right direction and it would be interesting to see how the new policy would be implemented on the reserves, where Aborigines had suffered generations of paternalism and deliberate destruction of their culture.

Unless the means of communication were made available to tribal people, by way of public telephones and government postal services, they would not be able to enjoy the basic elements of democracy, which we took for granted. With all the millions to be allocated, this should have been a number-one priority, if tribal Aborigines were going to be permitted to try and determine anything for themselves. If this was not done the tribal people would simply fall into the hands of others, as they were not assertive and were reluctant to stand up for themselves in the face of aggressive authority.

After the elections the Assistant Administrator wrote a 'please explain' letter concerning my venturing beyond Oenpelli without a permit. I wrote a detailed reply, and sent statements from the Gunwinggu elders, which he accepted.

In late December, Yirawala sent a telegram to say he was coming in to Darwin with Mary. I sent him two tickets for 2 January 1973.

When Yirawala came in he said he wanted to find out about the new government. He had talked with Borgordubhu and other elders and they were anxious to go back to tribal lands as soon as possible. He wanted to see his lawyer about land and money from the new government.

The lawyer told him that the Labor Government would make different laws. Aborigines would have to make different applications now. He would advise Yirawala of the changes and assist as best he could.

Yirawala sat tapping his foot, impatient for some positive action. 'I want new gov'ment give me land, help. Kick out mission, Welfare and balanda. You reckon new gov'ment help we?' The lawyer said we must wait and see.

As we were leaving, Yirawala said that another lawyer had been out to Croker Island to get him to sign some papers. He wanted to know if his lawyer had sent the man. The reply was in the negative. Yirawala frowned and said, 'That lawyer, him talk 'bout my land – me sick in bed, never understand meaning for that paper, lawyer.'

His lawyer advised him never to sign any papers that he did not fully understand and to refer the person to him in Darwin.

Yirawala and Mary stayed for eight days. He was anxious to get back and hold further talks with other tribal elders.

In mid-February 1973 the Minister for Aboriginal Affairs would be visiting Darwin to take submissions from various interested people. I wrote to Yirawala but he was unable to come in. He sent a message that I send in a submission on behalf of him and the other tribal elders, concerning land and finance.

I obtained an appointment with the Minister for 14 February and sent the submission in advance.

There was a long queue of people waiting to see the Minister. I recognised some of them as mission staff.

My interview with the Minister was not as productive as I had hoped. He said he had heard of me and my old Yirawala. After a brief conversation he leaned forward and said he was going to introduce legislation to class anyone as an Aborigine who identified as one, 'A Wooloomooloo [Sydney suburb] Aboriginal will be classed the same as old Yirawala.'

In my capacity as Yirawala's official secretary I wrote to the Director of Aboriginal Affairs in Canberra to request a vehicle for the Gunwinggu, to facilitate contact with scattered tribal elders and inform them of the coming land rights hearings and arrange for them to be present.

The Gunwinggu also wanted to know when they could go back to their tribal lands.

I wrote in March to the secretary of the Aboriginal Land Rights Royal Commission asking for details of the Northern Territory itinerary for the land rights hearings. I also sent details of the Gunwinggu land claim.

By early May when there was no response from the Territory or Federal Government about a vehicle for the Gunwinggu, Yirawala and I decided to make an appeal for public funds through the local media and mount a small exhibition of his paintings in the Northern Territory Legislative Council chambers. Only $50 was raised. Thirty dollars from the public and $20 from a mining company.

In mid-May I was advised that land rights hearings would be held at Maningrida on 12 June 1973.

I applied for a permit immediately, and heard of a new obstruction to my going: apparently there was no accommodation for me on Croker Island.

I wrote to the new Director of Aboriginal Affairs in Darwin, who suggested I make an appointment to discuss things with him. Our meeting resulted in a permit being issued for 24–28 May to discuss with the Aborigines the coming hearings of the Royal Commission into Aboriginal Land Rights.

When I arrived at Croker Island the missionary picked me up at the airstrip. I had to ride on the back of the truck all the way across the island, over a rough track.

I was tersely informed that I could only stay a few hours. A plane provided by Darwin Aboriginal Affairs would pick me up after lunch. This I was told had been arranged by radio that morning. I asked if the Aborigines had any say in the matter, and was told that the missionary's head Aboriginal councillors, Dick and Jumbo, had said they did not want me to stay.

When I repeated this to Yirawala, he jumped to his feet in anger and called out to David and Bobby. They all marched off to see the two councillors, who denied saying they didn't want me to stay. They signed papers to this effect and said I could stay, then they went off to tell the missionary.

Half an hour after, Jumbo came hurrying up to Yirawala's hut to say the missionary was very angry and I was summoned to appear before a meeting of the Mission Council. David, Bobby and Yirawala went with me.

The so-called 'meeting' erupted outside the council office. I was verbally attacked. The plane would still come for me.

Bobby Joran, always so calm and polite, was now provoked into anger at what appeared to be a situation where a stooge council might agree to anything; the people were never told what was happening.

Bobby also said that when he and his father came up to the office for any information, they were usually told to get out.

David Gumaraitj spoke in support of Bobby. He was told to shut up, but refused. 'Mission never tell us about Woodward land meeting. Mrs Holmes come to tell us and help us. Mission never teach us to work radio, or post-office business. Mission own everything, keep books, bank, letters, pension cheques.'

An Aboriginal councillor piped up, 'We need mission man to work radio, the mail, pension money, everything. He is boss because we don't know how to do it.'

David exploded. 'That what I am saying. We never been trained to take over.'

Bobby spoke bitterly. 'Yes, mission control everything. Now you trying to interfere with our land business. Aborigines never made row or fight over land, till white man come. You stick your nose into our land business. You got no right. Our land nothing to do with mission.'

Finally the missionary said he would now consult with his council to decide whether I could stay until Thursday. I reminded him that I had the signed paper from the two traditional owners and in line with the Federal Government's new policy of Self Determination, that might be enough.

As we walked away, Yirawala put his arms around his sons, then dabbed at his eyes with a piece of rag, 'First time we talk straight to balanda. We all stand up straight today, me and my sons.' He was proud of them.

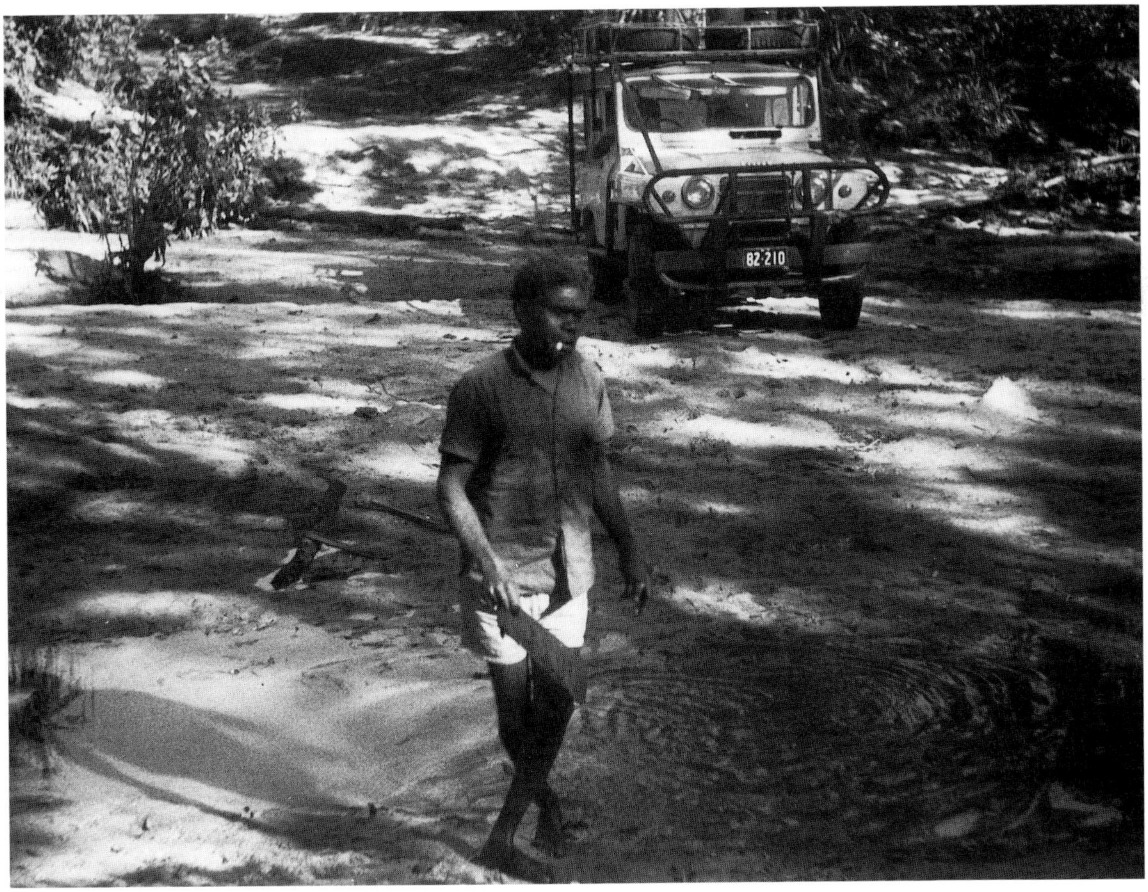

Albert testing a boggy track on the journey in May 1973 to notify and organise the Gunwinggu elders for the Woodward hearings (the Royal Commission into Aboriginal Land Rights).

An hour later the missionary drove down to Yirawala's hut and said I could stay, and that the mission could provide accommodation for me in a vacant flat. I camped on the beach near Yirawala's hut.

That night a meeting was held by lamplight with six of the Gunwinggu elders and others. All correspondence was read, interpreted and discussed. A statement was signed applying for government assistance to attend the land rights hearing at Maningrida Settlement. Tape recordings were made and Aileen Joran took notes. Yirawala nominated her as his bush secretary. He spoke passionately. They had one small victory today and there would be bigger ones, he said. The people must all stand strong together and fight for the land and money to make their own settlement.

Aileen wrote a letter for her husband, addressed to Aboriginal Affairs in Canberra, telling them about conditions on Croker Island and what the people really wanted. It was a very frank letter. David Gumaraitj also dictated a letter highly critical of the mission.

Yirawala dictated a letter to his lawyer, advising him of today's attempts to frustrate their meeting about the land rights hearings. He also said that he now knew that the lawyer who had come to Croker Island to get his signature on some papers, had come from the missions. He said he wanted a copy of what he had signed.

Bobby was nominated to come back to Darwin with me. We would visit Oenpelli and Goomadeer to organise transport to take the elders to Maningrida by 12 June.

Before the meeting broke up, a young Gunwinggu man named Albert volunteered to go with us on the journeys, to help with the driving and any problems which might arise.

Back in Darwin I went to see the Director of Aboriginal Affairs, asking for a vehicle to enable us to visit the Gunwinggu elders, to consult with them about the Maningrida land hearings in June, and to see if they wished to attend the hearings and have transport arranged for them. I requested petrol expenses and some money for Bobby and Albert, who had taken time off work. I applied for a permit for five days from 25 May. The Director agreed to supply a four wheel drive hire car for us. There was no word about money for the men, but at least we had a reliable vehicle.

We sent a telegram to the Border Store, asking Terry to get a message to the Oenpelli elders that we would be there in three days' time.

Chapter 9
Give us our land

When we arrived most of the elders were waiting for us. They were pleased to hear about the land rights hearing and anxious to be there, so we booked them in groups to go by chartered and commercial aircraft. They were given vouchers, provided by Aboriginal Affairs, which listed their names, status and pick-up dates. They said they would camp near the airstrip.

From Oenpelli we travelled to the Goomadeer River area, to make similar arrangements. Bobby and Albert had thoughtfully brought food. We found the Aborigines there in poor health. Children had sores and everyone was thin. Roorgoorla was very sick with infected eyes; one appeared to be ulcerated. The people said they were hungry and had been living on flour, tea and sugar. They welcomed the tinned meat that Bobby and Albert had brought. Bobby asked them about the vegetable garden growing near a swamp. The people said they could not touch it as it belonged to the mission.

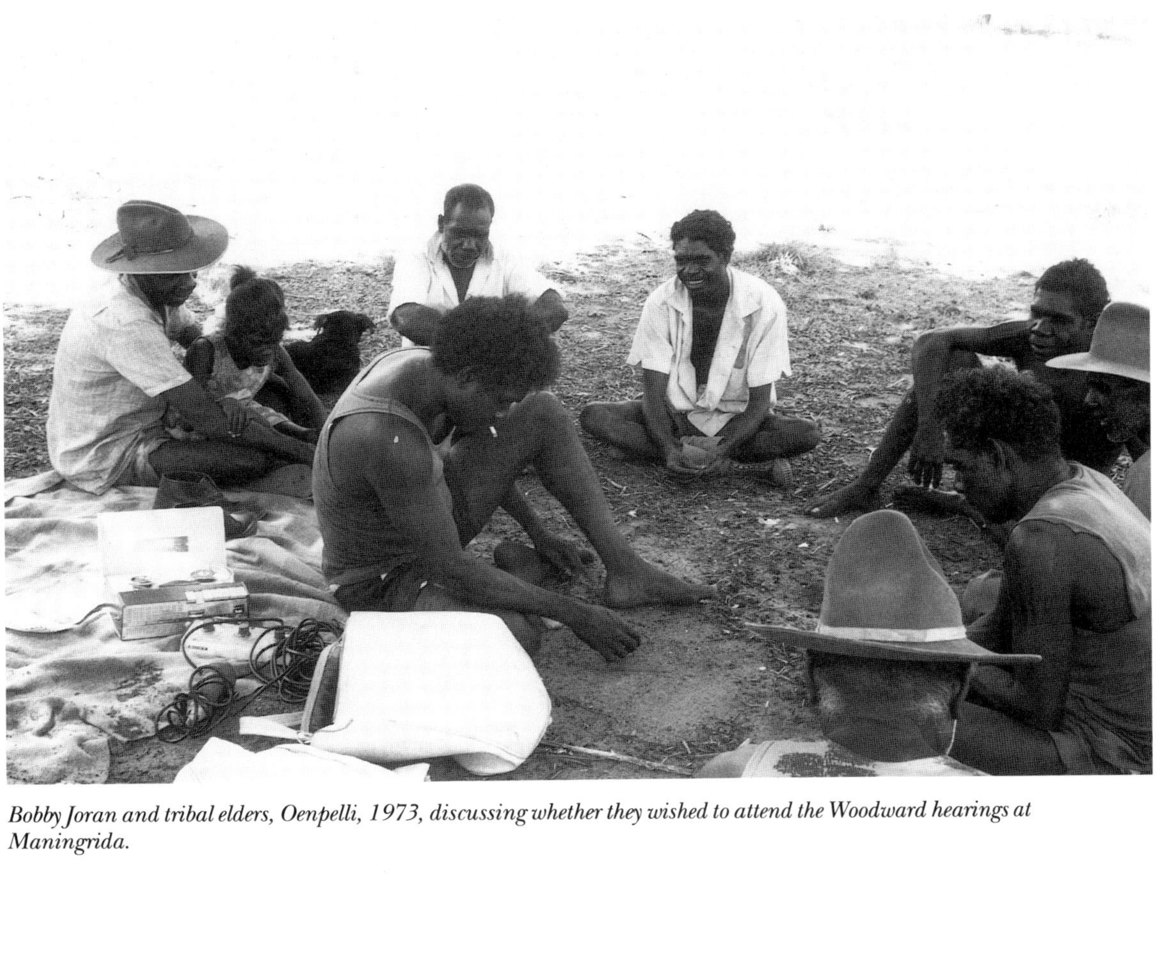

Bobby Joran and tribal elders, Oenpelli, 1973, discussing whether they wished to attend the Woodward hearings at Maningrida.

We had a meeting about the land rights hearing to be held at Maningrida, and most people were pleased; others seemed despondent and thought the forces against their being able to claim land would be too strong. Roorgoorla said he would not be well enough to go to the Maningrida land hearings, and nominated Captain to go in his place.

According to Roorgoorla, two young Gunwinggu men were claiming a large area of land in the Goomadeer area but were really working for the mission who already had leased the settlement land where we were. He thought the mission wanted to extend its leases.

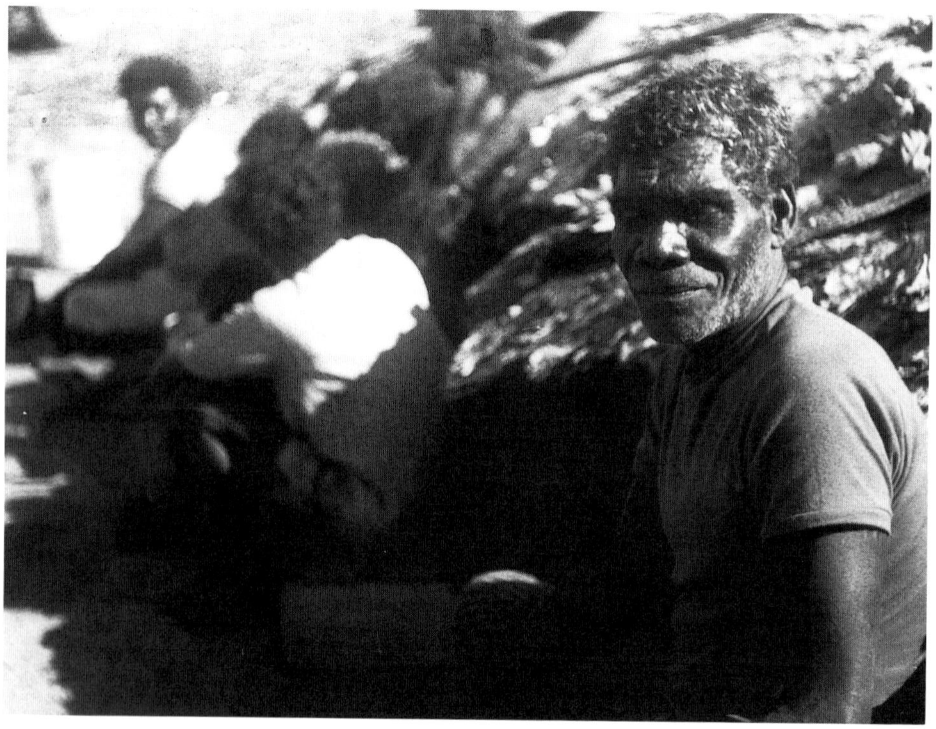

At Goomadeer Settlement, Captain was nominated by old Roorgoorla to go to the Woodward hearings in his place. We found the Aborigines at the settlement to be hungry and in poor health.

The people said those of them who worked to maintain the airstrip, using picks and shovels, were paid $20 a week.

Before we left, they queued up for some basic treatment for sores and infected eyes. The women asked us not to leave any tins around as children might cut themselves. If this happened there was no help, and transport was not available. We left them what food we had, plus some bandages, eye wash and simple medical items.

Bobby was very upset and angry and was anxious to report the situation to the Health Department in Darwin. He would again try to have old Roorgoorla and a sick child evacuated by air medical.

We arrived back in Darwin on 28 May. Bobby went straight to the Health Department, then to see Jim Bowditch at the *NT News*.

A story appeared in the *NT News* of 29 May 1973, under the heading, 'Yirawala's Tribe Wants to Appear at Land Hearings'. The article told of our journey and discussions with tribal elders, and also mentioned the health situation at Goomadeer, and that the people there had not been told about the land rights hearings at Maningrida. The article stressed that the Gunwinggu elders were anxious to be at the hearings and put their case, for which they needed financial assistance from the Government.

We contacted Aboriginal Affairs and submitted all the signed and witnessed documents

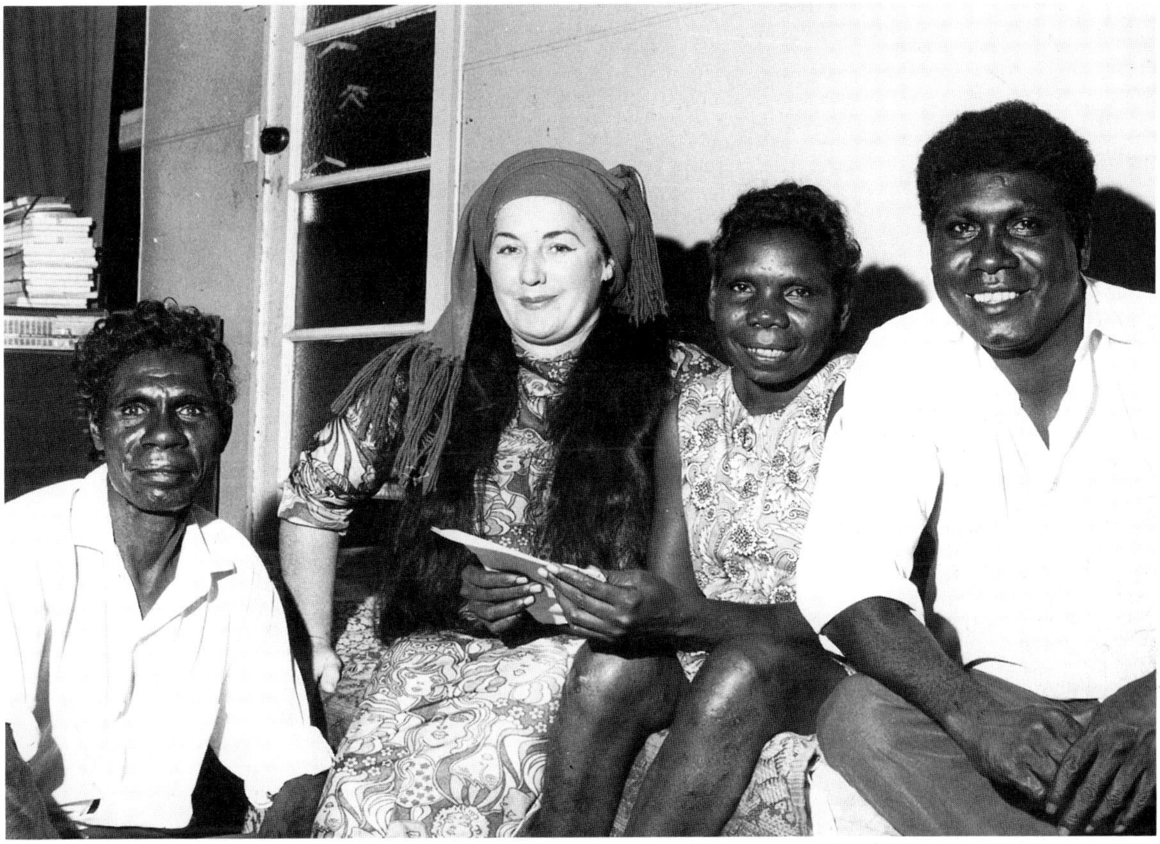

Left to right: David Gumaraitj (Yirawala's eldest son and heir), myself, Aileen Joran and Bobby Joran in Darwin, 1973. Aileen is holding the list and signatures of the Gunwinggu elders going to the Woodward hearings at Maningrida.

from the Gunwinggu elders requesting fares and charter planes to Maningrida. The full list of names, dates and pick-up points were included. At first there was a shocked silence, but they agreed to pay for the charters and fares.

When I applied for a permit to go to Maningrida I had to produce evidence that the Gunwinggu elders wanted me there to assist them. The proof that I submitted was not on nice stationery, neatly typed, but on pages torn from notebooks, stained with sweat and signed by men with anxious faces; some of them old, with trembling hands; most unable to write their names, for they were all tribal men. They made their marks with thumbprints, crosses and signs; they spoke on the tape recorder, desperately grasping at English words, trying to make themselves understood, hoping the white government officials would be patient and understanding.

A great deal of such material had been submitted to the Territory and Federal Governments. I wondered if they would understand or have patience with the complex tribal laws. What if it was all too time consuming and difficult?

It went off like a military operation, and by 10 June, two days before the hearings were to start, the Gunwinggu elders and tribal councillors had arrived at Maningrida. Present were: Yirawala, Kelly Borgordubhu, Peter Mahlunwunggu, David Gumaraitj, Bob Balil-Balil, Deedbarrkar, Joe Weedahrah, Frank Jollom, Captain, Thompson Naranolgi, Bobby Joran, Barnabus, David Malibumah, Joshua Wurunoonga, Goolberrberr, Silas Binjilulu, Mick Mundaingu, Jimmy Buryiller, Bomarah, Stephen Gongorlmah, Bobby Yainju, John Dulna-Dulna, Billy Yetj, Frank Minjiliwari and Bill Jumbinowah. They sat under a tree to discuss their submission. Bobby recorded everything and I made notes. Their original submission for their tribal land was read and interpreted for them and then fully discussed. They all agreed it was what they wanted. They added a further document, which they all

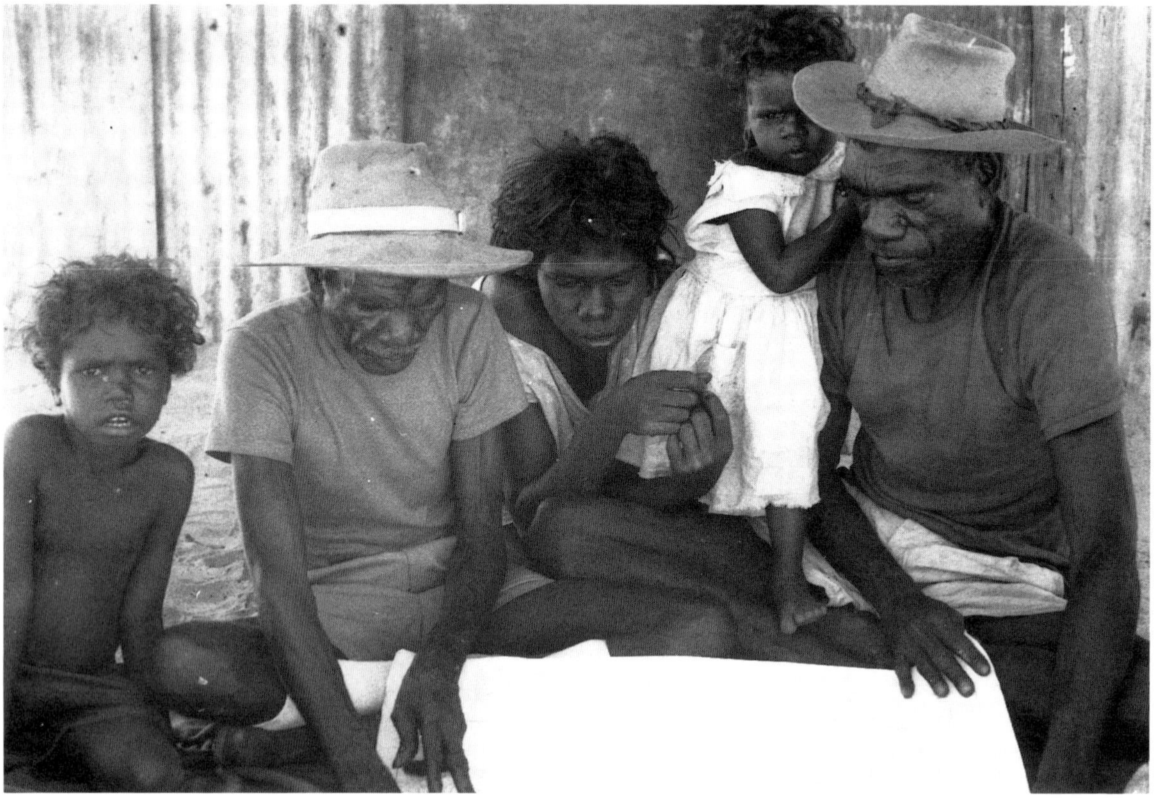

Maningrida, 1973. Yirawala and Peter Mahlunwunggu trying to pinpoint true Gunwinggu land area on a map of Arnhemland, before the Woodward hearings.

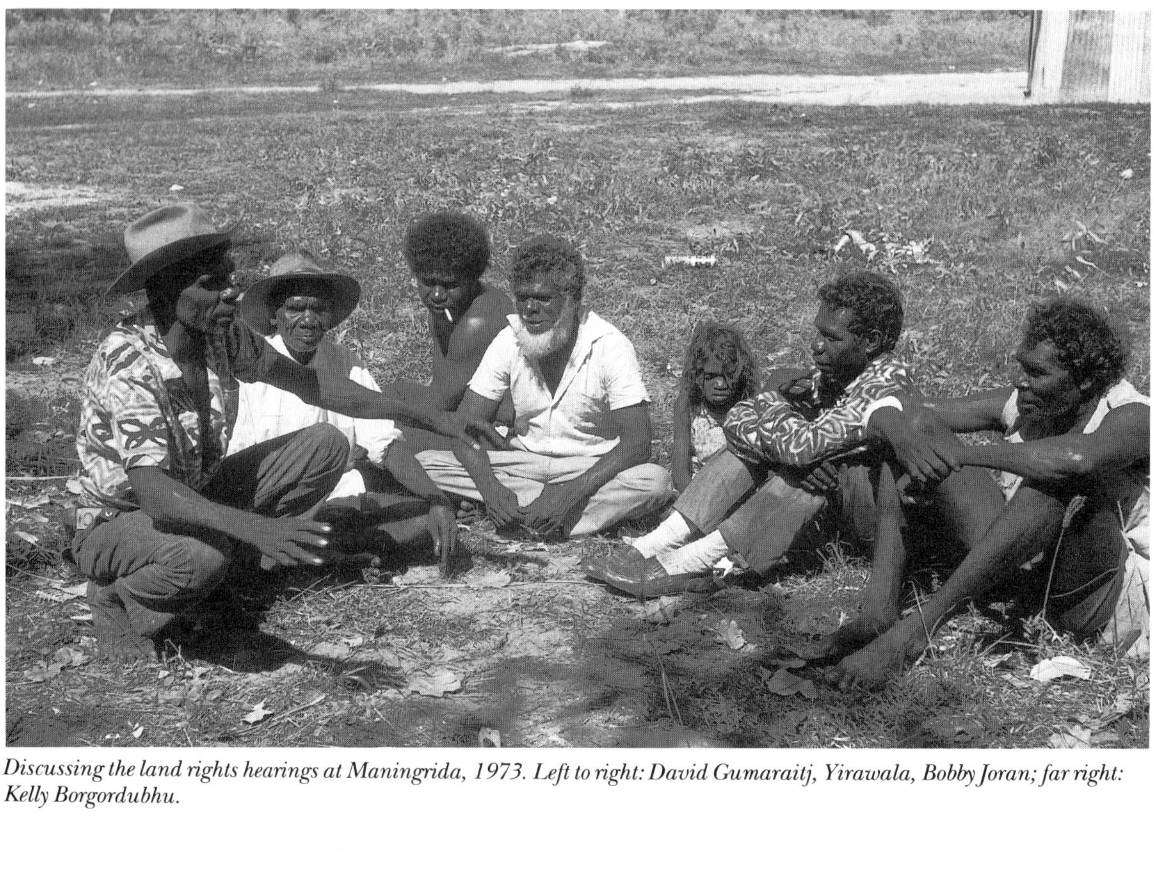

Discussing the land rights hearings at Maningrida, 1973. Left to right: David Gumaraitj, Yirawala, Bobby Joran; far right: Kelly Borgordubhu.

signed, emphasising that they were applying only for true Gunwinggu land which stretched approximately 50 kilometres from the Oenpelli side of Goomadeer River, then right across to the Liverpool and Mann Rivers, as marked on the Land Board Map.

The submission to the Commission on behalf of the council of elders of the Gunwinggu tribe read in part:

> This is our formal application for a pastoral lease and gardens on our tribal land ... The name of our lease shall be Marugulidban, which is our name for our tribal country.
>
> In our tribal group there are 400 people (including 100 school-aged children and a number of young, literate adults).
>
> About 200 men are capable of working hard. We have men experienced in (gardening, fishing, machine- and plant-operation, building, welding,) fencing, well digging, dams, cattle chutes, branding, general stock work, butchery and so on. Also we have men who can castrate bullocks, and overall experience with cattle work.
>
> A number of our men have been working with horses and cattle for years at Oenpelli and Croker Island also other places.
>
> There are many wild cattle in our country, we saw many last year when we went to our country; we shot a fine fat young bull for food.
>
> We saw some good grassed plains and wells with water all the year round, the wild cattle are fat. We know they are worth money, and would intend to round them up to start with. We can do this and follow them where a white man could not.
>
> We ask you for just a chance to do something for ourselves; we are not happy to sit down on Missions and Settlements with no land of our own and no future for the grandchildren. Also, we worry for somebody taking our country and spoiling our Dreaming sacred places.
>
> If we have this cattle station and vegetable and fruit gardens then we can stand up on our own and be proud people. We believe we can do this.
>
> We will employ our own lawyers, accountant and secretary and hold meetings every month to check up on how we are going.
>
> We will ask for $30,000 to start with, half of this to be a grant and half to pay back on easy terms. We will need money to buy iron posts, wire, horses, saddles, iron, etc, for our first huts; also a radio, small school and hospital, plus a lighting and water plant. We will need this money as soon as we get the lease.
>
> We want the lease to be for one hundred years with an option of renewal – or after that we ask for the land to be ours forever from the white man's law. Really the land is ours now.
>
> [Furthermore] we do not recognise Mission and Welfare Councils, and we want no interference from such bodies. We do not recognise part Aborigines as full bloods, or as having any rights on tribal land; we class them with full white and are called Balanda. We are not hostile to Balanda – we seek and need their help but want none of them taking up long term residence on tribal land or profiting from anything on tribal land.

They also said they did not want mining on their land.

On the day before the hearings a number of Aborigines and white people had arrived, including missionaries from Oenpelli and other areas, and the Member for the seat of Arnhem, accompanied by his wife. David wondered why the Member for Arnhem had come.

At 9 a.m. on 12 June, we all trooped up to the hall. As we mingled with Aborigines from other areas there were few friendly greetings. Each group kept to themselves. Tension was in the air.

Yirawala sat next to me. He was trembling and very anxious. Bobby sat on my left and had been elected as the Gunwinggu spokesman and interpreter.

The Aboriginal Land Rights Royal Commissioner, Mr Justice Woodward, sat on the raised platform with his advisors, one of whom was an anthropologist. When we were all seated a Maningrida councillor distributed a series of typed questions and answers. Bobby and I carefully studied the two pages. 'Are they wanting our answers or just telling us what is going to be done?' he asked.

Yirawala stared at the papers. 'What him say, this paper?' Other men also wanted to know the content of the papers and why they had not been given out earlier so that everyone could discuss them and understand them properly. It was too late to interpret them now. The anxious voices grew louder and Mr Woodward called for silence. The meeting had begun.

Mr Silas Roberts, a Maningrida councillor, introduced Mr Justice Woodward to the audience and explained something of why the commissioner had come to Maningrida. Mr Woodward cleared his throat and after acknowledging the applause, called for information about various areas of tribal land and the different language groups represented at the meeting. He called out the names of the tribes and asked their spokesmen to come forward to look at a large map spread out on the platform.

Slowly some men walked up to point out the boundaries of their tribal areas on the map. When the Member for Arnhem went up he was sent back to his seat. Thompson Naranolgi, a Gunwinggu elder, and Bobby went up for the Gunwinggu people.

Mr Woodward said the Federal Government wanted to give the land to the Aborigines, but wanted them to say what they wanted to do with the land and how they wanted it administered.

Mrs Kentish, the wife of the Member for Arnhem, got up to speak. She was not Gunwinggu, but was the daughter of a Maung woman.

Old men were not asked to speak, and there were no translators for different tribal groups. Everything was in English and the tribal elders were not following it.

Mr Woodward said that the Government could give land to one man, a group, or a family, and asked the opinion of the Maningrida council. Silas Roberts replied that the Maningrida council would look after it all. Settlement and mission councils wanted to control all the land. Mr Woodward nodded, and seemed to agree, and suggested that Aboriginal Affairs also be included, to look after things. He then asked about minerals. It would be easier if all the country was looked after by one community, as old men were scattered in different areas.

Silas Roberts then asked the Aboriginal audience how they would run the settlements.

Mr Woodward cut in, saying a variety of options could be considered, such as:

1 One council for the whole of Arnhemland, covering mining permits, tourists, etc.
2 Each big mission and settlement community to look after land in their area and control permits, forestry, and funds. The clan leaders would be the traditional owners, but the real owners of the land would be the village councils and boards.
3 Country could be divided up between families and clans, but that would be very difficult; surveyors would be needed and it could take years.

Mr Woodward was just putting forward some ideas for general discussion, but such discussion was not forthcoming. Tribal people could only discuss things when they fully understood the Government's ideas and proposals; they did not understand, as the meeting was conducted in English and according to white man's procedure.

Yirawala kept nudging me and whispering, 'What him say? What them all talkabout? We never understand.' He leaned across and spoke in language to Bobby, who shook his head. Yirawala was exasperated.

Mr Woodward asked the meeting, 'If mining companies want to come in, who should have the say?' Silas Roberts replied that the village councils should look after mining; they should decide in co-operation with the Aboriginals and the superintendents.

At this point a Gunwinggu man from Goomadeer got up and complained about white men's cattle grazing on their land. Yirawala was pleased that someone from his tribe had spoken. He whispered 'Gumuk!' (good), and said to me, 'Nobody ask we, old men — boss for country — speak for our land.'

Bobby kept getting up and trying to speak, without success so far.

A group of Aborigines from the Blythe River area said they wanted Welfare to run things.

Mr Woodward indicated that so far the Government did not know who to give the land to.

Bobby stood up again and just started speaking. He said all the Gunwinggu people wanted to go home to their tribal land and run it themselves. People could be sent south for better training to handle cattle, buffalo farming, fisheries, forestry and gardens. Mr Woodward said that the Government might not give land until a town had been built. He

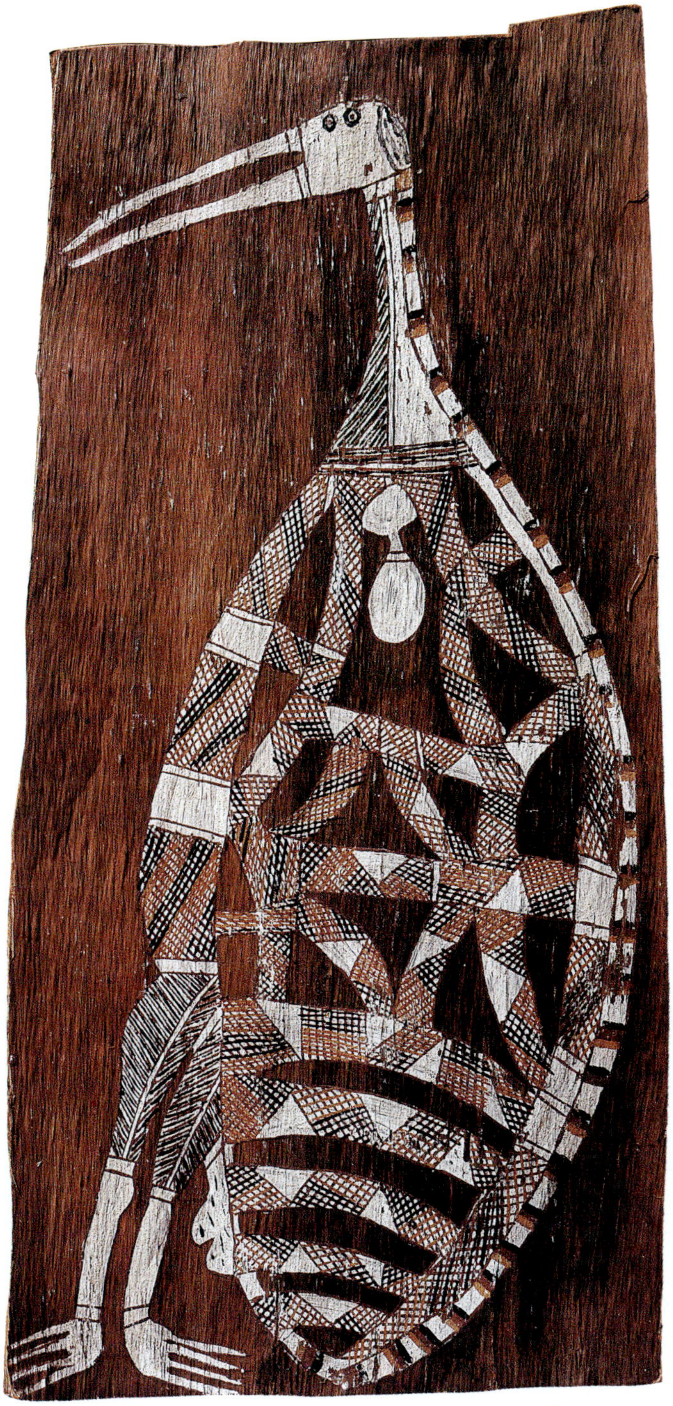

Plate 64 MARAIAN SERIES

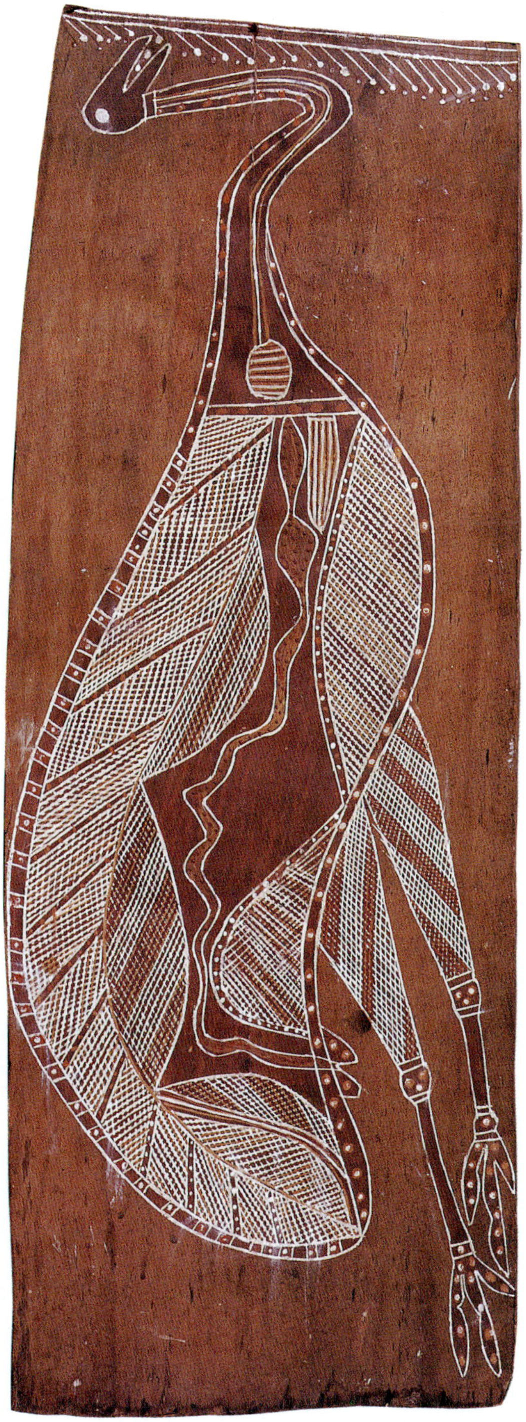

Plate 65 MARAIAN SERIES

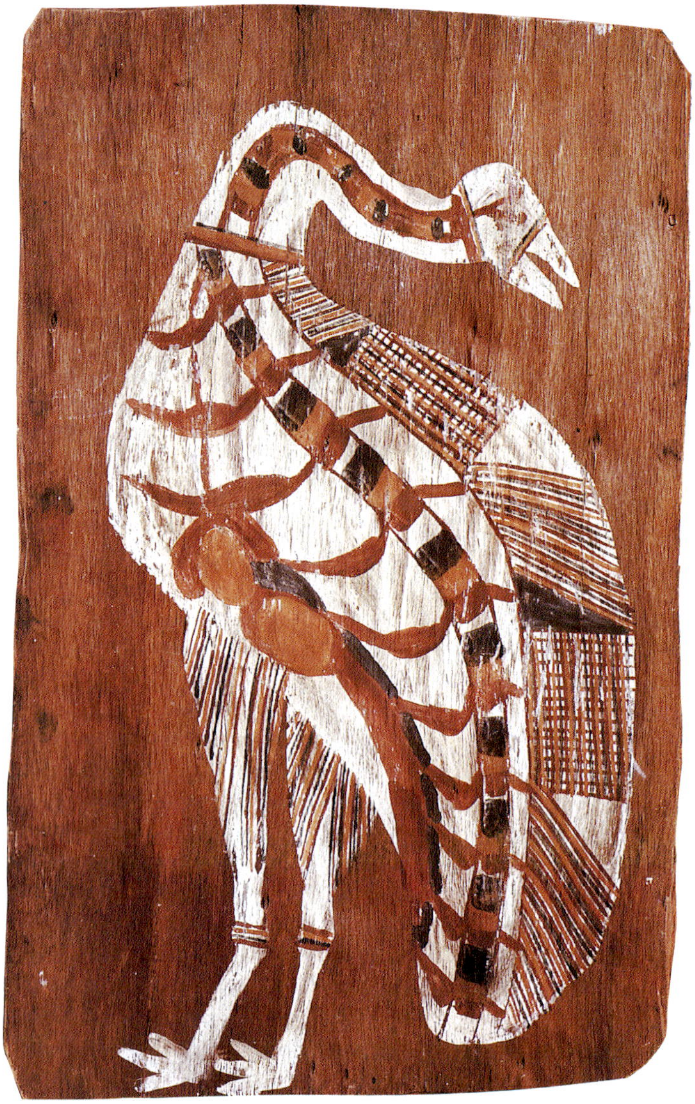

Plate 66 MARAIAN SERIES

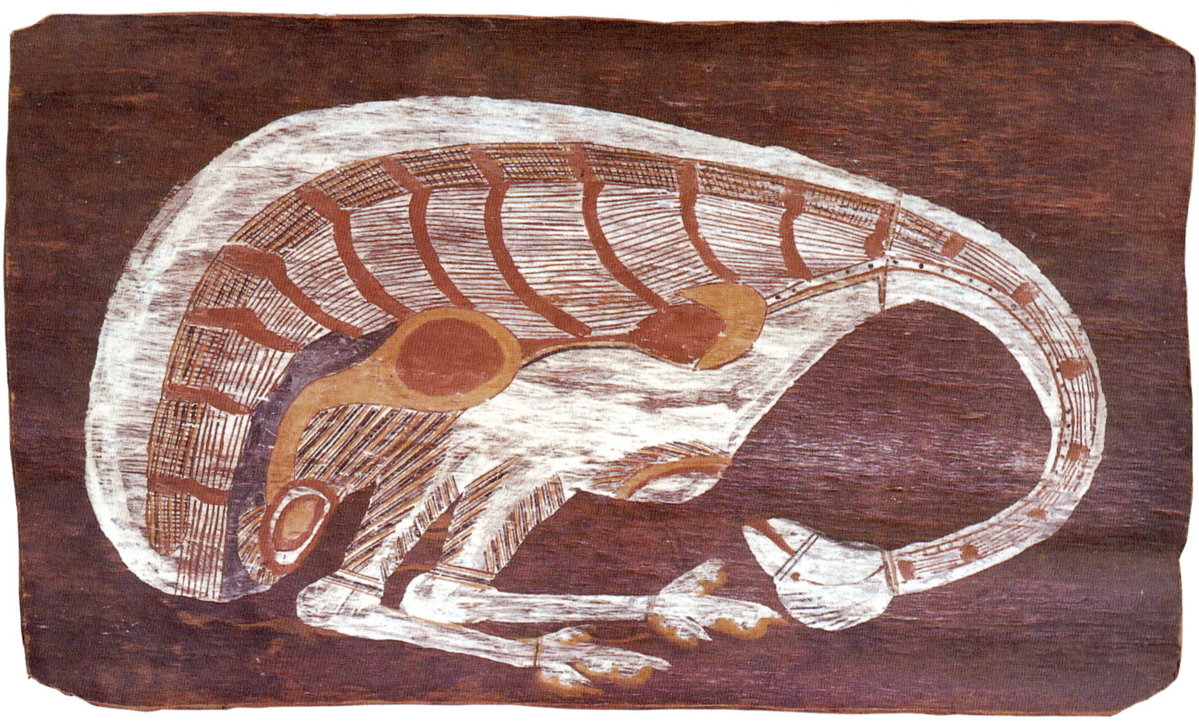

Plate 67 MARAIAN SERIES

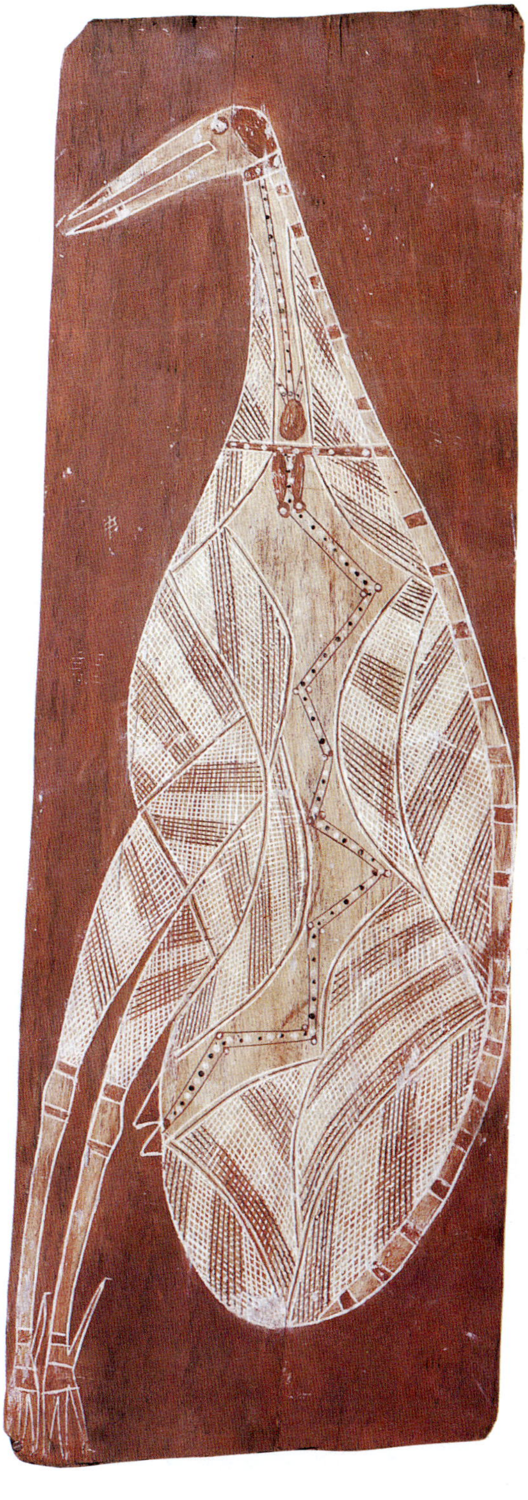

Plate 68 MARAIAN SERIES

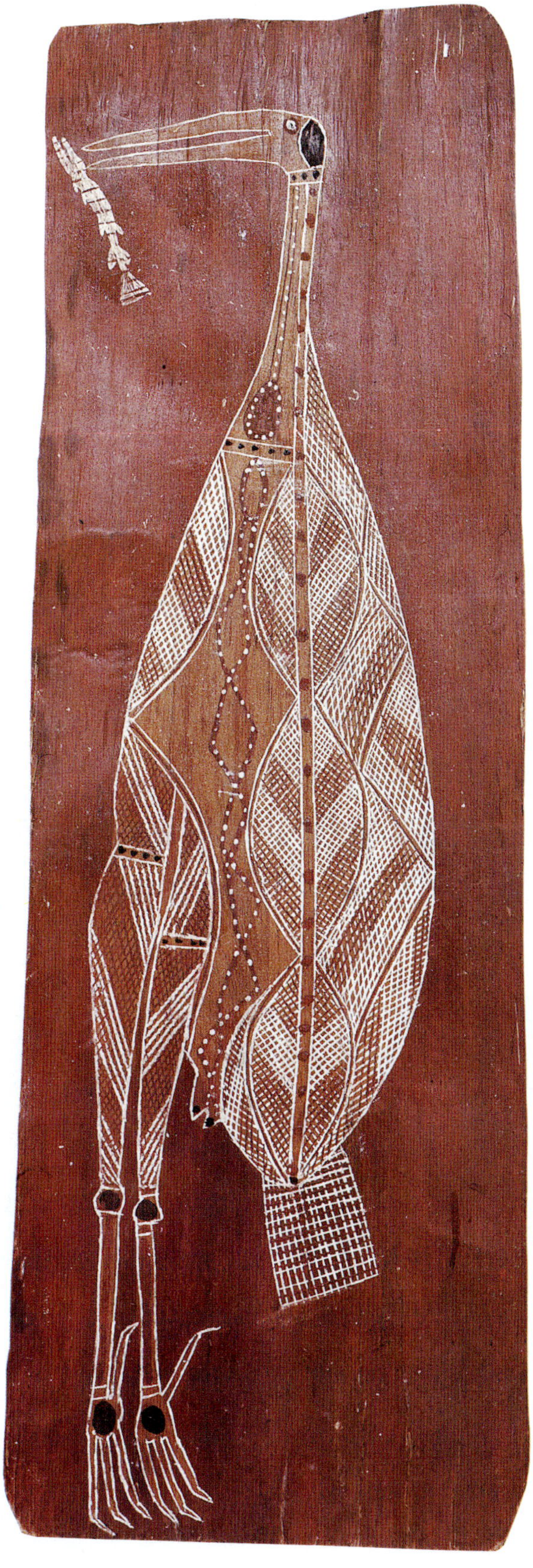

Plate 69 MARAIAN SERIES

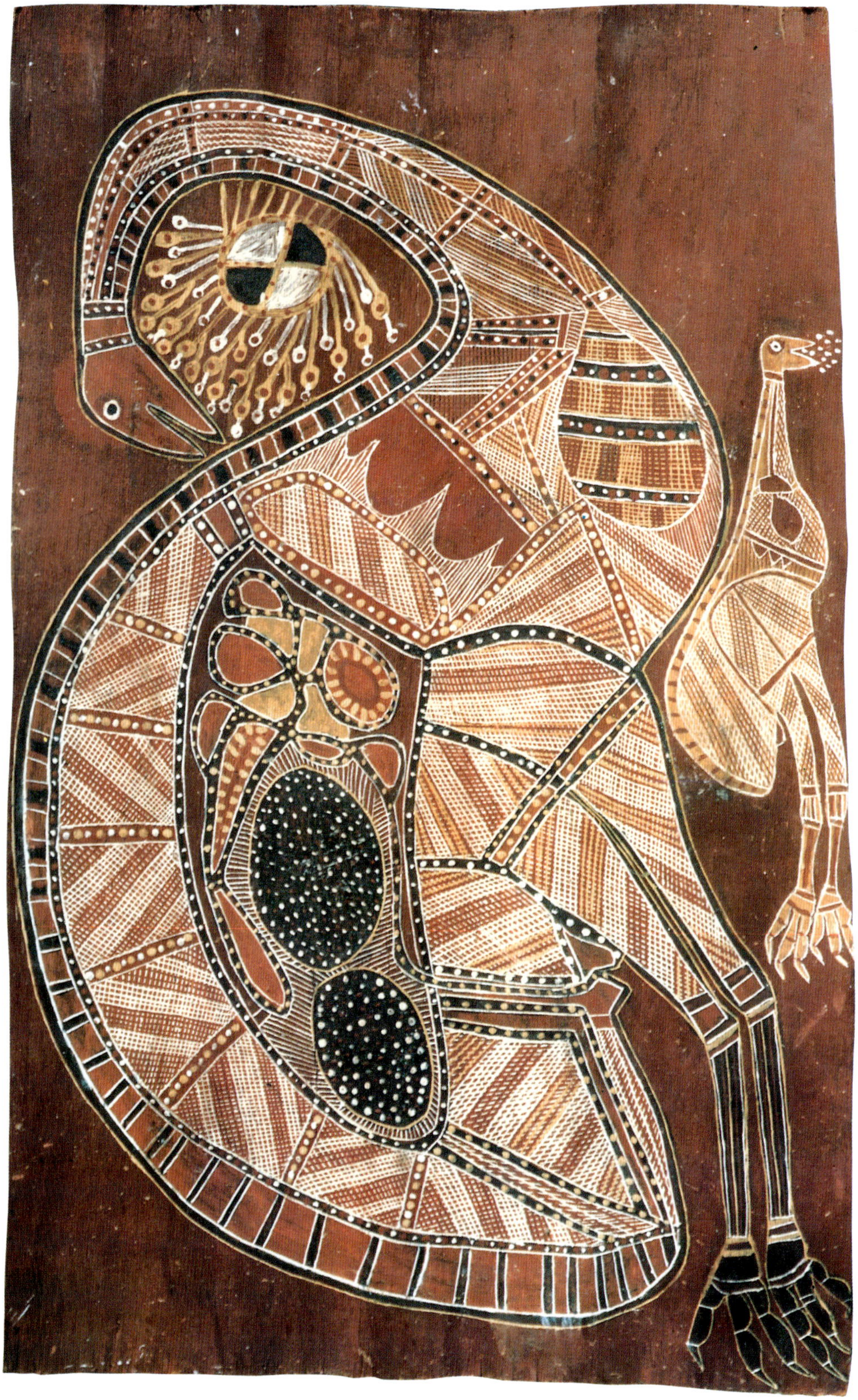

Plate 70 MARAIAN SERIES

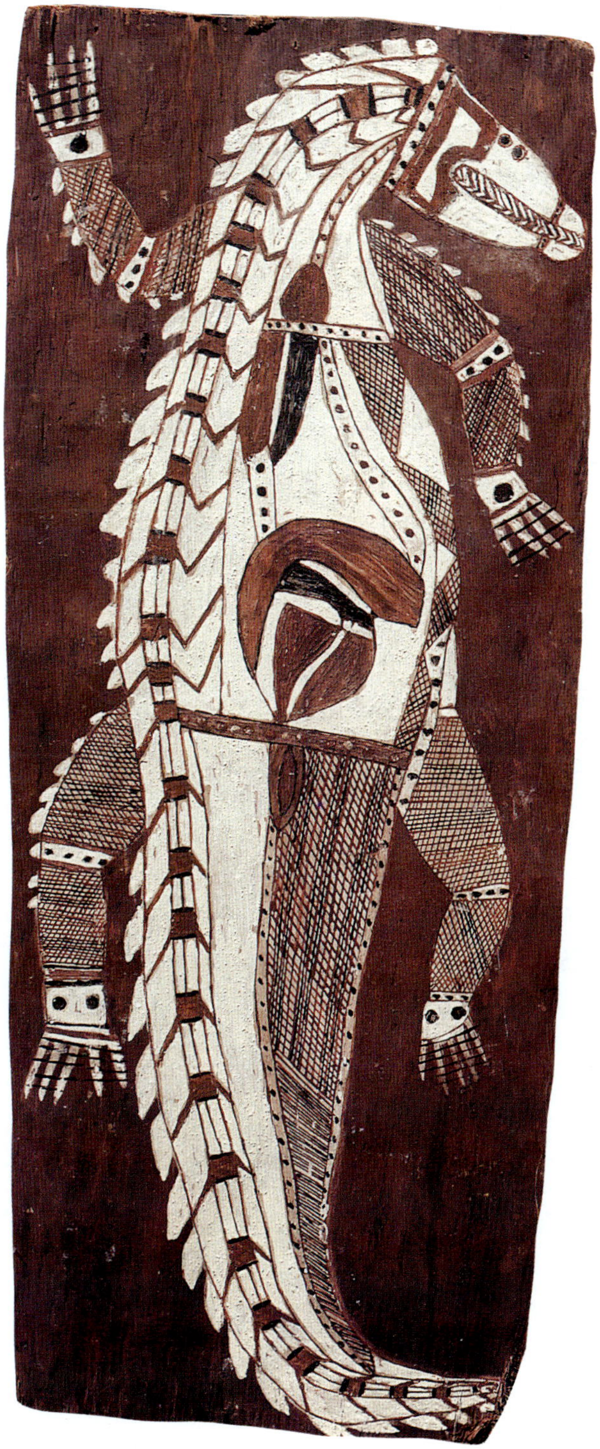

Plate 71 MARAIAN SERIES

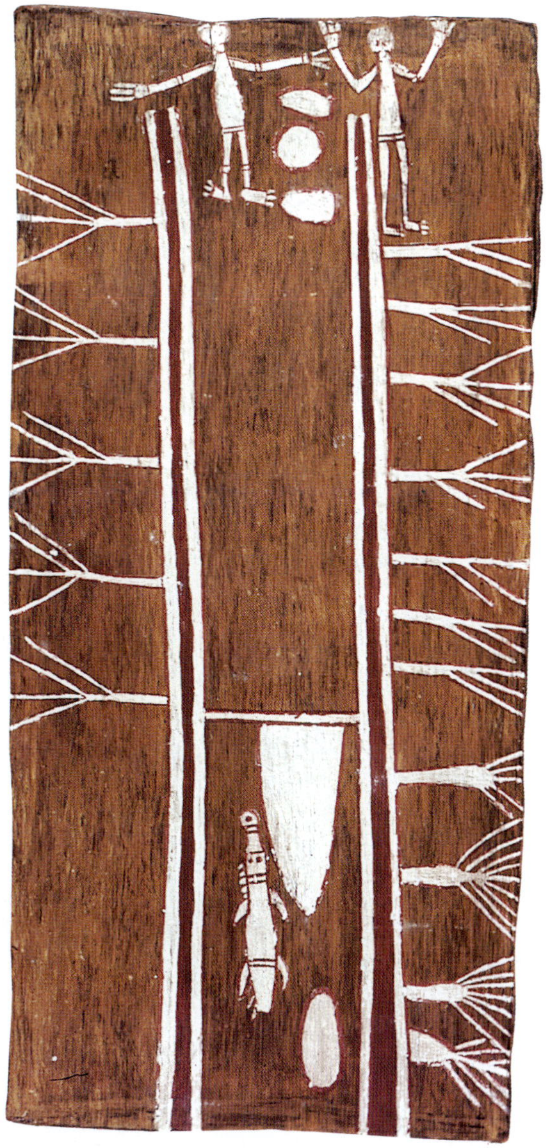

Plate 72 MARAIAN SERIES

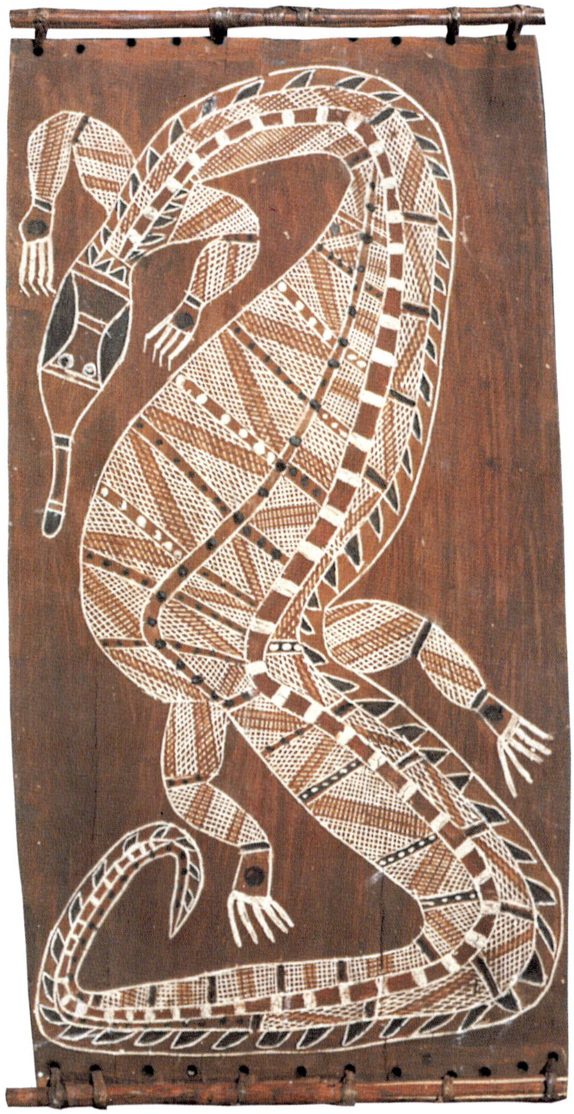

Plate 73 MARAIAN SERIES

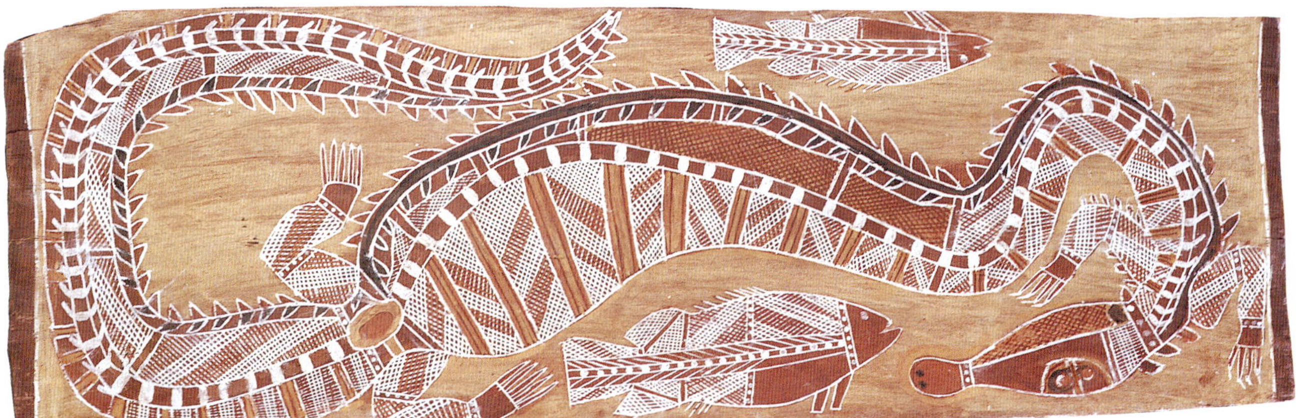

Plate 74 MARAIAN SERIES

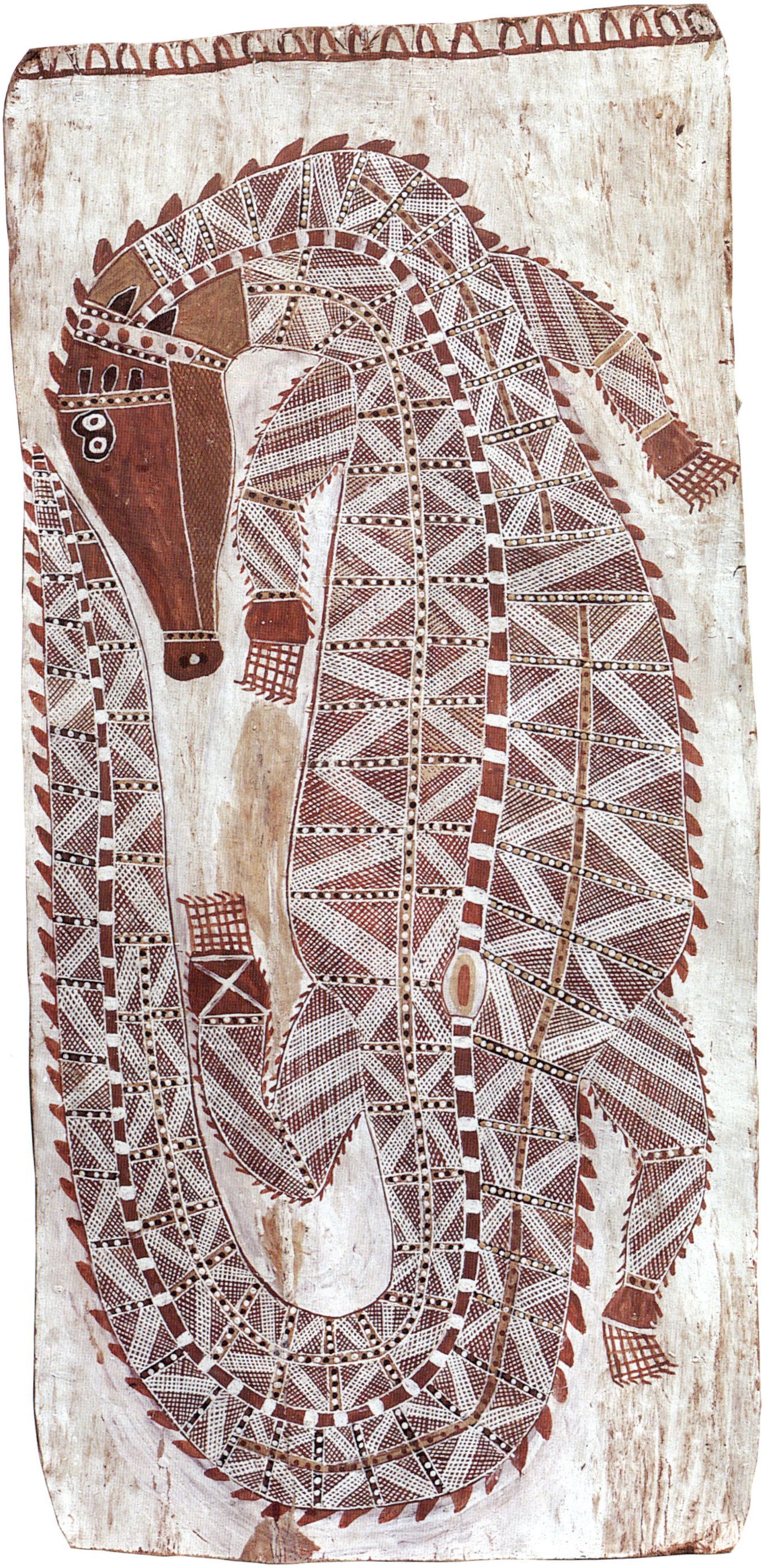

Plate 75 MARAIAN SERIES

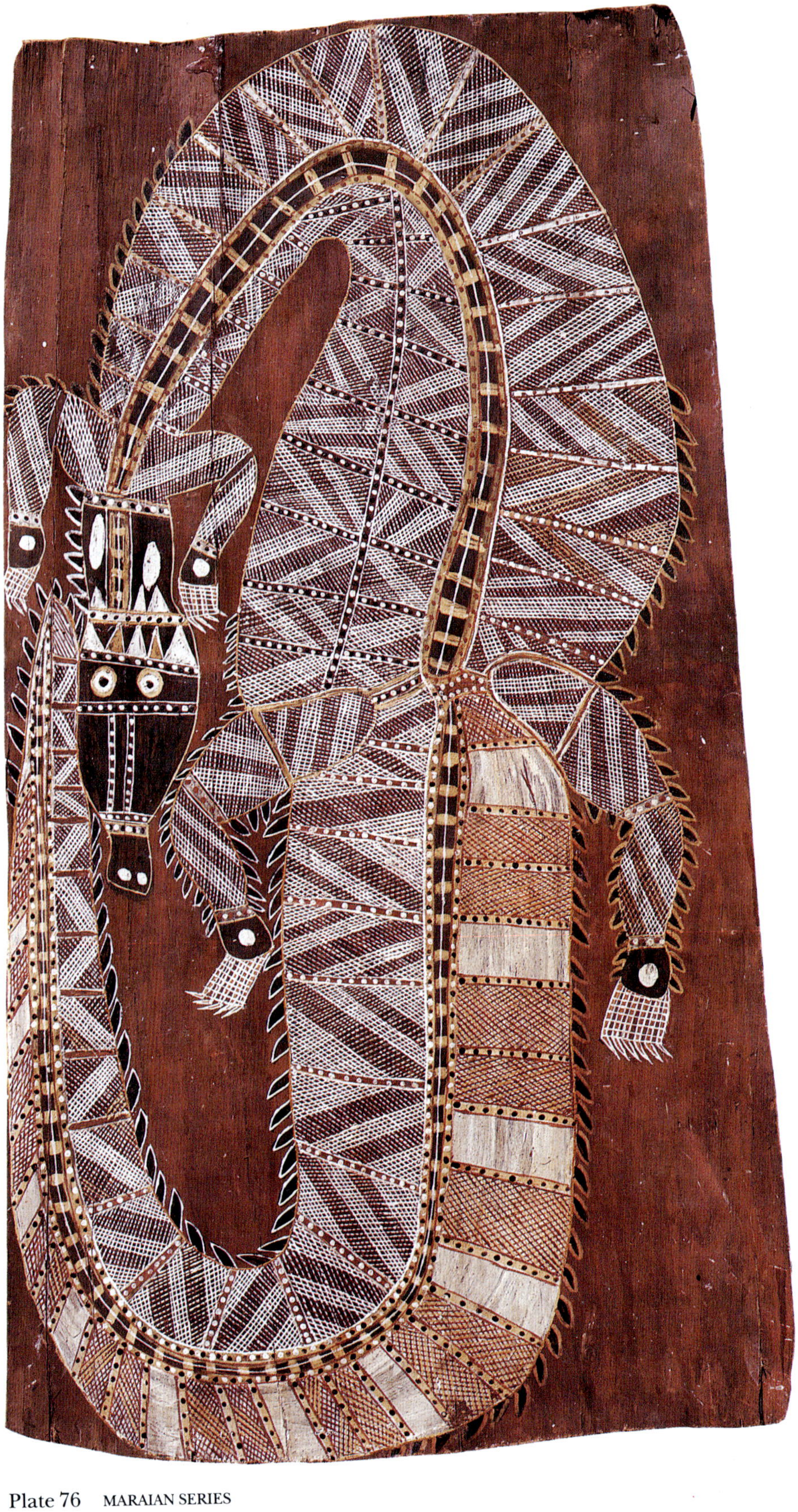

Plate 76 MARAIAN SERIES

asked Bobby, 'What do you say to that?' Bobby continued speaking about their plans to go home. Mr Woodward asked, 'Who would look after your council then?' Bobby replied that they could look after their own council and their own land.

Sam, the chairman of the Oenpelli mission council, then got up to speak. He said he was Gunwinggu and that he was claiming Goomadeer area. The mission wanted to look after all that land around Oenpelli, and all the Gunwinggu people wanted the mission. Yirawala angrily rejected this and said, 'Him Mialli tribe, not Gunwinggu.' Mr Woodward asked Sam how much land Oenpelli mission would control. Sam replied, 'About 11 263 square kilometres.'

Mr Woodward said that Croker Island, Oenpelli and Goulburn Island missions formed about forty council members, responsible for all the country from the Blythe to the Liverpool River.

A Rambarrnga man stood up and said that his people had mingled with whites, and in the Rambarrnga country mining, cattle and buffalo farming had been going on for a long time; now the Aborigines wanted their own farms and fisheries. He said they would like Maningrida council to look after it all.

Disgusted with the subservience to mission and Welfare control, Yirawala stood up, looking around at the audience in anger. 'You all got slack guts. Nobody stand up speak straight for land.' Bobby took his father's trembling hand and gently urged him to sit down. When his father was seated, Bobby stood up to speak again about their little settlement at Marugulidban. Mr Woodward asked him where his people would obtain supplies. Bobby replied, 'From Maningrida.'

Yirawala stood up to support his son, desperately grappling with the English words, trying to make himself understood. In his anxiety, Yirawala's whole body was shaking. Thompson Naranolgi stood up to help him, and said they wanted to establish a station on their own land where the Gunwinggu people could work and run things themselves. They did not want mission or Welfare control anymore. If given a chance they would succeed, but they needed money and help to start things off. They would employ white people as needed.

Mr Woodward made no comment about Thompson's speech, except to say something about there having been white and black conflict over the land.

The commissioner went on. The Government must know one man as owner of the land. It was hard for the Government to make Aboriginal law white man's law, and a way must be found to satisfy white man's law and yet leave some room for Aboriginal law. White man's law wants to know who has to give the permit for such activities as mining and forestry. With timber cutting, and cattle as well, who is going to run it and get the money? White man's law wants to know this. You could have Maningrida council owning land or saying people can live in their own country. The council could talk to the traditional clan owners. He repeated that if they wanted the country divided up between clans and families it would take too long.

A few Aboriginal spokesmen stood up. Groote Eylandt people wanted to claim Umbakumba. Tiwi people wanted Melville and Bathurst Island. Yirrkala council wanted control of Yirrkala and country all round. Millingimbi council wanted Millingimbi and lands all around. Elcho Island council said they wanted all of Elcho Island and others nearby. Mr Woodward said this might be too difficult and suggested bigger divisions and control would make things quicker and easier.

He asked questions about fishing enterprises. Maningrida said their boats were out of action. Goulburn and Croker Island councillors said they did not do much fishing but worked mainly looking after cattle and building houses.

Mr Woodward then asked who was working in forestry felling trees? Maningrida council replied that thirteen Aborigines were doing this work. Then Bobby spoke up, 'Did anyone ask the owners before they cut down the trees? I left the job because I did not like cutting down other men's trees.'

'If white people want to buy or lease land will you let them have it?' Mr Woodward asked. Voices in the audience said no.

'What if mining company want to come in. Yes or no?' Most Aborigines said okay. Only the Gunwinggu gave a unanimous and positive no. Sam, the chairman of the Oenpelli mission council, said yes, they wanted the mining, but the miners must consult him first.

Mr Woodward pointed out that once the miners are let in to the reserves, the Aborigines cannot stop them going ahead with mining. Perhaps Aborigines could have a share, because if the miners are given rights, Aborigines can't stop them.

At this point, Yirawala stood up and asked the platform to be fair and let all the men speak. The Gunwinggu submission was handed up to Mr Woodward to peruse (a copy had already been sent to him in Canberra).

Bobby again went up to point out the Gunwinggu land area on the map. He made it clear they only wanted their own tribal land and made no claim on Goulburn Island. Sam from Oenpelli interrupted him, in English. Bobby answered him in language. A short, sharp exchange followed. Then Bobby continued speaking in language so that his father and other elders could understand something.

Mr Woodward said they could speak in language. It was not interpreted to him.

Yirawala's voice was angry as he spoke to mission Aborigines. Other elders from the Gunwinggu and other tribes spoke together in language, which was their traditional way.

Sam from Oenpelli cut in, saying in English that they wanted Oenpelli, Goomadeer River area, Nimbuah, and areas all the way to the Liverpool and Mann Rivers, then to Coopers Creek and the East Alligator River.

Yirawala was making strange noises and started to speak. He was told to be quiet.

Mr Woodward then asked if the clans would look after their own places.

Yirawala and Bobby began talking together in language, then in English, that they did not want to be dominated by mission or government councils. They would run things through their tribal council, on their own land. Yirawala cried out, 'No mission. No balanda on our land.'

Sam spoke up, saying only the mission council could run things for the Aborigines.

Bobby said the Gunwinggu people did not want mission or Welfare control.

Mr Woodward asked me to speak. I explained that I was acting as a secretary and advisor and did not want land on the reserve. I outlined what the Gunwinggu elders wanted regarding land and assistance to develop it in their own way.

Sam spoke again, saying he did not want archaeologists, but mining was all right and the missions should stay as advisors to the Aborigines.

Yirawala rose to denounce him as not being Gunwinggu but was ordered to sit down. He was treated like a fool.

Mr Woodward asked some questions about the Gunwinggu people. Sam cut in saying two young Gunwinggu men were already running Goomadeer settlement. He mentioned five mission outstations from the East Alligator River to Coopers Creek, Goomadeer and Murganella forestry camp.

Mr Woodward said it would be difficult to work out ownership. Would it be possible for one council to look after all the places? Sam said yes, and then said he wanted to include Gumbulung people's country.

Bobby whispered to me, 'Looks like the mission wants the lot.'

The Maningrida council chairman, Silas Roberts, said the Aborigines only needed one council for everyone's tribal land. Mr Woodward then named different mission stations and asked Sam if they would all agree to that. Sam replied, yes, they would, but existing mission and Welfare councils should be retained.

At this point the superintendent of Oenpelli mission arrived with an anthropologist and sat down next to Sam.

Thompson Naranolgi went up again to look at the maps spread on the floor, just as the Oenpelli missionary rose to speak. The missionary said there seemed to be some confusion about Goomadeer settlement — it was not leased by the mission, they only advised the Aborigines, but did not own anything. The land was owned and run by a young Gunwinggu man named Tim. Mr Woodward asked, 'Has the mission sponsored the wrong people?' The missionary replied, no, they had not sponsored the wrong people. 'The Aborigines make all the decisions, not us.' Yirawala gave a derisive laugh on hearing this.

The missionary called Tim to speak. Tim got up and said it was okay for him to have that land at Goomadeer as all the Gunwinggu had said yes.

Yirawala made strange choking sounds and cried out that this was not true. Nobody took any notice of him.

Sam went out to the front, facing the audience, and strongly supported Tim's claim.

Bobby and Thompson then went up to the front, holding a copy of the Land Board map. They had intended pointing out once more the Gunwinggu area of tribal land. Sam confronted them, holding up his hands and saying, 'Let's just keep everything together. Forget about that map. It is an old map, anyway.'

Bobby and Thompson went back to their seats. Bobby looked at his copy of the map and remarked that this was the one issued to them at the meeting.

Sam continued to hold the floor, speaking about the virtue of the missions looking after the land.

An older Rambarrnga man got up to speak. He was nervous, but kept going. He said that most of the Rambarrnga elders were back home, too shy to come to the meeting, so they had asked him to speak for them. The elders wanted to know when they would be allowed to go back to their tribal land. They wanted to control their own land and council. There were about eight hundred people, he said.

There was no comment to his contribution, so he went and sat down again.

The Member for Arnhem got up next. He began by saying that the country and the people had been there a long time, undeveloped. Most development in the last thirty to forty years had fizzled out, apart from Howard Island mission. Now with government backing much could be done. Money was needed to make it go, he said, but at this stage he was not sure where the money was coming from. Clear titles for land were needed, which would mean proper surveys. This was vital, as well as the money. Title to land must be held before money could be loaned. Maybe there could be a new approach to develop reserves?

Mr Woodward pointed out that there could be difficulties with titles, as Aborigines did not want to sell their land. He paused, then said to the Member for Arnhem, 'You said that you did not want to claim land on Aboriginal reserves.'

The Member for Arnhem replied, 'No, not personally, but I am supporting my wife and her submissions for land on the reserve, and also her other relatives on Goulburn Island. I have a lot of land already, as much as I want in my life. I only want to assist the clans to be satisfied.'

While this was going on the Rambarrnga man was forlornly looking at the big map on the floor, which he could not read.

Mr Justice Woodward spoke to the whole meeting, 'Do you want Welfare council to look after your land?' Most said yes, except the Gunwinggu people.

Thompson Naranolgi got up and in a forthright manner accused Oenpelli mission of taking cattle from Gunwinggu land. He said the people did not like it.

Justice Woodward asked him, 'Do you want white men to help you look after your cattle and help you sell them?'

Thompson replied, 'No! We can do that for ourselves, and we want a lawyer.'

To that, Justice Woodward said, 'Solicitors are not much good at looking after cattle.'

Thompson continued, 'We would employ white men to work for us, that's all. The white men are in our country now, taking our cattle.'

The Oenpelli mission superintendent got up quickly to deny this accusation. He said they would be taking buffalo soon. This had been arranged through an Aboriginal company at Murganella.

Yirawala was clearly distressed. He was afraid that as usual the mission and Government held all the cards, and he knew that through lack of literacy and understanding of white man's way of running a meeting and making decisions, the Gunwinggu could lose their land. Most of the tribal elders did not understand the full implications of what was in progress. Yirawala spoke to Bobby, urging him to do something. Bobby was not lacking in courage but the forces against them were almost insurmountable.

Bobby stood up once more and addressed the Gunwinggu elders, asking them if they had anything to say. The men looked down and said nothing, because they were used to discussing things in their own language and then only making important decisions when everyone present was in agreement. This kind of meeting was new to them and they felt somewhat intimidated by the 'big white men' on the raised platform. In any case they would have been battling to get past Sam, who was a fluent speaker in English and held the floor most of the time.

Now Sam was speaking again, saying that he wanted no wildlife sanctuary on the Coburg Peninsula or the Wolwonga Reserve. He went on to talk about land around Deaf Adder Gorge, Jim-Jim and Jabiru and mentioned the mining companies associated with the areas.

Mr Justice Woodward asked, 'What do you want to do?' Sam replied, 'We want to go in there.' Mr Woodward asked, 'Do you want it back?' Sam replied, 'Yes.'

Mr Woodward asked if Aborigines could look after wildlife. Sam said, yes, if they were trained as rangers. He went on to say the Goulburn Islanders were worried about fisheries.

Captain, the Gunwinggu elder nominated by Roorgoorla, got up to speak about people being hungry and in need at Goomadeer mission settlement. He also talked about poor wages and conditions.

Sam called Captain a liar. Mr Woodward intervened and stopped this discussion.

Finally, Mr Woodward said that money could be requested to develop land but that he was mainly interested in who will look after the land, so he could make recommendations to the Federal Government. Copies of this report would be sent to all the leaders, then they could say what they thought about it.

Uninvited , the Member for Arnhem and the superintendent of Oenpelli mission got up to address the meeting and put their case.

The meeting wound up for the day and everyone filed out.

Chapter 10
A hand over our mouths

That night the Gunwinggu elders discussed the land rights meeting thoroughly. Kelly Borgordubhu said they had been severely handicapped by a lack of literacy and a better command of the English language. He was upset about the heavy mission representation and the Goulburn Island claim on a portion of Gunwinggu land. In the traditional way, this could never happen, he said. He asked me if the Royal Commission was going to abandon Aboriginal traditional laws relating to land ownership. I could only reply that we would have to wait and see.

Bobby held up the questionnaire forms that had been distributed to the Aborigines at the meeting. He said the men must thoroughly discuss each question and give their answers, so that they could present it all to the Commission next day. He switched on the tape recorder and I took out my notebook and pen. Bobby then began to read each question and interpret it in language. He recorded their answers.

Q 1 What are the main languages which are spoken at the village? [Maningrida]
A 1 Burera, Gunwinggu, Gunavidji, Jinang (not in order of significance).
Q 2 What are the names of the main tribes or clans which live at the village?
A 2 Gunavidji, Gunwinggu, Burera, Rambarrnga, Nagara, Jinang, Gunardpa, Gurragone. (These are general names only and do not show the clan groups at Maningrida.)
Q 3 Give a general description of the land held by those tribes or clans before the white man came.
A 3 Refer commission to Gunwinggu applications for land and Land Board maps.
Q 4 Should Aboriginal lands be managed and controlled by the village councils, or by the separate tribes or clans, or in some other way?
A 4 Lands should be controlled by clan leaders and tribal councils only, in the traditional manner. Village councils should not control Aboriginal lands.
Q 5 What lands are the people of this village [Maningrida] particularly interested in managing and controlling? Which of them should control and manage it [the land]?
A 5 The Maningrida village council should not control Gunwinggu land. We want to control our own council and manage our land in the traditional way.
Q 6 Should money for Aborigines from mining companies on Aboriginal lands go only to Aborigines who hold that land, or should some of it be divided up among other Aborigines?
A 6 The Gunwinggu say no to mining on their lands.
Q 7 Should money from leases of Aboriginal land be paid to all Aborigines who live in the area, or only to those tribes or clans who hold the land which is leased?
A 7 We do not want to lease our land to anyone. We also want to own our land, not just lease it.
Q 8 Should Aborigines be able to lease their land to white people or only to other Aborigines?
A 8 We do not favour leasing land.
Q 9 Should Aborigines be able to sell their land to anyone?
A 9 No — selling of land to be prohibited.
Q10 Should Aborigines be able to divide their land up among themselves, so that some men or families become the complete owners of part of that land?
A10 No — we are all traditional owners and share land.
Q11 What can be done about land for Aborigines who have left their land or their village to live in town?
A11 Don't know.
Q12 What if these people want to come back to their land or village later?
A12 That is okay. It is still their land.

Q13 Should children share in any payments that are received for Aboriginal land — by way of rents, mining royalties, or in any other way?
A13 This question does not apply as we do not want mining and do not want to rent or lease our land. In regard to any other moneys, our children share everything with us.

When all the discussion and answers had been dealt with, Yirawala said they might lose because they could not understand white man's law and writing. He said the pen was more dangerous than a spear. 'All kid got to learn balanda writing,' he said as he picked up my pad and pen. He began trying to copy my writing, then reverted to his own symbols and signs, in the shape of feathers, strokes and circles. He held the pad out to me. 'This mark and drawing, that my writing, Aboriginal way. Balanda him never understand, never know my law.'

At 9 a.m. the next day, we all trooped back to the hall only to find that Mr Justice Woodward had flown out to another settlement and would not be back. The Aborigines were very disappointed. Yirawala said, 'Him come — go — like bush fire.'

The Gunwinggu elders then held a meeting and elected a committee to advise them on land rights. They also decided to found a Land Association and register it.

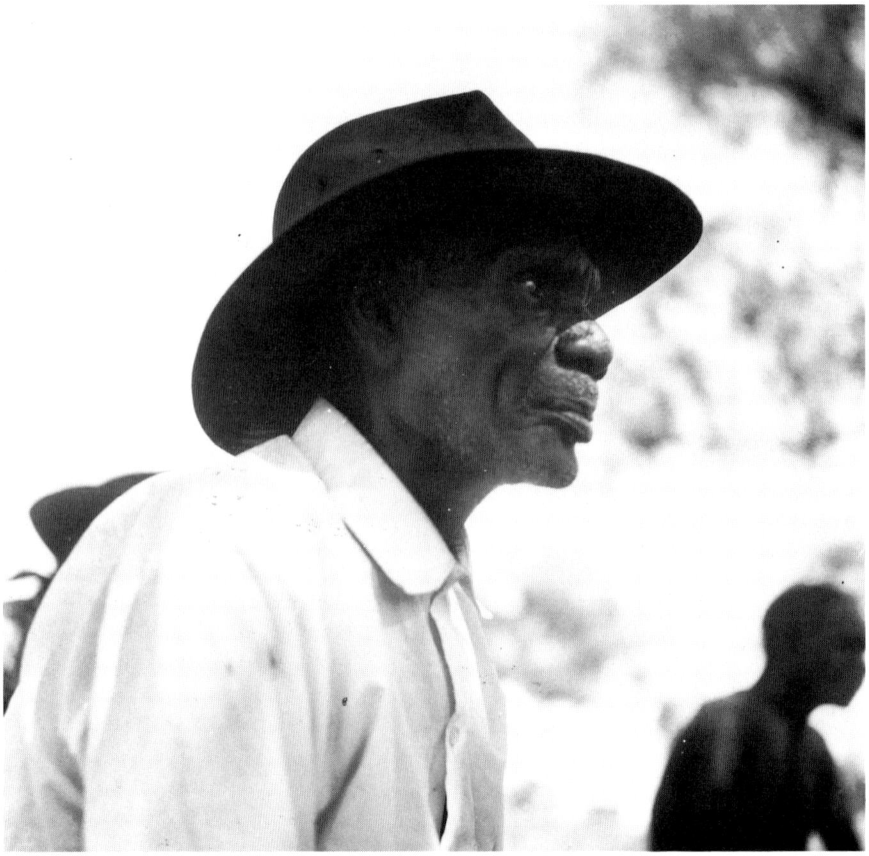

Yirawala and others waiting outside the meeting hall at Maningrida to put forward the Gunwinggu case for land, only to find that the Commission members had flown out early that morning. Of Mr Justice Woodward, Yirawala remarked: 'Him come — go — like bush fire.'

Mr Justice Woodward visited some twenty Aboriginal communities in the Northern Territory and held lengthy discussions with the tribes. He found that the Aborigines he visited had not been informed of the changes that were now in progress, so he urgently recommended that this situation be remedied with all speed.

Mr Woodward also found that tribal Aborigines were shy and had great difficulty in expressing their ideas and translating them into English. They also found it extremely hard to impart an understanding of their complex traditions of land ownership which have no parallel in European law.

Mr Woodward therefore recommended that the Federal Government should set up two regional land councils: one for Central Australia and the other for the Northern Territory's top end. The headquarters for the Central Land Council should be in Alice Springs, and the headquarters for the Northern Land Council should be in Darwin.

Land Councils should be made up of members from existing Aboriginal settlements, with one member to be elected from each settlement. He further recommended that legal advisors for the land councils should be paid by the Federal Government, and that all operational costs of the land councils should be met by mining royalties, channelled through government agencies.

The ownership of land on existing Aboriginal reserves and certain other lands in the Northern Territory should be granted to Aboriginal corporations, generally land trusts. It should not be possible to mortgage or sell the land.

The Northern and Central Land Councils should be incorporated to supervise the land trusts, to protect the rights of traditional owners, and to negotiate about any proposed commercial use of the land — especially mining exploration and development.

The land councils would administer leases and income from Aboriginal lands and also control permits to enter Aboriginal lands.

Aborigines should have the right to reject mining, mineral exploration or development and their views should be overridden only if the 'national interest' required it.

Existing leases and other rights should be maintained, and mineral rights remain reserved to the Crown.

Mission leases should remain undisturbed.

In February 1973, six months before the land rights hearings, the Minister for Aboriginal Affairs had announced plans to establish a council, made up of Aborigines from all States, to advise on Aboriginal problems. The new organisation would be called the National Aboriginal Consultative Council (NACC), and a committee would be elected later in the year.

The same year a Mr Robert Edwards of the Australian Council for the Arts flew to Darwin to set up the Aboriginal Arts Board.

Trying to explain all this to Yirawala was difficult. He could not understand why the new Government which had promised so much seemed to be making things more complex. The Government had started to sit down and talk with Aborigines, but then set up powerful organisations that by-passed the traditional tribal councils and made them redundant. He regarded the NACC and the land councils as white men's councils, pushing white men's ideas. He said, 'Mission and Welfare block our mouth for long time, now we got more hand stop us talk. Balanda got voice now, not we.'

Bobby wondered who would listen to them now and really help them to go home and make a settlement.

Yirawala's lawyer said they should still form their own organisation and register it. He offered to draw up some documents for them. Bobby and Aileen accepted, and said they would continue to write to Aboriginal Affairs to put their case for some funding and maybe a truck to enable them to make a start on establishing their settlement.

Yirawala said he wanted to contact the Prime Minister, the big boss of Australia. Maybe he would help them. They would send Mr Whitlam a message stick asking him for help to go home to their tribal land. I was asked to take the message stick and letters to the Prime Minister.

I flew to Sydney on a fly-now pay-later scheme and presented the letters and message stick to the Federal Department of Aboriginal Affairs, requesting they be sent to Canberra. (An article on this matter appeared in the *Sydney Morning Herald* of 27 June 1973.)

Explanations for the incisions on the stick were sent with the Gunwinggu's submission to the Aboriginal Land Rights Royal Commissioner.

In due course we received a reply from the Minister for Aboriginal Affairs. In part it said that he was asking the Northern Territory division of his department to keep in touch with the Gunwinggu group about their needs and to offer all reasonable help.

On 28 August Bobby Joran wrote to Mr Justice Woodward, referring to the Maningrida hearing saying that the people were worried about the setting up of two big land councils. He asked for the recognition of their group's existence and representation of at least one of their members on the Northern Land Council. He said they had started to go back to their tribal country and wanted a fair go. They did not want the mission, but real independence. The mission outstations still belonged to the missions.

The same month, Aileen, in her capacity of bush secretary to the Gunwinggu group, wrote to the Director of Aboriginal Affairs in Darwin, asking him for some positive help to enable them to go home to Marugulidban. They wanted a truck and some tents to start them off, also they would need some funding.

She said that Yirawala's eldest son, David Gumaraitj, had been injured mustering cattle and received no compensation. Also, most of the Gunwinggu people had lost their jobs on Croker Island. She felt that certain forces wanted them off the island.

Aileen said they would found their own organisation, called the Marugulidban Land Development Association, and register it. The people wanted recognition of their organisation and some help. She asked for some wages for her husband who was the assistant chairman and liaison officer for their group.

David Gumaraitj went to Marugulidban area in September, to talk to the few people there and to tell them that there would soon be a big Land Board meeting in Darwin, which would be convened by Aboriginal Affairs and attended by representatives from various councils. They did not know about it. He was elected to go to the meeting and learn what he could, then report back to them. He found the situation at Marugulidban very depressing. Marugulidban seemed to be just an outstation of Maningrida. The Gunwinggu were living in bough shelters and painting for the Maningrida warehouse. 'All they got is a painting camp there,' he said.

Also around this time, David dictated a letter to the NT Director of Aboriginal Affairs asking him for assistance to help his father to make a small house on the family land, as Yirawala was shaky now and would need shelter in the coming wet season. David also made reference to information that $12 000 had been allocated to the Marugulidban area. He said Yirawala, Bobby and Aileen wished to make an appointment with the Director.

The campaign of nuisance phone calls began again, this time more threatening. One man said if the Yirawala paintings were not handed over, he would come and take them. This was followed by obscenities and threats to kill me and my daughter. Amanda was terrified and refused to answer the phone. There were also problems with night prowlers. The police were contacted but drew a blank.

I knew that if we were to have any chance of holding onto the collection we would need powerful support. With this in mind I had been corresponding with Mr David Boston of the London Horniman Museum to arrange an exhibition of Yirawala's work. Contact with him had been arranged through Mrs Jacquetta Priestly and Lord Ted Willis. With such backing we could hope to build a bulwark against future attacks. We also felt it might encourage philanthropists in England or Australia to sponsor a Yirawala Teaching Museum, in Darwin.

David Boston was enthusiastic about the display and fully understood the significance of the Yirawala collection. We began to make plans. The Horniman Museum would cover all exhibition costs, but we would have to pay air fares and freight.

Bobby and I approached a major airline without success, then the Australian Council for the Arts, Aboriginal Affairs and other government departments. The Horniman also approached the Council for the Arts in Britain. Letters went back and forth but nothing positive eventuated, so we decided to arrange a non-selling exhibition at the Sydney Opera House, hoping to attract a sponsor for the airfares and freight. We applied for an exhibition space there and waited for a booking to be confirmed.

On Croker Island, Aileen and Bobby were organising a number of Gunwinggu people for the foundation meeting of the Marugulidban Land Development Association. A constitution had already been worked out, plus the aims of the Association. The documents had been drawn up by Mr Ron Withnall as instructed by Bobby and David.

The aims of the Marugulidban Land Development Association were:

1 To obtain title to the traditional tribal land known as Marugulidban, or Morgaleetbah, in Arnhemland in the vicinity of the Mann and Goomadeer Rivers.
2 To develop and use the land known as Marugulidban in the interests of the Gunwinggu people.
3 To develop and pursue on the land known as Marugulidban industries including pastoral, fishing and agricultural industries.
4 To preserve on the said land and elsewhere the Gunwinggu culture, sacred ceremonies and sites.
5 To ensure the well-being and advancement of the members of the Association and other members of the Gunwinggu people.

Six tribal people were elected to the committee. David Gumaraitj was elected president, Bobby Joran, vice president and Aileen Joran, secretary.

The meeting unanimously endorsed the constitution and the aims of the organisation. They were all very pleased and hoped for Federal and State recognition. Bobby and Aileen were instructed to convey the signed papers and minutes to Mr Withnall so that the Association could be registered. The members requested Aileen, Bobby and David to contact Aboriginal Affairs in Darwin for some financial assistance and a vehicle, even a second-hand one would do.

On 12 September Bobby and Aileen came to Darwin to see Aboriginal Affairs about the truck and some funds. Nothing was promised.

David had wanted to attend the Land Board meeting in late September, but so far their tribal council and association were not recognised. In any case, he was suffering from a chest infection and the injury he had received when mustering cattle for the mission.

I took him to the hospital and he was admitted. He asked me to phone Aboriginal Affairs and tell them of his family's needs and problems.

A spokesman for Aboriginal Affairs said if the family was in real need they had only to go to the mission office and ask for help, as adequate funds had been provided for all areas by the Federal Department of Aboriginal Affairs.

Early one morning we were sitting on the front verandah. Aileen and Bobby were labouring over yet another letter to Aboriginal Affairs, when a pyjama-clad figure came hurrying up the driveway. It was David, who said he had run away from the hospital because the doctor wanted to operate on his injured right hand. We kept him in bed for a few days then, at his request, sent him back to Croker Island.

Bobby and Aileen were looking at my file of letters and telegrams to and from Croker Island. There were copies of my letters and telegrams informing Yirawala that his pension cheques had been sent, then telegrams from him urgently requesting they be sent. Bobby said only a few cheques got through, and that there should be a proper, government post-office on the island. Aileen said things were dear at Croker Island and also they had to pay for services and pay rent for the little house.

Meanwhile, the National Aboriginal Consultative Council (NACC) was active all over Australia compiling an electoral roll of all Aborigines and Torres Strait Islanders over the age of eighteen, in order that voting for the NACC committee could take place on 10 November. There would be eight electorates in the Northern Territory.

As had been announced in February by the Minister for Aboriginal Affairs, the official role of the NACC was to consult and communicate with all Aborigines, Australia wide, and convey back to the Federal Government the concerns and wishes of Aboriginal groups.

The NACC candidates for the Northern Territory visited all Aboriginal groups on the reserves, seeking votes. Many tribal people did not understand what the electioneering was all about and were confused about the role of the NACC. Most tribal elders thought the NACC was unnecessary. Yirawala called it 'throwing mud in the billabong'.

David said when some people from the NACC came seeking their support, Yirawala had said, 'If you got land and money where you come from, you go there, ask Gov'ment, money, land — not here.' He was increasingly afraid that the tribal council would be rendered powerless, others would speak for them, and their voices would be lost. They would be in the hands of others, and any chance of obtaining their home country and funding would be gone. He wondered why the big government man had bothered to come to Maningrida and ask them what they really wanted.

On 3 October I wrote to Yirawala asking him to come to Darwin to sign a formal application to the Government for a truck. I also asked him to bring a few paintings. I received no response.

Three weeks later, on 24 October, the Director of Aboriginal Affairs replied to a letter from David. He offered to supply travel warrants for three people, David, Bobby, and Aileen to fly to Maningrida, then travel to Marugulidban to talk with relatives there. Yirawala went with them and was angry to find the men mostly sitting down, painting for Maningrida. The people were isolated, without communications or a vehicle, and still living in leaf sheds. He was so upset at the lack of any progress that he became ill and almost died.

Chapter 11
Gov'ment give me humbug, that's all

Yirawala's family flew back to Croker Island, then heard that Bobby and Aileen's eldest daughter, Christine, who was in Darwin Hospital with a kidney complaint, was now seriously ill. Bobby and Aileen sent word that they both wanted to come to Darwin to see her. Yirawala would come too. At the time I was also suffering hardship and could only pay one way for Yirawala, so I approached the Canon G McGowen of the Church of England for assistance. He kindly paid the parents' fares from Croker to Darwin, out of his own pocket. I also sought assistance from government welfare for food, as I would have to support the family for a while.

We visited Christine every day and she improved gradually, but she would remain a delicate child.

Yirawala was still upset about there being no progress in the home country, and he was finding Croker Island increasingly hard to bear. So, while in Darwin, he dictated a letter to Mr Ted Evans of Aboriginal Affairs urgently asking for a truck and help to go home to Marugulidban. Yirawala said his family could no longer afford to live at Croker Island. On their own land they would have no rent or any other charges to pay, and could live off the land.

After Christine's stay in hospital an application was made to Aboriginal Affairs for travel warrants. They agreed to pay for Aileen but not for Bobby or Yirawala to go back to Croker Island. When this was conveyed to Yirawala he exploded in wrath. He felt degraded about having virtually to beg for plane tickets for himself and his son. It was the last straw in a long history of refusals, frustrations and deprivation.

'Gov'ment give me humbug, that's all. Him never help me. Never give me truck, money, land, anything. No letter, no ticket for plane. We not dogs. What for Queen give me medal?' He was trembling with emotion. He slammed on his hat and started towards the door. Bobby ran after him, asking where he was going. 'You take me white man law house. I sit down level with law men, talk 'bout my land, money, help. We make big talk, sit down. Him law men, me big law man for r'own people.'

In desperation he would try and talk face to face with the Members of Parliament, face to face, man to man, on equal terms. He would tell them about his people's law and the battle for some dignity on their own land. They did not want handouts like beggars. They would work hard but needed help to start them off. He would go to the white lawmakers, and also to his friend Jim Bowditch on the local newspaper.

When we arrived at the Legislative Council Chambers we were allowed into the public gallery, where we sat for some time listening to the speakers droning on. Yirawala's face was set as he stared down at them. Bobby fidgeted uneasily.

When the session ended and the members began to file out, Yirawala went downstairs to meet at least one of them. He was calm and dignified waiting for someone to speak to him. We had to let an usher know that this was Yirawala's intention.

All the white men filed past him. The lawmakers had ignored him. Yirawala began to tremble and Bobby led him outside.

By this time some reporters had gathered round. They asked Yirawala what he was doing in the Legislative Council. For answer, he pulled the MBE medal from his pocket and held it aloft. Bobby told them that his father's presence was a demonstration against treatment he had received from officers of the Department of Aboriginal Affairs. He was protesting about no assistance with airfares to visit a sick grandchild and no finance or a truck to help them on their tribal land. He had received no help despite applications to the Government.

Yirawala's face was a mask of bitterness. He said, 'Queen give me a medal, what for? More better give me my land. Gov'ment give me humbug, that's all.' With that he walked away and we went to see Mr Bowditch on the *NT News*.

On the way home Yirawala broke down in tears and Bobby put his arm around him.

Newspaper articles appeared, and Aboriginal Affairs paid the fares.

Also in response to the newspaper articles, I received a phone call from someone offering to pay. The caller sounded angry and seemed to be blaming me for the situation that developed.

White authority believed that tribal people usually did not act on their own initiative. Somebody always put them up to it. Some stirrer.

The superintendent of the Croker Island Mission wrote on 6 November 1973 with the following information:

> Dear Madam,
>
> Yirawala recently requested the Minjilang Aboriginal Council to grant you a permit to visit Croker Island.
>
> The Council decided against granting a permit and said that if you want to talk to any Croker Island folk, you should fly them into Darwin. The Council also decided that it would not grant to you any permit in the future.
>
> The Dept. of Aboriginal Affairs Permits section has been advised of the Minjilang Council's decision.

In the same month, The Honourable Senator J L Cavanagh, the new Federal Minister for Aboriginal Affairs, wrote to me, in part to say that $12 000 had been approved to help the people at Marugulidban establish themselves.

I asked Aileen if she had received any letter about the money, or any money in fact. She said that to the best of her knowledge they had received nothing, and perhaps the money was sent to the Maningrida council.

Over the next few weeks inquiries to various elders revealed that none of them had heard about the $12 000. This was a big disappointment and something of a mystery.

Aileen, a girl of some spirit, said she would write to the Director of Aboriginal Affairs about a truck and the denial of a permit to me. It was more urgent than ever for me to come to Croker Island and Marugulidban for discussions. The men wanted to see me, she said. Aileen sent me a copy of her letter:

> Yirawala, Bobby and I came here to Darwin to ask for the truck. It is our idea that we ask for the truck. Mrs Holmes is not pushing us to ask for it.
>
> I am telling you the truth that Mrs Holmes is not pushing us. It is our rights to have Mrs Holmes as helper, because we are all citizens now. We've got to have her as our advisor, because she can explain the meaning of the hard words that we don't understand. I mean the words that we don't really understand; so we must have Mrs Holmes our advisor to explain of the word that we don't know. Also, we want Ron Withnall to be our lawyer.
>
> Mrs Holmes is our relation, and we have been together a long time, so whenever we want her to come and visit us at Croker, the permit must be given to her. It is our rights when we ask Mrs Holmes to come to Croker.
>
> Every time we came into Darwin we stay at her place and she give us food, without paying her money, and look after us properly.

The letter carried Aileen's and Bobby's signatures, and Yirawala's thumbprint and mark.

There was no reply to this letter. There was also no reply to any letters or telegrams that I sent to Croker Island, nor any acknowledgement of cheques, food, clothing parcels or Christmas presents. The pandanus curtain had been pulled down hard.

December and January passed with no word from Yirawala and his family.

In February 1974 I was disheartened to learn from a nurse based on Croker Island that Yirawala was painting full time for the mission and a dealer who was out there almost once a week. This was confirmed by David, who came seeking my help to purchase a used car. He said his father was very depressed about having no control over his land. Power had been stolen from the elders, the traditional custodians, and Yirawala found this unbearable. David said that Yirawala was short of money, and letters were still going astray, so his father had to paint. 'No man can stay strong all the time. My father is getting old now,' he said.

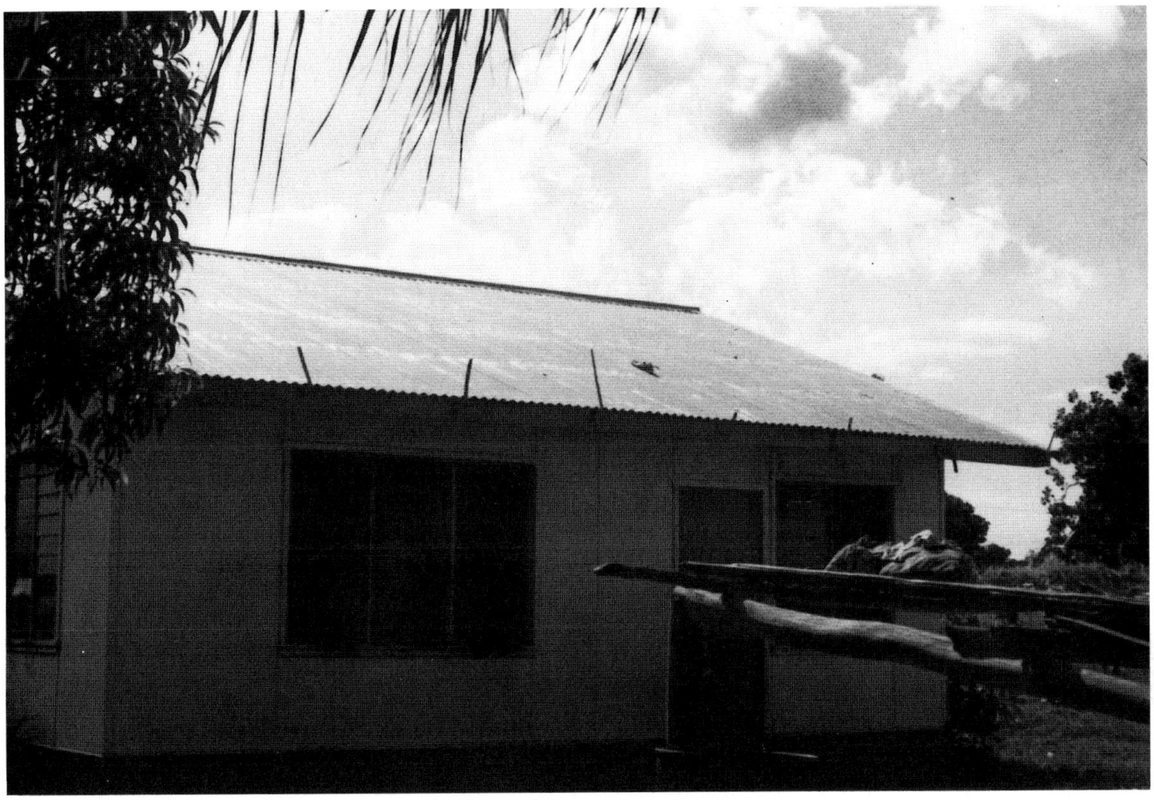

By 1974 Yirawala and his family were renting a new house, away from the beach.

Their hopes had been high the year before, when for the first time government men from Canberra had sat down with them and asked them what they wanted. Yirawala had summoned all his strength in the fight for the land, but felt now they had been betrayed. His strength was beginning to fail and he was sick of trying. He had taken refuge in painting, working hard seven days a week.

Yirawala's ideas for ownership of clan land and their own autonomy was totally unacceptable to the Federal Government. No Aborigines have title to the land on the reserves, it is all held in trust, so his claim to ownership of land by traditional title was revolutionary. He had tried to organise his people, but without any real functional literacy and an understanding of white man's law and institutions, they were seriously disadvantaged, and doomed to failure.

Aborigines could go and sit on their tribal lands if they wished, but without real ownership and assistance from the Federal Government to develop it they had lost control of their land.

Some Aborigines did go and camp on their tribal land, living in makeshift huts and bough shelters. Such groups were called 'outstations'. These did not give Aborigines their own autonomy, separate from mission or government control. Yirawala and his sons called these outstations, 'painting camps', where tribal elders mostly sat painting for distant craft stores. Agents from these warehouses came by boat and truck to pick up the bark paintings and artifacts at regular intervals.

During David's visit I received a letter from my brother in Perth to say that our mother had a stroke and was in hospital. I broke down. I had spent so many years away from her, fighting for what appeared to be a lost cause. David tried to comfort me. 'You try again for permit. You got family at Croker. You go talk with my father.'

I decided to write to Lazarus Lami-Lami, who now had more power within the Croker Island council. He was also a fully ordained Methodist Minister. I made an appeal to his Christian conscience. The result was a permit for two days to see Yirawala and his family.

The meeting with Yirawala was emotional. He said he felt ashamed about the lost paintings, but he had needed money and nothing had come from Darwin. One could check up eventually on these things but there was no remedy.

When Yirawala began to cry, Mary, Margaret and I cried too. We put our arms round each other. They wept for the loss of land and a sense of defeat. I wept for them and my mother.

That night we all sat together, around the fire, talking. Yirawala said he wanted the whole story written down in a book, so everyone would know about it. Somebody might learn something. He did not want the long struggle to have been totally in vain. He also wanted his paintings and stories in the book, to make white people understand what the land meant to tribal people. He made me promise to do this. 'You go, make book, all my fight, my drawings and story, make balanda understand.' Bobby said they did not want just a pretty picture book describing his father as an artist like a white man. I would put his father's Aboriginal book in mine so everyone would know. 'The balanda stamped on our fire, we give you some coals, you start another fire.'

Bobby asked about the Horniman Museum display in London. I told him that I still hoped it would go ahead, and when we had strong support we would probably be able to hold onto the collection; but if the Yirawala Teaching Museum in Darwin did not go ahead, I might be forced to send it to Canberra, or suffer having it seized. We discussed all this and Yirawala said that if the collection was forced from me, others would not really own it. They might have possession physically, but the ceremonial designs and stories were his alone and belonged to him and David Gumaraitj, his heir. The ownership of his intellectual property he bequeathed to his sons and made me a boss and a keeper for the painting designs. I had sole right to copy them, and nobody else. He also gave me all the sacred and non-sacred stories of his paintings, which had never been given to anyone else. Next day a document was drawn up to this effect, signed by Yirawala and witnessed by Bobby.

I did not want to lose my collection; I still hoped to exhibit at the Horniman Museum.

In April 1974 an article appeared in the local paper, about a dealer from America who was making another visit to the Arnhemland reserve. I discovered that he went to Croker Island.

The same month Aileen, Bobby and David wrote to the Federal Minister for Aboriginal Affairs, Senator J L Cavanagh about the pressure being applied to Yirawala by dealers. The paintings were lost to the Aborigines and for little money at that. They wanted something done about it. A letter was also written to Northern Territory Aboriginal Affairs.

The Minister for Aboriginal Affairs wrote to me on 26 April 1974, supplying me with some very interesting information in the last two paragraphs of his letter:

> Dear Mrs Holmes,
>
> I refer to your previous communications with me concerning your complaints about your inability to visit the artist Yirrawala at Croker Island.
>
> I am now advised by Mr Creed Lovegrove, the Acting Director of my Department in the Northern Territory, that he has also had correspondence and 'phone calls from you stating your

concern about the possible take-over of your paintings by [dealer's name].

On your behalf, Mr Lovegrove made approaches to the Minjilang Aboriginal Council, and they have indicated they are prepared to allow you to visit Croker Island for two days only, and that you must provide a guarantee to the Department of Aboriginal Affairs that you have made proper arrangements for your departure from Croker in the time specified...

The advice my Department has gained from Croker Island is that they treat Yirrawala and his production of artifacts, in the same way as any other person at Croker, and are prepared to purchase from him especially at those times when he has not received his pension cheque and is seeking an income by sale of artifacts.

Apparently they do not recognise any contract between you and Yirrawala, and therefore these paintings may subsequently be sold to [dealer's name].

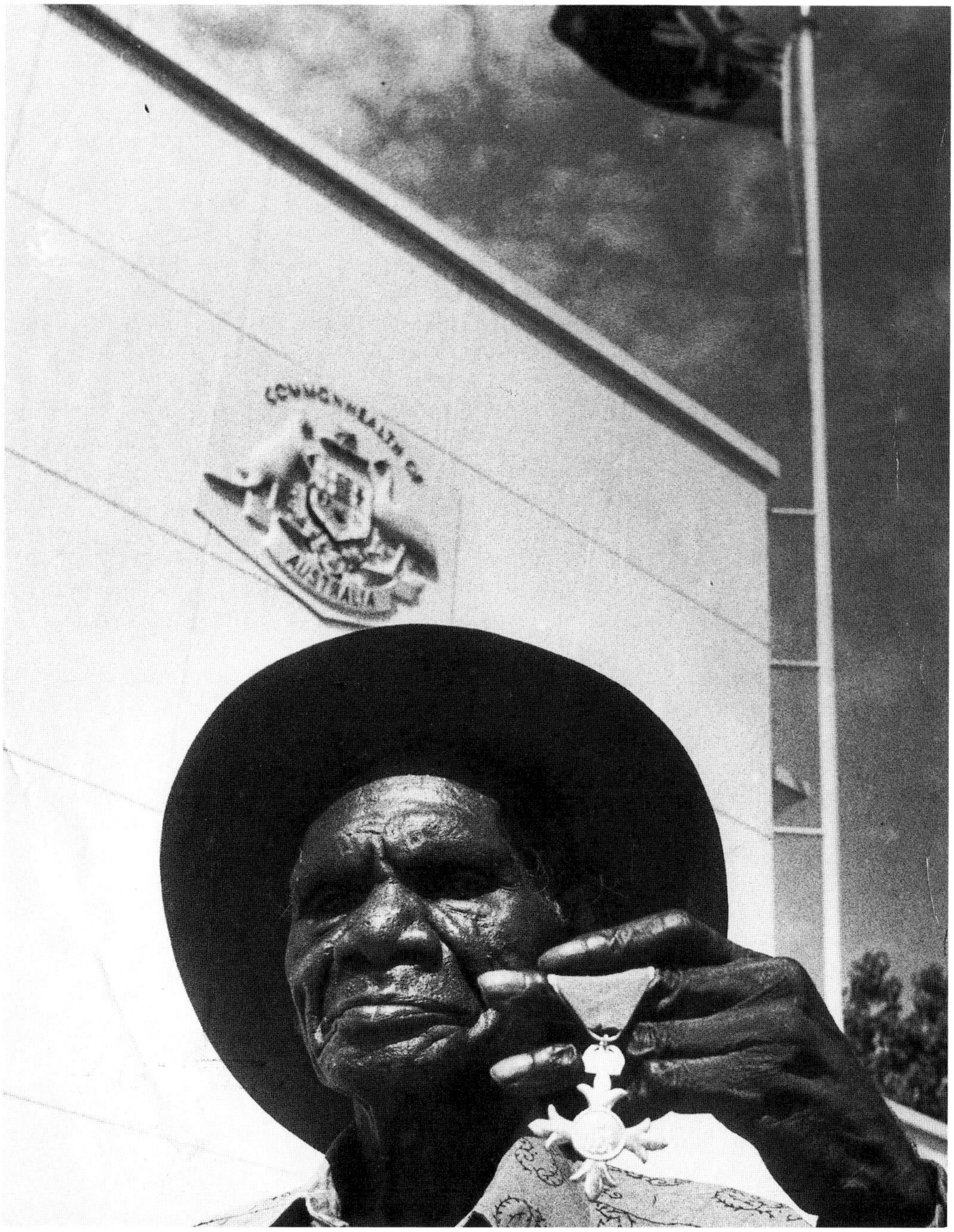

Gov'ment give me humbug, that's all. (NT News photo)

On 3 May I received a letter from David Boston of the Horniman Museum to say that the Yirawala exhibition was scheduled for next year, April 1975.

Shortly after this a messenger came from Yirawala to tell me to hold onto his cheques and bring them to him personally. I was not to send them to Croker Island.

On 5 May I received a letter from Senator Cavanagh in reply to my application for assistance to establish a Yirawala teaching museum. He said no funds were available and that they would soon be establishing government museums in Darwin and Alice Springs.

A week later a telegram came from Yirawala, asking me to send his pension cheques as he had no food or money. I sent them, by registered mail, with a covering letter followed by a telegram. A few days later he sent another telegram for his cheques. I immediately sent a telegram to the superintendent asking for an explanation. This did not solve anything, as telegrams continued to come from Yirawala, asking for his cheques. I rang the Department of Social Security and asked them to investigate. I heard nothing from them on this matter.

I had some heartening news on 11 July, when a letter came from Mrs Jacquetta Priestly, to say that the exhibition would indeed go ahead in 1975. Lord Ted Willis would be visiting Australia in November, which would prove helpful in smoothing out any difficulties. David Boston would be sending a formal request to Dr Battersbee of the Australian Council for the Arts, requesting their support for the London display. I wrote to tell Bobby Joran.

Later that same month, the superintendent on Croker Island sent a telegram informing me that Yirawala's pension cheques had been received.

In late July Yirawala sent a telegram to come and see him as he had some paintings ready for me. I could not get a permit and so the paintings were lost. I applied for a permit again in August and received it for one day only, so I had to go by charter plane.

Yirawala was very pleased to see me but regretted he had no paintings left. I gave him money as part of a kinship obligation. I mainly wanted to discuss the coming London exhibition with the family. It was decided that Bobby should go with me, as Yirawala was now too old. Yirawala was very pleased about the exhibition and told me to give his regards to the Queen. He asked me if I had started writing the book. I said as yet I had no time or peace of mind.

I showed him and Bobby the superintendent's letter stating that the pension cheques had been received. Bobby said that was good, but the people on Croker Island still needed proper facilities such as a public telephone service, post office and bank, like people had in Darwin.

On 20 August David Boston wrote from London to say that there would be a six months' delay in the showing of the Yirawala exhibition, as they were seeking the official backing of the Australian Council for the Arts. He went on to say that there were promising signs that a major airline might assist us. I felt some unease about whether the Australian Council for the Arts would give its support, and hoped the project would not be cancelled if their support was not forthcoming.

I wrote to the Director of the Australian Council for the Arts, explaining that the collection would be for display only and nothing would be sold or left in England. Bobby and I would accompany the collection and bring it back to Australia. I pointed out that the exhibition would only reflect honour on those making it possible. I did not receive a reply, but felt sure one would be sent to London.

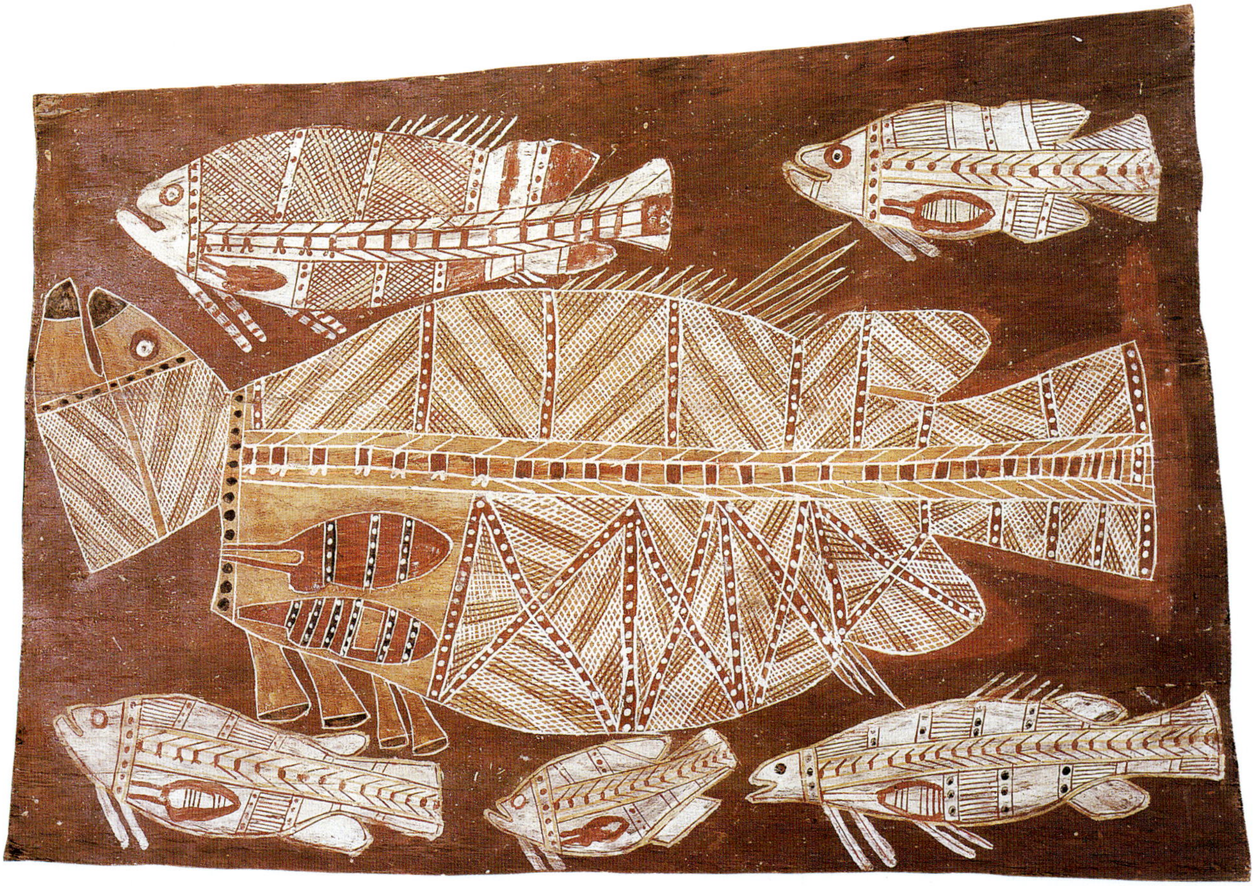

Plate 77 MARAIAN SERIES

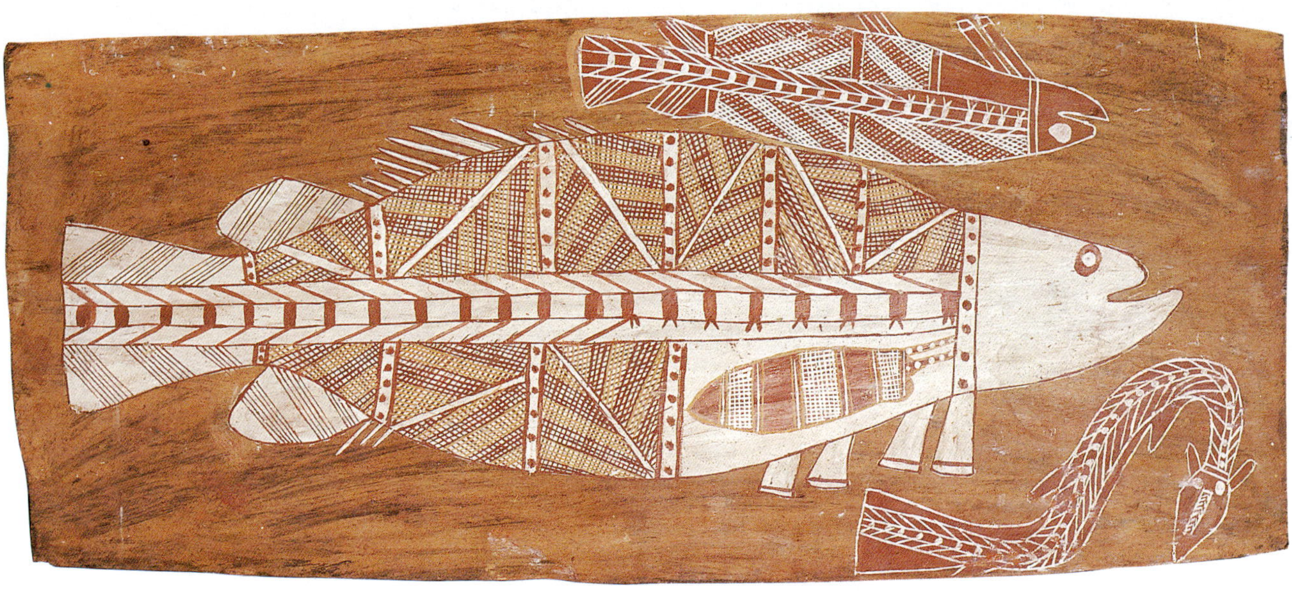

Plate 78 MARAIAN SERIES

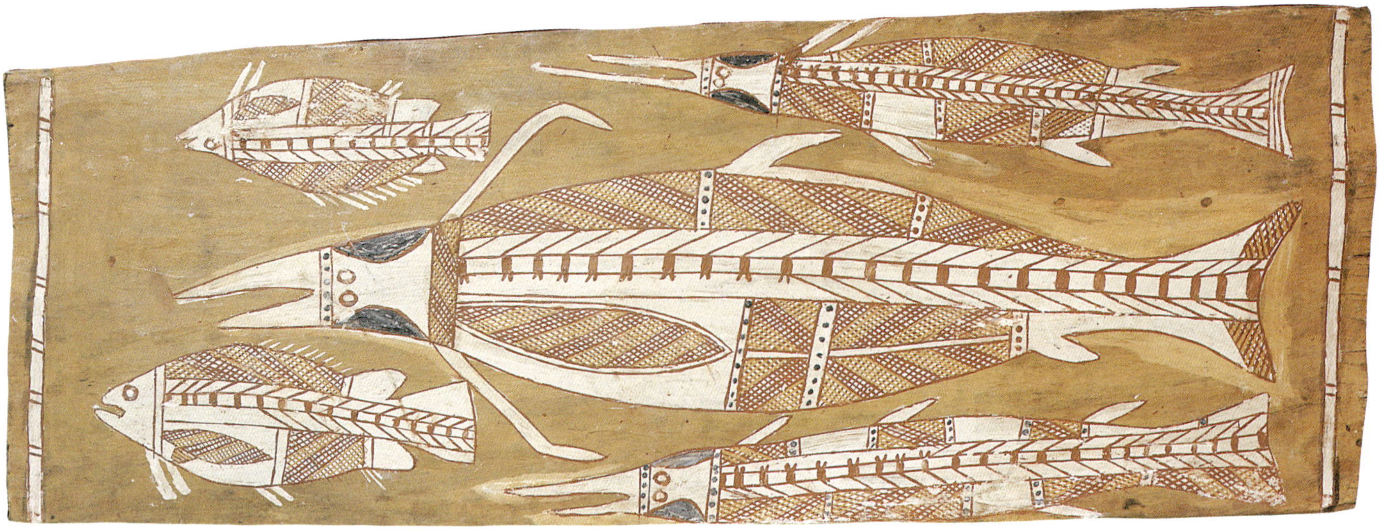

Plate 79 MARAIAN SERIES

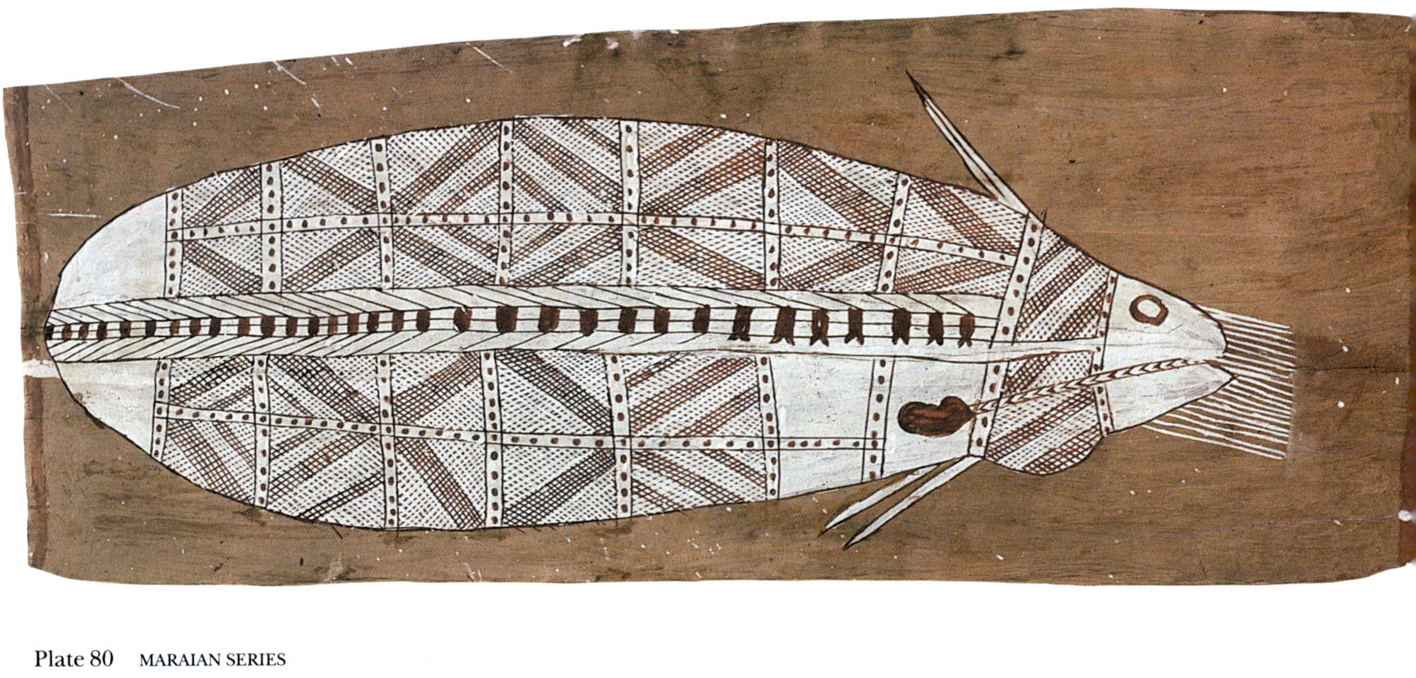

Plate 80 MARAIAN SERIES

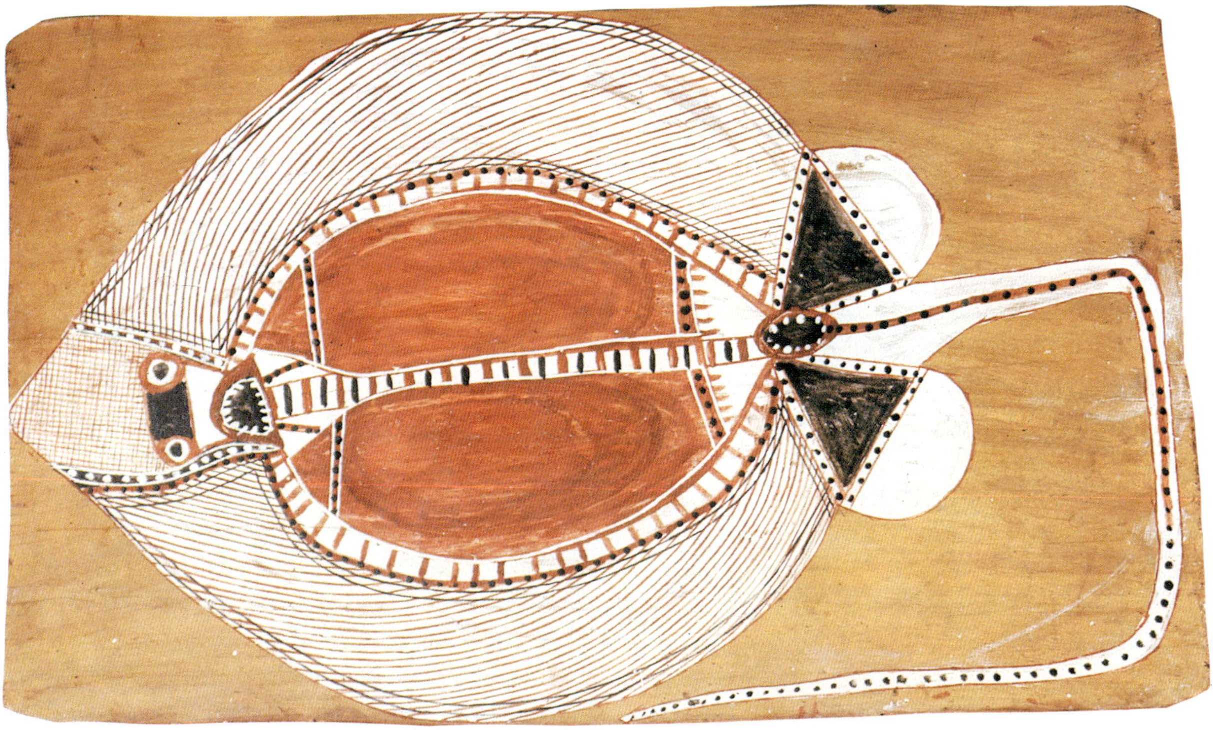

Plate 81 MARAIAN SERIES

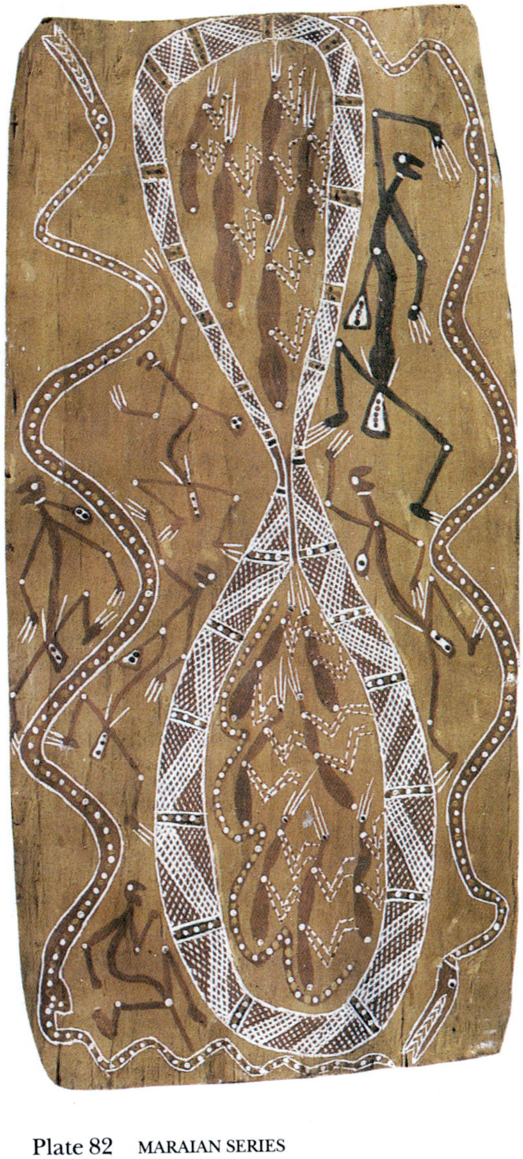

Plate 82 MARAIAN SERIES

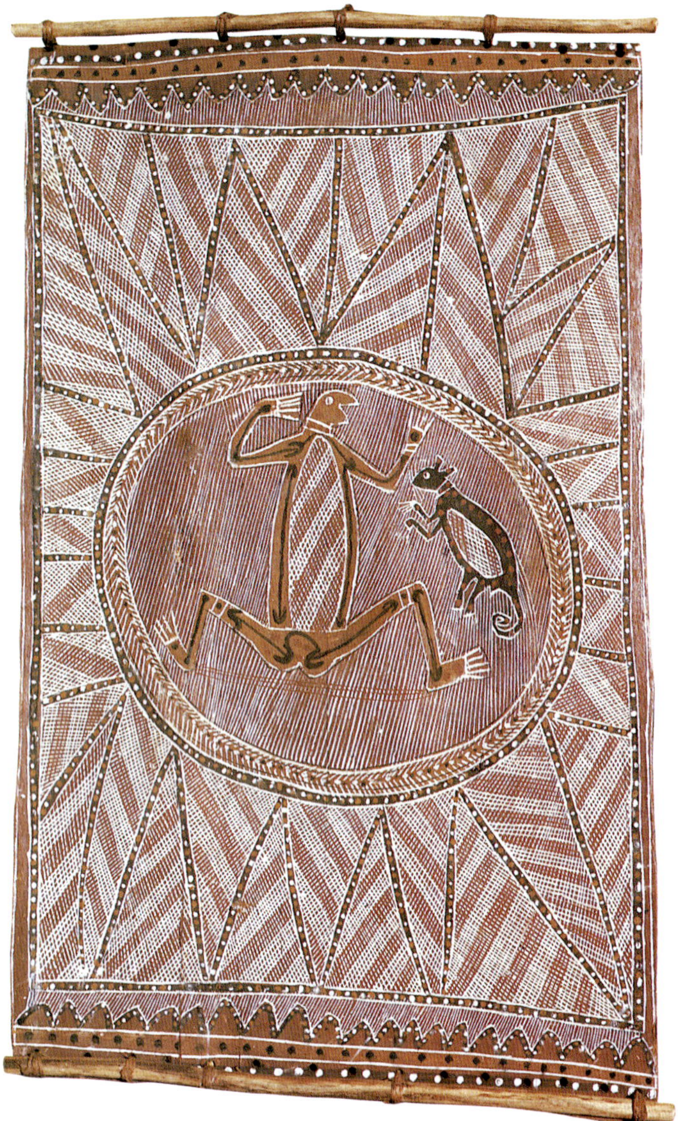

Plate 83 GUGURR THE MOON MAN AND MULITJI HIS DOG

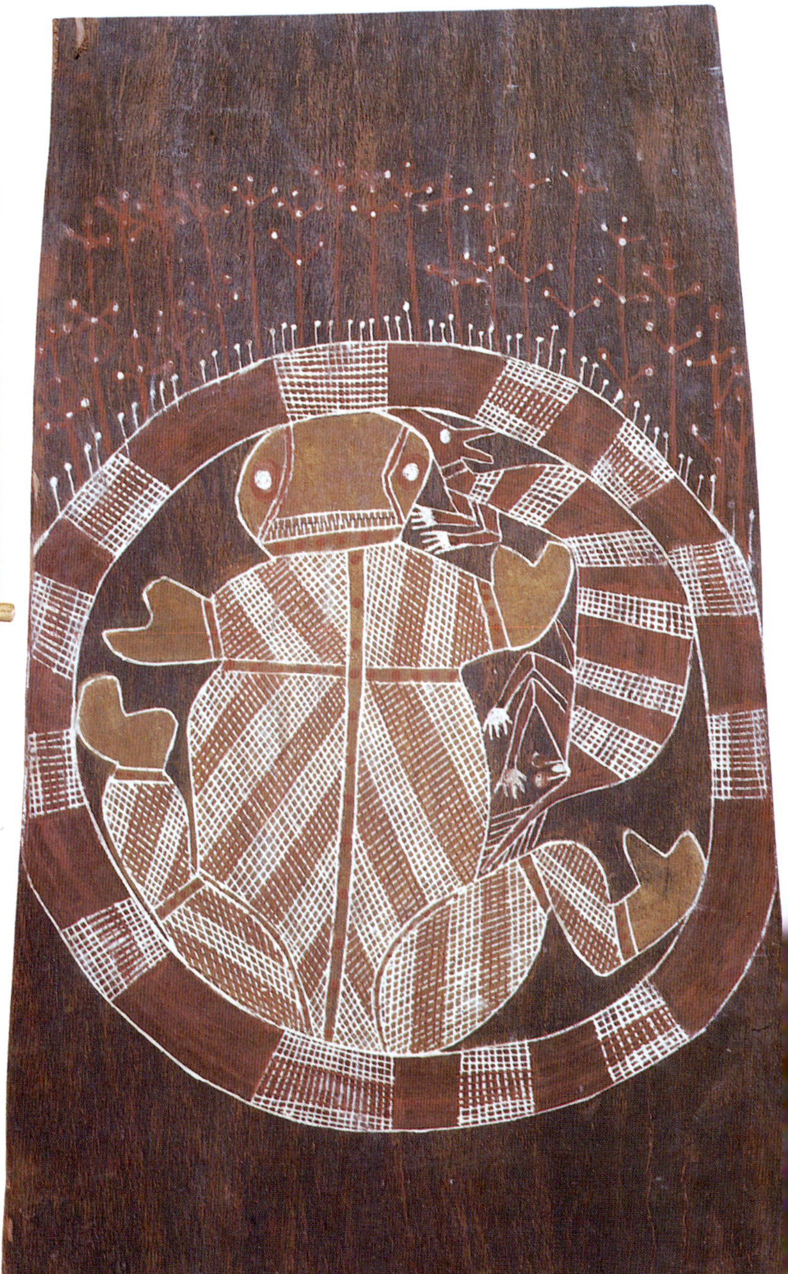

Plate 84 THE MOON MAN AND HIS DOG

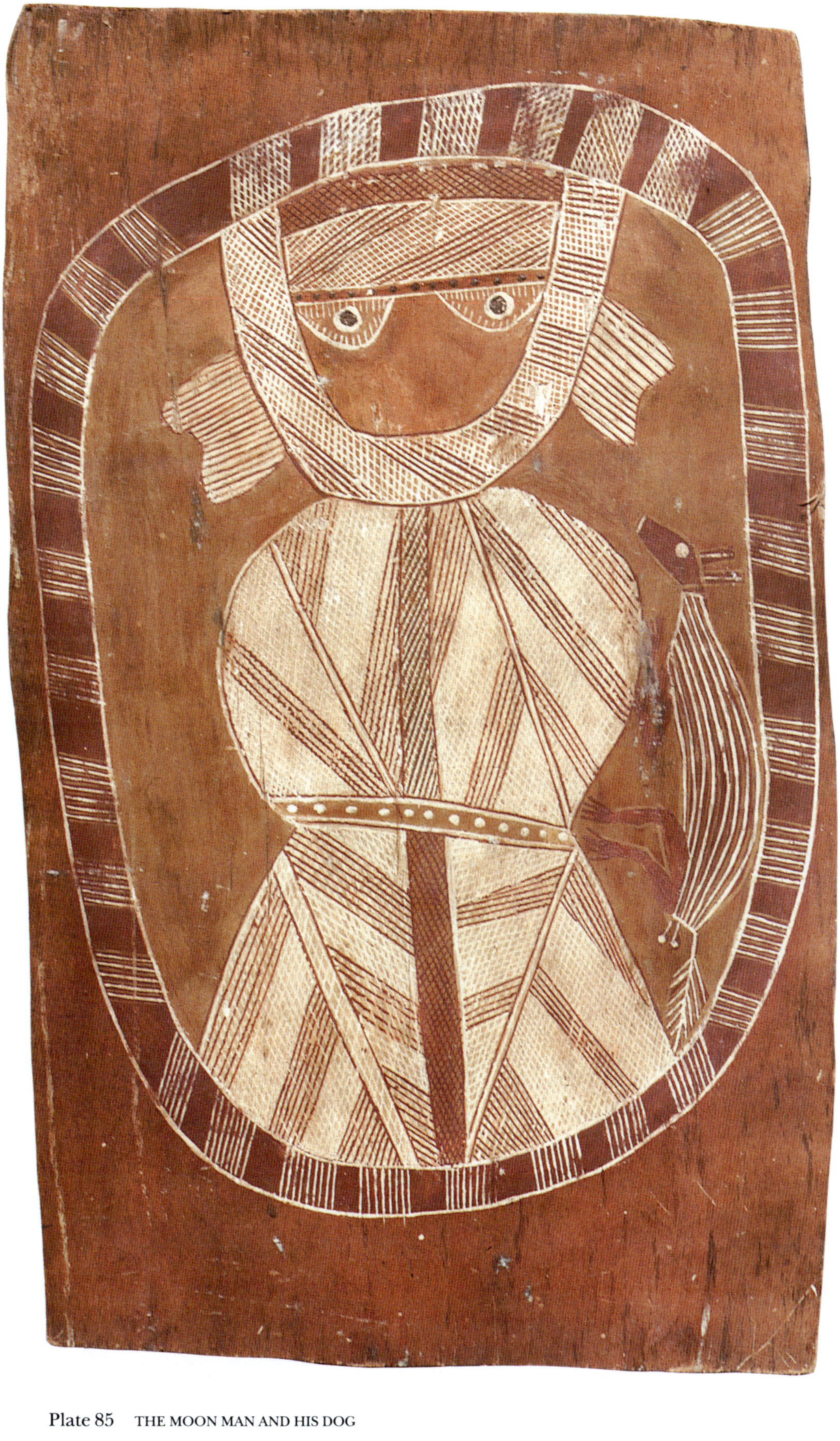

Plate 85 THE MOON MAN AND HIS DOG

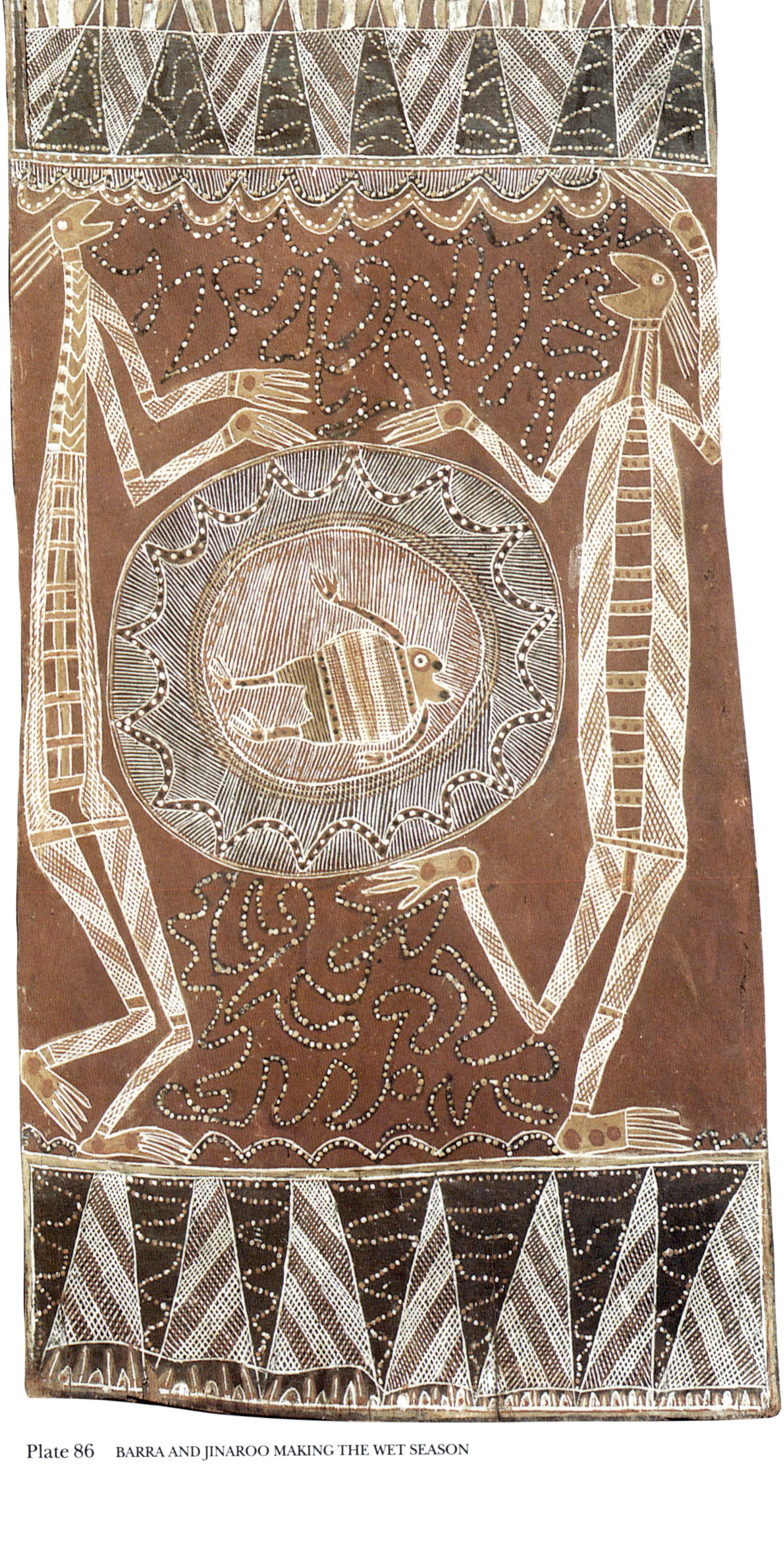

Plate 86 BARRA AND JINAROO MAKING THE WET SEASON

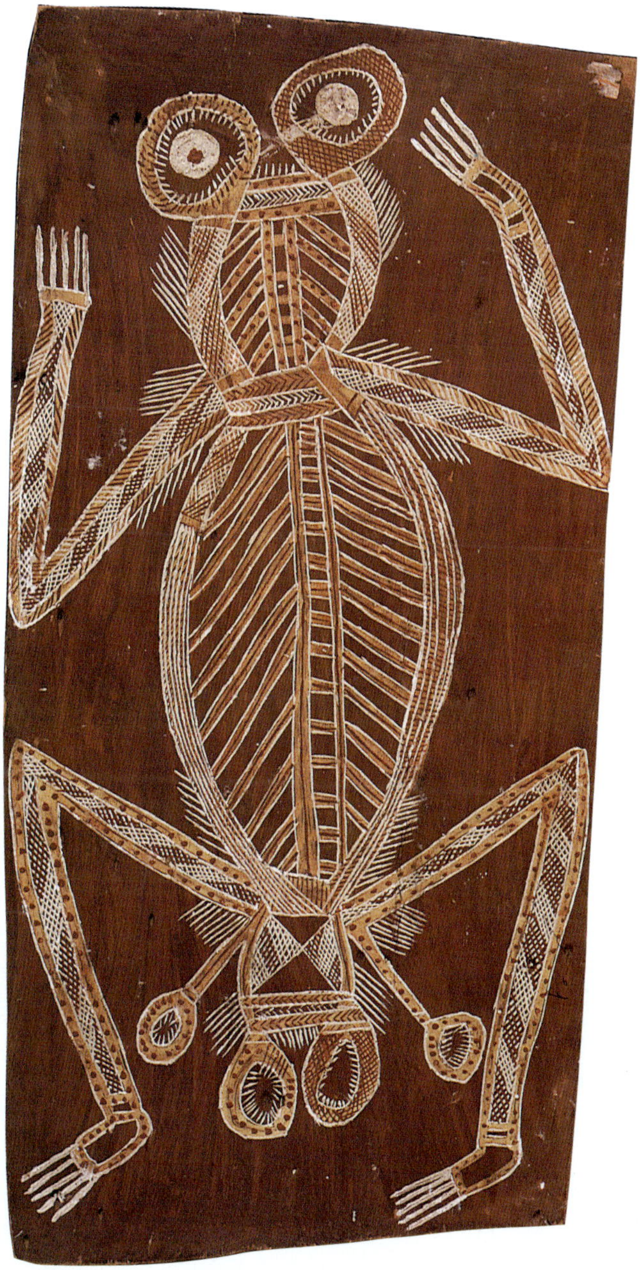

Plate 87 THE FROG KING

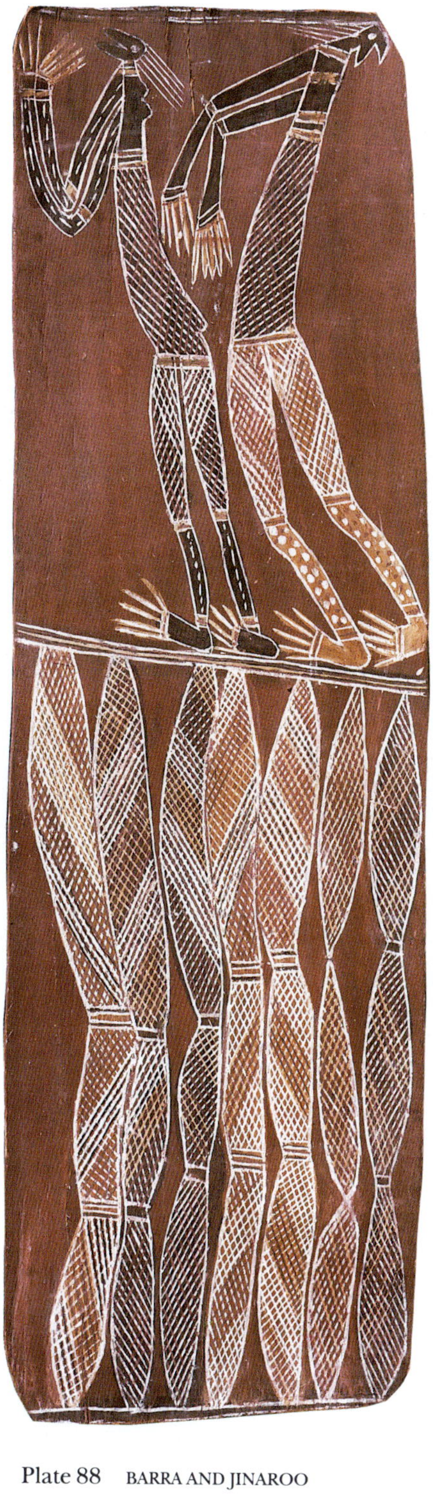

Plate 88 BARRA AND JINAROO

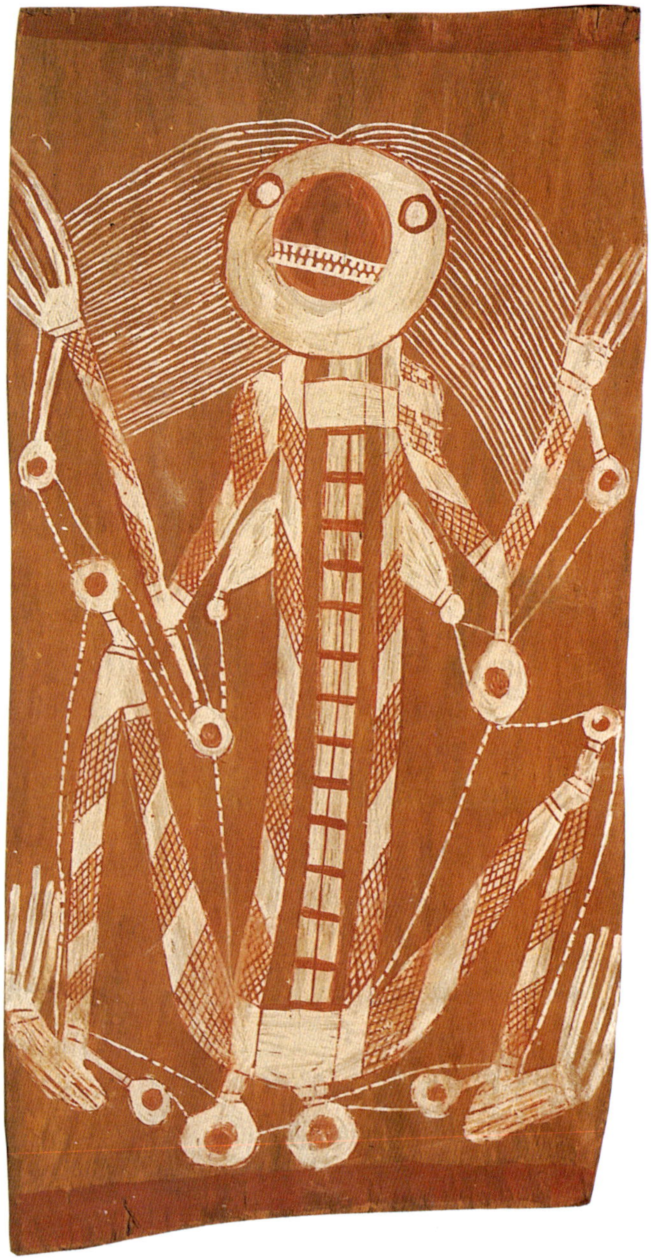

Plate 89 THE LIGHTNING

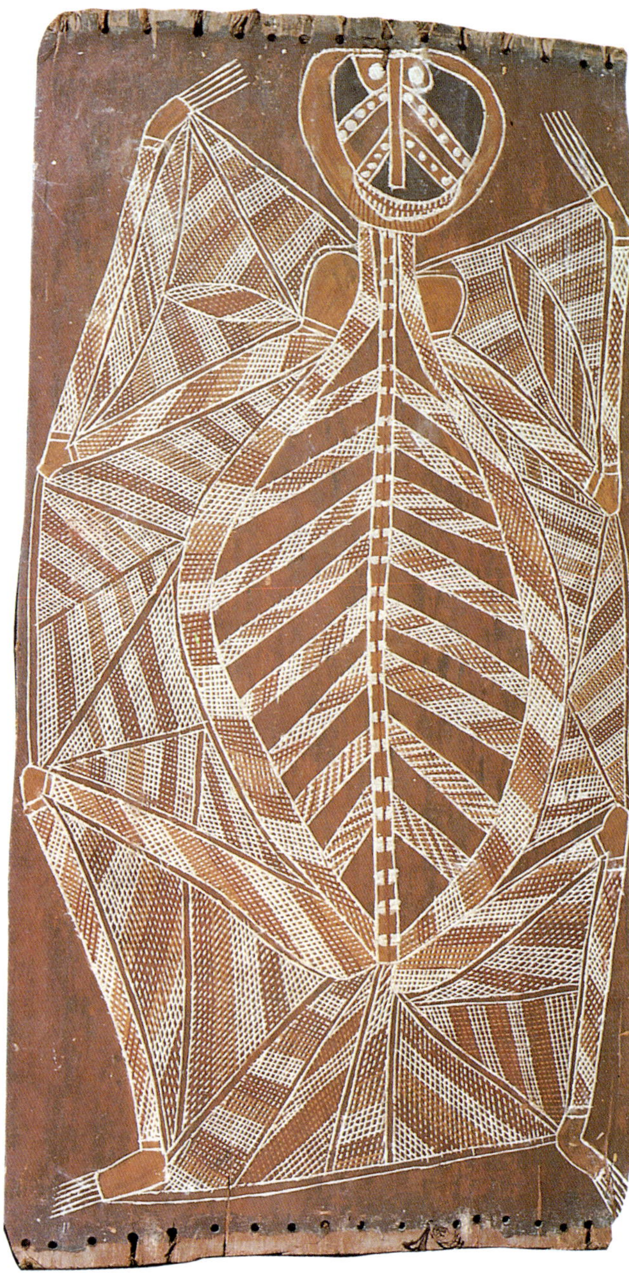

Plate 90 SHEET-LIGHTNING FIGURE

Chapter 12
Get up Barra, make big storms, drown the whole country

In late September Yirawala sent a telegram telling me to come and pick up some paintings he had made for me. I applied for a permit stressing that Yirawala had requested my presence and it was in line with our legal contract. The permit was not issued, and so once more the paintings were lost. Bobby and David came to Darwin with a document dated 9 October 1974 and signed by Yirawala and a number of Gunwinggu elders. They had written it themselves and it read as follows:

> We say no to the mining company. They never ask us here on Croker Island about our country. They only talk to the Council; but they never tell us.
>
> We do not want the mining company to dig for uranium at our country. We did not say yes that the mining company could look for uranium over there.
>
> The NACC never asked us. Government promise us our own land. We think promise broken. We ask the Prime Minister to listen to us.

The men had signed mostly with crosses and symbols, witnessed by Bobby Joran. As requested, the letter was sent to the Prime Minister.

David said they were really worried, as mining trucks were all over their country. One man told him the miners were also after gold and diamonds. Yirawala wanted me to try and stop them.

Bobby and I went to see a trade union official, who was sympathetic but said there was little that could be done apart from discussing the situation at their meetings and perhaps sending a protest to the Federal Government. It seemed that the organisations set up by the Federal Government were now the spokesmen for the tribal people.

On 28 October another telegram came from Yirawala, asking me to come and see him and also pick up some bark drawings. There was apparently some problem about accommodation at Croker Island, so I could not go. I sent a message to Yirawala asking him to come into Darwin. When there was no response I wrote a personal letter to the superintendent on Croker Island, asking for a permit for 18 November. There was no response.

I then received a telegram from Yirawala asking for money to enable him to fly to Maningrida. Bobby was still in town so I gave him the money and paid his fare home to Croker Island. He said that his father was very worried about the miners on their land and feared that the sacred sites could be destroyed and the Lumahlumah cave looted. He wanted to organise Peter Mahlunwunggu and others to guard the caves and sites.

For two weeks there was no word from Yirawala. David came in to Darwin to say Yirawala had gone from Croker Island in a small boat with another man, to see Paddy Compass on the mainland. We sent telegrams to various places but they had not seen him. I paid David's fare to try and find his father.

Meanwhile, I received a letter from the Prime Minister's Department to say that my letters concerning the proposed Yirawala art exhibition in London had been sent to the Australian National Gallery and the Australian Council for the Arts for their consideration, as these bodies advised the Prime Minister on such matters.

The AIAS also had an interest in the matter. It seemed that if these bodies were against the showing of the Yirawala collection in London, then it might not proceed, despite the invitation and guarantees given.

I knew the Australian Government wanted the collection, but they had not helped to save it or preserve it; on the contrary, as most of Yirawala's paintings had gone (and still went) into the dealer's maw without government concern or intervention.

If the Horniman Museum exhibition did not go ahead and through it the support from influential people, it would be extremely difficult for me to hold onto the collection. There was a limit to playing for time.

At the end of November Yirawala came to see me, having arrived by truck from the Oenpelli area. He said he had been to see Paddy Compass and they had been making 'business' (ritual) for storms, to stop the mining trucks. They had been to the place and power caves of Barra the thunder and lightning man. They had made strong magic with sacred stones to sing up big storms — maybe a cyclone.

Yirawala was happy and said he would paint Barra for me. 'Big magic, sing him drawing, make big storm.' He sipped his tea and smiled. 'We block mining truck, that's all. Gov'ment tell lie 'bout land for we.'

I thought it sad that they were resorting to magic when all else seemed to have failed.

Yirawala looked fit and well, speaking with passion against the mining men, whom he greatly feared. He warned me to look out in the coming wet season. If the frogs sang out very loud and persistently, I must pack everything away and maybe leave Darwin for a while. 'If frog sing out properly loud, you look out, take little girl, boy, my drawing other place. Big storm coming, you see.'

After lunch he began painting storm symbols, working quickly and singing as he made them. After that he painted Barra the wet season man and his triumph over Jinaroo the dry season man. The skinny, stick-like Jinaroo swayed backwards and held up his hands, trying to ward off the thunder man's strong winds, as thunder rumbled and lightning flashed over their heads. Barra sang up thunder and lightning to drive Jinaroo back into his cave. Barra's voice roared above the sound of thunder, 'Sit down old dry season man, it is my turn now to make big storms and bring in the wet, so all things will multiply. Sit down old man, until next year.'

Jinaroo protested in a high crackling voice that Barra had come too soon and he did not want to leave just yet. Barra lifted his arms and sang. The lightning man looked out from his black cave and hurled his spears at Jinaroo, who hopped about dodging them. Barra called up more thunder and summoned the king of all frogs to sing out for big rain.

Jinaroo began to retreat, still protesting feebly as Barra stamped on the edge of a sacred well and the great one-eyed king of all frogs rose to the surface, croaking loudly. All the frogs joined him in a deafening chorus. Jinaroo fled as a strong wind blew and a curtain of rain swept across the rocks and plains.

The crocodiles listened and all nature welcomed the rain.

Yirawala recorded the power words for making storms and the inside story for the painting. He said these must be kept and not be printed in our book. Only the non-sacred, alternative words and 'outside' stories could be used. No matter what happened eventually with the collection, the power words and 'inside' stories must not be given to anyone. If the Government ever got its hands on the collection, they were to be told nothing at all. He was very bitter about the treatment meted out to him and his clan. 'Him trick 'bout land. Tell me lie; never give help, money, truck, land. Only humbug him give me, that's all.'

He seemed to have recovered some of his old spirit and wanted to make a last effort to try to stop the miners coming through. He called on me to make a last effort as well.

I promised to do my best but I had not been well for some time and had seriously depleted my emotional and financial resources. He looked hard at me and put his hand on my forehead, nodding slowly. Yes, I was getting weaker and must have help. I would have to be very strong for the final fight. He said he had brought something special from Paddy Compass to make healing ritual and give me power and strength from the Dreaming. The ceremony would have to be performed at dusk, away from everyone as it was dangerous. He added that he would also give me power of the tongue to speak for them, and eyes to see.

That evening I sent the children off to a neighbour's house and made ready for the ritual.

In the far corner of my yard, screened by bushes, Yirawala had made a fire. He told me to sit next to him and wait for the sun to go down.

The wind shook the branches above us and the fire suddenly flared up as Yirawala began chanting. He held a small, finely woven dilly bag from which he drew something wrapped in paperbark. A small portion was dropped in the fire and we were wreathed in acrid smoke.

To prepare me he spoke in English first, telling me that this was Dreaming power from Paddy Compass to make us both strong to fight for the land and save the sacred caves. Paddy was scared that 'sickness places' (sacred and secret places) would be blown up by the mining men.

Yirawala's face appeared and disappeared in the swirling smoke as he whispered, 'We can ask gov'ment anything. We stand up all the way. He can't put me down. Paddy Compass send you promise. Him boss for cave, plenty dead body there. Him want you, look after all that Dreaming for him. Him help we two men, me and you. Him boss for secret cave, like magic, poison cave. Paddy Compass lift you high. You work for him. Him want you to learn.' At this point he placed some fatty substance in my hand and told me to burn it slowly and blow on it. He would sing the power words. These words were very secret, from Paddy, very strong and dangerous. He struck a match and handed me the flame, whispering in a deep voice, 'All the people he never learn, kid. Him never told him, only yourself, like. You keep yourself. Nobody know, only you.' After this Paddy Compass would follow us all round the country and we would win.

I held up the piece of fat and lit it. As it spluttered and melted Yirawala chanted, giving me a special name. His voice was very deep now as he explained, 'We callim yam; call yam him and nephew, two little boy him follow you. One old woman, old man and two kid, that your Dreaming. Him give you power.'

The burning fat gave off a strange odour as it melted. Yirawala caught the fat and rubbed if over my arms and chest, then in the centre of my forehead.Finally my tongue was touched with a bitter substance. Now I could speak and see.

As the chanting continued I suddenly felt afraid. I became very cold and shivered, although it was a hot evening. In the swirling smoke I seemed to see faces and forms swaying in the shadows. I felt that we were alone in the middle of a great black void and I was sinking.

Yirawala shook me and piled more wood on the fire as he called my special kinship names.

I recovered as the wind blew the smoke away, then small cicatrices were made on my arms and chest. Yirawala stood up and taking my hand helped me to my feet. The ceremony had ended. We went inside and I made some strong coffee. I felt as if I were floating.

When I had recovered fully, I confessed that I had left my tape recorder switched on and everything had been recorded. Yirawala sat silent for a moment then said it was all right as long as the tape was never played to anyone else, as it could make them sick. I should play it each night to give me power from Paddy's Dreaming.

Before Yirawala went home he finished four paintings and said he would have to finish the series on storms back at Croker Island. I told him to try and send a relative in future to bring paintings, as communications were so difficult.

He said we were both much stronger now and we would fight once more for land and rights, after Christmas.

After he went home two earth tremors shook Darwin and the massive build up of cumulus clouds increased. The heat was stifling and the ants were in feverish activity, cleaning out their nests. Streams of green ants poured along the verandah rail and up the trunks of trees.

Early in December there was a cyclone alert. The cyclone dispersed out at sea and the suffocating build up continued.

In mid December my husband came to visit us for Christmas.

On 22 December a heavy rain depression moved slowly around Groote Eylandt and developed into a cyclone. For two days Cyclone Tracy remained stationary behind Melville Island and we all thought it would disperse as the first one had done. Slowly and inexorably it began moving, on course for Darwin.

The cyclone warnings became more frequent and frayed the nerves as we obeyed instructions to remove objects from the yard, and tape windows, fill containers with water, and stock up on tinned food, candles, torches and other necessities.

However, we couldn't do everything required. Most of our time was taken up packing archival material in plastic bags and storing them under the house, which was built into the side of a hill. The collections were also stored under the house. We had no time to worry about other possessions such as furniture, furnishings and clothing.

We were worried but not frightened, because we had never experienced a cyclone before.

On Christmas Eve Darwin people were subdued as they moved about, shopping for presents and survival.

As daylight faded, most people hurried home to their families, where children played happily waiting for Father Christmas. Little lights on Christmas trees flickered uneasily in loungeroom windows as Darwin waited under the heavy black clouds that hung over the city, like the lid on a pressure cooker.

By 5 p.m. the cyclone warning sounded every few minutes and people battened down as best they could. A few people left town but most stayed to defend their homes. A number of Aborigines in Bagot Settlement had already left.

By 6 p.m. it was dark and still, not a leaf stirred; then the frogs began to croak, sporadically at first, then in a rising, frantic chorus as they emerged from the ground in thousands, in a frenzy of sound and movement, calling for rain and waiting to mate.

Frogs were everywhere, clinging to the wire door, staring with goggling eyes, and when you walked outside you slipped on them.

By 8 p.m. the north-eastern sky turned red, bathing everything in an eerie light. Then a distant moaning sound was heard, growing louder as short gusts of wind hurled small objects against the house.

By 9 p.m. the moaning turned to a shriek, as the monster pounced on Darwin. My husband, who had been under fire in World War II, took command, preventing me and my daughter from making a run for it. The house trembled and swayed. In the red glare we saw clumps of trees and debris, including small cars, rush past our smashed windows. Spears of timber tore through the walls like rockets, as we fought to hold the double doors at the end of the loungeroom, knowing that if they smashed in the whole house would go. We shouted into each other's ears to hang on and not let go.

As we repeatedly pushed the big jarrah dining table against the doors, the roaring blast hurled us back again and again. We were soaking wet and shivering as we held the table against the doors and our feet were cut and bleeding from broken glass. Cecil shouted at us to redouble our efforts as giant hands tried to tear our old house from the hillside.

I had been sick with fear and crying aloud to God to save us, then, in the deafening roar, all fear of death vanished, there was only the dogged will to hang on. Chunks of masonry and an iron girder smashed through the wall, sending driving rain and wind slashing at us and broken glass flying, but we hardly noticed as we struggled to hold the doors.

All night we fought to save the house and gradually the great wind gusts lessened.

In the grey light of dawn the wind had eased and we could lean over the table to rest. Through the broken louvred windows, we could see flickering red lights and hear the faint wail of ambulance sirens.

Looking around our damaged house I thought we must be one of the unluckiest families in Darwin — until we stumbled outside to a scene of devastation, and I saw that we were one of the luckiest. The houses across the road had gone. Only a few stumps remained.

Power poles leaned at crazy angles, festooned with tangled wires like giant spider webs. Most of the trees were uprooted as were most of the big trees in our backyard, and their bodies had been a buffer against the mass of debris from collapsed houses all around.

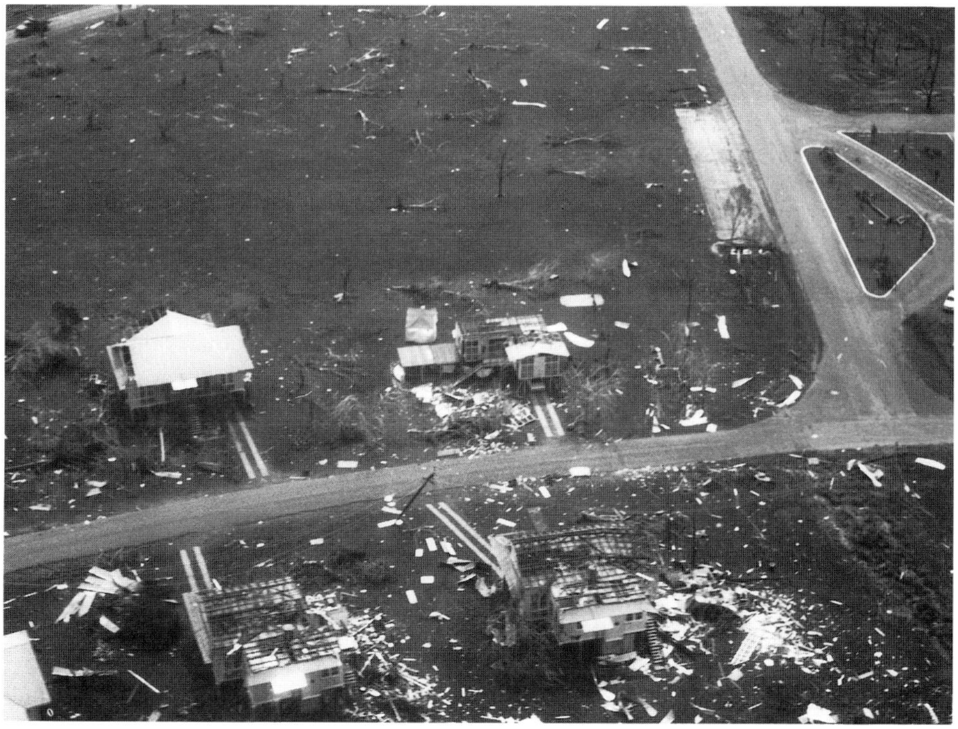

Darwin after Cyclone Tracy.

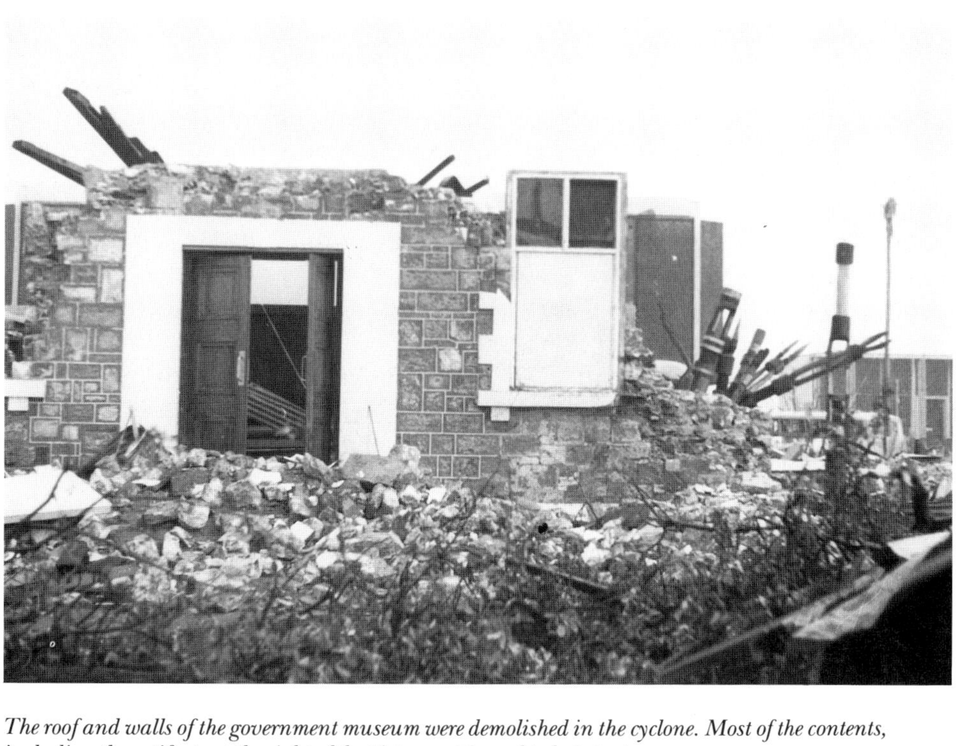

The roof and walls of the government museum were demolished in the cyclone. Most of the contents, including the artifacts at the right of the picture, appeared to be intact.

Our neighbour across the road had three little children and we thought they must have all perished. We went to investigate. Karl and his children crawled out from the wreckage. They had taken refuge in a bathroom under the house. He dug out a bottle of Scotch and offered us a drink. He told us that most of the other families had gone to shelter in government buildings.

Our old tropical house had stood up well and the collections and bags of archive material had survived. Upstairs, Yirawala's photograph still hung on the wall.

I had glass in my left eye and we drove to the hospital, where dented ambulances were disgorging their loads of dead and injured. In the hospital entrance the dead were piled on the floor, and the water running through the rooms was red with blood. Exhausted ambulance drivers stumbled through the slush. One of them broke down when he lifted out the dead body of a little girl. He was led away sobbing.

A handful of doctors and nurses were trying to cope. I sat in a chair as a doctor removed the glass particles from my eye. His hands were trembling and he dropped the cotton wool. He grabbed some more and a bandage from somewhere. A nurse came to write down my name but I could not remember it. She said not to worry.

We had no water or power, so we collected water from a creek on the golf course and boiled it on a fire outside.

That night we lay on plastic-covered sodden mattresses, sweating and being eaten by mosquitoes. I managed to get to sleep, but woke up with a raging thirst, intending to go out to the kitchen and get a drink. As I reached for the torch I glanced towards the doorway and fell back frozen with terror, unable to cry out. With all my strength, I tried to reach out and wake Cecil but could not move. There framed in the doorway was a fearful figure of swirling smoke, with large black holes for its eyes. It stood still in the sickly moonlight then drifted away into Amanda's room. Only then could I shake my husband and croak that somebody was in the house.

Cecil grumbled and blundered about over the bits of glass and debris, the torchlight stabbing the darkness. He shouted that there was nobody in the house and went back to bed. (Weeks later, when Yirawala came to Darwin, he kissed my daughter and me and unsolicited said he knew we were all right as he had come to have a look.)

Dr Jim Cairns, the Deputy Prime Minister, ordered the Navy to Darwin to re-establish communications and bring urgently needed equipment and supplies. Later Major-General Alan Stretton, Director-General of the Natural Disasters Organisation, came to take charge. Police from interstate were brought in to keep law and order. Non-commissioned sailors were detailed to clean up Darwin and we owe them a debt that can never be repaid. Later they were assisted by the Army.

After persistent representation to Naval Headquarters in Mitchell Street, I was invited on board HMAS *Melbourne* to take tea with Rear-Admiral Wells and record for him my eye-witness account of the cyclone. Sitting in his stateroom was like being on another planet. Everything was so immaculate, with the reassuring portrait of the Queen and the Duke hanging on the wall. Here was law and order which had not prevailed on shore.

I had asked to see him to obtain some help in saving my collections of Aboriginal art and artifacts. Although they were under the house, they were not wrapped and water was dripping through the floorboards onto them.

Rear-Admiral Wells was sympathetic and said certainly something of beauty and importance to the nation must be saved. He summoned a captain to detail some Naval personnel to wrap and secure my collection. But for this kindly intervention the collection would have been damaged beyond repair. The Navy lads not only wrapped the collections, but made temporary repairs to our roof.

After the cyclone I wrote at night by lamplight as the power was off. During the day we worked cleaning up, or queuing for food, ice, bedding and whatever was going. We also took turns day and night, guarding the house from looters.

Chapter 13
Money is water that flows away, the land is there forever

The cyclone slowed things up for mining activity, but only for a few months.

Early 1975 saw trucks and jinkers hauling heavy equipment and buildings into Arnhemland. Endless convoys of trucks roared and churned through the bush, lumbering day and night, then faster as new ribbons of bitumen split the forests. In the glaring searchlights of the road trains, bush creatures were blinded and crushed. They could only keep coming along their natural pathways in nature's scheme of things, until they were all gone. The carnage on the roads was terrible to see. Today, wildlife is scarce and the wonderful dawn chorus of birds is no more.

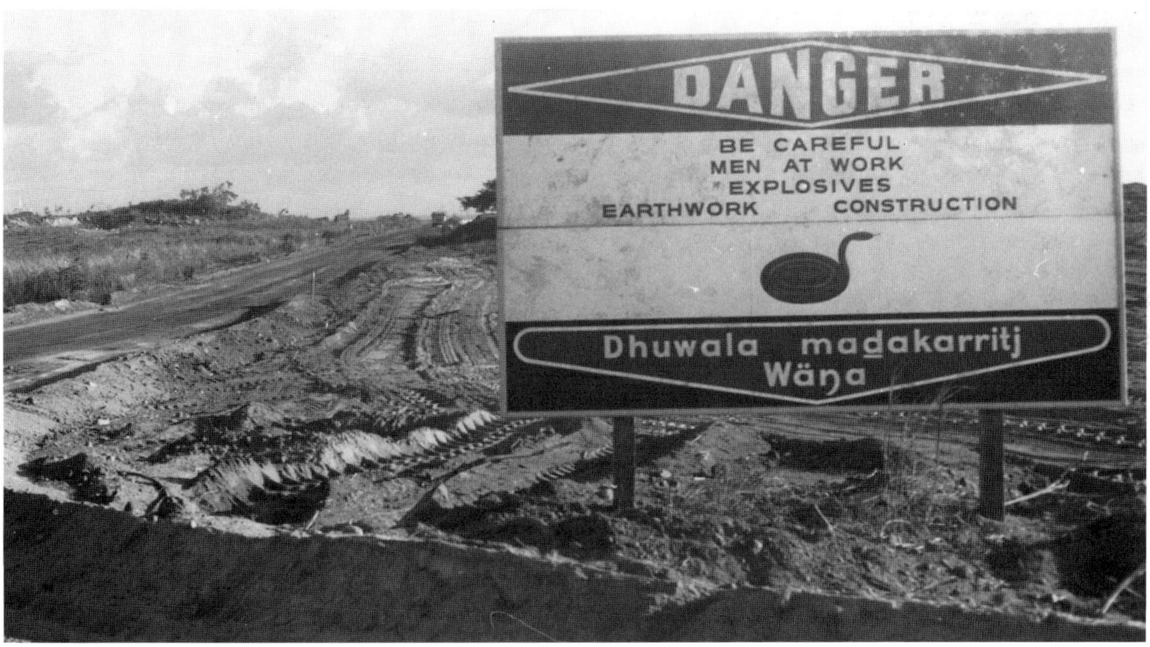

Mining area at Yirrkala, Gove. A warning to local Aborigines — at least, to those who could read.

Aborigines in the area were stunned and most were unable to grasp how this had happened. The awful events were beyond their control. Many just gave up, some trying to get something in the way of compensation from the white men, others finding forgetfulness in alcohol, as the breakdown of their traditional life and values accelerated.

Yirawala's worst fears were being realised. He and other tribal custodians of the land had lost all control over it. Now councils and committees were making decisions. Important documents were signed by a few so-called traditional owners, many of them illiterate, ignoring their traditional tribal law under which every member of a clan is a traditional owner and must be consulted. The traditional Aboriginal laws had been swept aside as an expedient.

Yirawala travelled around talking to groups of Aborigines, asking them not to sign anything about mining. David and Bobby assisted him in this work, which was made more difficult by an Aboriginal man, employed by a mining company, who travelled around telling Aboriginal groups that mining was good for them: they would get some money and be able to buy cars; mining would only make little holes in the ground, which would be filled in later and trees replanted. In any case, he said, the men might as well sign and get something because they could not stop the mining. The speaker was sophisticated in the white man's world, and had an understanding of tribal people.

We were sitting down in a camp not far from the East Alligator when Yirawala heard all this. He was angry and said the white men lied. Nobody could replant the forests that had taken so many years to grow, and what about all the animals and birds destroyed? Nobody could restore them to life or create once more all the different species of birds and animals in their natural habitat.

The men said this was true, but how could they stop the mining, as nobody listened to them anyway. They did not want to see the land laid waste and sacred sites endangered, but they felt helpless and without a voice.

One man said he would like to have a vehicle. Yirawala rounded on him and pointed to a rusted wreck amongst the trees. Cars break and rust away, but the land is there forever, always there, to feed us and look after us. The land is our mother. We do not sell her, he said.

David and Bobby supported him saying, 'Look what happened to that mob at Yirrkala. Big town built at Nhulunbuy and big bauxite mine at Gove, killing the country, poison the fish.'

Yirawala said, 'Hotel there. Big mob Aboriginal him drink, drink, lose land, Dreaming.'

Yirawala wept to see the carnage of the bush creatures. 'Ah, poor Dadat, my Dreaming bird, got no home. Poor bugger cockatoo no home. Rainbow snake might be him dead. Mining men blow up rock.'

On one trip we picked up some injured wallabies but they died before we got them back to Darwin. Bobby found a frog-mouth owl lying amongst the bushes with broken wings, gasping its life away. Speaking soothingly he picked it up and cradled it in his arms. He would not leave it lying there in the sun to die. He would take it home and bury it.

Sad and despairing, Yirawala said he would make no more trips in the area. It was more than he could bear. He would go home to Croker Island and talk with members of his family and clan about going home. Once there they would stop the miners coming through, even with spears in the old way.

My letters and the pension cheques were still going astray. I told Yirawala and his family to complain officially. I would do the same.

In response to a telegram from Yirawala, asking me to come to see him, I had for some weeks requested permits from Croker Island council without a response from them, and Yirawala made constant representation to the council. All my letters were now addressed to Lazarus Lami-Lami, as he was chairman of the council now, but I received no reply.

To my surprise I received a letter from the ex-superintendent, who said one of my letters asking for a permit to see Yirawala had been dealt with by the council a few days ago. He wondered if I had heard about it. I had not. I thanked him for the letter and was glad that his attitude had changed somewhat. He was now classed as a senior officer on the council. Some of his duties had been taken over by Aborigines.

On 26 March David Boston wrote to me from London to say that he was not confident of obtaining support for the Yirawala display at the Horniman Museum. A representative of the Australian Institute of Aboriginal Studies had been to see him but they had been unable to reach agreement. He refrained from giving details.

I had over the last few months written to the Prime Minister and Federal Government departments seeking support and a fairly small amount of money for our expenses. My letters had been met by refusals or silence. It seemed the Australian Government, for reasons best known to itself, was not enthusiastic about the proposed display and no help would be forthcoming from them or their statutory bodies. I also approached big companies, airlines and banks, all of which said they were short of money and could not help.

I had contacted the Sydney Opera House booking office and received a reply that a hall would be available on 26 July 1975 for an exhibition of Yirawala's paintings.

It was a last-ditch effort to find a sponsor to assist us with fares to London in October for the Horniman Museum display.

I continued to write to the Croker Island council for a permit to see Bobby and Yirawala concerning the exhibition. Finally I was granted a permit for three days, from 20 to 22 April. I took food, clothing and vitamin pills for Yirawala and also a half-Alsatian puppy that had been immunised against distemper.

My bitch had had six pups. The father, a full Alsatian, had been shot by the police as there was a fear that rabies might break out. When the police came to kill my two dogs, I rushed inside to get the rifle. They would have to shoot me first. One policeman laughed and said, 'Looks like she means it. Oh, come on. People have been through too much as it is.'

When I arrived at Croker I found Yirawala weak and unwell. He welcomed the food and vitamin pills and said he wanted to go to Darwin to see his doctor in a week's time; I must make a booking for him when he was ready and send the ticket out on the plane.

He was delighted with the puppy and lavished kisses on its head as it licked his face. 'My r'own dog. I call him strong name later.'

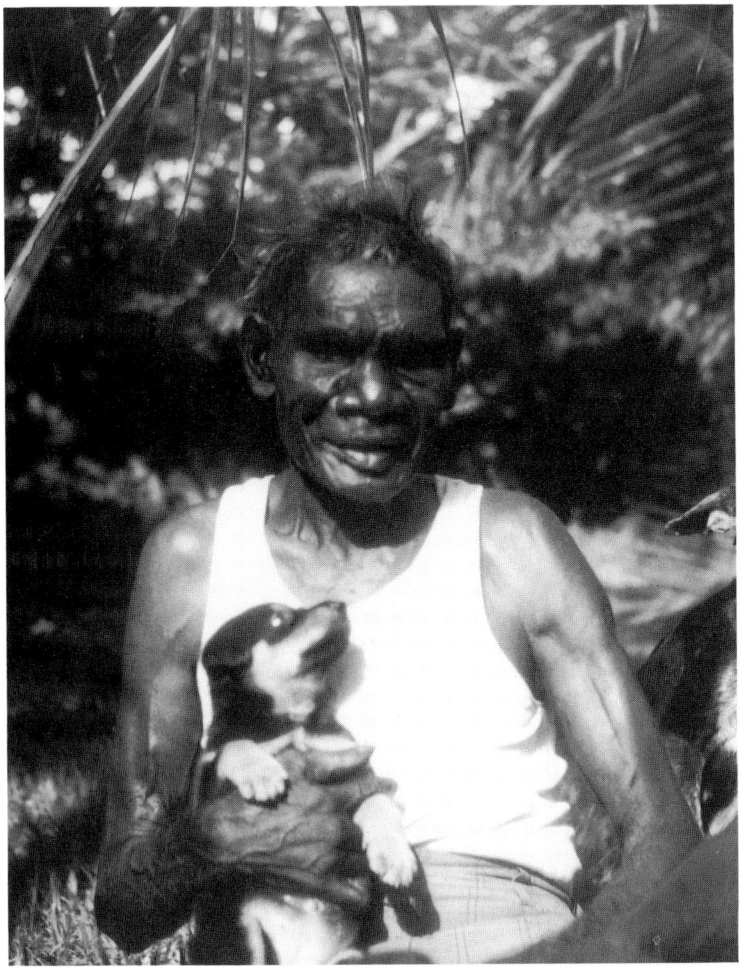

Yirawala holding the puppy I gave him. 'I call him strong name later.'

That night we discussed the London display and the coming exhibition at the Sydney Opera House. Yirawala and his family were pleased about these arrangements and nominated Bobby to go with me on both occasions.

One week later word came from Yirawala to make a booking for him for 28 April. The ticket was sent out on the plane but he didn't come in to Darwin. He said later that nobody took him to the airstrip.

Communication still remained a major problem, so in the hope of overcoming it, I began sealing my letters with red-sealing wax, stamped with my father's seal in the shape of an eagle.

I was worried about Yirawala and requested the Croker Island council to assist with arrangements to fly him to Darwin.

Then, in early June, I received a telegram from the ex-superintendent to say that Yirawala was coming in to Darwin on a visiting Uniting Church aircraft.

There was also an official Church letter to certify that 'Billy Yirawala is to have a medical examination at Darwin Hospital' and would be staying with me. This was a breakthrough, but I wondered why white authority called him Billy. He said it was a 'rubbish balanda name', and he found it offensive.

In Darwin the doctors said Yirawala was suffering from stress and weakness. He also suffered headaches and his eyesight had worsened. We should continue with vitamin tablets, nourishing food and plenty of rest. For the first two weeks Amanda and I had to bathe him until he was strong enough to do it himself. He had let his whiskers grow and one morning said to us that he would shave them off. He laughed, 'Might be I give you a fright, by and by.'

One evening as we sat on the front verandah, watching the flying foxes slide across the red sky, he said like them he was going home. When he was strong again he would go with his family group to hold the home country, no matter what the government said. 'Can't wait too long. Me getting little bit old. You help me. We talk later on.' He then asked me to make more tape recordings so people would know his story and remember him. He caught my hand urgently. 'You catch him whole story — make book, teach balanda, 'cause him never understand.'

His voice was sad, but tinged with bitterness when he spoke of the Government's treatment of himself and the tribal people.

Yirawala stayed a few weeks with us and gradually he picked up, but he would never be as strong as before.

In July, when Yirawala had returned to Croker Island, Bobby came in to Darwin to make ready to go to Sydney. TAA kindly assisted us once more with concessions.

The Opera House exhibition created great interest. The opening night was attended by a number of distinguished people, including the Director of the Australian National Gallery. Bobby Joran opened the exhibition and gave a moving speech about his father and the reason for holding the exhibition. Some people who came to the display gave Bobby donations but no sponsor came to our rescue, despite all the publicity.

On the way back to Darwin, Bobby expressed his disappointment with the Government and the public. It seemed we had exhausted all avenues. I decided that I would add to the mortgages, if possible, to meet the cost of freight and fares to London.

When we arrived home there was a letter from London. David Boston had cancelled the Horniman Museum exhibition. This was a bitter blow to our hopes of getting out of the net. I did not blame David Boston. A combination of disapproval from various Federal government institutions had rung the death knell.

There was also a letter from the House of Representatives Standing Committee on Aboriginal Affairs regarding the inquiry into alcohol and Aborigines. I had given evidence verbally and in a written submission concerning the problems of alcohol amongst the tribal people. The Standing Committee requested a perusal of the transcripts and a list of corrections.

In part, my submission read: 'If nothing is done to prevent the uncontrolled consumption of alcohol on the Aboriginal reserves [then] we are just going through a

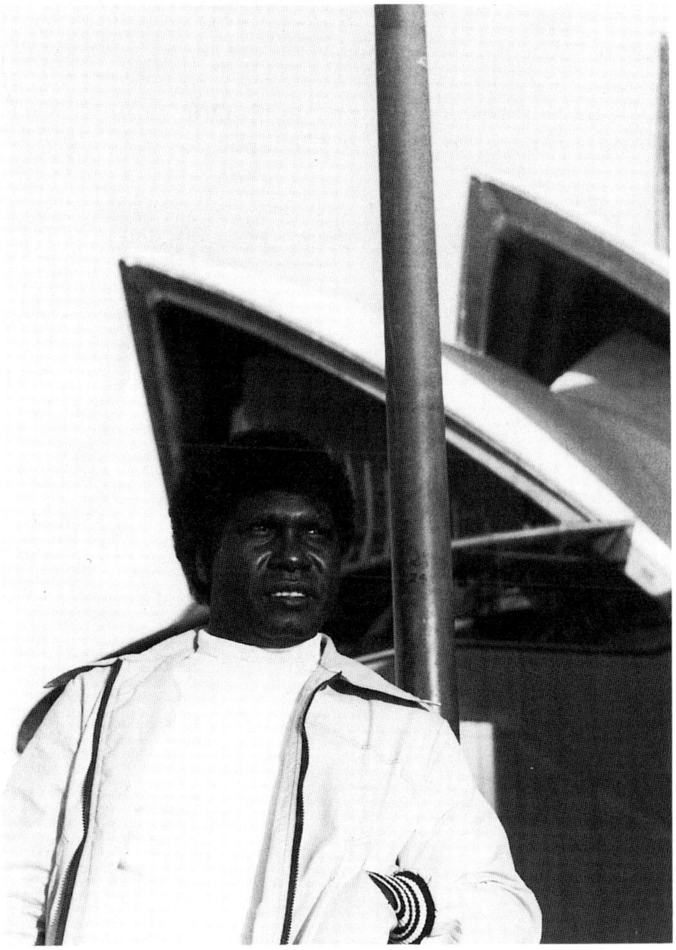

Bobby Joran outside the Sydney Opera House exhibition, 1975. The exhibition created great interest, but no sponsor.

window-dressing exercise and if it continues we can only call it velvet-gloved genocide.'

On 5 August Yirawala sent a message that he wanted to see me. I applied for a permit which was issued for one day, 9 August.

When I went down to his little house he was seated on a blanket near the door, with his sons and some of the clan elders. He patted the blanket for me to sit beside him and told Mary to make a billy of tea. 'We make big talk,' he said, as the pup, now half grown, scrambled all over me, whining and licking my face. Yirawala laughed. 'Him know you, alright.'

As we drank tea, David said his father had decided they were all going home next year in the dry season time. We must start planning now about trucks, tents, tools and building materials to start their small settlement at Marugulidban. Some men were there already and had cleared some small areas for huts. They had also finished levelling the airstrip, with picks and shovels. How much longer would it take to get money from the Government to assist them?

Yirawala put down his tin mug and said, 'We try again, ask gov'ment for help. If not we try union men. You go see him.' He spoke in language for a while to the men and they responded with 'Gumuck!' (good).

The discussion continued for two hours, concerning possible ways of raising money. The men were adamant they did not want mission and Welfare domination. Yirawala said, 'We block mission, Welfare, mining mob. Him not allowed.' His face was stern.

Aileen and I would write more letters to the Government in Canberra and I would ask

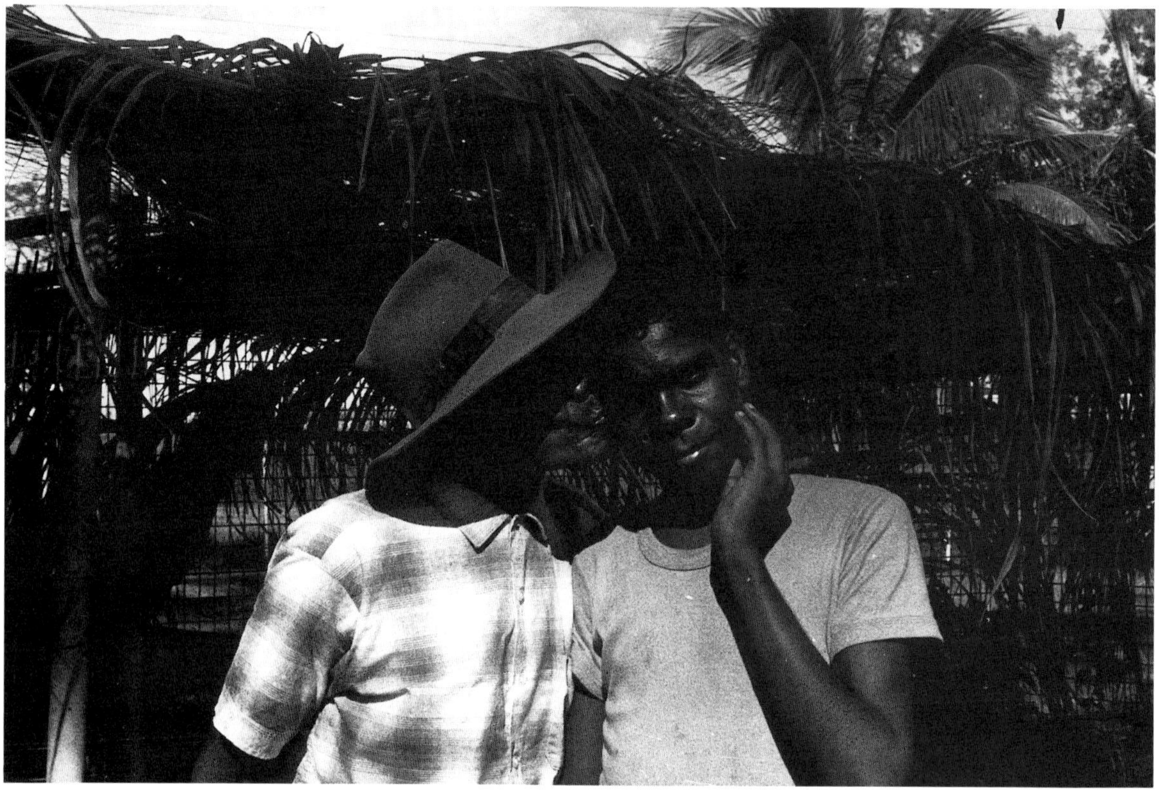

Yirawala kissing Danny. 'We are going home, all family, relations.'

the trade unions for assistance to buy a truck and the goods needed for the settlement.

The Government could not stop them from sitting down on their land, but obtaining assistance that would enable them to stay there and found their own settlement was another matter.

As I was leaving Bobby said they might come to Darwin for a short time if they could get a lift on a charter.

In mid-September they came in for two days. Yirawala said that mining men had been seen in the Marugulidban area and he must get there soon. He wanted to build a fence, because that was something white men understood. If Aborigines were just sitting down in leaf shelters they would be pushed back like the kangaroo. Had the Government promised help, or the trade unions?

My answer was no, not yet but I would keep on trying. Yirawala looked so worried and disappointed, I said half joking, 'Well, I have no money, only the collection. The Government has been after it for years.'

Bobby and Yirawala talked in language for a few minutes. Bobby said that would be a last resort, but if everything failed we would have to talk. His father could wait no longer than next April. He must go home and rally the elders to make their settlement, and hold onto it.

After that we talked about the book that I must write to tell their story. Yirawala said, 'All my drawing, put in book, tell straight story for balanda. Only you makim, got story my drawing. I give you whole lot, nobody else got story, can make book. When me die, you boss all my story, drawings, nobody else can copy.' Bobby agreed: his father wanted me to write the book and only I had the right to reproduce Yirawala's paintings now and when he dies. I was the owner of the copyright.

I asked Bobby to dictate this in his own way according to Yirawala's wishes. As he spoke I wrote it down in my diary and they both signed it.

After they went home I received a letter from Spike Milligan to say he had tried to raise support for the Horniman exhibition in London. He had even approached the Australian High Commission, without success. Spike had not heard it had been cancelled.

The collections were still stored in a room under the house, and my roof was still letting in water as I waited for a new roof from the Darwin Reconstruction Commission.

The collections were damp and urgent assistance was needed to build airy shelves under the house and erect a waterproof ceiling.

I wrote to The Honourable Mr Les Johnson, the new Federal Minister for Aboriginal Affairs. He was sympathetic and in late September, on a visit to Darwin, he came to see me to discuss the Yirawala collection and a means of preserving it.

I suggested a loan of $8000 for preservation and security of the Aboriginal art and artifacts. I also told him about Yirawala's plans to go home to clan country and his need of government help. The minister said my requests would be considered and he would advise me in due course.

I was elated. At last, here was a man of some sensibilities and understanding. My hopes were high of receiving assistance and being able to keep the Yirawala collection. I decided to wait for something more positive before telling Yirawala.

On 30 September I gave an anti-mining submission to the Ranger Environmental Inquiry in Darwin.

In the second week of October Yirawala and Bobby came to Darwin for more discussions about a truck and to discuss the mining inquiry. Men from Oenpelli had told them big talks were in progress about uranium mining. I told them that I had put in an anti-mining submission on their behalf. Yirawala thanked me but said it was probably more government humbug. He said he was very tired now and needed more good medicine. I took him to the doctor, who prescribed a cough mixture and vitamin tablets.

Three weeks after he went home Yirawala sent a message for food and more cough medicine. I sent them on the next plane. His young son Danny Noloman had also requested some music cassettes.

Unfortunately I did not hear further from The Honourable Mr Les Johnson, as Sir John Kerr, the Governor-General of Australia, sacked the Whitlam Labor Government on 11 November and appointed a caretaker Liberal Government led by Mr Malcolm Fraser.

The Liberal Party won the next federal election (and remained in power until 1983).

The new Liberal Government's policies on Aborigines differed from those of the previous government, but much of Labor's legislation remained, including the Northern and Central Land Councils. They retained most of their power, except the right to veto mining. Now they could only make deals.

In early December Yirawala sent word that he wanted to come in and see a doctor. I set wheels in motion to bring him in on 15 December.

He slowly descended the aircraft steps and stumbled at the bottom. He looked very tired and his eyes were inflamed. He said he wanted to see a good doctor, for his eyes and his body.

We were unable to get an appointment with the eye specialist at the public hospital, so I took him to see a private opthalmologist.

After examining Yirawala's eyes, the doctor recommended a cornea transplant, which would have to be performed down South. Yirawala said, 'You told me before — operation. Nobody cut my eye.' The doctor said that if he didn't want an operation nobody could force him. In the meantime he prescribed eye drops and glasses. The doctor said he would check Yirawala's eyes in six weeks' time, when he was scheduled to visit Croker Island.

After the visit to the specialist, Yirawala asked me to see my local GP, who was a kindly, caring man. He said Yirawala's blood pressure was all right, but he seemed to be run down and would need building up again. He prescribed tablets and other medicines. Yirawala said he was a 'properly number one doctor.'

At home Yirawala asked if there was any news from the Labor Government men about a truck and some assistance to go back to Marugulidban. I explained that Labor was now out of power, and chances were now very slim of obtaining anything. He looked very downcast and asked, 'Welfare men, him all come back, like before — and mission?' I did my best to explain that many changes made by Labor would remain, but the Aborigines now would have less say about exploration and mining on their land. He sat thinking for a while, then said I would have to help them to go home next year.

We went shopping for food, clothing and presents for his family. I gave him a mattress and blankets to take home. He said he would sing out for me after Christmas, when we must have big talks about his journey home.

After he left I wondered how we could raise the money for a vehicle, tents, tools and other things needed for him and his family to go back to their tribal home country. I was hard pressed with two mortgages and a broken house.

In a way Cyclone Tracy had done me a favour. I was about to be sold up by the mortgagees, the bank and a newspaper corporation. When the disaster occurred, there was a year's grace for people with heavy debts. Now the pressure was on again to pay up.

Even if I had wanted to sell my home, the price would have been inadequate, almost giving it away.

The carpet baggers were still out in force, almost a year after the cyclone, crawling through the wreckage of people's homes, offering desperate people small sums of money for their properties. Many people, still in shock and seeing little hope for the future, did sell. Some had beach-front property in what was called the 'Surge Zone', a dangerous area to live in the event of cyclones and tidal waves. Much of this land went for a song to the speculators.

One morning I had been cleaning up debris in the front yard, when a man with a briefcase came crawling through the fallen trees. He gave a toothy grin and said, 'I give you three thousand dollars as she stands.' I said, 'Just a minute,' and went inside to get the rifle. I pointed it at him, my hands shaking with anger. He scrambled back through the trees, yelling, 'Sorry, lady. Sorry!'

For some time Darwin residents were nervy and on a short fuse, especially women on their own.

In January 1976 Danny wrote to say his father had received the box of food and the pension cheques, and Aileen and Bobby had gone to Snake Bay to attend her brother's funeral ceremony.

In early February I wrote a submission to Mr Barrie Dexter, the Secretary of Aboriginal Affairs, in Canberra. My submission outlined the meaning of Aboriginal traditional art as being related to the tribal land, and how, because of little understanding by white people, the clans were beginning to break down now. My submission went on to say that this break down could be avoided to some extent by the setting up of educational institutions which would involve important Aboriginal art and artifacts and thereby generate Aboriginal pride. To this end I offered my services and the use of my films, tapes, art and artifacts.

However, I still sought an alternative to letting the Yirawala collection go to Canberra, hoping for a last-minute miracle to enable me to retain the collection in Darwin.

There was also the question of Yirawala and his urgent desire to go home to Marugulidban with his family. There was also the certainty that if mortgages were not paid the house would be sold.

There being no immediate response from the Secretary of Aboriginal Affairs and no certainty that help would be forthcoming, in late February I went to see Yirawala and Bobby to discuss things.

On arrival I found Yirawala unwell. He asked me if I had brought any vitamin tablets or 'good medicine' with me, but I had brought only money and food. I had not known he was sick but said I would send them out to him when I returned to Darwin. He said he had headaches and often felt weak. I asked if he wanted to come back with me and he said no, he was waiting for a relative from Maningrida. He would go in to Darwin in about two weeks' time to see his doctor there.

He was lying on his bed and smiled at me. 'Me alright. You send good medicine, make me walk about. I come to Darwin later on.' He motioned to Bobby and me to sit on the bed. 'We make 'portant talk.' He said the doctor would make him strong again and he would be going home soon. 'You get me new Toyota truck — put Dadat and country there.' He meant that he wanted his little red and green parrot, his Dreaming, painted on it and also the name Marugulidban.

I told them I had no money at all, only debts. The only way to buy the Toyota, tents and equipment was to let the collection go to Canberra. They had been after it for a long time.

We all sat in silence for a while, knowing all else had failed and we were beaten.

My tears began to flow. It was a heartbreaking decision, from which I never really recovered.

Yirawala sat up and put his arm around me. He said the Government was too strong for us. 'Gov'ment tell lie. Nobody help we, only you try. You can't cry. Might be Gov'ment look after drawings, him never own, no!'

For some minutes he spoke with Bobby in language, after which Bobby explained to me that his father said, yes, the collection could go to Canberra as long as the Government gave a proper legal document that they would never sell it or break it up. Yirawala wanted his name and mine on the collection, because he had made it and I had saved it. The Government could look after the paintings but they did not own the designs and stories. The meanings were never to be given to them and they could not reproduce the paintings in books. Only I could do that. He had given me the sole right. I would write the book about his life and works and show everyone, so they might at last understand.

Yirawala's eyes blazed with some of the old fire as he sat on the edge of the bed and pulled out a box. Inside was the MBE medal. His voice was bitter. 'Gov'ment give me humbug, that's all. Him give me medal. Never give me land, help. Him never help you.'

Bobby said if the Government did the wrong thing we would take them to court and get the collection back.

Yirawala put his hands on both our heads and said, 'You two men help me properly, all the way. I go home soon, stop mining men, might be with spear, all Gunwinggu men.' They would protect the Lumahlumah caves and other sacred sites.

Out of the misery and grief, at least Yirawala would get his vehicle and goods, go home and make a stand. That is what he desperately wanted to do. This was the only way it could be done.

I left Croker Island with a heavy heart. There was still a faint hope that Mr Dexter would accept my proposal and help would be given to Yirawala as well.

On 28 March a message came in from Yirawala: he wanted to come to Darwin in two days' time to see the doctor. I immediately sent a ticket out to Croker Island for him. He did not come. Three days later Danny sent me a letter:

> Thanks for telling me all about Yirawala's fares, because Mr —— told that old man that he's not going on that plane that day.
>
> But we didn't get the medicines only the letter and the cheque but not medicines. I'll find out at the office about Yirawala's medicines.

I learned later from Bobby that his father was sad about my losing the collection but was glad to be going home at last. He went around telling everyone that he was going home and would stop the mining company. He seemed to be getting stronger, then he began to fade again at the end of March. He had wanted to come in for medical treatment prior to going back to the home country.

I received a telegram from the Secretary of Aboriginal Affairs, to say that he could see no way at this stage of assisting me to establish an Aboriginal teaching museum, because of financial restraints.

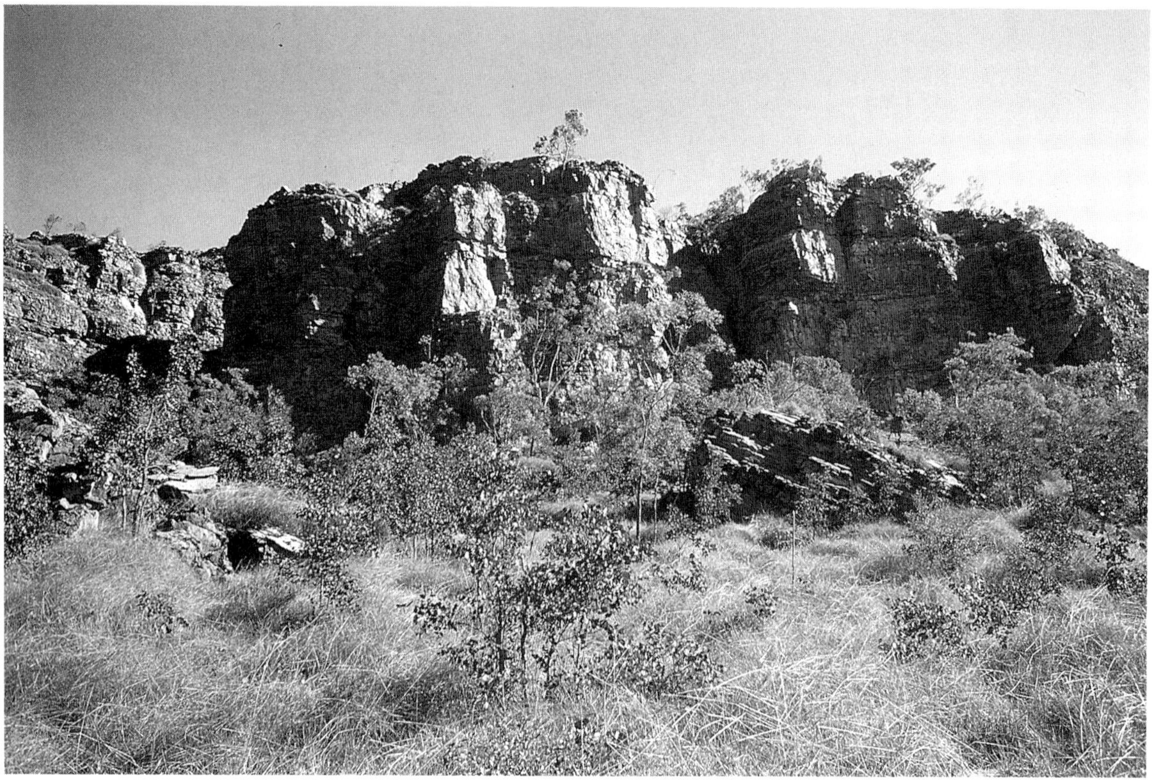

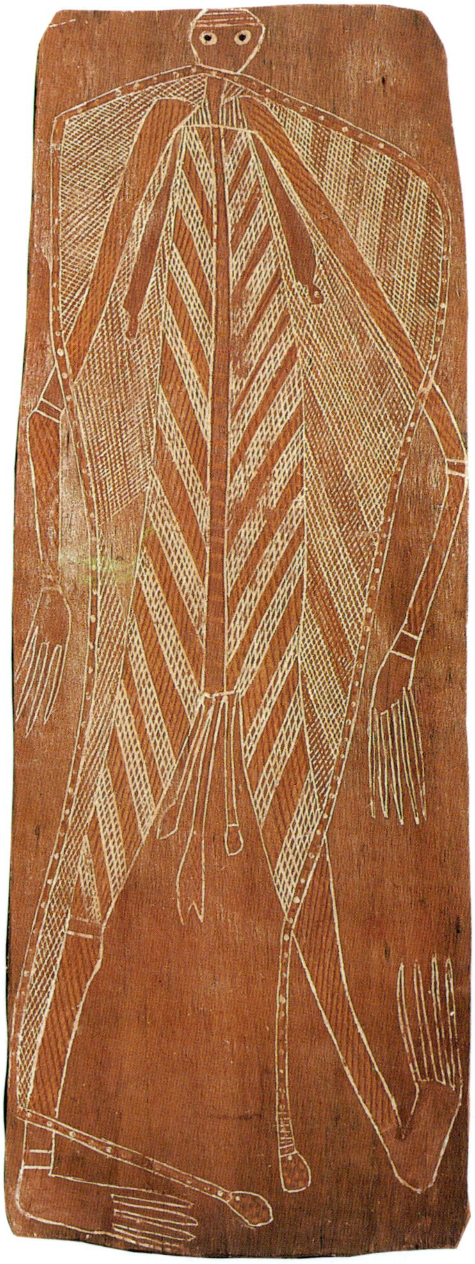

Plate 91 NAMORREN THE LIGHTNING MAN

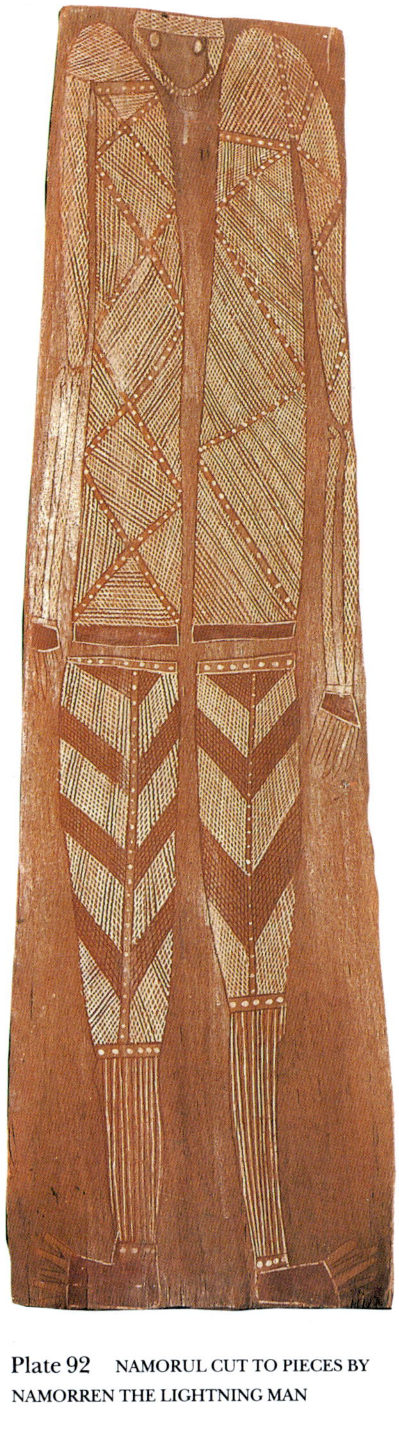

Plate 92 NAMORUL CUT TO PIECES BY NAMORREN THE LIGHTNING MAN

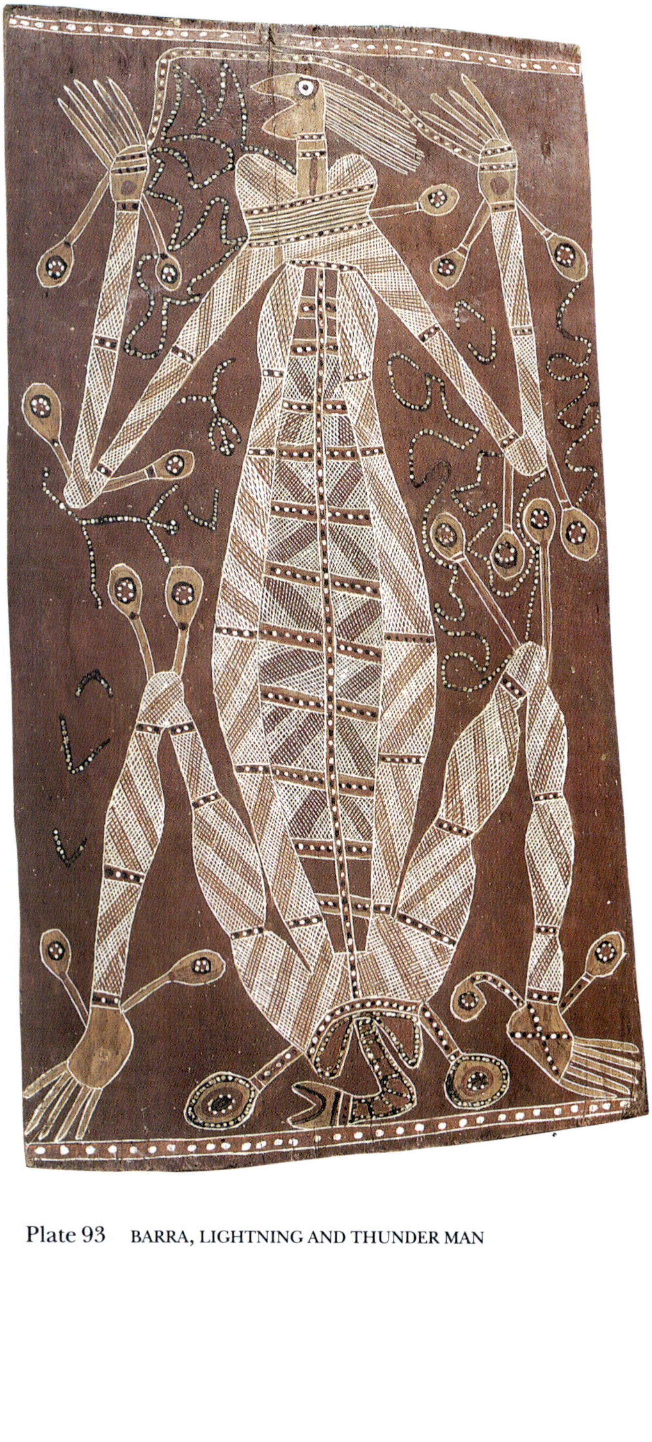

Plate 93 BARRA, LIGHTNING AND THUNDER MAN

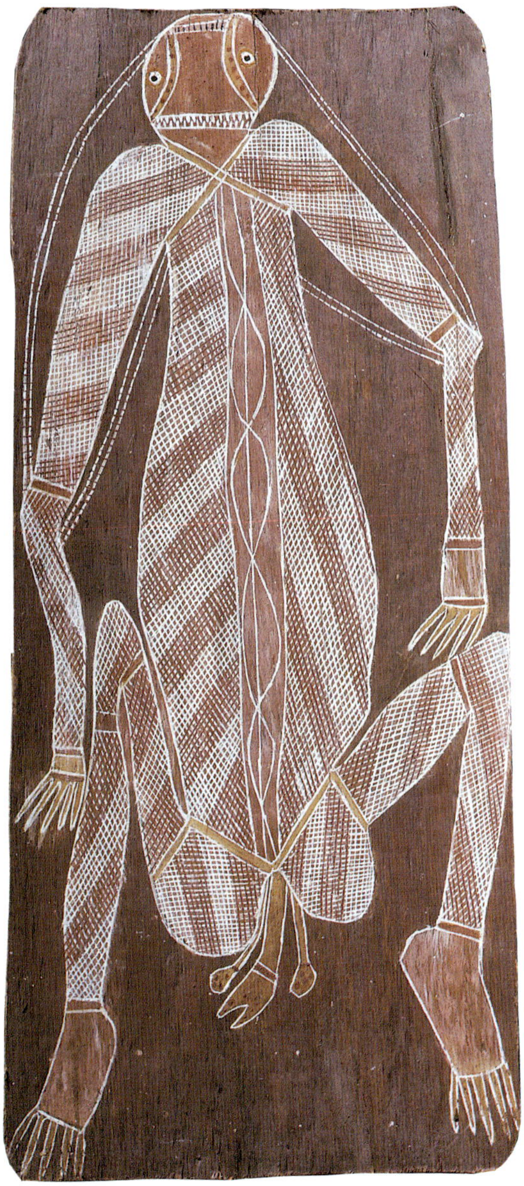

Plate 94 THE LIGHTNING MAN RESTING IN HIS CAVE DURING THE DRY SEASON

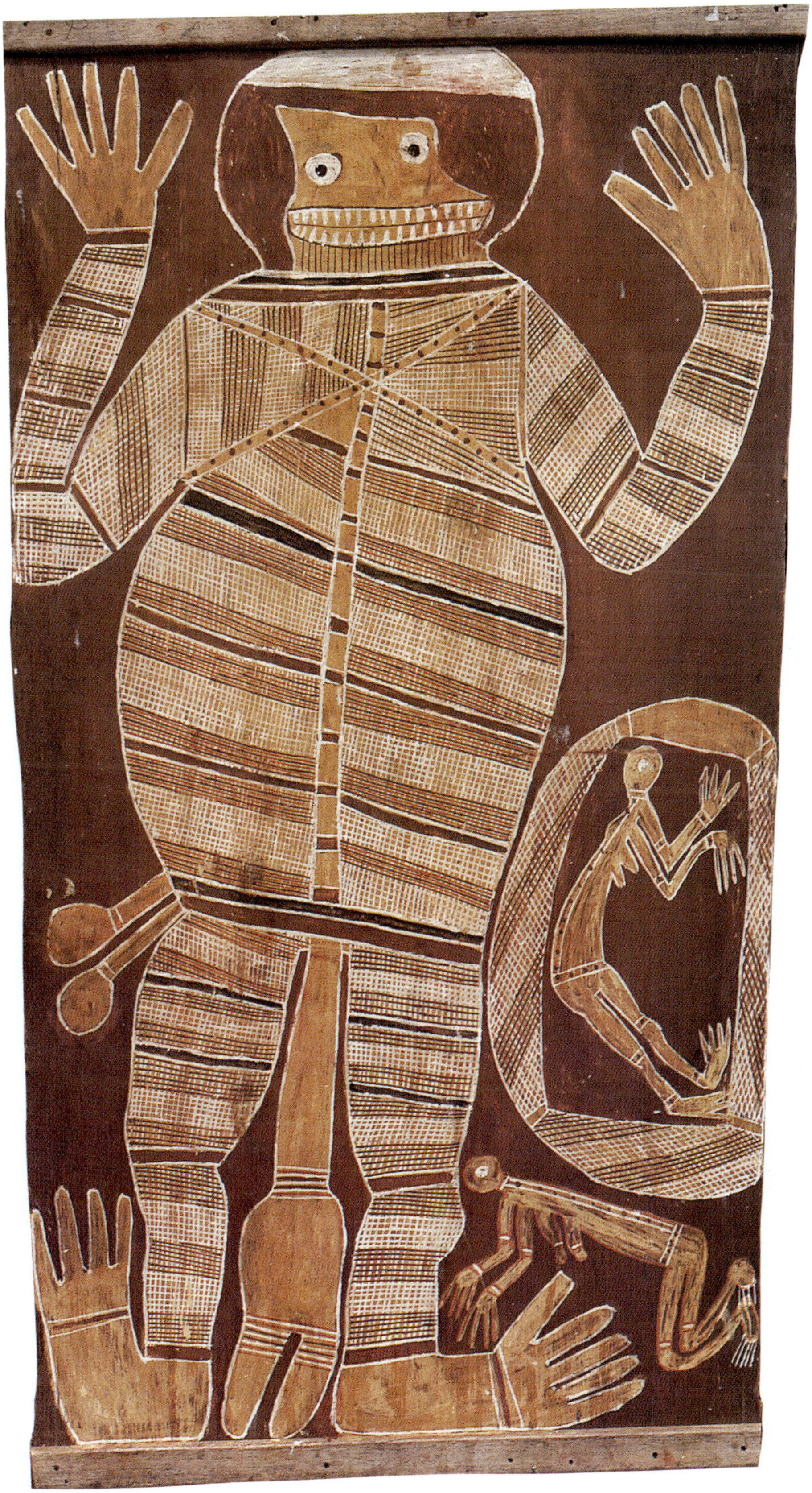

Plate 95 BEW-BEW THE GIANT, OR THE ORIGIN OF THE DIDJERIDU

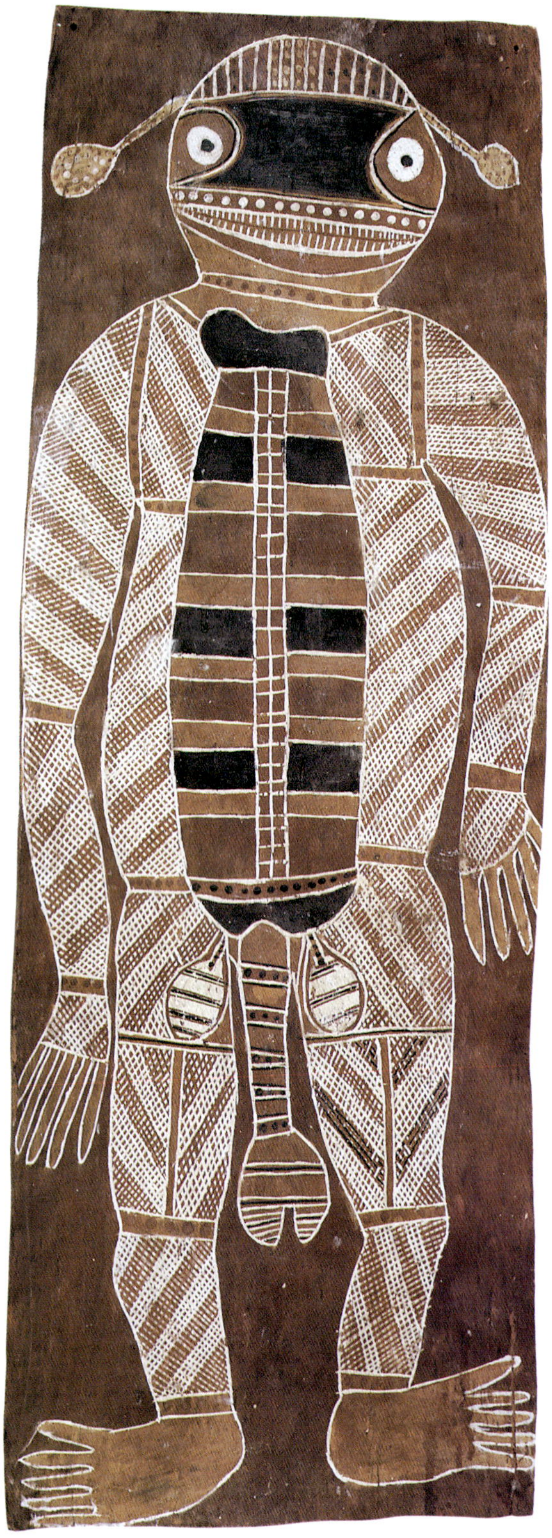

Plate 96 BOOMA-BOOMA THE BIG MAN

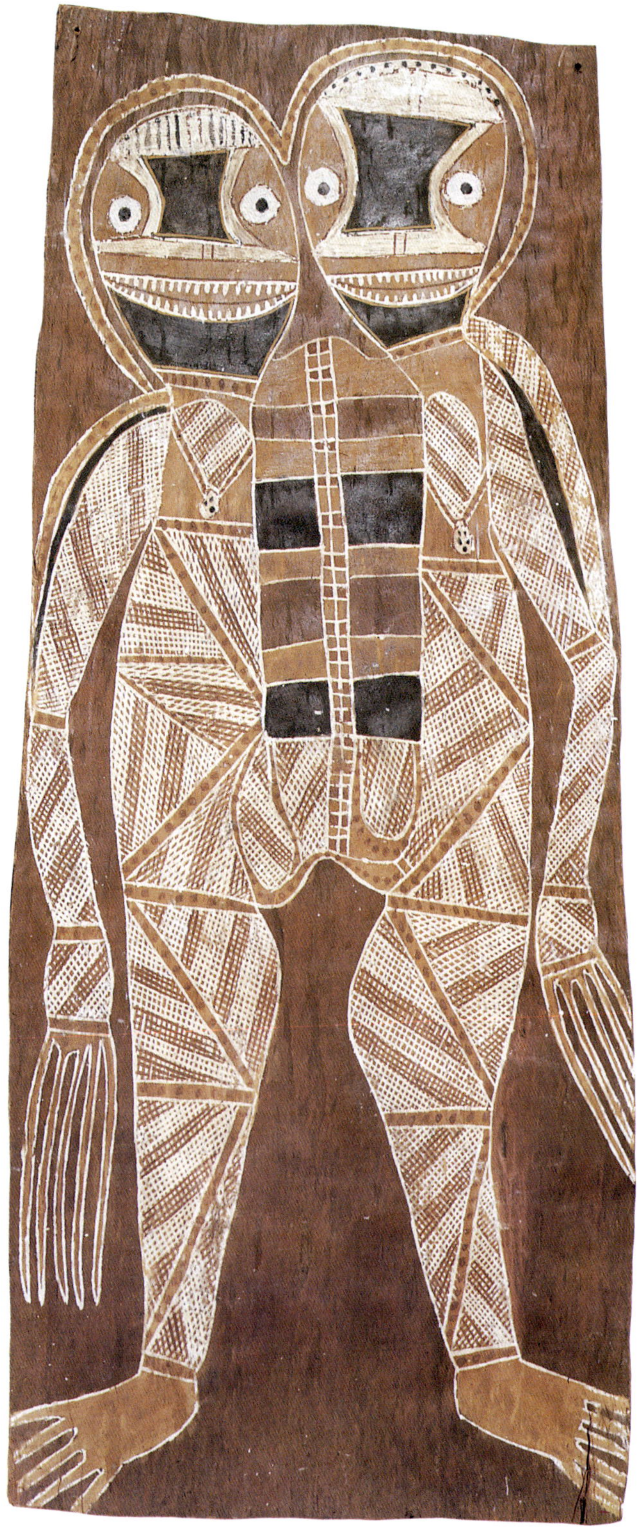

Plate 97 TWO-HEADED MONSTROUS WOMAN

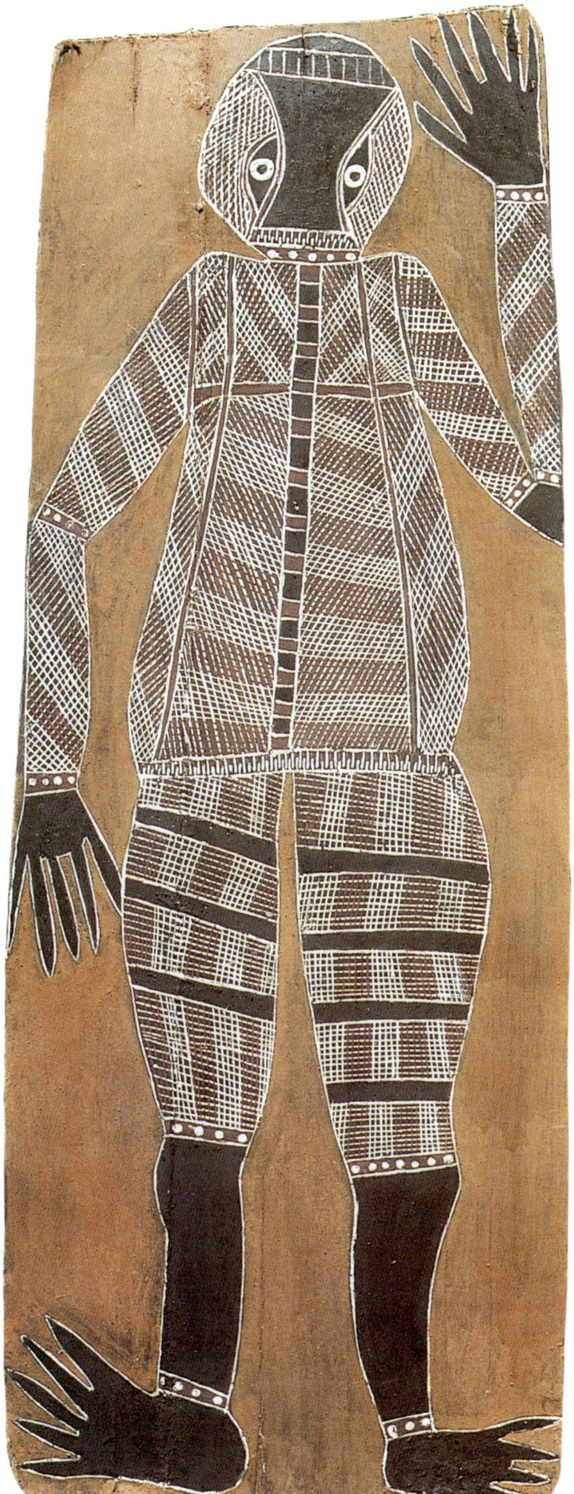

Plate 98 NAMARALTO, OR GORRORELLI

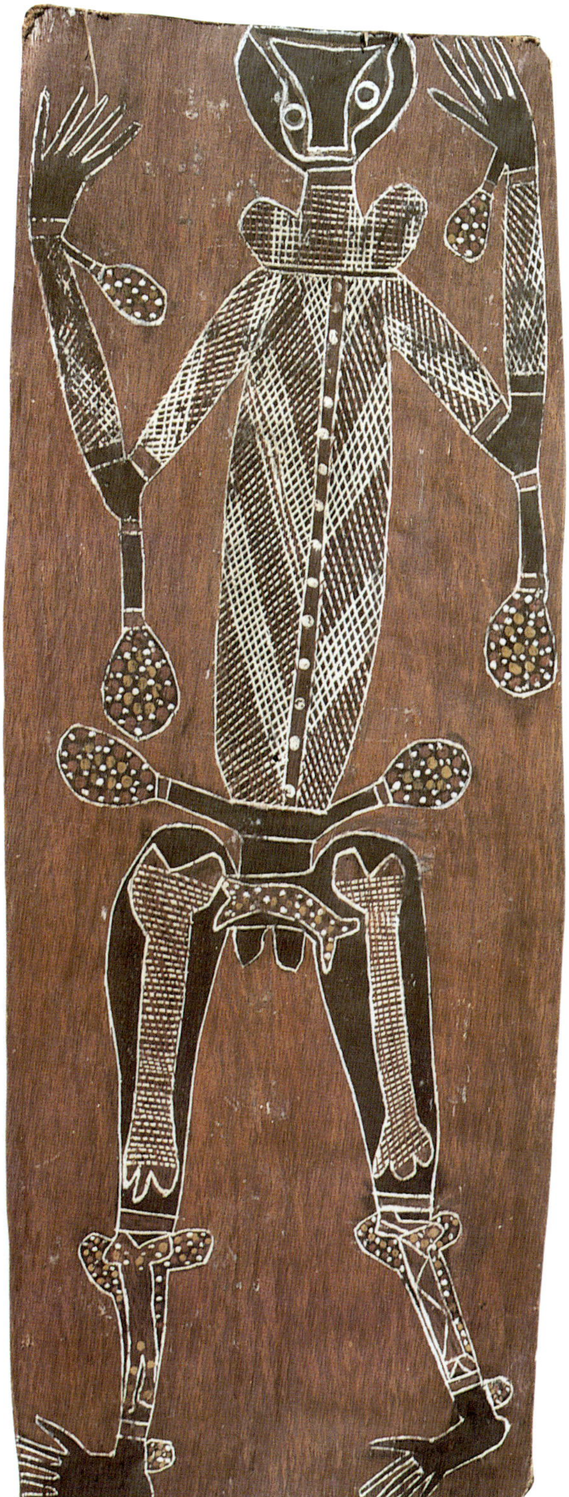

Plate 99 BOLIG-BOLIG THE HONEY MAN

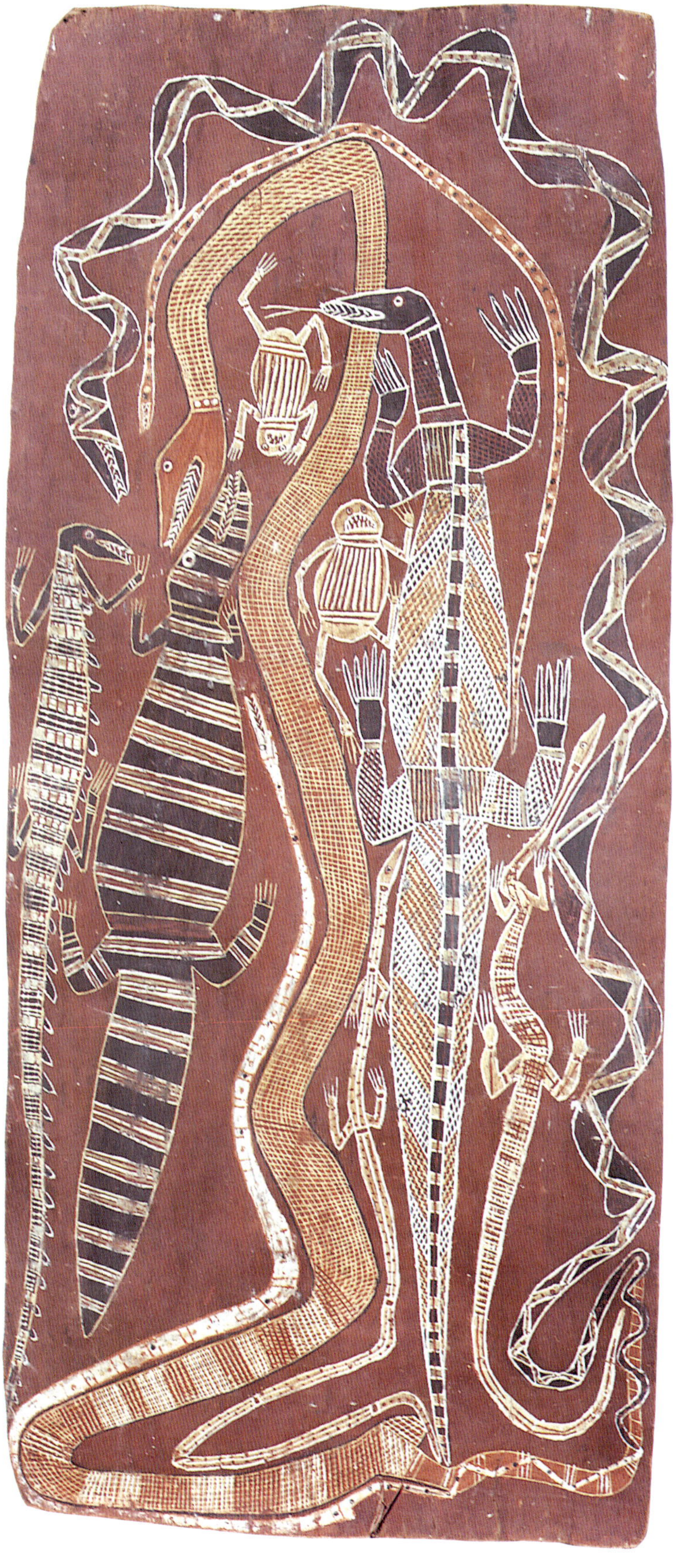

Plate 100 DAADBI AND GULAWAN

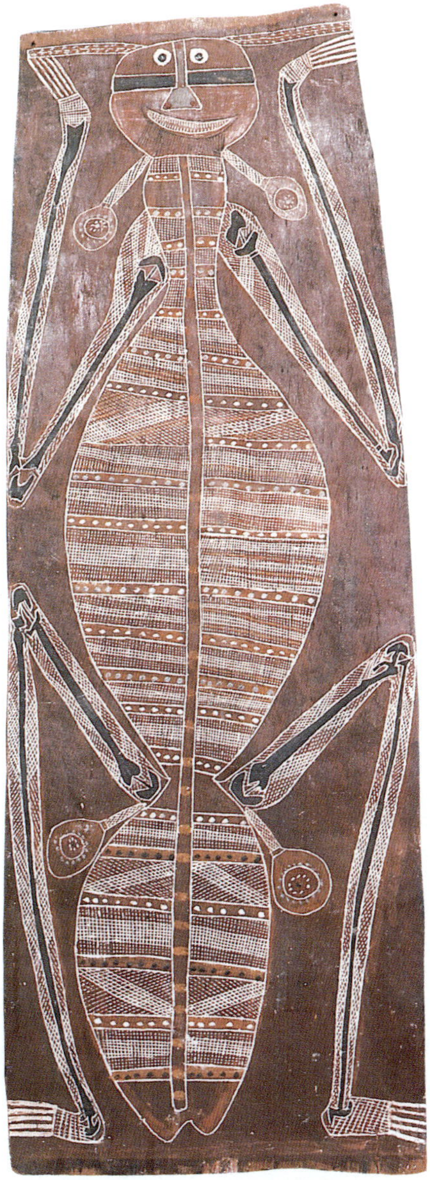

Plate 101 THE PRAYING-MANTIS MAN

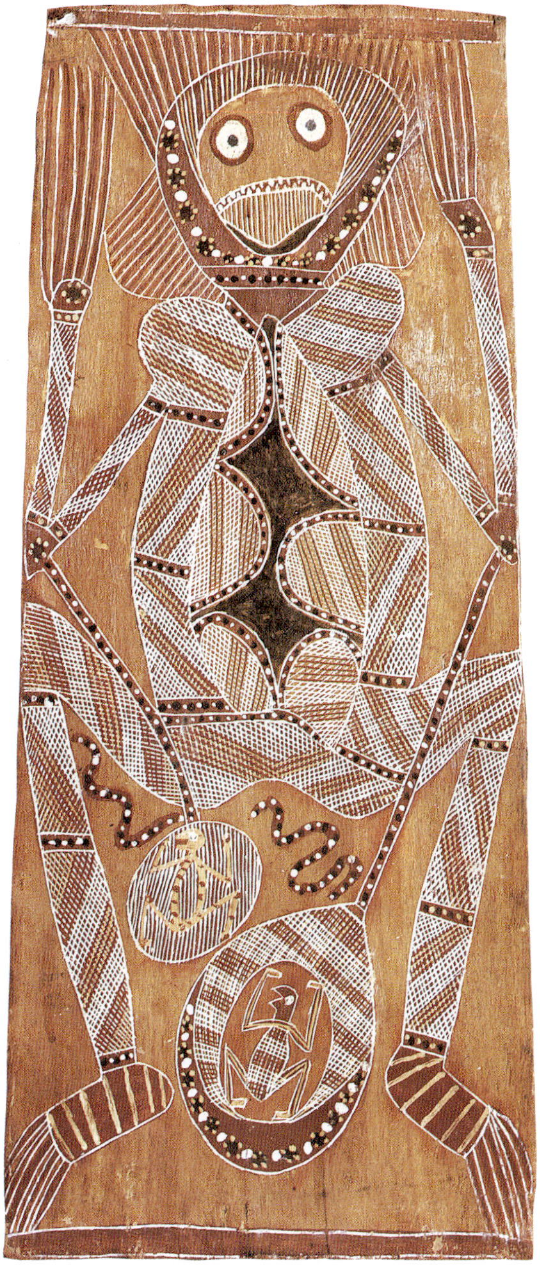

Plate 102 NAMARRGINE THE BIRD MAN

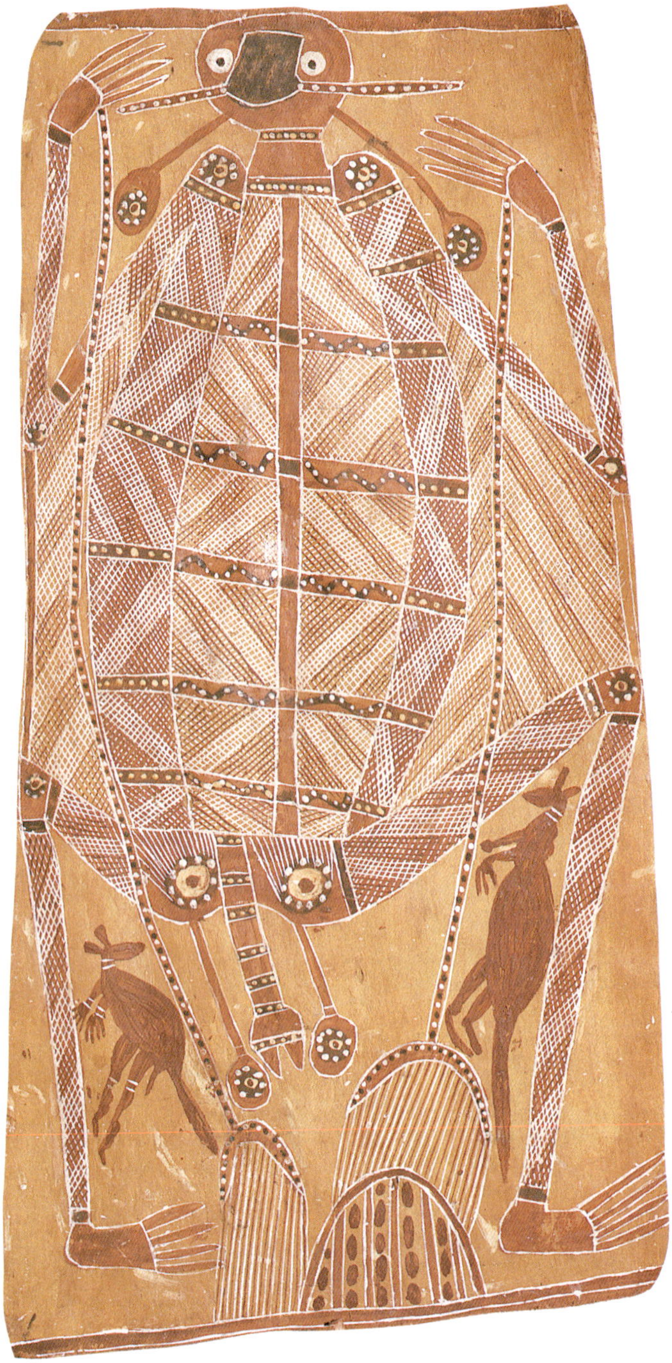

Plate 103 NAMARRGINE THE BIRD MAN

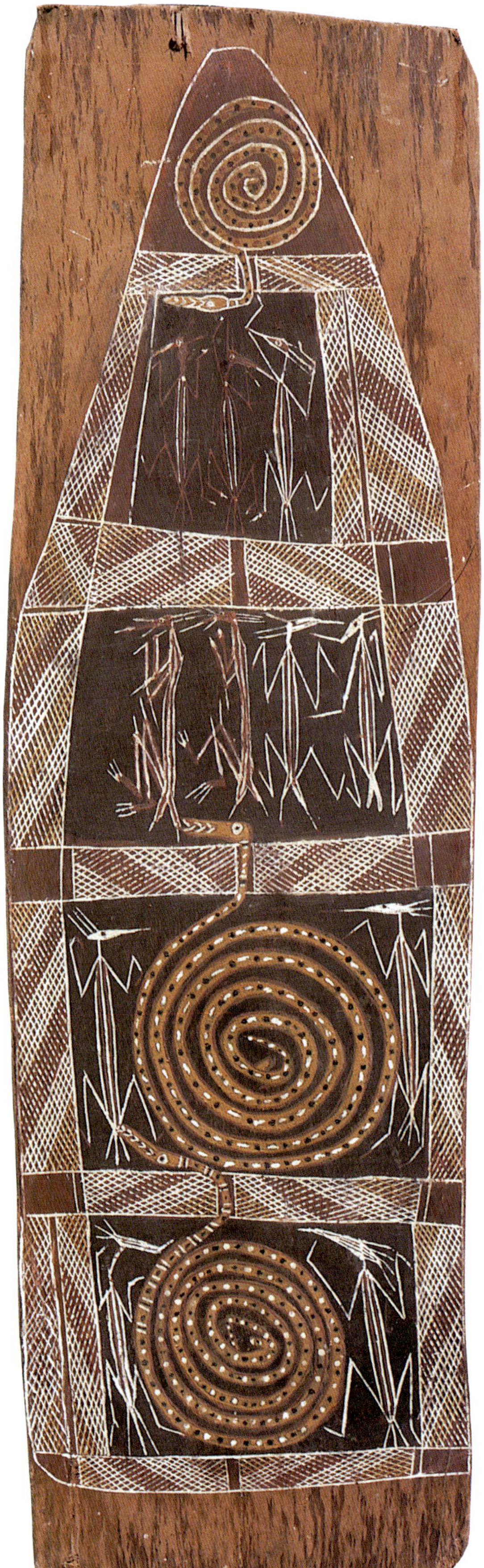

Plate 104 THE SNAKES AND THE MOSQUITO PEOPLE

Chapter 14
My fire has gone out, my spirit is going home

Five days later my husband came from Sydney to visit us, then, on 12 April, Bobby came to Darwin to say that Yirawala was sick with some sort of stomach upset, perhaps food poisoning, but the new health worker on Croker Island was not a nursing sister, just a nursing aide. He had asked her to call a medical plane but she had not thought it necessary. She gave him some white-coloured medicine instead. I immediately rang Air Medical and asked them to evacuate Yirawala. They reminded me that only a nurse on the spot could do that and so far no request had come from Croker Island. I rang the Darwin Mission Headquarters and asked them to contact Croker Island about Yirawala on their next medical schedule.

Later Mission Headquarters informed me that Yirawala was all right, but I was very uneasy and called the Mission Headquarters again, asking them to contact the superintendent at Croker Island.

I received a telegram: 'Yirawala still sick but has improved a great deal since Bobby saw him on Monday.' It was signed by the superintendent's wife, Croker Island.

I booked a charter plane and told Bobby to bring his father in to Darwin. I would meet the plane and take him straight to hospital.

At sunset Amanda and I waited for the plane to return from Croker Island. We had made up a bed in the back of the Landrover in readiness.

We watched the plane land. The pilot opened the door and closed it again. I ran up to him, demanding to know why he had not brought Bobby and Yirawala in. He said, 'The old bloke was too crook' and in any case his was 'not a medical plane and not equipped to carry seriously ill people.' He had waited for some time at Croker Island and had to leave. He was afraid of losing the light.

I raced home and sent a telegram to Bobby saying I knew Yirawala's health had worsened and to urgently get him in to Darwin. After this my phone went dead, unaccountably.

I went across the road and asked a neighbour if I could use his phone to send a telegram. The telegram was addressed to the Superintendent, Croker Island, Outpost radio Darwin: 'Yirawala urgently needs medical attention please assist with evacuation.'

On Friday 16 April Bobby and the superintendent sent a telegram to say that Yirawala had a relapse and was very sick.

I rang the Air Medical again, in desperation begging them to send out a plane. They repeated that no request had come from Croker Island. I decided to go out there by charter and bring him in. It was the Easter weekend and no charter was available until midday on Sunday.

A terrible feeling of dread took hold of me. I began vomiting, doubled up with stomach cramps, as if I had been poisoned. Cecil took me to the hospital, where the doctor said there was nothing wrong with me, except acute stress. I was in tears and said to Cecil, 'Yirawala is dying.' He told me not to be silly.

At 9 a.m. on Sunday morning there was a knock on the door. A taxi driver stood there with two telegrams. Somebody at the local Post Office had some compassion. Since my phone was still out of order, the Post Office had sent the telegrams by taxi.

One telegram read : 'Yirawala passed away early today Saturday.' The second one said: 'Double funeral Yirawala and Yaragu 3 p.m. today Sunday 18.4.76.'

Amanda started crying hysterically and I collapsed. Cecil brought me round and gave me a brandy. He tried to comfort me and Amanda, and was deeply moved by Yirawala's death. He said permit or no permit we would all go out to the funeral.

Flying over the Arafura sea my tears kept flowing. My heart ached in a black void of pain. Oh, God, how cruel and unjust, that he should die on the eve of going home to the tribal land he loved so much and sought to defend to the last. Now, only his spirit would ever go home. A courageous voice had been silenced. A great intellect extinguished and a noble heart stilled. His fire had gone out.

The plane landed on the mission airstrip and we were picked up in a truck. As we drove to the camp I said to the driver, 'Why didn't you call the Air Medical plane?' He turned his head away and made no reply.

As we walked towards the canvas awning where Yirawala's body lay, grieving relatives came to meet us, clinging onto our hands and throwing their arms around us as we mourned together. A large crowd of grieving people swayed to and fro. Some cried aloud in their pain and cut themselves until blood flowed. Others intervened to prevent serious injury. Lines of men painted white surged backwards and forwards as the song men beat the clapsticks and sang the death dirges.

David Gumaraitj and Brisbane supported Yirawala's youngest sons, Danny and Andrew, holding them in their arms.

Bobby was supporting his older sister, Margaret, preventing her from gashing her head. He put his arms round me and we wept together. His eyes were filled with pain and he trembled all over. I asked him about the medical plane and he said they had begged for it, even threatened, to no avail.

Mary and Margaret sat under the awning, holding the shrouded body of their dead husband. They pulled me by the hands to sit down with them to mourn, then they placed the body of Yirawala in my arms which was more than I could bear. I felt cold as if I was falling into a deep well. The sound of the clapsticks grew terribly loud then everything started to fade. They removed the frail body and I recovered. Only a faint giddiness remained.

Suddenly, out from the crowd stepped an old man, his tall frame etched against the sky, white hair blowing in the wind. He leaned on a twisted walking stick, his sightless eyes turned towards the body of Yirawala, his dearest friend and fellow painter. Mijau-Mijau had made many bark paintings, until an eye disease robbed him of his sight. Now he stood with bowed head, tears streaming unchecked, gnarled hands clutching his walking stick. He moved slowly forward and people made way. When he reached the awning he lifted his head and a loud cry of anguish burst from his lips and his body shook like a storm-smitten tree. His family led him away.

A surge of wind from the sea threw sand and ashes against the tin huts and rattled the iron roofs and the cries of the mourners and mortuary songs were blown on the wind to the distant trickle of mission staff making their way to the little church for the Easter Sunday service. Faintly I could hear the organ and the Christian hymns for Jesus who was crucified and rose again.

David Gumaraitj said that Yaragu, Yirawala's nephew, aged only 50 and always a strong man, had taken ill the same time as Yirawala and died the same day. Yaragu's body was with his relatives under a separate awning. Both men would be buried in a small graveyard on the hillside. Bobby was the grave digger for his father. Two trucks stood ready to convey the bodies to their last resting place.

As I talked with David and Bobby a Methodist Minister in full dress came to discuss Yirawala's burial arrangements, and offered to perform a Christian burial. David recoiled angrily, saying his father was not a Christian and would be buried according to his own religion. Bobby almost lost control, his face working with sorrow and fury. 'Haven't you done enough to him?' Then fiercely, 'Don't any of you touch him.' The Minister approached Yaragu's family and they somewhat reluctantly agreed to a Christian burial.

A Christian burial for Yirawala would have been the final indignity and would have made it impossible for his family to lift his bones at a later date and convey them back to the family cave. His spirit would never return to its Dreaming place, but wander forever in a dark nether world, lost and alone.

The sad procession of trucks and mourners wound their way to the burial place where two graves had been dug, only a few feet apart.

Bobby was standing in the grave, shovelling out the last of the sand and waiting to receive his father's body, which was wrapped in Yirawala's bedding. A coffin was not requested.

Yirawala's relatives sang and danced the whale and fish mortuary songs with spears in their hands as his body was gently carried from the truck and placed on the ground. The last rites were chanted by Kelly Borgordubhu, Peter Mahlunwunggu and other tribal elders.

Nearby, the Minister gave the Christian burial service for Yaragu, and mission staff stood around singing hymns, with Bibles and sunshades in their hands.

The hymns and mortuary songs mingled as the bodies were lowered into the graves.

David and Kelly passed Yirawala's body to Bobby, who laid it to rest. Other men assisted to shovel the sand amid the sound of singing and crying.

Danny broke down by the grave and was comforted by Brisbane, who put an arm around him and led him away. Andrew, the youngest son, was comforted by Margaret Monanggu, his mother.

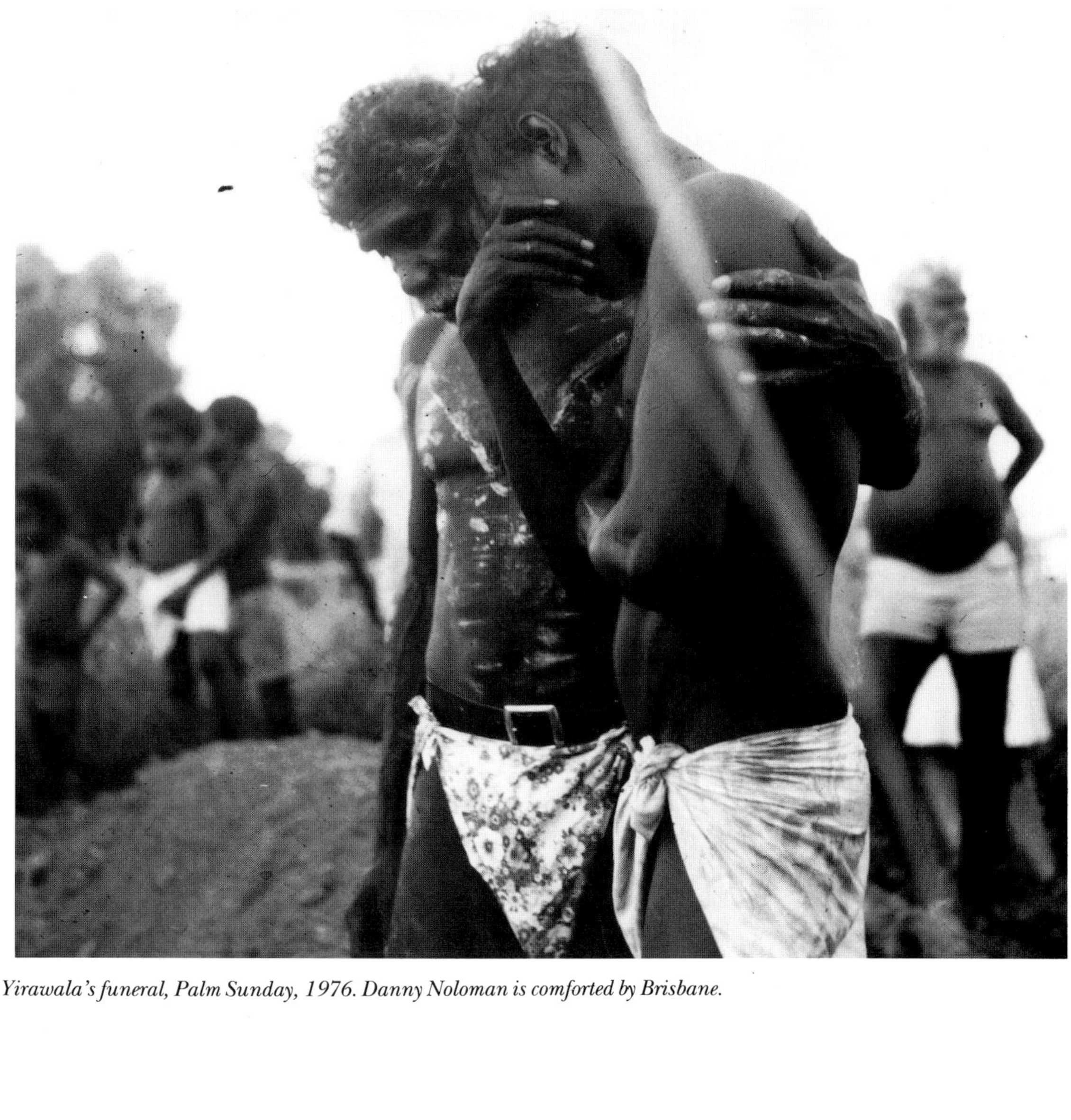

Yirawala's funeral, Palm Sunday, 1976. Danny Noloman is comforted by Brisbane.

Before we left Croker Island, Bobby said that the day before he died, his father had said, 'If me die, you, David, my sons, take over, go home in truck make station Marugulidban. Stop mining mob.' The sons promised to carry on. The dream would not die.

Bobby said he would come in to talk things over in two or three weeks' time, in between ceremonies for his father.

After the funeral Cecil went back to Sydney, where he was writing film scripts.

A week after Yirawala was buried we heard strange noises in the night, sounds of soft footsteps, sighing, and an occasional cough, then crying and whispering. Sometimes there was knocking on the walls and doors but nothing visible, until early one morning, just as it was getting light, Amanda came running into my room very frightened. She said something woke her up, something very cold on her face. She saw a flickering shadow and heard a faint voice say, 'Only mummy and you worry for me.' She slept in my room after that.

I sent messages to Kelly Borgordubhu and other elders at Oenpelli and Croker Island, asking for help to send the spirit home.

Bobby Joran came in to organise men to smoke the house and land and perform the appropriate ritual. After supper he went downstairs to sleep. I heard a loud cry and he came leaping up the stairs stuttering out, 'He's there, sitting on the bed, like smoke. I can see right through him.' That night he slept on the dining-room floor with the lights on, after which he went away to organise elders from Oenpelli and elsewhere to cleanse the house and people from contact with the dead man.

While we waited for the men to arrive Mr Dexter Daniels, an Aboriginal friend from Roper River, came to see us. I told him not to sleep in the room under the house as it might be haunted. He laughed and said he didn't believe it.

In the night there was hammering on the front door and Dexter calling out to be let in. He was shaking and said he was asleep until somebody touched him on the shoulder. He looked down and in the half light saw a long thin hand but no body. He also slept upstairs with the lights on.

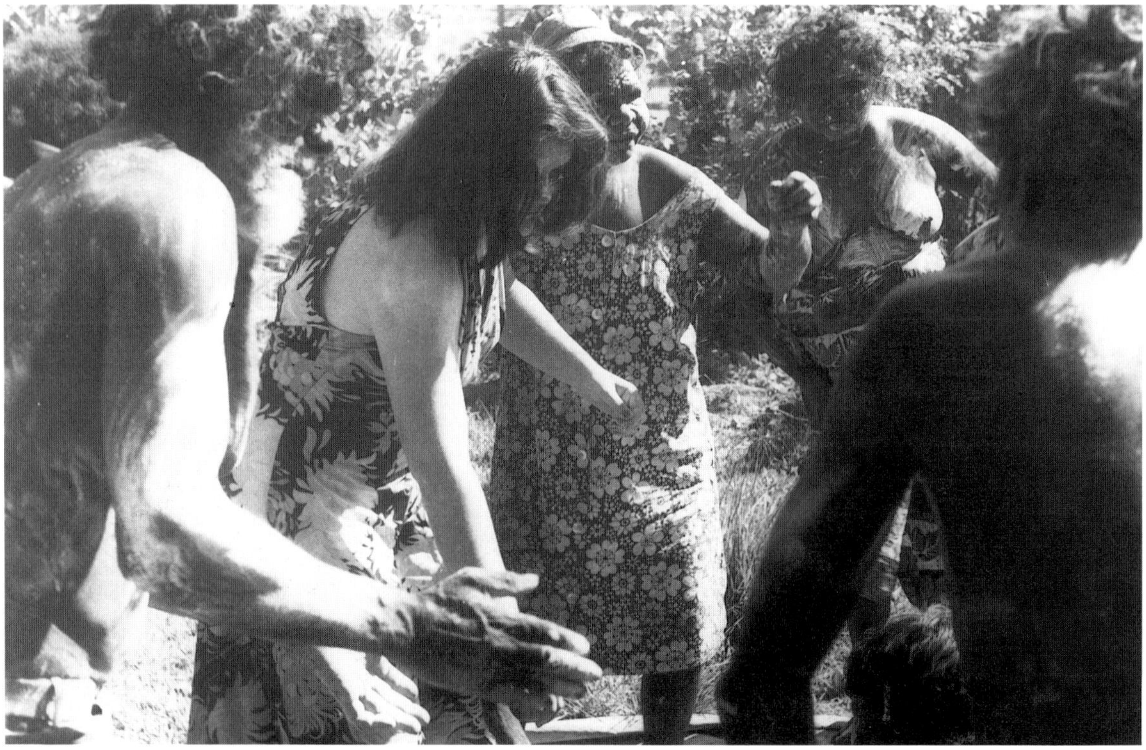

Ceremony to send Yirawala's presence to its home country. Amanda dancing with women after being ritually washed and painted in sacred 'well'.

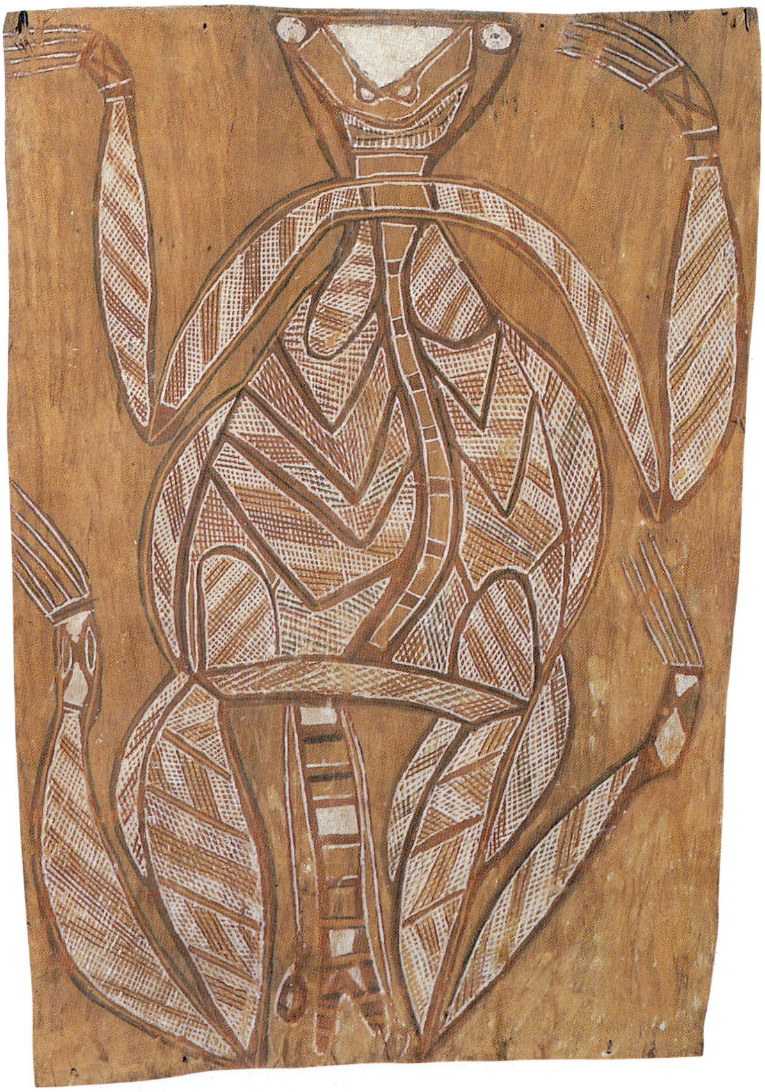

Plate 105 MOWANI THE CANNIBAL GIANT

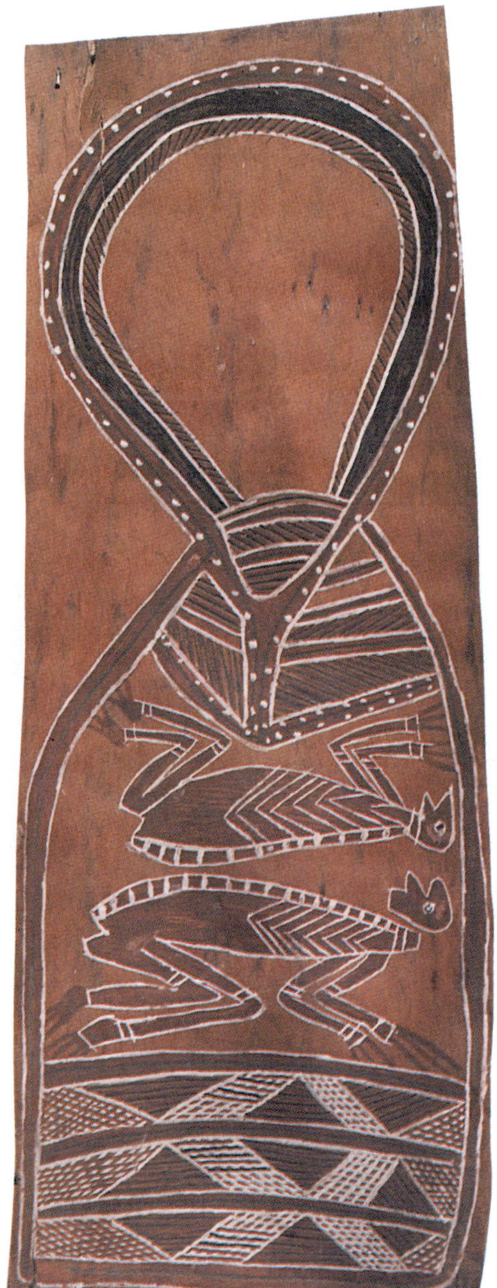

Plate 106 GIRLS IN DILLY BAG

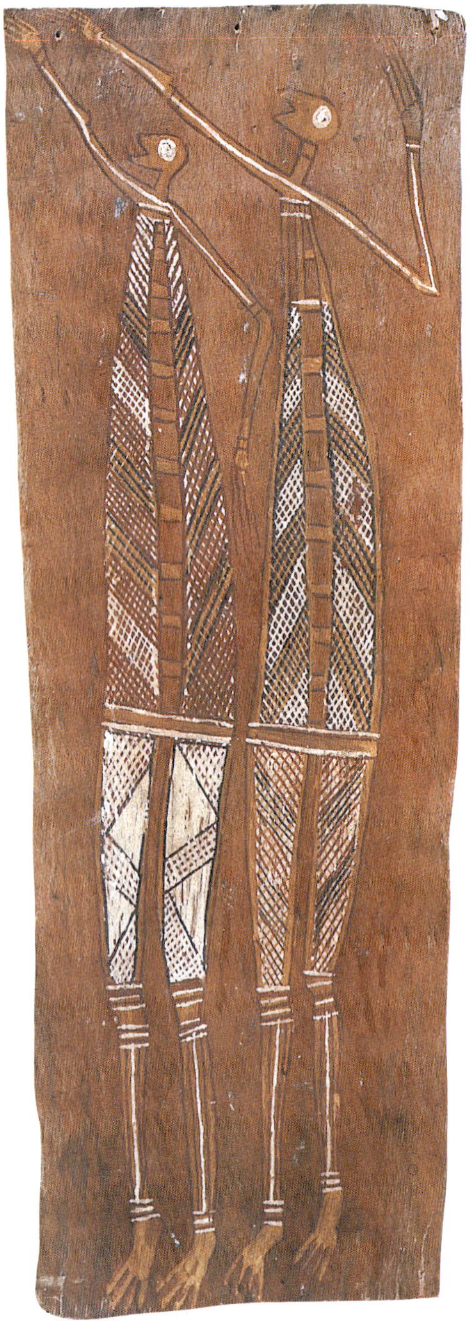

Plate 107 BAT AND WAGTAIL POINTING THE WAY TO MOWANI

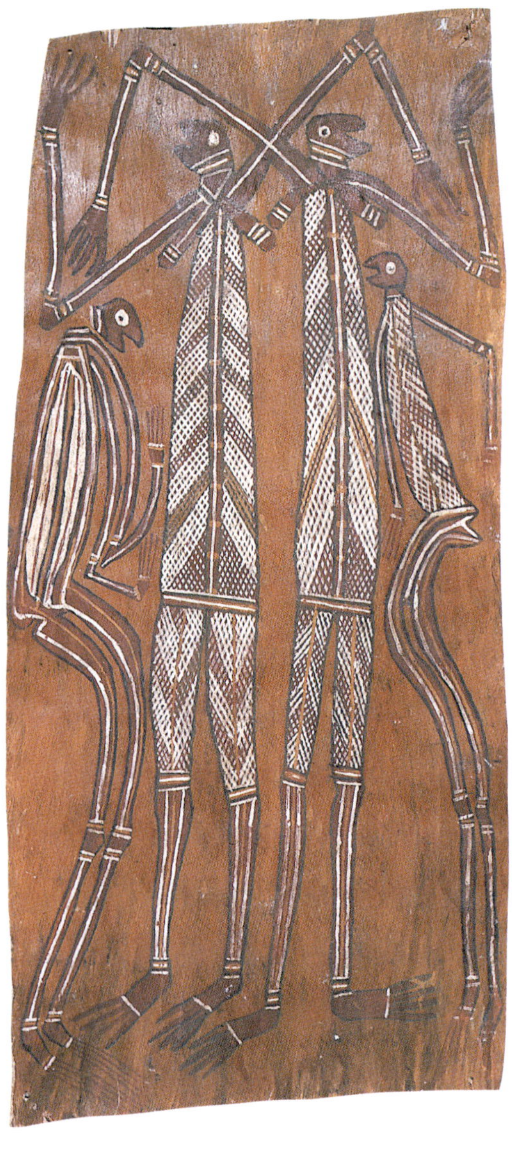

Plate 108 SPIRITS OF THE DEAD MOTHER AND HER BABY RETURN TO HER MOTHER AND GRANDMOTHER, WHO MOURN OVER THEM

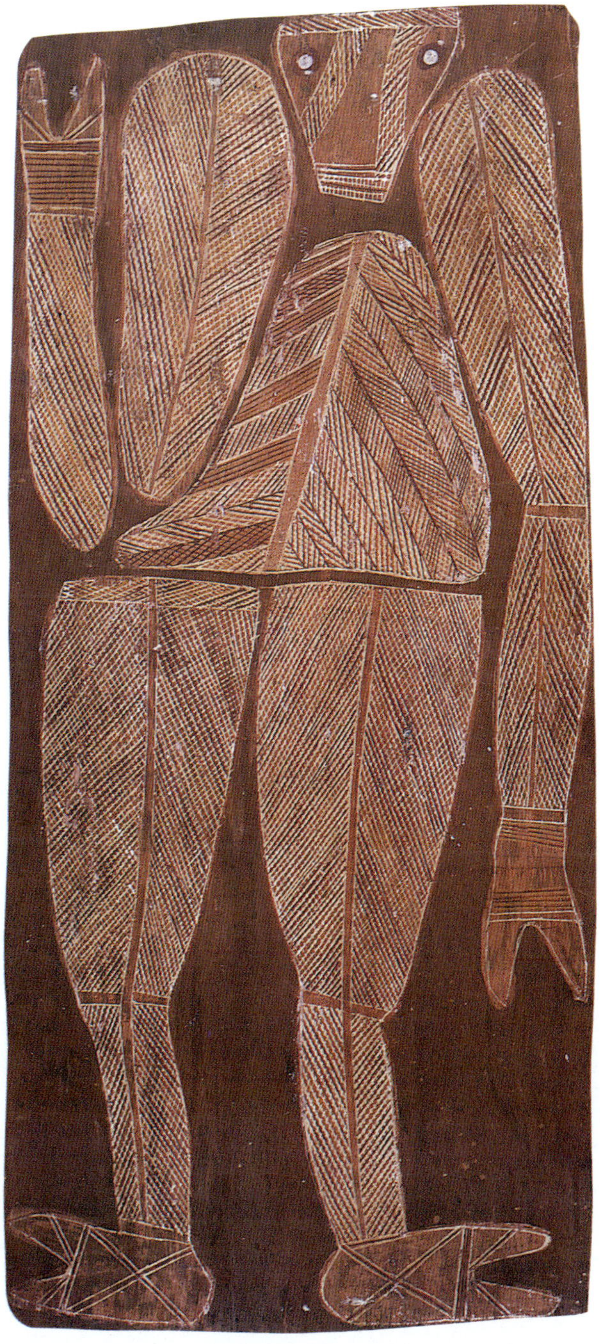

Plate 109 MOWANI THE GIANT DEAD AND CUT UP

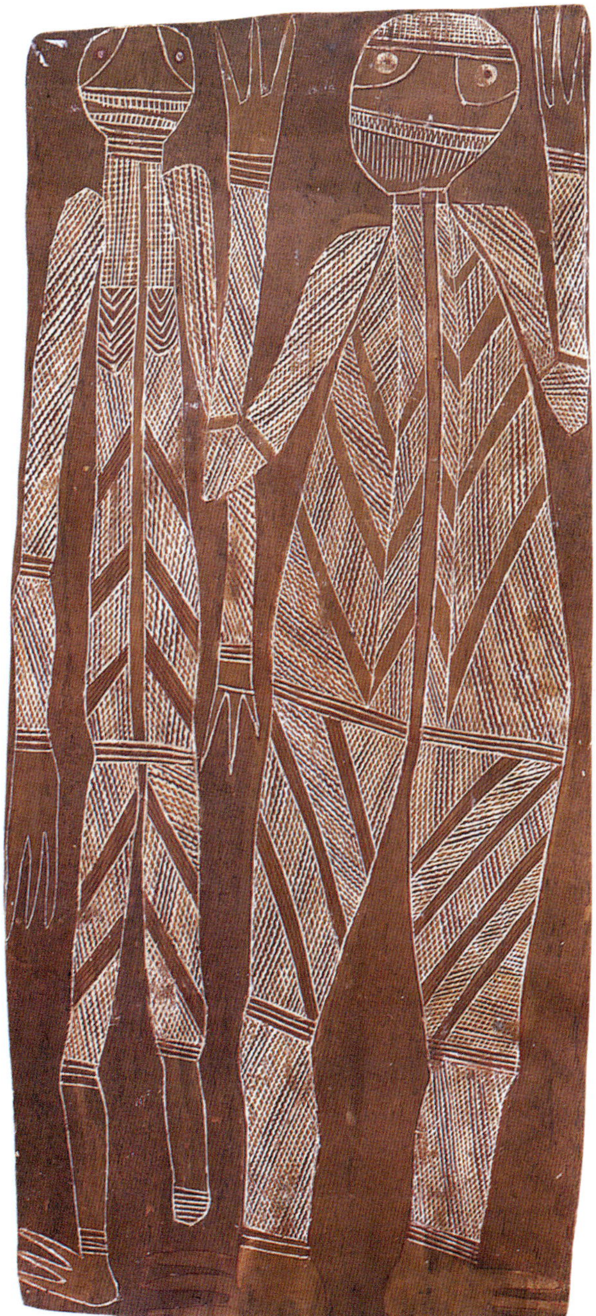

Plate 110 BAT AND WAGTAIL AFTER THE BATTLE

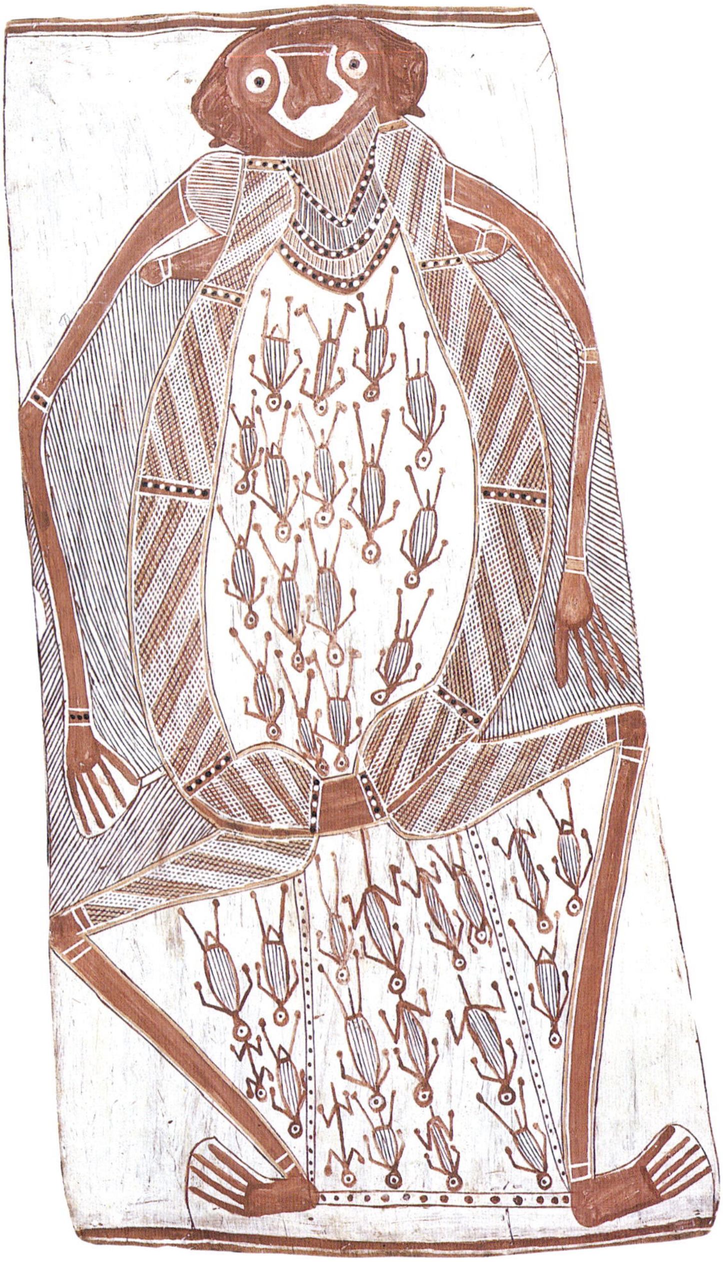

Plate 111 MARALAITJ THE EARTH MOTHER GIVING BIRTH TO THE TRIBES IN THE BOUCAUT BAY AREA

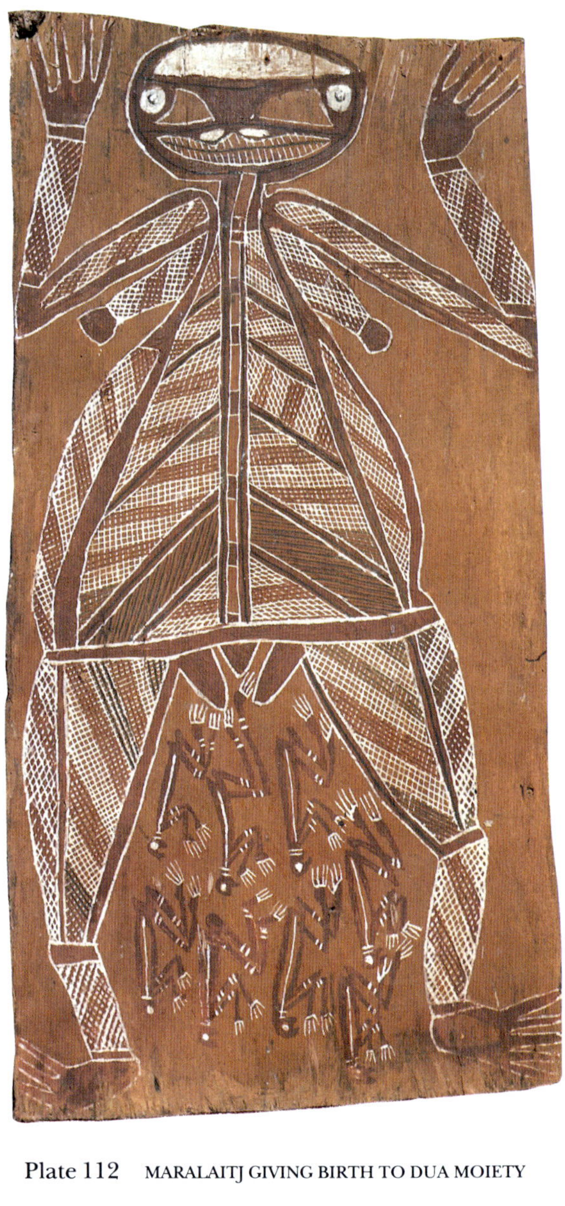

Plate 112 MARALAITJ GIVING BIRTH TO DUA MOIETY

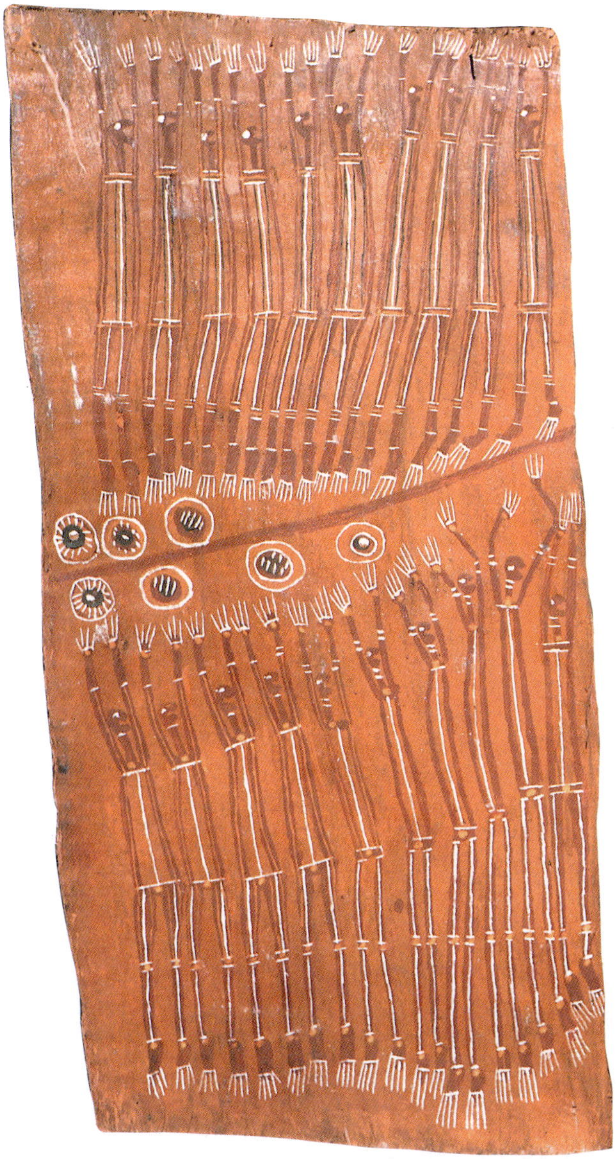

Plate 113 JIRITJA MOIETY DIVIDED INTO SKINS

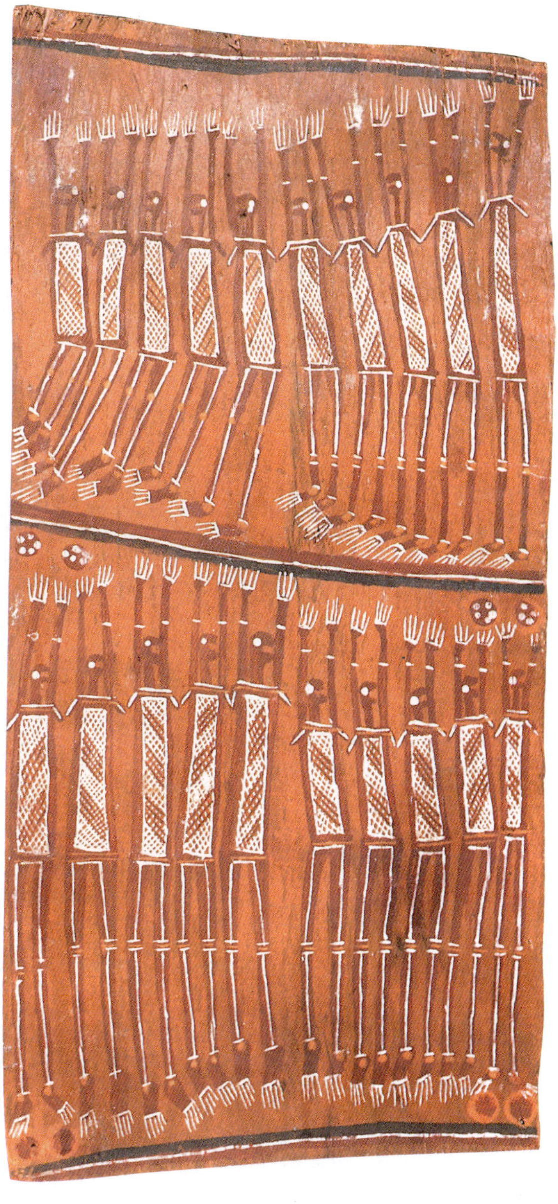

Plate 114 DUA MOIETY DIVIDED INTO SKINS

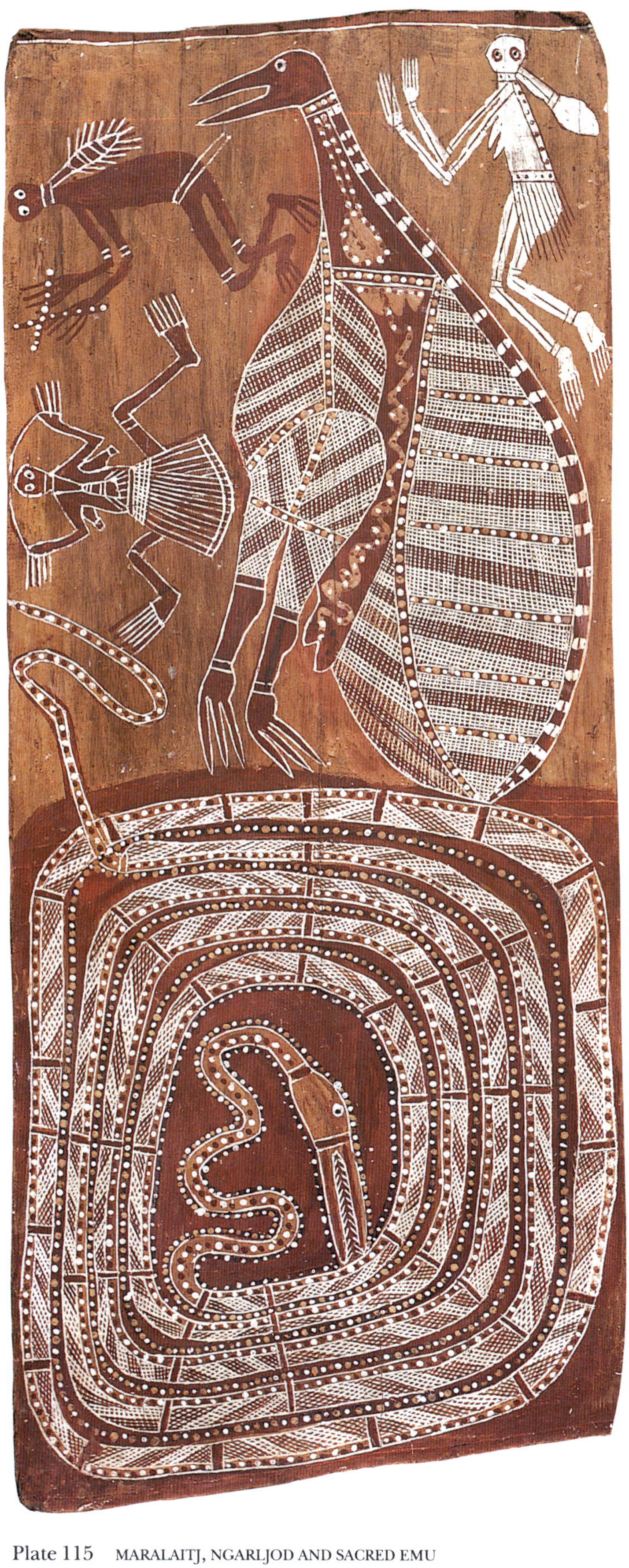

Plate 115 MARALAITJ, NGARLJOD AND SACRED EMU

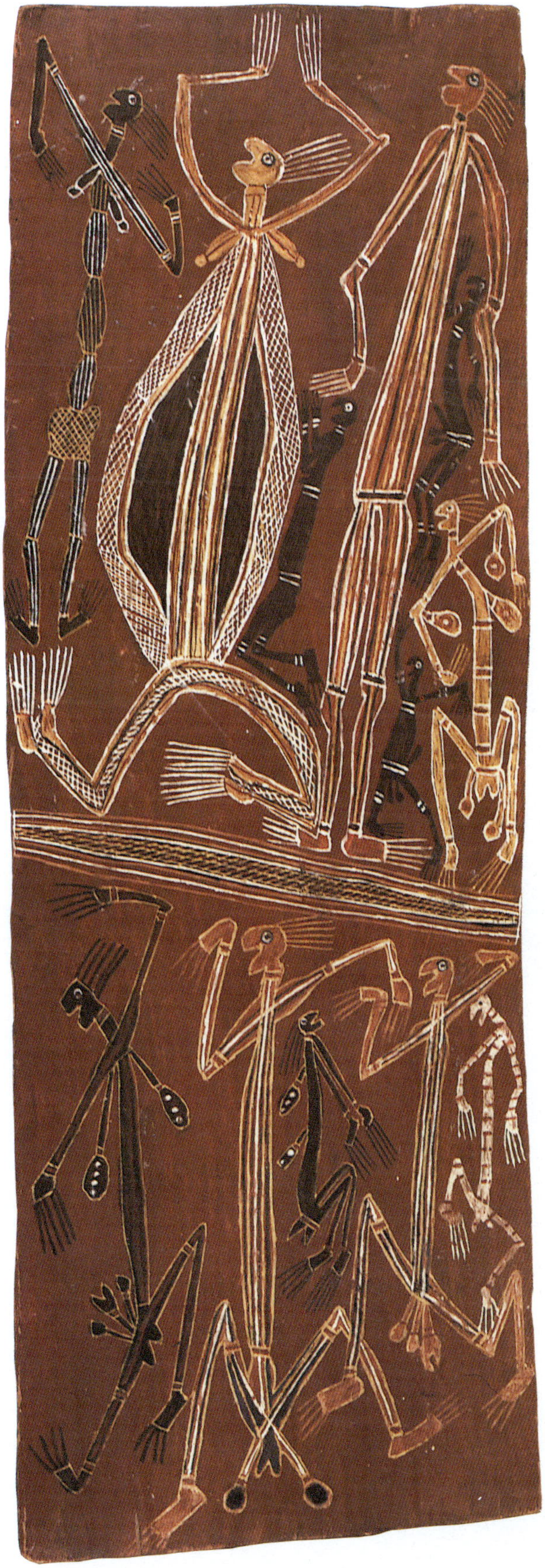

Plate 116 MARALAITJ AND HER WOMEN: FERTILITY DANCE

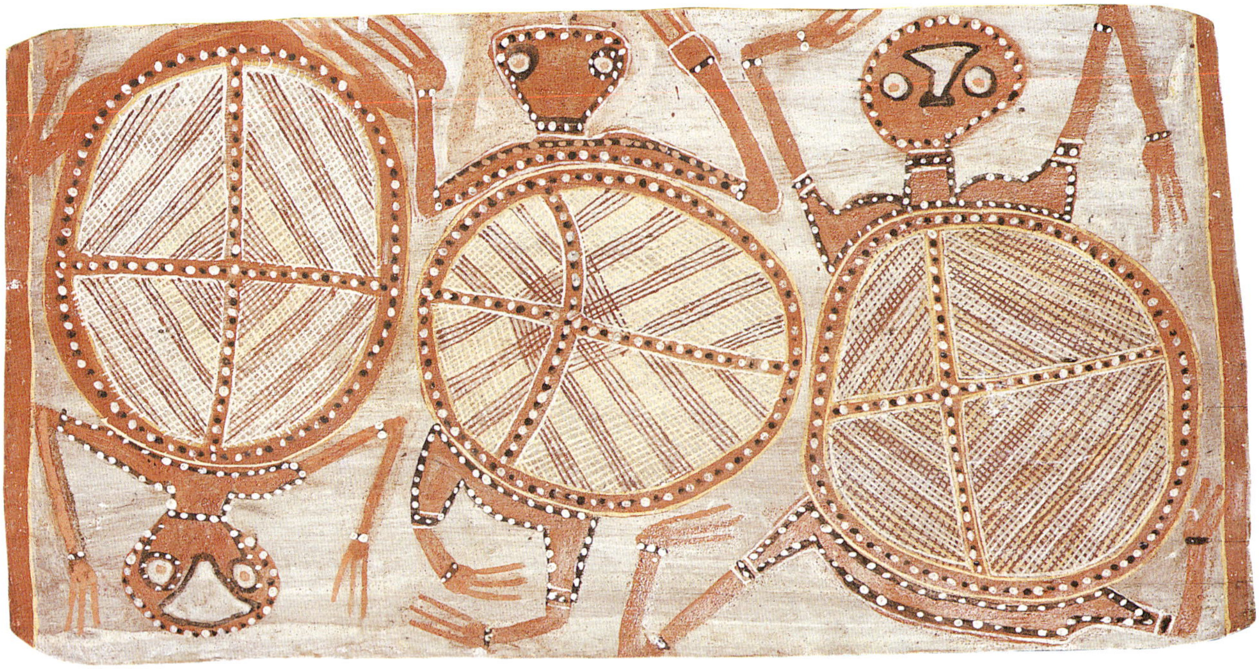

Plate 117 BABY-DREAMING WATERHOLES

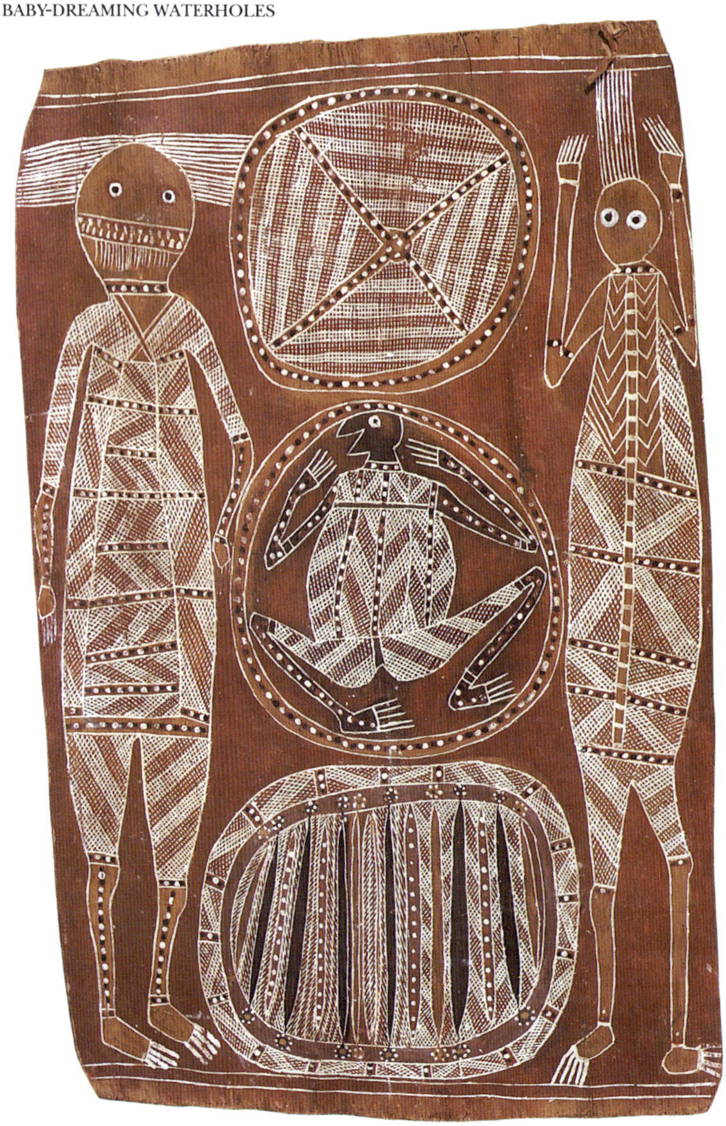

Plate 118 BABY-DREAMING WELLS, AND CREATOR BEINGS

No Aborigines would come near the house and we waited impatiently for Bobby and the elders to come.

A few days later two truckloads of painted men arrived. They unloaded piles of ironwood leaves and placed them around the house and land. The men chanted as they lit the leaves, and acrid smoke blew in and around the house. An old man with burning bundles of leaves sang and gestured to the four corners. Wreaths of smoke blew around the remains of Yirawala's hut and hung like ribbons in the tree branches. The old medicine man was telling the spirit to go home to its Dreaming and be at peace.

Men and women danced around the house, then a symbolic sacred well was made on the front lawn. Amanda and I in turn stood in this 'well' and were ritually cleansed with smoke and water. This was accompanied by calling Maraian names and singing. Then Yirawala's sons danced, followed by various old men. Gradually the singing and dancing reached a crescendo and the sticks beat faster. At a given signal the men grabbed smoking torches of ironwood leaves and poured up the stairs into the house, chanting loudly and rhythmically stamping in every room until the house shook. Old men called out above the noise then the men emerged from the back of the house, calling and crying aloud. The ceremony was over.

After the ceremony to send Yirawala's spirit home to its Dreaming, David Gumaraitj sat on the steps covering his face and weeping. Bobby was comforted by an uncle. The women had remained outside the house. They had come separately via Bagot Settlement.

Next day David and Bobby talked to me about their father's last wishes. They had decided to make a preliminary journey into Marugulidban in early June, but would need a vehicle and equipment by then. I told them that I was negotiating with the National Gallery but it might not be finalised for a few months. I suggested that in the meantime they could ask for some assistance from the Northern Land Council.

Professor Elkin was grieved to hear of Yirawala's sudden death. He wrote the following epitaph:

> In honoured tribute to Yirawala, MBE, Gunwinggu tribesman, keeper of sacred symbols, myths, rituals and of cave galleries of rock paintings, the title deeds of his people's land.
>
> Artist of renown, painter of priceless Maraian series, the sacramental expression of the Dreaming, spiritual source of life in nature and in man, seen only with the inner eye.
>
> Yirawala, head man and defender, man of understanding, 'properly clever man'.
>
> To your Dreaming in your own land we commend your spirit.
>
> Goodbye old man.

In June I learned that David was ill and without a job, so I wrote to the Croker Island council, asking them to assist him in obtaining an invalid's pension and ensure that he was sent to Darwin for hospital treatment. I undertook to look after him when he came in.

Bobby said David was very depressed but might get better when they were able to carry out their father's wishes.

In July Bobby came in to Darwin to select a new long wheel base Toyota Landcruiser and arrange for Yirawala's Dreaming bird, Dadat, to be painted on the side with the name Marugulidban.

When this was done he said the elders wanted the truck sent by barge to Croker Island where a ceremony would be performed to emphasise the significance of the truck and to honour his father.

When the Toyota was unloaded at Croker Island, Bobby drove it to the ceremony ground where Kelly Borgordubhu, a ceremony 'boss' (leader), welcomed the truck with a line of painted dancers.

As the ceremony progressed Kelly went over to Mary Malilba, one of Yirawala's widows, and cut her hair off. A symbolic sacred well was dug. Kelly painted my face white and I stood with Yirawala's sons and grandchildren in the 'well' for ritual washing as Maraian names were called.

One month later David, Bobby and Danny brought the Toyota to Darwin where it was

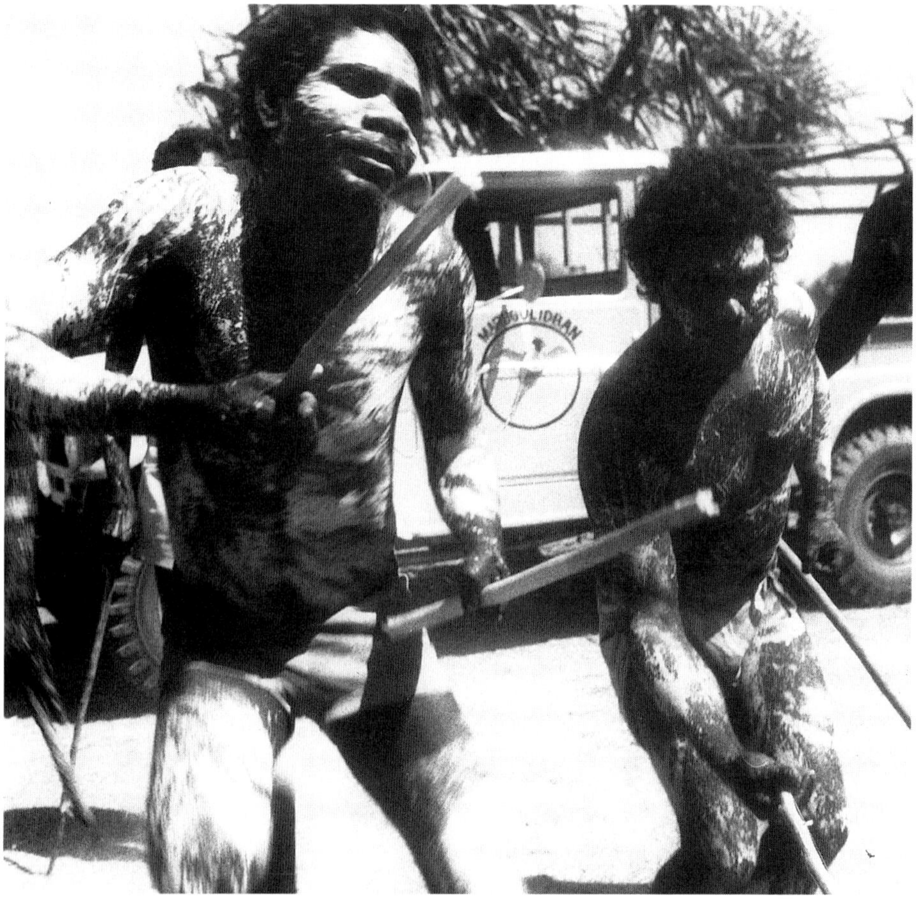

Croker Island, 1976. Ceremony to welcome the Toyota truck that symbolised the going home to Marugulidban. Yirawala's Dreaming bird, Dadat, was painted on the truck door.

loaded with goods and supplies for a preliminary journey home.

David and Bobby were happy, and resolved to carry on for their father. They would go to Marugulidban and have meetings to organise the people and plan their settlement. They would be back in two to three weeks' time.

As they progressed through the country, Bobby sent telegrams. The last one was from Oenpelli. After that I heard nothing for two months.

One morning in early October, Bobby knocked on the door. I made breakfast for him, which he ate in silence. He looked very tired and upset so I waited for him to speak. Suddenly he put his head down on the table and cried. He said he had lost his spirit and his father's dream was over.

There had been a lot of jealousy at Maningrida about the new Toyota and they had not been able to get past there to go to Marugulidban. There had been little sympathy for the founding of a settlement which would establish its own council and autonomy. What was really just a painting camp in the bush could have been turned into something better, not just an outstation 65 kilometres from Maningrida, but this would not have suited those wishing to perpetuate the existing situation. The finest painters of ceremonial designs were Gunwinggu elders camping in the Marugulidban area.

Yirawala had wanted them all to live off their own country, with their own autonomy, and when the religious leaders painted, it would be for instruction and their own museum.

Bobby said that there were some people at Maningrida who didn't want anyone to interfere about the craft and make their own station.

Somebody had smashed up the Toyota truck and now it lay in the mechanic's garage at

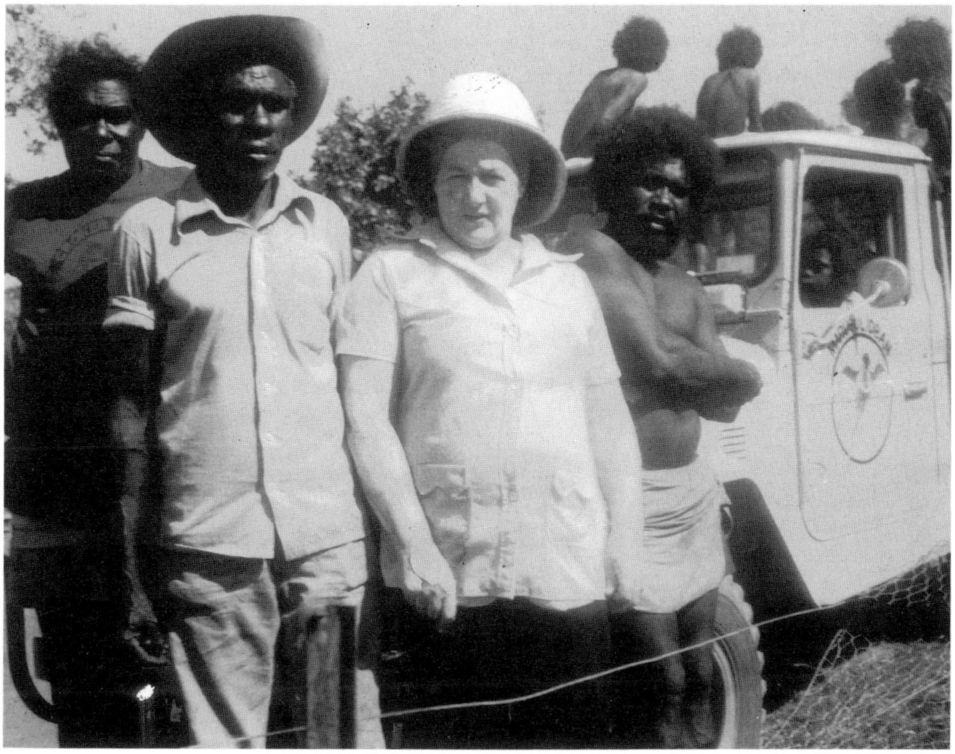

At the ceremony to welcome the truck. From left to right: Kelly Borgordubhu (at rear, who took over as ceremony number-one boss after Yirawala), David Gumaraitj (eldest son and heir of Yirawala), myself and Bobby Joran. My face has been painted white as a symbol of mourning.

Maningrida. The damage was estimated to be $3000 to $4000 worth.

I undertook to pay for the repairs when the truck was brought in to Darwin.

Bobby said he would wait for David to come in and then they would discuss the next move.

As the Toyota had been profaned and could not now be used as their father had wished, David and Bobby decided it must be repaired and sold. They would buy a long wheel base Landrover with the money.

We went to see the garage where the vehicle was stored and David discussed things with the garage mechanics. After that he said he wanted to say goodbye to the Toyota.

It was raining as we went to a shed where the truck was stored, covered with a tarpaulin. David lifted the canvas and a large green frog jumped onto his hand, whereupon he burst into tears, then leaned over to kiss the painted Dreaming bird.

David said the dream was over and there were also divisions amongst the people now.

The Landrover was finally purchased and a telegram sent to Bobby Joran to come and pick it up. A reply came back to say that he would be at our house at 6 p.m. on Friday.

Then, on Wednesday, two days before Bobby was due, the *NT News* reported that Bobby had been murdered on Melville Island. I went straight to the police station and said there must be some mistake. The sergeant said there was no mistake, Bobby was dead.

On Friday the gate bell rang just after 6 p.m., but nobody was there.

There was some confusion about the exact cause of his death. A medical certificate said that he died of a heart attack.

We flew his body home to his family on Croker Island.

Men carried his coffin from the plane. His mother, Mary Malilba, fell to her knees and gave a terrible long drawn out cry as they approached. Men cut themselves and bit the hafts of spears in the grief of losing one so young, so noble.

All night Mary lay across the coffin of her son. Lines of painted mourners danced backwards and forwards like the waves of the sea washing over us; this and the harmonious singing brought some comfort to sore hearts.

As the morning star rose, David bore his brother away to bury him by a stream, saying goodbye all alone.

Bobby Joran (Kadjiba) was 30 years of age when he died. A man of honour, high minded in the fight to save the tribal land and people. A warrior with a strong arm who bore his father's shield and hurled his father's spears.

Even though cut down, their spirit lives on, their message engraved forever on the sands of time. The fire they lit is an immortal flame that illuminates the Aboriginal fight for true self determination.

Yirawala lives on in his powerful magical drawings and in the book I promised to write, to make the balanda understand.

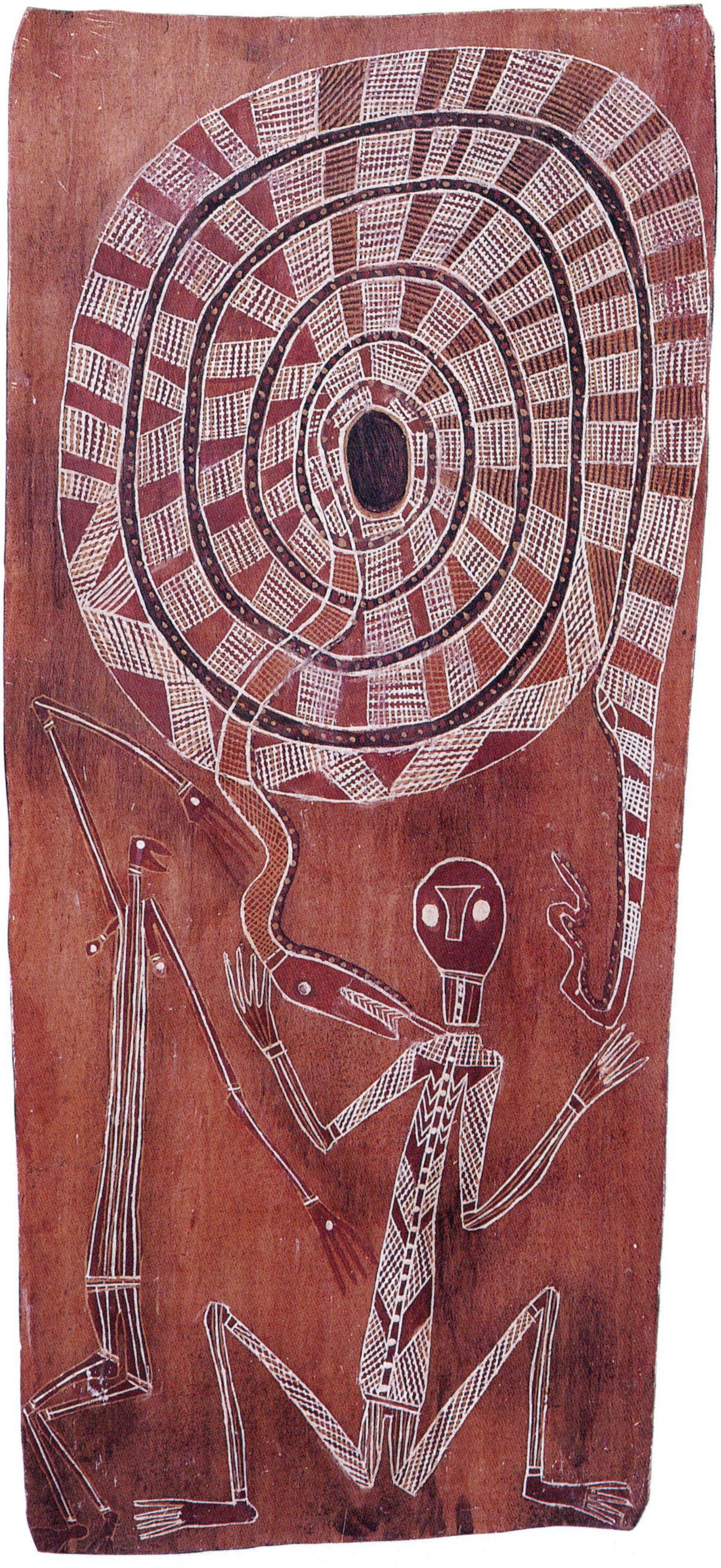

Plate 119 NOWYRAN THE BIG CARPET SNAKE

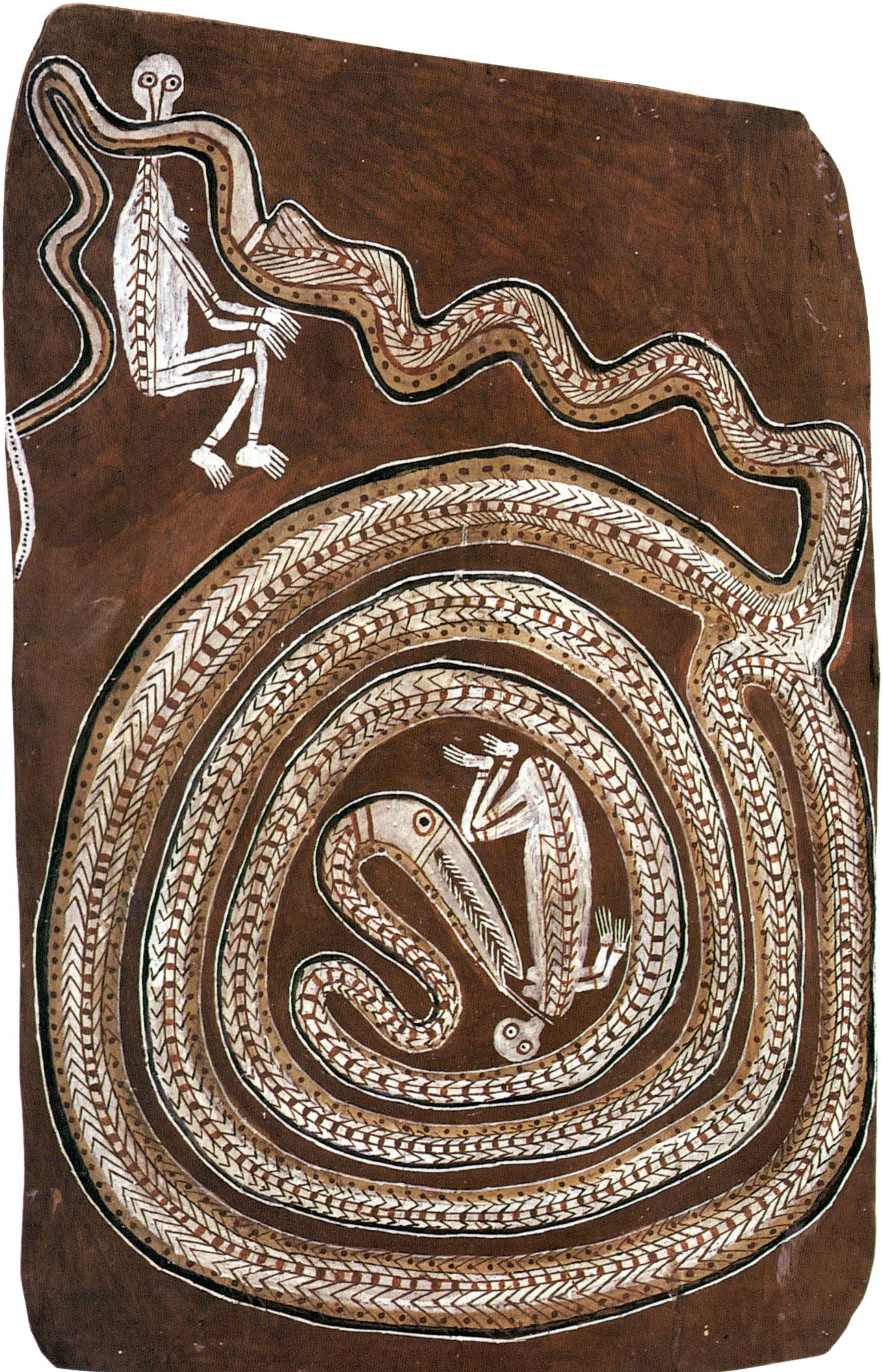

Plate 120 LUMAHLUMAH'S DAUGHTERS

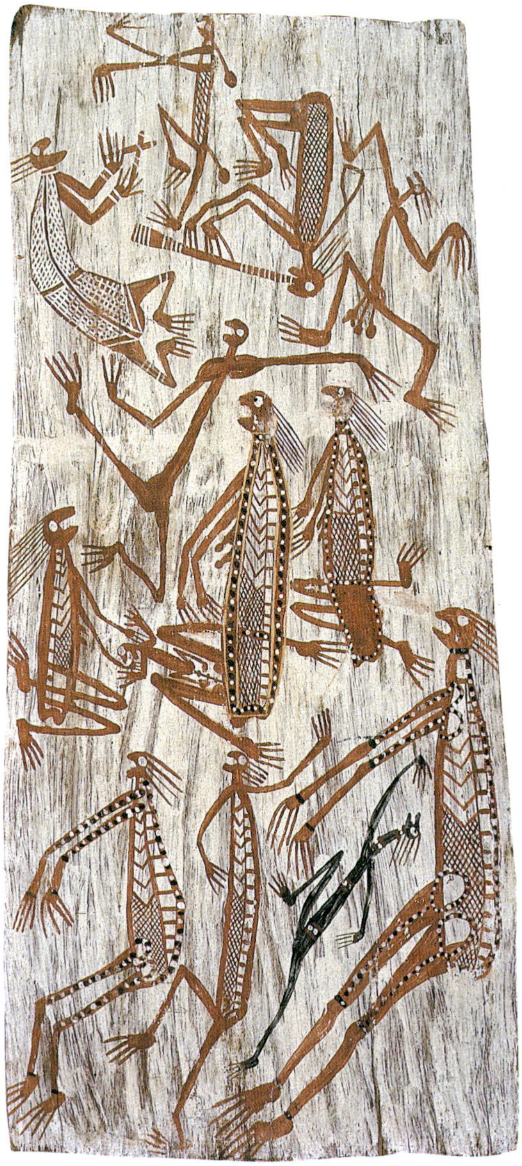

Plate 121 MIMI GIVING BIRTH

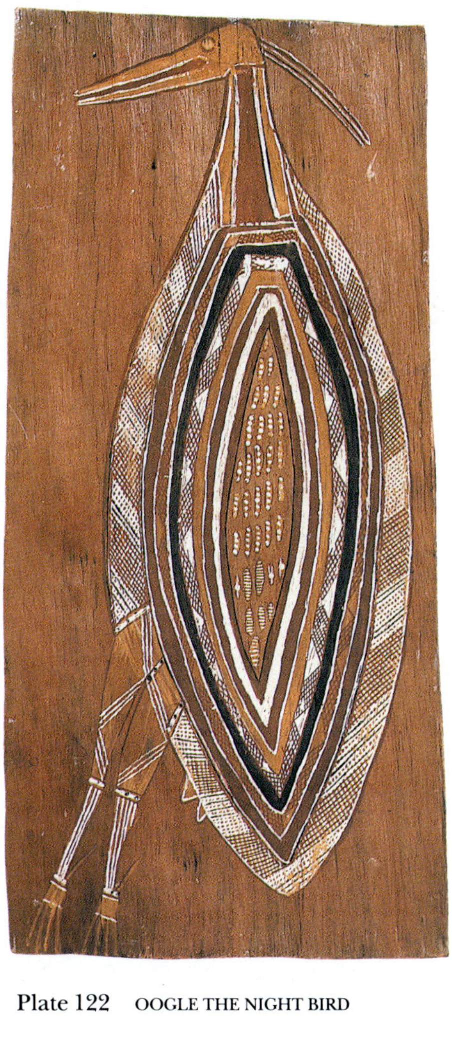

Plate 122 OOGLE THE NIGHT BIRD

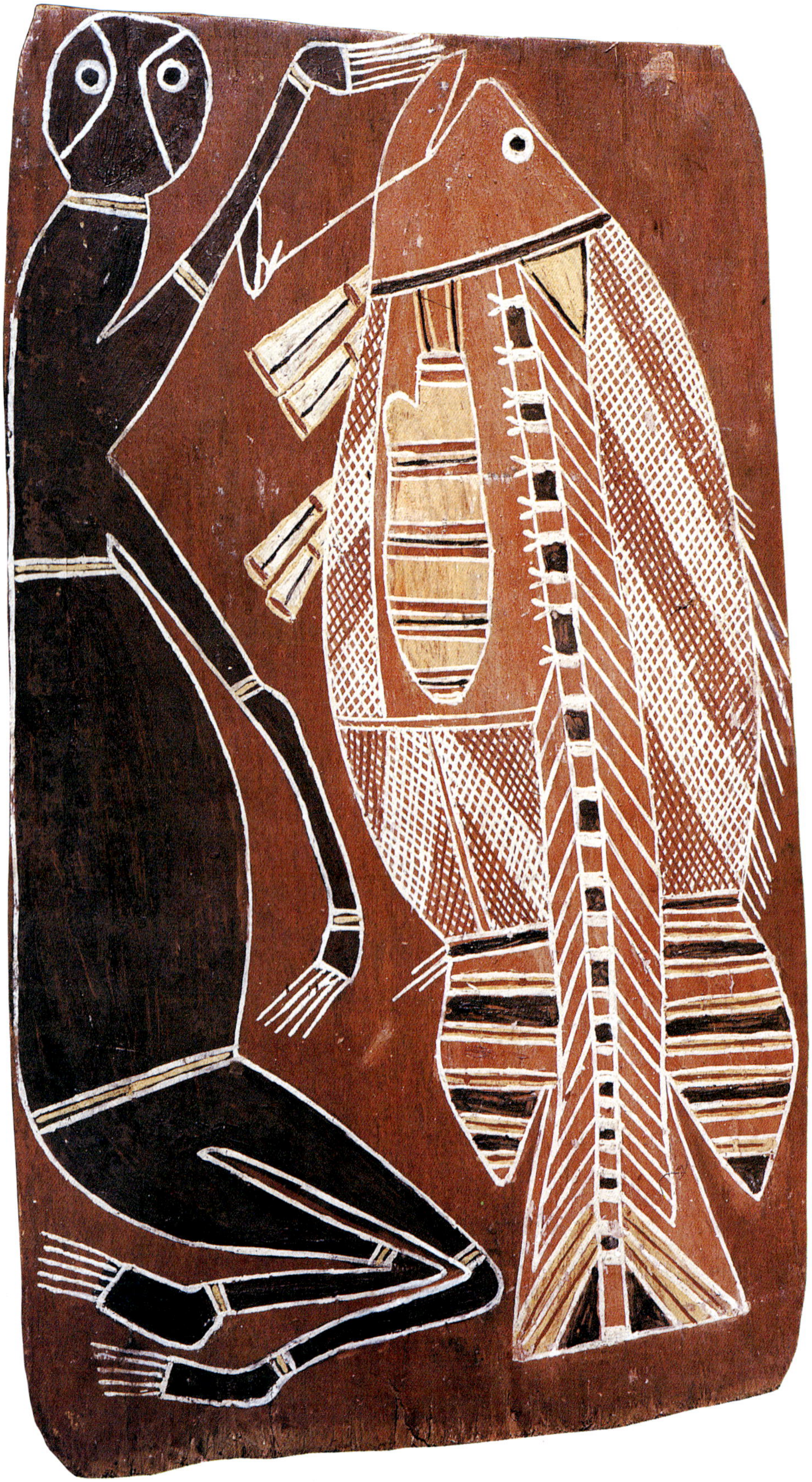

Plate 123 GEECHNOCH THE LAZY MAN

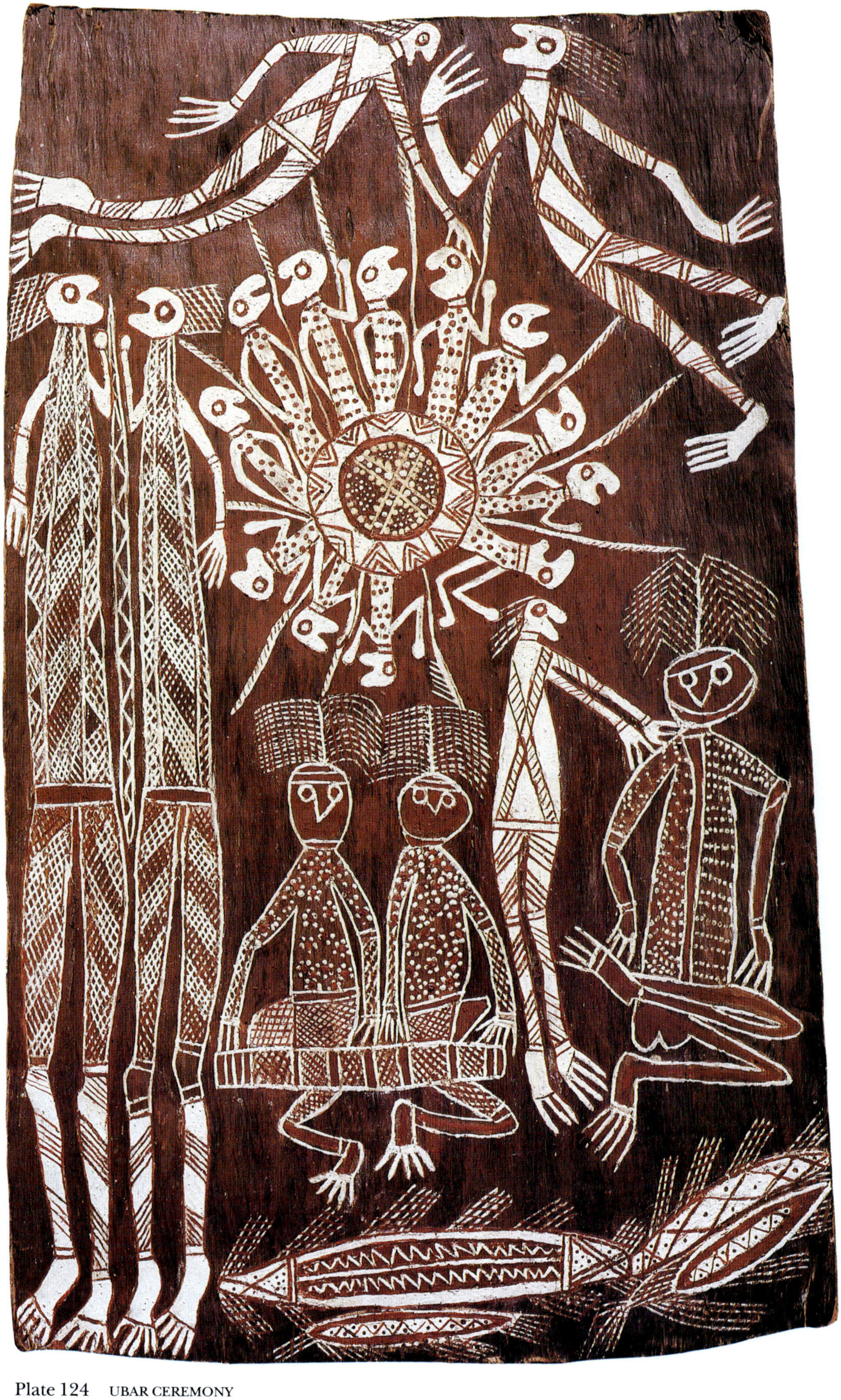

Plate 124 UBAR CEREMONY

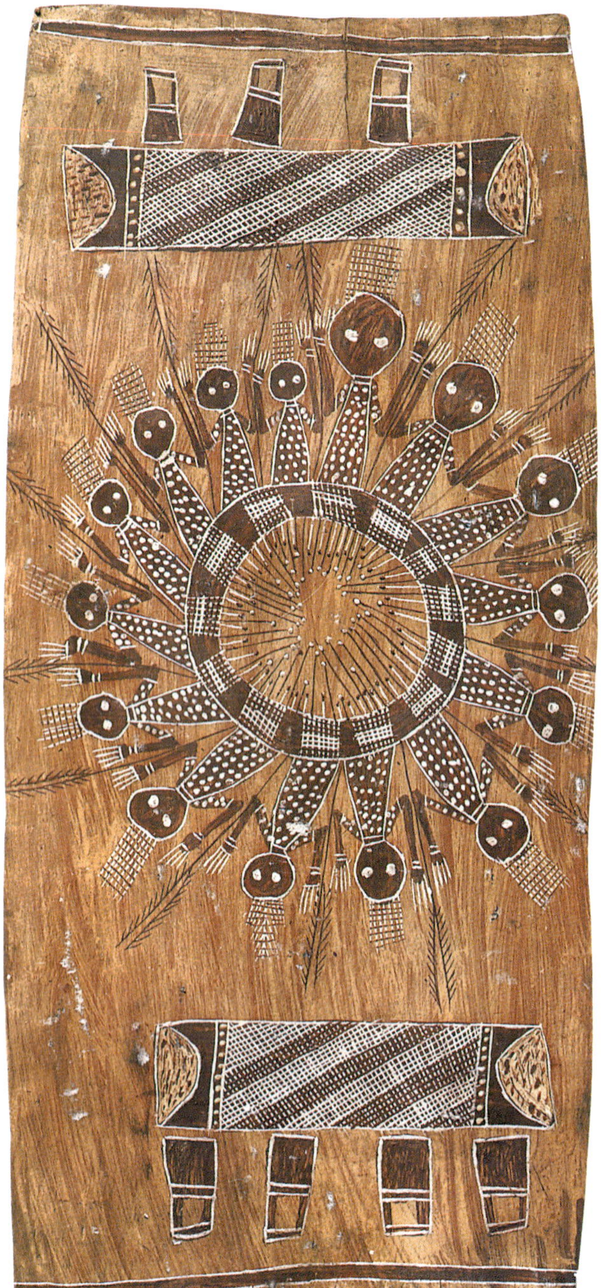

Plate 125 UBAR CEREMONY: DRUM AND WALLABY DANCE

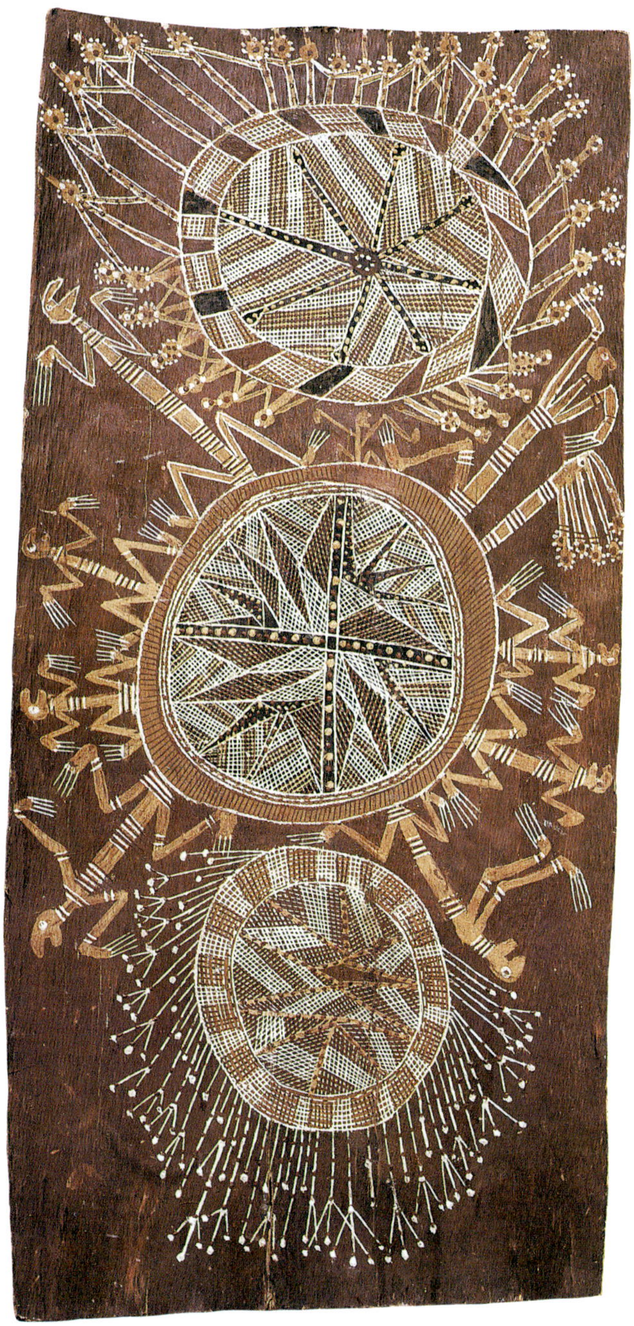

Plate 126 UBAR CEREMONY: DRUM AND WALLABY DANCE

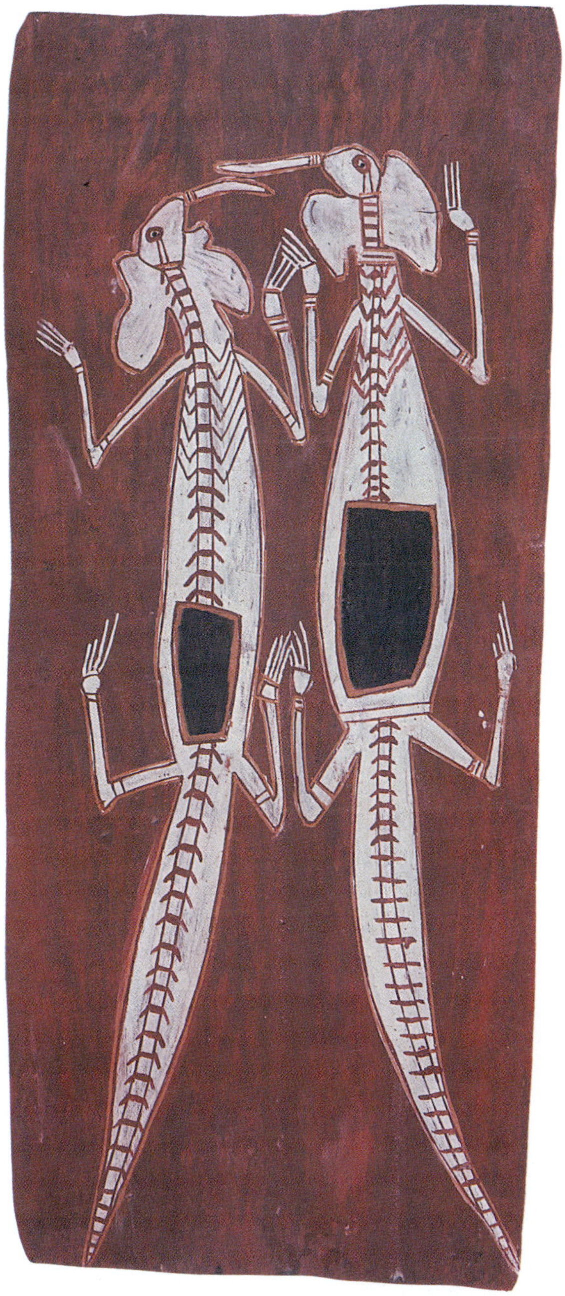

Plate 127 UBAR CEREMONY: FRILL-NECKED LIZARD DANCE

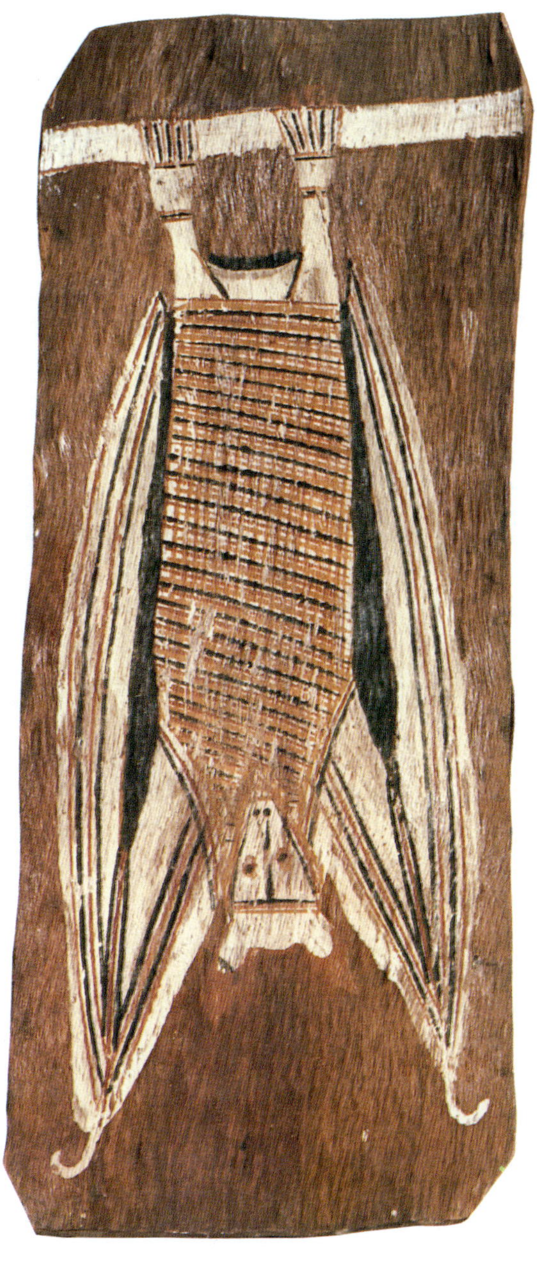

Plate 128 UBAR CEREMONY: DUA FLYING FOX

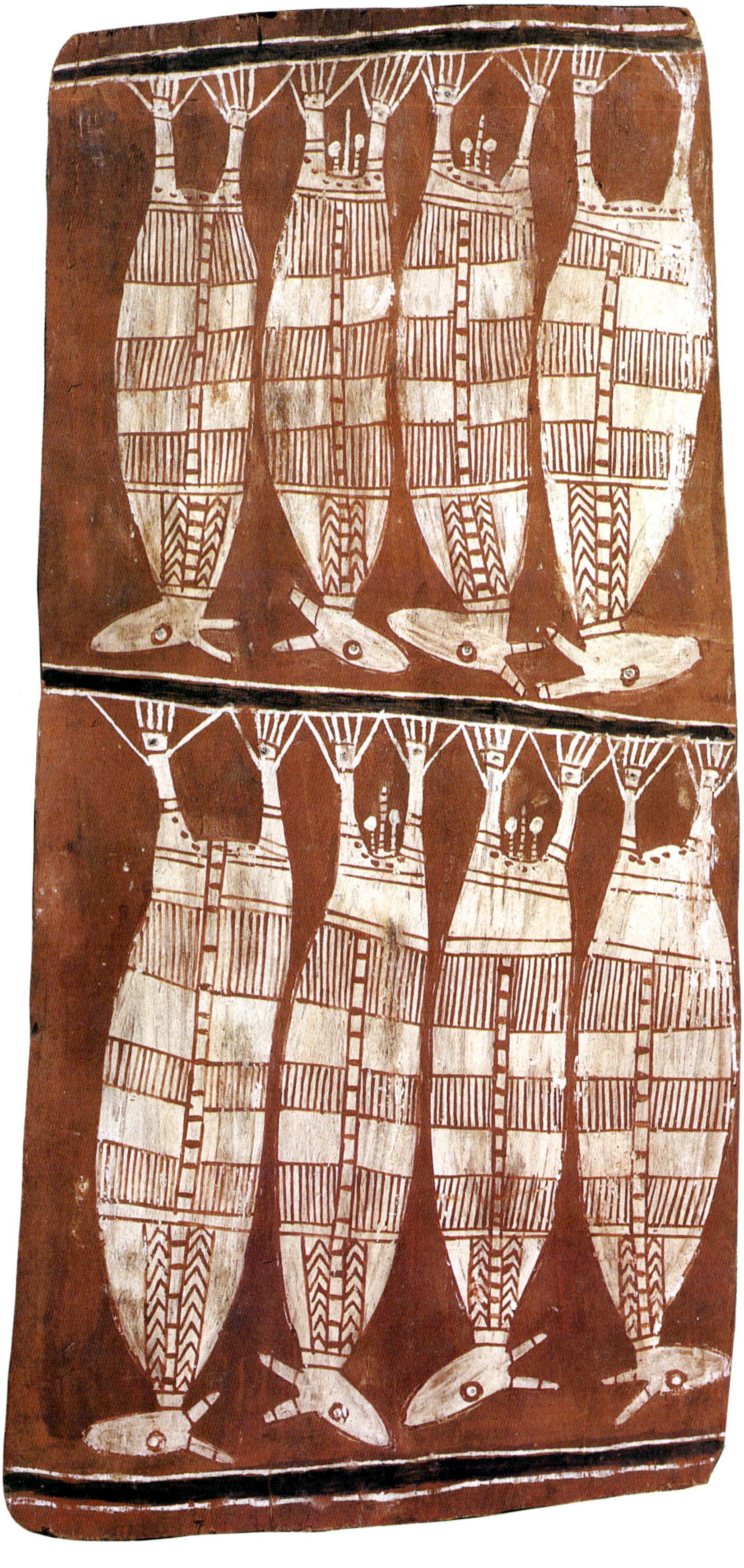

Plate 129 UBAR CEREMONY: FLYING FOXES

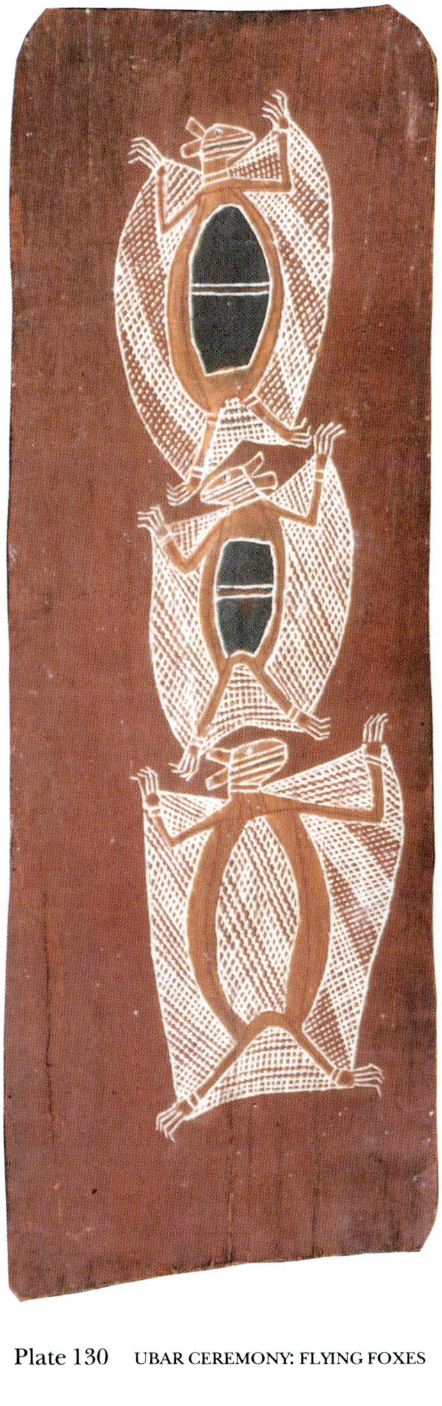

Plate 130 UBAR CEREMONY: FLYING FOXES

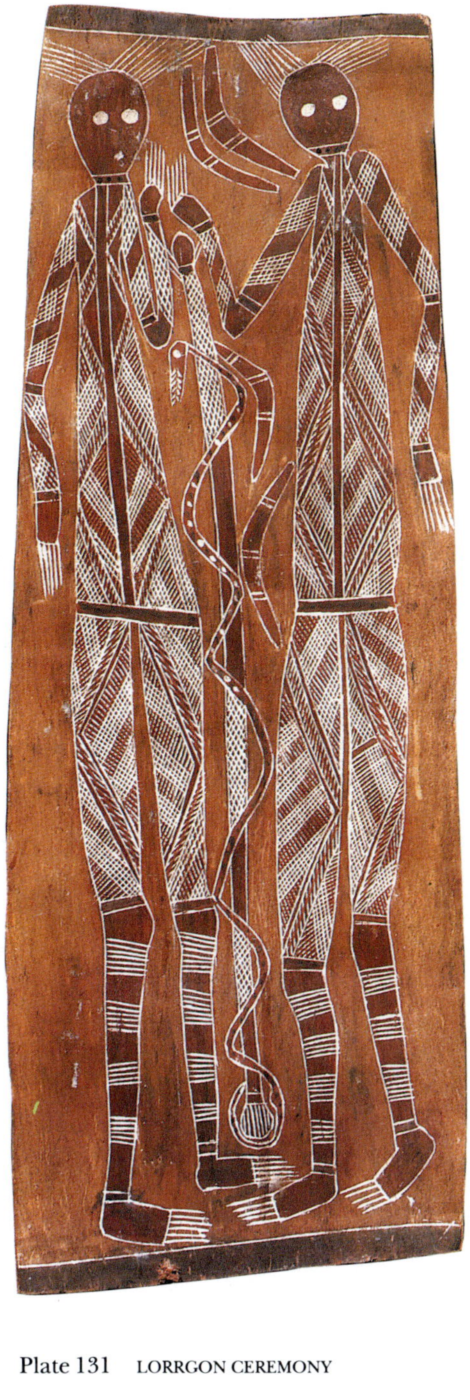

Plate 131 LORRGON CEREMONY

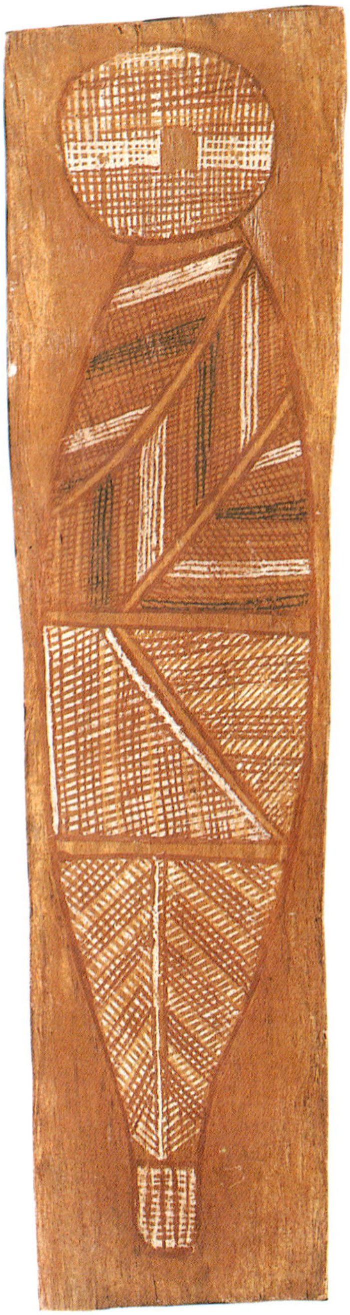

Plate 132 LORRGON CEREMONY PLACE

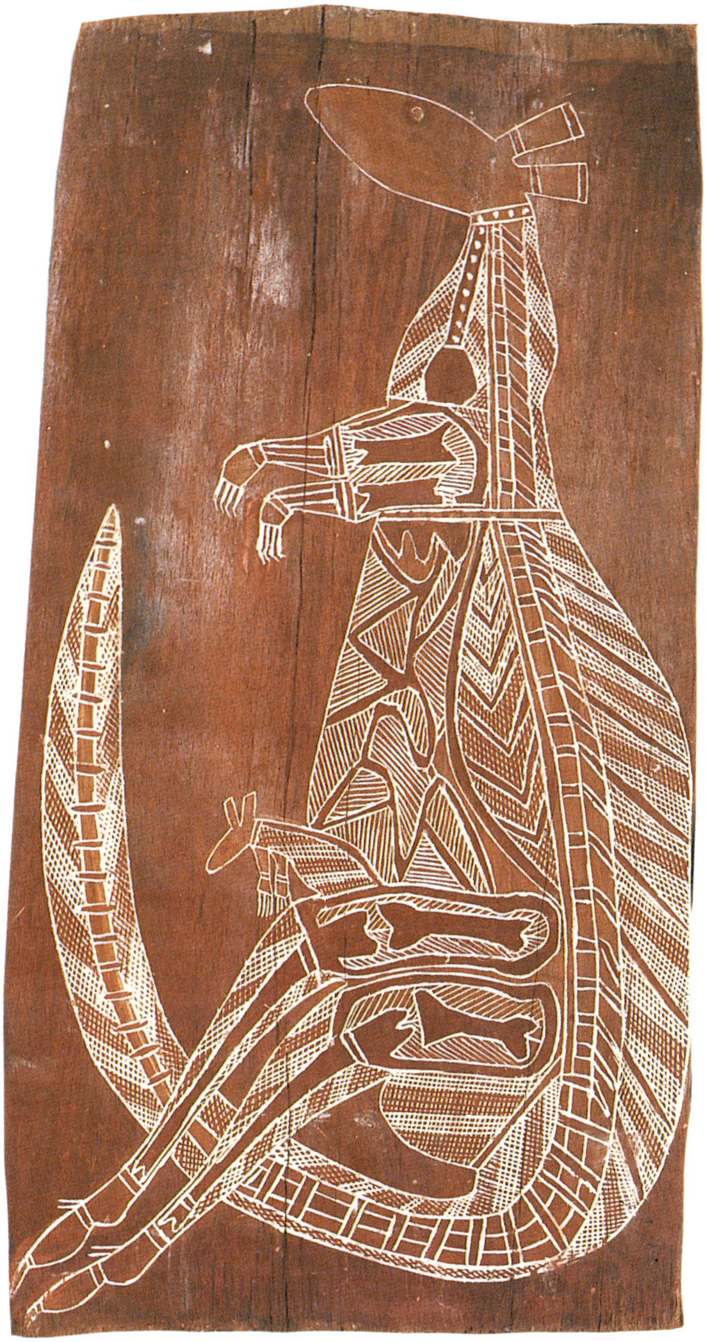

Plate 133 LORRGON CEREMONY: BIRTH OF KUNDAAGI

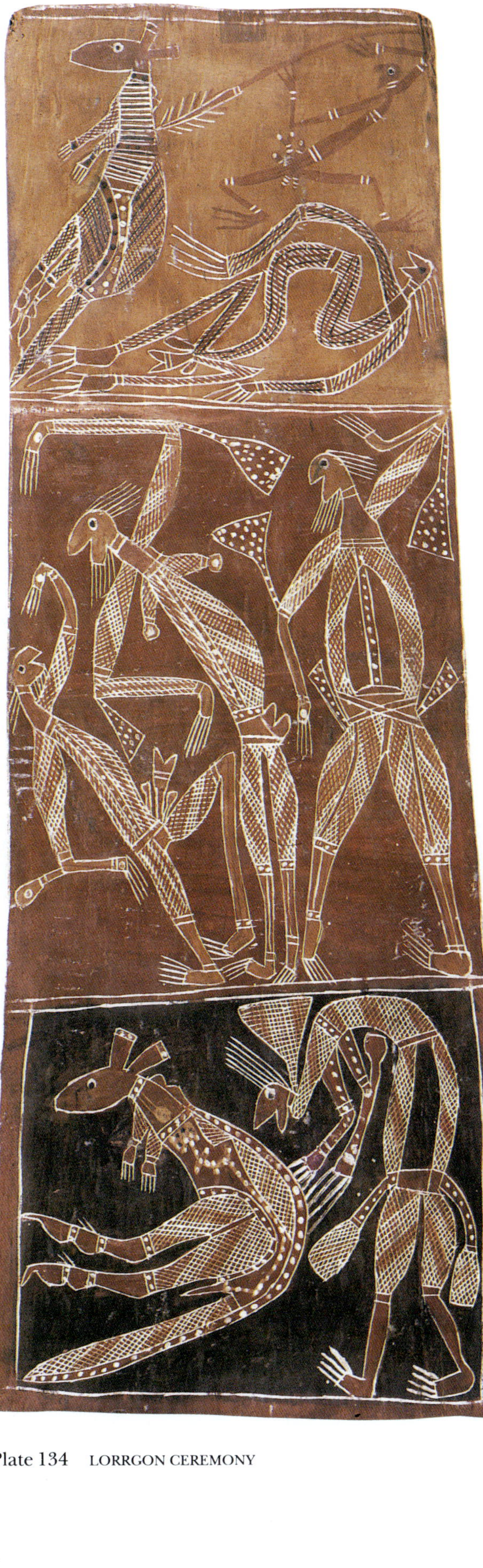

Plate 134 LORRGON CEREMONY

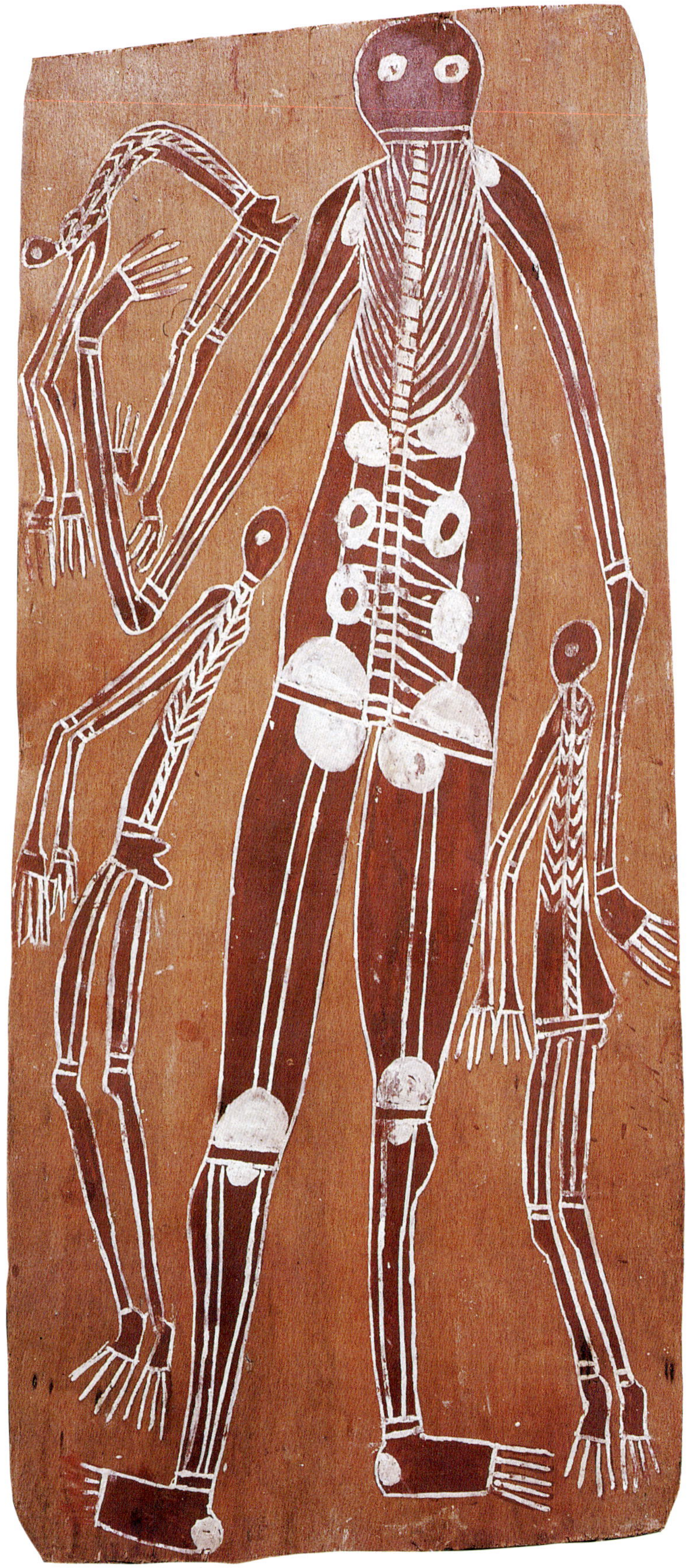

Plate 135 LORRGON CEREMONY

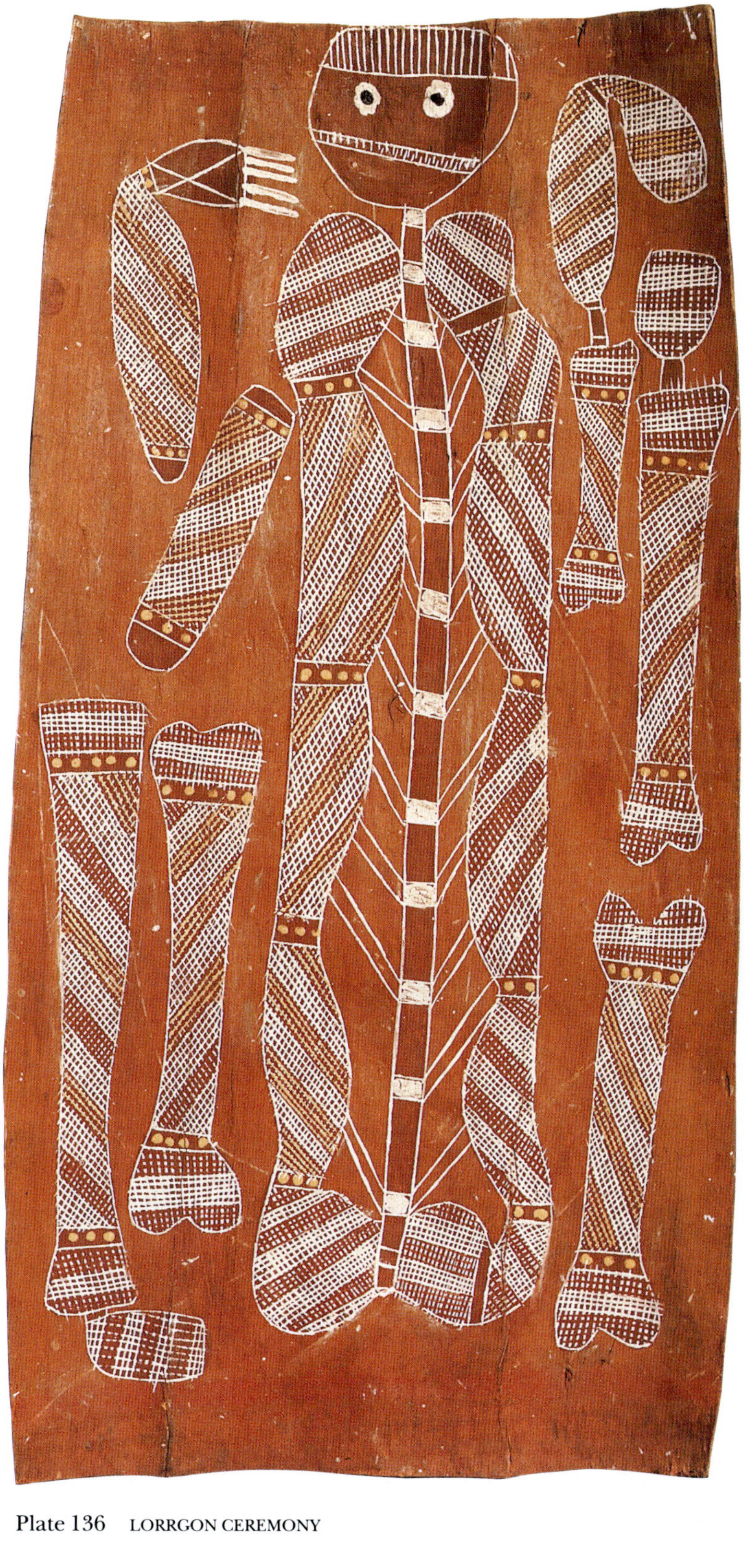

Plate 136 LORRGON CEREMONY

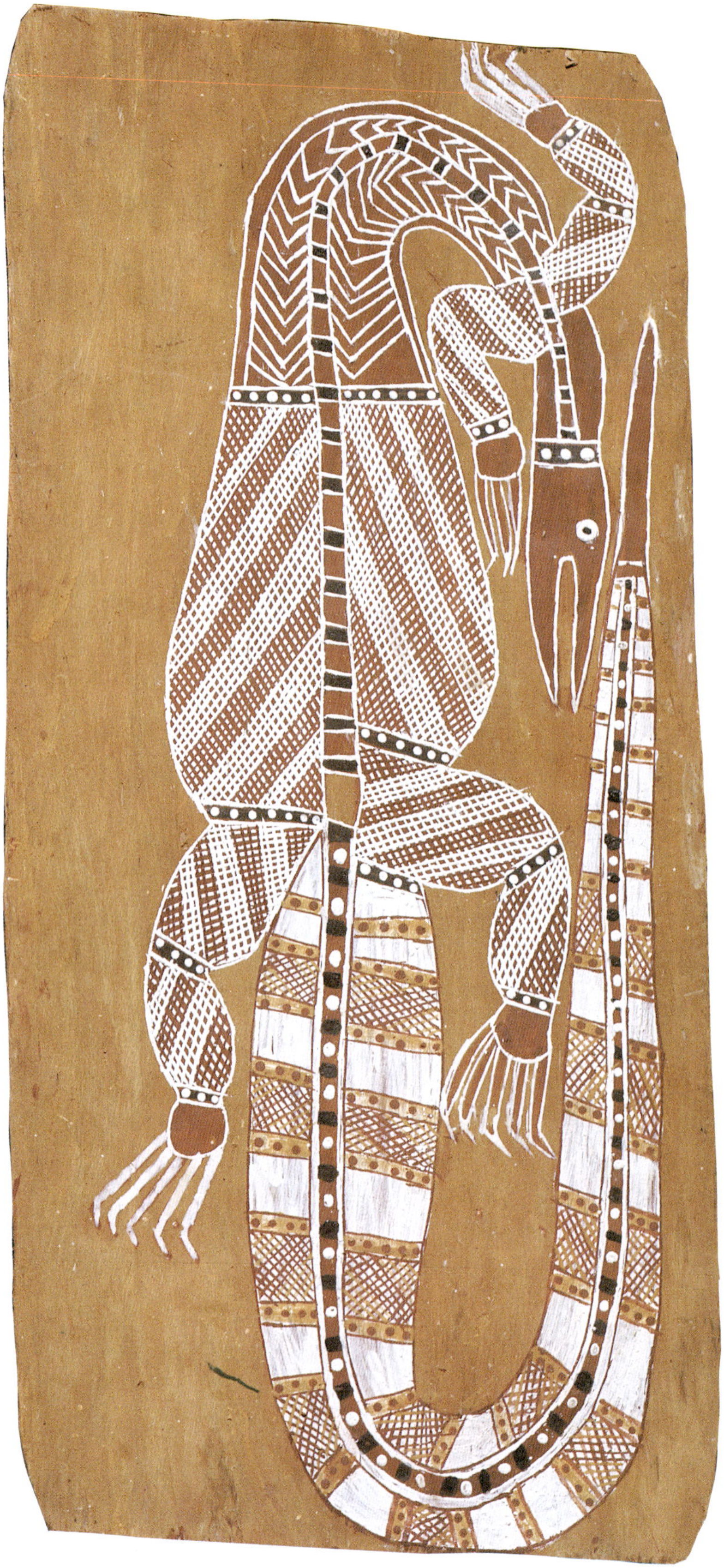

Plate 137 LORRGON CEREMONY: GOANNA

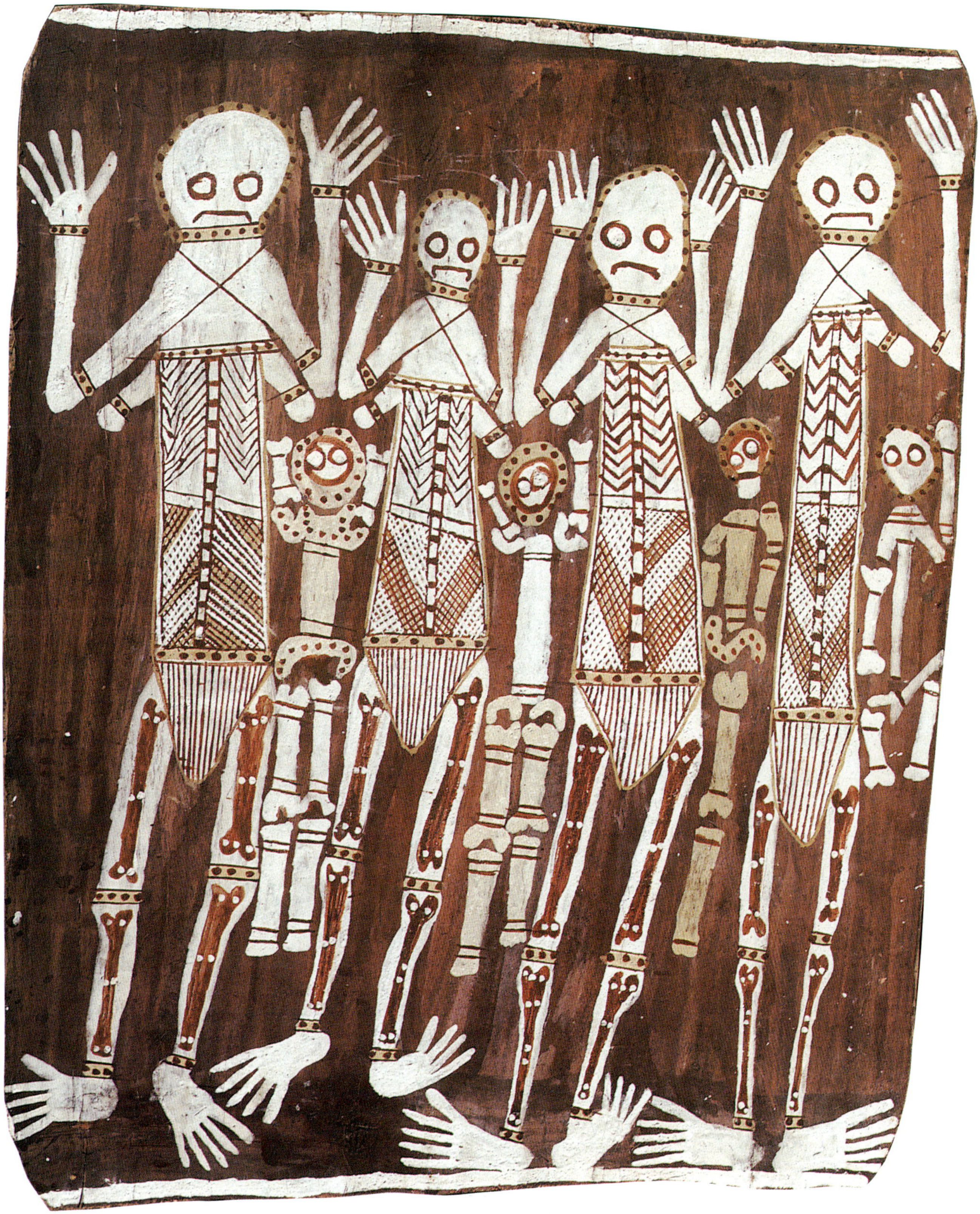

Plate 138 LORRGON CEREMONY: DANCE OF SKELETONS

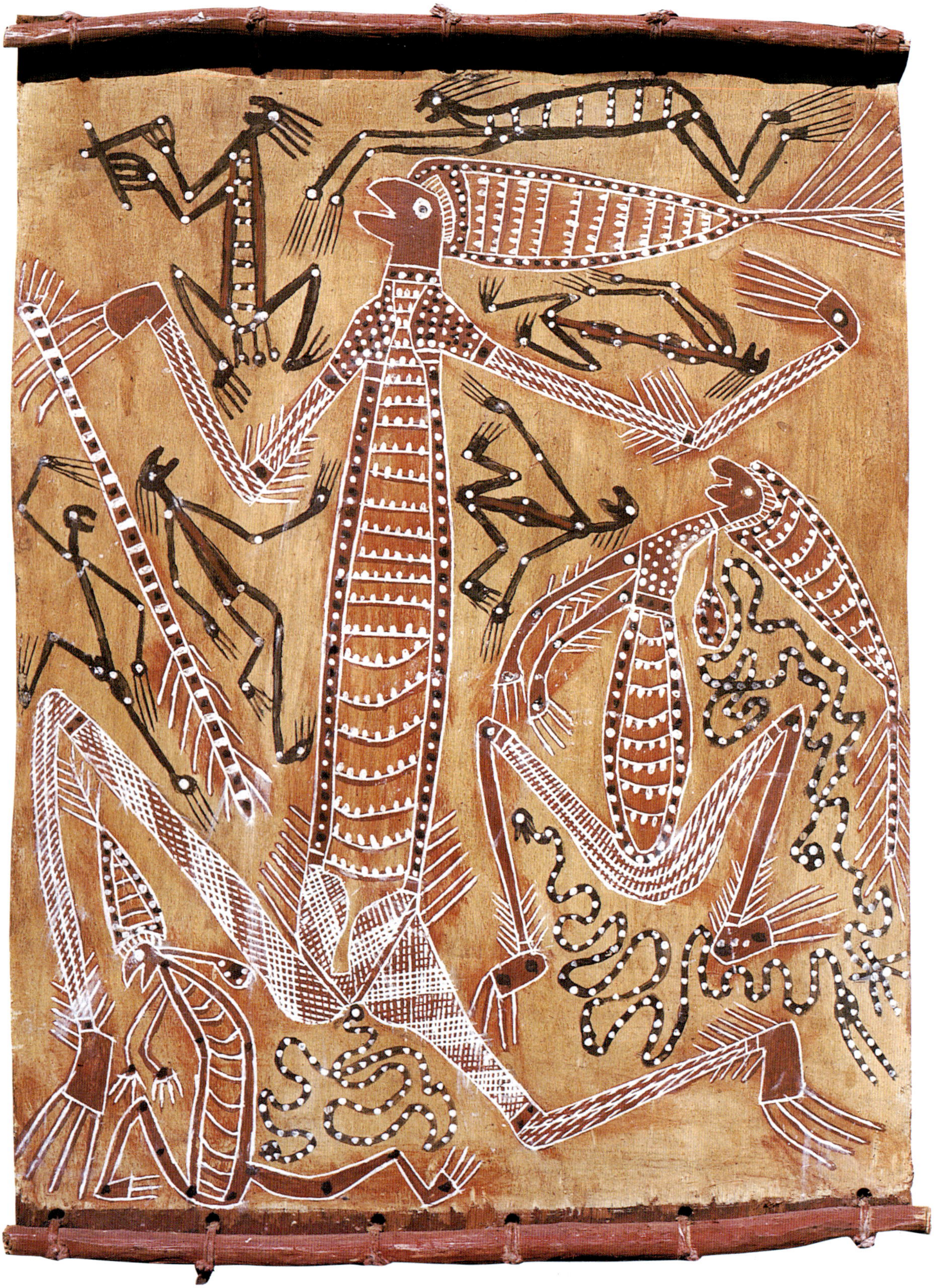

Plate 139 LORRGON CEREMONY: RED PLAINS KANGAROO DANCE

Part II
The paintings

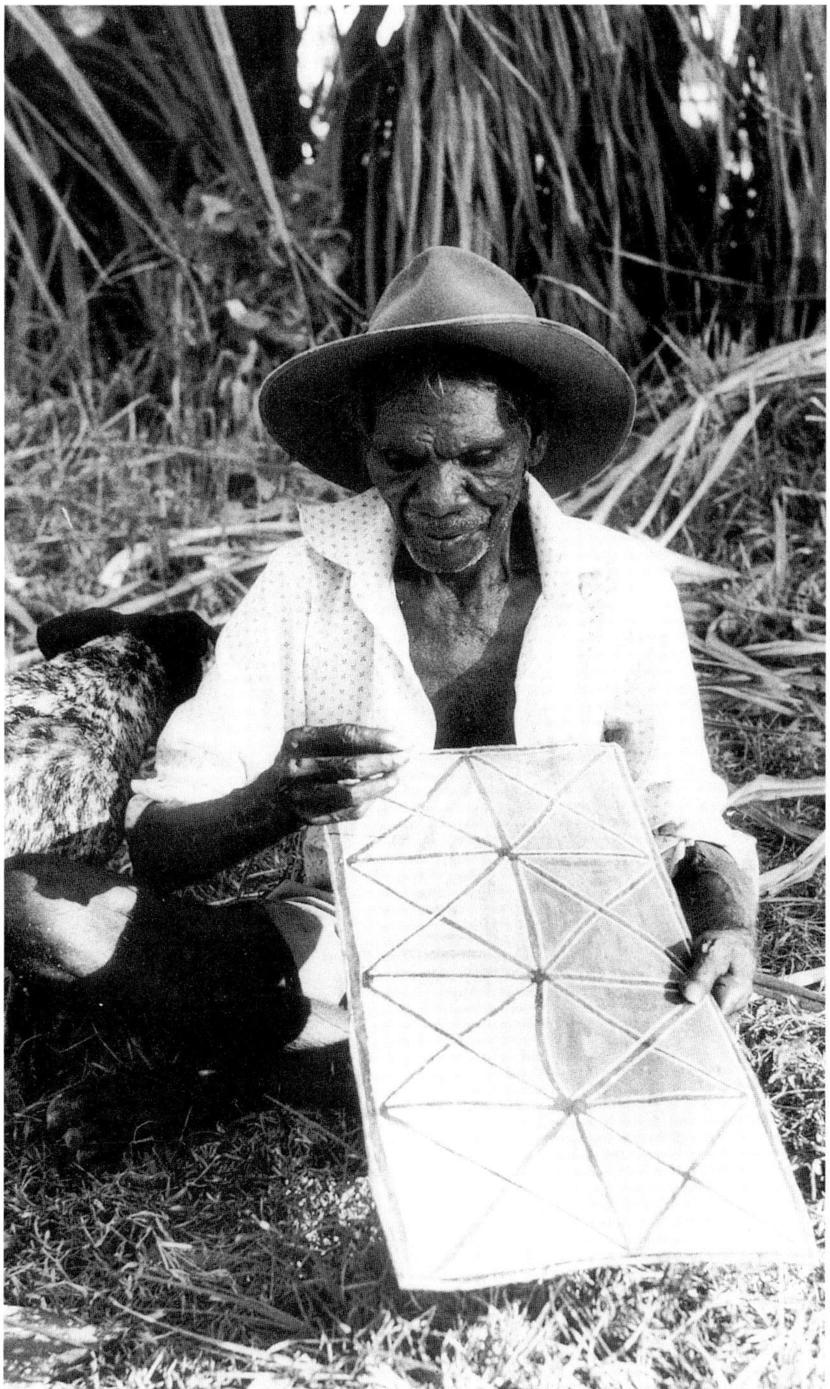

Previous page:
Yirawala explaining something of the Maraian design.

Chapter 15
Art or religion?

The traditional designs were painted by Aboriginal elders to preserve and perpetuate Aboriginal historical events and religion. The mythological journeys and miracles performed by totemic and cult heroes are portrayed in pictures, songs and the dances of re-enactment, all of which summon power and life from the Dreaming, where the spirits of man* and the natural species are incarnated. The heroic past and the Dreaming are thus brought into the present. Such painting is in the service of ritual and is the sacramental expression of the Dreaming.

A traditional painter inherits the prescribed ritual designs and the ochre colours which belong to his family and clan. He uses only what he has inherited, and would never attempt to copy the work of another or use his colours. Such an act would be considered a serious crime in traditional Aboriginal society.

Aboriginal intellectual property of ceremonial symbols and designs, with the accompanying songs, stories and dance, are bequeathed through patrilineal descent from one generation to the next. Such knowledge is power, owned by certain tribal elders who must in turn pass it on to their sons as they climb the ladder to manhood by way of initiation and participation in a variety of man-making sacred ceremonies. The complex process of teaching and learning takes years. A learned tribal man is an older man with greying hair. When the final mysteries are revealed, the heirs all knowing can paint the prescribed dogma, which must remain unchanged so that the religious truths and power from the Dreaming are not profaned and lost and thereby endanger the survival of man and the natural species.

Aborigines believe in the pre-existence of spirits in the home country of the clans. After death the correct painting of religious symbols and performance of mortuary ritual ensures that the new ghost will return to where it was first incarnated. It will return to its Dreaming.

Spirits waiting to be born dwell in certain sacred baby dreaming waterholes, in the form of tiny fish and minute life, darting about beneath a mantle of water lilies. A spirit child enters the mother's womb when the human father makes a dream to call it from the water. The conception is mystical. The father finds the baby spirit for his wife, who gives it flesh and blood.

When the father dreams of a spirit child he also dreams of its association with some natural species in the father's country, this then becomes the child's conception totem.

Traditionally, when an Aboriginal person died their possessions were burned. In recent times valued items such as a car, boat or rifle are smoked and sung to cleanse them of contact with the dead person.

The burial ritual ensures that a new ghost will find the right road to the spirit world and a guarantee of life after death. Without the prescribed rituals the spirit of the dead could not return to its Dreaming, but would wander forever in a limbo land.

* In this context I use the term 'man' to mean all human beings, male and female.

If the Dreaming places are destroyed the spirits can never return. (This in part explains why a true Aborigine fears the coming of mining, wood chipping or similar exploitation of the land.)

In certain caves, the bones of the dead are interred. In others there are galleries of rock paintings, sacred signs and signatures of hands. These are the title deeds of the land, bequeathed from generation to generation for thousands of years and signed by vanished hands.

Some caves are called 'danger places' and contain sacred objects of stone and wood. These represent the life force of the creator beings who give life to man and nature, through the veneration of the objects. Some objects may represent the phallus of the creator, others his bones and symbols of power over the elements. The keepers and guardians of these places would never wittingly agree to their destruction.

Some drawings in caves are painted one on top of another. These are increase drawings (i.e. drawings to ensure the increase of the species); their magic assists the hunters to catch the particular species depicted. When such prescribed drawings are made they are sung to give them power.

Drawings of creator beings, totems and sacred symbols are never painted over, only retouched occasionally by the keepers of the cave.

Commercialisation of Aboriginal paintings, carvings and artifacts began in the mid 1950s and early 1960s, when warehouses were established in Darwin and out on the Aboriginal reserves.

The dealers' concentration began at Yirrkala, Millingimbi and Elcho Island; later it extended to the Tiwi Islands, Goulburn Island, Croker Island, Port Keats, and areas around the town of Katherine in the Northern Territory.

It was a golden age of great painters and religious leaders: Mauwulan, Mathaman, Birigitji, Gawarin, Mauw, Naritjin, Djowa, Bungawoy, Bininyuwuy, Namaradali, Noganyari, Yirawala, Gumaraitj — to name a few.

All of these elders were important but owned different designs and stories to Yirawala. They and other men of high degree were custodians of sacred creation designs, songs and meanings. Some men were keepers of sacred objects containing the life force from the Dreaming. Their paintings and objects were not 'art and craft', but religious and historical records of the clans passed down unchanged since time immemorial from one generation to the next.

Apart from a few paintings and designs on paper collected by a few anthropologists, the great religious books of such men in the form of bark painting and objects were lost, scattered all over the world in fragments. Apart from the series held in the Australian National Gallery and reproduced in this book, no other series was saved. Most of these men are now dead.

The Aboriginal religious fabric was torn to shreds in the dealers' feeding frenzy. Competition was fierce. At Yirrkala and Millingimbi the biggest dealers were given priority. The best was reserved for them by arrangement with craft managers.

Block-buster exhibitions were held in Australia, America and Japan. Overseas dealers sniffed the wind and in various guises came to Australia.

As demand increased, dealers scrambled to fill the overseas exhibition halls. By this time they had turned their attention to all parts of Australia, including Central Australia, where sacred stone tjuringas were sought.

The life force of the tribes flowed out of Australia unchecked, under the heading of 'art and craft'. There was a government Sacred Objects Ordinance, but obviously there were ways around it.

With heavy commercial pressure being applied, ancient prescribed designs were bound to be modified, even altered to suit the market.

In the early 1960s when my husband and I were at Millingimbi to film the Djalambu ceremony for the AIAS archives, the outdoor radio–telephone rang. A strident voice demanded a large number of bark paintings and carvings to be sent within a few days as the southern exhibition had sold out. The craft advisor hurried about exhorting the painters to hurry up. As it was they were sitting in a row as if they were in an assembly line. Some painters began filling in with dots instead of the fine time-consuming cross-hatching. Others made various short cuts.

Some dealers observed that paintings showing male and female genitalia were not much in demand. Overseas and local buyers did not want these abandoned figures cavorting across boardrooms or putting the china ducks to flight on loungeroom walls. So, the order went out to chop off the phalluses and put nappies on the naughty figures. Most of the painters complied. Yirawala refused to change the designs taught to him by his father. Let phalluses flourish and be damned, was his attitude.

A few years later, when buyers and collectors became better educated concerning traditional Aboriginal designs, they sought the old-style paintings as being more authentic and better value for money. Dealers, agents and craft advisors made some attempt for the restoration of the genitalia, but apart from a few tacked on as an afterthought, there was no going back.

By 1969 Aquadhere glue had replaced the bush-orchid juice traditionally used to size the bark. This glue, when mixed with ochres, made the paintings more durable for the trade.

The dealers demanded bigger bark paintings. Originally bark drawings were made mainly for instruction, so they were not large. Under pressure, some painters did not cure the bark properly, resulting in cracking and curling later on.

Traditionally, bark painting belonged to Arnhemland; elsewhere religious designs and symbols were incised on stone objects and wood, and concentric designs were made in the sand during ceremonies.

The work of new Aboriginal painters made for commercial interests can truly be called art, and its value is according to the demand created through promotion by the commercial art galleries. The paintings have no ceremonial significance.

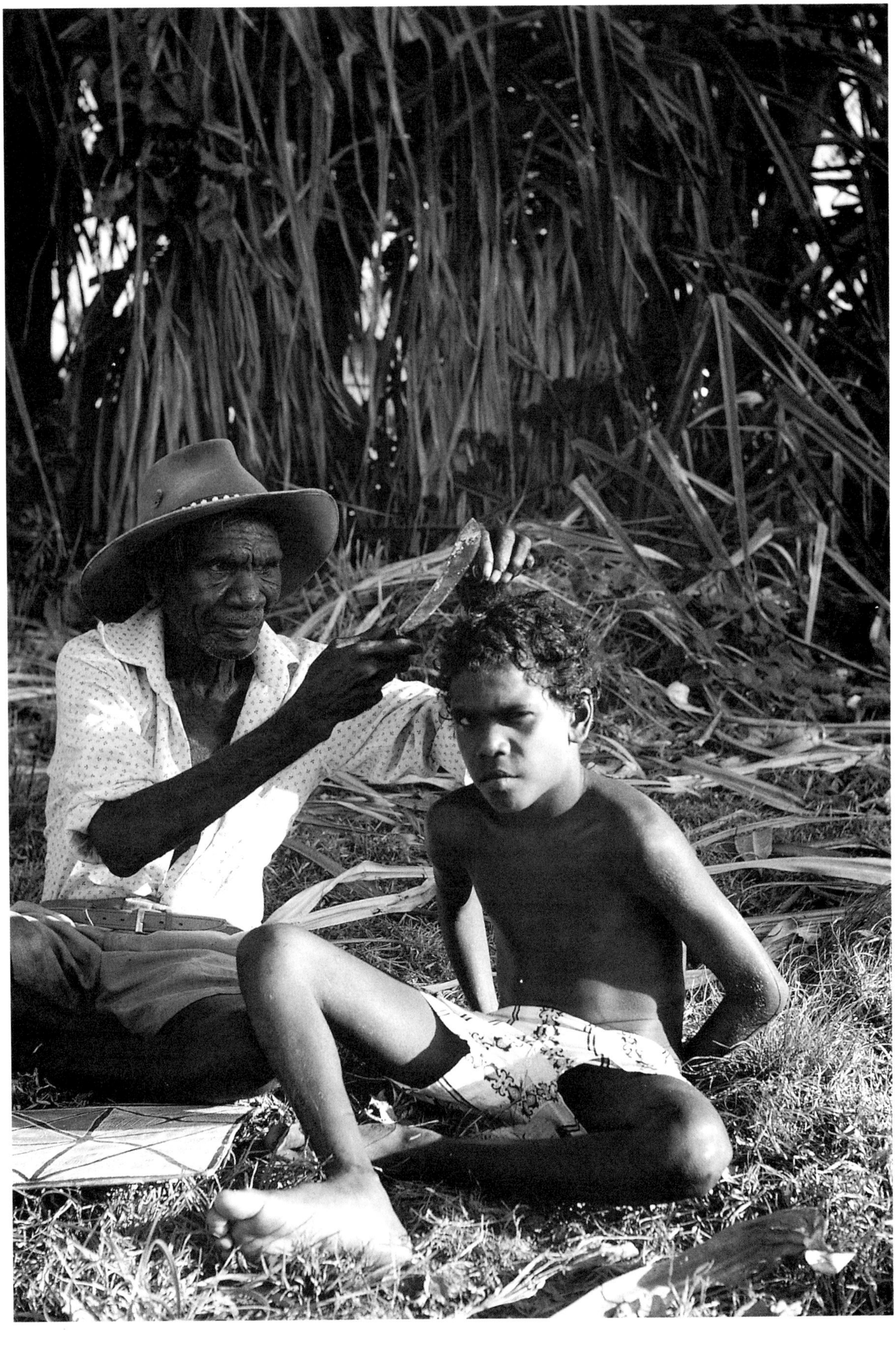

Chapter 16
The ceremonial series

Under Yirawala's guidance the author collected the ceremonial series of 139 bark paintings and recorded the meanings on tape. 'You keep whole lot meanings yourself, nobody else,' he said. 'Later on you make big book all my drawing. Tell balanda true story, because him never understand.'

The ceremonial series is now in the Australian National Gallery, Canberra, and his explanations (the 'outside' or non-sacred stories and meanings) are now in this book.

Plates 1–82 THE MARAIAN SERIES

Maraian means sacred, powerful and spiritual. The word Maraian may be used by anyone. Secret power names used by fully initiated men are sacred, as are the signs and symbols and the songs belonging to them.

The Maraian ceremony ensures the general well-being of man and maintains the link between the living and the dead, past and present, the seen and unseen. It can be likened to a festival of souls.

During the ceremony Maraian designs are painted on men's bodies, accompanied by singing and the calling of power words. The designs represent the spirits of natural species from the time long past and the present.

On the men's ceremony ground a leaf shelter, called a 'shade', represents the doorway to the spirit world. Inside it are stored the sacred ironwood sticks which have been taken from certain waterholes by the old custodians. In the 'shade' the old men repaint these sacred objects, singing prescribed secret power songs which summon the spirits from the Dreaming. The spirits 'take on flesh'. The natural species emerge from the 'shades' on the ceremony ground and perpetuate their kind.

Dua and Jiritja moieties participate in the ceremonies, owning different parts of the big stories.

If a mistake is made in sacred Maraian ritual the punishment is death, for the survival of man and nature is at risk, and a link to the Dreaming would be broken.

After the ceremony men return to their camp, some with the designs still visible on their bodies. The important thing is that the uninitiated have not seen or heard the ritual dances and songs which gave power to the body designs performed on the sacred ceremony ground.

The Maraian is performed at the end of the dry season and helps to make rain.

In the Dreaming time a cult hero named Lumahlumah came from Indonesia way. He followed his Dreaming path all over the country, making songs and dances, performing some miracles and naming natural species. Lumahlumah was a giant and the people called him the big Maraian man.

Opposite: Yirawala cutting off hair from his son's head to make a paintbrush.

Lumahlumah first saw the morning star and named it; he made a song for the dead as he saw the star rising and leaving the earth.

One day Lumahlumah outlived his usefulness and began eating people, many people, until the tribes all around the coast got sick of it and decided to have a big intertribal meeting to solve the problem. Messengers were sent all along the coast, to Rowland Bay, Johnson Bay, Maningrida, Cape Stuart and Blythe River, summoning the fighting men to Cape Stuart.

Many men gathered, thousands of men, for a council of war. The decision was to go in canoes, find the giant and kill him. The men were a little bit frightened so they sang and danced to make themselves brave, and when the great fleet of canoes set out next day, the men were still singing and shouting war cries, for Lumahlumah was a big giant, full of power and magic.

Lumahlumah lived on an island near the Crocodile Islands. As the canoes grounded on the beaches, the men ignited their bark torches and threw them into the bone-dry grass and brush. Behind the flames, the great circle of men moved in towards the centre of the island. There they saw the monstrous singed figure of the giant, who was roaring with pain and anger, brandishing his clubs and bellowing his battle cries.

The noise of the giant was like claps of thunder and for a moment the attackers paused, but the cries of their leaders sent them on, wave upon wave to fight. Many men died but the weight of their numbers had weakened the giant, who was filled with spears. His blood stained the earth all around.

Lumahlumah fell on his knees as the head men rushed in to finish him off. The giant lifted his arms and said, 'Do not finish me off yet; wait, I have Law to give you, important Law.' The giant began to sing Maraian, and cut his chest with a certain sacred design. The amazed warriors listened to the giant's song and learned the designs painted on his body and all the sacred rituals for the regeneration of man and all nature.

Lumahlumah said, 'I give you life, you and all the birds and animals. You are all one, depending on each other. Keep the Law and do not profane the sacred songs and drawings that I give you. Take my remains to a cave and guard them well, for I am your life.'

Plate 1 MARAIAN SERIES
Lumahlumah holding sacred sticks.

Plate 2 MARAIAN SERIES
Lumahlumah showing power in his body.

Plate 3 MARAIAN SERIES
Lumahlumah's sacred incarnation waterhole, showing the centre of power, the centrifugal force radiating out, and the sacred poles in the waterhole. In these poles dwell the dormant spirits, the totemic beings who, when singing and dancing and painting invokes them, emerge from the poles in the sacred 'shade' house on the ceremony ground, to sanction the ceremony that gives life and regeneration to man and all nature.

Plate 4 MARAIAN SERIES
Men of the Dua and Jiritja moieties in canoes, on their way to kill the giant. Dua moiety in the top half and Jiritja below.

Plate 5 MARAIAN SERIES
Lumahlumah being speared by mainland warriors, after they have trapped the giant by fire in the centre of the island.

Plate 6 MARAIAN SERIES
Lumahlumah starting to fall when the attack led by tribal elders is heavy.

Plate 7 MARAIAN SERIES
Lumahlumah calling out to the warriors, 'Do not finish me off yet; wait, I have Law to give you, important Law.'

Plate 8 MARAIAN SERIES
Lumahlumah saying, 'Now my body and organs are sacred, full of power. Take my remains to a cave and guard them well, for I am your life.'

Plate 9 MARAIAN SERIES
The body of Lumahlumah cut up by the tribal elders as instructed.

Plate 10 MARAIAN SERIES
Dua and Jiritja men taking bones of Lumahlumah.

Plate 11 MARAIAN SERIES
Messenger birds before the body was dismembered.

Plate 12 MARAIAN SERIES
Men dancing as the spirit of Lumahlumah rises and drifts away.

Plate 13 MARAIAN SERIES
Lumahlumah's two wives weep over his body and see his ghost rising.

Plate 14 MARAIAN SERIES
Some of the most sacred designs that were given to the four ceremonial leaders of the tribe. Around the neck of the left-hand top figure (Binning) is a sacred red feathered dilly bag, which contains sacred power stones that represent some of the organs of Lumahlumah. These stones give power for the regeneration of life in man and nature, and are brought out towards the end of the Maraian ceremony — part of the most high and secret revelations that only a man seeing his fifth or sixth Maraian ceremony may see and learn about. (Sometimes a man may be 50 years of age before he sees all the mysteries of his religion; only then is he recognised as a full tribal man, a responsible elder.)

Plate 15 MARAIAN SERIES
Sacred designs given by Lumahlumah to the four elders, who sing sacred songs in the doorway of the 'shade' (or leaf house, which is synonymous with the doorway to the spirit world).

Plate 16 MARAIAN SERIES
Maraian totemic centres of life.
Top-left panel: Sacred poles.
Top-right panel: Green ant Dreaming.
Middle-left panel: Body cuts; the final revelations.
Middle-right panel: Kangaroo increase.
Bottom-left panel: Cult heroes singing Maraian.
Bottom-right panel: Elder and Mimis dancing and singing Maraian.

Plate 17 MARAIAN SERIES
'Cheeky yam', Maraian symbol of increase. Such religious objects are painted and sung in one stage of the ceremony, for the perpetuation of their kind.

Plate 18 MARAIAN SERIES
Custodians of the sacred poles for Maraian, bringing the emblems from the waterhole for the ceremony.

Plate 19 MARAIAN SERIES
Maraian ritual dance with white fish sacred poles.

Plate 20 MARAIAN SERIES
Custodians of the sacred objects in worshipful contemplation of the objects in the 'shade' on the ceremony ground.

Plate 21 MARAIAN SERIES
The fish dance. Men lie down in rows and shake to symbolise the dying struggle of a fish or whale. This is synonymous with a man dying.

Plate 22 MARAIAN SERIES
Totemic increase site and cave of Lumahlumah.

Plate 23 MARAIAN SERIES
Daughters of Lumahlumah going forth with creator staffs to follow their Dreaming path on the mainland.

Plate 24 MARAIAN SERIES
Power symbols of Maraian. These sacred poles are painted and sung at a high stage in the ceremony, for fully initiated men. (Paintings like this can be seen but the chants and power words cannot be revealed.)

Plate 25 MARAIAN SERIES
'Cheeky yam' Dreaming. The yam is also a sacred pole, seen here walking at the end of its Dreaming journey.

Plate 26 MARAIAN SERIES
Body painting (Dua moiety). A stage in a man's initiation as he is taught more of the sacred law and religion.

Plate 27 MARAIAN SERIES
Body painting (Dua moiety) for a man; a higher stage in the Maraian ceremony.

Plate 28 MARAIAN SERIES
Body painting (Jiritja moiety) for a man's chest and upper legs. A higher stage in the Maraian ceremony.

Plate 29 MARAIAN SERIES
Maraian body painting, given by the giant, Lumahlumah, in the Dreaming. This design links the living with their pre-existence (which is the Dreaming).

Plate 30 MARAIAN SERIES
Maraian body painting, originally on the body of Lumahlumah when he taught the designs and ritual to the early time tribal elders.

Plate 31 MARAIAN SERIES
Maraian painting for Lumahlumah. The last design that is marked out with Maraian string attached to symbols over the grave of a man of very high degree.

Plate 32 MARAIAN SERIES
Designs of stages of the Maraian.

Plate 33 MARAIAN SERIES
Maraian sticks, symbols of the bones of Lumahlumah.

Plate 34 MARAIAN SERIES
Maraian body painting (Jiritja moiety) for a man seeing his third and fourth Maraian ceremony.

Plate 35 MARAIAN SERIES
Maraian body painting (Dua moiety) for a man seeing his third and fourth Maraian ceremony.

Plate 36 MARAIAN SERIES
Dua and Jiritja young men, painted Maraian for second and third stage of their initiation.

Plate 37 MARAIAN SERIES
Sacred Maraian dilly bag which contains foreskin of a circumcised boy.

Plate 38 MARAIAN SERIES
The totemic being for yams has observed a mistake in the sacred dancing in the Maraian ceremony. This old man is very angry and his tongue is 'hot', like a snake, as he calls for punishment of the offender.

Plate 39 MARAIAN SERIES
First and third panels: Maraian body painting.
Second panel: Men dancing and singing Maraian ritual. One man makes a mistake.
Fourth panel: The dancer who has made the mistake is killed.
Fifth panel: Lumahlumah's body painting for Maraian.

Plate 40 MARAIAN SERIES
Bone fish, one of the first dances in the Maraian, synonymous with bones of a man and Lumahlumah.

Plate 41 MARAIAN SERIES
Maraian white fish, a dance in the first section of the ceremony.

Plate 42 MARAIAN SERIES
Sacred pole and wand with white barramundi, a dance of importance in the ceremony.

Plates 43 & 44 MARAIAN SERIES
White barramundi, first seen by Lumahlumah, who made a song and dance and named the fish. This is an important dance in the ceremony.

Plate 45 MARAIAN SERIES
In the Dreaming Time, Nutmungi the turtle walked about like a man following his Dreaming path. One day he saw a beautiful young girl and wanted her for his wife, but so did the ant-eater man. The two men quarrelled over the girl until it came to blows. Fiercely the two men fought. The ant-eater man hurled many heavy rocks at Nutmungi, bruising him all over; Nutmungi, in return, hurled spears until the ant-eater man was covered in spikes. The battle raged on until both men were badly wounded. The ant-eater man crawled away into the bush and turned into a small ant-eater animal (an echidna), and Nutmungi staggered away and fell into a waterhole where he turned into a turtle.

The pattern on his shell is said to have been caused by bruising from the stones the ant-eater man threw at him.

Plate 46 MARAIAN SERIES
The echidna who fought with Nutmungi the turtle man (Jiritja moiety). These are dances in the Maraian for the survival and continuation of the natural species.

Plate 47 MARAIAN SERIES
Echidna (Dua moiety). A dance in the Maraian.

Plate 48 MARAIAN SERIES
Daadbi the poison snake and Barrap-Barrap the little sea bird that was eaten by the snake. This drawing shows Daadbi before he evolved into an ordinary snake. In the Dreaming he was both male and female, a giver of life. The design also indicates the dual role of the earth mother and the snake in the creation time.

Plate 49 MARAIAN SERIES
Daadbi the poison snake in pursuit of Barrap-Barrap the little sea bird. Now Daadbi has become a proper snake.

Plate 50 MARAIAN SERIES
Maraian increase dance for scrub fowl. The male and female fowls support the sacred increase dilly bag.

Plate 51 MARAIAN SERIES
Kundaagi the red plains kangaroo with two frill-necked lizards. These dances also belong to the Ubar and Lorrgon ceremonies. The kangaroo men dance in lines, Dua and Jiritja in turn.

Plate 52 MARAIAN SERIES
Kundaagi the red plains kangaroo and the Mimis. The Mimis pursue Kundaagi and the other kangaroos and wallabies. Kundaagi is speared by the Mimi.

Plate 53 MARAIAN SERIES
Kundaagi cooked by the Mimis. They ate him but did not break up his skeleton or burn it, for that destroys the spirit.

Plate 54 MARAIAN SERIES
After eating Kundaagi the Mimi spirits make magic to restore flesh to the kangaroo, that is, to 'lift him up.' Life is restored to the kangaroo by the sacred life-giving songs and dances. The ritual songs and dance regenerate man and nature, and give life after death.

Plate 55 MARAIAN SERIES
Male black kangaroo (Dua moiety) wearing ritual head dress. This ritual can only be seen by a man going through his fourth Maraian ceremony.

Plate 56 MARAIAN SERIES
Grey kangaroo (Dua moiety). A dance in the Maraian.

Plate 57 MARAIAN SERIES
Yellow wallaby (Jiritja moiety), first seen and named by Lumahlumah. In the Maraian this animal is a symbol of endurance for young men, as well as a symbol of increase. In the Uwar ceremony, initiates undergo an ordeal near the symbolic country of the wallaby.

Plate 58 MARAIAN SERIES
Yellow kangaroo (Jiritja moiety), an important dance and ritual in the Maraian.

Plate 59 MARAIAN SERIES
Mother wallaby feeding on bush fruit. This is a ritual dance and song for increase of animal and plants. (Wullur, white rock wallaby.)

Plate 60 MARAIAN SERIES
Totemic kangaroo showing power signs on body. Nearby is the 'shade' (spirit) of an ancestral being. In the Dreaming, the kangaroo walked about as a man. Man and nature are one, the same, dependent on each other.

Plate 61 MARAIAN SERIES
Turkey dance in the Maraian. The turkey was pursued by Mimis who wanted his body fat. Turkey told them to leave him alone because he was a man like them. So saying, turkey turned into a man.

Plate 62 MARAIAN SERIES
Bush turkey and goannas. Turkey is feeding on bush fruit in the country of the goannas. These are important songs and dances in the Maraian ceremony.

Plate 63 MARAIAN SERIES
Wimbrel, a bird that lives on small water life. This is a dance and song in the Maraian. (Dua moiety.)

Plate 64 MARAIAN SERIES
Wimbrel. (Jiritja moiety.)

Plate 65 MARAIAN SERIES
Emu eating fish, bush fruit. Increase for both. Dances and songs in Maraian.

Plate 66 MARAIAN SERIES
Male emu (Dua moiety), watching near its mate; waiting to take his turn on the eggs.

Plate 67 MARAIAN SERIES
Female emu (Jiritja moiety), about to lay the eggs. This is an important ritual for the survival of the bird. The eggs are symbolised by sacred stones, kept by certain male custodians.

Plate 68 MARAIAN SERIES
Female Jabiru (Dua moiety). In the Dreaming she followed a Dreaming path, crying out as she came along it.

Plate 69 MARAIAN SERIES
Stork or Jabiru eating fish.

Plate 70 MARAIAN SERIES
Emu and her young (Jiritja moiety). This painting is a powerful increase design, and inside the bird can be seen the eggs (the sacred stones).

Plate 71 MARAIAN SERIES
Maraian crocodile (Dua moiety). Sacred ritual belongs to it. The 'stones' in its body are its tongue and eggs, which are kept by old custodians who have inherited the sacred songs, ritual and designs associated with them.

Plate 72 MARAIAN SERIES
The ceremony ground for the Maraian; the section where the stones are brought out and through the appropriate songs, painting and dance, power is sought from the Dreaming and the totemic beings are summoned to sanction the ceremony.

Plate 73 MARAIAN SERIES
Golomomo, the freshwater (or Johnstone) crocodile, about to emerge from a waterhole and follow the creeks and rivers. The wet season is the time for the increase (mating and procreating) of the crocodile.

Plate 74 MARAIAN SERIES
Maraian freshwater crocodile and barramundi in the Dreaming waterhole.

Plate 75 MARAIAN SERIES
Salt-water crocodile (Jiritja moiety) swimming up from a deep billabong to begin her travelling to mate in the wet season. Very sacred power designs and meaning.

Plate 76 MARAIAN SERIES
The great 'boss' crocodile dancing and singing for big rains and power. In his head he carries great power centres, which are also destructive forces of magic.

Plate 77 MARAIAN SERIES
Maraian Barramundi. The large white barramundi (head cut off) is cooked. The white barramundi is a sacred section of ritual in the Maraian and it was first seen and named by Lumahlumah in the Dreaming time.

Plate 78 MARAIAN SERIES
Barramundi increase painting. Maraian ceremony.

Plate 79 MARAIAN SERIES
Maraian increase for barramundi and kingfish.

Plate 80 MARAIAN SERIES
Maraian increase painting for cuttlefish.

Plate 81 MARAIAN SERIES
Stingray Dreaming (Jiritja moiety). The stingray followed a Dreaming path all round the coast and over to Groote Eylandt.

Plate 82 MARAIAN SERIES
Maraian, sacred green ant and snake Dreaming. In the Jabiluka, Kakadu National Park areas.

Plate 83 GUGURR THE MOON MAN AND MULITJI HIS DOG
This is the origin of the Liverpool River, and how it was made in the Dreaming time.

When I told Yirawala that the Americans had put a man on the moon, he looked at me without surprise, saying that the Gunwinggu people already had a man and a dog up there. 'That not so big thing, my people put man and dog there long time ago. I tell you story now.'

Gugurr was a creator being in the Dreaming time. He was travelling a long way with his dog, Mulitji. They had gone far into the inland and were very thirsty. Mulitji had run ahead of Gugurr, sniffing for food and water, and finding none began to whine desperately. Suddenly Mulitji began sniffing in a certain place in the middle of an area of hot dry land, then started to dig frantically. Gugurr went over to investigate. The excited dog nipped him on the neck, then dug with greater energy, whining all the time. Gugurr bent down and began to help Mulitji to dig.

Man and dog worked hard, and soon a trickle of water oozed from the sand. They kept digging until more water flowed, then suddenly a great spurt of water burst from the earth, filling the hole and crumbling the sides until a mighty stream of water rushed across the land, cutting a deep path on its way to the sea.

Gugurr and Mulitji were trapped in the water, trying to stay afloat but often going under as they clung to each other for support and comfort. Gugurr said, 'Mulitji, we cannot get out, we are finished.' The little dog cried out as though agreeing, then Gugurr said, 'But we will never be forgotten because when we die our shadows will be on the moon and stay there forever. People will see us there and remember us always for the water we have brought, and they will know that this place where we die will remain as a whirlpool in the river.'

To this day Gunwinggu people see the 'shades' of Gugurr the moon man and Mulitji his dog as shadows on the moon. The people are reminded that Gugurr and his little dog made the mighty Liverpool River.

Plate 84 THE MOON MAN AND HIS DOG
Gugurr the moon man and his little dog Mulitji on the moon.

Plate 85 THE MOON MAN AND HIS DOG
Gugurr the moon man at the height of his power, during the full moon.

Plate 86 BARRA AND JINAROO MAKING THE WET SEASON
Every year in late October, Barra the wet season man argues with Jinaroo the dry season man. Barra is the big boss of storms and he comes to take over from Jinaroo, who is always reluctant to go. Jinaroo pleads for time, saying that Barra is too early and the wet must be a long way off. But Barra lifts his arms and sings, 'I am Barra, big boss of the storms. It is my turn now to sing and dance to bring in the wet, so all things will multiply. Sit down old dry season man until next year. It is my turn now. I will stamp on the edge of the waterhole and call up the king of all frogs to sing out for big rain.'

Barra stamps on the bank of this important waterhole and sings loudly, calling out for the one-eyed king of all frogs who, hearing the sacred Maraian calling, emerges from the water and begins the ceremony for the making of rain, to regenerate man and all nature.

The first creature to hear the frog king is Golomomo, the great salt-water crocodile, who rises from a deep inland billabong and waits for the flowing torrents that will link up the waterholes in the river bed. The sky darkens as Barra and the frog sing and thunder shakes the earth.

The king crocodile is moving, listening to the thunder, leaving the deep waterholes, following the river, mating and singing; life goes on forever.

All over Arnhemland the frogs dance and sing, a great chorus of frogs which always heralds the coming of the wet season.

The designs on the top and bottom edges of the painting represent clouds, rain and wind. The looped edging represents lightning.

Yirawala said that if the wet season is late then he or some other old man of power will go to the frog's waterhole and stamp on the edge, singing and calling the power names.

I had sometimes heard Yirawala call out, 'Get up Barra. Make big storms.' This when very little rain falls during what is called a 'dry wet'. Food is plentiful when the rains come.

Plate 87 THE FROG KING
The frog king is dancing and singing for the increase of all natural life. The emphasis on genitalia is to emphasise his role in procreation and the continuation of life.

Plate 88 BARRA AND JINAROO
Barra the wet season man is on the left of the painting and Jinaroo the dry season man is on the right. Jinaroo feels utterly dejected because he is reluctant to go. The lower panel is the strong winds before the rains.

Plate 89 THE LIGHTNING
This totemic being sings and makes magic for lightning. It is both male and female. The strings and dots represent linked power bags, lightning stones that are magic. The hair is rain.

Plate 90 SHEET-LIGHTNING FIGURE
Related to other lightning figures. The place of sheet lightning is in Gunwinggu country, in the place of stones (this includes stones of different and unusual shapes). By calling power names and striking a lightning stone near Liverpool River, storms may be called up.

Plate 91 NAMORREN THE LIGHTNING MAN
Long ago in the Dreaming time, a number of Gunwinggu men went out hunting and stopped to rest near a waterhole. The older men told the younger ones they must not use the waterhole to wash in or something terrible would happen to them.

One young man named Namorul was defiant and said to himself, 'I will go and wash the sticky honey from my hands. I am not frightened by these old stories.' So he went to the pool and washed. Later his two brothers asked him why he had defied the older men, and said they were afraid for him, for what he had done was against tribal law. Namorul laughed and said, 'Rubbish. Look at me. I am all right. Nothing hurt me because I was not afraid. I am strong and I did what I wanted to do. That is the only way.' His brothers told him that they were still afraid for him, and he should listen to what the older men said. But Namorul laughed and walked away.

That night the sky grew black and a bright streak of lightning shot through the night like a giant spear and struck Namorul, severing his head and slicing his body down his backbone to his genitals.

Soon the fate of Namorul was told to all the tribe, and has been passed down the years to young people, especially those who are defiant of older people. Namorren the lightning man, they warn, does not act alone, but is summoned by a medicine man who sings him up and bids him do his work.

Plate 92 NAMORUL CUT TO PIECES BY NAMORREN THE LIGHTNING MAN

Plate 93 BARRA, LIGHTNING AND THUNDER MAN
Bringer of the wet season. The little bags tied to his arms and legs are 'power bags' containing magic stones for making storms. The stones are painted and sung in a certain sacred place in Gunwinggu country.

Plate 94 THE LIGHTNING MAN RESTING IN HIS CAVE DURING THE DRY SEASON
In this area there is a waterhole surrounded by heavy trees and brush. People may pass this place in peace but they must not pull grass or break any bush, because this would profane the pool of the lightning man and water sprites, and all the people might die by lightning bolts or drowning. This cave is not far from the whirlpool area in the Liverpool River where the moon man and his dog drowned.

Plate 95 BEW-BEW THE GIANT, OR THE ORIGIN OF THE DIDJERIDU
One day Wandjuk Marika, from Yirrkala, came to visit us and play a big didjeridu that his father Marwulan had painted. Yirawala said that Wandjuk was a good didjeridu player and the instrument had a very interesting origin, according to the Gunwinggu. Yirawala said he would make a painting about it. This is the story...

Long ago in the early time there lived a big man name Bew-Bew. This giant lived on the mud flats at the northern end of Goulburn Island, in a cone-shaped hut of mud and sticks. Entrance and exit were through a hole in the top. The name of this hut is boonji, which means 'blind', having no door.

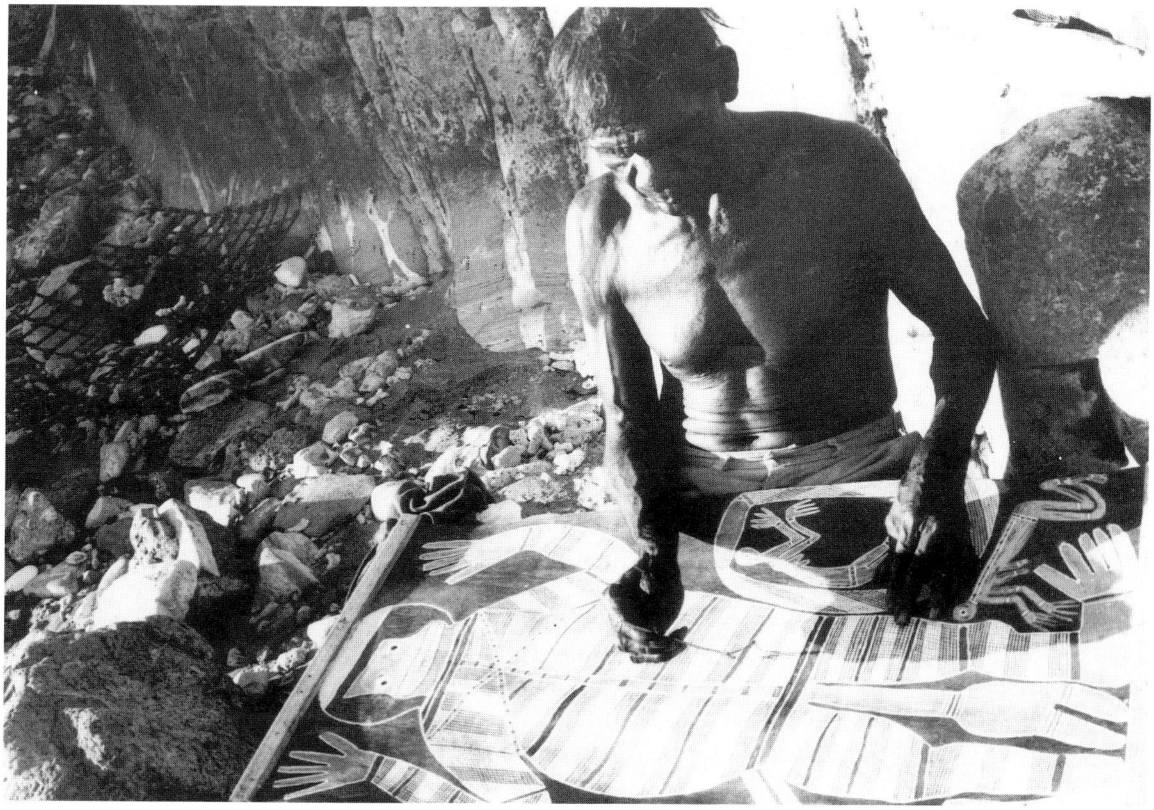

Yirawala on Mindil Beach, Darwin, painting Bew-Bew the lecherous giant.

(The house was fashioned this way as a protection against mosquitoes. A smoke fire allowed the occupant to sit virtually unmolested by the savage flying legions of sandflies and mosquitoes. The wood burned for such smoke protection was Cyprus pine, which is still used to ward off these insect pests.)

A rope ladder hung from the hole in the top so that the giant could lower himself to the floor. This ladder is called an arrowk.

Bew-Bew lived on food from fresh water: lily roots, goose eggs, tortoise and fish.

One day two young girls went walking away from their camp, looking for nut trees. They became lost and wandered into Bew-Bew's camp. The giant was delighted and said, 'Welcome my wives'. He captured them and put them in his house, pulling up the ladder so they could not escape. The giant brought food and water for the young girls, who were very frightened. They pleaded with Bew-Bew to release them but he only laughed.

In the night the giant became amorous but the girls resisted him, the older girl pleading for her sister more than herself. The elder sister said they did not want Bew-Bew as a husband and in any case they were too small for him. The giant only smiled and took both girls by force.

Next morning the girls were sick and could not stand so Bew-Bew went hunting to find delicacies to restore them. The giant returned with lily roots and fish but the girls could not eat. Bew-Bew scratched his thick head and thought he must be giving the girls the wrong food and this was why they had no appetite. He decided to go far afield and get fresh goose eggs for the girls, so they might eat and be happy wives. The giant climbed the ladder, carefully pulling it up after him, and went blundering off into the forest.

The younger girl was still very sick but her sister desperately exhorted her to make the effort to escape, otherwise they would surely die. The elder sister tried to climb the walls but kept falling back, so she told her sister to stand up so that she could stand on her shoulders.

Desperately lunging from the shoulders of her sick sister, the older girl managed to grasp the rim of the hole and pull herself through, then reached down to grab the hands of her sister and hauled her out.

The younger girl could not walk so her sister carried her back to their own people, who had been searching for them. When the girls told of their terrible ordeal with Bew-Bew, the people were enraged, vowing instant revenge on the giant.

In the afternoon the giant returned with baskets of goose eggs, calling out the equivalent of 'I'm home'. When he found the girls had escaped, he hurled the eggs to the ground, bellowing with rage. Snatching up his clubs of tree trunks, he went rampaging through the bush looking for them.

Now the tribesmen expected this, and had been frantically digging for some hours a vast pit on the only pathway to their camp. The pit was covered with dirt, branches and leaves so that it looked like ordinary ground.

They had scarcely finished covering the pit when they heard the giant's roaring and crashing, his knocking down trees in his path and bellowing for his two wives. 'Give me my wives. I will smash and kill you all.'

The tribe stood beyond the pit watching Bew-Bew come towards them. Close to the pit the giant paused in surprise — so he began bellowing for his wives and stamping about so that the ground shook. Then he jumped onto the trap and fell into the pit.

Many people had been hiding in the bush in case the trap did not work but now everyone came running up to look at the threshing monster, who was soon filled with spears and looking like a porcupine.

The giant was groaning and moaning as the people hurriedly began filling in the pit on top of him. In a sudden spasm, Bew-Bew reached down and put his penis in his mouth and commenced blowing it. The noise sounded like 'didjenbraw, didjenbral, didjenbraw'. The men paused to listen and liked what they heard. They tried to imitate the sound but found it was physically impossible for normal men.

Some of the men persisted, and others went into the bush, looking around for something to make the sound. Small trees were cut down and found to have some hollow branches, which were cut in lengths and then held to the mouth. At first no sound came when the men blew into the hollow pieces of wood, then one man made sounds which with practice sounded like Bew-Bew's penis.

So the giant gave them something useful (the didjeridu) before he died.

Plate 96 BOOMA-BOOMA THE BIG MAN

Booma-Booma was an evil giant who hunted at night, mainly stealing children and eating them. The hungry giant was attracted by a crying boy or girl. Mothers would endeavour to silence crying children by saying that the giant would come and take them if they persisted.

Booma-Booma had a very large phallus and was also engrossed in stealing young girls and women for his pleasure.

He had no wives and lived alone, deep in the bush, near a certain stony hill. (This is also the camp of a fearsome giant named Namaralto.)

One night Booma-Booma stole the baby son of Wullurr, a great warrior and tribal elder. Wullurr was so grief stricken and enraged that he declared war on the giant. Waving his spear and woomera, Wullurr danced and called for revenge on the cruel giant.

Early next morning Wullurr and his fighting men began their journey. In the late afternoon they came to the country of Booma-Booma. Wullurr crept through the trees to scout the land, creeping through the dark, dank undergrowth until he heard the sound of snoring. Lying next to the remains of a cannibal feast was the giant, fast asleep.

Wullurr went back to get his men and together they crept into the lair of Booma-Booma. The men gazed in fear and horror at the big ugly giant but Wullurr, shouting his battle cry, hurled a spear into the giant, followed by blows from his club. The other men attacked and the battle raged until the giant fell down dead.

With triumphant shouts the surviving men built a big fire over Booma-Booma's body, determined to reduce it to ashes. As the fire finally died down, the men danced with joy to see only a great pile of ash. But suddenly the hot ashes stirred and a flaming red hot skeleton rose up and turned into a two headed woman. She crawled from the ashes saying, 'You cannot kill me. I am immortal. My old body is finished but I will live again.' The skeleton had taken on new flesh after death.

Yirawala said that this story was very old and was magic.

Plate 97 TWO-HEADED MONSTROUS WOMAN
After Booma-Booma was burned.

Plate 98 NAMARALTO, OR GORRORELLI
A giant who lives in the stony hill country on the way to Gumardir River. (Even today, people do not go through this area after dark.)

Plate 99 BOLIG-BOLIG THE HONEY MAN
At certain times of the year in Arnhemland, particular trees give out a fine sugary powder on their leaves. This powder must be collected very early in the morning, as it disappears with the warm light. When this happens people say that Bolig-Bolig the 'sugar bag' (wild honey) man has beaten them to it.

Bolig-Bolig loves wild honey and carries it about in little finely woven bags on his waist and arms. This spirit man is the giver of honey.

Plate 100 DAADBI AND GULAWAN
Daadbi the poison snake was always looking for a new home and was not above taking someone else's. One day the snake was travelling along his path and came upon a very snug-looking house, a hole in the ground, sheltered from wind and rain, and hidden by overhanging bushes.

Daadbi began crawling inside and found that Gulawan the goanna was at home and prepared to defend what he had made. The goanna ordered the snake to leave at once, but the snake offered to fight him and the goanna accepted.

Outside the hole, the goanna and the snake were locked in battle, threshing and biting each other. Daadbi laughed, thinking that the poison from his bites would soon kill Gulawan. But the wily goanna smeared the poisonous bites with his own excrement and spittle, then carried on fighting. Soon their relations joined in the battle. The snakes were beaten and driven off.

This painting is used for healing magic. Yirawala said that Aborigines used certain parts (the liver and part of the bowel) of a big goanna's body for poison bites.

Plate 101 THE PRAYING-MANTIS MAN
Long ago there lived a man who was a social misfit in the tribe. He took no responsibility and was a thief, stealing stores of honey and berries. The old men were tolerant at first, since the man broke no serious laws, but when he did not mend his ways as promised, the elders decided something must be done.

Mook-Mook the owl man was a powerful magician for sickness and death, so he was consulted. Mook-Mook said that since the man was always in a begging position, asking for food and help, then so he should remain. The elders were mystified until the owl man explained. He told them that soon a certain bright star would come closer to earth and in the star was great power which could be used when certain singing and ritual was performed by him. The owl man said he knew the ancient words to release from the bright star a ray of power that would change the unwanted man into something manageable.

The days passed, and the misfit ignored further warnings to stop begging and behave like everyone else. Then one night everyone noticed a very bright star slowly descending closer to earth. The time was at hand for the magical singing so the owl man went to a certain hill and began invoking the power from the star. All night Mook-Mook sang and danced as the star glittered then descended somewhere on earth.

In the camp the people saw a startling change coming over the misfit nuisance. As power from the star was directed onto him, he began to grow feelers on his head; then his arms and legs became longer and longer, and he took up a stance like a praying mantis. He grew wings after he called out plaintively, 'Give me wings — I want my wings, I am only half finished.' Later he was a proper praying mantis and crawled away up a tree to wait for insect food.

In the painting the praying mantis is half finished and is calling for his wings.

Plates 102 & 103 NAMARRGINE THE BIRD MAN

Namarrgine was an evil magician responsible for stealing the spirits, which he trapped and kept in bags until he was ready to devour them.

He preferred stealing the spirits of babies. At night his fingernails and toenails would grow quickly, until they were long snake-like extensions. These long nails would then crawl like snakes over the ground and pluck babies from their resting places.

Namarrgine lived with a tribe until he began killing people, then he was driven off into swamp country. He takes the form of the black swamp bird that wanders around at night calling, 'Kowk, kowk, kowk'.

When a child is crying a lot, a mother may warn it to be quiet in case Namarrgine is out walking. If a child is very thin and its skin going blackish grey, people observe that Namarrgine has taken its spirit already and they are afraid.

In Yirawala's country we had noticed an evil-looking half man, half crocodile in a small cave by itself. Yirawala said that this was also Namarrgine, waiting for victims.

Plate 104 THE SNAKES AND THE MOSQUITO PEOPLE

In the Dreaming time the clan of the mosquito Dreaming lived near the mangrove swamps at a place called Marugulidban (which is Yirawala's clan country) about 80 kilometres inland from the mouth of the Liverpool River. Because the area was full of danger from reptiles and insects, the Mosquito people built conical houses on stilts of pandanus palm trunks, with sleeping platforms inside. Each hut had a hole in the top and in each floor platform to provide an entrance and exit and to allow smoke to escape. The hole at the base was always closed at night.

One night three great pythons came, attacking the Mosquito people as they slept. The people had no chance and were all killed.

The shape of the painting is consistent with the ranga shape and the cross hatching is Maraian.

Plate 105 MOWANI THE CANNIBAL GIANT

Mowani was a giant from the Jun-bar-bar family of giants, who were all greedy cannibals. One day Mowani was recovering from a feast of human flesh, when he heard the distant sound of stone striking wood. The giant smiled wickedly for he knew the sound: the cracking of the small hard nuts found in his country. Mowani rose and picked up a large club.

Two sisters were cracking the nuts. They had been told to look for nut trees only in their own country close to the camp, but they wandered on and on. At first they were unaware they were lost and went on collecting nuts. The younger girl was using two stones to break open the nuts from a fully laden tree, and was told by her sister not to make such a noise as they might be in someone else's country and some hostile thing might hear them.

The elder sister was pregnant and was resting on a lower tree branch when Mowani appeared. There was no escape and the giant knocked her down, killing her instantly. The other girl was captured and stuffed into the giant's dilly bag with her dead sister.

Back at his camp Mowani made an oven of stones and cooked the dead girl, thinking to leave the younger one until the next day. After eating the girl and her baby, Mowani went to sleep. The young girl chewed at the bag and escaped, running home to tell her people.

The girl's tribe knew that Mowani was very savage and before attacking him they must first send spies to have a look. Since no ordinary man could go, magic was made and the first two spies were turned into the owl Ngokaok and the storm bird Wirriwirriyak. The third spy was turned into the bat Nabarmingming, and the fourth became a willy wagtail bird named Jigaritj-Jigaritj.

Plate 106 GIRLS IN DILLY BAG
The spies flew over the camp, and bat and wagtail saw that Mowani was very sick from eating the girl and her baby. The giant was staggering about and surely this was the time to attack. Bat and wagtail flew home to point the way for the attack on Mowani.

Plate 107 BAT AND WAGTAIL POINTING THE WAY TO MOWANI

Plate 108 SPIRITS OF THE DEAD MOTHER AND HER BABY RETURN TO HER MOTHER AND GRAND-MOTHER, WHO MOURN OVER THEM
Painting no. 4 in Mowani series.

Plate 109 MOWANI THE GIANT DEAD AND CUT UP
Painting no. 5 in the Mowani series. The people attacked and killed Mowani the giant, but the heroes were the bat Nabarmingming and the willy wagtail man Jigaritj-Jigaritj.

Plate 110 BAT AND WAGTAIL AFTER THE BATTLE
Painting no. 6 in Mowani series. This painting shows wagtail and bat after the fight with Mowani the giant. Jigaritj-Jigaritj the wagtail man is on the left and Mabarmingming the bat is on the right. (Wagtail has lost a foot.)

Plate 111 MARALAITJ THE EARTH MOTHER GIVING BIRTH TO THE TRIBES IN THE BOUCAUT BAY AREA
The old earth mother came from Indonesia way and on the mainland met two old men, with whom she copulated. The creator heroine followed her Dreaming path, giving birth to tribes in different places. Each time she was in labour, she cried out 'kah, kah, kah', meaning 'many children'.

The painting shows the mother goddess giving birth to Dua and Jiritja moieties. The Dua were born first.

Plate 112 MARALAITJ GIVING BIRTH TO DUA MOIETY
Maralaitj giving birth to the Dua moiety. This creator ancestor of the Northern tribes was blown from the direction of Indonesia onto the mainland, where she met Ngarljod the rainbow snake who brought her two old men for husbands. Maralaitj gave birth the first time at the sacred waterholes in Gunwinggu country.

After following her Dreaming path and giving birth to the first tribes, Maralaitj and the rainbow snake placed spirit children in certain baby Dreaming waterholes. The snake and the woman are closely associated.

Plate 113 JIRITJA MOIETY DIVIDED INTO SKINS
This painting shows the Jiritja moiety people and the skins (sections and sub-sections). Maralaitj first placed them in moieties and skins.

Plate 114 DUA MOIETY DIVIDED INTO SKINS
The painting shows Dua moiety people divided into skins (sections and sub-sections). Each group is represented by their symbol (circles, dots and lines).

Plate 115 MARALAITJ, NGARLJOD AND SACRED EMU
Sacred increase ritual being performed by the deep waterhole of the snake. It is increase for man and for the depositing of spirit children in baby Dreaming wells. The white figure is the everlasting spirit of Maralaitj.

Plate 116 MARALAITJ AND HER WOMEN: FERTILITY DANCE
The central figure in the top panel is Maralaitj, pregnant and dancing with her women. She is performing women's business (ceremony) for women and although men may see this painting they may not know the 'inside' sacred women's story and songs. In the bottom panel, Mimi women join in the dancing that is perpetuating life itself.

Plate 117 BABY-DREAMING WATERHOLES
Dua and Jiritja sacred incarnation wells, from whence come the spirits of babies to impregnate their mothers, and to where they return after death. The wells represent incarnation and reincarnation, giving life and an assurance of life after death.

Plate 118 BABY-DREAMING WELLS, AND CREATOR BEINGS
The central circles are three important increase centres for reincarnation and incarnation. The top circle (well) has the sacred Maraian life force design. The central waterhole is the embryo of a human being. The third well is the storage place for creator staffs and rangga where totemic beings dwell. The figures on either side are creation heroes.

Plate 119 NOWYRAN THE BIG CARPET SNAKE
Nowyran is the biggest carpet snake in Australia and lives only in one rocky area of Arnhemland, in the Gunwinggu country

In the Dreaming time, Nowyran was once a man and also a magician of great power but was forced to leave his original camp because of a quarrel over a woman, a young promised wife who refused to go to him. Nowyran was so upset and angry that he went away into the rock country to brood over wrongs inflicted on him by the girl. After some weeks of sitting by himself, Nowyran sang a magic song and turned himself into the great rock python.

One night Nowyran was repeatedly awakened by the persistent crying of a child and he became angry. The child's mother tried desperately to stop him crying for she feared he might be heard by some hostile being. The following three nights the little boy kept on crying until Nowyran, unable to bear any more, slithered down from his high rock pile and attacked the child, biting off his head as the mother screamed and tried to save her son. Nowyran ate the boy.

Plate 120 LUMAHLUMAH'S DAUGHTERS
A regional variation of the Wawiluk story of the two creator women who broke the Law and were eaten by the snake. In this painting the snake has killed the two women for profaning a sacred well with menstrual blood. The women died at the end of their Dreaming path and had finished their work.

Plate 121 MIMI GIVING BIRTH
The central section shows a Mimi giving birth. Supporting her at the back is her grandmother, and waiting to receive the child is her mother.

The Mimi woman is in the traditional birth posture, squatting over sterile ash obtained from burning a certain wood. Leaves are burned to give off a strong perfume that helps to ease the pain. After the birth, male and female relatives dance with joy to celebrate.

Plate 122 OOGLE THE NIGHT BIRD
This bird belongs to an old-time ceremony which is no longer performed. The bird dance was for the increase of small inland fish. Here the bird is full of fish.

Plate 123 GEECHNOCH THE LAZY MAN
Geechnoch was a lazy man who scrounged food from others. Each day when the men returned from the hunt he would beg for smaller fish from the nets, or for portions that nobody wanted. The men fed him like a dog and held him in contempt, giving him food only when it pleased them. When they gave him nothing, he wandered round the camp pleading

for scraps. The men laughed and said, 'If you are so hungry, go and get your own fish.'

One morning Geechnoch was so hungry he asked the men if he could go fishing with them. They rejected him and when he tried to follow, threatened him with spears.

Geechnoch sat down and cried in a squeaky voice. He decided he would show the men what he could do. He would go that very night and catch fish.

Next morning Geechnoch showed the men all the fish he had caught. The men only laughed and asked who had given them to him. Finally they believed he had caught them, but heaped ridicule on him as 'the man who goes alone at night to catch fish'. So he became more of an outcast than ever.

Geechnoch sat down and cried again, his voice sounding strange. That night he went to catch fish and never returned.

At night the men heard a strange sound in the swamps, a night bird fishing, calling out 'kowk, kowk, kowk', as it wandered about. The men said, 'Ah, poor thing, that is Geechnoch, turned into a bird that fishes at night.'

Plate 124 UBAR CEREMONY
The two figures at the top are messengers to invite elders from other tribes to the Ubar ceremony. Below the figures are initiates of the Dua moiety. On the left a Jiritja man is painting a Dua man. On the right are two Dua moiety men with the Ubar log drum that is beaten during the ceremony. The sound of the drum represents the voice of the primary 'old woman' creator ancestor. Beneath the seated figures are 'cheeky yams' increase objects. On the far right, two men sing a welcome to the invited people.

Plates 125 & 126 UBAR CEREMONY: DRUM AND WALLABY DANCE
Top and bottom of this painting are the Ubar log drums and the pandanus beaters. In the centre are the initiates performing the rock wallaby dance.

Plate 127 UBAR CEREMONY: FRILL-NECKED LIZARD DANCE
Female and male frill-necked lizards. This is a dance in the Ubar ceremony. Men painted as lizards climb trees and mime the actions of the frill necks. Men with spears chase the 'lizards' up and around the trees.

Plate 128 UBAR CEREMONY: DUA FLYING FOX
The flying fox is a fruit-eating bat with a fox-like head and is about as big in body as a large rat. The flying fox dance is an important part of the Ubar ceremony. The dancers mime a Dreamtime hunt when men with torches first caught the bat.

The flying fox was once a man following his Dreaming path. When he became a flying fox he taught the first Aborigines how to make the woomera. He gave the men the hook from his wing to fit to the end of their throwing sticks so that they could throw their spears with greater leverage and accuracy.

Plate 129 UBAR CEREMONY: FLYING FOXES
Showing male and female, Dua and Jiritja flying foxes, hanging upside down in a tree.

Plate 130 UBAR CEREMONY: FLYING FOXES
The top two flying foxes are Dua Moiety and the bottom bat is Jiritja Moiety. Here the flying foxes are in motion, frightened by the flaming torches of men hunting them.

Plates 131-139 THE LORRGON CEREMONY
The Lorrgon ceremony is a mortuary ceremony, and the full big ceremony is performed when a tribal elder dies.

The bones of the dead are interred in a hollow log coffin after having been removed from the ground in which they were buried for nine to twelve months and perhaps carried about for a time by female relatives before they reach their final resting place in the log coffin. It is painted with totemic emblems and stands upright in a symbolic sacred well.

Dua and Jiritja moieties participate in the ceremony, performing dances representing totemic beings: animal, goanna and Mimi spirits of the Dreaming.

This ceremony is the rites of passage in the deceased person's lifecycle. The sacred rituals ensure that the warrow (true spirit) will return to the totemic well from whence it came. The performance of the ceremony is an affirmation of life after death.

When a person dies, two spirits are released. One is the warrow and the other the morkoi (trickster spirit) who lives in jungle country. If the ceremony is not properly performed, the morkoi could lead the warrow astray and it would never return to the totemic well. When the correct rituals are performed, the ancestral ghosts are summoned and guide the new ghost home to the well.

Yirawala and other old ceremony bosses carried a large dilly bag containing the bones. The final act of placing the bones in the log coffin was accompanied by beautiful chanting, rising and falling in harmonious chorus, rich and deep, full of power and feeling. The painted dancers clustered round the log, calling the ancestral spirits and totems. Now the new ghost would go with its ancestors, sustained on the journey by Bunba, the butterfly spirits who gather nectar from the flowers to feed the new ghost. The ancestral spirits may also collect sugar-bag (wild honey) on which to feed.

As the ghost departed from the log the faces of the singers reflected satisfaction, then sadness as the chanting became more muted, ending on a high note.

Finally relatives sat in symbolic sacred wells scooped out of the sand, and ate special food. This communion integrates the living and gives comfort to them.

The long interval between the ground burial and the final interment in the hollow log has been a gradual adjustment to the death. The carrying about of bones by female relatives has also given some comfort.

Plate 131 LORRGON CEREMONY

The Lorrgon is a mortuary ceremony, and the full big ceremony is performed when a tribal elder dies. Two messengers, tribal elders, hold the sacred staff which 'awakens the dead'. The men beat boomerangs together and sing sacred ritual which is very beautiful to hear.

Plate 132 LORRGON CEREMONY PLACE

This ceremony ground and 'shade' (leaf house for sacred objects) links the living and the dead.

Plate 133 LORRGON CEREMONY: BIRTH OF KUNDAAGI

The skeletal painting is of the birth of Kundaagi, the red plains kangaroo who is an important figure in the Lorrgon ceremony.

Kundaagi was killed and eaten by the Mimis, who did not break up his bones or burn them; instead they lifted up the skeleton and put flesh on it. This is symbolic of a death and a rising.

Kundaagi's mother first found her son's bones and placed them in a wooden container which she took away to the ceremony ground and there the Mimis lifted up the skeleton and the first Lorrgon ceremony was performed to restore life to Kundaagi the kangaroo.

Plate 134 LORRGON CEREMONY

A painting in three panels.
Top panel: Mimis chasing Kundaagi the kangaroo.
Centre panel: Mimi performing increase magic for man and natural species.
Bottom panel: Mimi stealing Kundaagi's body fat.

Plate 135 LORRGON CEREMONY

Totemic being as a skeleton then putting on flesh, but still an invisible spirit. Beside him Mimis and spirits dance for the regeneration of man and nature.

Plate 136 LORRGON CEREMONY
The body of an ancestral hero broken up for preparation in the mortuary rituals (synonymous with Lumahlumah).

Plate 137 LORRGON CEREMONY: GOANNA
The big Lorrgon goanna is painted on the hollow log coffin as the secret songs are sung and the boomerangs are clapped. The goanna crawls into the log coffin.

Plate 138 LORRGON CEREMONY: DANCE OF SKELETONS
During one section of the Lorrgon ceremony when the living commune with the dead, the skeletal spirits rise up and dance so that they too participate and 'take on flesh' (are resurrected).

Plate 139 LORRGON CEREMONY: RED PLAINS KANGAROO DANCE
In this part of the Lorrgon ceremony 'kangaroo' dancers re-enact the travelling of Kundaagi the kangaroo in the Dreaming time, and how he was tracked and speared by the Mimi who assisted to raise the kangaroo up again (life after death). The wild little figures are Mimis dancing increase for kangaroos and man.

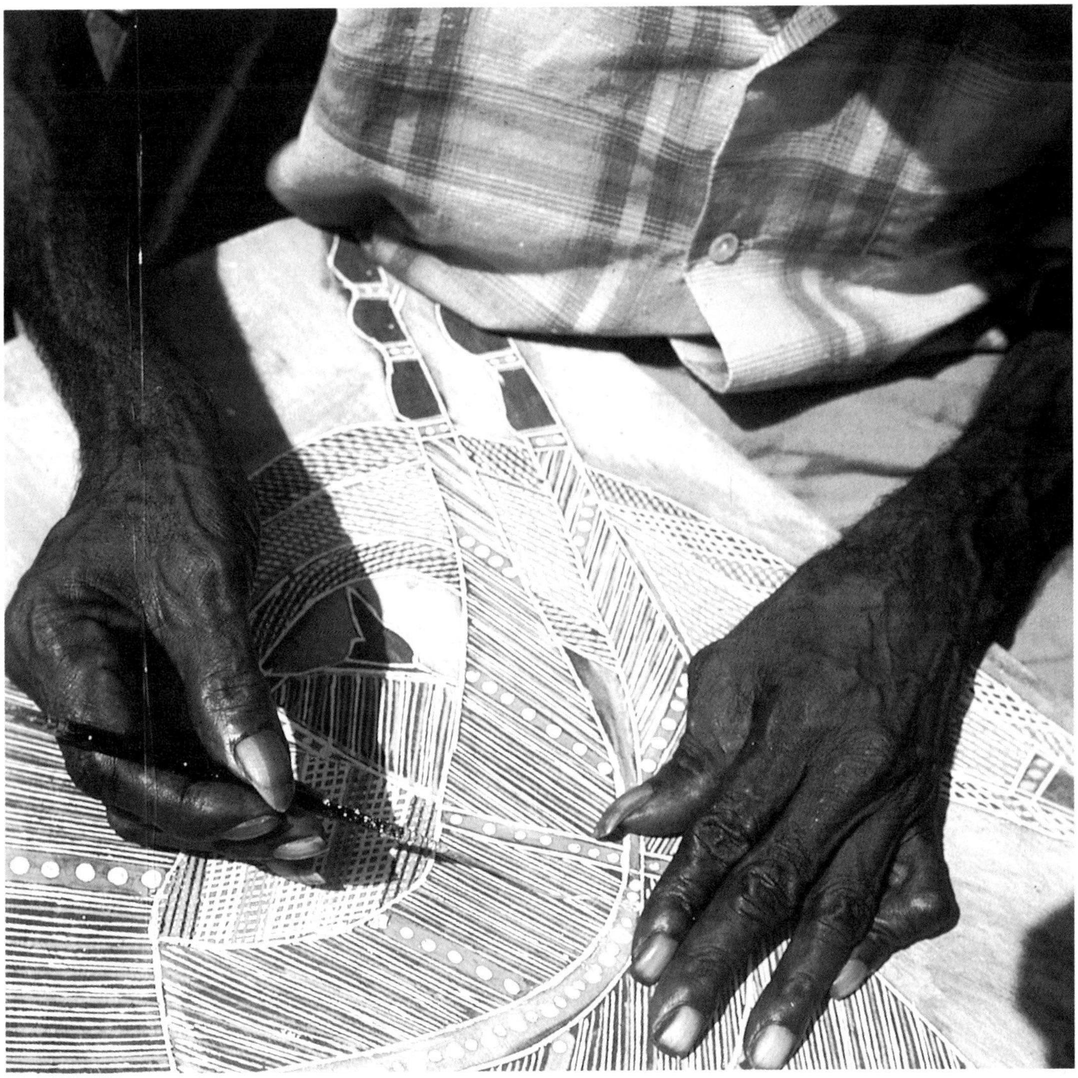

Epilogue

Late in life Yirawala set out to teach white people through lectures and displays of his religious drawings.

While thus engaged in teaching us about his religion and law, he was unaware that although Aborigines were made citizens of Australia by Federal legislation in 1967, this did not give recognition under Australian law to tribal marriages or customary laws of inheritance.

Yirawala had inherited his father's intellectual property, that being the sacred designs, symbols, songs and stories. As a chosen heir he was carefully instructed in tribal law, power designs, symbols, songs, ritual and stories as he progressed through various stages of ceremonial life, until he was shown the final mysteries at the age of forty-five. His learning continued until he became a 'clever man' (medicine man and healer), master of mysteries, keeper of sacred symbols, and defender of the faith.

Yirawala's drawings were not art but religion and history, and in the customary manner he began teaching his eldest son, David Gumaraitj, the religious designs so that the tribal records would be preserved and perpetuated. He in turn would pass it on unchanged to the next generation.

All this is Aboriginal business and has nothing to do with white man's law, yet, because Yirawala died without having made a white man's will, his intellectual property (i.e. the copyright inherent in his sacred symbols and designs) was later disposed of to commercial interests.

Yirawala's estate came under the Northern Territory Intestate Aboriginals (Distribution of Estates) Ordinance 1961-1967,* administered by the Public Trustee of the Northern Territory.

On 24 September 1976 the Director of Northern Territory Aboriginal Affairs caused a document to be issued to the Public Trustee in Darwin, in which the dependents of 'Billy' Yirawala were listed, and which concluded: 'As far as can be ascertained this person was not legally married and did not leave a will. At the time of his death, "Billy" Yirawala was cohabiting with Margaret Marranggu [Monanggu] and Mary Malilba.' (There was no mention that he was also an MBE.)

Yirawala's property distribution took place three years after his death, in March 1979. At the time the estate was listed as being only money in the bank, which would be distributed to the consorts and children. At the time copyright (Yirawala's intellectual property) was never mentioned as being part of his estate. It was included later, in 1980, when the Aboriginal Artists Agency of Sydney applied to the Public Trustee in Darwin for exclusive licence to reproduce Yirawala's paintings. This was granted to them. Then, in 1986, the Aboriginal Artists Agency applied to the Public Trustee to purchase Yirawala's copyright outright for the sum of $2500.00, after which the two widows would receive no payments and could make no

* Repealed in 1979. However, the old Act still applies to all tribal Aborigines who died before 1979. At the time of writing this book (February 1992) there is still no recognition of Aboriginal customary laws of inheritance.

claims. It was to be a once-only payment.

As I was in possession of certain documents relevant to Yirawala's will and copyright I challenged the validity of the copyright sale.

In July 1990 an out-of-court settlement gave me eight years' exclusive use of Yirawala's copyright, and thereafter my permission must be sought prior to publishing or causing to be published any reproductions of Yirawala's paintings.

In his lifetime Yirawala had assigned copyright to me verbally before witnesses, on tape, and through four small, sacred Maraian paintings bearing his handprints. He had signed an entry in my diary which was witnessed by his son Bobby Joran. He also made statements that he had made me boss to look after his painting designs and all the sacred and non-sacred stories for them, and these stories had only ever been given to me.

My responsibility was to ensure that the drawings were not trivialised in any way and always presented as religion, not merely as art. Yirawala had seen sacred drawings from other old men reproduced on table mats, postcards, posters and T-shirts. I must see that this did not happen to any of his drawings.

I had also promised Yirawala that I would write a big book about his life and work. He wanted the whole religious series of paintings shown with their non-sacred explanations, and the full story told of his struggle for land and human rights. He wanted white people to understand.

Until the out-of-court settlement regarding copyright I was prevented from having this book published. It is written according to his wishes.

Late in 1976 the Yirawala ceremonial series of 139 paintings was deposited in the Australian National Gallery, Canberra.

Yirawala had said the Government could look after the paintings but could never own the designs, symbols and signs and were never to be given any explanations because the Australian Government had not recognised Aboriginal religion and ownership of tribal land, nor helped him and his clan to go home to their land and determine their own future as they wanted.

He earnestly hoped that one day his series of paintings would be recognised as religion and treated with respect and understanding.

When this book is published, I will have kept my promise and discharged my responsibility. Then I can return home in peace to Darwin to the old house under the poinciana trees where memories linger.

I will go once more to Arnhemland
And drink from the shining waterfalls.
In cool shaded places
I will pick the cosma like flowers
And weave a wreath to float out on the waters
In memory of him.
I will whisper farewell to the lorikeets
As they fly crying and calling
Through deep gorges,
Where shy black kangaroos linger.
I will climb to the caves in reverence
And hold the spirit hands,
Pretending not to see the shy bush mice
Peeping from nooks and crannies.
Far away I will see Nimbuah, the mighty rock,
The old man of dreams
And hear once more Yirawala calling,
To tell the spirits that he is home.

The author

Sandra LeBrun Holmes was born on Boolcoomatta Station in the far west of New South Wales, where her father worked as a coachbuilder, blacksmith and wheelwright.

As a very small child she watched Aboriginal camp dances, and from the children learned a few simple steps. They played games and marked her face with clay in innocent communion.

In 1929, when the Great Drought overtook Boolcoomatta Station and the owner lost it to the bank, the workers had to move on. The author's parents loaded their possessions and children into a T-Model Ford truck and set off for Kalgoorlie, in Western Australia, with the dog on the running board. The Aborigines came to see them off. The author called to her playmates but they looked at the ground, tracing patterns in the red dust with their toes. It was a sad parting.

In Kalgoorlie the local Aborigines were despised and badly treated, living in lean-tos of bag and tin; the adults begging in the back lanes until white people set dogs onto them. The author's mother said that the Aborigines owned all the land before the white man took it from them.

The author joined the air force during World War II. When the war ended her thoughts turned back to the plight of the Aborigines. She decided to journey all over Western Australia to document their condition as best she could. She wrote to Professor Elkin at the University of Sydney and he encouraged her to go and listen to the Aborigines. He sent her a letter of introduction to the Director of Aboriginal Welfare in Perth, which enabled her to obtain permits to enter Aboriginal reserves.

In the early 1950s she bought a large Philips table-model tape recorder, which had to be powered from a twelve-volt battery via an inverter and transformer. Having little money, she obtained lifts from transport drivers, commercial travellers and itinerant dentists and doctors, often using their vehicles' batteries to run her recorder.

She recorded the songs and stories of tribal groups in the deserts and in the north of Western Australia, and also carried recorded messages from one group to another as she travelled the country. She recorded statements about their plight, with particular reference to the loss of their children. Many parents had their children taken away and placed in missions and settlements where they would be assimilated into white society and given a new identity and a new religion.

In telling of their loss, some mothers wept and men sang dirges as for the dead. They were dispossessed of their land, religion and children. One man mourned that all his law and knowledge would die with him, as there was nobody to 'take over' when he died.

In sorrow and anger, the author determined to make all this public. She hired halls and gave talks but few people wanted to know. After these failures she made masks and costumes and presented Aboriginal songs and dances as a means of attracting people to listen. They liked the songs and dances but did not want to know the rest.

In the mid-1950s she left the State, seeking a wider audience and somebody to make a film about the plight of Aborigines in Western Australia, and so met her then husband, Cecil

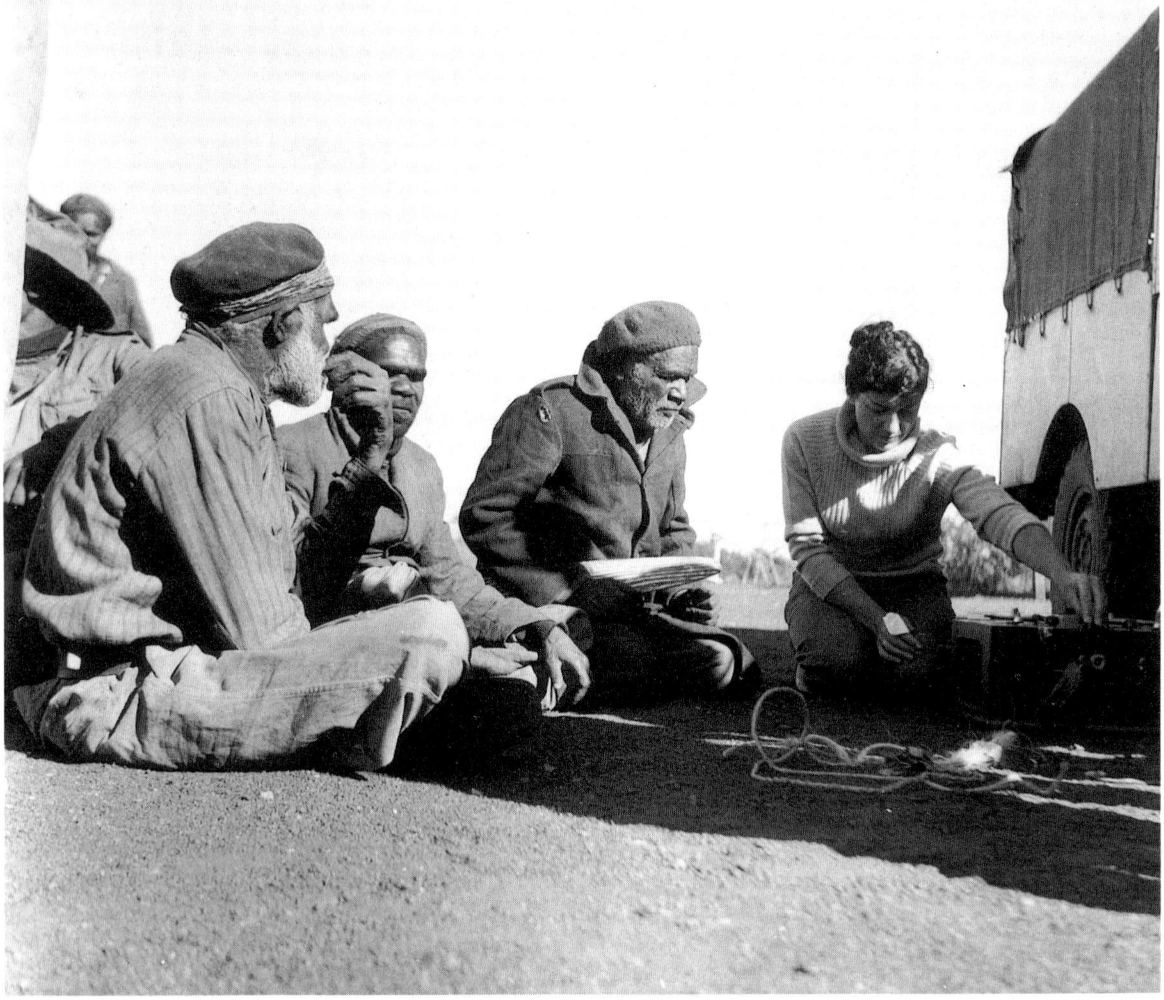

Recording Pintubi elders at Laverton, Western Australia, in 1952.

Holmes, a writer and film director. Efforts to raise money for such a film failed, but she continued to speak about the plight of the Aborigines and, encouraged by Professor Elkin, studied anthropology at the University of Sydney.

In 1963 the author went with her husband to live in Darwin, where she became an accredited anthropological researcher for the Australian Institute of Aboriginal Studies (AIAS) and assisted her husband in filming sacred ceremonies for the AIAS's archives (for restricted viewing). She believed that through this work she was assisting to preserve Aboriginal religion and culture.

She became involved with Aboriginal rights, the struggle for citizenship and land rights. She also made two important collections for Australia: the Yirawala Collection (in the Australian National Gallery, Canberra) and the Holmes Tiwi Collection (in the Northern Territory Museum and Art Gallery, Darwin).

Sandra LeBrun Holmes has three children: Adrian, Clinton and Amanda.

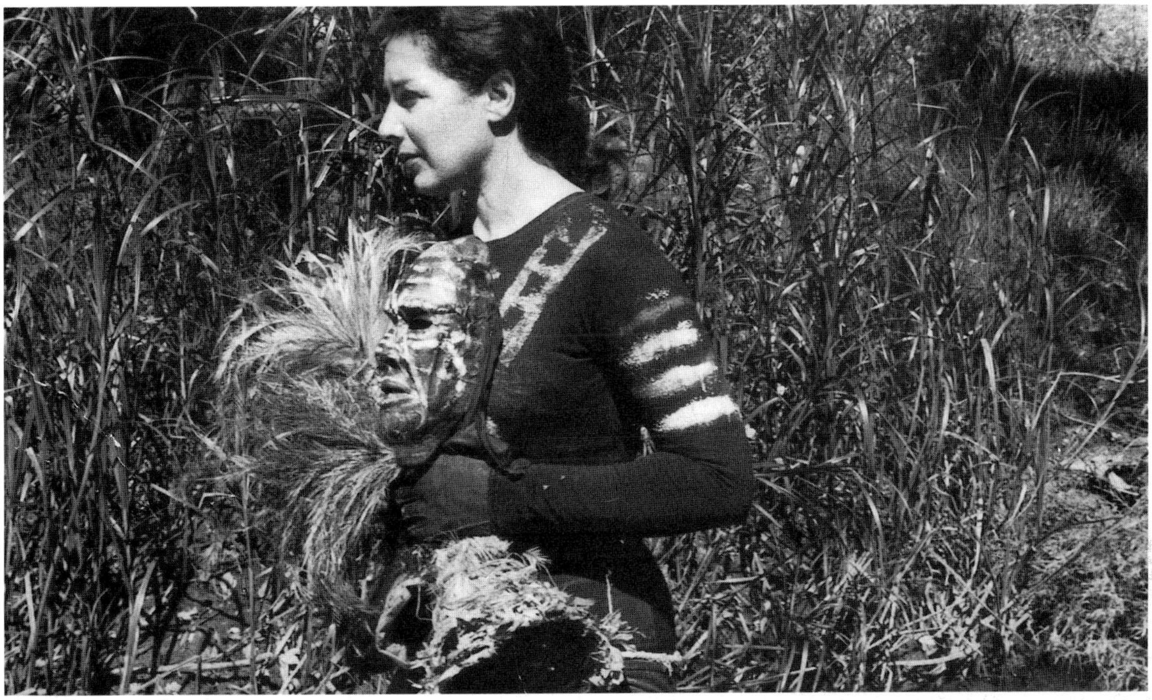

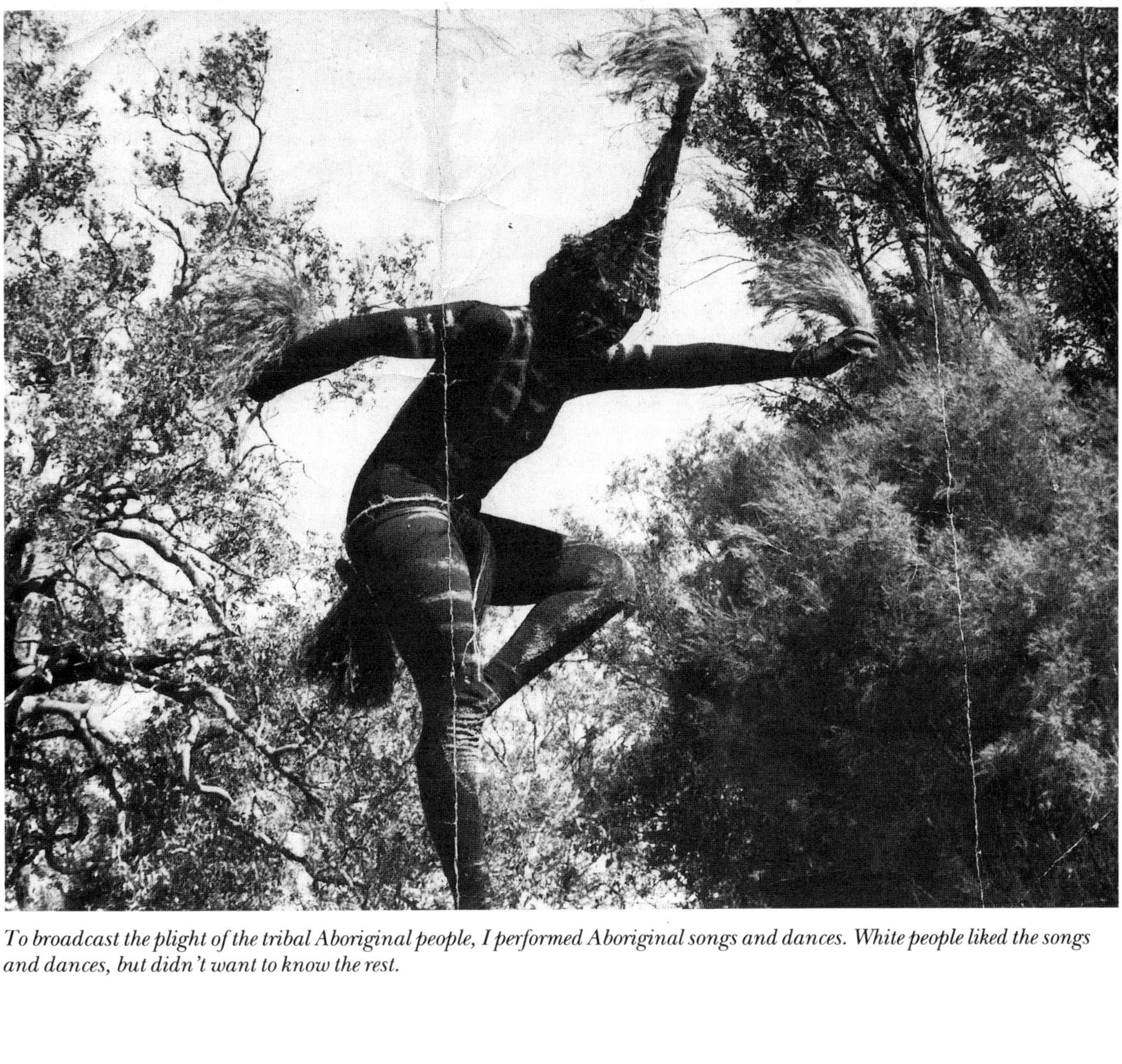

To broadcast the plight of the tribal Aboriginal people, I performed Aboriginal songs and dances. White people liked the songs and dances, but didn't want to know the rest.

Other works by the author

FILMWORK

People of Pindan (documentary on Aboriginal mining co-operative, WA), sound recordist and liaison (1956).

Lotu (documentary, New Britain), sound recordist, field researcher and liaison (1958).

Djalambu (film for AIAS of Aboriginal mortuary ceremony, Millingimbi, Arnhemland), sound recordist, researcher, liaison, mix supervisor (1960).

How Shall They Hear (historical documentary for the Methodist Overseas Missions, NSW, on mission work amongst tribal Aborigines), researcher, liaison, sound recordist and mix supervisor (1960).

Faces in the Sun (documentary about four tribal leaders faced with changing ways), researcher, Aboriginal liaison, sound recordist (1960).

The Uwar Ceremony (for the AIAS's restricted-viewing archives, film of sacred ceremony, Goulburn Island), researcher, Aboriginal liaison, sound recordist, continuity (1964).

The Lorrgon Ceremony (for the AIAS's restricted-viewing archives, film of sacred mortuary ceremony), researcher, Aboriginal liaison, sound recordist (1965).

The Nagarren Yubidawara Ceremony (for the AIAS's restricted-viewing archives, film of sacred ceremony, Roper River, West Arnhemland), researcher, advisor, Aboriginal liaison, sound recordist (1965).

Return to the Dreaming (documentary on Yirawala and his sons visiting their home country), sound recordist, advisor, liaison (1971).

The Goddess and the Moon Man (documentary on the Tiwi religion; Prize for Excellence and Contribution to the Humanities, Tashkent International Film Festival, 1980), director, writer, producer, editor, sound recordist (1979).

Yirawala the Picasso of Arnhemland (documentary on the life and works of the great painter and tribal leader; prizewinner at the Moscow International Film Festival, 1982), writer, director, editor (with Amanda Holmes), producer, sound recordist (1981).

FIELDWORK

Anthropological research (filming, documenting, recording and photographing) of Aboriginal ceremonies, religion, designs and oral histories, from Yirrkala Mission, Mainarou Station, Beswick, Bamjilli, Roper River, Katherine, Goulburn Island, Elcho Island, Croker Island, the Tiwi islands and Bagot Aboriginal Reserve, for the AIAS (1964-78).

WRITINGS

Yirawala: Artist and Man, Jacaranda Press, Brisbane, 1972.

Articles published in: *Aboriginal Affairs Magazine, Millah-Wah-Millah, Northern Territory News, People, Reserve Bank Magazine, Travel Leisure Magazine, Walkabout.*

LONG-PLAYING RECORDS

Music and Sounds of Melanesia, EMI, 1957.

Land of the Morning Star (Aboriginal music, Arnhemland), EMI, 1962.

The Hunter of the Black (Dame Mary Gilmore's recollections of Aboriginal massacres when she was a child, and Dame Mary reading her own poems on the Aborigines), Festival Records, 1989.